D1341966

Drafting and Negotiating Computer Contracts

Drafting and Negotiating Computer Contracts

Second Edition

Rachel Burnett
Paul Klinger

Tottel
publishing

Tottel Publishing, Maxwelton House, 41–43 Boltro Road, Haywards Heath, West Sussex, RH16 1BJ

A CIP Catalogue record for this book is available from the British Library.

ISBN 1 84592 000 7

1-84592-024-4

Typeset by Columns Design Ltd, Reading, UK
Printed and bound in Great Britain by William Clowes Limited, Beccles, Suffolk

Foreword to the Second Edition

I am very pleased indeed that the second edition of this book has now been published. The authors have an enormous amount of combined practical experience. It is interesting that their careers are both firmly rooted in technical backgrounds within the industry itself as well as in legal practice, which has undoubtedly influenced their innovative and commercial approach to contract negotiation.

It is still a matter of great concern that major IT projects fail too frequently. A thoroughly negotiated contract which anticipates and prescribes what is to happen when foreseeable difficulties arise is an important means of preventing many problems in the first place, and enabling those which do nevertheless occur to be effectively managed.

I am confident that this book will prove of immense value to IT professionals and their legal advisers, and will be recognised as a 'must have' in their libraries, just as the first edition has been.

I have enjoyed reading this book and from my academic perspective, found it informative and insightful. I have no hesitation in commending it to its readers, and I congratulate the authors on producing such a valuable work of reference.

Wendy Hall CBE
September 2004
University of Southampton
Wendy Hall is Professor of Computer Science at the
University of Southampton and President of the
British Computer Society 2003–4

Foreword to the First Edition

I warmly welcome the publication of this book, as I believe it addresses an area of central interest and importance in the computer field. Writing computer system contracts is a peculiarly fraught experience due primarily, I think, to the intangible nature of the product. I refer in particular to the software component of a system, which determines how that system will respond in practice to its users and which controls the services delivered. Software quality is very hard to assess – the real 'product' is its behaviour when actually in service, and this is generally not possible to predict with certainty during the development process.

It is an inescapable fact that, except perhaps in a few very specialised areas, software can never be assumed to be free of errors, and indeed the general view is that all software, and hence all computer systems, must be assumed to contain an unknown number of errors which are as yet undiscovered. Nevertheless, we are surrounded by computer systems, often of great complexity, and we rely on the operation of such systems in very many of our activities, from flying an aircraft to using the washing machine.

This central issue in computer systems engineering leads to severe problems in effective project management and in quality control. The record of achievement by the computer systems industry over the years in delivering products to specification, on time and within budget, is notoriously poor, and has often led to client dissatisfaction and indeed to litigation. A well-constructed and effective contract is not easy to establish in this difficult area, and this book provides, both for lawyers and for computer systems specialists and their clients, much helpful guidance.

In such a book, a wide range of computer-related contract formats must be covered and analysed. The discussions of areas such as the specification-driven approach widely used in the last two decades, consultancy contracts, software licences, intellectual property issues, fixed price and time and materials charging and indeed many other areas must produce practical and widely-acceptable guidelines for writing these contracts.

I particularly welcome the discussions on more recent approaches to contracting. These are moving away from the requirements for a full specification prior to development, which can be cumbersome and even confrontational, to more collaborative fast-prototyping and joint development approaches. I think these newer approaches to building computer systems have much to offer and they may well provide more effective routes towards the goal of delivering products which truly meet the requirements. Successful systems have been built in this way, on the basis that only the client can really understand the requirement, but in general contracts cannot effectively specify it either in computer or legal terminology, and so a 'partnership' is the best approach. Recent technical advances, for example in very high level application-specific programming systems, can give more effective support for fast prototyping and so make the use of such an approach more realistic and feasible.

Personally, I found this book interesting, informative and a pleasure to read. The subject, I think, is of crucial importance to the development of our use of computer systems and I hope it will be widely read and consulted both by lawyers and by computer systems engineers.

John Buxton
October 1993
Kings College, London
John Buxton is Professor of IT at
King's College, London, and
Chairman of Room Underwriting Systems Ltd.

Preface to the Second Edition

The focus of our book remains as before: to offer a perspective to drafting and negotiating computer and other IT contracts which is practical rather than narrowly academic, drawing on our own experience in the industry. Since our first edition, the computer and telecommunications industries have continued to evolve and expand, and in parallel the Internet has become the most dominant feature of the information society. We have therefore added new chapters, to consider application service provision (ASP), website development and e-commerce agreements. Another new chapter examines leasing arrangements because, particularly in connection with hardware supply transactions, leasing is frequently the preferred means of financing. The rest of the book has required substantial revision to take into account the commercial and legal developments over the last decade.

Although our prime purpose is to discuss and analyse the negotiability of the various types of contracts commonly encountered in relation to the supply of computer products and services, we have responded to the many requests we have received to provide precedent formats by including with this edition a CD containing examples of the contracts reviewed. These precedents are in Microsoft Word format and may easily be customised. However, we would strongly urge any reader who is contemplating use of the precedents, first to define the details of the actual transaction for which the precedent is consulted – perhaps with the help of the checklists in Chapter 23 – before consulting the precedent wording, and second, to obtain up-to-date specialist legal advice. This is essential in order to ensure that, in any individual case, the precedent will be appropriately adapted and that it reflects the current legal position in this rapidly changing area of the law.

We would particularly like to thank the following: Professor Wendy Hall CBE, President of the British Computer Society, Head of Computer Science at Southampton University, for her endorsement of the manuscript; John Briggs and Richard Mackay for their advice concerning the financial aspects of leasing; and Harry Kelly and Adrian Robinson for sharing their considerable practical experience of e-commerce, which we have used in the discussion of the e-commerce agreement example in Chapter 20.

As previously, any surviving errors are all our own work.

We are grateful to all our clients, their customers and suppliers, and to our professional colleagues, for continuing to present the arguments forming the basis of this book.

The law is stated as at October 2004.

Rachel Burnett
Paul Klinger
London and Guernsey
November 2004

Preface to the First Edition

Now that we are undergoing the information revolution, where society has come to depend on information and the technologies by which it is communicated and used, the computer industry continues to advance at an unprecedented rate, far outstripping the rate of growth of any other industry, in terms of both technological advances and new applications.

A distinct body of law relating to the supply and use of computer products and services is evolving. There are numerous forms of legal agreements designed to address the issues arising in computer-related business transactions. Some precedent materials are now available to assist those whose work involves drafting and reviewing computer contracts. Nevertheless, the industry has not reached the stage of maturity where standard forms of agreements are in common use. To a large extent this reflects its dynamic and innovative approach to business, with the variety and multiplicity of transactions. Moreover, very little assistance is available in respect of the negotiation of these contracts or of their administration. In this book, we focus firmly on these aspects.

Each major category of computer contract is discussed, but, rather than provide absolute precedent wording, we have chosen to offer examples of the principal clauses normally found in each type of contract, using them as a basis for discussion about negotiability. We have concentrated as much as possible on the commercial factors which typically confront the supplier and the user when a computer contract is under consideration.

We have deliberately sought to avoid an academic standpoint and to give the work a practical flavour, founded on our respective backgrounds working within the computer industry and for computer users, initially as systems analysts and consultants and, since the early eighties, as practising lawyers. We hope, therefore, that this book will be useful to computer and system suppliers and users as well as to those professionally engaged in advising them.

We would particularly like to thank the following: Professor Colin Tapper for his thorough review of the manuscript and his invaluable suggestions for its improvement; Professor John Buxton for his practical advice on the manuscript and for the helpful observations on industry practice; Antony Smith for his comments in connection with Chapter 3; Lindsay McNish for his comments in connection with Chapter 4.

Any surviving errors are all our own work.

We would also like to thank our various secretaries who have contributed to typing the manuscript, and especially to thank Gwen Clarke for her general secretarial support and organisation and for tackling the whole of the final manuscript so patiently and efficiently.

Finally, reflecting the empirical experience we have gained over the years, we would like to thank our clients and our professional colleagues for their significant contribution towards the development of the arguments – and to the suppliers and customers of our clients without whom some of the arguments would not have been considered in the first place.

Paul Klinger
Rachel Burnett
November 1993

About the Authors

Rachel Burnett's career started as an IT professional after graduating from Exeter University. She was originally with the Post Office/British Telecom, and subsequently worked at Sainsburys, Midland Bank and Brooke Bond Oxo in system development and project management. She worked on some of the largest and most complex storage and retrieval systems in Europe at that time, and was part of the team that designed and implemented the first online computer system for foreign exchange dealers.

Rachel studied for her law examinations while she was still working full time in IT, joining Paul Klinger's successful niche IT law practice as a solicitor in the 1980s. Moving on to City of London law firms, and after several years as a City partner, she now runs her own IT practice, acting for users and suppliers. Her clients include service providers, software publishers, system integrators, and other value added intermediaries in the IT supply chain.

She is Vice-President (Forums) of the British Computer Society, a Court Assistant of the Worshipful Company of Information Technologists, and was Chair of the Institute for the Management of Information Systems 2000–03. She is an Associate of the Institute of Linguists.

Rachel is author of *Outsourcing IT: The Legal Aspects*, published by Gower, and editor of the *IT Law Guides* series published for the Institute of Chartered Accountants of England and Wales on a variety of legal topics.

Paul Klinger has spent his entire career in the IT world. He trained originally as a systems analyst with Burroughs Machines Limited (later to become part of Unisys) but after five years left to take a law degree at the University of Leicester, qualified as a solicitor and became an in-house UK legal counsel at Digital Equipment Limited.

The distinctive feature of Paul's legal career, innovative in 1981, was to establish a private practice specialising in IT law and offering an in-house style of legal service to numerous start-up companies in the computer and telecommunications industries, as well as providing IT related legal services to customers of these industries. Paul's clients have included Aspective Limited, Autofile Limited, Centerprise International Limited, ComponentSource Limited, Cray Systems

Limited, speed-trap Limited, Sun Microsystems Limited, Telematics International Limited and for many years Silicon Graphics Limited and Inc., culminating in an appointment as its European Legal Counsel. He has had extensive experience of the international issues facing multi-national companies in the IT sector and has travelled frequently within Europe and to the US and Australia. He has also managed several corporate financing, acquisition and disposal transactions from an in-house perspective.

Now based in Guernsey in the Channel Islands, Paul serves as a non-executive director or legal adviser to a number of Boards, and provides his specialist legal services on a consultancy basis to both users and suppliers.

Contents

Glossary

Generally speaking, these terms are quoted in full on their first occurrence and by abbreviation subsequently.

ADR	Alternative Dispute Resolution
APR	Annual Percentage Rate
ASP	Application Service Provision
CE	Communauté Européenne
CIF	Cost, Insurance and Freight
CPU	Central Processing Unit
DPP	Delivery Duty Paid
EC	European Community
ECJ	European Court of Justice
EEA	European Economic Area
EFTA	European Free Trade Association
EU	European Union
FAST	Federation Against Software Theft
FCA	Free Carriage Abroad
FM	Facilities Management
GAAP	Generally Accepted Accounting Practice
ICC	International Chamber of Commerce
IP	Internet Protocol
IPR	Intellectual Property Right
ISO	International Organization for Standardization
ISP	Internet Service Provider
IT	Information Technology
LAN	Local Area Network
MOA	Memorandum of Agreement
MOU	Memorandum of Understanding
MSP	Managed Service Provider
OEM	Original Equipment Manufacturer
PC	Personal Computer
RFQ	Request for Quotation
SSP	Storage Service Provider
TTBER	Technology Transfer Block Exemption Regulation
TUPE	Transfer of Undertakings (Protection of Employment) Regulations 1981, SI 1981/1794
TV	television
UCTA	Unfair Contract Terms Act 1977

UK	United Kingdom
UNCITRAL	United Nations Commission on International Trade Law
UNIDROIT	International Institute for the Unification of Private Law
US	United States
VAR	Value Added Reseller
VAT	Value Added Tax
WASP	Wireless Application Service Provider
WIPO	World Intellectual Property Organization

Table of Statutes

Table of Statutory Instruments

Table of Cases

CHAPTER I

Introduction

A. General

This book is addressed to the information technology ('IT') industry and its users. The target readership includes members of the sales and purchasing departments respectively of the industry and its customers, IT and information systems directors, and directors of IT suppliers and service organisations. In view of this aim, unnecessary legal language or jargon has been deliberately avoided, and explanations and interpretations are commercial. Nevertheless, the hope is that this book will also be useful for lawyers, accountants, management consultants and other advisers servicing this significant sector of the economy.

The intention is to provide a practical guide to drafting and constructing an IT contract and to the principles of IT contract negotiation. Creating a good contract relating to IT products or services requires an understanding of the commercial objectives of the transaction and of the reasons for the legal principles which should underpin it. As a prerequisite to successful negotiation, it is necessary to have an awareness of the legal and market environments which influence the ways in which IT contracts are made. It is essential, also, to appreciate the need for adequate systems of legal risk management, order administration and contracts administration.

This book is not an academic treatise on this important new area of contract law, nor should it be regarded as an exhaustive statement on the techniques of negotiation. The approach is, rather, to explain, inform and guide in simple and useful terms, with the hope that those who refer to it will find it a helpful preparation for IT contract negotiations.

B. The IT industry

Change is endemic in the IT industry and IT is itself a continuing vehicle for progress. The emphasis of commercial computing has changed from its early function of support in merely providing information faster or in automating processes. Computerised production techniques and automated manufacturing processes are in increasing use throughout industry. Word processing and spread-sheets are used throughout business, and at home too. It is only recently that the computer has become pervasive – a web of interconnected devices in constant use, embedded into everything. No longer is it a passive device used occasionally. Now computing is 'ubiquitous', with distributed interactive systems, networks connecting large numbers of components of various kinds, including small devices which can be embedded in many things and sensing technologies to relate to the physical environment. Computing reaches everyone as a background part of everyday life, taken for granted in the activities and interaction that it supports. Nevertheless, mainframe computing remains significant.

IT industry growth used to derive spectacularly from start-ups creating innovative products, often a breakaway team working in a garage or shed who became millionaires when their company was sold shortly afterwards. But the trend in today's cautious climate of slow growth or recession is towards consolidation and integration, and away from novelty.

IT expenditure is consistently above inflation, and reported gloom is based on inflated expectations rather than objective statistics. E-commerce is thriving, and the unrealistic emphasis on the demise of the dot.coms reeks of *schadenfreude*: 'boom and bust' is an economic phenomenon which follows the introduction of revolutionary technologies (it happened with the railways). The IT industry is not merely about dot.coms. Nevertheless, user decisions about proceeding with a major transaction, such as procurement or outsourcing, are taking longer to make. Cost cutting is now as important as investment, and will be automatically expected in the business justification for a project. This is illustrated by the savings made through sending entire processes offshore and where the technology (both high speed connections and software tools) facilitates this. Using services in India, the Far East or Eastern Europe, enables companies to stay competitive.

This is in line with the general move towards decentralisation. Hardware was often built far away from its local markets. Now software is too. Companies no longer need to retain all their service functions internally, or to have them situated geographically nearby. Expertise can be imported temporarily for specific purposes or for projects with limited time spans. Outsourcing and the use of independent consultants are increasingly common.

Negotiation of hardware supply has declined as it has become a low margin commodity with falling prices, few risks, and likely to be supplied on standard terms and conditions. Software itself has largely become commoditised. Routines and modules are coded separately, and may be combined with other software in various ways, and then possibly customised, utilising various skills and services. Numerous software components can be re-used with little adaptation. Their immediate availability lends itself to online trading. With application service provision ('ASP'), software applications can be delivered electronically on a one-to-many basis, the hosting and maintenance being carried out remotely on a central system. The service providers can exploit economies of scale for many users. Meanwhile the number of service-related industries and activities is increasing.

C. Contractual relevance

There are two overriding features of this vigorous industry as far as its contractual context is concerned. The first is the need to adapt to, and provide contractually for, new and expanded products and services as IT evolves. The second is the need to protect intangible assets which are continually being redefined, within a legal environment which is itself evolving.

1. Contractual background

The IT industry did not concern itself with protecting its software assets until, in 1969, IBM started charging separately for consultancy, training, maintenance – and software. From then on, a distinct software industry has evolved, with a need to consider hardware and software issues separately, as well as in combination as systems, together with an extensive range of services: not only maintenance and support of hardware and software products, but such diverse activities as consultancy, outsourcing, disaster recovery and escrow arrangements, which are discussed further in their respective chapters.

In reaction to developments in the IT industry, various legal responses, methods and techniques are evolving. Most of these are essentially rooted in contract, and comprise the subject matter of the discussions in the individual contract chapters that follow, for example on limiting and excluding liability or on confidentiality issues. Legal recognition of intangible proprietary assets, such as software and data, is being strengthened and extended, protecting the rights of ownership and providing sanctions regarding unauthorised access, use and modification.

Contracts are directed towards the supply of products and services, risk-sharing arrangements between the parties for specific purposes, the development, testing and licensing of applications, and the implementation of a remarkable number of distribution arrangements. A whole array of ancillary agreements has been created to cater for areas such as confidentiality and compliance with standards and regulations.

2. Trends affecting IT contracts

ROUTES OF SUPPLY

There are many channels of supply, distribution and marketing, from the manufacturer to the eventual end user and varying routes to procurement, often cross-border. This has implications for the different kinds of contracts being created between the parties, some of whom within the chain will be both customer in buying or licensing from one or more vendors, and also supplier, putting together the different elements of a product and adding value for onward supply. This supply is also becoming more and more international – in India, the Far East, different parts of the US and Europe. The international business context brings the law and jurisdiction clauses of the contract, and its enforceability, into sharp focus.

FLEXIBILITY AND CHANGE CONTROL

The increasing modularity, compatibility and interoperability of software and associated services should benefit the contract outcome. Yet uncertainty and complexity still beset systems integration. Change control procedures have always allowed the supplier to evaluate and cost variations proposed during the contract lifetime, building in timescales and other formalities. This is even more relevant now where flexibility and scope for change are intrinsic to the transaction, for example where the supplier is taking responsibility for business process re-engineering.

INFORMATION

Technology has transformed the collection, collation, dissemination and use of information and turned it into a commodity that may be profitably traded, for example through online commercial databases. Moreover, it is easily accessed and downloaded on the web.

Unlike the supply of technological products and services, the provision of information is affected by disintermediation: direct access by a user to information (such as legal information) that otherwise would require an intermediary (such as a solicitor). The effect of this is a greater recognition of intellectual property rights, particularly for data, graphics and other material protected by copyright. Owners of rights in software are appreciating the need for its protection by contract as an economic asset, and in order to prevent unauthorised access, use and modification, the better to exploit it commercially.

The risk is that ease of storage of information may render it far less accessible. For example, it will be possible within the life span of a person born in this decade to store a lifetime's memories on a chip the size of a grain of sand. Nevertheless, there are possibilities of better decision making and easier collaboration.

PARTIES TO THE CONTRACT

As in most areas of business, suppliers and customers have different commercial perspectives. The position is more difficult when dealing with IT-related products and services. This is partly because of their complex character. However, there has also been the ability of suppliers to be sufficiently innovative to dictate the terms on which they are prepared to enter into transactions, to a much greater extent than is usual for suppliers generally in commercial transactions; and often because the purchaser has to rely on one supplier's solution as the only viable way of meeting its needs. On the other hand, there are many small IT companies run by their founders where technical and entrepreneurial sophistication go hand in hand with legal naivety. Overall, however, suppliers have become alive to driving a bargain in an aggressively competitive environment and are also constantly refining and enhancing their products to keep them marketable.

At the same time, customers are more knowledgeable about their technological demands and more insistent on their legal rights. They have been assisted by technical standards, quality assurance procedures and project management methodologies, which provide criteria for assessing levels of service and reliability. More informed negotiation takes place as purchasers assume greater power in determining the terms of a transaction.

Systems will often continue to be supported and enhanced by the supplier when they have gone live. A well-managed ongoing relationship between the parties has to be co-operative, yet at arm's length. Such tensions should lead to more balanced contracts, where risks, rights and obligations have been allocated fairly between the parties. Conversely, it is not unknown for IT contracts to become unnecessarily longer and legalistic, to no one's advantage.

D. Legal trends

The first book on IT law was written in 1978.[1] As the industry has grown and diversified, IT law has developed. It extends traditional areas of law such as contracts, negligence, intellectual property and competition law into a distinct body of law applicable to IT, covering such specific areas as IT misuse, security and digital rights.

1. IT-related law

New legislation, often resulting from EC Directives, is changing the content of commercial contracts generally, but some new statutes and regulations are especially applicable to IT contracts. As for any commercial contract, statutory interest is now payable on debts. Contracts for consumers are subject to a raft of laws, for instance, for distance selling. E-commerce is becoming highly regulated. In transactions involving personal data, data protection indemnities will be sought and given. The rights of third parties that may be affected by the contract, such as the software licensee's end users, will normally be expressly excluded.

Developing case law has led to other changes to the IT contract. Several disputes have been litigated involving problematic IT projects, originally entered into with enthusiasm and optimism by both supplier and customer. The courts have generally taken a pragmatic approach, and it seems as if the individual circumstances, and the behaviour of the parties, have weighed heavily in the interpretation of the legal principles applicable.

UK intellectual property legislation has arguably not varied dramatically since the Copyright Designs and Patents Act 1988 became law. Updating has mostly been through efforts at harmonisation throughout the EU: for example, with regard to trade marks, aspects of copyright relating to software and online protection, the creation of the rather odd database right – and the unresolved argument about the extent of patents for software. The decisions in IT-related cases on copyright infringement are no real surprise to the industry (except occasionally as a salutary reminder that freelance programmers will retain rights in their coding if nothing different is explicitly agreed).

2. Law for the IT industry

An IT company will require trading terms and conditions, establishing its business styles and terms, to include its commercial limits of liability. It will have procedures for negotiating significant contracts. Occasionally, the company may become embroiled in disputes.

With continual technological advances, and as more sophisticated ways are found of sharing development and marketing risks, there is scope for new kinds of contracts to structure the transactions and to allocate responsibilities and rights between the parties. Joint ventures and marketing agreements are common ways of investing both the financial resources and the know-how necessary for development.

The rights of owning and using intellectual property rights must be allocated and protected. The law regarding patents and copyright has been extended to accommodate technological developments, incorporating revisions, enhancements, modifications and teamwork both within one organisation and between different companies and people.

Where systems are large, complex, expensive and critical, failures in development, integration or implementation especially matter. As a result, disputes are often aggressively pursued in the courts and by arbitration and other types of formal negotiation. There may be complicated questions of fact, much detail and a multiplicity of contracts and sub-contracts.

Nevertheless, the supplier must be concerned to limit exposure to liability. In the IT industry, guaranteed performance levels, promises of 100 per cent reliability or open-ended commitments to resolving all problems are, at least, costly options, and at worst will be impossible to fulfil. The risks have increased with the greater use and greater complexity of software, which may consist of millions of lines of code. There is potential for enormous liability where software is used in aeroplanes, for air-traffic control, robotics and medical systems. The use of software with other systems over which the supplier has no control, and which could slow performance or restrict the volume capacity, or, worse still, affect the results, must make the supplier wary of what commitment can be given.

E. Principal objectives of this book

This book has two principal aims. The first is to give guidance in the negotiation of a range of IT contracts. The second is to provide practical advice in structuring and drafting various types of IT contracts. In each of these cases, the perspectives of supplier and customer will differ, and will be discussed accordingly.

The commentary on the key terms and conditions focuses on the scope for realistic negotiation.

1. To give guidance in negotiating IT contracts

Some general principles are always applicable when negotiating.

Preparation is fundamental to the outcome. An agenda can shape the negotiating process, although it should itself be negotiable. Objectives should be pre-defined. Negotiation is for the purpose of achieving a result. Each side should learn the other side's initial preferred offers and positions. Timing needs careful consideration in terms of how much leeway there is, when to begin, how to pace the negotiation. In the negotiation itself, when to speak and when to listen is a matter of sensitivity. Silence can be a helpful tactic. Many people find other people's silence disconcerting.

Contracts are negotiated in a commercial world. Theoretical principles have to take account of practical constraints. One constraining factor is the commercial weight of the parties. In an unbalanced relationship, there are limits to the extent to which the weaker party can realistically negotiate. A large organisation may lay down inflexible sets of requirements, and a small company supplying its products may feel obliged to go along with these. Yet there may be certain provisions that would be a high risk commercially for the less powerful company to accept, such as termination of the contract without payment for failure to deliver specially developed software by a fixed date. If the supplier does not succeed in negotiating more acceptable terms, it will be necessary to make a commercial judgment about whether the business is worth the risk.

Where the contract under negotiation is dependent on an already existing contract with a third party, the earlier contractual limitations can restrict the flexibility of negotiations. A tight timescale may inhibit the ideal contract being achieved. Further instances of constraints might be statutory limitations, technical boundaries or financial restrictions.

For effective negotiation, the authority to negotiate must be present for both parties. However, even if there is no actual authority to negotiate, an ability to handle objections can be acquired by a representative, whether seller or buyer, who understands and can explain contractual requirements to an opposite number in a convincing manner. The impersonality of an unseen third party can sometimes be used as an advantage in discussion of the terms and conditions.

Every organisation should have well-defined rules for the conduct of negotiations and ought always to be aware of professional advice before constructing a contract or conceding a legal point. There should always be reasons why a provision is in a contract in the first place, or for any objection to a contractual provision. Ideally negotiation will seek to meet the objections through understanding why they are made, and finding a solution that will be mutually acceptable while retaining the spirit of the original. The relative importance of the provisions must always be considered in a negotiation. Some will be more easily conceded than others in order to achieve the common objective of a good result for both parties.

This book will therefore concentrate on the principal terms and conditions for each major category of contract, examining the extent to which there may be scope for negotiation and suggesting possible solutions for reconciling contrary points of view. All serious contract negotiations are conducted on the premise that there will be a contract at the end of the day. Thus, from the outset, there is always some measure of goodwill on which to build.

The aim must be to achieve the best terms possible by compromise as necessary in all the circumstances. A good negotiation is one where both parties walk away each feeling it has gained. There is every opportunity under normal conditions for changing the shape or structure of a deal to enable both parties to gain substantially, for example by maintaining the asking price but providing flexible payment terms, or by conceding sole ownership of a jointly-developed product in exchange for exclusive use in a defined market at an attractive price.

2. To provide practical advice in structuring and drafting IT contracts

The introduction to each of the IT contract chapters sets the example contract in its commercial context. The considerations applicable to the supply of standard products are in contrast to those applicable to the provision of bespoke solutions. The different types of contracts are kept distinct for the purposes of discussion. However, it is not uncommon for complex contracts to include a number of apparently disparate features, so that supply, licensing and support, for instance, might be combined for one transaction.

The objective for which the contract is being drafted should be analysed in sufficient detail for the overall contract structure to be drawn up, with all of the matters requiring thought and decision being clearly identified.

A contract may be built up logically, commencing with explanatory and contract-specific clauses applicable only to the contract under consideration, then its operative clauses, taking some kind of logical approach, perhaps chronological to match the particular contract-related activity, and finally the general housekeeping-type clauses found in almost every contract. The process of contract drafting is in some ways analogous to the development methodology for a software product.

The reasons for many commonly encountered clauses and provisions and their meanings are explained, distinguishing clauses included for commercial reasons from those included for legal reasons.

In addition to the negotiation of the contract, the mechanisms for ensuring that it works should be put in place. Administrative procedures should be integral to the contractual process. They should not be regarded as an afterthought. They are important for effective working contracts.

F. Structure of the book

Some important principles of contract negotiation are addressed in **CHAPTER 2**, because it must remain true that success or failure in negotiation will be the single most important factor in determining whether or not a satisfactory form of contract is achieved. No matter how comprehensive and attentive to detail a contract is, it will count for little if poor negotiating techniques result in the erosion or elimination of key terms.

Before looking at the process of creating a contract, some basic background information is provided. The legal environment is going to influence the contractual context, and this is considered in **CHAPTER 3**. A brief look at some of the more important principles of English contract law is contained in **CHAPTER 4**, since this is the framework for contracts being negotiated, made, performed or terminated.

CHAPTER 5 explains the method for construction of an IT contract.

The substance of the book contains practical examples of the principal types of IT contracts and clauses, in **CHAPTERS 6 TO 21**.

For each type of contract considered, an example skeleton comprising clause headings is presented to show the overall structure of the contract.

Those clauses that are specific to the contract in question are then each discussed by means of typical wording and comments on negotiability.

In almost every contract some clauses should be incorporated as a matter of course. These deal with 'housekeeping' issues, and some typical examples are therefore considered in **CHAPTER 6**. Although at first sight there may not appear to be much that is worthy of negotiation, it is important to recognise that some significant issues can arise, even here. For instance, at the very beginning of an agreement where the names of the parties are to be found, there is a need to consider whether a given party should properly be expressed to include, for example, its subsidiaries and/or its associated companies and/or its agents and/or its sub-contractors.

A number of other clauses of an administrative character are to be found in most (not necessarily all) IT contracts, for example relating to duration, payment terms, limitations of liability, termination, and so on. A representative selection of these clauses is discussed in **CHAPTER 7**.

Before the concluding checklists in **CHAPTER 23**, **CHAPTER 22** contains important advice on risk management, order administration and contracts administration. This is a much-neglected area. A surprising number of companies, large as well as small, pay scant attention to these aspects of the contractual process. While virtually all sales organisations have defined procedures for booking and acknowledging orders and entering them into the system for purposes of production, delivery, invoicing and calculating commissions, far too many fail to scrutinise orders from a contractual standpoint. This frequently results in contracts being made on the purchaser's terms and undermines all of the time and expense put into the development and presentation of a supplier's own terms and conditions of business. These remarks apply also to purchasing organisations that fail to impose or negotiate their standard terms and conditions because of their casual practices in placing orders and in dealing with acknowledgments and acceptances.

Once the contract has been negotiated and is in force, important areas of contract administration are often ignored by many. Thus, obligations of confidentiality go unchecked and unmonitored, as do other ongoing but not very visible contractual terms. For example, in a continuing agreement, such as a distributorship or a discount agreement, the consequences of failing to comply with such obligations as a commitment to offer prices and other terms at least as favourable as those offered to other customers, or to purchase a minimum quantity by a given date in order to continue to qualify for an agreed level of discount, or to submit regular reports in an agreed format in order to continue as a distributor or dealer, can be extremely expensive. Yet exposure of this type is often not considered nor catered for by the managers of the relevant functions, who are generally more preoccupied with their day-to-day responsibilities.

In conclusion, to reiterate the purposes of this book: it is not intended, for any of the types of IT contracts discussed, that the structure suggested or the clause contents should merely be copied to produce a standard contract. It will depend on the circumstances and perspectives of any particular transaction which clauses would be relevant and appropriate, and what those clauses should state. In some instances, clauses have been included for the purposes of discussing their viability, not because it would necessarily be correct for them to appear automatically in an IT contract, as illustrated or otherwise. Guidance and advice is given in order to show what should be considered, what might be included, what could be omitted, and how modified wording would affect the construction and negotiation of IT contracts.

Finally, there are hard copies of the example precedents from the accompanying CD. It is important to recognise that the characteristics of an individual agreement are going to reflect the parties' particular needs and intentions. As with any legal precedent, use of the examples as a basis for drafting calls for careful consideration. Each clause should be reviewed to determine its suitability for use as drafted or as amended in the particular situation. Other clauses which do not feature in the examples may need to be included. Another important point to keep in mind is that the law may have changed in some way since the precedent was drafted. Appropriate professional advice should be sought to confirm its continuing validity.

G. Conclusion

Law can be most effectively used in the IT industry as a positive resource in constructive and strategic business planning.

As IT contracts evolve, the legal challenges include:

- protecting valuable intangible assets such as software and databases:
  - as they are continually redefined through revisions, enhancements and additions;
  - with further layers of complexity as access to the Internet increases;

- managing risk in an international business environment;

- facilitating flexibility in a regulatory environment; and

- adapting legal responses to technological innovation and consolidation.

1   Colin Tapper *Computer Law* (4th edn, 1989) Longman.

CHAPTER 2
Principles of contract negotiation

A. Introduction

Negotiations feature in every aspect of daily life. They are essentially the bargaining process between two or more parties seeking to secure predetermined objectives, usually with a clear sense of purpose. Although mostly associated in the mind of the average person only with business transactions of one sort or another, negotiations take place constantly between husband and wife, parent and child, buyer and seller, employer and employee, branch office and head office, prosecution and defence, in fact in every situation where two or more parties need to reach agreement on anything at all. The results of negotiations govern relationships in all situations and determine the extent of a person's achievements in life and a business's achievements in the market place.

Given the significance of negotiation, it is a strange anomaly that many people possess poor negotiating skills, which in turn often lead to unsatisfactory results in their various dealings. This is one area, however, where training can make a substantial difference, providing skills and techniques where none previously existed and supplementing the natural abilities present, but not always recognised, in some individuals.

The goal of every negotiation must be to achieve a result which, even if it falls short of the original objective, can be considered a satisfactory advancement towards it. Compromise is an essential feature of most successful negotiations: each party needs to walk away afterwards feeling that he or she has gained. Each party will have a subjective point of view and any consensus reached will generally be associated with perceived advantages or with minimising the perceived disadvantages, whether or not they are real. Because decisions are reached on a subjective basis, there is much scope for a skilled negotiator to make inroads into the other side's position and to accomplish more than would be considered reasonable or realistic if examined objectively. Indeed, in the business context, having regard to the prevailing commercial circumstances and whether these favour buyer or seller, the only real measurement of success is the extent to which a negotiator is able to achieve a result against the commercial odds.

Where then does the power lie in a negotiation? Achieving a consensus in IT contracts can appear difficult in the context of apparently entrenched starting positions. Each party has a view about an ideal form of contract, but historically the computer industry has come to the table with a powerful position: the most successful products have tended to be in short supply, with the result that suppliers have had a tendency to insist upon the application of their own standard terms and conditions of supply. Steadily increasing competition, characteristic of a maturing industry, has made considerable inroads into this traditional position, particularly for PCs and networking products which are in common use, and in connection with the extensive range of service offerings now available. Nevertheless, the comparatively few major equipment suppliers, all big companies themselves, remain generally unwilling to be flexible unless dealing with major customers. Significance will always be attached to higher monetary value and may also apply when there is considered to be a strategic or prestigious value to the business. Standard IT contract terms and conditions frequently originate in the United States, although the position is gradually changing, but it is still the case that there has been limited examination by the English courts of many of the principles involved. Furthermore, small suppliers of hardware products are usually acting as resellers or distributors for the large manufacturers and have limited ability to vary terms and conditions, restricted in some instances by contractual obligations and in others by an unwillingness to accept risks in the form of potential liabilities which go beyond the levels of warranty and indemnity offered by the manufacturer.

Software developers are often much smaller than many of their customers and much more vulnerable to dictated commercial terms, but customers frequently end up with an unsatisfactory result nevertheless, because they fail to appreciate the importance of having a close involvement in the process of creating software tailored to their requirements. If things go wrong, the results of delay and expense, possibly exacerbated by the supplier's precarious financial position, can be disastrous.

An understanding of the process of negotiation is essential and the following areas deserve particular consideration.

(a) The relationship a negotiator has with his or her own organisation

Anyone entrusted with the responsibility of negotiating contracts should have a clear understanding of his or her levels of authority for the purposes of commitments to be made during negotiations, and should have unrestricted access to those responsible for making decisions which the negotiator is not empowered to make. Anything less, and negotiations are liable to procrastinate and even fail for lack of progress. Confusion in the camp can be of benefit only to the other side, which astute negotiators will certainly exploit. (Although there are certainly frequent instances in business negotiations of unempowered participants being used in the early stages, if this is done it should be a deliberate and carefully considered tactical ploy, not a failure by the party concerned to think through properly how it is to achieve its goals.)

It is important, therefore, to ensure that negotiators are well trained, not only in the techniques of negotiation, but also in both the immediate and broader business goals of the organisation. Properly briefed, a negotiator is then in a position to develop an appropriate plan, designed with timescales, prices, quality issues and all other relevant matters in mind, and to enlist the support and assistance of others within the organisation who may help to achieve a successful outcome.

(b) The reasons for having a negotiation

An understanding of these is a prerequisite to obtaining the right result in terms of the organisation's business goals. There will usually have been a broad decision to do business with the other party and therefore to want the negotiation to produce a positive result. For this reason, although often not recognised by sales personnel, there can be as much pressure on the buying side to produce a successful outcome as there is within the selling organisation. Occasionally, a buying organisation will embark on negotiations with several prospective vendors, but it is a poor use of resources all round for any detailed negotiating of terms and conditions to take place until a general decision to proceed with a particular supplier has been made.

From a sales perspective, it is not enough that there is a business opportunity to be pursued. Negotiations are costly, particularly when specialist departments or outside advisers are involved, and the usual risk-versus-reward analysis needs to be made. Negotiations can range from a telephone discussion on a number of key points, through to one or two meetings designed to enable quick final decisions to be made by both sides, up to a full-blooded negotiation, where every detail is hammered out in a full form agreement to be signed by senior executives of both parties. This latter type of negotiation can often take many months and involve several senior members of each organisation involved. Justification for a negotiation therefore needs to take into account the value of the business to the supplier, in terms of profitability, prestige, strategic importance related to future opportunities, or in difficult times even the chance to keep a workforce together and active, with an eye to improved prospects when there is an upturn in business generally.

Negotiations need not only be about the winning of new business. Particularly in the IT industry, where many contracts continue for a long period of time, a number of interim reviews will take place and negotiating skills can be just as important in ensuring a continuation, expansion or modification of an existing contract as they will be in gaining a new one. It is common for large ongoing contracts to incorporate quite detailed change control procedures, necessitating continual negotiations by project managers on detailed content and, at least where major changes are contemplated, the re-involvement of other members of the original team, for example finance and legal representatives.

(c) The need for careful preparation

A checklist of key points can be useful. Most specialist books on negotiation offer their versions of these. The following list is representative of the matters which need to be considered, in particular when preparing for a full negotiation of a major contract:

- **Clear objectives: a general or strategic plan**
  For example, a useful opening strategy for suppliers is to relate requests for changes in standard terms and conditions to pricing. On analysis, almost all standard terms can be amended on a costed basis, so that there need be no difficulty about agreeing to a longer warranty period, extended payment terms, a larger cap to limits of liability and so on. Even movement on things like intellectual property ownership and rights can be priced in theory, although generally the sums involved will make no rational sense to the buyer. As price will then become a focus itself for the negotiation, this approach can be effective in reducing the list of points for ongoing discussion and can on occasion dissuade a purchaser from pursuing some requested changes.

- **Appointment of a team leader and team**
  Too many negotiations take place on an impromptu basis, with the membership of the negotiating team varying from one meeting to the next, and with different individuals taking leading roles on different aspects without effective overall control. Pre-determined team leadership is essential and the leader, whether or not present at all meetings, should have the necessary authority to conclude a binding agreement (subject only to Board approval where the internal rules of the organisation require this, as many do for really substantial transactions).

- **Recognition of the balance of power**
  Negotiations have to be conducted with a sense of realism. Success needs to be measured against what would otherwise be the predictable outcome in the particular circumstances. A small supplier seeking business from a major purchaser is not going to be able easily to impose its own terms and conditions or normal ways of doing business. Every retained condition is going to have to be justified on the basis that it is necessary and not catered for by the purchaser's terms. On the other hand, the small supplier with a unique product may find itself in the stronger position when it comes to the negotiating table. This demonstrates the importance of having good and up-to-date knowledge about the competition, and wherever possible vendors should endeavour to obtain good intelligence about those of their competitors who have also made the short list.

- **Strengths and weaknesses of the participants on both sides**

  Very often, when a negotiation commences, several of the individuals involved have already come to know each other through their earlier discussions and perhaps previous dealings. Knowledge about strengths, weaknesses, particular areas of interest and personal goals can be helpful in planning the course and emphasis of the negotiation. Sometimes unfinished business from previous transactions may be resolved as part of a package generating new business. On other occasions, the balance of advantage will be served by isolating the old from the new. Business judgments such as these must be made and fed into the negotiation plan.

- **Relationships of the participants with their own organisations**

  Knowledge about the way individuals are regarded within their own organisations can be very valuable. Are they the people with 'clout' or are they regarded as relative nonentities? It may seem unkind to evaluate people in this way, but it is all part of understanding the true context of the negotiation. Also, what is the political influence of the individual's department within the organisation? Suppliers may find themselves negotiating with professional buying teams, but, underlying them, the real power is being wielded by the intended users of the system. This underlines the importance of gaining a full and accurate understanding of the opposing party's structure and business methods and styles in advance of serious discussions.

- **Scope for flexibility**

  Knowledge about the other side's business, its organisation and goals, the past history of dealings between the parties and the probable motivations of the other side for the proposed contract, are all examples of indicators as to the rigidity or flexibility of approach likely to be brought to the table by the other side. Such information can also be used to structure a proposal, for example a cash-rich customer may be attracted by a discount for payment in advance (supported if appropriate by a bank guarantee from the supplier's bank, this too being costed into the proposal); in another case, some sort of rentalised arrangement over time could be anticipated to appeal. Any proposal that demonstrates an awareness and understanding of the other party's circumstances and preferences is bound to stand a better chance of gaining acceptance.

- **Latest available information about the other party**

  This should include a company search, a financial appraisal and finding out about the other party's current organisational structure. Many companies employ credit managers these days and many of these have online access to computerised reporting services, so reasonably up-to-date information about financial strength can be obtained quite easily, and can be invaluable in some of the decision-making which will need to take place in the negotiation. Decisions will be based on such things as information about payment terms and credit limits, parent guarantees and whether or not it is desirable to include a change of ownership or control as a ground of termination.

- **Tactical possibilities, particularly at the outset**
  Is the other party likely to adopt an aggressive stance, or should one be adopted? Aggression in negotiation needs to be very carefully and sparingly used (that is, deliberate and controlled, perhaps because there is an opportunity to turn a previously suffered wrong to advantage, never in the form of uncontrolled anger), but it is another weapon in the armoury and might be appropriate in certain circumstances, depending upon the answers to some of the matters considered above, and in particular where there is unfinished business to be resolved.

- **Forward thinking and the development of alternative solutions**
  There must be a visionary element to negotiation. If likely areas of challenge can be identified and analysed, answers can already be formulated for anticipated questions, and if a range of outcomes can be visualised, the advantages and disadvantages of each one can be used to help steer the course of the negotiation.

- **Identifying concessionary areas**
  By the time serious negotiation gets under way, the parties often have a good idea about which of the areas are of greatest contention. In the context of a business's objectives, some issues are going to be sacrosanct whilst others will be of secondary importance. The latter should be identified and held in readiness for use as concessions when the trading of terms and conditions begins in earnest. For this reason it is essential to establish *all* areas of difference before making any concessions: to do otherwise exposes the conceding party to repeated use of the 'just one other thing' syndrome. Final positions should be reserved until there is confidence that everything is on the table.

- **Documentation**
  A carefully prepared agenda and well-constructed preparatory notes are prerequisites for each meeting, and especially for the first meeting.

- **Rehearsal with team**
  This level of preparation will obviously be inappropriate for use on every occasion, but its value cannot be over-estimated as a means of identifying all of the key issues and sharpening the arguments, and should be considered a very important part of the preparation for a major negotiation. It also serves to pull the team together on the project and help them relate to each other in the most effective way. Rehearsals may range from a formal get together in a pre-meeting to the first main meeting with the other side, through to a review of presentations intended to be made to the other side.

- **Reservation of sufficient time**
  One of the greatest pressures that can mitigate against success in a negotiation is shortage of time. Where this affects one side but not the other, it provides the latter with a distinct advantage. For any negotiation of consequence, sufficient time must be allowed for thorough preparation and for a negotiation with the other side which is not dictated by its time limits.

At the end of a long day, the person who wants to get home or on to another engagement is prone to make concessions and patience is then able to reap its reward.

B. Negotiating guidelines

As with preparation, a checklist of key points can be a helpful reminder. If reviewed by a negotiator on a regular basis, the list will become familiar. It is not offered or intended as an absolute set of principles but it does represent the chief considerations which should be borne in mind for the conduct of a major negotiation:

- **The team leader is the principal spokesperson**
  Generally but not always the team leader will be the most senior member of the team, having the authority to commit his or her organisation. Any constraints on this ability need to be made clear to the other side at the outset, and similar knowledge needs to be gained about the status of the other side's team leader. In addition to acting as principal spokesperson, the team leader's role is to control the team and to steer the course of the negotiation as much as possible. Team discipline should be such that kicks under the table because a team member has spoken out of turn and imprudently simply do not happen.

- **Use lawyers sparingly**
  Whether legal advice is obtained from an in-house source or from an outside adviser, it is a good policy to keep legal consultations in the background. As a general rule (and of course there will be exceptions, as with all rules) a lawyer should not be a member of the negotiating team unless it is known that the other side proposes to include a legal adviser in its team. Legal involvement in commercial discussions can tend to prolong them and frustrate commercial managers whose objective is essentially to close a deal. This is not to suggest in any way that a lawyer should not be consulted in the background. Commercial managers need to understand all of the terms and conditions being put forward, including legal implications which are frequently not apparent to the lay person, and it is an important part of the lawyer's role to ensure that the members of the negotiating team are fully aware of the legal issues and able to make informed business decisions. During the negotiation, any failure to agree points which the negotiating team has been advised should be regarded as non-negotiable can be referred back for further legal advice and suggestions about how the legal objections may be overcome. Sometimes it is helpful for the legal representatives of the parties to talk to each other in order to hammer out a solution which can be recommended to their respective principals, but this need not require the presence of the lawyers at the negotiating table. There is a strong argument for suggesting that, where it is necessary for a lawyer to be present at the negotiation, he or she should act as the team leader. If that role is not an

appropriate one in the circumstances, it must raise a question about the need for the legal presence in the first place, with its attendant implications of cost and formality.

- **Ensure all relevant materials and information are to hand**
  The thorough preparation recommended earlier will have produced all of the required information, organised and summarised for ease of reference. This documentation should be properly labelled and grouped for ease of reference. Numbered copies to identified individuals can be an important means of control where confidentiality is of particular importance.

- **Use of an agenda to lead the discussion**
  A surprisingly large number of meetings take place without a formal agenda having been prepared or agreed between the parties. This results in a good deal of wasted time and an unstructured discussion which can result in important areas being overlooked or given insufficient consideration. Ideally, agendas should be prepared and agreed in advance of a meeting, but with the flexibility to cater for last minute items in a review of the agenda at the beginning of the meeting. Development of an agenda helps to confirm or question in the minds of the parties the need for the meeting, and enables preparation for the meeting to be better directed. However, if an agenda has not been agreed in advance, the first task of the meeting should be to agree upon one. Occasionally there can be a tactical advantage in preparing an agenda but not showing it to the other side prior to the meeting, but generally such conduct is both unhelpful and discourteous.

- **Ensure the presence of decision makers**
  Unless it is an agreed preliminary meeting, planned as part of the overall process to identify the main problem areas for the negotiation proper, a lot of discussion will prove to be fruitless if the team leaders are not empowered to make decisions on behalf of their respective organisations. Time and again, lengthy negotiations take place at a detailed level, although any 'agreement' which is reached is then subject to ratification and approval by others who, if diligent, will want to review all of the arguments which resulted in the terms being placed before them. The negotiator is thus put into a position where someone from the other side is putting forward their understanding of its organisation's position, with the likelihood that issues thought to have been resolved come back to the table. This scenario can prolong a negotiation substantially, with all the attendant cost and business planning implications.

- **Adopt a constructive and persuasive attitude**
  Belligerence has no place at the negotiating table. Patience is needed and terms and conditions which are considered non-negotiable should be explained in a reasoned and logical manner. Constructive suggestions will always be far better received than intemperate criticism or unreasoned rejection of the other party's terms.

- **Use facts and arguments economically**

  It is often unnecessary to present the whole case in defence of a particular point, or even any of it on some occasions. If this is the position, hold back the unwanted information however much preparation has gone into it. It should be remembered that the whole purpose of the preparation was to win the point in question and if it has been conceded anyway, that particular objective has been achieved. Further, it cannot be assumed that all facts and arguments available for presentation will be convincing; the more that are presented, the greater the likelihood that some of them will be exposed as inaccurate, incomplete or unsustainable.

- **Aim high**

  This advice is generally included in published materials which advise on the conduct of negotiations and is no less sound for it. Most negotiators will assume that the other side will start out by asking for more than it expects to get anyway, and it is virtually impossible to negotiate upwards, from a previously conceded position. Aiming high is, therefore, more likely to produce an end result close to the original objective.

- **Always keep the objectives in mind**

  It is natural for people engaged in discussion to go off at tangents from time to time, as related points occur or because of one person's particular field of interest. The greater the numbers at the negotiating table (and those actually present should always be limited to the minimum number of representatives considered necessary to achieve the objectives) the more distractions there are going to be. It is vital therefore that the original objectives are always kept in mind, so that discussion can be steered back towards them and arguments structured to support them at every opportunity. Since both parties often have hidden agendas, a combination of determination and tact will be required to secure a successful result. It is a major responsibility of the team leader to ensure steady and logical progress towards the end goals and to keep the team members focused and on track.

- **Use concessionary areas wisely and tactically**

  It is essential to bring all of the issues on to the table before any concessions are granted. Unstructured discussions particularly tend to result in concessions being given on a point-by-point basis, without keeping the overall objectives in view. This can result in having to give away much more than was originally intended in order to reach an agreement. Once it is confirmed that all of the issues causing concern have been tabled, it is possible to make a proper assessment of the situation and to plan suitable trade-offs, with the aim of conceding less important points in order to secure agreement to points which are considered fundamental.

- **Make time count**

  Whatever the realities of the situation, it exposes a weakness to let the other side see that there are significant time constraints, except where it can be used to pressure the other side into making a decision, for example when a limited availability product is being sold and delay will increase the delivery lead time significantly. Letting the other side see that they themselves have no time can also be used as a negotiating advantage. Whilst it is desirable that negotiations be concluded in as short a time as possible, to minimise costs if for no other reason, there should be an availability and willingness to continue the negotiation for as long as it takes to achieve the original objectives. Let the other side be the ones to press for a conclusion.

- **Dealing with impasse**
  Sometimes impasse is unavoidable. Lengthy discussions simply fail to produce an acceptable compromise. If this point is reached, it is a good idea to agree to 'park' the issue and continue with the negotiation. When all aspects have been covered, any outstanding issues can then be re-considered in the context of what has been achieved overall. This will sometimes enable a concession to be made which will resolve the impasse. If not, the meeting will have to close so that internal discussions can take place to explore ways around it. Because the parties have decided at the outset that, in principle, they wish to do business with each other, it is rare for an impasse to result in a complete failure of the negotiations. The usual solution is to escalate the issue, if necessary so that it is discussed Chief Executive to Chief Executive. A Chief Executive is quite likely to make a winning concession that a subordinate would never have been permitted to make. A contingency plan can usefully be set up in advance, setting out the issues which should be escalated in the event of an impasse.

- **Using adjournments and postponements**
  It is never a good idea when negotiating as part of a team to explore ideas or to argue about an organisation's policies and practices in the presence of the other side. Knowledge may be assumed which is not there, and there may be ramifications to points put forward which are not realised by the speaker but which should not be revealed to the other side. 'Time-outs' are a perfectly acceptable device to enable a team talk to take place. Generally, the host organisation will be the one to withdraw to another room, either for an agreed period of time or until the other side sends a message that it is ready to resume. If a short adjournment (no more than half an hour) is not going to be sufficient, it may be necessary to postpone the meeting to another date. For this reason, time-outs should not take place until all of the issues have been tabled and the negotiation is foundering because a particular problem or series of problems cannot be resolved. (An exception is where a team member is persistently taking a line which has not been agreed, or is guilty of imprudent and potentially damaging behaviour.) Just like injury time at a football match, time-out also provides an opportunity to make a quick assessment of progress and to revise tactics in response to the way the negotiation is evolving.

- **Treatment of others**
  It is essential to cultivate a sensitivity to the status of others and their roles in their own organisations. Not every member of a team is going to hold a senior position within its organisation but each person's role must be

assumed to be regarded as important by the other side for the purposes of negotiation. The objective should therefore be to make such people allies and not provoke hostility by treating them or their comments dismissively.

- **Silence is golden**
  There comes a point in any negotiation where the other side is called upon to make a decision. Whatever the decision to be made, whether it is to place an order or to agree or concede a point, *once the question has been asked, wait for the answer.* Extrovert and enthusiastic sales people in particular find it hard to resist the temptation to say something further. Long silences are difficult to tolerate and there is a temptation to fill the space with sound. All this is doing, however, is to let the other side off the hook, providing them with additional thinking time and an excuse to say no or to counter with another question. It has been said that, when these decision-making points are reached and the question is hanging in the air, *the first one to speak loses!*

- **Maintain ethical standards of behaviour**
  This is most certainly not to be confused with 'softness'. It is perfectly possible to be a tough negotiator without in any way straying from the bounds of propriety or behaving in a less than courteous fashion to representatives of the other party. However, ethical conduct requires that an offer made and accepted is not withdrawn; it requires that when a concession has been granted, it is not immediately followed by a demand for a further concession on the same point; it requires that there are no disclosures of third party confidences; it requires that there are no illegal practices such as bribery; it requires truthfulness and honesty at all times; and it requires consistency of treatment between competitors.

- **What happens next?**
  The ideal position is that the negotiation has concluded successfully and it only remains for final agreements to be prepared, checked and signed. If this is not the case, a meeting should conclude with an action plan and timescale for both parties to pursue outstanding issues, and for a further appointment to be set as soon as possible after a reasonable time has been allowed for the agreed actions to be carried out. If such matters are left open, this provides an opportunity for further delay or prevarication, or worse still, a complete change of heart.

The extent to which specific guidelines should be followed is going to vary widely between one negotiating situation and another. Many of the ideas discussed above are not going to be consciously checked off on each negotiating occasion, but they should be sufficiently familiar to be followed in practice as a matter of course, and adapted as appropriate to meet the needs of the negotiating situation.

C. Training

(a) The benefits

Instinctive skills in negotiating are exceptional, although many people who would not consider themselves to possess particular negotiating skills manage to conduct their daily affairs in ways which enable them to achieve their objectives when dealing with other people. Whatever the inherent level of skill, training can produce levels of competence which will produce personal satisfaction and career achievements for the individual, and business success for his or her employer. Flair and quick, creative responses to problems can sometimes win the day, but more often success is due to thorough preparation, attention to detail and discipline in the negotiating environment. These are skills that can be learned or improved upon through the medium of training.

(b) Who should receive training?

In any business, all those involved in direct dealing with customers or suppliers should receive appropriate amounts of training to equip them suitably to meet their particular responsibilities for their employer. Training should therefore extend to pre- and post-sales support personnel, sales executives, buyers, sales and purchasing management, and senior management. Those in more junior positions should also be encouraged to acquire interpersonal skills which will enable them to deal more effectively with customers or suppliers. They are often in a position to introduce or confirm the administrative and product development processes of their employers and can help to set realistic expectations about what can be achieved by their organisations. A positive and constructive approach should be emphasised. Those in more senior positions are charged with the responsibility of doing business in accordance with their organisation's policies and practices and more emphasis needs to be placed on decision-making techniques and the actual process of conducting a business negotiation.

(c) Methods of training

There are many. The most common one probably continues to be experience gained on the job, observing colleagues and being permitted to undertake certain aspects under supervision. Whilst it may be true that more formal methods of tuition are no substitute for the real thing, there are obvious dangers. Experiences of being 'thrown in at the deep end' will no doubt develop some individuals' skills but others will fall by the wayside. This exposes the employer to financial risks arising from incorrect representations, lost concessions and disclosure of information which was not intended to be disclosed.

At the other end of the spectrum, carefully directed reading of the company's own product and procedural materials and publications about negotiation and interpersonal skills can be supplemented by appropriate video and cassette training, to allow basic knowledge to be acquired at the individual's own pace and in his or her own time. There are some excellent products available on the market today. Following on from this, use should be made of lectures, seminars and courses. These can be external or internal, the latter being particularly useful if numbers warrant them, as material can be tailored to an organisation's particular requirements and discussions can take place on subjects that would be regarded as confidential to outsiders. Knowledge can be tested in an informal manner with the use of multiple-choice questionnaires dealing with, for example, a company's standard terms and conditions, or products, or development and production methods, in each instance focusing on issues which tend to result in problems for the company if not presented and solved correctly.

Mock negotiations, especially with the aid of video recording and playback, can be a very entertaining and useful means of testing knowledge and negotiating skills, as long as feedback is immediate and constructive.

The majority of these methods are not in any way dependent upon the size of an organisation and even small companies will benefit from investment in this area.

(d) Subject matter of training

This should of course be related to the needs of the organisation. In the context of IT contract negotiations, for those actively involved in negotiation it should certainly include company policies and procedures, internal rules and constraints, actual levels of authority, relevant terminology and concepts, principles of contract law, preparing for negotiation, techniques of negotiation and good administration. The latter is important because, aside from good practice and compliance with legal obligations, a properly retained record of a negotiation may prove to be a critical factor in any subsequent negotiation with that same party. This includes use in dispute resolution, particularly where there is no written contract, or an incomplete one: far too frequently the case.

D. Standard terms and conditions

In most significant IT contract negotiations, it is common for both parties to want to start from their own standard terms and conditions of supply or purchase, as the case may be. It is less usual for contracting parties to agree at the outset that they should sit down and write a contract from scratch. This is principally on grounds of cost. The supplier in particular will have priced its product and service offerings on the basis of its terms and conditions and needs to be able to use its terms and conditions as a benchmark against which to judge the customer's demands and, where applicable, the impact of these on anticipated gross profit margins. This is a persuasive argument for most customers but some will feel strongly that they are the buying entity and accordingly should be in a position to dictate terms. Invariably, this will cause a supplier to incur additional cost, because one way or another the finally agreed scope and extent of the supplier's service obligations must be recorded in the contract documentation. If a supplier is foolish enough to contract beyond its capabilities or resources and if a customer is foolish enough to allow or insist on this, the parties will only have themselves to blame when the inevitable disaster occurs.

(a) Why have standard terms and conditions?

Aside from the relationship between terms and conditions and product prices, and the significant costs associated with writing an original contract, suppliers and customers alike gain the following advantages:

(i) They guarantee consistency. Suppliers are on shaky legal ground these days if they do not behave consistently towards their customers, essentially offering the same terms and prices to all those customers who have similar requirements. Unfair trading practices can be challenged, especially where there is any real dominance in a particular marketplace. Customers often expect the reassurance, by means of an express term of the contract, that no one else is obtaining better terms and will not do so for the duration of the contract.

(ii) They ensure that all relevant areas are covered. IT contracts generally contain a large number of detailed provisions, reflecting the issues which the parties ought to address before proceeding. Respective responsibilities, qualifications and exceptions need to be agreed, as well as the other commercial, operational and legal terms of the contract. Standard terms also serve as a checklist so that, even in a negotiation where it is agreed that the other party's terms will form the basis of the contract, there is a means to hand of ensuring that no matter of substance is overlooked.

(iii) They take full account of the business interests of the proposing party. Terms and conditions should not be included in standard forms if their absolute relevance to the organisation requiring them has not first been established by that organisation. The company must be committed to its published terms and conditions or there is little point in having them. Indeed, they can have a negative effect on customer relationships if each one cannot be defended on clear commercial and legal grounds. The reasons given may not be accepted by the other side, but they will at least be respected and will form the basis of a responsible dialogue, more likely to result in concession or compromise than in impasse.

(iv) They make certain that proprietary interests are identified and protected. Software products in particular are not protected adequately by the general law and licensing terms need to be spelled out in the contract. Any third party rights need to be reserved in products being supplied and rights generally need to be identified, defined, asserted and acknowledged.

(v) They make sure that limitations and any exclusions of liability are clearly stated. In a negotiated contract there is much less likelihood of such limitations or exclusions being held to be unenforceable, but there is a steadily increasing volume of case law which emphasises the need to be able to demonstrate a reasonable and rational justification for such departures from statutory principles. Both parties need to understand where the limits lie, and whether those liabilities which are offered and accepted, and those which are residual, can be covered by an appropriate type and level of insurance.

(vi) They protect policies and rights. Where the supply or purchase is of relatively low value, neither party is likely to be able to commit resources to a negotiation, on grounds of both cost and availability of staff. Standard terms, for suppliers in particular, are a means of ensuring that even low-value, low-volume product sales continue to reflect and safeguard their pricing policies and proprietary rights, provided that they are capable of being defended on grounds of reasonableness.

(b) Whose terms and conditions should apply?

In any contract negotiation, the first goal should be to gain this initiative. Suppliers are often able to establish their terms in computer contracts because few customer organisations will have terms which specifically address issues relating to computer products. On the rare occasions when standard purchasing terms and conditions even address software licensing, they are unlikely to anticipate all of the particular terms of licence which are being offered by the supplier. Special aspects, such as export and re-export restrictions on products of United States origin, will not be covered at all, and detailed provisions covering intellectual property rights will rarely be included, at least in a form acceptable to the supplier. This said, on any contract of substance, it is seldom in the interests of either party to agree wholesale to a set of standard terms and conditions. There will always be some objectionable provisions and, if the overall circumstances justify a negotiation, the opportunity should be taken to resolve all perceived issues. Although statute laws for the most part are strongly orientated towards the protection of buyers, the overriding principle illustrated by the maxim 'caveat emptor' ('let the buyer beware') continues to be sound advice.

No term or condition on any contract of substance should be accepted without the context and application of the clause being carefully considered. What is the clause actually saying? What exposure or risk does it create? What other parts of the contract does it affect? What points can be put forward as legitimate objections to the clause, either as phrased or in its totality?

(c) The 'Battle of the Forms'

It is essential for negotiators and order administrators to understand and apply the basic legal principles governing the making of a contract. There is little to be gained from undertaking the expense of preparing and publishing standard terms and conditions (of supply or of purchase) if administration procedures are so slack that they result in the other party's terms and conditions being accepted by default.

E. Government and other standard form purchasing contracts

Government and other standard form purchasing contracts are identified as a distinct category because suppliers are generally required to quote, tender and contract on the basis of the standard forms put forward, with a very limited opportunity to negotiate many of them. Contracts with major purchasing organisations tend to be large and/or prestigious, giving the organisation the initiative at the outset of negotiations. Of course, occasionally the supplier is in the happy position of offering a unique and important product, enabling it to establish its own terms and conditions of supply with rather more success than normal. However, even in the majority of cases where the size of the opportunity and the competitive situation induces suppliers to accept the standard terms put forward, there is still scope for some negotiation. Internal users of products can be very influential in the choice of supplier and it is not unknown for tender specifications to be drawn up (often with the assistance of an incumbent or user-favoured supplier) in such a way that they are capable of being accepted without qualification by only one or two suppliers with products which can fully comply. Whatever the situation, contract opportunities do not disappear solely on the grounds that purchasing terms and conditions have not been accepted without qualification. If a product or service is selected on its merits, there is almost always scope for negotiation of terms and conditions.

The published standard forms tend to be well known to specialists in government and other public sector contracting. Typically, a whole series of standard terms and conditions may be invoked as contract documents. Terms and conditions can be very numerous and contained in a multiplicity of documents. They are wide ranging and also tend to incorporate several provisions contractually obligating the supplier or contractor to comply with various statutes relating to such matters as the Official Secrets Act, the Race Relations Act, the Health and Safety at Work Etc. Act, and others, as well as requiring declarations in relation to such matters as equal opportunities and corrupt gifts. Having the force of contract provides grounds for termination for breach, in addition to the statutory or criminal penalties which may apply.

Provisions are often included which have no relevance to the contract under consideration and it is necessary to scrutinise each provision to determine its applicability, as well as to see whether its terms are capable of being complied with. Great care is needed to check all officially sourced terms and conditions used in a contract, to ensure that the supplier is capable of meeting the requirements of the contract. This is particularly important in areas such as acceptance testing, achievement of performance standards and 'up-time' guarantees, where there can be onerous consequences for non-performance by the supplier.

The security aspect which is present in many government contracts and other agreements with customers, who in turn have dealings with government, should alert suppliers to the need to brief their employees appropriately. Employees should be instructed not to sign confidentiality or security agreements in order to gain admission to customer sites, without first referring these back to head office for approval. It is unacceptable for any employee to be asked to sign a document which has not first been agreed with the supplier, and the supplier also needs to explain the import of such documents to its employees, giving these individuals the option to accept or decline the personal responsibilities established by such documents.

The Office of Government Commerce works with government to improve procurement and project or programme management processes[1]. It publishes operational and business guidance for suppliers on contract management and management of risk, as well as information and guidance on the myriad procurement regulations which have derived from EU procurement rules.

Notwithstanding the Government Procurement Code of Good Practice, a common feature of contracts with government or other quasi-official bodies tends to be a rather inflexible approach to contract negotiation, although single source products or very strong user group support can alter the balance in favour of the supplier. Strong competition certainly inhibits the prospects for negotiation (and the need to maintain equality between prospective suppliers is often invoked as the reason for inflexibility). When negotiations do take place they tend to be costly and time consuming, simply because of the sheer volume of provisions which need to be reviewed and agreed. This sometimes results in sending letters of intent, to encourage suppliers to commence performance in parallel with continuing negotiations. Letters of intent are generally unenforceable documents, depending on their precise wording, but suppliers need to ensure that at least they have binding contractual commitments ('authorities to proceed') in relation to preliminary work before it is undertaken.

Invariably a tendering process takes place, which may be in stages and quite extensive, before reaching the contract proper. The Government Procurement Code of Good Practice will apply and this Code is intended to ensure that the whole procurement process is fair. To enable costs to be kept within bounds, detailed contract negotiations should be reserved for the final stages when the supplier has been selected or short-listed.

As discussed in **CHAPTER 4**, it is necessary to take the greatest care when submitting tenders. Tenders may be 'invitations to treat', but they are more likely to be offers which, if accepted without qualification, will lead to binding contractual commitments. Suppliers should be very careful not to sign a declaration which is frequently included in tender documentation, confirming their acceptance of the various terms and conditions recited in the request to tender. It is also extremely important that all documents that are intended to form a part of the final contract are individually understood and approved before being permitted to become a contract document. Carelessness in this area can result in onerous obligations that at the very least may render a contract unprofitable to a supplier – which is of no long-term advantage to either party.

Where contracts are placed frequently which do not individually have a particularly high value, but which are cumulatively significant to both parties, this presents an opportunity to negotiate an umbrella agreement designed to operate for a stated period of time and usually renewable. The carrot to the purchaser is the prospect of a cumulative volume or value discount and it is usually possible to agree relatively short-form interim terms, pending conclusion of the main negotiation, after which the completed agreement will be agreed to apply retrospectively to the contracts commenced or performed while negotiations were in progress.

The Chartered Institute of Purchasing and Supply offers model forms of contracts to purchasing organisations. From a supplier's perspective, current versions are more balanced than older versions, but they remain firmly weighted in favour of the purchaser and include requirements which, almost certainly, will not have been contemplated when a supplier's standard product prices were being established. They will not necessarily be appropriate to the supply of specialised or unique products or services.

1   www.ogc.gov.uk.

CHAPTER 3
The legal environment

A. Introduction

Different territories have different laws and different ways of balancing opposing interests and of organising justice. Each political society has its own system of law. This book is written on the basis of English law, as affected by the laws of the European Union ('EU'). (It is strictly correct to refer to 'EC' law, since it stems from the original EC Treaties, and to refer to the 'EU' as the unit formed by the member states.) In the United Kingdom ('UK'), as in the other member states, it is necessary to take into account the increasing effect of EC legislation. These requirements are not restricted to transactions where one of the parties is in another member state, but may affect local business arrangements too. Yet in today's internationally oriented business climate the influences of foreign laws cannot be ignored either. This will clearly be the case where a contract involves a foreign element, perhaps because the products concerned are being imported or exported, or where a distributor's territory encompasses more than one country.

This chapter considers the basic features of the English legal system, its differences from other legal systems, and aspects of trading internationally, in the context of IT contracts. The EC legislative institutions are introduced. Two illustrations of the fundamental effect of EC legislation on IT businesses and contracts are discussed:

(1) the intellectual property rights of copyright, database right and patents; and

(2) competition law.

These and other EC laws will often be at the root of particular issues in other chapters, for example on e-commerce.

Institutions, structures and processes which it is easy to take for granted, are not universal. Such variations need to be borne in mind when preparing or negotiating a contract with international aspects.

B. Legal perspectives

The UK comprises Great Britain (the collective name for England, Scotland and Wales and the small adjacent islands excluding the Channel Islands and the Isle of Man) and Northern Ireland. In the UK there is one legislature, the UK Parliament, and three separate legal systems: England and Wales, Scotland, and Northern Ireland. The Scottish legal system has evolved from origins quite different from those of the legal system of England and Wales. The legal system in Northern Ireland is similar to that of England and Wales but has evolved in response to the unique political situation there. In the legal context, 'England' is synonymous with 'England and Wales'.

Common law – England and Wales, and the US

The legal system in England and Wales is a 'common law' system, in contrast with 'civil law'. There is neither a written constitution nor a comprehensive legal code. The principal difference is that the common law developed by custom, originally before written laws, by the pragmatic application of facts, creating case law. This judge-made law is one of the oldest sources of law.

Thus the sources of law are legislation – Acts of Parliament (statutes) and delegated legislation – and law made by the courts that create precedents through decisions made in actual cases, which may then be applied to subsequent cases where the facts are analogous. There is a hierarchy of courts within this system of judicial precedent. For a binding precedent to apply, the court must be more senior to or at the same level with the court in which the subsequent case is heard, and the facts of the cases must be sufficiently similar. A decision of the highest court – the House of Lords – is binding on every other court in the hierarchy. It is bound by no other court, except by the European Court of Justice on matters of EC law. It is not bound by its own decisions.

The United States (US) inherited the English legal system and shares the heritage of the history and values of common law, but the systems have developed independently. There are great differences in constitutional principles and political institutions. The US governmental system is complicated. The individual American states have separate laws, with an overlay of federal law, although on the whole there is a common legal tradition and culture. The Constitution of the US governs the nature and extent of federal legislative jurisdiction. Court and administrative structures vary from state to state.

As in the UK, statutory law in the US is subject to interpretation through case law. However, American law is based on the American Constitution as the supreme law, and statutes can be struck down by the courts if the courts consider them to be incompatible with the Constitution.

In US law there is a very broad distinction between intra-state and inter-state trade. Under the American constitution, the former is the sole province of the state concerned, while the latter may be regulated by the Federal Government in Washington DC. Thus, where goods and services are bought and sold purely within one state, that state has the sole right to enact laws regulating the conduct of such trade. Once goods and services cross state boundaries, then they fall under the jurisdiction of the Federal Government.

The US law of contract is not unlike the English law of contract. It used to consist only of case law but, in the last 50 years, statute law has become increasingly important. New laws have been created, and others have codified areas of contract case law, so that today there is a mix of original legislation, codes and cases.

The Uniform Commercial Code, the provisions of which apply mainly to traders, enables parties to stipulate which law should be applicable to their contract. Case law is also taken into account. Normally the law chosen must be related to the particular legal transaction. It has been adopted by all states except Louisiana and the Virgin Islands, although there are variations. Essentially, it codified English common law in relation to commercial business, with only a small distinctively American component.

As in Europe, there are laws in the US to encourage competition and prevent anti-competitive practices. These laws are referred to as 'anti-trust'. These developed from about a century ago when it was perceived to be necessary to break up the oligarchies which had formed in big business. State law also contains provisions about unfair competition and consumer protection.

Civil law systems

Civil law is derived from Roman law and is the basis of law in many countries, including many European countries, and also Scotland. It has developed from broad legal principles, and there may be a written civil code, such as the Napoleonic Code as the basis of French law.

Acts of Parliament consist of specific words, intended to apply definitively to the situation for which they are implemented. In contrast, in continental legal systems, legislation is often drafted more broadly than in England, with the intention of setting out the guiding principles to be followed. Legal precedent from court cases is far less significant. Courts in civil law jurisdictions do not develop new remedies or interpret the law as creatively as English courts may do in applying law to the particular facts of actual cases.

The Scottish legal system derives from civil law (it is not codified however), but also contains elements of common law, as the House of Lords is the final court of appeal in the UK for Scottish cases (apart from criminal cases), interpreting Scots law through English legal principles.

Thus, in situations where a commercial project or transaction involves parties from different jurisdictions, the legal principles and their application may well be viewed differently by each party. In the implementation of the Eurotunnel project, the English Chairman of Eurotunnel said: 'It is the story of the resolution of conflicts of legendary proportions between civil law in France and common law in England'.

Contract formalities

The rules as to whether a contract is validly formed differ between jurisdictions. What constitutes an enforceable contract under another legal system may not be a contract which could be enforced under English law. In English law, it is in general necessary for there to be some feature of 'bargain' in a contract, known as 'consideration'. A promise to carry out an action that has no element of bargain and is not made under seal is not valid under English law; in legal terminology there is no 'consideration' for the promise. This is discussed further in **CHAPTER 4**. Thus, a commitment to keep an offer open for a certain length of time is not binding as such under English law. However, it could be binding under other legal jurisdictions, Scottish law being one example.

There are material differences between the Scottish and English law of contract, as well as in the terminology. Different rules apply to making a contract which is legally binding and to proving that a contract was made. A unilateral, voluntary obligation promised or undertaken by one party and communicated to the other can be binding in Scottish law. In both systems there are rules relating to when a contract has to be in writing.

English law requires a positive acceptance to a contractual offer. In other jurisdictions, a contract can be created without this step. In England, if post is agreed to be a method of accepting a contract, the acceptance takes effect from the moment the letter is posted, even if the letter is delayed or lost in the post, and a contract will be brought into effect. This is the same as in the US. Most countries in Europe have other rules, and a contract would therefore be formed at a different time, or perhaps not formed at all if the letter did not reach its destination. In Germany, a posted acceptance is valid when it is delivered. In France, a posted acceptance takes effect when it is read by the addressee.

Again, the formalities for creating a legally binding contract may vary; requirements for witnesses to the signing of the document, and other ingredients required to make a document legally effective, may differ.

Exporters should also be aware of the terms which may be implied into a contract under local law, which do not need to be expressly set out in the contract to apply. For example in France, the court automatically has a discretion to consider the good faith of the parties' performance of the contract, as a result of the Civil Code requirement for parties to carry out a contract in good faith. In general there is no implied duty of 'good faith' in English contract law.

Harmonising international trading contracts

International trade is facilitated by Conventions and Treaties made between nations, which reach consensus on the subject matter and then incorporate the points of agreement in their national legislation. The various Treaties establishing and modifying the European Community in its different forms and creating and expanding the European Union are examples of this.

The United Nations Convention on Contracts for the International Sale of Goods, the Vienna Convention, was drawn up by the United Nations Commission on International Trade Law ('UNCITRAL'), which was established to help remove barriers to international trade[1]. Now UNCITRAL devotes its efforts to harmonising international trade law, for example by reports and recommendations, drawing up voluntary codes and model laws, publishing information and working with other organisations with similar interests, such as UNIDROIT – the International Institute for Unification of Private Law, and ICC – the International Chamber of Commerce.

This Convention applies to contracts for the sale of goods between parties having their places of business in different states if either state is a contracting state, or when conflicts lead to the application to the contract of the law of a contracting state[2]. Although 'goods' are not defined, it does not apply to contracts where the greater part of the obligations consist of labour or other services[3]. It covers contract formation, delivery, conformity of the goods, payment, remedies, breach and damages. In order for the Convention to be acceptable in countries representing a variety of legal traditions, it does not cover all aspects of sales law, for instance not the point at which risk transfers.

It has been ratified (in whole or in part) by over 60 states since 1988 accounting for over two-thirds of world trade, including France, Germany, Italy, and Australia. Neither the UK nor Japan is a signatory. In the US, the Convention overrides the Uniform Commercial Code where there is conflict – because the Convention is federal law – in respect of the contractual matters to which it applies.

The parties may choose to opt out, by specifying clearly in the contract that it should not apply, for example:

> This Agreement will be governed by and construed according to the laws of [...]. Pursuant to Article 6 of the 1980 United Nations Convention on Contracts for the International Sale of Goods, the parties agree that the Conventions will not apply to this Agreement.

It is also good contractual practice if the Convention does apply, to say so expressly, for example:

> The terms of this Agreement will be governed by and construed according to the 1980 United Nations Convention on Contracts for the International Sale of Goods.

Which law applies?

Determining which law governs a contract and which courts have jurisdiction to deal with a dispute, will depend on the exact circumstances of forming the contract, the wording in the contract, the effect of the contract, the status of the parties, and the locations involved. In practice, there will therefore be a number of considerations, including the value of the transaction concerned.

The governing law and jurisdiction should always be stated in contracts where there is any possibility of an international element. This clarifies what may otherwise be a complicated issue. English law and jurisdiction can be specified for contracts which are effective beyond England and Wales. This choice of law will be respected within the EU with certain exceptions, particularly those relating to consumers. However, certain other countries and states claim the right to impose their own domestic laws in any event.

A UK vendor trading with businesses outside the EU, for example with the US, may be subject to the jurisdiction of the laws of the state where the business is situated. Terms and conditions of software originating in the US may have a clause relating law to an American state, even though the contract was made in the UK for software to be used in the UK. The user will therefore not obtain the benefit of English legal protection, for example limiting exclusion of liability, and may unwittingly become subject to conditions which appear to be totally unreasonable from an English law perspective.

This underlines the importance of expressly agreeing jurisdiction in the contract, whether or not the contract is being made with a European party, so that as far as possible the parties remain in control.

Governing law

Laws governing the contract affect the interpretation of the contract, aspects of contractual performance, and whether there has been a breach of contract. Each country will have its own set of rules on what happens should conflict arise over the laws which govern the contract.

Within the EU, the Rome Convention 1980[4] determines which legal system applies to the contract. The initial principle is that the parties are free to choose the governing law and state this in the contract[5]. Therefore, if there is a 'choice of law' clause in the contract (the practical considerations of the 'choice of law' provision

35

in a contract are discussed in **CHAPTER 6**), then the legal system which has been selected will apply. Otherwise, the contract will be governed by the law of the country with which the contract is most closely connected[6]. However, the choice of law may be displaced by mandatory rules of another jurisdiction or by other rules in respect of particular kinds of parties or transactions, for example those relating to employees or consumers.

In e-commerce contracts within the EU, EU providers of commercial electronic services are subject to the laws of the member state in which they are 'established', with certain limitations[7]. This is known as the 'country of origin' approach. 'Established' refers to the geographical location from which the business pursues its economic activities, not the technological location. Contracts relating to copyright are one of the exceptions to this, in that any legal requirements applicable in the customer's jurisdiction must be taken into account.

Jurisdiction

The jurisdiction for a contractual dispute is the legal forum that has the right to hear the dispute, rule on it and enforce it. It is not necessary that it should be the same law as the governing law of the contract, although clearly there are many advantages if it is. The forum is not bound to apply its own law if the governing law of the contract is different.

Where jurisdiction has not been expressly chosen in an international contract, the jurisdiction applicable will depend on whether a Convention is in effect between the nations whose jurisdictions are involved. In the EU, the Brussels Regulation[8] applies for all member states except for Denmark[9].

The basic rule is that a defendant in a civil and commercial action may be sued in his or her country of domicile. For companies, 'domicile' means where the company is incorporated or where its central administration or principal place of business is[10]. Residence and a 'substantial connection' with the UK constitutes UK domicile for an individual. A claimant may take action in the courts of the place of performance of a contract – where the goods or services were, or should have been, delivered or provided.

However, consumers may bring proceedings in their own jurisdiction or in the supplier's jurisdiction at their option, but may themselves be sued only in their home courts.

Where the jurisdiction is one to which the Brussels Regulation does not apply, the rules will be in accordance with any bilateral or multilateral Convention or, if there is none, the rules of the particular jurisdiction.

C. The European Union

The EU came into being in 1993 with the ratification of the Treaty on European Union signed at Maastricht by its then member states. This controversial Treaty combined previous European Community Treaties as amended, with the addition of further policies and statements.

The original objectives were to raise the living standards of people within the member states by eliminating all obstacles to intra-Community trade and merging the national markets into a single Common Market. This was therefore designed to facilitate the free movement of economic resources (comprising people, services, capital and goods), throughout the member states. To this has been added economic and monetary union.

EU institutions

Four important EU institutions are the European Commission ('Commission'), the Council of the EU, formerly the Council of Ministers ('Council'), the European Parliament and the European Court of Justice ('ECJ').

The Commission is the executive and administrative arm of the EU. Its main purposes are to research policies, and to draft and present proposed EC legislation to the Council of the EU. It also negotiates on behalf of member states in multilateral and bilateral trade matters and in agreements with non-member countries. It consists of Commissioners and an EU civil service. The Commissioners are appointed by mutual agreement from the member states for a five-year term, although they are required to act solely in the interests of the EU.

In the decision-making processes, lobbying is important and consultation is encouraged with those affected by the proposals put forward for legislation at all stages of the EC policy-making and legislative processes. Lobbying has a better chance of being effective at the initial stages of proposed legislation. The Commission seeks assistance from experts in the field concerned. Officials rely on information and learn from practical experience in the industries covered by their proposals.

The Council is the principal legislator, although before adopting legislation it consults with the European Parliament and other relevant advisory bodies.

The European Parliament is an elected body, with elections every five years, membership depending on the size and importance of the member states. Members sit by political groupings rather than by national interests. Voting is on a majority basis. Its functions include an amending role in legislation; a budgetary role in the right to amend 'non-compulsory' expenditure; and it may censure the Commission. It has specialist committees where draft legislation will be scrutinised.

Within each committee a 'rapporteur' is appointed to study a proposal in detail and to prepare a draft report which will be discussed. This is another opportunity for lobbying on any particular matter.

The function of the ECJ is to keep a check on the balance of powers between the EC law-making institutions and the member states. It has jurisdiction to give rulings on the interpretation of the original Treaties. It is a forum for actions brought against member states themselves by the Commission or by other member states, against Community institutions by individuals, and for references to it from national courts on points of EC law. It consists of independent judges, assisted by Advocates General. Most issues involving member states or an EC institution are heard by a full court, although relatively simple issues will be heard by a bench of three to five judges. Decisions are made by majority vote with no scope for dissenting judgments and the procedure is inquisitorial (a civil law concept, not adversarial as is the common law approach). Cases are first assigned to an Advocate General, who will provide a reasoned Opinion for the court – but the Opinion does not have to be followed.

There is also a Court of First Instance, which has limited jurisdiction, including competition cases, and there is a possible right of appeal to the ECJ.

EC law

The purpose of almost all EC legislation is to harmonise the varying regulatory and legislative environments of its member states, who must apply the law as set out in the Treaties or in EC legislation. National legislation resulting from the EC law must match the requirements of the EC Treaties or legislation, no more and no less, unless permitted under the individual EC law.

Primary legislation in the EU consists of the Treaties themselves and other agreements of equivalent status. These agreements and any subsequent amendments to them are subject to ratification in national parliaments and in the European Parliament.

Secondary legislation comprises all the types of laws that can be made by the Institutions. Recommendations and Opinions may be made by the Council or by the Commission, but have no binding effect. A Decision of the Council of the EU or of the Commission is directly binding on those to whom it is addressed, which may be a state, a commercial enterprise or an individual. A Regulation is binding and directly applicable in all member states.

A Directive is normally proposed by the Commission and ratified by the Council. It is brought into effect in each member state by means of its own national legislation, to achieve the result by any date for implementation set out in the Directive. In the UK, this is either through an act of Parliament or by statutory instrument.

D. Intellectual property rights

'Intellectual' property is the ownership of intangible works involving some extent of creative effort, such as music, literary works, dance, design and so on, in contrast to real property such as freehold ownership in land or personal property such as jewellery. Software is one kind of intellectual property. It is not a disk or tape which is important in software, but the intellectual creation itself which has the value of invested effort. Intellectual property rights enable their owner to have some control over the use, publication and copying of the subject matter. Legally and practically they have an economic value. Profits may be made from their commercial exploitation. In IT, the intellectual property of a company may be its prime, or even only, asset.

Each legal jurisdiction has its own laws, which may vary substantially, for protecting intellectual property rights, as for laws in respect of other kinds of property. UK laws differ from those in the US or anywhere else. Several EU Directives have already been implemented in member states' legal systems as part of the process of harmonising various aspects of intellectual property law in the EU.

It is important that proper account should be taken in a contract of any intellectual property rights, and this is especially important for an international transaction. Reliance should not be placed on national laws, which may be restricted in the protection they afford the owner of the intellectual property, or in some cases are non-existent.

The intellectual property rights of copyright, database right and patents deserve special attention in the context of IT contracts. The two guiding principles of which organisations should be aware are: first, to protect intellectual property which they own and may wish to exploit, and second, to be properly entitled to use intellectual property which they do not own.

Copyright

Copyright is the main way at law in which intellectual property rights in software are protected. It is the right to authorise or prohibit copying of a work. It prevents the expression of an idea from being copied. It does not prevent the idea itself from being appropriated, nor does it prevent the independent creation of the same form of expression. If completely coincidentally two programmers, each acting independently, developed a program which in both cases happened to be written in the same lines of code, there would be no breach of copyright. The earlier expression would not be protected. There would have been no copying by either party.

Copying includes storing any work in any medium by any means and in any form, including electronically. Viewing or downloading any material from the Internet constitutes copying. When a copyright work is digitised, different layers of copyright may exist: copyright in the original work itself, such as the copyright of the creator, and copyright in the digitisation, that is the copyright of the person creating the digital image. If a work is digitised and then the digitisation is enhanced or manipulated, there could be another layer of copyright. Multimedia will have its own copyright and there will be copyright in the individual layers, such as third party graphics. Each copyright owner's consent and licence will be needed before legitimate use. For such digital works, there may be automatic digital rights management systems embodied in or attached to the work, providing a fast and easy tool for users to secure licences for the use of particular content – and for rights owners to collect information about usage. These new licensing systems, combined with other technology are a means of maintaining control over who gets access to digital material, and what they may do, for example in ensuring that works are copied only in limited ways or over a limited time.

The Berne Convention[11] is the most widely observed international treaty relating to copyright, to enable trade in intellectual property to be carried out between the signatory countries. The Convention originated in 1886, long before computers were invented or software first created, and software is treated for copyright purposes in the same way as 'literary works' under the Convention. 'Literary works' does not refer to any merit in the work, and includes text, novels, instructions, lyrics and newspaper articles. No formalities are necessary to obtain copyright protection. The US joined the Berne Convention in 1989. Another copyright convention, the members of which include the US and a number of Latin American countries, is the Universal Copyright Convention. This applies to works created within the territory or by a national of any of its members throughout all of the member states. It requires a copyright notice on published works. In some jurisdictions, a deposit of the work or its registration is necessary before protection applies. For works which were first published outside the country requiring such formalities, a formula consisting of the symbol (©), the name of the copyright owner and the year of first publication is deemed to meet the requirements. This formula is used far more widely, as it is a harmless method of indicating copyright ownership.

The Software Directive[12] harmonised copyright protection for computer programs throughout the EU, implemented in the UK by regulations which amended the main copyright laws[13]. The Directive requires programs to be protected by copyright as for literary works, following the Berne Convention. Under the Directive, a 'lawful acquirer', a licensee of the program, is permitted to carry out any form of copying which is necessary for the program to be used, and in order to make a security back up, without having to obtain express consent. Error correction will be permitted, but this will be only for the purpose of enabling the program to run. It will not affect the need for proper maintenance and support arrangements to be made. A lawful licensee is entitled to analyse the underlying code, copy and translate the program and investigate the functioning of the program to determine its ideas and principles, without the consent of the copyright holder, to the extent necessary to achieve the interoperability of an independently created program with other software, subject to compliance with a number of conditions: 'reverse engineering' or 'decompilation'. The information necessary must not already be 'readily available'. Moreover, only those elements of the program necessary to achieve interoperability may be copied.

The World Intellectual Property Organisation ('WIPO') is an organisation that promotes intellectual property rights internationally. It created a legal framework to facilitate communication and exploitation of online copyright works and to safeguard the rights of copyright holders in two Internet Treaties[14] which came into force in 2002. The US Digital Millennium Copyright Act of 1998 is based on the Treaties. In the EU, the Copyright Directive[15] enacted the provisions of the Treaties. In the UK, implementation was by means of the Copyright Regulations[16] amending copyright legislation. Copyright holders of online material – authors, performers, broadcasters, etc – have exclusive rights to control reproduction or copying and distribution of their work, and the right to control electronic transmission, including 'on demand' access by the public from a place and at a time individually chosen.

One mandatory exception is that temporary and transient incidental copying like browsing and caching must be permitted if it forms an integral and essential part of a technological process; and has no independent economic significance. For example, there will be no liability for browsing the Internet on a home PC, or for Internet service providers acting as intermediaries. There are also several optional exceptions which each member state was able to choose whether or not to implement. One was for 'fair dealing', permitting copying for non-commercial research and private study.

One of the key requirements of the international copyright treaties was that all signatory states should offer legal protection to copy control technologies – those that control access, copying and use of copyright works, such as encryption technologies. These enable record companies and webcasters to control their rights – to prevent a user from unauthorised copying. Equally it is necessary to constrain the manufacture and sale of products and services that get round the copy control systems Thus the law seeks to use technology in enforcing copyright law, making it illegal for example, to circumvent a technological protection measure – access to protected digital works is legal only through software or hardware approved by the creator of the digital format. This encourages the application of digital rights management methods as a means of protecting the interests of all parties.

Copy protection was seen to be increasingly important for digital media, to support legal rights. As a result, through the Copyright Directive, all member states have to allow the use of technological measures, such as encryption, to protect copyright works. They must prohibit devices intended to circumvent copy control systems (such as a pirate chip which interfaced with Sony Playstation technology to extend its unauthorised use[17]); or which remove or alter electronic rights-management information to identify ownership, such as electronic watermarks.

The creator of the work, or the employer if the work was developed in the course of employment by an employee, is the first copyright owner and no formality is necessary to establish this right, although in the US, copyright registration provides a more reliable form of protection. Ownership may be transferred by assignment, one of the few agreements which requires certain formalities to be effective. In IT, services of freelance contractors and consultants are commonly commissioned. The contractors will retain copyright in the software, website structure, documentation or manuals which they develop, even though they may be paid for writing code to a specification according to instructions from their client, unless the terms of their written service agreements, or other forms of contracts, provide otherwise. If the intellectual property is created by a contractor, and express terms are lacking, that contractor will own the legal rights and the commissioning client will not have full legal ownership, only an 'equitable' interest in that it has paid for the development. This is of limited practical benefit. The company may be able to enforce its equitable interest (and right of use) against the contractor by taking legal proceedings, but will not be able to assign ownership of the intellectual property rights to a third party, or grant licences to use the programs, text or data without the consent of the contractor – and will almost certainly have to pay for that consent.

It is useful for a commercial enterprise to own copyright in work which it is exploiting in order to make profits out of it. If not, copyright ownership is usually not really necessary. Instead, the right to use the material is what counts, normally for internal use within the licensee's organisation. However, if a team of contractors is working together on developing software for a software project, the most practical way of dealing with the results may well be for it to be in the ownership of a single party. For website material or for software which the user may need to develop further using the services of different contractors from the original developer, there is also often a good argument for the user to own the copyright.

The few software-related cases on copyright infringement which reach the English courts often concern ex-employees or former consultants using software commercially which is alleged by the former employer or client of the consultant to have been copied. One High Court case was over infringement of software which had been developed for stock control and labelling for pharmacy shops[18]. The defendant had previously worked at various times as a contractor and an employee of the company claiming copyright infringement in their software. Later, working with his own company, he had developed software, also for pharmacy shops. With the assistance of experts, the court compared against the original programs those programs alleged to be infringing by copying the general scheme of the earlier programs, even though a different programming language had been used. Several elements of similarity were found, some resulting from copying three features of the original programs. The issue of fact was then whether this represented a 'substantial' enough part of the original, this test being necessary to prove infringement. It was decided that even though the evidence was that there had been no direct, deliberate copying of lines of code, there had been infringement in those three features of the software, but other similarities were not significant.

In another case, the defendants, a new company called Tradition, recruited a programming team previously employed by Cantor Fitzgerald (the claimants), inter-dealer brokers in bonds in London[19]. Within three months, this team had produced front office software for their new employer in the same programming language as Cantor Fitzgerald's systems. They admitted some copying of source code, including downloading it, which in itself was copyright infringement. However, only a very low percentage of code was actually copied. Wholesale copying was not proved. The judge considered that the Tradition programmers wanted to use the code to see what they had done before, in order to write better and different programs, not to copy it. The interrelationship of the originality of the work and the substantiality of the part of the work copied was again significant, as in the pharmaceutical software case mentioned above. Whether a part is 'substantial' must be decided by its quality rather than by its quantity, and by the skill and labour in the design and coding. So Cantor Fitzgerald failed in their claim of infringement in respect of all the modules which Tradition denied copying. One of the problems for Cantor Fitzgerald was that there were no terms in their employment contracts about copyright, confidentiality and restrictive covenants to bind their ex-employees.

There are also certain 'moral rights' for individual authors, including the creator's right to be identified as the author and the right to have the integrity of the work respected by preventing its distortion[20]. However, these must be asserted on initial publication, and do not fully apply to software nor to those works where copyright vests in the employer.

Copyright in software, as for literary works, extends for 70 years beyond the author's death[21]. There is a 50-year period in respect of computer-generated works, commencing from the end of the calendar year in which a work is 'made', that is, brought into existence. It takes some imagination to envisage the length of the copyright period in itself as being of any relevance for software.

Database right

Collections of information are becoming increasingly important, and electronic databases have become essential to handle information storage and retrieval on a large scale. A database right applicable in the EU prevents unfair extraction or re-utilisation of databases[22]. These are defined as a collection of independent works, data or other materials arranged in a systematic or methodical way and individually accessible by electronic or other means. For example a telephone directory is a database, as is an anthology of poems in book form, or – from the first database case to reach the courts in England and Wales – fixture lists of races and associated data compiled and published by the British Horseracing Board.

The individual materials in the database themselves may be subject to copyright. And if the database is original in terms of its structure or in the collection and presentation of the materials, that is to say that if the collection of material is arranged in such a way that the compilation is the author's own intellectual creation, then it too will be protected by copyright. However, 'intellectual creation' is a higher standard, as it applies to databases, than is required for other copyright material.

If there is not enough originality of selection or arrangement for the database to qualify for copyright protection according to these criteria, it may nevertheless be protected by the database right.

The right prevents extraction or re-utilisation of all or a substantial part of database materials or the repeated extraction or re-utilisation of an insubstantial part of database materials by anyone without the owner's consent. The term of the database right lasts for 15 years from the beginning of the year following completion of the database. 'Completion' is a significant term in relation to databases, many of which are frequently modified, updated and improved, especially many electronic databases, which are the subject of constant change. The making of these is never actually completed in the way in which written or printed work is completed.

The 'maker' of an EU database is the person who takes the initiative in obtaining, verifying or presenting its contents, and assumes the risk of investing in that obtaining, verifying or presentation. This is a different criterion from the person first entitled to copyright, the author. If the database is made by any employee in the course of employment, then, subject to any express agreement to the contrary, the employer will be regarded as the maker – as for copyright.

A 'maker' must qualify for the database right, by being a national of, or habitually resident in, an EEA state (European Economic Area state – the EU member states together with Norway, Iceland, Liechtenstein); or a corporate body or partnership which was incorporated or formed under the law of an EEA state and with its central administration or principal place of business within the EEA, or its registered office within the EEA and its operations linked on an ongoing basis with the economy of an EEA state.

Patents

A patent is a monopoly right granted for a term of 20 years for an invention which is capable of industrial application. The details of the invention are recorded in public registers. It gives the inventor, or the inventor's employer who has made significant investment in research and development of technologies and processes for industrial application, the chance of a return on that work and investment. The owner of a patent has the exclusive right to prevent others from making or dealing in the invention, and can authorise exploitation, deal in it itself or license or assign the right. The owner must stay alert to infringement, whether intentional or inadvertent, and be prepared to enforce the patent where necessary in the courts of the territory in which it has been granted. Moreover, no evidence of 'copying' is required. Unlike copyright or database right, it is irrelevant whether anyone else is deliberately or inadvertently dealing in a similar invention.

In applying for a patent, secrecy is vital. If the idea for the patent is disclosed, except under the terms of a non-disclosure agreement or to anyone professionally bound by equivalent rules of confidentiality, the application will fail.

To be patentable in the UK, the invention must be new, involve an inventive step, be capable of industrial application, and must not be one of the statutory exceptions, one of which is 'software as such'. However, software inventions with a technical effect may be patentable, such as hardware incorporating software which is machine-dependent or a system for co-ordinating communications between networked programs and data. In the UK and also within other European countries, 'schemes, rules or methods for doing business' are not patentable. Many other countries do not grant patents for software inventions, or grant patents only within limited circumstances. On the other hand, the US readily grants patents for software, including software for business methods. There is a rapidly increasing number of US computer-implemented 'business method' patents. Controversy continues to rage in the EU on whether software itself should be patentable, partly to close the increasing differences with the US in this area, although US patents are more often challenged in the courts.

Because patents are national rights, separate applications must be made to all national patent offices where patent protection is required. However, in Europe it is possible to make one application to the European Patents Office in Munich for patents in those countries which are signatories to the European Patent Convention. The grant is for a collection of individual national patents, not just one, because consequences may differ between countries in enforcing patent rights. Each will be subject to the national laws of all the countries concerned, and a valid patent has to be expensively translated into the languages of each country. Moreover each country's approach to patent litigation is different. This means that proceedings often need to be taken in a variety of jurisdictions – with attendant costs, expenditure of effort and time, and complexity. Proposals have been put forward to establish a single European Patents Court for litigating European patents, for the signatory states to the European Patent Convention.

A single Community Patent, which is enforceable throughout the EU, should be an inexpensive and simple alternative way to protect new inventions. Yet this is easier said than done. Negotiations have been ongoing for the last 30 years without agreement being reached.

E. Competition law

The objectives of EC competition law are to create an open and unified market throughout the EU; to avoid abuse by dominant companies of their position; to achieve fairness in the EU market place; and to maintain the competitive position of

45

the EU in the global economy. What follows is a very brief outline of EC competition law. UK competition law, which closely relates to EC competition law, is also discussed.

This is a complex area of law, which has the added difficulty of inherent conflict with intellectual property law: for example, a patent, a statute-based monopoly, versus the perceived need to promote competition. If it may be applicable to an IT contract, specialist advice is essential. It is important to apply the law correctly. Sanctions include imprisonment for cartel activity, fines, disqualification of directors and the contract being unenforceable.

Articles 81 and 82[23] contain the major provisions governing anti-competitive market behaviour which may affect trade between member states. As Articles, they are directly applicable in member states, and cannot be ignored whenever contractual circumstances fall within their ambit. Any contractual provision purporting to restrict trade in a way prohibited by arts 81 or 82 would be legally unenforceable.

National Competition Authorities and national courts will apply the EC competition rules using their own national procedures (in parallel to national competition law) whenever there is an effect on trade between member states. They will be able to award damages to companies who have suffered from other companies' breaches of competition rules.

Article 81

Article 81(1) of the EC Treaty prohibits agreements or concerted practices which have as their object or effect the prevention, restriction or distortion of competition within the EU, and which may affect trade between member states. An agreement containing restrictions caught by art 81(1) will either fall within the exemption criteria set out in art 81(3), and therefore be valid and enforceable, or will not meet those criteria and will be prohibited. Article 81(3) permits agreements which improve production or distribution, or which promote technical or economic progress, provided that they allow consumers a fair share of the benefit, contain only indispensable competition restrictions, and do not eliminate competition. It is for the parties to the agreement to prove that it meets these criteria. The standard of proof is high.

However, the Technology Transfer Block Exemption Regulation ('TTBER')[24], together with a set of guidelines[25], sets out the rules for exempting certain intellectual property agreements from the application of the competition rules in art 81(1). These include agreements for the production or provision of licensed products, including patents, know-how and software copyright licences. Simple agreements for the distribution of packaged software by a licensee without added value are excluded.

A block exemption is a regulation which automatically confers exemption on certain agreements which contain potentially anti-competitive clauses, but which comply with all of the block exemption's requirements. This is in order to recognise that, in certain circumstances, although competition may be harmed, the benefits overall of a particular arrangement will outweigh the harm. Research and development costs for a product can be high, and an exclusive arrangement such as a distribution agreement, which is valuable to the distributor, may be a way of recouping some of the initial costs invested by the principal party.

For the TTBER to apply, the combined market share threshold for competitors must not exceed 20 per cent of the relevant technology or product market, and for non-competitors, 30 per cent for each party. Restrictions on prices, outputs or sales, and market or customer allocation restrictions, are prohibited in any event.

The parties to an agreement have themselves to assess its legality on the basis of the TTBER rules and guidelines to decide whether it is not anti-competitive, and is therefore legally enforceable, by establishing that the pro-competitive effects of the agreement outweigh the anti-competitive effects. Again, they have a high standard of proof to meet.

The rules differ depending on whether the parties are competitors or not, and the exemption will apply only where the parties have low market shares in the relevant technology and product markets. The parties are held to be competitors if, in the absence of the agreement, they would have been actual or potential competitors in any relevant technology, geographical or product market affected by the agreement. Other restrictions differ for agreements between competitors from agreements between non-competitors. For competitors, sales restrictions are generally not permitted, nor are restrictions on the ability of the licensee to use its own technology or to carry out research and development. For non-competitors, certain contractual restrictions are permissible, such as restricting the territory where, or the customers to whom, the licensee may passively sell the contract products with a number of exceptions; a restriction of sales to unauthorised distributors is one such exception.

There are practical difficulties in interpretation; assessing whether a particular technology transfer agreement is within the scope of the TTBER; whether the parties to the agreement are defined as competitors for the purposes of the TTBER; the need to review the market shares of the parties from time to time to check that the agreement is still covered by the TTBER. Thus there is a clear case for taking expert advice if it looks as if art 81 is relevant to an agreement.

Article 82

Article 82 seeks to prevent 'abuse of a dominant position' in a particular market which adversely affects trade between member states, by a company in a dominant position within the EU. A dominant company distorts the competitive structure in its market and would find no difficulty in making a competitor company's position untenable. It is therefore not permitted to take advantage of its market power to exploit those with whom it deals. This can occur with a dominant company's refusal to supply existing customers with products, or excessive pricing, or discriminatory terms.

'Dominant position' relates to the particular market in which the company operates and the calculation of its market share, including any other relevant factors such as superior technological knowledge and sales network. Defining the market is not always easy, especially in a technology context. It may relate to a small market in specialised products. A company may be dominant where a market is dependent on its particular supplies such as spare parts or compatible products.

The EC fined Microsoft Corporation €497m in 2004 for abusing its dominant market position[26]. This was the largest fine imposed up until then on a single company for violating European competition rules. Microsoft had refused to supply interface protocols in relation to group server operating systems and media players, preventing their use for the development by competitors of products which would be interoperable with Windows PCs and servers. Microsoft had also tied its Windows Media Player with the company's Windows 2000 PC operating system. The effect of this was to stop competitors' activities in the market, effectively reducing consumer choice and increasing prices.

The Commission required Microsoft to disclose full interface information to enable other workgroup servers to be interoperable with Window PCs and servers, and to keep the information up to date. This would enable competitors to develop products to compete with Microsoft in the work group server operating system market. Microsoft was ordered to end its unlawful tying practices and offer PC manufacturers two versions of its Windows client PC operating system, one being an unbundled alternative version without the Windows Media Player. The rationale behind this was the overwhelming dominance of Microsoft, whose operating systems equip more than 95 per cent of PCs worldwide, the indispensability of the interface information, and prevention of the elimination of competition in the market concerned. The decision is being challenged by Microsoft in the European Court of First Instance.

The Microsoft case is the first in EC competition law where a major computer company has been fined for anti-competitive behaviour. The Commission had applied art 82 to the IT industry when it investigated IBM's activities in the computer industry in the 1970s and 1980s[27]. IBM had a significant market share in central processing units. It was alleged to have abused its dominant position in the supply of central processing units and basic operating and system software for IBM computers System 360 and 370. It had not provided other manufacturers with the technical information they would have required in order to make competitive products which could be used with System 370. IBM gave undertakings to supply competing companies with interface information, not to bundle memory, and to make available certain formats and interface protocols available to competitors. However, this was effectively a settlement, not a formal decision by the Commission or the ECJ.

The Microsoft decision followed an earlier case[28], in the requirement for Microsoft to grant a compulsory licence of its interface information. In the previous case, television network companies had been using their copyright to create a monopoly in the market for television listings. The ECJ held that it was an abuse to prohibit the use of copyright information about TV programme timings where this information was essential to allow competition in the market for TV listings magazines.

An ECJ judgment in a case subsequent to the Microsoft decision also considered issues associated with compulsory licensing[29]. The companies involved in this case both collected data about pharmaceutical sales in Germany. IMS Health complained that NDC Health Corporation had infringed its copyright in its database. NDC denied the claim, but asserted that in any event the database was an 'industry standard', and that customers required data to be in that format. Thus it wanted to use the IMS database to supply the same customers as IMS's with a different product. If IMS enforced its rights to prevent NDC from entering the market, this would infringe art 82.

The judgment clarified that a refusal to grant a licence could be regarded as 'abusive' and therefore in breach of the law in certain highly exceptional circumstances: if the owner is dominant; if the refusal to license is not objectively justified; if all competition in a market might be eliminated; if the use of the intellectual property is 'indispensable' to enable the company wanting the supply of products or access to services to carry out its business, creating new products or services where there is a potential customer demand.

A judgment on appeal in the Court of First Instance that Michelin had abused its dominant position by its system of loyalty rebates and bonuses for its dealers is also relevant by analogy to the IT market[30]. The quantity rebates offered were standardised and based on objective criteria – the rate increased with the volume of purchases made – but were calculated and paid annually. The delay in payments prevented dealers from estimating the true unit price of Michelin tyres and caused uncertainty until they were paid. The service bonuses induced loyalty to Michelin by dealers, by encouraging them to give priority to Michelin instead of other tyre manufacturers. These practices strengthened Michelin's market position and reduced competition on the market for truck and bus tyres.

Where a supplier is dominant, discount schemes must therefore be operated so as to pay rebates to customers within a short time. There should not be uncertainty in the levels of bonuses and impact on overall pricing. They should be objectively justifiable.

49

Competition law in the UK

The UK competition law regime is governed by the Competition Act 1998, complemented by provisions in the Enterprise Act 2002. The Competition Act is modelled on the EC competition regime, but is directed at trade within the UK. Agreements are assessed according to their economic effect rather than on their form.

The 'Chapter I' prohibition broadly mirrors art 81 of the EC Treaty. Agreements which prevent, restrict or distort competition and which may affect trade in the UK are prohibited[31]. This includes price-fixing, market sharing, and the imposition of supplementary conditions which are unrelated to the subject matter of the contract – for example, in an agreement between two computer vendors, a requirement for one of them not to advertise or promote certain other components which are not part of the contract itself.

Certain agreements may be excluded from these provisions, so long as price-fixing or market-sharing is not involved, or the agreement is not part of a network of agreements with a cumulative effect in the market concerned. This includes those agreements where there is not an 'appreciable effect': agreements where the combined turnover of the parties does not exceed £20m or the parties' joint market share in the relevant market does not exceed 25 per cent[32]. An individual exemption may be granted, if the agreement contributes to improving production or distribution, or promotes technical or economic progress. Nevertheless, it must not impose unnecessary restrictions or eliminate competition[33]. The exemption may be for a defined period of time and subject to conditions[34]. A block exemption may be ordered for certain classes of agreements[35]. Parallel exemptions will apply to agreements covered by EC exemptions.

The 'Chapter II' prohibition mirrors art 82 of the EC Treaty. Abusive conduct by undertakings which are dominant in their market within the UK is prohibited if it may affect trade in the UK, with a similar test for dominance[36]. In general terms 'dominance' means a market share exceeding 40 per cent. This includes predatory pricing – for example, drastic cuts in prices to squeeze out competitors; price discrimination, for example in order to reward loyalty of certain customers; the imposition of unfair trading conditions, such as overly strict quality controls; unfair discount structures; placing limits on production or technical development; applying differential trading conditions for different companies; requiring the other party to accept extraneous obligations, such as not to stock the components of a rival manufacturer.

Additionally, if an agreement is capable of having an impact on trade between member states of the EU or the EEA, EC competition law will also be applicable.

The UK courts must ensure that there is no inconsistency between the principles applied and decisions reached, and the principles laid down by the EC Treaty and the decisions of the European courts[37].

The Office of Fair Trading ('OFT'), established under the Enterprise Act 2002, is responsible for applying and enforcing competition law, to make markets work well for consumers[38]. It has wide powers of investigation and enforcement. It can investigate a market if it appears that competition has been prevented, restricted or distorted by the structure of the market or the conduct of undertakings or their customers. Thus it can:

- launch investigations;

- conduct dawn raids;

- demand documents and information;

- order companies to stop anti-competitive behaviour; and

- impose significant fines on infringing businesses.

In addition to a fine of up to ten per cent of turnover, and incurring significant costs in undergoing an OFT investigation, an offending company may be subject to third party claims for damages. Moreover, the directors concerned may also be liable under the Enterprise Act, which makes it a criminal offence to participate dishonestly in price-fixing, market sharing, bid-rigging, or agreements to limit production or supply. The penalties are imprisonment of up to five years and an unlimited fine. Directors may be disqualified for up to 15 years.

A number of areas have been reviewed in this chapter in order to demonstrate that where there is an international aspect to a contract, it should not be automatically assumed that English law will be sufficient. Indeed EC legislation will also be relevant to many contracts without any apparent international aspect.

1	www.uncitral.org/en-index.htm.
2	United Nations Convention on Contracts for the International Sale of Goods 1980, art 1.
3	United Nations Convention on Contracts for the International Sale of Goods 1980, art 3.
4	Rome Convention On The Law Applicable To Contractual Obligations, implemented in the UK by the Contracts (Applicable Law) Act 1990.
5	Rome Convention On The Law Applicable To Contractual Obligations, art 3.
6	Rome Convention On The Law Applicable To Contractual Obligations, art 4.
7	Electronic Commerce (EC Directive) Regulations 2002 SI 2002/2013, implementing E-Commerce Directive (EC) 2000/31; www.hmso.gov.uk/si/si2002/20022013.htm.
8	Council Regulation (EC) 44/2001 on Jurisdiction and the Recognition and Enforcement of Judgments in Civil and Commercial Matters ('Brussels Regulation') implemented in the UK by the Civil Jurisdiction and Judgments Order 2001. As a Regulation, this applies directly in the UK.
9	Jurisdiction between Denmark and other member states continues to be governed by the Brussels Convention on Jurisdiction and the Enforcement of Judgments in Civil and Commercial Matters (1968), the 'Brussels Convention', which was implemented in the UK by the Civil Jurisdiction and Judgments Act 1982.
10	Brussels Convention, art 60.
11	Berne Convention for the Protection of Literary and Artistic Works as revised by the Paris Act 1971.
12	Directive on the Legal Protection of Computer Programs (EC) 91/250, OJ 1991 L 122/42, implemented in the UK by the Copyright (Computer Programs) Regulations; SI 1992/3233.
13	Copyright, Designs and Patents Act 1988.
14	WIPO Copyright Treaty 1996 and WIPO Phonograms and Performances Treaty 1996.
15	EC Directive 2001/29 on the Harmonisation of Certain Aspects of Copyright and Related Rights in the Information Society.
16	Copyright and Related Rights Regulations 2003, SI 2003/2498: www.legislation.hmso.gov.uk/si/si2003/20032498.htm.

17 *Kabushi Kaisha Sony Computer Entertainment Inc v Edmunds (t/a Channel Technology)* [2002] All ER (D) 170 (Jan) (the case preceded the Copyright and Related Rights Regulations 2003); *Kabushi Kaisha Sony Computer Entertainment Inc v Ball* [2004] EWHC 1984 (Ch), [2004] All ER (D) 51.

18 *John Richardson Computers Ltd v Flanders and Chemtec Ltd* (19 February 1993, unreported).

19 *Cantor Fitzgerald International v Tradition (UK) Ltd* [2000] RPC 95.

20 Copyright, Designs and Patents Act 1988, ss 77–89.

21 Directive on the Copyright Term 1993/98, Duration of Copyright and Rights in Performances Regulations 1995, SI 1995/3297, amending the Copyright Designs and Patents Act 1988.

22 Directive on the Legal Protection of Databases OJ 1996 L77/20, implemented in the UK by the Copyright and Rights in Databases Regulations 1997, SI 1997/3032.

23 Of the EC Treaty 1957, as renumbered by the Treaty of Amsterdam.

24 Commission Regulation (EC) 772/2004 on the application of art 81(3) of the EC Treaty to categories of technology transfer agreements.

25 Commission Notice – Guidelines on the application of art 81 of the EC Treaty to technology transfer agreements (2004/C101/02).

26 Case Comp/c-3/37.792 Microsoft; http://europa.ey.int/comm/competition/antitrust/cases/decisions/37792/en.pdf.

27 *EC Community v IBM* [1984] 3 CMLR 147.

28 Joined Cases C-241/91P and C-242/91P *Radio Telefis Eireann (RTE) and Independent Television Publications Ltd (ITP) v EC Commission* [1995] All ER (EC) 416.

29 Case C-418/01 *IMS Health GmbH & Co OHG v NDC Health GmbH & Co* [2004] All ER (EC) 813, ECJ.

30 Case T-203/01 *Manufacture française des pneumatiques Michelin v European Commission* [2004] 4 CMLR 923, CFI.

31 Competition Act 1998, s 2.

32 Competition Act (Small Agreements and Conduct of Minor Significance) Regulations 2000, SI 2000/262.

33 Competition Act 1998, s 9.

34 Competition Act 1998, ss 4 and 5.

35 Competition Act 1998, s 6.

36 Competition Act 1998, s 18.

37 Competition Act 1998, s 60.

38 www.oft.gov.uk.

CHAPTER 4

Contract law

A. Introduction

In this chapter various aspects of contract law are considered. The elements involved in forming a contract are analysed. Laws which qualify the terms set out in the contract are discussed, with some examples of how they have been interpreted in the courts. Failure to comply with the contract and bringing the contract to a premature end, and in the latter case the remedies available, are examined. Finally, the different means of formally resolving disputes, through the courts or otherwise, are summarised.

The legal context of contracts in the legal system of England and Wales is not something which is fixed and immutable. English law evolves whenever a new court decision or new Act of Parliament changes assumptions previously held about legal principles or about the ways in which those legal principles should be applied.

This evolution is haphazard. From one direction, legislation made in Parliament, through acts (statutes) or through delegated legislation, such as statutory instruments, sets out general rules without giving specific examples. From the other direction, cases decided at court establish general principles from particular facts.

English contract law developed in a major way during industrialisation in the nineteenth century. The law as decided by judges in cases tried in the nineteenth-century courts to deal with new and changing commercial conditions still applies today, affected and overlaid by legislation and later case decisions. Sometimes the case law is codified in legislation, such as the Sale of Goods legislation.

A contract is an agreement between two or more people or organisations, 'parties' to the contract, which creates rights and obligations for those parties. These obligations can be legally enforced by a party who is entitled to their benefits.

The general legal principles concerning contracts apply to IT contracts, as to all other contracts: buying a box of paper clips or selling computers; having a new kitchen fitted or having a complex manufacturing IT system supplied. But there are features, provisions and techniques applicable only to IT contracts which would not be relevant to agreements operating in different areas of commerce and industry, quite apart from the terminology unique to IT transactions.

The IT market is highly competitive. Now that there is less willingness to write off losses and greater insistence on enforcing legal entitlements, greater care is needed in drafting and negotiating IT agreements. The commercial structure underlying an IT contract is often complex, where the rights and obligations of organisations not parties to the contract ('third parties') must also be taken into account. One single contract may be tied up with various other third party transactions, and involve different elements of services, hardware, software, licensing or sale.

A contract enables the parties to achieve their strategic and commercial aims, apportioning risk and costs. By crystallising the agreement, it is a focus for discussing important issues and clarifying expectations. It can provide a framework for continuing to work together in a technology environment with a continuing relationship between the parties, perhaps involving a system with ongoing support requirements, or variable services, or enhancements and additions.

As well as rights and obligations within a contract, there may be other rights which are enforceable at law by an injured party. Certain wrongs such as negligence, deceit or defamation are legally known as 'torts' and can give rise to an action by the injured party for damages independently of any contract. Taking the tort of negligence as an illustration, a plaintiff must establish that the defendant owed a duty of care to the plaintiff, that the defendant was in breach of that duty of care, and that the plaintiff suffered damage from that breach. Physical damage to the claimant's property by the defendant, when the claimant is someone so closely and directly affected by the defendant's acts or omissions that the defendant should have thought about it, is one example of breach of duty of care. Another example is that, whether or not there is a contract, a supplier owes a duty of care to anyone who might reasonably rely on the products or services being supplied. Failure to follow this duty of care may constitute negligence which will be grounds for liability for any reasonably foreseeable direct loss resulting from the failure.

This duty of care can therefore extend to a third party outside the contract or to the other party to the contract alongside and in addition to the contractual relationship.

B. Making a contract: what it involves

A contract made under English law is a particular kind of legally enforceable agreement. It is normally a bargain made between at least two parties, with an offer by one party which has been accepted by the other party, with some benefit gained by or detriment suffered to either of the parties. This benefit or detriment is known as 'consideration'. If disagreement subsequently arises, it becomes necessary to analyse these elements of offer, acceptance, consideration, taken for granted at the time of making the contract, to establish what the form and the terms actually were.

1. Offer

An offer, the initial element of a contract, must be definite. An offer of a computer for sale subject to the 'usual leasing facilities provided on usual market terms', is too vague. It would not count as a valid offer.

However, an offer can be made by implication, without having to be stated in words. Behaviour can constitute an offer. A customer taking goods from the shelves of a self-service store and presenting them at the cashier's checkout is making an offer to purchase the goods, without having to say anything. The preliminary stage to an offer is legally known as being an 'invitation to treat', effectively the first step in negotiations. There is a case well known to lawyers resulting from a situation in which drugs, specified as poison, were displayed in a Boots the Chemists shop in Edgware[1]. The drugs had to be sold under the supervision of a registered pharmacist. The case was brought over a dispute about whether a registered pharmacist had to be in the shop at all times when the shop was open. It was decided in the courts that a registered pharmacist did not have to be permanently in attendance, because the goods on display on the shelves were not yet in the process of being sold. It was not an offer which was being made by the shop but 'an invitation to treat'. The customer makes the offer by taking the goods and presenting them at the checkout. This case demonstrates how legal principles are derived from actual situations.

To be valid, an offer must be communicated, whether to one individual or in general terms. A renowned case in this connection was brought against the makers of a medical preparation known as the 'carbolic smoke ball' in the closing decades of the nineteenth century, the Carbolic Smoke Ball Company. The company placed an advertisement in the *Pall Mall Gazette* extolling the virtues of the preparation[2]. It promised £100 as a reward to anyone who caught influenza after sniffing the carbolic smoke ball three times daily for two weeks according to the printed directions supplied with each smoke ball. The advertisement included a statement that £100 was deposited with a bank, to show the company's good faith in the matter. The preparation did not work for Mrs Carlill, who used the preparation, caught influenza and took the company to court. The court decided that it was perfectly possible for an advertisement to make a definite offer to anybody who read it, and that the company was liable to pay Mrs Carlill. The company had certainly communicated the offer which Mrs Carlill had accepted by buying the carbolic smoke ball. Normally, however, a computer store or a mail order catalogue advertising technological products will be making an invitation to treat, not an offer.

2. Acceptance

In response to a clear unequivocal offer, there must be a clear definite acceptance.

An acceptance must be communicated, although not necessarily in writing. Silence is not acceptance, although performance, such as accepting delivery of a consignment of PCs, will be. The *Carbolic Smoke Ball* case illustrates this as well. The Carbolic Smoke Ball Company put up various resourceful defences to avoid having to pay Mrs Carlill the £100. The court rejected them all and Mrs Carlill won her case. The offer by the company was made to all the world in order to contract with those members of the public who performed the condition on the faith of the advertisement. Mrs Carlill used the smoke ball three times a day as directed from November 1891 to January 1892 when she caught influenza. The offer had contained the implication that performance of the condition by following the instructions for sniffing the smoke ball was sufficient acceptance. There was no need for Mrs Carlill to go to the trouble of notifying the Carbolic Smoke Ball Company that she had accepted the offer. By using the preparation as prescribed, Mrs Carlill had accepted the offer by performance.

In this connection, if post is an acceptable method of communicating acceptance and nothing else is stated in the contract, the moment the letter is posted in England constitutes acceptance under English law even if the letter is delayed or lost in the post. This is a special 'postal rule'.

The offeror can withdraw an offer by communicating the withdrawal at any time before acceptance. The postal rule does not apply here, and the offeree must actually receive the notice of withdrawal for it to be effective. This could theoretically mean that an offer could be accepted even though a withdrawal notification was on its way.

With new technologies, such as fax and e-mail, the rules on offer and acceptance continue to apply, so that in general, and in the absence of specific requirements, an acceptance is effective when it is received. An example of online contract formation is set out below in this section.

An offer may be prescribed to be available for a set period, such as 'This offer remains open for 30 days'. However, in the absence of a binding collateral agreement to the contrary, the offeror may withdraw the offer at any time, even within the 30 days, so long as this is before the offer has been accepted – or rejected. Once it has been rejected, an offer cannot be subsequently accepted by the party to whom it was made.

If a supplier's proposal includes a statement that the terms remain open for 30 days, and two days after being sent to a prospective customer the supplier discovers that the proposal had been underpriced, the supplier is entitled to withdraw the proposal immediately so long as the customer is informed, and provided that the customer has not yet accepted the original offer. Once the offer is accepted, both parties would be bound, unless a patently obvious mistake could be shown to have occurred.

The acceptance must be unqualified and correspond to the offer. Many apparent acceptances introduce new terms. These new terms, in law, amount to a counter-offer, which is not acceptance, and which does not create a contract. Accepting an offer for computer equipment on sale at a fixed price by stipulating that payment would be made in three instalments would be a counter-offer to which the original offeror must then respond by acceptance for a contract to be created. A request for further information, perhaps by querying some details about the equipment concerned to establish the real meaning of the offer, will keep the original offer open.

Where tenders are invited for the supply of goods or services, the request is the invitation to make an offer, the invitation to treat. Each tender submitted is an offer. The party inviting tenders can accept any of the tenders submitted and in so doing will create a contract. A customer may invite tenders to supply a computer system. A number of tenders may be made in response. In due course the customer accepts one tender and if nothing else is stated, a contract will thereby be created. The contractor will provide a computer system and the customer will accept and pay for it on terms in accordance with the contractor's tender. Consequently, a contractor making a tender should include a statement making it clear that any order placed will be subject to the contractor's terms and conditions, unless it is willing to bid on other terms stated in the invitation to tender. The prices quoted in a tender will be the prices applicable to the contract.

Where tenders are invited to supply goods and services 'as and when demanded', the trader who submits a tender is making a standing offer. Here, there is a separate acceptance each time an order is placed with the contractor who submitted the tender, and a distinct contract is made on each occasion. It also follows that the standing offer can be withdrawn at any time, except as to goods or services actually ordered.

An offer lapses after a reasonable time. A counter-offer or conditional acceptance is a rejection, following which the offeror does not have to keep the offer open any further.

3. Legal enforceability

There is a presumption in commercial and business agreements that the parties intend to create a legal contract. This presumption need not apply if the parties both agree otherwise. 'Subject to contract' is a well understood formula for preparatory negotiations, to indicate that the discussions are not yet at a stage where binding commitments are being created.

In one case, a preliminary issue arose for decision by the court about whether there was a concluded agreement, in a dispute about the development of software under time constraints for a unit-linked mortgage plan system. It was stated in the Court of Appeal: 'when experienced businessmen use the words 'subject to contract' in a proposal, they mean more – and must be taken to mean more – than that the acceptance must be in writing. At the lowest, they are guarding themselves against being contractually bound without further action on their part'[3].

It will depend on what both parties intend and the words they actually use. An agreement which is still tentative is not binding but a *provisional* agreement may be. In a case concerning the purchase of a mushroom farm, an agreement had been signed ending with the words: 'This is a provisional agreement until a fully legalised agreement drawn up by a solicitor and embodying all these conditions herewith stated is signed'. The courts decided that because of the word 'provisional', the agreement was intended to be binding, and it remained in force until the provisions were embodied in a formally drawn up document. It was not 'subject to contract'[4].

In a dispute between a company trading in hardware and software and a husband-and-wife team who over four years had developed an accounting system[5], the question arose, on an initial application in an action for breach of contract and infringement of copyright, whether there *was* a binding contract. A meeting had taken place at which handwritten notes were drafted with deletions which were not very legible, including provisions about the charges to be made for the accounting system; that the company Systemics would market the product; that source code would be handed over to Systemics, and that copyright would pass to Systemics.

Mr Healey of Raindrop Data Systems sent a letter the day following this meeting, to say firmly that it was not a binding agreement. Systemics argued that the document was a preliminary draft anticipating the typed-up version.

The court considered the matter and took into account prior agreements which had been made. The judge described the document in dispute as 'compendiously to be described as rather scruffy. It is full of erasures, additions, and it is entirely in manuscript, and not very legible manuscript at that'. Nevertheless, it was decided that there was an arguable case that there was a binding and legal agreement in force.

A letter of intent may be contractually binding if, in combination with its surrounding circumstances, the elements comprising a contract are present. However, a simple agreement to negotiate, a 'lock *in*' agreement, is not an enforceable contract. There is no definite agreement. Negotiations put the parties in an adversarial position. At any time during negotiation, one side might decide to break off. It is impossible to say whether that party is entitled to do so, and therefore it is not possible to state whether an agreement to negotiate has been complied with. There is always room for doubt. Thus a simple provision in a software development contract to the effect that the parties will agree on the terms and conditions of a joint marketing contract once the software has been developed will not have any legal value of enforceability.

A 'lock *out*' agreement is an agreement not to negotiate with anyone else. Perhaps a special offer is being made to a customer. This can be enforceable provided that there is consideration for the agreement, and if it is for a fixed period of time. A 'reasonable' length of time is not good enough in this context. But this kind of agreement is not usually effective. The customer agreeing not to negotiate with any other supplier has only to wait until the period of time has expired, and then obtain the goods elsewhere.

In a case in the House of Lords[6], the prospective purchasers, Martin and Charles Walford, went to court when the owners of a photographic business, Mr and Mrs Miles, sold it to a third party.

The Walfords had offered £2m, and the main terms of the sale were negotiated 'subject to contract'. The Walfords asked Mr and Mrs Miles not to negotiate with anyone else. Mr and Mrs Miles had separately agreed that if they received a comfort letter from the Walfords' bank, they would not negotiate with any other party.

The comfort letter arrived but, two days later, Mr and Mrs Miles decided to sell the business to a different company, who matched the £2m.

The Walfords lost their claim. The agreement *to* negotiate was not enforceable. The agreement not to negotiate would have been enforceable, but was not because it did not state a fixed time.

However, in this case, Mr and Mrs Miles were liable for £700 damages for misrepresentations they had made. 'Misrepresentation' is considered later in this chapter, at Section C.

One IT case to mention in the context of contract formation is between the Co-operative Group and ICL (as it then was at the time of this case and the other cases to which it was a party referred to in this chapter). The system to be supplied by ICL was for a platform for merged Co-operative stores involving integration and further development. There was no written agreement. The Co-op terminated what they said was an unwritten contract, and claimed £11m damages.

The case went to the Court of Appeal. In the court of first instance (the first court to hear the case), ICL had successfully argued that there was no contract of any sort between the parties, because there was deadlock over a key issue of liquidated damages. The judge said that he found it difficult to understand how the Co-op's case could ever seriously have been put forward. He said the claim by the Co-op 'bordered on the nonsensical'.

However, the Court of Appeal said that 'put bluntly the judge's findings are obviously unfair. The judge's view makes no commercial sense whatsoever'. The words 'wounding and sarcastic' were used of the judgment. The Court granted a re-trial. Note that this was not a comment on the merits of either party's case.

What is clear here is that there was no written contract which the parties could rely on when problems arose – let alone any agreed dispute management provisions. The effects are that both parties expended an enormous amount of costs and effort without achieving any result remotely satisfactory to either party. The Co-op eventually decided to drop the case. It is an unequivocal lesson to make any agreement formally in writing, and to set out clearly the rights and obligations of both parties.

4. 'Consideration' and 'Privity of Contract'

'Consideration' is a concept applying to contracts under English law. 'Considera-tion' has been defined as some 'right, interest, profit or benefit accruing to one party, or some forbearance, detriment, loss or responsibility given, suffered, or undertaken by the other'[7]. It involves the feature of bargain or reciprocity between the parties. A promise made without any such bargain is not binding under English law, unless it is made under seal as a deed, that is, with greater formality than applies to an ordinary contract.

The consideration must consist of some advantage or promise to be carried out at the time of making the contract or in the future, not for something which has already been done or which has already happened. There must be some value to the consideration, but the value given by one party does not need to be equivalent to the advantage gained by the other. Usually one party will be in a stronger negotiating position than the other, depending on whether it is a buyer's or a seller's market, or for reasons such as prestige, commercial power or state-of-the-art technology. This will not mean that simply because one side has achieved a better bargain than the other, there is no consideration. The courts will look closely at inequality of bargaining power in the actual creation of a contract only where it is entirely one-sided. They will be reluctant to find that there is such inequality where both parties are commercial organisations.

Where one party to the contract waives any of the rights to which it is entitled under the contract, it is possible for it to change its mind and enforce them later at any time by giving reasonable notice – unless some benefit for doing so is obtained from the other party, that is, unless there has been some consideration.

For example, a customer orders and receives £20,000 of equipment. Subsequently, the customer tells the supplier that it is about to go into liquidation and cannot pay £20,000 but can manage £15,000 if the supplier will accept this in full payment. If the supplier agrees, preferring to have £15,000 rather than to take the equipment back, and at that time the customer is not worth suing, the waiver of the £5,000 would be gratuitous. The customer did not confer any benefit in return for this waiver, because the threat is that the customer would otherwise not pay anything. If the supplier later discovers that the customer can once again afford the balance, it would be entitled to recover it. If a new element had been introduced, the customer offering £15,000 plus an introduction to a third party who would purchase the supplier's products, there is consideration, and that would constitute a complete settlement of the transaction.

If the parties choose to vary what they originally agreed, again, there must be consideration for the variation to be effective. However, this will usually be found in mutual new rights and obligations.

The Court of Appeal confirmed damages awarded to Boots the Chemist in a case where it was held that the defendant, Amdahl (UK) Ltd, had been under an obligation to repurchase computer equipment and was in breach of contract by refusing to do so[8]. The decision turned on whether any agreement was reached through correspondence, whether evidence of intention to create legal relations was present, and whether variation of the original contract was with sufficient consideration. It was decided that a binding agreement had been reached through correspondence, and because the variation was capable of benefiting either party and had an element of detriment to Boots' acceptance of the benefit, this alone constituted sufficient consideration.

The 'consideration' rule relates to those commitments which are legally enforceable. Until recently, 'privity of contract' was a further rule applied under English law relating to enforceability. The effect of this rule was that where a contract was made by one party with a second, for the benefit of a third, neither the first nor the third party might be able to enforce the rights granted under the contract. For example, Purchaser A might place an order with Supplier B for products of a particular description to be delivered to Company C as a gift. If the products delivered turned out to be completely different from those ordered, Purchaser A could not recover worthwhile damages because it had suffered no loss itself, whereas Company C could not sue Supplier B for breach of contract because it was not a party to the contract. In a large IT system project, typically involving the customer, main contractor and a number of sub-contractors, none of them would have any direct remedy for contractual breaches caused by any of the others, unless there was a contract in effect between the innocent party and the party at fault.

In certain situations the application of this rule led to such unjust results that laws have been devised to overcome the effect. For example, various laws now enable parties injured in traffic accidents to exercise rights directly against the insurers of drivers at fault.

Alternatively the third party may bring an action in negligence against the defaulting party. But success in such an action is more uncertain then in a breach of contract case. It is more difficult to establish the evidence necessary to prove 'negligence' at law. 'Collateral warranties' are another legal device used to overcome the problem, a mechanism common in construction industry contracts but rarely encountered in IT contracts, as warranties which would give a third party a direct contractual link.

However, this 'privity of contract' rule has now been amended[9], bringing the law into line with most EU member states. If the contract expressly says so, or if the contract confers a benefit on a third party, that third party will be entitled to the same rights and can enforce the contract as if a party to the contract. The third party must be clearly identified in the contract, by name, description or as a member of a defined class. The third party does not become a party to the contract. It is not itself subject to any contractual obligations.

Certain contracts are excluded, such as employment contracts. Another exception is where on a 'proper construction' of the contract, it appears that the parties to it did not intend the terms to be enforceable by the third party.

The effect of this in practice for most IT contracts is that the application of the rule will be expressly excluded. This is partly to avoid later argument about the parties' intentions. Moreover, in many commercial situations, if third parties are to gain rights, this will frequently be as part of a nexus of mutual responsibilities and obligations. These will preferably be specified in a contract directly involving the parties concerned. For example, a software developer may enter into a contract with a reseller. As a result of this contract, the developer's software may be supplied by the reseller to end users. If nothing is stated in the contract between the developer and the reseller, the end user may seek to enforce its rights against the developer. However, the developer will be concerned that the end user should be properly licensed by means of a licence directly from the developer, or a sub-licence from the reseller. In either case the end user will have obligations as well as rights in using the software, such as restrictions on copying.

5. Trade customs

Trade customs can be implied into a contract on the basis that they do not need to be expressly stated: they are assumed to be part of the contract because they are so well understood by the parties in the course of their normal business. If there is a divergence between the parties' understanding, and no express terms make matters clear, the courts will look at what is customary in the circumstances of the practice of the particular business. For an IT contract, therefore, what is usually done and expected in the IT industry would be considered.

In a case in the early nineteenth century, the number '1,000' applied to rabbits was interpreted by the custom of the country as meaning '1,200' rabbits[10].

In one case in the knitting machine business[11], distributors had purchased a prototype machine, which was delivered to a customer for trial. Not long after, spare parts were required, but would have taken four months to be supplied. The customer therefore returned the machine. This led to a claim by the distributor against the manufacturer, alleging that spare parts for the machine should have been available within a reasonable time. They said that this was 'implied by reason of the usage of the trade and because a machine for which spare parts are not available is or very soon will be useless'. The courts looked at 'usage of the trade' – trade custom. Evidence showed that neither party had made any enquiry about spare parts and that availability of spares was not part of the transaction. It was decided in the Court of Appeal that it was not enough to provide a trade custom to show that it was 'usual' or 'normal' for spare parts to be available. No trade custom about the ready availability of spare parts of this machine had in fact been proved, whether or not the machine was tried and tested.

6. Formalities

Little formality is needed for a contract to be made under English law. Provided that the features of offer, acceptance and consideration are validly present, a contract does not have to be an incomprehensible 50-page parchment document in Gothic writing tied up with green ribbon with 'hereinbefores' all over the place. And if those features necessary for contract formation are not present in such a formidable document, it will not be a contract, whatever it looks like.

Most contracts do not have to be in writing to be binding and enforceable. A contract can be inferred from letters or from what was said. It can be an oral agreement made over lunch. It can be made by a customer's order and subsequent delivery of goods. It will still be a binding contract. The risk resulting from this is that a party may be bound by the terms of a contract without having had any intention of allowing them to apply. Nor does a contract have to be signed to be valid so long as the terms have been agreed and negotiations are not continuing.

Of course the question of evidence of what was actually agreed is more straightforward if there is a written signed document, but production of a document is not necessary. Many arguments over contracts in court turn not on the *meaning* of the terms, but on what were the terms actually agreed. The intention of the parties at the time is important in assessing whether a contract was actually made. Where the intention is not obvious, that is to say where one of the parties is arguing that there was not a binding contract in force, the court will look at the circumstances in which the contract was claimed to have been formed[12]. Where all the commercial terms have been agreed, even if there is no formal written contract, a binding contract may well have been created[13].

If a contract is signed, and afterwards the parties realise that there is a genuine mistake and it does not represent what they both intended at the time it was made, for example through a typing error, the written terms can be rectified and a court can order its enforcement. It is up to the party who seeks the change to prove what had really been meant.

The rules of contractual interpretation where elucidation is necessary are that words will bear their ordinary, literal sense, and legal or other technical words will bear their legal or technical meaning.

The court will look at evidence for what the parties originally intended if the terms are in conflict or if the parties intended terms to apply which have been omitted.

In one case, each side had genuinely believed in its own interpretation, as to whether books were sold in sets of four, or as individual units. The order acknowledgement read: 'Quantity: 40,000 copies of each of 4 titles in slipcase. Price: £1.20 per copy CIF UK Warehouse'. The case concerned the objective construction of the words. 'Each' was held to define the unit concerned. If each individual book had been an item priced at £1.20, then 'and 40,000 slipcases' would have replaced 'in slipcase'[14]. The price therefore was held to apply to each set of four, not to the individual book. Incidentally, 'CIF' stands for Cost, Insurance and Freight, and is part of the INCOTERMS, international commercial terms, discussed in **CHAPTER 9**. It is one of the shorthand acronyms which allocates responsibility and risk for the goods between seller and buyer during transport of the goods.

7. Online contract formation illustration

The process of contract formation can be illustrated by means of an online retail transaction.

Kodak offered through its website a digital camera package, as a 'special deal' at £100. The price should have been £329. Customers who placed an order received an automated confirmation by e-mail. Before the customers were charged and the goods sent out, Kodak tried to withdraw the offer by claiming that a mistake had been made. However, eventually Kodak agreed to comply with the orders.

The general view here is that the advertisement on the website constituted the 'invitation to treat'. A customer made the offer by completing the order form including details of credit card information. The retailer then accepted the order by confirming it. It is irrelevant to the principle of acceptance that the confirmation was generated automatically[15].

In any particular case, the retailer's terms and conditions displayed on the site may add further specificity to the contract formation.

Moreover, other rules discussed later overlay this analysis. For example, information such as price must not be misleading, as being a representation made by the retailer or under the Consumer Protection Act 1987, the Unfair Terms in Consumer Contract Regulations, and other legislation designed to protect consumers and encourage trade. If the price is false, action may be taken under Pt III of the Consumer Protection Act 1987 by the Trading Standards Authority. This would be a criminal offence and liability to fines would ensue. Regulations under the E-commerce Directive[16], requiring certain information such as price to be displayed, reinforce the requirements of contract. Also under the E-commerce Directive, acceptance occurs when the retailer has responded to a customer order and the response is available to the customer (eg on the customer's mail server).

Incidentally, an online vendor should consider implementing systems to provide automatic alerts in respect of unusual trading.

8. Shrink-wrap licence example

The 'shrink-wrap' licence is another practical illustration of some of the principles involved in the formation of a contract. This form of licence is widely used with high-volume, low-value software usually sold through mail order or retail. Software is supplied on disks with user instructions and a licence form in a packet sealed by means of outer shrink-wrap packaging, hence the name. The terms should be visible through the shrink-wrap, giving permission from the supplier for the user to use the software subject to all the conditions included in the licence. A warning states that opening the package means acceptance of the licence terms.

The problem for the supplier is that the contract is made at the time the software is acquired. The customer makes the offer to pay for the software at the stated price, to the dealer at the cash desk or by mail order, without prior knowledge of the terms and conditions, and without taking into account the terms and conditions of the licence, thus without agreeing to them at that time. The customer's payment is accepted in exchange for the software. Yet all the terms of a contract should already have been communicated by the supplier and agreed by the customer, by the time of the purchase, and they will not have been.

A registration card may be included for the user to return to the supplier which will request the user's signature as evidence of agreeing to the terms and conditions – which will be available to the user by this time, on opening up the package containing the software, the terms and conditions, together with the registration card, and any other information. The card may say that updates of the software will be provided to the user, if the card is completed and returned. This would be 'consideration' for a new contract under the offer made by the licensor. Few registration cards are ever returned. It is possible that the return of the registration card may create an enforceable contract. If it is appropriately worded, by its return, the customer will have accepted the terms and conditions, and a contract will be made.

One argument for its contractual validity could be that the shrink-wrap licence can be regarded as a trade custom. But the general belief is that the 'shrink-wrap licence' agreement does not constitute an enforceable contract if the registration card is not returned, except where there is a clear notice drawing the licensee's attention to the terms and conditions of licence prior to purchase.

The first UK case on the enforceability of shrink-wrap licences was in 1996 in the Scottish courts[17]. Adobe had ordered standard Infomix software by telephone from Beta. This was supplied with a shrink-wrap licence in a sealed package stating

65

that opening it 'indicates your acceptance of these terms and conditions'. Adobe did not open the package and returned the software. Beta refused to accept its return and sued for payment.

The court held that the contract in this case, as a software contract, incorporated elements of both purchase and licence. The contract was conditional upon acceptance by the purchaser of the licence terms intended to benefit the third party owner of the intellectual property rights. Those terms were enforceable. It was stressed that this court decision turned on its particular facts. For instance, as the software had been ordered by telephone, the terms and conditions had not been brought to the customer's notice before delivery. Moreover, Scottish law differs from English law, and the decision might well have been different if it had been litigated in an English court.

C. Legislation affecting contractual terms

Those conditions set out in a printed commercial contract are only part of the general legal framework. Statements made before the contract was created may be taken into account. In addition, certain other terms will be implied by law into a contract.

1. Statutory implied terms

Some terms do not have to be expressly stated in a contract to be applicable. Under the Sale of Goods Act 1979, modified by the Sale and Supply of Goods Act 1994, and the Supply of Goods and Services Act 1982, certain terms are implied into contracts relating to the sale of goods or the supply of goods or services.

The most important obligations under the legislation relating to the sale of goods in the course of a business concern the quality. In general, goods must correspond with their description, be of satisfactory quality except for defects specifically drawn to the buyer's attention or where the buyer has had the opportunity of examining the goods, and be reasonably fit for their purpose.

Under the Supply of Goods and Services Act 1982, in a contract for the supply of goods and services in the course of business, the services must be carried out with reasonable skill and care within a reasonable time; and for a reasonable price (although a price or rate will usually be contractually agreed).

Some of these implied terms may be overridden by the contract terms insofar as it is fair and reasonable to do this.

'Fitness for purpose' is problematic in relation to software. The concept applies to the supply of goods, not to the provision of services. Suppliers of computer products routinely exclude this term – which would otherwise be implied into the contract. Their rationale is that the concept of 'purpose' is open-ended as far as software is concerned. Its use need not be confined to one sole purpose. All the circumstances and potential uses cannot be anticipated by the supplier.

In one case, *St Albans City and District Council v International Computers Ltd* in 1996, Sir Iain Glidewell in the Court of Appeal expressed an opinion as to whether software was 'goods' or 'services'[18]. He felt that a term that the software would be fit for the purpose was incorporated into the contract. He said that in the absence of an express or contrary term, a contract for the supply of a computer program intended by both parties to perform specific functions is one of those rare cases where the court will infer an implied term under common law that the program will be reasonably fit for the intended purpose. He said that software had the legal attributes of goods when sold or hired as a packaged application. Then, implied terms such as 'satisfactory quality' and 'fitness for purpose' will apply. When the software is part of an application development contract, it does not have such attributes. But the contract nevertheless includes an implied term that the software is fit for the purpose intended. This would apply unless there is a contrary term in the contract which is either a non-standard contract or reasonable within the provisions of the Unfair Contract Terms Act, which is discussed in the next section.

He regarded a disk containing a program which is sold or hired as being 'goods'. If the program was defective, the goods were defective. It follows that it depends on how the software is transferred whether it can be defined as 'goods' and therefore subject to the sale of goods legislation. In this case, the software was licensed and the customer did not receive a disk. An employee of the supplier visited the customer's offices and loaded the software on the system. The judge held that in the absence of any express terms of quality or fitness for purpose, the contract is subject to an implied term that the software will be fit for purpose. According to this interpretation, there will therefore be an implied term of 'fitness for purpose' even if software is downloaded from the Internet. If there is a contrary term in the contract, and the contract is standard form, it must be reasonable to be effective.

If the provision is not specifically excluded, the customer who finds that the system being developed turns out to be unsuitable for its business requirements – a not uncommon situation in software procurement – may well find it of assistance, even if the system would be satisfactory in other respects by conforming to its supplier's specification.

However, software cannot be guaranteed always to work. It has been accepted by the courts that even software which had not excluded the condition of 'fitness for purpose' would not necessarily be error-free[19]. It was stated in that case:

> 'it is important to remember that software is not necessarily a commodity which is handed over or delivered once and for all at one time. It may well have to be tested

and modified as necessary. It would not be a breach of contract at all to deliver software in the first instance with a defect in it'.

In a later case concerning packaged software supplied to a firm of stockbrokers, the judge said in reaching his decision: 'I am in no doubt that if a software system is sold as a tried and tested system it should not have any bugs in it ...'[20], but this is not a view which is generally shared in the IT industry or in other case law.

2. Protection against unfair terms

If there are no provisions in the contract to limit or exclude a supplier's liability, the supplier will be liable for all losses to the other party resulting from a breach of that contract, and which could have been foreseen. The sums which could be awarded as damages if the breach of contract is established are potentially enormous, given the increasing supply of systems critical to running a business. Normally, however, there will be limits and exclusions of liability set out by the supplier in the contract.

However, various laws protect consumers against the imposition of unfair terms. The Unfair Contract Terms Act 1977 ('UCTA') is a long established law which restricts exclusions and limitations of liability in certain circumstances, and which has been invoked in a number of cases concerning claimed breaches of IT contracts. Liability cannot be restricted for death or personal injury resulting from negligence. Liability cannot be restricted for negligence causing other loss or damage except insofar as it is reasonable to do so[21].

If one of the parties is a consumer or the contract consists of standard terms of business, liability cannot be restricted for breach of contract except to the extent that the clause concerned is 'reasonable'.

Thus a contract clause attempting to exclude all liability for loss or damage of any kind would be unreasonable and therefore not enforceable. In a consumer contract it might also give rise to criminal liability.

What is 'reasonable' depends on the facts in every case, but the kinds of factors taken into account in assessing the reasonableness of excluding certain provisions are defined in UCTA[22] and include: the relative bargaining positions of the parties; any inducement to agree to the term; whether the order was special or on standard terms; whether or not the standard terms were imposed on the injured party; and the availability of insurance.

It is therefore commercially realistic for liability to be excluded or at least limited within legal limits by a supplier. Insurance cover should also be taken out to mitigate the effects of any liability which is found.

The onus of proof that a provision is reasonable is on the supplier. The supplier may therefore agree to certain limited obligations in a contract, such as liability for damage to property caused by negligence of its employees up to the level of its insurance cover, effectively in return for excluding other conditions and warranties not specifically spelled out in the contract, whether expressly or by implication, statutory or otherwise.

The courts regard absolute exclusions of liability in contracts more rigorously than limitations. They will look at limitations of liability in the overall contractual context, including aspects such as price, risk and insurance by either party.

In the past few years, there have been a number of cases between customers and suppliers of software and systems. The interpretation of the terms of the contracts, and especially the provisions limiting the suppliers' liability, has been reviewed under UCTA. The cases have turned on the particular facts applicable, but some principles have emerged.

In the case mentioned earlier brought by St Albans City and District Council against ICL[23], and also another case brought by South West Water against ICL[24], it was held that UCTA could apply, even though the limitation clauses themselves had been negotiated by the parties. These were landmark decisions for the computer software and services industry about the application of UCTA to standard form information technology contracts.

In the *St Albans* case, a computer system was supplied by ICL to St Albans City and District Council – as indeed to other local authorities – for the assessment of administration of the Community Charge to meet the deadline for its introduction in 1990. The software contained an admitted error in calculations. This led to financial consequences at the Council. There were breaches of obligations in the contract to provide reliable software.

The software had been supplied on ICL's standard contract terms. There was a clause in the contract which limited ICL's liability to an amount far less than the amount being claimed by the Council.

It was agreed that the clause had been discussed between the parties. However, the wording had not changed as a result of that discussion. It was held that if a contract is entered into on the basis of standard terms, even if the clauses had been negotiated beforehand, the terms remained standard, and thus could be scrutinised under UCTA. This came as a surprise to most people. In this case, ICL's standard clause limiting its liability for defects to £100,000, was struck from the contract, on the grounds that it was unreasonable.

In the *South West Water* case, in respect of ICL's failure to deliver a customised customer service system, ICL again sought to rely on various clauses in the contracts to limit its liability. There was a turnkey contract (held to be inappropriate for a project which did not rest on simple acceptance on delivery) and a project management contract. Both contracts took the format and some wording from the contract proposed by South West Water in its invitation to tender, and were adapted to include limitations of liability from ICL's standard system supply contract.

Yet – as in the *St Albans* case – the judge concluded that the parties had 'used a standard ICL contract which was only slightly adapted'. It did not help ICL that the parties had extensively negotiated other aspects of the contracts or that the contracts contained extracts from the terms and conditions of both parties – because the limitation clauses themselves had been taken from ICL's standard terms without amendment. Astonishingly, this turned out to be enough for it to be held that the parties had contracted on ICL's standard terms for the purposes of UCTA. The judge held that the limitation clauses denied South West Water an effective remedy. All the limitation clauses fell together as unenforceable. As a result South West Water was entitled to recover damages from ICL, which was faced with accepting unlimited liability.

The lesson here for suppliers is that if the project is out of control, this should be admitted, or else the courts are not likely to regard the arguments favourably.

What makes an exclusion or limitation term in a standard contract 'unreasonable'? The considerations include the context of the negotiations, the availability of insurance and the relative bargaining strength of the parties.

In the *St Albans* case, the reasons for regarding the limitation of liability clause as unreasonable included the context of the negotiations – for example, a statement made by a salesman that he could not hold the price if the contract was not signed – and the fact that ICL had worldwide insurance which covered far more than the amount claimed.

In another case[25], the customer for the hardware and software was an insurance broker. But the evidence was that the supplier was in a better position to obtain insurance against defective performance. This is generally the case. Additionally, the insurance broker would have had difficulty obtaining alternative software. These were the relevant factors in deciding that the exclusions and limitations of liability were unreasonable.

THE SUPPLIER/CUSTOMER RELATIONSHIP

In the cases against ICL, St Albans City and District Council and South West Water were both substantial organisations with legal representation. So it was another surprise to learn how the courts regarded the relative bargaining strengths of the parties, one of the factors to be taken into account under UCTA.

However, where the customer was also in the IT business, this affected the interpretation of 'reasonableness' as between the parties. Watford Electronics, a vendor of computer products, purchased software for its mail order business from Sanderson. The system failed to perform satisfactorily and was ultimately replaced. Watford Electronics sued Sanderson[26]. The Court of Appeal held that the contractual term excluding indirect and consequential loss was reasonable under UCTA, because:

- both parties were commercial organisations of equal bargaining power;

- Watford got a substantial reduction in the price;

- Watford understood the significance of the limitation clause. They discussed risk and the cost of insurance in negotiations. Watford's own terms contained similar exclusion clauses – and Watford was itself in the IT business.

Lord Justice Chadwick said:

'Where experienced businessmen representing substantial companies of equal bargaining power negotiate an agreement, they may be taken to have had regard to the matters known to them. They should ... be taken to be the best judge of the commercial fairness of the agreement which they have made; including the fairness of each of the terms in that agreement'.

Unless satisfied that one party has in effect taken unfair advantage of the other – or that a term is so unreasonable that it cannot properly have been understood or considered – the court should not interfere. Here it could not be said either that there was unfair advantage or that Watford had not properly understood or considered the limitation clause.

An earlier case elaborated the respective responsibilities of both customers and IT suppliers of packaged software[27]. The focus was on co-operation between the supplier and customer – in fact, in this case, the *lack* of co-operation by the customer.

Standard software was supplied by BML (Office Computers) Ltd on its standard terms and conditions, to Winther Brown, a distributor and reseller of wooden and carved mouldings and other decorative items to DIY stores. The contract included a requirement that purchasers of standard software should satisfy themselves that the software met their requirements.

As soon as the software was implemented, Winther Brown began to complain about it not working properly. They claimed damages for lost profits, waste of staff time, and the cost of a new system.

However, the court found that BML had made genuine efforts to meet Winther Brown's complaints and had performed substantially what it had contracted to do. Winther Brown's complaints were caused by its practices, and were trivial or not proved. Its expectations were far too optimistic. BML was certainly in breach of minor elements of what it had contracted to deliver. But here it seemed that the judge was so irritated by the behaviour of the customer and the unprofessional attitude of its expert, that he made it clear that BML's overall performance was perfectly acceptable.

The judge said that in the legal and IT world it was 'well understood that the design and installation of a computer system requires the active co-operation of both parties ... The duty of co-operation ... extends to the customer accepting where possible reasonable solutions to problems that have arisen'. So, for relatively unimportant items, the customer might have to be prepared to compromise.

The judge held that a term could be implied in contracts for the supply of a standard package software system that the customer should:

- communicate clearly any special needs to the supplier;

- take reasonable steps to ensure that the supplier understands those needs; and

- devote reasonable time and patience to understanding how to operate the system.

Correspondingly, the supplier should:

- communicate to the customer whether or not these precise needs can be met and if so how – if not, the appropriate options for meeting them should be set out; and

- take reasonable steps to ensure that the customer is trained in using the system.

In addition, the customer and supplier should work together to resolve the problems which in the judge's words 'will almost certainly occur'.

It is necessary therefore for a customer to be proactive in co-operating when problems arise.

3. Misrepresentation

A supplier is not free to make unwarranted claims which persuade a customer to enter into the contract[28]. There is liability at law for false statements or misrepresentations of fact. Even if made innocently, the misrepresentation by the supplier may be used as a valid defence in any action brought on the contract. Alternatively, the injured party may bring its own action once the misrepresentation is discovered.

Clauses exempting liability for misrepresentations made during negotiations can only be relied on so far as they can be regarded as fair and reasonable in the particular circumstances.

The IT supplier Wang knew that Pegler wanted a tried-and-tested IT solution for its plumbers' goods business[29]. Wang failed to supply it. Wang had made a pre-contractual misrepresentation that its standard software was a perfect fit and a low risk solution. The implementation failed for many reasons, including Wang's extensive breaches of contract. The court held that Wang might be able to rely on standard terms intended to exclude liability for some foreseeable lapse, but not in the context of misrepresenting what they were supplying. Then the exclusion of liability was unreasonable.

In the case brought by South West Water against ICL[30], ICL entered into the contract, having represented that they would sign a back-to-back contract with their sub-contractor. ICL's sales people knew at the time that this would not happen. The sub-contractor had warned ICL that ICL was seriously underestimating the resources required to carry out the project and refused to enter into a contract. South West Water would not have signed the agreement with ICL had it not expected a back-to-back contract to be in force.

The relevant contract between South West Water and ICL had a clause excluding liability for pre-contractual representations or warranties. The judge held that this was unreasonable under UCTA. The ambit of the clause was too wide, purporting to cover innocent, negligent or fraudulent misrepresentations and was therefore unenforceable in respect of ICL's fraudulent misrepresentation, following an earlier decision in a non-IT case[31].

Clauses in standard form contracts which attempt to exclude pre-contractual representations cannot be relied on, particularly if the misrepresentation is known to be untrue when it is made.

D. Carrying out a contract or ending it

It is entirely possible for a contract to continue to be effective without any expiry or termination, for so long as the obligations and rights of the parties stay in force. However, it is always advisable to consider, at the time of formulating the contractual requirements, the circumstances in which one party may justifiably bring the agreement to an end.

1. Performance

The most satisfactory conclusion to a contract is by the obligations being carried out, so that the contract is discharged. The supplier provides the products or services and the customer pays for them. This is 'performance' of the contract, which must be substantially according to what was agreed. This means that in principle, if there is an agreement to carry out certain work in its entirety for an agreed fixed price, and there are no other terms about this in the contract, the work must be completed before payment has to be made.

This is illustrated when an IT contract is for the provision of a whole working system and the supplier fails to deliver it. There will be a total failure of consideration. Even though the supplier may have delivered hardware and provided services, there will be no entitlement to payment.

However, in a complex software development project, even where the timescales have slipped unacceptably, and the end of the development is not in sight, much useful work may have been done by the analysts and programmers, to the customer's eventual advantage. If the contract can be construed to be 'divisible' or 'severable', as when there is payment by instalments on completion of milestones, payment will be due from the customer on completion of each milestone. This exception to the general principle will depend on what the parties intended. It is, therefore, most important for a software supplier to avoid any implication that all the work has to be completed precisely and exactly on a long-term, complicated development. The supplier should ensure that the work is broken down into sections, self-contained as far as possible, within the framework of a software development contract.

In the case of *Wang v Pegler*, referred to earlier[32], no system was delivered to Pegler. The judge described Wang's performance as 'disastrous'. The direct conse-quence of the high damages (and costs and additional expenditure) awarded against Wang was that Wang went into voluntary liquidation.

In the *South West Water* case discussed earlier[33], South West Water succeeded in its claim that it had received no benefit over the two years since the contract was signed where ICL could not deliver as originally promised, and where the target date had changed more than once. ICL had delivered hardware and project management and training services. But it was held that there was no value to South West Water in receiving any of this, because of the failure to deliver the software. South West Water was entitled to terminate the contract and to restitution of all the sums it had paid, which ICL had to return.

Nevertheless, where the obligations have been 'substantially' performed by the supplier, then the supplier can sue for payment of the price. The amount due will be offset by a claim for damages by the paying party with regard to the part of the contract which is outstanding.

If the supplier is in breach of contract, the purchaser will not necessarily be able to claim damages to put it into the position it would have been in, but for the breach – that is to say, the cost of a replacement system. If the entire cost is perceived as being unreasonable, damages will be awarded only to compensate for the loss.

One case to illustrate this is about a tangible swimming pool rather than an intangible computer system, but the House of Lords specifically stated that the principle extended beyond construction law[34]. The specification for the pool was for a maximum depth of 7 ft 6 in. The actual maximum depth was 6 ft 9 in (6 ft under the diving board). The cost of a new pool would have been £21,560.

The decision made in the Court of First Instance was changed in the Court of Appeal and changed back in the House of Lords, where it was held that the replacement cost was out of all proportion to the benefit. The pool was serviceable and the variation did not affect the value of the property. The concern was to compensate for losses truly suffered. The claimant, a keen swimmer, was awarded £2,500 for loss of amenity.

2. Part performance

If the party not in default has accepted that the contract has been only partly performed, payment can be due for what has been accepted. The accepting party must have had an actual choice whether to accept less than the total contract obligation. For example, the Sale of Goods Act 1979[35] states that the buyer may reject a quantity of goods less than the contract amount agreed with the seller, but if the buyer does accept the delivery, payment will be at the contract rate. But if the contract was for a building on the buyer's land, which was only half-built, the buyer would be put in a position where he could not choose whether to accept or not. In such a case[36], the builder was not entitled to recover for the work involved in the building, but was able to recover the value of the materials used.

3. Agreement to discharge the contract

If the parties both decide during the course of a contract that they no longer wish the contract to stay in force, they can agree to discharge it. This is, strictly speaking, a further agreement, and must therefore be supported by 'consideration', as discussed earlier. Where both parties still have rights and obligations to carry out, relinquishing those rights will constitute the consideration. But where one party has carried out its side of the bargain and is releasing the other party from its obligations, it must get something out of the agreement, rather than be making a gratuitous promise, for there to be consideration. Otherwise the release must be under seal (ie by deed).

4. 'Frustration'

There is a general rule of contractual liability that if a party wishes to protect itself against subsequent difficulties in performing its part of the contract, it should specifically provide for this in the terms and conditions. It is not the fault of the other party, who should not suffer because of non-performance of what has been agreed, whatever the reason. It is a question of who is to bear the risk of the occurrence of the event.

Exceptions to requiring performance are made only in certain cases, based on supervening events outside the control of the parties. It must be an event quite beyond what the parties intended in entering into the agreement, making it impossible to carry out. There is a court decision[37] to show that disappointed expectations making the performance of a contract more onerous than had been anticipated (so that it takes much longer to carry out), such as the development of a computer system, would not constitute this sort of exception. In that case, the building of houses took 22 months rather than eight, because of the lack of labour but the obligations remained.

If the contract is frustrated, all sums paid under the contract are recoverable, and all sums payable cease to be payable. The court may allow the party to whom the money was paid or payable to retain or recover a sum equal to expenses incurred, or to keep a sum equivalent to any benefit gained by the other party, if there are no other provisions in the contract.

An IT contract will normally contain special terms to deal with possible situations which the parties realise may arise. There is also a provision common to many agreements called 'force majeure', discussed in **CHAPTER 6**, to cover situations which would make the contract impossible to carry out.

5. Termination

The contract itself will often contain explicit termination provisions to bring it to an end. Termination may be at the option of one of the parties under certain specific conditions.

TIME LIMIT

There may be a time limit in the contract itself, for its expiry, after which it will no longer be in effect.

NOTICE

The contract may permit either party to terminate on notice to the other party. Generally speaking, it is always advisable to consider including this, rather than risk being permanently bound by the terms of a contract when circumstances may change in an unforeseen way. Yet it will also be giving the other party the opportunity to terminate without a particular reason, and the commercial sense of the transaction may make this undesirable. The provisions for termination on notice do not have to be mutual. For instance, a software licence may be granted without the owner having the right to terminate merely on notice if the software is necessary to the licensee's business, but the licensee may have the right to terminate if it no longer wishes to use the software.

INSOLVENCY

There is usually a provision in a contract for the supply of products or services permitting termination by one party on the grounds of the other party's insolvency. For example, there is no point in the supplier continuing to provide products or services where there is no prospect of payment being made.

BREACH OF CONTRACT

A clause is normally included in a contract to permit the injured party to terminate it in the event of breach by the other party whether or not this will be followed by court action. Breach of contract by one party which causes loss to the other party will entitle that other party to bring an action for damages and possibly other remedies depending on the nature of the breach. If the breach consists of a term in a contract which is so fundamentally important that the whole transaction would be drastically affected if it is not carried out, the contract may be treated as 'discharged' by the injured party. This term is called a 'condition'. Other terms are 'warranties' or promises, which are not regarded as so fundamental to the contract. Breach of a warranty entitles the injured party to damages but not to repudiate the contract. These definitions and their consequences depend on the facts of the contract, not by what names the individual terms and conditions may be given, and may be implied rather than being expressly stated.

6. 'Time of the essence'

The implication in a contract will normally be that an obligation should be performed in a 'reasonable time'. A term making time 'of the essence' should be expressly included in the contract if it is required.

Essentially, this specific provision requires timely performance of the contract. In other words, where the goods are not delivered or the services are not performed by the specified date stipulated, the non-defaulting party will be entitled to terminate the agreement and seek damages for any resulting loss.

If a supplier agrees to a 'time of the essence' provision, for example to deliver software by a particular date, any delay to such delivery would entitle the customer to reject the software, terminate the contract, and seek damages for any resulting loss.

Where no contractual obligation over time is specified, a reasonable slippage in the anticipated date for delivery or for implementing the services might be acceptable. But if there is undue delay, the other side is entitled to serve a notice to the effect that the services must be provided or the goods delivered by a certain date which must be within a reasonable time. This notice will then have made time 'of the essence'.

For example, in a software development agreement where there are milestones for payments, notwithstanding that there are dates set out which the software house must aim for, a delay in meeting these dates will not be as crucial as where the contract specifies 'time of the essence'.

For a supplier to commit itself to deadlines unnecessarily by accepting 'time of the essence' conditions is unrealistic in complex software development or for delivery of a system where it would not be in control of the supply of all the component parts.

Clearly there will be times when a date is genuinely critical to a customer, who will need a commitment spelled out. In such cases, the supplier should ensure that sufficient margin has been built in to its schedule for it to be absolutely confident of meeting it – and to allow for the enhanced risk when pricing the work.

E. Remedies

1. Remedies for breach of contract

If one of the parties to a contract is in breach by not complying with the terms of the agreement, perhaps by failing to carry out an obligation or by doing something that it had agreed not to do, the injured party will be entitled to a remedy at law for the loss or damage caused to it.

Court proceedings arising out of breach of contract must generally be started within six years of the date on which the breach of the contract occurred. There are certain refinements to this. If there has been some concealment or fraud which has prevented the claimant finding out about the right of action, the six-year period will start from the time when it was discovered, or when it reasonably should have been discovered.

The six-year period may be extended if acknowledgment is made by the party causing the breach. If a debt is acknowledged or part payment is made, the six years will start from the date of the acknowledgment or part-payment.

Damages are the most common remedy sought for breach of contract. The amount of damages which will be awarded is a question of fact arising out of the circumstances of the case, the law consisting only of general principles. Thus, the amount of damages must relate to the loss suffered. There is generally no 'punishment' in English law for breach of contract. Damages are compensation to the aggrieved party as an attempt to put that party into the situation that it would have occupied had the contract been carried out as the parties had originally intended.

The injured party may claim not only for loss actually suffered, but also for the loss of the benefit which the performance of the contract would have brought.

Damages may be assessed on the basis of what it would cost to have the work carried out by a third party. A supplier's loss of profits may also be recovered unless the goods in question are in such short supply that no real loss will have occurred because of the general demand for the goods.

A consequence of this concept of compensation is that the injured party should always take steps to mitigate loss. If goods have not been delivered as agreed, the injured party should try and purchase the goods elsewhere. On instalment contracts, where default is made in meeting a milestone or in making a payment, the injured party can bring an action for damages for breach, but may not treat the whole contract as discharged for that reason alone. Each party should carry out an evaluation at the start of a case of what the damages are likely to be, to assess the commercial risk of progressing it.

Damages to compensate the injured party for the injury itself are general damages, which have to be assessed on the particular circumstances of the breach. These are unliquidated damages in contrast to liquidated damages, which consist of the amount of the actual losses.

A 'liquidated damages' clause in a contract for a fixed sum payable for a foreseeable breach, such as breach of a restriction on employing any staff of the other party, should be a genuine pre-estimate of the potential losses arising from the breach. An arbitrary amount or a figure which the courts take to be a penalty will not be enforceable. The courts would always look at the sense of what had been agreed, rather than assuming that the name given in the contract to the sum demonstrated whether the compensation really consisted of a genuine sum as a pre-estimate or as a penalty. Nevertheless, it is wise not to call any pre-arranged term in the contract a 'penalty'.

Not all damages necessary to put the injured party in the exact position it would have been in if the contract had been performed will be recoverable. They must arise as natural consequences of the breach and not be too 'remote'[38]. They must have been reasonably foreseen by the parties at the time of making the contract. If special difficulties would arise if the contract is breached by one party, and those difficulties are not made known to the other party, no damages would be payable on their account in the event of breach.

IT suppliers' contracts often routinely (and understandably) exclude consequential loss. In *British Sugar plc v NEI Power Projects Ltd*, the judge held that 'consequential loss' meant loss that the claimants might prove over and above losses arising naturally and directly out of breaches of contract. This was upheld on appeal[39].

Loss of profits may well result naturally and directly from breach of contract in an IT contract. The supplier should now specifically exclude this as damages, rather than assume that it is consequential.

Where there is a breach of contract, the injured party can request the court to treat the contract as discharged, to 'rescind' or cancel the contract, if it is possible to restore the parties to their original positions (the noun is 'rescission'). There must be substantial failure in carrying out the terms of the agreement in order to justify setting the contract aside. Each party will be released from its obligations. Alternatively the injured party might prefer to rely on damages to recover the original losses and still require performance.

In some other situations, amounts of money will not compensate a claimant sufficiently. For example, in a non-disclosure agreement, if the confidential information is being publicised, what is required is for further disclosure to be prevented. Software piracy is another instance where speedy action to stop unauthorised access to the software will bring the most effective result.

An injunction or an order for specific performance is a remedy ordered by the court to stop a breach of contract or to require some positive act to be carried out in accordance with the contract. An *interlocutory* injunction is an emergency remedy which may be applied for on the way to a full court hearing of all the issues. But an injunction or an order for specific performance is a remedy only granted at the court's discretion. The standard of conduct of the party making the application to the court is one of the factors taken into account. The court may decide that damages would in fact be sufficient and, consequently, not grant the injunction. Even here, the court may award damages instead. If the obligations are not sufficiently well defined, such as ongoing complicated support arrangements, specific performance may not be a suitable remedy.

An 'Anton Piller' order is a special kind of injunction (the procedure is now set out in the Civil Procedure Act 1997, s 7). It is granted in certain circumstances where it is believed that the defendant may destroy incriminating materials. It is applied for without the defendant's knowledge − 'ex parte' in legal terminology. It is exceptional; the standard rule in legal proceedings is that a party should be informed of the case against it. But if the defendant knew that he was being accused of, say, copying software, he would destroy the copies, and there would no longer be any evidence against him. So an Anton Piller order permits the solicitor of the party bringing the action to search the defendant's premises under strictly defined rules, and seize the incriminating materials. The defendant would be aware that the order had been made only when the solicitor arrives at the door − although at that point the opportunity must be given for the defendant's own solicitor to be contacted.

Thus an Anton Piller order could allow the removal of computers believed to contain pirated software, and suspected back up discs, tapes and documentation. FAST, the Federation Against Software Theft, has been able to use Anton Piller orders in its fight against software piracy.

The constraint on a party who successfully but improperly applies for an Anton Piller order will be liability for the defendant's costs and damages.

2. Quantum meruit/Unjust enrichment

In the IT industry, work involved in software development, service provision or system integration, often goes ahead before the terms of any contract have been agreed by the parties.

When one party has provided a benefit to the other at its own expense without any contract in place, the courts may decide that it would be unjust for the receiving party to keep the benefit. There may be an action for the recovery of reasonable remuneration for services. The legal principle is known as 'quantum meruit', which means payment in proportion to the worth of the work done, or 'unjust enrichment', a more flexible term used recently.

- The defendant must have been enriched by willingly receiving a *benefit*.

- The plaintiff must have sustained *expense* through providing that benefit, without intending it to be a gift.

- It would be *unjust* to allow the defendant to retain the benefit.

In a case between Vedatech Corporation and Crystal Decisions (UK) Ltd[40], just such a situation arose. Vedatech assisted US and European software companies in introducing their products to the Japanese market, through sales, support training and services. Crystal (at that time called Holistic) had developed successful software which they wanted to supply in Japan.

Following a meeting between representatives of Vedatech and Holistic, a draft agreement should have been drawn up. It never was. Vedatech claimed that there was an oral contract. However, it was held that what was agreed at the meeting was too imprecise to form a 'concluded bargain'.

This is regrettably not uncommon in IT negotiations. Discussions may not be recorded or formalised in any detail, and yet will form the basis for work to be carried out, often over many months by the supplier. Sometimes all goes well. But frequently, disputes arise over what precisely was agreed − if anything − over particular points, or even major issues − and what should be paid.

Vedatech was not in the same position as would have been the case if there had been a proper contract. However, together with a team of people providing services, it had contributed a way into the Japanese market for Holistic's benefit. It was, therefore, a question of what Holistic should pay.

The judge said:

> 'The amount depends on all the circumstances. These particularly include the position taken by the parties in the failed negotiations for a contract − they give some guide to the value of the benefit. Often a fee on the basis of time will be appropriate ... But things may be different where a party provides a benefit on the express basis that he is to have some "share in the action" '.

81

In an earlier case[41], the manager of a goldmine introduced gold mine concessions to the owner at the owner's request. It was held that there was no contract. However, the manager was entitled to reasonable remuneration on the implied contract to pay him quantum meruit. The basis for this entitlement was a sum calculated on the basis of 'reasonable participation', a percentage of the profits, as had been contemplated by the parties.

This principle was followed in this case:

> 'because Vedatech were asked to and did undertake risk ... they are entitled to some reward if that risk proved beneficial'.

Vedatech was therefore held to be entitled to claim reasonable remuneration for the work done for Holistic, assessed not merely on a time basis, but on a time and success basis. In general, parties cannot claim for unjust enrichment in respect of work done in preparation for a contract. However, exceptional circumstances may apply when a claimant has been led to believe that it would benefit under a future contract.

This is illustrated by another case involving an IT-related company, ICL Pathway[42]. Countrywide Communications undertook free PR work for ICL in order to obtain a tender, after assurances that if the tender was awarded, Countrywide Communications would be granted a sub-contract for the PR work. ICL obtained the tender, but did not grant Countrywide Communications the sub-contract. It was held that only exceptionally could a party claim for the cost of work carried out in anticipation of a contract. Thus when it would amount to a 'denial of justice' a court could find for a sub-contractor's claim in quantum meruit. The relevant factors were:

- Would the services normally be performed free of charge?

- What degree of risk had the claimant undertaken that the services would not be recompensed?

- Did the defendant obtain real benefits from the claimant?

- Was there a conscious decision to renege on previous assurances, so as to involve an element of fault?

These cases demonstrate that although lack of an enforceable agreement can cause uncertainty, effort and expense, there may be some entitlement to payment for services rendered. It is much better to have a contract with clear terms as to what is expected and what is to be provided – and at what charges.

F. Adjudication

The majority of disputes are settled by means of commercial negotiation without recourse to the formalities of law. Many IT contracts which become subjects of disputes have not been negotiated and are on one party's standard terms, or the terms are unclear in that the parties do not agree on what formed the contract, or they are incomplete at the time of signature (especially the schedule contents).

Litigation, by means of taking formal legal court proceedings, is not the only means of resolving a dispute over a contract which has not been able to be resolved informally. Alternatives are arbitration and Alternative Dispute Resolution, the latter commonly referred to as 'ADR'.

1. Litigation

Litigation is always possible where there is a dispute and a provision in a contract which attempted to exclude litigation in the event of a dispute would not be valid.

It may take several years for some cases to reach a hearing at court, although during the course of the litigation, it is normal for the parties to try to reach a settlement. Most disputes where court proceedings are issued are settled by the parties themselves without getting as far as an appearance at court. However, immediate action at the outset can expedite matters. 'Summary judgment', a procedure where there is no real defence to a claim, can be an effective and relatively inexpensive method of achieving a quick result. Injunctions, discussed in the Remedies section above, are often required at short notice and can be very effective.

Under English law, the losing party is often obliged to pay the legal costs of the winner as well as its own. This can act as an incentive towards settlement. Legal costs can sometimes exceed the damages being claimed. The focus of the dispute will change, as the parties face the prospective financial risk of losing the case and paying damages, together with their own and the winner's costs in addition.

There are procedures available to each party to assist resolution. A claimant may apply to have a preliminary issue of fact or question of law determined, or seek an interim payment. A defendant may make a payment into court. If the damages awarded at trial are equal to or less than the payment, the claimant will have to pay the defendant's costs from the time of payment in. The defendant may apply for an order that the claimant gives security for the costs of the proceedings. If the claimant loses and is ordered to pay the defendant's costs, the defendant is secured against the risk of the claimant's inability to pay or evasion of payment (for instance if the claimant is based abroad).

2. Arbitration

The Arbitration Act 1996 gives the parties much autonomy in conducting arbitration and allows the arbitrator significant powers. The parties are free to decide how the dispute should be resolved, subject to certain public interest safeguards. The disputing parties choose a neutral person – or more than one – to resolve the dispute by a binding and enforceable decision or award. If they do not agree a procedure for arbitration, the rules will be taken from those set out in the Act.

The choice of arbitrator enables the parties to select a neutral adjudicator acceptable to both sides who has expert knowledge of the area in dispute (which they may prefer to do if technical knowledge is important for judging a case). It is also important, however, for an arbitrator to be knowledgeable about arbitration procedure, to be able to deal with any legal points which emerge, and to make a decision which cannot be challenged in the courts. The arbitrator is required to act fairly and impartially.

A neutral location for the arbitration proceedings must be found and paid for. The arbitrator's fees must be paid and, even if the matter is settled beforehand, the arbitrator may nevertheless be entitled to some payment. A time convenient to everyone, both to the arbitrator and to the parties, has to be found. The time can actually be chosen to suit the parties, whereas litigation does not operate in this way – the time is to suit the judge and the system, not the individuals concerned. However, the disadvantage of this is that an arbitration timetable can proceed much more slowly than litigation, where the existing commitments of the parties, witnesses and arbitrator have to be taken into account. Where there is more than one arbitrator, typically three will be the agreed number, and one of the practical disadvantages is in the increased costs through payment of their fees. There is also likely to be more difficulty in finding dates suitable to everyone, certainly where an early hearing is desired.

There can be greater flexibility in the legal rules of evidence and procedure, but the conduct of arbitration depends entirely on the nature of the agreement to arbitrate. Statutory rules apply, unless there are other provisions in the agreement. An arbitration hearing may be less formal than a court hearing. Evidence is often given in the form of documents, indeed it is possible to make an award based entirely on written submissions. There is an appeal to the courts from an arbitration award only in very limited circumstances. An arbitration award is therefore more final than a High Court decision. It is enforceable by the courts in exactly the same way as a court judgment.

Arbitration is claimed to be more flexible, quicker and cheaper than litigation but this is by no means automatically the case. It may be more expensive and slower, and with no effective right of appeal. It used to be the case that an arbitrator who was suitably qualified and experienced in understanding the nature of computing disputes would be preferable to a judge. However, judges are now better educated about information technology.

For international trade, arbitration is often a preferred route for settling disputes. The 1996 Arbitration Act increased the popularity of London as a venue for international arbitration. Other advantages include the English language, English contract law, the availability of experienced arbitrators, the presence of quality international law firms, specialised and general arbitral associations and the commercial importance of the City of London.

3. Alternative Dispute Resolution

Through Alternative Dispute Resolution (ADR), a framework is created for the parties themselves to negotiate a solution which they both find mutually satisfactory, normally with the assistance of a neutral third party, sometimes also with experts. The process is relatively informal, cheap, flexible and voluntary (although if it is unsuccessful, this will, of course, increase the costs). There is no continuing obligation and it can be stopped at any time. The neutral third party's role is based on consent, and the process stays under the control of the parties. The costs are usually divided between the parties. It is important that senior management is involved. Their time is another factor to take into account. There are a number of ADR techniques which can be modified as required by the parties. The neutral mediator has no authority to make any decisions for the disputing parties, but will have training in skills to help them resolve their dispute by negotiated agreement without adjudication. Unlike an arbitrator or judge, the mediator may participate in developing proposals and making suggestions for settlement. The mediator will meet separately and perhaps redefine the main issues in conflict, drawing out the strengths and weaknesses of each issue. In this way, the parties can explore different possibilities of compromise.

ADR changes the emphasis of the dispute from an outcome of 100 per cent success or failure to a co-operative process controlled by the parties themselves to achieve a workable settlement. Its success depends on the willingness of the parties being ready to resolve their dispute in a mutually satisfactory way. The mediator cannot impose a solution. The parties do not have to agree until both are satisfied.

Decisions are not binding, and should there not be an outcome on which both parties are happy to rely, any confidentiality agreed about the procedure will not have any effect if the matter subsequently proceeds to a court hearing. The conciliator or mediator will not be in a legally privileged position regarding disclosure of information learned during the course of the ADR. However, an unsuccessful ADR process conducted on a formal 'without prejudice' basis will not be permitted to be referred to in subsequent litigation.

CHOICE OF DISPUTE RESOLUTION FORUM

In deciding which of the different forms of dispute resolution would be most appropriate, the relative merits should be considered in terms of timescales and formality, and according to the type of dispute. Considerations for deciding on one means rather than another will also include the number of parties involved; the technical depth of the dispute; its complexity; questions of speed, cost and privacy. For IT-related disputes, the parties concerned are likely to need or wish to have a continuing business relationship whatever the result of the dispute, and this is another factor to be borne in mind – for example, a supplier continuing to support its system licensed to a customer, where no other maintenance organisation would have the expertise.

However, among the recommendations in Lord Woolf's report 'Access to Justice', implemented in 1999, greater use of ADR was proposed within the litigation process. The courts are required to encourage the use of ADR in appropriate cases and to facilitate it through case management. Thus, the courts may halt the litigation timetable for the parties to try and settle the dispute through ADR. This forms part of a procedural protocol with the overriding objective of enabling the courts to deal with cases justly[43]. This includes active case management.

Indeed, the courts are now actively considering whether ADR should have been used in attempting to resolve a dispute which is litigated. In one case, the Court of Appeal advised both parties to consider the use of ADR, in granting leave to appeal to a claimant against a judgment in favour of the defendant. The claimant's appeal was dismissed. However, the defendant was not awarded costs because it had refused to mediate[44].

The courts recognise that skilled mediators may achieve results which go beyond the powers of the courts. The latter may give legal rulings which do not assist the practical resolution of a problem. In a dispute between neighbours about a water supply pipe, the judges in the Court of Appeal were unanimous in finding it unsatisfactory that it had not been mediated[45]. A joint expert had reported that the best solution was for each property to be fed by its own pipes. The recommendation had not been followed.

Cable & Wireless and IBM entered into an agreement for IT services to be supplied worldwide[46]. One of the clauses provided rather imprecisely for a reference to ADR. When a dispute arose, Cable & Wireless characterised the ADR reference as an 'agreement to negotiate' because of its lack of certainty, which would therefore render it unenforceable (the earlier discussion on enforceability refers). However, it was held that for the court not to enforce a contractual reference to ADR would 'fly in the face of' public policy. It should therefore be enforced.

However, in two cases, the Court of Appeal did not penalise the successful parties who had refused to mediate[47]. In one the defendant believed (correctly) that it had good prospects of success and in the other there was an undetermined point of law. Nevertheless, the court stated that lawyers should routinely consider with their clients whether disputes were suitable for ADR. Matters to consider by the court in whether to award costs sanctions against a successful party who had refused mediation included:

- the subject matter of the dispute;

- the merits of its case;

- previous settlement attempts;

- costs of mediation;

- risks of delaying trial by mediation; and

- whether the mediation would have had prospects of success.

Thus ADR is becoming an integral part of litigation and the overall dispute resolution process. The courts may expect it to be considered in the course of the development of the case, and if it is not, in certain defined circumstances the successful party may not be awarded costs.

1   *Pharmaceutical Society of Great Britain v Boots Cash Chemists (Southern) Ltd* [1953] 1 QB 401, [1953] 1 All ER 482.
2   *Carlill v Carbolic Smoke Ball Co* [1892] 2 QB 484, [1891–94] All ER Rep 127, CA.
3   *Fraser Williams v Prudential Holborn Ltd* (1993) 64 BLR 1, CA.
4   *Branca v Cobarro* [1947] 2 All ER 101, CA.
5   *Raindrop Data Systems Ltd v Systemics Ltd* [1988] FSR 354, Ch D.
6   *Walford v Miles* [1992] 2 AC 128, HL.
7   *Misa v Currie* (1876) 1 App Cas 554, HL.
8   *Boots the Chemist Ltd v Amdahl (UK) Ltd* (2000) unreported, CA.
9   Contracts (Rights of Third Parties) Act 1999.
10 *Smith v Wilson* (1832) 3 B & Ad 728.
11 *L Gent & Sons v Eastman Machine Co Ltd* [1986] BTLC 17, CA.
12 *Spectra International plc v Tiscali UK Ltd and World Online Ltd* [2002] All ER (D) 209 (Oct).
13 *DMA Financial Solutions Ltd v Baan UK Ltd* [2000] MCLR 40.
14 *Reader's Digest Children's Publishing Ltd v Premier Books (UK) Ltd* [2002] All ER (D) 134 (Mar).
15 *Thornton v Shoe Lane Parking Ltd* [1971] 2 QB 163, CA.
16 E-Commerce Directive (EC) 2000/31 implemented in the UK by Electronic Commerce (EC Directive) Regulations 2002, SI 2002/293.
17 *Beta Computers (Europe) Ltd v Adobe Systems (Europe) Ltd* [1996] FSR 367.
18 *St Albans City and District Council v International Computers Ltd* [1996] FSR 251, CA.
19 *Saphena Computing Ltd v Allied Collection Agencies Ltd* [1995] FSR 616, CA.
20 *SAM Business Systems Ltd v Hedley & Co* [2002] EWHC 2733 (TCC); [2003] 1 All ER (Comm) 465.
21 Unfair Contract Terms Act 1977, s 2.
22 Unfair Contract Terms Act 1977, Sch 2.
23 *St Albans City and District Council v ICL Ltd* [1996] FSR 251, CA.
24 *South West Water Services Ltd v International Computers Ltd* [1999] BLR, 420.
25 *Horace Holman Group Ltd v Sherwood International Group Ltd* [2001] All ER (D) 83 (Nov).
26 *Watford Electronics Ltd v Sanderson CFL Ltd* [2001] EWCA Civ 317, [2002] FSR 19.
27 *Anglo Group plc v Winther Browne & Co Ltd* [2000] ITCLR 559.
28 Misrepresentation Act 1967.
29 *Pegler Ltd v Wang (UK) Ltd* [2000] ITCLR 617, QBD (T&CC).
30 *South West Water Services Ltd v International Computers Ltd* [1999] BLR 420, QBD (T&CC).
31 *Thomas Witter Ltd v TBP Industries Ltd* [1996] 2 All ER 573.
32 *Pegler Ltd v Wang (UK) Ltd* [2000] ITCLR 617, QBD (T&CC).
33 *South West Water Services Ltd v International Computers Ltd* [1999] BLR 420.
34 *Ruxley Electronics and Construction Ltd v Forsyth* [1996] AC 344, HL.
35 Sale of Goods Act 1979, s 54.
36 *Sumpter v Hedges* [1898] 1 QB 673, CA.
37 *Davis Contractors Ltd v Fareham UDC* [1956] AC 696, HL.
38 *Hadley v Baxendale* (1854) 9 Exch 341.
39 *British Sugar plc v NEI Power Projects Ltd* [1998] IT CLR 125, CA.
40 *Vedatech Corp v Crystal Decisions (UK) Ltd* [2002] EWHC 818 (Ch), [2002] All ER (D) 318 (May).
41 *Way v Latilla* [1937] 3 All ER 759, HL.
42 *Countrywide Communications Ltd v ICL Pathway Ltd* [1999] All ER (D) 1192.
43 Civil Procedure Rules 1999, r 1.1.
44 *Dunnett v Railtrack plc (in administration)* [2002] EWCA Civ 303, [2002] 2 All ER 850.

45 *Martin v Childs* [2002] EWCA Civ 283, [2002] All ER (D) 250 (Feb).
46 *Cable and Wireless plc v IBM United Kingdom Ltd* [2002] EWHC 2059 (Comm), [2002] 2 All ER (Comm) 1041.
47 *Halsey v Milton Keynes General NHS Trust; Steel v Joy* [2004] EWCA Civ 576, [2004] NLJR 769.

CHAPTER 5
Construction of a computer contract

A. General

The objective of drafting, constructing and negotiating a contract is not to write the most elegant contract, or one which can be considered 'watertight' from at least one party's perspective. It is, every time, to achieve a good quality working document which gives each party what it essentially requires and which enables the parties to do business without undue hindrance or delay. It is founded on the assumption that the parties *want* to do business together and the task of the draftsperson is to facilitate this in a suitably commercial manner.

Point scoring and indulgence in esoterics should never be permitted to transcend commercial objectives, and all draftspeople and negotiators would do well to keep in mind the commercial wishes of their principals.

There are numerous IT contract categories. The purpose of this book is to demonstrate ways in which the most commonly encountered IT contracts can be developed and negotiated. Ways of doing business and therefore the contracts to deal with the transactions are still evolving. For example, outsourcing, in the sense of the wholesale transfer of computer equipment and IT staff to the supplier who takes over the running of the customer's systems, is now a major contract area. Yet it used to be almost unheard of other than as bureau services, which were common in the early days of computing. Outsourcing contracts themselves have changed in style, content and scope over the last few years, and will continue to do so in line with progress in the outsourcing business itself.

The process of drafting, constructing and negotiating has a structure that can be applied to new forms of contracts that are generated.

Definitions should be an early consideration in drafting a contract.

The final part of this chapter sets out how this book may be used to assist the drawing up of a contract.

B. The development process

IT contracts are more often generated by suppliers than by their customers. This is not surprising since it is the suppliers who are regularly doing the selling and offering their products and services, on related terms of business. It is their business. For most customers, the transaction will be more likely to be a 'one-off'.

However, customers should want to take some initiative where software development, outsourcing, website services or other specifically designed or tailored services are involved. Large IT users will also find it useful to create special purchase agreements, as government departments and other public authorities already do. There are available model forms of contract, for example those created by the Chartered Institute of Purchasing and Supply, but these are not often encountered in practice, partly because suppliers will tend to reject outright the attempted imposition of such terms by smaller users, and also because the industry has not yet settled down to a situation in which standard terms and conditions meet the requirements of the business arrangements being made. Where software may be worth hundreds or millions of pounds, licensed for many different reasons, one standard licence form will not work. The range and values of products and services vary so much.

There is growing emphasis on the use of systematic methodologies for developing software systems, providing project planning, estimates for resource requirements, project control and documentation, and quality assurance. The stages of development are defined and monitored. The process of creating a computer contract, regardless of its purpose and whether it is written from a supplier or customer perspective, can be seen as analogous to the process of developing a software product.

Stages

	Software Development	IT Contract	
	Feasibility Study/Response to Tender	Review of Transaction Principles	
	User Requirements/Concept Paper	Statement of Structure of the Agreement	
	Detailed Specification	Clause Headings/Skeleton Agreement	
(	Code	First Draft	)
Iterative (	Testing	Review	) Iterative
(	Recoding, Debugging, Modifications	Negotiations	)
	Acceptance and Implementation	Signed Agreement	
	Support – ongoing debugging/modifications	Performance and Contract Administration	

For certain types of contracts there may also – or alternatively – be a negotiation process analogous to iterative prototyping. This enables requirements to be flexibly altered through trial and error, as more experience and a better understanding of the application and its objectives is gained.

This is admittedly simplistic but it serves to illustrate the process which should be adopted to ensure a satisfactory result.

Each stage in the process should be subject to the agreement of the other party before the next stage commences.

Taking this analogy one stage further, the advantages of using pro forma languages for describing the structures and processes of software systems (as for example, in testing systems used in aeronautics to predict failures before the systems are implemented) also apply to the use of clear formal language in a contract. Such language helps to remove ambiguity, facilitates communications, and ideally provides a framework appropriate to the business for future contracts for similar kinds of transactions, where the issues important to running the business concerned can be taken into account. Just as formal specification, refinement and verification in software development will improve the integrity of the application, so can the use of formal procedures in contract drafting and negotiation lead to a contract which accurately reflects the interests of the parties concerned.

C. Points of construction

Many computer contracts are quite complex in terms of their subject matter, often involving difficult intellectual property points. The products and services being provided also need to be very carefully described, including all associated conditions and exceptions.

The observation of a few ground rules will be found to be helpful. First, however, consideration should be given as to whether the task of constructing a contract can be justified by the initiating party in terms of expense, including the time of all those who will need to be consulted.

- Is the contract a high value one?

- Is the contract critical in its impact on the business (of the initiator)?

- If the user – is the contract for a product or service of a value where the supplier will not consider terms other than its own standard offering?

- Will it be more economic to analyse and negotiate the other party's document? (But it is a false economy to assume that this will automatically be less expensive in terms of resources and effort.)

- Is there a level of technical content which can be generated or described by only one party in the first instance?

Assuming that it remains desirable to develop a contract document:

(a)   Concentrate first on the essence of the contract:
   —   a detailed description of the product or service being offered or sought;
   —   identification of any conditions of eligibility for the service;
   —   specific list of any exclusions, to avoid any implication to the contrary; and
   —   enumeration of the responsibilities of each party in connection with the performance of the contract or the provision of the service.

(b)   Consider all vital areas, for example:
   —   guarantees of acceptability and performance;
   —   delivery conditions;
   —   confidentiality requirements; and
   —   establishing and protecting intellectual property rights.

(c)   Produce a full skeleton contract by adding in the other special and general clauses which will be needed. Keep the order logical — incorporate contractual events in sequential order, for example:
   —   Parties
   —   Purpose(s)
   —   Definitions
   —   Term, if applicable
   —   Any rights granted
   —   Exclusions
   —   Obligations of supplier — product development, preparation and delivery-related
   —   Obligations of customer — acceptance and payment-related
   —   Supplier's warranties
   —   Supplier's limits of liability
   —   Intellectual property rights
   —   Termination
   —   Standard contract provisions.

(d)   Produce the first fully worded draft:
   —   Keep the language simple and clear but comprehensive. Avoid jargon as much as possible (whether legal or technology-based). Would a layperson reading it understand it without having to refer to third parties or to reference materials? This is not always attainable with some of the more technical provisions but it is a practical aim.
   —   Use short-form clauses wherever possible and keep the paragraphs and sentences brief. The contract itself should not be lengthy for the sake of it. In all forms of contract drafting there is a temptation to try to anticipate every conceivable contingency. This generally results in documents which are very difficult to read and to follow, which is of no help either in contracts administration or in the event of a dispute. A contract is not a statute.

- Be consistent in the use of clause, paragraph and sub-paragraph numbers and letters, typeface and format.
- Use punctuation minimally but sufficiently to make reading easy. There is no reason not to use commas or semi-colons in a contract where these are grammatically correct. Beware of creating ambiguities – if in doubt, spell it out!
- Presentation is worth thinking about. There is no reason why a contract should not be agreeable to look at – it is more likely then to be read and understood. Headings and indentations can help achieve this. A 'Contents' page listing the clauses and their page references at the beginning of the contract can be helpful. It may be that terms and conditions on the back of an acceptance of order form cannot be in large print, but they should certainly be readable if they are to have any effect. The courts themselves refuse to accept formal documents such as writs, statements of claim, and affidavits for formal court proceedings which are in a typeface of less than 11 points.

(e) Discuss and agree as the negotiation progresses. If a point is worth negotiating, its inclusion or absence in the contract should be established at the time the issue is raised. It is not constructive negotiation, apart from the inherent discourtesy to the other party, to return later on to matters which should have been resolved at an earlier stage. Furthermore, if the contents themselves are not at issue it is neither constructive nor courteous to amend the other party's draft purely so that it conforms more closely to the drafting standards of the modifying party.

(f) Try not to deal with issues in isolation because each one will be only part of the strategy for reaching the final objective. For example, if software ownership is being assigned, the intellectual property indemnity and software warranties should be dealt with at the same time, as these are all aspects of the software assignment. The opportunity to negotiate trade-offs will also be lost if issues are resolved one at a time.

Strong methodologies are needed to ensure high quality systems. Similarly, formal procedures are important in drafting, negotiating and administering high quality contracts.

D. Definitions

Every expression, phrase or term frequently used in the contract should be defined within a 'Definitions' clause, to help the reader and to avoid unnecessary repetition.

Whilst an agreement is easier to read if full explanations are incorporated in the text at the relevant place, this would considerably lengthen the document. Any expression which needs to be used several times should be included as a definition. Definitions should be presented in alphabetical order for ease of reference.

One principle of the 'Definitions' clause should be 'the fewer definitions, the better' if the contract clauses are to remain reasonably easy to read. On the other hand, it is desirable to avoid cross-referencing within the contract as much as possible. In some contracts, definitions are denoted in the text only where they first appear. This is a matter of preferred style, but a 'Definitions' clause does have the practical advantage of avoiding the need to hunt through the document to locate the first use and meaning of a definition.

Definitions are sometimes found as a detachable schedule to an agreement for ease of reference, rather than at the beginning of the agreement. However, it is preferable that they should be a demonstrably intrinsic part of it.

In subsequent clauses, the defined terms will be given capital initial letters. Where capital initials do not occur for terms so defined in the example clauses, this is because the reference is to a more general example. For instance, 'Software' may be defined specifically with a capital initial to refer to software being customised under the terms of the contract, but will remain undefined and therefore in lower case when referring to other software with which the developed software is intended to be used or integrated. A reference may be made in a clause later in the contract to 'software' without a capital initial, meaning software not confined to the customised software identified in the definition.

Where there are many details specific to the agreement, such as a timetable, especially where they are likely to be amended, it is best to define the term by reference to a schedule where the details will be set out separately and can be replaced as a result of negotiations, or under the change control process in the contract. Subject to this, definitions should be self-explanatory as presented.

The temptation should be avoided to expand definitions so that they become, in effect, operative conditions of the contract. For example:

' "Inappropriate Material" is material which is provided or made available or procured by or through the Supplier in breach of clause X of this Agreement'.

This is at worst an underhand method of stating the requirements, but is in any event confusing and may be meaningless.

Definitions sections are generally approached with little enthusiasm. They tend to be regarded as one of the more tedious elements of contract drafting – this is a great mistake. Whenever a new form of agreement is required for which there are no useful precedents, the definitions are the springboard essential to the contract construction process. This is especially true for a complex bespoke agreement, but it is also very important in drafting a standard form document.

The contract draftsperson really needs to start by gaining a thorough understanding of what the contract is intended to achieve. The more technical the subject matter, the more important it is to ensure that the essential meanings of the product and service descriptions are conveyed to a reader who may not be familiar with the technical aspects. The best way of reaching this comprehension is to develop a series of definitions which collectively describe the key elements of the transaction in question.

Business promoters of new products and services sometimes give insufficient thought to all the ramifications of what they are seeking to do in introducing new products and services. It is therefore useful for both the contract draftspeople and the business managers to work through the details and implications. Debates on any subject tend to produce additional perspectives and ideas, so that any specific problems can be overcome.

For example, definitions which describe specific service features often involve the invention of new expressions and acronyms. These can each be tested separately with the business people concerned, to make absolutely sure that each one says what it means, and means what it says.

Additionally, there will be a host of relatively standard definitions: for example, the identification of the parties, explaining what a term such as 'net price' means, and so on. Ideally a definition should be sufficiently descriptive to invoke the meaning to be conveyed.

With a list of definitions established, the full contract structure can be developed. As each clause is drafted, it will be found that the whole drafting process has been eased by the use of the definitions now available for ready reference. Familiarity with the fundamental concepts of the new contract makes the entire process of drafting much easier.

Contract-specific definitions have been included in the various agreements considered in the following chapters. Some definitions are very pertinent to the contract in question, for example 'Specification' in connection with Software Development, and these are considered in the relevant chapter. Others are of more universal application.

E. Using Chapters 6 to 21

CHAPTERS 6 TO 21 are designed to highlight the negotiable aspects of example clauses in IT-related agreements.

CHAPTER 6 reviews a number of standard clauses which will be found in all kinds of contracts, sometimes known as 'boilerplate' clauses, and which should be considered for inclusion in IT contracts as a matter of course.

CHAPTER 7 collates for discussion in one place a number of clauses which are common to many IT contracts.

In **CHAPTERS 8 TO 21**, the first part of the chapter, Section A, is an introduction to the type of agreement being discussed. The other sections provide a structure of one example of that agreement, as a skeleton list of clauses. The clauses being specifically discussed in that chapter are marked with an asterisk. The end of each structure usually consists of the 'General Contract Provisions' which are those clauses discussed in **CHAPTER 6**. Other examples of clauses which are not asterisked are to be found in **CHAPTER 7**.

For some example structures, proposed schedule contents are included, and other documents intended to be attached as appendices. 'Exhibits' or 'Annexes' are other terms which may be used for details which are an important part of the contract. It may be convenient to have schedules from an administrative perspective where these provide material varying a company's standard terms and conditions, describing the software concerned in the agreement, identifying the contact representatives of each party, listing the hardware being supplied, and so on. Schedules are also a better place to incorporate information which is likely to change during the course of the contract, given that there are suitable procedures in the contract for updating it, such as a functional specification or acceptance test procedures. It is more practical to replace a schedule than to have additions or modifications to the main body of the contract. Normally in a contract, schedule references would identify the schedule by number or alphabetically, but for ease of use in the example clauses and their discussion, this has been avoided, and the schedules referred to by name.

The next section in the chapter gives an example clause for each clause which was marked with an asterisk in the agreement structure, and discusses it in terms of negotiability. In a few chapters, clauses from a second example agreement are also discussed.

'Clause' is the term applied to a whole clause being discussed. The term 'paragraph' has been used throughout this book for referring to sections within a clause, but in a contract, 'sub-clause' is technically found as an alternative. ('Paragraph' is the normal term for a clause in a schedule.) In the US, the preferred terms are 'section' and 'sub-section'.

Although the primary purpose of the proposed clause wording is as an example for discussion, rather than as a precise precedent to be used in drafting a similar contract, square brackets have occasionally been used in order to identify alternative options within the wording, or where the clause itself is optional.

CHAPTER 6

Standard 'housekeeping' provisions

A. Introduction

The clauses in this chapter deal with the administrative mechanics of an agreement, and should be considered for inclusion in any agreement, whether an IT contract or not. On the face of it, there might seem to be little in this area which could be contentious. This is not necessarily the case however, and this short chapter illustrates some of the issues which can arise and which contracting parties ought to consider. The selection of clauses is not a closed list, but represents the most commonly found clauses in this category.

One unfortunate habit still evidenced in too many agreements is the apparently compulsive desire to state the obvious or unnecessary, such as clauses which inform the reader that the masculine includes the feminine, that singular includes plural, and so forth. These particular examples are catered for by statute[1], so that it is normally quite unnecessary to be confronted with such information, which is bound to lengthen an agreement. Complex agreements are difficult enough to read and digest without being side-tracked or put off by unhelpful legalese. It may, however, be useful to include expressly a provision which will apply automatically at law whether it is set out in the contract or not, for the purpose of reminding the parties that it should not be forgotten.

Agreements often also include a clause relating to headings, to advise the reader that clause headings in the agreement do not form part of the agreement. Why not? Any heading which does not logically relate to the content of its clause is not the right heading to use. If a heading accurately describes the clause which follows, there is unlikely to be any difficulty if the agreement should ever be subject to interpretation by the courts.

Wherever possible when drafting an agreement, these miscellaneous administrative clauses should be grouped together under a single heading such as 'General' or 'Contract'. This is to avoid too many separate clauses in the agreement, since the very number of clauses can be daunting to the reader. Depending on which clauses are included in the 'General Clauses' section, they may logically be either at the beginning or at the end of the Agreement. As the general clauses are not the most interesting or a unique feature of an agreement, the end is preferable.

B. Typical standard 'housekeeping' clauses

The following are typical clauses found in an agreement:

- Entire Agreement and Variations
- Severability
- Waiver
- Relationship of the Parties
- Rights of Third Parties
- Assignment
- Notices
- Force Majeure
- Governing Law and Jurisdiction
- Arbitration/Alternative Dispute Resolution (optional).

C. Specific clauses

1. Entire Agreement and Variations

This Agreement [and the documents referred to in it] constitutes the entire agreement and understanding between the parties and supersedes any previous agreement between the parties relating to the subject matter of this Agreement [other than the Non-Disclosure Agreement dated ....]. Each of the parties acknowledges that in entering into this Agreement, it does not rely on and will have no remedy in respect of any statement of fact or opinion not recorded in this Agreement (whether negligently or innocently made), except for any representation made fraudulently. No variation of these terms and conditions will be valid unless confirmed in writing by authorised signatories of both parties on or after the date of this Agreement.

The first sentence excludes other contracts, either previous contracts or any related contracts. The second sentence refers to representations. The third clarifies the need for any amendments to be in writing and signed at the same time or later than the date of the agreement, to eliminate any doubt over their validity.

'The purpose of an entire agreement clause was to preclude a party to a written agreement from threshing through the undergrowth and finding a chance remark or statement on which to found a claim'[2].

Where a written contract is made following discussion and negotiation, it is important that the parties know what has finally been agreed, and what the boundaries of that contract are. This is the main reason for having the contract in printed words. However, during the course of the discussions and negotiations leading to the contract, many statements will have been made by each side to the contract, orally or in writing, and any of these statements may have played a part in persuading the other party to agree to the deal.

It is not always easy to know whether this kind of statement, known as a representation, has become an integral part of the contract or not. If it is intrinsic to the formation of the contract but it turns out not to be true, the injured party who relied on it in making the agreement will have remedies at law, the extent of which will depend on whether the representation was made innocently, recklessly or fraudulently.

Certainly a purchaser should not assume that presentations by sales representatives, benchmark claims or glossy promotional brochures are bound to be entirely accurate and reliable. At law, vendors are allowed some scope in boosting their products; 'mere puffs', as a nineteenth-century judge described sales talk that would not be taken seriously as encouragement to proceed with a purchase.

Preliminary discussions will cover a range of issues open for argument, not all of which will eventually lead to agreement. Those representations which are to be considered part of the contract must be included in the contract. But this need not require the details to be set out in the main body of the contract document, so long as they are incorporated into the agreement by a clear reference. For example, in a software development agreement, a functional specification document may be referred to in the 'Definitions' section of the agreement as being incorporated, as an appendix to the agreement.

Similarly, it will be advisable for a purchaser who has raised preliminary important matters with the supplier to ask for a letter of confirmation from the supplier setting out the terms. This letter should incorporate any statements made to the purchaser which influenced the decision to enter into the contract, such as system performance times, the number of satisfied users, compatibility with existing systems, and delivery as and when requested. It should then be referred to in the body of the contract and incorporated as a schedule or an appendix. If the letter is dated earlier than the agreement and not incorporated into it, it will be assumed that it did not contain any commitments which were contractually binding. In the case of a letter dated at the same date or at a later date than the agreement and signed by both parties at the correct authorised level, the proposed wording of this clause will permit the terms of the letter to be treated as varying the contract. This is how any variations agreed between the parties will be brought into effect.

Invitations to tender and the written responses in the form of actual tender submissions are often expressed to be documents forming part of the contract in cases where the detailed contract provisions are negotiated and an agreement signed after the award of the contract. This gives suppliers a further opportunity to check that all of the material in the tender submission is accurate before finally committing to it. It may be difficult to resist a requirement that all documents connected with the invitation and any preliminary responses to a tender be treated as contract documents. Yet any documents which were submitted prior to the tender itself may not be sufficiently precise to be included safely as contract documents. Decisions about what should form part of the transaction may well have been modified.

This clause should therefore be included in every written contract and the parties should be aware that everything which matters to them and which is relevant to the transaction needs to be stated in the contract. There is then no conflict of evidence over uncertainty of what might have been agreed verbally or informally.

It must be noted that including this provision will not automatically guarantee that pre-contractual representations become irrelevant. In the event of any dispute, a view will be taken by the courts on whether it is fair and reasonable in the circumstances for the clause to be relied on[3]. If the contract has been extensively negotiated, the parties are more likely to be bound by the terms, including this clause, than if this clause is merely one of a set of standard clauses.

Suppliers should take care to verify the contents of their sales literature, particularly for the accuracy of technical performance claims, and ensure that their sales representatives are thoroughly familiar with the products or services being offered, and that customers take the opportunity to try out the system or software for themselves before entering into the contract. An invitation to contact names at random from a customer list for reference purposes will further emphasise the customer's responsibility for the final purchase decision.

IT cases involving misrepresentation are discussed in **CHAPTER 4**.

2. Severability

> If any of the provisions of this Agreement is judged to be illegal or unenforceable, the continuation in full force and effect of the remainder of them will not be prejudiced [unless the substantive purpose of this Agreement is then frustrated, in which case either party may terminate this Agreement forthwith on written notice].

The purpose of this clause is to provide for the exclusion of a term or condition which turns out to be ineffective, without affecting the rest of the agreement.

If a whole contract is illegal, no part of it can be rescued and, as a general rule, neither party will be entitled to benefit. It would be against public policy. For example, a provision for defrauding the Inland Revenue as part of the payment terms would clearly be illegal.

However, there may be less obvious instances where it is not appreciated by the parties that a particular clause would not be upheld by the courts on grounds of illegality.

It may also happen that a subsequent court decision on a provision which was agreed in good faith by the parties at the time of the agreement means that the provision will no longer be acceptable. The inclusion of this severability clause in the contract will facilitate the performance of the remainder of the contract, unless the provision in question is one which affects the very purpose of the contract, when it would be pointless to attempt to implement the remainder of it. In such a case, the right of termination needs to be available.

If a contract consists of a number of commitments, made in good faith, but some of these are legal and others turn out to be illegal, it may be possible for the illegal commitments to be removed so that the legal part of the contract may be enforced. In this case, only the offending clauses would be void, and the rest of the agreement will still create rights and obligations for the parties. It is in both parties' interests for an agreement to be effective so that each side can enforce its obligations for business to continue to be done, and this clause is an attempt to achieve this objective.

3. Waiver

> No forbearance or delay by either party in enforcing its respective rights will prejudice or restrict the rights of that party and no waiver of any such rights or of any breach of any contractual terms will be deemed to be a waiver of any other right or of any later breach.

If one party leads the other to believe that a right will not be enforced, this right may be lost. This often happens when goods are not delivered as promised, but the buyer keeps asking the seller for a new date. This means that the buyer has accepted that the expected date will not be met. This wording is to the effect that if either party does not enforce – that is, it 'waives' – a contractual entitlement at any time, it will not lose the right to enforce it later. For example, one side makes a voluntary concession on one occasion not to charge the interest which is stated in the contract to be due on late payments. With this provision in place, the other party's obligations in respect of paying this interest will remain.

If the clause is not included and particular rights are not enforced by one party, the other may be led to believe that it does not need to carry out its side of the bargain. It can happen in contracts where the parties are geographically far apart. The first party may simply not be aware of the other's breach of contract over certain of its obligations in the agreement; yet the second party may incorrectly assume that the breach no longer matters, and that the rights in respect of the breach have been waived by the first party.

4. Relationship of the Parties

> The relationship between the parties is that of independent contractor. Neither party is agent for the other, and neither party has authority to make any contract, whether expressly or by implication, in the name of the other party, without that other party's prior written consent for express purposes connected with the performance of this Agreement.

Where the agreement is between two parties each acting independently, this fact may need to be expressly stated, to avoid any implication that one party is acting as agent for the other. This matters because an agent, representing his or her principal, has the authority to create contracts between the principal and other parties, and thus obligations which the principal has to abide by, whether or not the principal was aware of these in advance. An agency may be inferred by another party whether it in fact exists or not.

Distribution agreements in particular may give rise to this implication, but many kinds of agreements may be made where subsequent actions might lead an outsider to assume that there was an agency relationship when this is not in fact the case.

It is therefore useful when there is no question of agency or other connected relationship for this to be made clear between the parties to the contract, for the benefit of each of them.

5. Rights of Third Parties

> [Subject to clause (X)... (specify which clauses the third party may enforce) a] [A] person who is not a party to this Agreement has no right to benefit under or to enforce any term of this Agreement.

A third party has the right to sue to enforce a contractual term if the contract expressly says so, or if the contract confers a benefit. The identity of the third party must be clear in the contract, whether by name or as a member of a class, for example, 'Distributor's Customers'. The third party will be entitled to the same remedies as if a party to the contract. This will be subject to all other terms of the contract, such as limitations of liability. The parties could, for example, provide that a term would be enforceable by a third party only if certain procedural steps were followed.

Thus, end users might have an enforceable interest in a software licence agreed between the software owner and the distributor.

Any potential issues arising from commitments in favour of third parties should therefore be considered carefully.

If it is clear from the construction of the contract that the parties did not intend the third party to be able to enforce the contract, the third party will not be able to do so. But there may well be arguments over the implications arising from the contract. If it is not intended to grant third party rights, it will therefore usually be advisable to include specific wording in the contract to prevent third party rights arising by accident unless it is entirely clear that the Contracts (Rights of Third Parties) Act 1999 will not apply, either because the contract falls outside the provisions of the Act (for example because it is an employment contract) or because there is no possibility of the court interpreting the contract as one which confers third party rights. A contract between the parties directly affected will generally be a more practical solution.

In practice, the potential exposure would arise only if the contract contains a contractual provision expressly allowing non-parties to sue, or if a term confers a benefit on a third party *and* for some reason the third party does not receive the benefit and wishes to take action. It will also of course depend on the relevant third party's awareness of the missed benefit and the contents of the contract.

6. Assignment

> Neither party will assign this Agreement [or any benefits or interests arising under this Agreement] without the prior written consent of the other party [which will not be unreasonably withheld or delayed] [except that assignments will be permitted to [subsidiary and] associated companies [of the Supplier/ Customer] [as defined in the Companies Act 1985] provided that the transferee compan[y][ies] shall undertake to be bound by and perform all of the obligations of this Agreement as if originally a party to it].

An 'assignment' of a contract means that the contract stays in existence, but the rights are transferred by the assignor to another party, the assignee. Unless there is an express prohibition against assignment in the contract, or the contract is of a type which cannot be assigned, such as a contract for personal services, either party can assign the benefit of the contract as a whole, or any of the benefits arising from the contract, to a third party. Thus a supplier may transfer its right to be paid to a factoring organisation.

When a contract is first negotiated, each party should have taken into account the other's standing, financial soundness, long-term viability and capacity for carrying out its part of the bargain. An assignment by one party would transfer its rights under the agreement to a third party. The other party to the agreement will want the opportunity to decide whether or not this should be permitted to happen. There may be reasons for not consenting. The third party may be a competitor. There may have been previous unsatisfactory dealings with the other party. There may be questions of confidentiality to consider.

The true meaning of 'assignment' in law is often overlooked or misunderstood by contracting parties. The legal position is that only benefits can be assigned, not burdens or obligations. This is logical because assignees have a contractual relationship only with the assignor, and not with any other parties to the agreement. Thus, if a supplier assigned its contract to an alternative supplier, the customer would not be obliged to look to the assignee of the supplier to perform the agreement. That responsibility would remain with the original supplier. However, provided that the customer has been given notice of the assignment, it will still be obliged to pay for the goods or services supplied to the assignee, payment being a benefit to the original supplier which that supplier would be free to assign in the absence of any contractual prohibition. A typical example of such an assignment would be to a factoring company. Conversely, if the customer was not contractually prevented from assigning the contract to another party, the supplier would have to deliver its goods or services to the customer's assignee. But the supplier could continue to look to the original customer for payment. If there is to be a complete transfer of those benefits and obligations it must be done by way of a tripartite agreement involving the other original contracting party as well as the assignor and the third party to whom the burden is being transferred. Such tripartite agreements are known in law as novation agreements.

The right may be limited by a provision that the contract cannot be assigned without the consent of the other party or by assignment being permitted only to a named assignee or a defined class of assignees.

However, in circumstances in which one of the parties is a subsidiary company belonging to a group of companies, it may be acceptable to permit assignment within that group without the other party first having to seek formal consent. Any decision about this should particularly take into account the financial status of the proposed assignee, so that an automatic permission is at least conditional on there being no reduction in security for the other party.

The words in square brackets 'or any benefits or interests arising under this Agreement' enable an individual benefit arising under the contract to be assigned as well as the contract as a whole. For example, if a customer's business were to be sold, the customer could assign the right to sue the supplier for breach of contract.

When the question of assignment arises, it is often an opportunity for the parties to re-negotiate certain of the terms, and to 'novate' the contract by creating a novation agreement to replace the original contract, for both the parties to the original contract and the new party. This has the advantage of making it entirely clear which parties are to be involved. The new party to the contract will then also take the obligations as well as having the benefits transferred to it.

7. Notices

> Any notice given under this Agreement by either party to the other must be in writing and may be delivered personally or by [recorded delivery] [first class] [registered] post, and in the case of post will be deemed to have been given two working days after the date of posting [where the addresses of the parties are both within the United Kingdom or seven working days after the date of posting where the notice is addressed to or is posted from an address outside the United Kingdom]. Notices will be delivered or sent to the addresses of the parties on the first page of this Agreement or to any other address notified in writing by either party to the other for the purpose of receiving notices after the date of this Agreement.

The purpose of this clause is to clarify the circumstances in which notices given under a contract are to be brought to the attention of the party concerned. 'Notices' to be given under an agreement will include any variation of the contract (in writing and agreed by both parties – see the section above on 'Entire Agreements and Variations'); notice that one party intends to bring the contract to an end; notice by one party that the other is in breach. Each of these kinds of notices is important, and there should be no conflict about whether the notice has been sent or received.

Where legislation requires or authorises documents to be served or sent by post, and a properly addressed and pre-paid letter has been put in the post, service by post is deemed to have been effected, unless the contrary is proved, when the letter would have been delivered in the normal course of post[4].

For the courts, service by post is deemed to have been effected, unless the contrary is proved, at the time when the letter would have been delivered in the ordinary course of post[5]. This is (optimistically) deemed to be the second working day after posting for first class post[6].

'Deemed notice' will be overridden if there is evidence, such as the return of a recorded delivery letter to the sender, that the notice was not delivered[7].

If nothing different has been agreed, communications may be addressed to a company at its registered office[8]. A notice to be served on an overseas company[9] may be left at or sent by post to an address which has been delivered to the Company's Registrar. If none has been delivered, it may be sent to any place of business established by the overseas company in Great Britain.

This example clause tries to be fair to both sides, varied as to what are appropriate methods of notification, and according to whether the contract is within the UK or international, and for what is convenient.

A clause defining the way notice is given can extend over several pages, taking into account various methods, such as fax, electronic mail and covering international communications, including the title of the authorised recipients for each party and their address details, but a reasonable balance should be attained.

It is more difficult with fax or e-mail to ensure that the correct destination has been reached and the nominated party notified. It has been held that transmission of a faxed document takes place when the complete document has been received by the recipient's fax machine[10]. It is irrelevant if it remains in memory before being printed. Sometimes a contract will state that notice may be sent by fax but must still be confirmed by post to be effective. But in practice fax is less used now, and e-mail is not advisable as a means of sending formal notices for security reasons. Again, the risk is of proving that an important communication has reached its destination. Personal service or post alone may be perfectly adequate.

8. Force majeure

> Neither party will be liable to the other party for any delay in or failure to perform its obligations (other than a payment of money) as a result of any cause beyond its reasonable control, including but not limited to any industrial dispute. If such delay or failure continues for at least 90 days, either party will be entitled to terminate the Agreement by notice in writing without further liability of either party arising directly as a result of such delay or failure.

This clause is known legally as 'force majeure', the term deriving from the French Napoleonic Code. Its object is to provide a mechanism for suspending performance of the contract or even for terminating it without liability on either side in the event of unforeseen circumstances. While the events continue, the party affected will not be required to perform its obligations or be liable for failure to perform. In negotiation, each party is likely to have in mind its particular concerns. A customer will not wish to offer a supplier an easy escape route for failure to deliver on time. A supplier will not want a customer's legitimate excuses for non-performance to extend to failures to make payments. This can lead to extensive debate over what contingencies should be included. It is desirable to limit these circumstances to those outside the reasonable control of the party concerned.

A pragmatic approach is advocated under which force majeure circumstances should be narrowly and briefly defined unless the particular contract circumstances call for something more. Some force majeure clauses make difficult reading, and the events are listed at great length, including 'act of God, civil commotion, riot, war, government act, fire, explosion, accident, flooding, hurricane, impossibility of obtaining raw materials, delays by third parties'. But all of these would be 'any cause beyond reasonable control'. It is not necessary for them all to be listed.

On the other hand, if there is doubt about whether a specific event should be included, then it should be listed. One event with the potential to cause delay about which there may be doubts as to 'beyond reasonable control' is 'industrial dispute' which should therefore be specifically included. Another instance would be the default of sub-contractors or suppliers who are independent of the parties to the contract – although the counter-argument is that under effective supervision, this would not be an event beyond reasonable control.

'Act of God' is a term often used in contracts of insurance as an exclusion. The principle is that a defendant should not be legally liable for an event so extraordinary that it could not have been foreseen.

A case in the Court of Appeal concerned the termination of a crew management agreement for a cruise vessel on the grounds that the agreement relating to the hire of the cruise vessel was frustrated because of warlike hostilities in the area of charter – between the ports of Cyprus, Israel, Egypt and the Red Sea[11]. The agreement contained a force majeure clause that the associated company whose obligations the defendants guaranteed, was not liable for any failure to perform its obligations by reason of any cause beyond its reasonable control. Evidence was given by academic experts in security and hostilities that the threat of terrorism made the operation of ships in the area dangerous. However, the test should have been that if the obligations under the Agreement were to be enforced, would it amount to a radically different performance from what had been agreed? The worsening security in that area was hardly surprising let alone radically different. It did not constitute force majeure.

There should be a provision for termination by either party if the force majeure circumstances continue, say for more than three months. It is not reasonable to expect the operation of a contract to be suspended indefinitely.

9. Governing Law and Jurisdiction

> This Agreement is governed by and construed in accordance with the law of England and Wales and [subject to the arbitration provisions] the parties submit to the [non-exclusive/exclusive] jurisdiction of the courts of England and Wales.

Within the English legal system, it would be normal to expect to see a clause establishing that English law and jurisdiction will apply, where there is any possibility of an alternative legal system. A contract may be made between parties located in different jurisdictions. A foreign parent company of one of the parties may be able to exercise some control over it. End users may be in a foreign territory. The 'offer' part of an e-commerce contract may be made in one country and the 'acceptance' in another – and theoretically the services may be carried out or the goods delivered in a third. The rules can become complicated in determining which law applies to a contract and which courts have jurisdiction to deal with a dispute. Thus it will depend on the exact circumstances of forming the contract, the wording in the contract, the effect of the contract, the status of the parties, and the locations involved.

There are two aspects to the choice of law for a contract: first, the law which is to govern the formation and provisions of the contract; second, the legal forum in the event of a contractual dispute.

It is very important to state the governing law and the jurisdiction applicable to the contract where one of the parties is in a different jurisdiction from the other. English law and jurisdiction can be specified for contracts effected beyond England and Wales. This is discussed further in **CHAPTER 3**.

Thus, if there is an express choice of law clause in the contract, that choice will govern it, given that there is some sort of connection between the transaction and the legal system. The terms and conditions will be drawn up on the basis of those laws. If there is a disagreement on the meaning of a particular word or phrase, and there are different interpretations under different laws, the legal system selected will apply. Certain contractual provisions may be permitted or forbidden, depending on the legal system.

From a practical viewpoint, if a dispute does arise, seeking advice in a foreign country and going to court in a foreign jurisdiction will be inconvenient and expensive – even where the language is apparently the same. Awards of damages and costs may be subject to entirely different legal principles. Enforcement of a judgment may also prove much more difficult.

Jurisdiction may be expressed as being 'exclusive' or 'non-exclusive'. Jurisdiction is defined as being 'exclusive' for the purpose of barring a party from taking legal proceedings in a jurisdiction other that specified. As a general rule, if a clause provides that the courts of a foreign country should have exclusive jurisdiction, proceedings which are commenced in England in breach of the clause will be prevented. However, even a clause which purports to provide for the English courts' exclusive jurisdiction may not completely remove another court's discretion in the matter. A non-exclusive clause keeps open any right which a party may have to issue proceedings in a jurisdiction other than that specified. Either party may then take legal action first in the preferred jurisdiction.

10. Arbitration/Alternative Dispute Resolution

(a) Any dispute arising in connection with this Agreement shall in the first instance be referred to a main board director of each party for discussion and potential resolution within 7 days of the date of referral. No party may initiate any legal action until this escalation procedure has taken place unless one party has reasonable cause to do so in order to avoid immediate damage to its business or to preserve any right of action it might have.

(b) Any dispute between the parties about any matter relating to the performance of this Agreement (other than in relation to the payment of any money) [including any question regarding its existence, validity or termination] which cannot be resolved by the parties within 60 days of notice of the dispute being served by one party on the other:

- *Arbitration Option* will be referred to the arbitration of a single arbitrator agreed between the parties, or on failure to agree within 30 days of a written request by one party to the other, appointed on the application of either party by the then President of the [British Computer Society/Society for Computers and Law/The Law Society[12]] at the time of the application in accordance with and subject to the provisions of the Arbitration Act 1996. The place of arbitration shall be London. The costs, charges, and expenses incurred in respect of such arbitration including the legal costs of each of the parties will be at the discretion of the arbitrator;

- *Alternative Dispute Resolution Option* will first be referred to mediation or other alternative dispute resolution procedure as agreed between the parties, each acting in good faith. If the parties are unable to agree a procedure or any aspect of a procedure, they will seek assistance from the [Centre for Effective Dispute Resolution[13]]. Unless otherwise agreed, the parties will share equally the costs of mediation, and the use of mediation will be without prejudice to the rights of the parties in all respects if the mediation does not achieve an agreed resolution of the dispute.

This clause is optional.

The first paragraph allows for negotiation by the parties themselves at a senior level. Discussion by people who have not been involved in the details of the dispute may be helpful to resolve matters. However, an opening must be left for invoking the court's jurisdiction immediately, for example in the event of a breach of confidentiality or alleged intellectual property infringement,

There are different formal legal means for resolving disputes: litigation, arbitration or Alternative Dispute Resolution ('ADR'). These methods are discussed further in **CHAPTER 4**.

Making a decision at the time of negotiating a contract as to ways to resolve a dispute, and having a contractual provision accordingly, may enable a solution to be reached more effectively and more quickly. If there is a breach of contract, a method agreed in advance for attempting to reach an amicable settlement can save a great deal of time, trouble and expense.

Litigation is confrontational, public and can divide the parties even more as the process goes on than at the start of the dispute.

An arbitration provision enables the parties to use arbitration procedures rather than court proceedings for resolving a dispute. Although the jurisdiction of the court cannot be excluded in a contract, the law permits arbitration to be specified as the method of adjudication. A decision made by the arbitrator will normally be binding on the parties.

Suppliers sometimes include an arbitration clause in their standard terms and conditions. One reason is to take advantage of the fact that arbitration proceedings take place in private. Other considerations are that in international contracts, arbitration is often perceived to be a mutually acceptable neutral forum. There is scope for appointing an arbitrator, whose decision both parties will respect, who they believe has expertise relevant to the subject matter of the dispute.

Arbitration is similar to litigation in being adversarial, but it is more flexible in that there is no obligation to conform to legal rules of evidence and procedure, and in the choices of timing and decision maker. It may give more opportunity than litigation for a relationship to be sustained where there is ongoing business between the parties.

Suppliers usually exclude payment of money due from the arbitration or ADR procedure as there are well-defined court procedures for debt collection.

There should always be a fallback provision in the clause for a third party to appoint an arbitrator if the parties themselves cannot agree. Otherwise, the effect of the clause would be negated, and the parties would have to make an application to the court for the appointment with consequent delay, which is unlikely to suit both of them, and creates a situation that the wording of the arbitration provision should have avoided. The third party selected to make the decision on who is to be the arbitrator can be anyone who the parties agree at the time of drafting the clause should be appointed, a time when agreement is more likely to be reached easily than at the point when the dispute has arisen. The choice is often the President or Chairman of a respected professional or trade association, such as the Institute of Arbitrators, the British Computer Society, the Law Society or the Society for Computers and Law.

If the arbitration option is selected for an international contract, two of the best known arbitral associations are the International Court of Arbitration of the International Chamber of Commerce (ICC), based in Paris[14], and the London

Court of International Arbitration (LCIA)[15]. In the US, there is the American Arbitration Association (AAA)[16]. There are also specialist organisations, such as the World Intellectual Property Organisation (WIPO) in Geneva[17].

Unless there are other provisions set out in an arbitration clause, statutory rules apply to the conduct of an arbitration. It is possible to set out detailed rules of procedure, venue, and anything else the parties know in advance that would assist in limiting further arguments and would help towards resolving the dispute. Clearly costs may be an issue.

Litigation and arbitration as means of solving disputes can be expensive in both costs and time. An absolute win/lose result does not always provide the most effective method of resolving complex disputes.

Alternative Dispute Resolution (ADR) is being used increasingly. It has proved particularly popular in the US where litigation costs and damages awards are much higher than in the UK. It essentially involves a neutral mediator which may offer a better resolution mechanism than litigation or arbitration within the IT industry. If the contract concerns an ongoing business relationship, for example, where both parties have an interest in settlement and are in equivalent bargaining positions, ADR may be less disruptive as a means for resolving any conflicts which arise.

The Centre for Dispute Resolution, the Chartered Institute of Arbitrators[18] and the Academy of Experts[19] are three respected organisations which offer ADR services and trained mediators, amongst others, and it will be helpful to name one in the clause.

It is always possible to choose arbitration or ADR as an option whether this is specified in the contract or not. Once a dispute has arisen, however, it is not an ideal time to attempt to agree a procedure for resolving it.

1   Law of Property Act 1925, s 61.
2   *Intrepreneur Pub Company Ltd v East Crown Ltd* [2001] 41 EG 209.
3   Under the Unfair Contract Terms Act 1977 or s 3 of the Misrepresentation Act 1967, concerning misrepresentations inducing contracts.
4   Interpretation Act 1978, s 7.
5   QB Master's Practice Direction No. 41 [2A–110] referring to s 7 of the Interpretation Act 1978.
6   Service of Documents, Part 6, Rule 6.7 www.dca.gov.uk/civil/procrules_fin/contents/parts/part06.htm#rule6_7.
7   *Re Thundercrest* [1995] 1BCLC 117.
8   Companies Act 1985, s 275.
9   Companies Act 1985, s 695.
10   *Anson v Trump* [1998] 1 WLR 1404.
11   *Globe Master Management Ltd v Boulus Gad Ltd* [2002] All ER (D) 39.
12   www.bcs.org.uk; www.scl.org; www.lawsociety.org.uk.
13   www.cedr.co.uk.
14   www.iccwbo.org.
15   www.lcia-arbitration.com.
16   www.adr.org.
17   www.wipo.int.
18   www.arbitrators.org.
19   www.academy-experts.org.

CHAPTER 7

General administrative provisions

A. Introduction

The following provisions discussed here govern the administrative and compliance aspects of a transaction. They are likely to be required in one form or another in most of the wide range of IT contracts, and are therefore discussed once in this chapter. The clause headings will be found in many of the contract structures set out in the chapters which follow, normally without being further elaborated in those chapters.

In each instance the clause considered is by way of example, as there may be a variety of alternative possibilities appropriate to particular contractual circumstances. The important point is for each party to recognise the need to consider the issues covered by the example clauses when structuring or responding to a draft contract. The assumption is made that words in the example clauses with capitalised initials will have been defined in the 'Definitions' clause of the contract. This clause is discussed in **CHAPTER 5**.

- Duration

- Charges

- Variation of Charges

- Expenses

- Payment Terms

- Title

- Intellectual Property Rights Indemnity

- Indemnities and Limits of Liability

- Integrity of Data

- Employment Restriction

- Confidentiality
- Publicity
- Insurance and Guarantee
- Data Protection
- Export Control
- Termination for Cause.

B. Specific clauses

1. Duration

> This Agreement commences on the Commencement Date and will continue for an initial period of 12 calendar months, after which it will remain in force unless or until terminated by either party giving at least 90 days' notice of termination to the other party to expire on the anniversary of the Commencement Date [or on any subsequent anniversary of the Commencement Date] [or at any time thereafter], or by the Customer giving 90 days' notice within 30 days of receipt of notification of a change in prices by the Supplier as permitted by this Agreement, and otherwise subject to the other termination provisions in this Agreement.

This clause allows for termination by either party on notice. There will be other provisions, discussed later in this chapter under 'Termination for Cause', for termination by either party where there is a reason to do so, for example because of breach of the contract by one party, or because of insolvency.

The clause will be unnecessary in connection with a single delivery of products, but one like it will usually be required in an agreement for the continuing supply of products or services. It is in the supplier's interest to keep an agreement automatically in force where there are recurring payments to be made. It may also be in the customer's interest where it is relying on the continuing provision of products or services. However, sometimes it will be permitted only to one party to terminate on notice. Thus, where software is required by the licensee on a long-term basis, the licence may be terminable on notice by the licensee but not by the licensor. Where the licensee depends on the continuing use of software for its business, it will not wish to be put in a position where the licensor may decide to withdraw the licence without cause.

As far as the customer is concerned, any right of termination should extend to the right to terminate the agreement on the grounds of any unacceptable price increases made by the supplier. The customer should ensure that any such increases proposed by the supplier are coupled with an option for the customer not to renew, or to terminate the contract. For example, if payment is to be made annually in advance, the right of termination should be exercisable from expiry of the notice of a price increase, that is, from the date it takes effect. Alternatively, and preferably, a contractual limitation should be negotiated in the charging clause, or in a variation clause such as the example clause on Variation of Charges below, covering the frequency and the extent of any increases in contracts which continue in force. This will be particularly important in those cases where it is impracticable or impossible for a customer to obtain the contracted products or services from an alternative source.

The more precise the definition of time, the better. If nothing further is stated in a contract, 'month' will mean 'calendar month'[1]. However, a calendar month does not have to begin on the first day of the month. A month 'from 18 August' ends 31 days later. A month 'from 18 September' ends 30 days later. 'Working days' is a more useful term than 'days', particularly where a small number of days is concerned, so that public and national holidays are excluded: for example to enable the Christmas holiday period to be taken into account for giving notice or for sending notices by post.

The surrounding wording can also be important. There is, for example, a difference between:

'This Agreement will last for one year from 18 August 2004';

and

'This Agreement will commence on 18 August 2004 and last for one year'.

'From' normally means that the date referred to is excluded. In the first example the year will begin immediately after midnight on 19 August and end immediately before midnight on 18 August 2005.

'On' means that the date referred to will be included, and so in the second example the year starts and ends one day earlier than in the first example.

If an agreement contains one date, but is signed by the parties on a different date, the date which counts, in the absence of any wording to the contrary, will be the date contained in the agreement. If there is no date in the agreement, it will commence on the date of the signature made by the last party to sign.

2. Charges

(a) The Charges payable by the Customer to the Supplier for the [Products/ Services] are [set out in the Schedule/shown in the Supplier's current Product Price List and are valid for 30 days from the date of the Order or until the date of delivery, whichever is the earlier] [including the charges for delivery within the United Kingdom]. [If the Products remain undelivered on the expiry of 30 days from the date of the Order, the Supplier reserves the right to alter the prices to those then current in its Product Price List at the date of delivery. The Supplier will be responsible for the cost of insurance during carriage within the United Kingdom.]

(b) All prices are exclusive of Value Added Tax and any similar taxes. All such taxes are payable by the Customer and will be applied in accordance with UK legislation in force at the tax point date.

In any commercial agreement, this is a significant clause for both parties. Pricing is often an intricate provision in a contract and the above is one comparatively straightforward example. This is not to suggest that it should be acceptable to the customer without modification. As ever, the commercial strength of the negotiator may prove more significant than the negotiating skill of the other party and it is the progress which can be made against the tide which is the true measure of success.

For product supply, the customer needs to consider many questions. First and foremost, what does the quoted price include? Carriage? Insurance? Import duties? Which party is to be responsible for insurance in transit? This may be stated expressly as in this example. Alternatively, the 'INCOTERMS' trading conditions are discussed in **CHAPTER 9** in connection with the contract on product supply. These conditions define a number of acronyms used as shorthand for the allocation of responsibilities for delivery, payment and insurance, especially for international supply contracts.

Second, how long will the price remain valid? Can it be related back to a fixed price quotation, that is, to a fixed price provided that an order was placed within a specified period? Next, what are the projected delivery timescales and will the price remain firm until that time? While the supplier may be unwilling to accept any financial liability for late delivery, the customer should at least seek to negotiate a right of cancellation without liability after the scheduled delivery date has passed or an unacceptable price increase has been announced. On the other hand, the price ruling at the date of delivery may turn out to be unattractive in a falling market. The customer will rarely be allowed to have its cake and eat it, and so as accurate as possible a reading of the market situation will be useful.

A pricing clause may need to be structured to accommodate stage payments. When a large system comprising many elements and combining several products and services is ordered, or when significant development work is being undertaken, suppliers often require payments along the way, to fund development work and to finance interim deliveries. Where the system or development is very large, it is to both parties' advantage to break it down into modular stages, so that milestone instalment payments can be made by the customer once the defined deliverables have been delivered and accepted. Customers should be concerned to retain some part of the price until they can be satisfied that all elements of the system are performing in their intended environment following installation as required under the contract and preliminary implementation by them. Much negotiation will concern the number and percentages of payments, and when they should be made, and over the definition of the deliverables and their acceptability criteria at the milestone stages. Suppliers may have counter-arguments – sometimes over retentions, particularly where a customer has participated closely in all aspects of development. While retentions quite properly offer some level of guarantee to customers which reassures them, many suppliers can testify to the difficulty of obtaining retained payments from customers in circumstances where there are no sustainable grounds for withholding them. A ten per cent retention is one tenth of the price to the customer, but it may represent the lion's share of net profitability on the transaction to the supplier. Both parties must be adequately motivated if the contract is going to succeed.

Some pricing models used in the IT industry involve an element of 'risk sharing' transparency. This can mean that no charges are paid initially by the customer, who pays when the target has been achieved. A more limited version of this is encountered with service levels as the measurable criterion, when the supplier's failure to meet them will mean reduced profits for the supplier represented as liquidated damages or service credits. This is further discussed in **CHAPTER 17** in relation to outsourcing. However, it is unsatisfactory for both parties to risk everything by making the price for delivery of a large system payable only when the whole system has been implemented. Although the supplier may have invested resources, including training or management services, and even supplied certain hardware, if the contract is for the provision of an entire system with no interim points of self-contained delivery, the customer may not have to pay if the system is never delivered. From the customer's perspective, it also will have invested time and effort, yet will not have the system it needs. The situation discussed in **CHAPTER 4**, concerning two cases where there was a complete failure to deliver a working IT system and therefore failure of contractual performance, is a salutary lesson in this respect[2].

Pricing may be fixed or be based upon the cost of time and materials. The latter is not popular with customers because of its potentially open-ended nature. Nevertheless, it is often not realistic, or even in the customer's best interests, to demand a fixed price. This is especially true in a complicated system integration contract, where neither party can state with certainty what the final product is going to be, no matter how much specification work has been done in advance. Practical problems and new ideas are going to emerge as development progresses, and this will force choices to be made, and the need to prioritise price as against time or additional features; functionality and performance capability, and so on. A fixed price at the outset may lead to higher prices being charged for amendments subsequently settled on a time and materials basis.

One solution sometimes possible here is to contract on the basis of time and materials, subject to estimated ceilings, with a mechanism for early warnings of increases in estimates, so that an informed choice can be made by the customer as to whether to pay more, or whether to forgo some aspects, as preferred. Further, the actual rates and frequency of payments of time and materials charges remain to be negotiated. Can these be fixed or can restrictions be placed on increases, for example, not to increase rates more frequently than once annually and not by more than the prevailing rate of inflation, as evidenced by a defined index rate (see the clause on Variation of Charges below) and not during the first year of the agreement? Are payments to be made monthly in arrears or to coincide with certain pre-determined milestones? Is it appropriate for the customer to sign off time sheets, copies of which might then be attached to invoices as evidence to support payment demands? (If so, the customer should be required to sign these in a timely manner and not unreasonably withhold signature, but be willing to use an escalation process in the event of any dispute.) Can an element be held back on retention? If the contract is one for services, are these to be paid for by lump sum or by periodic payments and, if the latter, at what intervals?

In contracts for system supply where third party products are being supplied by a lead supplier (prime contractor), what scope, if any, is there for the customer to receive such products at cost, or at a discount on the supplier's standard mark-up? If the customer is already dealing with a sub-contractor, can the customer obtain a bigger discount than the supplier, but allow some of this to the supplier for its administrative and risk-bearing role?

In relation to clause (b), the price payable for the supply of goods or services includes taxes which would be chargeable, unless the tax is stated to be separately payable in addition[3]. Contracts should therefore expressly state that value added tax and similar taxes are also to be payable, since a customer would otherwise be able to refuse to pay the tax for which the supplier would nevertheless still be liable.

The commercial customer has an opportunity to offset or pass on these taxes, and they cannot be included as part of the price at the rates in force at the time of quotation, or even order, because legislative or regulatory changes in tax rates frequently take effect from midnight on the day of announcement. The tax point date will generally be the invoice date, but might be the date on which payment is actually made.

3. Variation of Charges

> The Supplier will be entitled to increase its charges on the [anniversary of the date of this Agreement] [Commencement Date] and thereafter not more than once in any successive period of 12 months by giving not less than 60 days' notice to the Customer, provided that any such increase expressed as a percentage [does not exceed any percentage increase in the Retail Prices Index published by the Department of Employment for the 12 months immediately preceding the date of the notice] [does not exceed the rate of the Supplier's salary inflation reported in its accounts for the immediately preceding year].

This is one example of a price variation mechanism which is quite commonly used. The alternatives in square brackets are two examples of indices which might be referenced. Sometimes a split between the Retail Prices Index and a mutually agreed computer salaries index is used, for example the National Computing Centre's Annual Salary Survey which is made across job categories and industry sectors, or the Employment Index published by Computer Economics, to provide more of a balance. There have been times when salaries in this sector, especially for technical personnel, have far outstripped inflation, and for service-orientated companies in the industry the salary bill is easily the biggest overhead. But many customers coming from less dynamic environments will not be happy to agree to costs increases above the anticipated norms.

A clause on variation of charges might also deal with other circumstances of permitted variation such as increased customer requirements as and when these are agreed, or exceptional currency fluctuations, or the peculiar situation of hardware supply where the costs are more likely to fall than rise, although the specification is more likely to be increased in the time lag between the making of the contract and its delivery.

To provide as much price stability as possible, some suppliers promote a 'snake' device, that is, a provision which serves as a limited hedge against currency movements. Thus, an exchange rate will be agreed and any movements above or below the rate within a stated percentage either way will be borne by the parties, each taking a limited risk if the rate moves against it. Should the rate fall outside the chosen parameters, it will be grounds for a general re-adjustment which will have the effect of increasing or decreasing the price to the customer purely as a result of the exchange rate movement, and with no bearing on the supplier's costs of production and sale. For example, a supplier of products manufactured in the US might agree an exchange rate of US$1.50 to the £ sterling, plus or minus ten per cent. If the actual rate fell below $1.35 or above $1.65, the set rate of $1.50 would be reviewed and amended by agreement. Exchange rate-motivated price adjustments, since they do not reflect any change in the supplier's costs, should not be considered part of the permitted periodic price review.

4. Expenses

(a) All prices quoted in this Agreement are exclusive of expenses reasonably incurred in the performance of this Agreement by the Supplier.

(b) Expenses include but are not limited to:
(i) travel to the Customer's sites when applicable;
(ii) magnetic media;
(iii) data connection charges;
(iv) couriers;
(v) freight;
(vi) accommodation and subsistence charges;

and any other expenses reasonably incurred by the Supplier in connection with this Agreement.

(c) Expenses must be [agreed in advance] [supported by receipts or other documentary evidence as appropriate].

The customer and supplier should agree what is allowable as an expense and any permitted rates and allowances, to be included in a schedule if necessary. Mileage costs could be related to those recommended by one of the motoring organisations; or air and rail travel may be limited by a ceiling figure or made equivalent to the standard full cost of a journey in a particular class. To borrow a phrase from tax legislation, 'reasonably and necessarily incurred' may usefully be stated. Any chargeable expense should be demonstrated to be necessary, as well as reasonable in extent. Negotiation may also establish a requirement for claims to be supported by receipts, and perhaps a requirement that any expenses in excess of a stated sum should be agreed in advance by the customer.

5. Payment Terms

(a) [The total price for the Products/The initial licence fee and support charge will be paid to the Supplier against invoice [on or before delivery].] [The Customer will be invoiced [quarterly/half-yearly/annually] in advance for the Charges payable.] Expenses and other charges will be invoiced monthly in arrears. All invoices are payable [20] days after receipt [other than the invoices for the support charge which are payable [immediately] [by Clearing Bank standing order].

(b) Payments which are not received when payable will be considered overdue and remain payable by the Customer together with interest for late payment from the date payable at the statutory rate applicable as well after as before any judgment, and independent of such judgment. This interest will accrue on a daily basis and be payable on demand.

(c) Notwithstanding the above provision for late payment, in this event the Supplier may at its option, and without prejudice to any other remedy at any time after payment has become due, terminate or temporarily suspend performance of this Agreement.

(d) If the Supplier becomes entitled to terminate this Agreement for any reason, any sums then due to the Supplier will immediately become payable in full.

It is important for a supplier to minimise the risk of non-payment or late payment. The only possible justification by a customer for withholding payment in respect of goods or services received, a serious breach of contract, is a justifiable allegation of failure on the part of the supplier to perform in accordance with the contract.

In the construction industry, where the risk of non-payment is relatively high compared with other industries, the following provisions are not uncommon: monthly advance payments against a bond provided by the contractor; an undertaking by the contractor to set money received aside in a deposit account, interest accruing to the contractor; bonds or guarantees by the customer's parent company, referred to below in the clause on Insurance and Guarantee; payment by letter of credit against production of certificates; direct payment agreements with funders.

These mechanisms are not in wide use in the IT industry but might become more familiar as risks of insolvency increase, and as the sums involved grow larger.

Strangely, some customers become agitated during negotiations by the concept of any contractual consequences for late payment, particularly the right to terminate in the absence of other grounds such as suspected insolvency. But suppliers are not bankers and should not be expected to carry the cost of late payment.

Where both parties are acting in the course of business, defined broadly enough to include government departments, professional bodies and public authorities, irrespective of size, the creditor can claim statutory interest for the late payment of a commercial debt[4]. This does not apply to consumer contracts. Statutory interest is currently the Bank of England base rate plus eight per cent. The rate will be set each 30 June and 31 December for the following six months. Creditors may also claim entitlement to debt recovery costs up to £100.

Interest runs from the date the debt is created under the contract. If the contract does not state a date, interest runs from 30 days after the obligation giving rise to the debt is performed, or 30 days from the date on which the debtor is notified of the debt, whichever is later. The parties to a contract are free to agree a different interest rate, but only if the contract provides an alternative 'substantial remedy' for late payment. If it does not, the interest rate and payment period will be open to challenge. Representative bodies on behalf of small businesses may challenge in court unfair standard contract terms which attempt to oust or vary the right to statutory interest. Factors likely to be considered include:

- the usual practices in the sector;

- the relative bargaining strengths;

- the length of the credit period; and

- the theoretical cost of borrowing for the purchaser and the supplier.

Suppliers should consider noting on their invoices that they are aware of their rights to statutory interest and debt recovery costs.

Similar legislation applies throughout the EU. Beyond these boundaries, this legislation does not apply to contracts where English law governs by choice only, but does apply to contracts which should have been subject to English law, but have been made subject to the law of another jurisdiction.

The provision in paragraph (b) of the example for interest to accrue after judgment is in case the judgment may be given for a single sum and for payment terms which include both the principal debt and the ancillary interest. By means of this wording interest will continue to run, which may be useful if it takes a while to recover the judgment debt.

In practice, few suppliers actually invoice late payment charges unless the business relationship with the customer is considered to have broken down irretrievably.

6. Title

(a) Title to the Products is vested in the Supplier. Only when all prices, taxes and charges due under this Agreement have been paid in full, will title to the Hardware Products pass to the Customer. [The Products must be retained in their original packaging and remain clearly marked as the Supplier's until payment is made.]

(b) No title or ownership of the Software Products or of any third party software licensed by the Supplier to the Customer is transferred to the Customer.

(c) In the event of non-payment, the Supplier may repossess any Products for which payment has not been received when due. [For such purposes, the Supplier, its agents or authorised representatives will be entitled at any time without notice to enter upon any premises in which the Products are reasonably believed by the Supplier to be kept.]

The norm in the computer industry is for title to pass on sale in respect of hardware products, but rarely on software products, which are generally licensed and not sold. In standard supply and purchasing agreements, provision is often made for title to pass on delivery, but English law on retention of title effectively allows a supplier to hold on to title until payment for the products in question has been received in full, provided that the clause is clear and unequivocal. This concept is not recognised or accepted in a number of other jurisdictions, notably the US, but it is a reasonable form of security in return for **extend**ing credit payment terms.

It is worthwhile for suppliers to consider what risks in particular they are seeking to eliminate. Since the purpose of retention of title is to enable goods to be repossessed if they are not paid for, the main target is the insolvent customer. This clause is an attempt by the supplier to be able to retrieve the products on the basis that it still owns them. The risk is that if title has passed, the supplier will have lost both the products and the payment for them. The supplier wants to establish a position whereby it is not merely an ordinary unsecured creditor in respect of unperformed contractual obligations, and that its goods are not available for disposal by a receiver or liquidator. This is best achieved by a straightforward statement that title will not pass until payment has been received in full. Where a customer is a reseller who has sold goods on for which the supplier has not been paid, the law gives innocent third party purchasers good title. Some suppliers then attempt to establish prior rights to the proceeds of such sales and, while this is legally possible, it involves cumbersome administrative procedures, possibly including registration of interests at Companies House, and will not be practicable for many suppliers for their normal contractual situations.

Some retention clauses are extremely convoluted, and attempted enforcement of them has established a body of law based on the outcome of litigated cases. There are many areas of ambiguity, but it is clear that suppliers who attempt to cover every possible contingency run the risk that their laboriously drafted words will fail for lack of clarity or even because attempts are made to go beyond accepted legal principles and practices.

Individual decisions on the approach to be taken should depend on the typical trading circumstances and the value of the average products being sold. Suppliers do have other means of protection available to them. It will often be commercially unrealistic to require resellers to keep products in their original packaging, and not to sell goods on until they have been paid for, or to require them to notify their end-user customers formally that, initially at least, prior title is vested in their own supplier. But credit control checks on resellers can be made especially stringent in order to minimise the risk of losses and so that credit limits can be kept relatively low. Sophisticated search and investigation facilities are readily available from credit control agencies on subscription and these can be effective tools in helping suppliers to assess credit risks. If some suppliers decide to take a more relaxed view of their reseller customers' financial capabilities in order to establish as wide and rapid a distribution of their products as possible, they should also be willing to take on the greater element of risk involved.

Whatever the clause says, it is the first instinct of a receiver or a liquidator to challenge it and to seek to retain possession of goods. Applications for interim injunctions which prohibit the sale on of goods prior to a full court hearing of the issues can be an effective means for a supplier to secure acknowledgment of its rights by a receiver or a liquidator, who will often not have or not be willing to expend the funds necessary to fight the issue, particularly if precedents can be pointed out of similar circumstances where other receivers or liquidators have failed.

The right in paragraph (c) of the example for the supplier to enter premises where products are kept in order to repossess them is useful as a matter of contractual statement, but it is of limited value because an entry cannot be forced without court authority. Repossession of goods is almost always a second-best result for a supplier. The supplier must be able to identify the products and relate them to specific invoices. There will not often be the opportunity to sell goods at the same price to another party unless they remain unopened, but it is a means of mitigating losses, particularly as it is rare for a supplier to end up with full payment in a receivership. Sometimes, however, a receiver or liquidator will be able to realise a better value for goods which incorporate the supplier's products and may elect to honour an outstanding contract, or at least to bargain a compromise price with the supplier.

In practice, the supplier must immediately notify the administrative receiver or liquidator of the defaulting customer. An administrator, however, has greater statutory protection from creditors. If the products are recovered, VAT cannot be claimed on the bad debt.

Even where retention of title cannot be established by a supplier, a receiver or liquidator will often seek a specialist supplier's help in disposing of highly technical products on a shared revenue basis.

Occasionally, retention of title clauses purport to apply until all outstanding debts have been paid off by a customer, in other words a revolving situation when title might never pass. Such provisions are of very doubtful effect and overly complicate the supplier-customer relationship. As such, suppliers should not use them and customers should resist them.

Some title clauses also deal with the question of risk of loss, that is, which party should bear such risk and from when. Price often includes carriage and insurance until delivery, after which risk passes to the customer even though title may have been retained. Since the customer is in possession of the goods, it is reasonable that it should bear the risk of loss from this time, but a prudent supplier will maintain fall-back insurance until such time as it has been paid in full.

Retention of title is rarely of value in connection with service agreements because usually there are no goods capable of being retained.

7. Intellectual Property Rights Indemnity

(a) The Supplier is either the sole and exclusive owner or an authorised licensee or user of all intellectual property rights and interests including but not limited to patent, registered or unregistered design right, copyright, database right, trade mark or service mark ('IPRs') that may subsist in (i) the text, data, information and branding and (ii) in the programs, formats and layouts comprised in or relating to the Products, and such IPRs are the valuable commercial property of the Supplier or its licensors. Because of this value to the Supplier, the Supplier, at its own expense, will defend or cause to be defended or, at its option, settle any claim or action brought against the Customer on the issue of infringement of any [United Kingdom or Republic of Ireland] IPR by the Products ('Claim'). Subject to the other conditions of this clause, the Supplier will pay any final judgment entered against the Customer with respect to any Claim, [and fully indemnify the Customer in respect of all costs and expenses relating to the Claim] provided that the Customer:

   (i)   notifies the Supplier in writing of the Claim immediately on becoming aware of it;

   (ii)   grants sole control of the defence of the Claim to the Supplier [subject to the Supplier providing the Customer with such security for costs and other liabilities as the Customer reasonably requests]; and

   (iii)   gives the Supplier complete and accurate information and full assistance to enable the Supplier to settle or defend the Claim.

The costs and fees of any separate legal representation for the Customer will be the Customer's sole responsibility.

(b)   If any part of the Products becomes the subject of any Claim or if a Court judgment is made that the Products do infringe, or if the use or licensing of any part of the Products is restricted, the Supplier at its option and expense may:

   (i)   obtain for the Customer the right under the IPR to continue to use the Products; or

   (ii)   replace or modify the Products so that any alleged or adjudged infringement is removed; or

   (iii)   if the use of the Products is prevented by permanent injunction, accept return of them and refund an amount equal to the sum paid by the customer for the Products [subject to straight line depreciation over a five-year period].

(c)   The Supplier will have no liability under this clause for:

   (i)   any infringement arising from the combination of the Products with other products not supplied by the Supplier; or

   (ii)   the modification of the Products unless the modification was made or approved expressly by the Supplier.

IN NO CIRCUMSTANCES WILL THE SUPPLIER BE LIABLE FOR ANY COSTS OR EXPENSES INCURRED BY THE CUSTOMER WITHOUT THE SUPPLIER'S PRIOR WRITTEN AUTHORISATION AND THE FOREGOING STATES THE ENTIRE REMEDY OF THE CUSTOMER IN RESPECT OF ANY IPR INFRINGEMENT BY THE PRODUCTS.

The supplier will have warranted elsewhere in the agreement that to the best of its knowledge and belief the products do not infringe any ownership right of any third party. The supplier of the hardware or software products is actually using this clause to assert title, its own or its licensor's. It is a warranty from the owner that it is not expecting the customer to be put in a position of using the products without the right to do so. Subject to certain conditions imposed for its protection, the supplier will take over the claim. If a third party should come along with a claim, the owner undertakes to take the claim over from the customer and to indemnify the customer. The owner does this because it is in its interests to do so, in order to defend its own intellectual property rights, not the customer's, and also because litigation in this area is generally very complex and it will be important to the owner to have absolute control over the defence strategy.

At the same time, an owner will use this clause to limit its liability if the case should go against it, if in fact it has (inadvertently or otherwise) supplied products which it was not entitled to supply, and which may no longer be able to be used by the customer. Unlimited liability could result in considerable damages where these extend to consequential losses resulting from the need for the customer to acquire use of alternative systems. Moreover, the circumstances may also amount to a fundamental breach of the contract as the supplier would be supplying products which it actually had no right to supply, because it did not have either good title or a licence to supply the products. This would entitle the customer to repudiate the contract as well as to pursue the damages claim.

The supplier will seek to confine the scope of the indemnity to the territories of supply, where the customer is entitled to use the products. The customer will seek a worldwide indemnity. The customer needs only to focus on the jurisdiction in which it is entitled to use the products. It is therefore unreasonable to expect any extension to this. Most suppliers will reasonably limit any widening of the scope of the indemnity only to countries where they are in business or distributing.

Any other liability will be excluded by the final clause.

In recent years, customers' legal advisers have sought to try and negotiate the details of the first part of this clause without any clear understanding of the issues involved. For example, in paragraph (a), it is important to a supplier's defence strategy that it learns of any claim 'immediately'. At paragraph (b) it is not to its advantage to share control of the defence – the customer is not defending its own intellectual property.

The customer must understand liability in the context of intellectual property right infringement. It is in the last resort a low level of risk – although they will get very little money back compared with the consequences of a prohibited future use. The clauses are almost universally accepted, not least because it is unlikely that the courts will order a customer to stop using the products. They are more likely to confine remedies to damages payable by the infringer to the infringed. Some inroads can sometimes be made to improving the level of liability to the customer when high value agreements or unique products are involved. However, customers should certainly seek to ensure that the indemnity which protects them from the financial effects of a successful third party action is not limited in any way and is not part of the overall limits of liability contained in the clause on indemnities and limits of liability discussed below.

8. Indemnities and Limits of Liability

(a) The Customer agrees that it has accepted these terms and conditions in the knowledge that the Supplier's liability is limited and that the prices and charges payable have been calculated accordingly. The Customer is advised to make its own insurance arrangements if it desires to limit further its exposure to risk or if it requires further or different cover. [The Supplier will be willing to provide reasonable assistance to the Customer if the Customer requests the Supplier to make enquiries about increasing cover on the Customer's behalf provided that the Customer recognises that this will result in increased charges being passed on to the Customer.]

(b) The Supplier will indemnify the Customer for direct physical injury or death caused solely either by defects in the Products or by the negligence of its employees acting within the course of their employment and the scope of their authority.

(c) The Supplier will indemnify the Customer for direct damage to property caused solely either by defects in the Products or by the negligence of its employees acting within the course of their employment and the scope of their authority. The total liability of the Supplier under this sub-clause will be limited to [one million pounds] for any one event or series of connected events.

(d) Except as expressly stated in this clause and elsewhere in this Agreement, any liability of the Supplier for breach of this Agreement will not exceed in the aggregate of damages, costs, fees and expenses capable of being awarded to the Customer the sum of [£50,000] [the total price paid or due to be paid by the Customer under this Agreement].

(e) Except as expressly stated in this Agreement, the Supplier disclaims all liability to the Customer in contract or in tort (including negligence or breach of statutory duty) in connection with the Supplier's performance of this Agreement or the Customer's use of the Products and in no event will the Supplier be liable to the Customer for special, indirect or consequential damages or for loss of profits or arising from loss of data or unfitness for user purposes.

[(f) The Customer will indemnify and defend the Supplier and its employees in respect of (i) any third party claims which arise from any Supplier performance carried out on the instructions of the Customer or its authorised representative; and (ii) any losses or expenses incurred by the Supplier as a result of the Customer's failure to license its own customers in accordance with the terms of the licence from the Supplier and to facilitate the enforcement of these licences.]

(g) The Supplier shall not be liable for any damages arising from negligence or otherwise unless the Customer has established reasonable backup, accuracy checks and security precautions to guard against possible malfunctions, loss of data or unauthorised access, and has taken all reasonable steps to minimise its loss and has carried out tests to determine the suitability of the Products for the purposes for which they are required.

(h) The Supplier makes no representations and gives no warranties, guarantees or undertakings concerning its performance of the Services except as expressly set out in this Agreement. All other warranties, express or implied, by statute or otherwise, are excluded from this Agreement.

This clause is characteristic of what tends to be offered by the IT industry to its customers. The whole subject of indemnities, limitations and exclusions of liability is fraught with danger for a supplier because several statutes and interpretations by the courts have combined to create a good deal of uncertainty about where the boundaries lie. Go too far, and some or all of the provisions will not work. Customers are best advised to work on the assumption that whatever is negotiated or imposed by the clause will work, and therefore to negotiate on the basis that what is agreed will be satisfactory for their purposes.

There is a further danger for a supplier who may well have relied upon the effectiveness of this clause as an important factor in its product pricing, or even the commercial decision about whether or not to take the business. If there is such a significant failure on the part of the supplier to perform the contract that the customer becomes entitled to the legal remedy of rescission, that is, to nullify the contract, then the protection which might have been afforded by the clause could be lost. This will open up the possibility of recovering consequential losses by the customer. These could far outstrip the value of the contract to the supplier.

The limits and exclusions of liability set out here must be regarded as reasonable to be enforceable if the Unfair Contract Terms Act 1977 ('UCTA') is found to apply to the contract, as discussed further in **CHAPTER 4**. Paragraph (a) is an attempt to justify the provisions by relating the supplier's business terms to the prices chargeable, and indeed the costs and potential costs of the supplier's business approach are bound to affect the charges. It reminds the customer that there is a possibility of increasing insurance cover.

Paragraphs (b) and (c) concern the limits of liability for negligence or defective products. Paragraph (b) reflects the statutory position under UCTA which prohibits exclusion of liability for death or personal injury. The limit of liability stated in paragraph (c) is required to be regarded as reasonable if the clause is not to fail if UCTA is found to apply to the contract. It is normal for it to be related to a supplier's public liability insurance cover for such losses. The reference in paragraphs (b) and (c) to employees acting within the course of their employment and the scope of their authority is intended to confine the supplier's liability to the types of situations in which it would be held vicariously responsible at law for the acts of its employees. Some customers will argue that any damage or loss caused by a supplier's employee should be within the scope of the clause.

Paragraph (d) imposes a limit of liability for breach of contract. Again if UCTA applies, this limit must be reasonable. However, the risk for the customer in the transaction is not intrinsically related to the price payable, and it may be more appropriate in some circumstances to link the limit of liability to insurance cover.

At paragraph (e), 'direct losses' are those which directly result from an event, for example if there is an electrical fault in a machine and it is destroyed by fire, the cost of replacing the machine would be an example of direct damage. 'Indirect damage' is rather more remote. It will be less foreseeable in an incident, for example a cable connection to another building and some transmission of an electrical fault causing a fire there which burnt the building down. 'Consequential losses' are sometimes referred to as economic losses. As the term implies, they include all of the consequential losses of an incident to a company. The arguments in court usually turn on whether the losses may be categorised as 'direct', and therefore covered. Exclusion of liability for 'consequential losses' will not exclude loss of profit or any other type of loss which is foreseeable, and any such specific foreseeable losses are best specified for exclusion separately[5].

It is normal for consequential and indirect losses to be totally excluded from IT-related agreements, and the supplier should ensure that this is done in all of its contracts. It is therefore almost universally the case when reviewing suppliers' contracts that these will contain an exclusion of indirect and consequential losses along the lines of paragraph (e). Most customers accept this position. Perhaps they are aware that it is standard within the industry or they assume that it is completely non-negotiable, or they consider themselves to be adequately pro-tected by their own insurances. Sometimes they may take the view that in a sufficiently serious breach of contract situation, the exclusion would not be upheld. All of these assumptions have some foundation. However, if the issue is of such concern to a party that it becomes a significant point of principle in contract negotiations, it is better to agree a specific solution acceptable to both parties than to leave the issue in a state of uncertainty. In this instance, a discussion with the supplier's insurance company will be likely to produce a solution in the form of a quotation for the particular contract – specific insurance cover on terms acceptable to the parties for a premium which they can agree to share or which one party will bear in order to facilitate the transaction.

These examples have been confined to addressing limitations of liability of the supplier in favour of the customer. The customer indemnities in paragraph (f) relate to failures of the customer to act in accordance with the contract. Many such clauses adopt a similar approach, although they may vary greatly in the scope of the limitations set out: for example in distribution agreements such clauses, or perhaps a separate additional clause, provide for equivalent indemnities from the customer to the supplier, especially where end users may be involved. The general idea contemplated by the words in the square brackets in paragraph (f) is that if the customer's customer (who may be an end user or a sub-distributor) causes any loss to the supplier, the customer should indemnify the supplier against all such loss. There may be no limitations or exclusions in relation to this liability. The implications for the customer are considerable. For example, suppose that a distributor customer licenses a single software package to an end user, very likely by means of a shrink-wrap licence on a product purchased in retail circumstances. The end user illegally copies the product in great volume and disappears to South America with his ill-gotten gains. In theory, with an open-ended and unqualified indemnity, the distributor customer will be faced with an enormous liability to the supplier. This is an illustration of the extreme importance to customers of understanding and negotiating contracts. These sorts of clauses tend to be encountered when very large suppliers deal with much smaller customers and adopt a 'take it or leave it' approach to negotiations. The supplier may seek to reassure the distributor customer that it would never sue a distributor because of the future business potential of the relationship or that the clause would only ever be invoked against the distributor customer if the latter had been guilty of wrongdoing. The distributor customer may also be reminded that problems in this area are rare and it may assume that such a stringent contractual provision would not be enforced by a court because, if the distributor customer had itself complied with its contract with the supplier and licensed the product in the manner required, any other result would be patently unfair.

The general difficulty is that the customer has no real way of knowing what interpretation its supplier, or indeed a court, is going to place on the contract terms. Every attempt should be made to negotiate appropriate qualifications to an indemnity of this kind so that its scope is at least confined to circumstances where the distributor customer can be shown to have acted wrongfully itself. Even the concept of 'wrongful' is a negotiable point. Should it be confined to fraud or extended to reckless or negligent behaviour?

Paragraph (g) suggests some practical ways in which the customer can ensure that its arrangements are conducive to security and to its systems and avoid losses and damage, and limit the possibility of making a claim.

Finally, paragraph (h) is an attempt to exclude any promises or representations by the supplier not specifically set out in the contract, and as with the other paragraphs, this may also be subject to the 'reasonableness' test.

In the event of a dispute over the contract, depending on the value and type of the transaction, and the timing of the dispute, many customers would initially choose to have products replaced under warranty, or to re-negotiate the timescales or system content, and few will be interested in testing the validity of the limitation clauses. For consumers, the Unfair Terms in Consumer Contracts Regulations 1999 will additionally apply, and further to the rights of individual consumers a number of bodies such as the Office of Fair Trading and the Consumers' Association have the power to take action and remove or amend unfair contract terms.

9. Integrity of Data

(a) The parties agree that the Customer is the best judge of the value and importance of the data held on the Customer's computer system, and the Customer will be solely responsible for:

    (i) instituting and operating all necessary back-up procedures, for its own benefit, to ensure that data integrity can be maintained in the event of loss of data for any reason;

    (ii) taking out any insurance policy or other financial cover for loss or damage which may arise from loss of data for any reason.

(b) The Supplier disclaims any liability arising from loss of data from the Customer's computer system for any reason and the Customer agrees to indemnify the Supplier against any third party claims which arise from loss of data for any reason.

This clause often meets resistance from customers, principally in relation to the insurance provision which tends to be viewed as a requirement, although it is really advisory, and particularly in respect of the indemnity of the supplier in paragraph (b).

The supplier's argument is that appropriate back-up procedures minimise any damage which might result from loss of data from a computer system. The more sensitive or critical the data, the more frequent the back-up procedure should be, and only the customer can make this judgment. If back-up procedures are adequate in the particular circumstances, it will not be much of a problem to restore the situation if the data is lost and this is the reassurance that the supplier seeks. Working on a system fault and trying out various remedies can sometimes result in loss of data but this provision will prevent the supplier from exposure to a claim for damages, even if there is negligence on its part, where the responsibility for the protection of data is acknowledged to be solely that of the customer.

Only the customer (or the owner of the data, and possibly any data subjects where personal data is concerned) has an insurable interest in the data held on its system. Such insurance appears not to be available to suppliers, although public liability policies may cover the position: a supplier willing to accept liability would need to verify this.

The indemnity in respect of third party claims is intended to protect the supplier from negligence actions, which rely on general duties of care and do not require a contractual relationship between claimant and defendant. A party who owned data erased from the customer's system or who could show direct losses as a result of lost data, precluded by a contractual term from suing the customer or seeing the supplier as a financially more promising target, might be tempted to sue the supplier in negligence. Adequate back-up procedures would normally have eliminated the basis for such a claim.

On the other hand, customers in a strong negotiating position will not wish to tolerate an indemnity obligation in circumstances where a claim could succeed only because of its supplier's negligence. There is also room for argument about the extent of any indemnity: should there be a financial cap, or should the customer be able to participate in or control the defence strategy if it is going to have to pay the final bill? Comparisons with other indemnities and limitations of liability negotiated elsewhere in the agreement should ensure some consistency of approach.

10. Employment Restriction

[Recognising the commercial importance of the Products and Services] Without in any way restricting the right of a person freely to accept employment, while this Agreement is in force and for a period of 12 months from its termination for any reason, the Customer will not solicit the employment or engagement of services, whether directly or indirectly, of any person employed by or acting on behalf of the Supplier who was assigned to work [on the Customer's System] [at the Customer's site] over a period of three months or more in the preceding 12 months [and who was assigned to provide Services in connection with this Agreement]. [If the Customer is in breach of this condition, the Customer, recognising that the Supplier will suffer substantial damage, will pay to the Supplier by way of liquidated damages and not by way of penalty a sum equal to [twice] the gross annual [salary] [fees] paid to that person by the Supplier in the immediately preceding 12 months.]

This clause appears in various guises in many types of IT contracts. Sometimes it is expressed to be for the benefit of both parties. Employees or contractors of either a supplier or a customer may be tempted by the perceived working conditions of the other party when working closely together. The issue is an important one because specialist skills in the industry tend to be in short supply. As a result, employees are harder to find and more expensive to recruit; their earnings and fringe benefits tend to be high when compared with their counterparts in other industries.

From a supplier's viewpoint, many of their employees work closely with customers over long periods of time and on occasion there is a tendency to forget who the actual employer is. Suppliers will be concerned to ensure that they do not lose staff as a result of taking on customer contracts.

On the other hand, it is necessary to have regard to the sorts of public policy interests which suggest that workers should not be limited in their employment opportunities and that employers should not face artificial restrictions when approaching the labour market. The courts will enforce a restrictive clause such as this one only if it can be demonstrated to be fair and reasonable in the particular circumstances, protecting the legitimate interests of the employer, consistent with what is adjudged to be the general public interest, and not in restraint of trade.

131

Both parties should have regard to these principles when negotiating an employ-ment restriction in order to be reasonably confident that the clause finally agreed would be upheld in the event of a dispute.

A number of considerations arise. It will be helpful to identify the roles and functions which could cause a problem: 'key personnel' in the operation of the services, for example. Should the provision be mutual? Major projects afford opportunities for the capabilities of customer staff to be appraised by suppliers. Should a clause of this nature be included at all? If the customer has outsourced a specialist application but has no need or intention to employ in-house specialists, and if the customer is not operating in a major vertical market of the supplier, there may be no need for a restriction clause.

If the clause is breached and is not rendered unenforceable in the particular circumstances, the question of damages arises. 'Liquidated' damages are pre-agreed as to the amount, or the method of calculation of the amount. English law does not recognise 'penalty' levels of compensation for breach of contract. The damages must be realistic in terms of loss suffered, not carrying any 'punishment' element. It is tempting to pre-agree a liquidated damages position in order to avoid later argument. But this forces a generalised position which may not suit every situation. Liquidated damages may be appropriate to protect against the poaching of maintenance engineers in a maintenance contract, but may be less satisfactory in a general consultancy contract where several different categories of specialist personnel, from junior programmers through to project managers are likely to be deployed. However, if it is necessary to apply for an injunction, the inclusion of a pre-estimate of damages in the contract will not be helpful – the argument that the loss is not possible to calculate cannot be made.

Assuming a breach to have been established, agreed liquidated damages will be upheld provided that they are not regarded as a penalty and therefore unenforce-able. But a claimant is allowed only to recoup actual losses and not to profit beyond those. The parties therefore need to consider both aspects: what liquidated damages are appropriate in the particular circumstances; and whether the amount of liquidated damages is fairly assessed as a pre-estimate and in no way a penalty.

This said, low levels of liquidated damages, often used in order to play safe, may be well wide of the mark when all the sums are done. Given the relative scarcity of good quality computer professionals and the expenses of recruitment costs, lengthy training and bringing the person up to speed in the employing organisation, it should not be too difficult to justify a payment related to annual salary costs. Using the example of the maintenance engineer, a comparatively low paid professional in the industry, it may be perfectly defensible and realistic to agree (or to impose in standard terms and conditions) a liquidated damages sum equivalent to two years' salary. The loss of an experienced engineer can result directly in disruption or even loss of business.

In many senses, the retention of staff is a commercial and management issue, and contractual devices will not prevent an employee wanting to change employment. Moreover, in a continuing relationship between supplier and customer, legal action on this account is often not desirable.

11. Confidentiality

The parties recognise that under this Agreement they may each receive trade secrets and confidential or proprietary information of the other party, including but not limited to information concerning [products, customers, business accounts, financial or contractual arrangements or other dealings, transactions or affairs, reports, recommendations, advice or tests, source and object program codes and development plans]. All such information, which is either marked 'Confidential' or stated at the time of disclosure and subsequently confirmed in writing to be confidential, constitutes 'Confidential Information'. Each party agrees not to divulge Confidential Information received from the other to any of its employees who do not need to know it, and to prevent its disclosure to or access by any third party without the prior written consent of the disclosing party. This obligation will survive the termination of this Agreement for a period of three years or until such earlier time as the Confidential Information concerned reaches the public domain other than through the receiving party's own default.

A non-disclosure agreement is discussed in **CHAPTER 8**. However, in the context of many agreements, some contractual commitment to confidentiality is called for, such as agreements for maintenance and support where the maintenance engineer is working on the customer's premises, perhaps with sensitive customer data available, or in a disaster recovery scenario, where the customer's data is being processed at a different site. In many situations, confidentiality will not matter, or will be important only to one of the parties to a contract. For example, in a contract to supply products, the customer is more likely to have a concern about the issue than the supplier.

Several aspects of this clause are negotiable, including the definition of 'confidential information', the duration of the confidentiality period and exceptions or exclusions. These and other issues are considered in **CHAPTER 8**.

12. Publicity

[This Agreement is confidential. Neither party will publicise [the existence or] the contents of this Agreement.] Neither party will use the name or any trade mark or trade name, whether registered or not, of the other party in publicity releases or advertising or in any other manner, including Customer lists, without securing the prior written approval of the other [not to be unreasonably delayed or withheld].

Negotiated contracts are going to include concessions by the supplier which will not have been given to all of its customers. It is, therefore, reasonable for the contents of the agreement to be subject to an obligation of confidentiality. Confidentiality in respect of the *existence* of the agreement may be more difficult. Such information is more likely to reach the public domain from a variety of sources and the supplier may wish to publicise the customer relationship in return for special concessions made during negotiations. The customer may be willing to be included on a general customer list but unwilling to allow special significance to be attached to the relationship, particularly where it implies the endorsement of a product. It may be appropriate to restrict use of customer trade marks and logos even if there is agreement by a customer to be included on a list.

A supplier seeking approval for publicity should try to prevent unreasonable withholding of consent and especially delay in decision making. Large companies tend to have laborious processes for approval, and an opportunity for publicity which may in fact be of mutual benefit may be missed if decision making is slow.

13. Insurance and Guarantee

(a) The Supplier will insure and continue to be insured against all losses, claims, demands, proceedings, damages, costs, charges and expenses for injuries or damage to any person or property which are the result of the fault or negligence of the Supplier in carrying out the Services, including but not limited to employer's liability, public liability, property damage, professional indemnity and motor insurance.

(b) The Supplier, if the Customer so directs, will ensure that the beneficial interest of the Customer is noted on the face of the insurance policy. The Customer may, at its option, require proof of insurance as a condition precedent to the commencement of the Services, and evidence of payment of the last premium from time to time.

(c) This Agreement is conditional upon and will not be effective until the Supplier procures from its parent company [a guarantee executed by the parent company and signed by such persons who (in accordance with the laws of the territory in which the parent company is incorporated) are acting under the authority of the parent company in favour of the Customer guaranteeing the performance of the supplier's obligations under this Agreement.] [an irrevocable bank guarantee/a standby letter of credit in favour of the Customer payable on demand by the Customer upon any termination of this Agreement for [£.........]. Such guarantee will be in the form set out in the Schedule and will take effect from the date of this Agreement.

This provision is comparatively unusual, and will probably be capable of being imposed only by a large customer on a small supplier.

The first paragraph is of a general nature, and for the most part is referring to insurances which any business is required to carry by virtue of statutory requirements. If such a clause is negotiated into the contract, it would be appropriate to include much more specific requirements such as minimum values and situations for which the customer requires the supplier to hold insurance.

The paragraph will not be acceptable to some suppliers because they will not have insurances covering the specific contract, and may be unwilling to provide full details of their general insurances. The principal reason for this reluctance is that most general business insurance policies will provide levels of cover which are much broader than the specific levels of liability contained in suppliers' terms and conditions. If a customer has sight of these the natural instinct is to want the full extent of the protection available, but a supplier's premiums and aggregate claims potential are to some extent dependent on it having more restrictive provisions in its standard terms and conditions. This also allows a supplier a safety net if it incurs actual liabilities beyond the contractual limits, which are always subject to the customer's interpretations of relevant statutory provisions.

Noting the customer's interest on the insurance policy is an added safeguard if this can be agreed for a major contract as it brings the customer into a direct relationship with the insurance company. Nevertheless, many insurance policies specifically prohibit disclosure of their terms and conditions to a third party. However, it would be sensible for a customer to have the right to require proof of insurance at any time during the life of the contract.

If a customer is so concerned about the ability of a supplier to meet losses that it needs confirmation of insurance arrangements, it should also consider some form of third party back up, as in the alternatives at paragraph (c).

If the supplier defaults in its contractual obligations, the customer's right of action under the contract will be enforceable only against the assets of the supplier as a party to the contract. If the supplier has no assets (not uncommon for software houses whose products and services consist of customer-specific software), the customer will have no satisfactory redress in the event of being substantially let down. However, where there is security given by a third party, often an associate or parent company of the supplier, at the time of entering into the contract, a customer will be able to enforce its rights against the assets of that third party to the extent set out.

Arrangements can be made with a supplier's bank in certain circumstances for a letter of credit or performance bond in specific language and terms to be issued. A customer will be entitled to payment of a pre-determined sum, usually related to the contract value, in the event of serious default in performance by the supplier.

One difficulty for some suppliers in arranging this sort of protection is that the value of a bank-provided bond will fall within the overall credit facilities extended to the supplier.

Parent company guarantees or payment in advance (such as in the security of a bond) are not unusual in other industries, but are infrequently encountered in the IT industry. The customer is looking for a third party to guarantee performance – a parent company or bank. Basically a sum of money would be made available for the customer in the event of the supplier's insolvency. This would not actually solve the customer's difficulties in not obtaining contract performance, but would provide financial compensation.

14. Data Protection

> The parties agree that they will at all times comply with the provisions and obligations imposed by the Data Protection Act 1998 and the Data Protection Principles set out in that Act in storing and processing personal data. All personal data acquired by either party from the other will be returned to the disclosing party on request. Each party agrees to respond promptly to the other in dealing adequately with all enquiries received relating to data protection. Each party agrees to indemnify the other against all losses, costs, expenses, damages, liabilities, demands, claims, actions and proceedings which the other party may incur arising out of any breach of this clause.

This is a general provision wherever personal data may be involved as part of the transactional arrangements. More detailed clauses will be appropriate for transactions in which personal data form a significant part of the arrangements.

The Data Protection Act 1998 regulates the holding, processing and use of personal data by imposing obligations on those responsible for the processing – data controllers – which include compliance with the Act's eight Data Protection Principles. These Principles comprise a basic code, balancing the need for personal data to be processed and the protection of basic rights and freedoms, including the right to privacy. They cover all aspects of processing the personal data, in terms of accuracy, fairness, lawfulness and related security measures. There are extra rules relating to 'sensitive' personal data, such as those relating to race.

The Act gives rights to the 'data subjects', those who are the subjects of the personal data. They may find out what personal data are held about them, have incorrect personal data amended or erased, and take action for compensation if they suffer because personal data are inaccurate or wrongly disclosed. The Act is enforced by the Information Commissioner and there are criminal sanctions for failure to notify the Information Commissioner that personal data are held and for failure to comply with enforcement procedures. The Information Commissioner's office is the independent supervisory authority for both the Data Protection Act and the Freedom of Information Act 2000. The Information Commissioner reports directly to the UK Parliament.

A data controller is responsible for the personal data. If a contractor is used to process personal data on its behalf for any reason – for example in outsourcing or for data recovery – the data controller remains ultimately liable and will therefore be responsible for ensuring that the contractor's security standards are suitable for the personal data. The data controller must enter into a written contract for this purpose and monitor the data processor's procedures. The data controller must be confident that it has taken all reasonable steps to maintain the security of the personal data. Guidance is available from the Information Commissioner[6].

The Data Protection Act is the result of an EU Directive[7] which all member states are required to implement into national legislation. Accordingly all these countries have equivalent laws to protect personal data. The eighth Data Protection Principle restricts cross-border transfers of personal data. Personal data must not be transferred to any country outside the European Economic Area (the EU member states plus Norway, Switzerland and Liechtenstein) without an adequate level of protection for the data. The European Commission can produce a 'Community Finding' that a particular country's laws do provide this level of protection, and has done so for Hungary, Switzerland, Canada and Argentina, for instance. Alternatively, the data controller who wants to export personal data must obtain the consent of the data subject, or ensure through contract that its own legal obligations are also imposed on the foreign recipient of the personal data.

Model contract clauses are available[8] where the data controller is transferring personal data to a data controller or to a data processor to a country outside the EEA which is not regarded as having adequate data protection laws. These clauses are extensive and rather legalistic and their wording is not mandatory.

Whereas the EU is working with comprehensive legislation for privacy issues, the approach in the US combines legislation, regulation and self-regulation. The 'Safe Harbor' framework was developed by the US Department of Commerce in consultation with the European Union. It consists of a set of privacy principles which meet the European Commission's requirements for data protection. American companies may choose to self-certify against the Safe Harbor rules, and thus to enable personal data to be securely and safely transferred to them. They must confirm annually that they continue to meet the requirements. The US Department of Commerce keeps a list of these companies at its website and provides useful guidance[9].

The basis of the clause as worded above is that there is a contractual as well as legal obligation – which must be complied with in any event – in processing personal data. Negotiation may focus on the extent of the indemnity which, however, is typically uncapped.

15. Export Control

> Having regard to the current statutory or other United Kingdom Government regulations in force from time to time and, in the case of Products manufactured in the US, to the United States Department of Commerce Export Regulations in force from time to time, and regardless of any disclosure made by the Customer to the Supplier of an ultimate destination for any Products, the Customer will not export or re-export, directly or indirectly, any Products without first obtaining all written consents or authorisations which may be required by any applicable Government regulations. The Supplier will assist the Customer to apply for the requisite consents or authorisations if so requested.

Any technology intended for, or which could be used or adapted for, military use will be subject to export control restrictions in relation to transfer abroad, including by electronic means[10]. Hardware, software or technical information to which export controls are applicable must have an export licence issued by the Department of Trade and Industry. The penalty for breaching the terms of the licence or for not having a licence may be fines or imprisonment. Dual-use items (including hardware and software) are also subject to controls when they are exported from the European Union[11].

This type of clause, typically appearing in contracts for US-sourced computer equipment, focuses attention almost exclusively on the US regulations. A number of British purchasers take exception to this. The requirement for this export controls clause is because there is some variation in the prohibited countries listed in the respective US and UK regulations.

The resistance is generally motivated on sovereignty grounds and will rarely be based on any actual intention to re-export to countries prohibited by US regulations. However, if there is no contractual condition imposing such regulations, there can be no absolute guarantee about conduct.

This clause gives prominent reference to the UK regulations, whilst also emphasising US regulations. It could be argued that this would constrain purchasers even more although, of course, they would be bound by the UK regulations in any event.

There is no absolute requirement in the United States Department of Commerce export regulations requiring American manufacturers to make it an express condition of contract with their customers that the regulations must be observed. American manufacturers, however, are required to draw the attention of their customers to these regulations, and to report any actual or suspected breaches. Since their general export distribution licences could be adversely affected, in addition to other significant penalties for deliberate or reckless violation of the regulations, there is naturally going to be some sensitivity to any request for the removal or modification of the export control clause.

Some distribution agreements by American suppliers go so far as to require an indemnity from the distributor in respect of any violations of export regulations by the distributor's customers. This is an extreme requirement which should be strongly resisted. Unless it can be shown that the distributor was careless or worse in establishing the 'ultimate destination' for products supplied, there is no justification for an indemnity. If the products in question are low unit value distributed in high volume to a large number of customers, it is highly unlikely that the distributor will have any means of knowing whether or not such products are going to end up at a prohibited destination.

If agreement of the clause genuinely does prove to be an insurmountable difficulty, there are some alternative forms of wording which could still enable an American or American-parented supplier to demonstrate its reasonable efforts to the authorities to ensure that the US regulations will not be infringed, or that they have at least been drawn clearly to the customer's attention.

For example:

> The Customer confirms that the Products identified in this Agreement are solely for the Customer's own use within the United Kingdom and are not intended for re-export.

This will be acceptable to some American organisations as representing an absolute undertaking not to re-export goods obtained under the contract mentioned. However, the wording could be construed as amounting only to a declaration of intention at the time of agreement and failing to cater for a subsequent change of mind.

Alternatively:

> The Customer is advised that United States Department of Commerce Export Regulations may apply to some or all of the Products and that these regulations prohibit the re-exporting of applicable products to certain destinations. In any event, Software Product licences are not transferable without the prior written consent of the Supplier.

This 'demotes' the clause from being mandatory to advisory in nature. While purists will argue that such wording has no place in a contract since it does not constitute an obligation, its inclusion will be of assistance to US suppliers in their dealings with their Department of Commerce.

Another solution for a major customer who has refused to sign a contract containing the standard clause is to omit the clause altogether, but write a letter in the same terms as the clause advising the customer of the regulations.

The negotiation of special wording with smaller customers is unlikely to be considered appropriate by most suppliers. Customers who are significant on the grounds of their expenditure or prestige may justify the effort of finding a compromise.

16. Termination for Cause

(a) This Agreement may be terminated immediately by notice in writing:
- (i) by the Supplier if the Customer fails to pay any sums due under this Agreement by the due date without prejudice to any other provisions relating to late payment in this Agreement;
- (ii) by either party if the other party is in material or continuing breach of any of its obligations under this Agreement and fails to remedy the breach (if capable of remedy) for a period of 30 days after written notice by the other party;
- (iii) by either party if the other party is involved in any legal proceedings concerning its solvency, or ceases trading, or commits an act of bankruptcy or is adjudicated bankrupt or enters into liquidation, whether compulsory or voluntary, other than for the purposes of an amalgamation or reconstruction, or makes an arrangement with its creditors or petitions for an administration order or if a trustee, receiver, administrative receiver or general officer is appointed over all or any part of its assets or generally becomes unable to pay its debts within the meaning of Section 123 of the Insolvency Act 1986, or equivalent circumstances occur in any other jurisdiction.

(b) Any termination of this Agreement under this clause will be without prejudice to any other rights or remedies of either party under this Agreement or at law and will not affect any accrued rights or liabilities of either party at the date of termination.

(c) On termination of this Agreement, including the Software Licence, the Customer will be obliged to satisfy the Supplier that it has erased the Software and all copies of any part of the Software from the System and from its magnetic media and that it has no ability to reproduce the Software in any way, and it will further be obliged to return to the Supplier immediately all related documentation and all copies, books, records, papers or other tangible things in its possession belonging to the Supplier.

Some supply contracts do not expressly provide for termination for cause, leaving this as a matter to be determined by the application of the general law. For the avoidance of doubt, a specific termination provision is desirable. This example deals with the right to terminate the contract for unremedied failures to perform and with insolvency. The parties' rights are reserved in respect of the other consequences which could result from premature termination, for example, the right to claim damages, or a right to obtain performance of the contract elsewhere at the expense of the defaulting party, or a right to make a final purchase of products at the special contract price, or the right to manufacturing data and drawings.

Where ongoing performance is necessary after the supply of products has been completed, there is scope for additional specific provisions and this is where negotiation is likely to take place, that is, to state some of the rights or consequences of termination, or to incorporate more detail about the circumstances entitling the defaulting party to bring the contract to an end. Such negotiations are likely to be confined to higher value and more complicated supply contracts where termination is but one of many issues to be resolved.

A right to terminate is often encountered to take effect immediately in the event of any breach without any opportunity for the breach to be remedied. The circumstances in which such a provision could be regarded as reasonable are going to be unusual, and it is desirable for an opportunity to be provided which will allow a defaulting party a chance to put things right. The effect of such a clause is also going to be different towards the end of a contract than in the early stages, and it would be unfair for a party who has performed, say, 90 per cent of a contract to be subjected to termination for a minor breach.

Paragraph (c) will be appropriate for contracts which include the supply of software, and an obligation to return materials belonging to the supplier may also be justified in contracts which do not include the supply of software. Sometimes a reciprocal provision will be needed to ensure the return of a customer's property.

1   Law of Property Act 1925, s 61; Interpretation Act 1978, s 5 and Sch 1.
2   *Pegler Ltd v Wang (UK) Ltd* [2000] ITCLR 617, QBD (T&CC); *South West Water v International Computers Ltd* [1999] BLR 420, QBD (T&CC).
3   Value Added Tax Act 1983, ss 10(2) and 42(2) implementing the European Communities Council Sixth Directive. VAT law in the UK is principally the Value Added Tax Act 1994, which has been amended by subsequent Finance Acts, and there are also many statutory instruments setting out detailed rules.
4   Late Payment of Commercial Debts (Interest) Act 1998 (as amended), implementing EC Directive 2000/35.
5   *British Sugar plc v NEI Power Projects Ltd* [1998] ITCLR 125, CA.
6   www.informationcommissioner.gov.uk.
7   EC Directive 95/46.
8   http://europa.eu.int/comm/internal-market.
9   www.export.gov/safeharbor.
10 Export Control Act 2002 and associated Orders: Export of Goods, Transfer of Technology and Provision of Technical Assistance Order; The Trade in Controlled Goods (Control) Order; The Trade in Controlled Goods to Embargoed Destinations Order.
11 Regulation No 1334/2000.

CHAPTER 8

Non-disclosure

A. Introduction

Through the use of computers, information has become something to be processed and traded in its own right, like any other commodity. However, unlike many commodities, the value of certain information is proportional to its exclusivity, such as a technical process, financial projections, or a customer list. Increasing specialisation has made the protection of confidential information a critical matter to any organisation. This is particularly true in the computing industry, where there is so much innovation that any competitive edge does not last long. Trade secrets are immensely important.

1. Use of non-disclosure agreements

The essential purpose of a non-disclosure agreement is to ensure that confidential information remains confidential and is not broadcast to competitors, disseminated to the general public, or exploited in competition with the owner.

A non-disclosure agreement is useful for the times when outsiders need access to an organisation's confidential data, for example for the purpose of preliminary discussions and evaluations: where a purchase of a company is contemplated, a joint venture is planned, or where close evaluation of a computer system by a prospective purchaser is being undertaken; for the development of new products; or where technical information about engineering and manufacturing processes is being imparted.

A purchaser may wish to impose non-disclosure terms to cover its own proprietary information where prospective suppliers are investigating existing processes and procedures to determine how their products and services will meet the purchaser's requirements.

When companies are acquired and sold, the examination and valuation of intellectual property assets has become a key task in the 'due diligence' exercise, a careful enquiry by a company's purchaser, designed to identify, test and quantify this part of the purchase in relation to the price.

In all these circumstances, the use of non-disclosure agreements is widespread, to provide some protection and to show that no general disclosure is intended.

A standard confidentiality clause is provided in **CHAPTER 7**, and this will be appropriate in many circumstances for including in those contracts where confidentiality is a required feature. Nevertheless, a comprehensive agreement will be called for in situations covering specific subject matter disclosed for a specific purpose. A non-disclosure agreement should cover the subject matter, exceptions to the confidentiality in respect of people or information, the strength of the obligation, and its duration. The more detail, the better the protection that will be achieved.

2. No general law of privacy

There is no general law of privacy under English law, and therefore information disclosed in confidence will not necessarily be protected by law. Confidentiality clauses and non-disclosure agreements are necessary for protecting commercially confidential information.

Commercially sensitive information is not necessarily a trade secret which the courts will protect automatically, whether it consists of a commercial method, customers' details or marketing techniques. In one case in the courts, reverse engineering of a coin discriminator, where information had to be decrypted, was held not to constitute a breach of confidence. Anyone could purchase the discriminator. The information had not been received in confidence simply because it required decrypting to find out how it was made[1].

A right to informational privacy has now been established in principle, based on an evolution and expansion of the law on breach of confidence in relation to the Human Rights Act 1998, and the interpretation of legislation in a manner compatible with the European Convention on Human Rights, balancing the right of privacy against the right to freedom of expression, case by case[2]. There are also legal obligations to protect 'personal data'. Principles set out in the Data Protection Act 1998 govern the use of such information which relates to a living identifiable person, and which is processed automatically or held in an on-automated filing system. A recipient of personal data must abide by the principles in ensuring that such information is kept and processed fairly and with care, and is held no longer than necessary for the purpose.

3. Remedies for unauthorised disclosure

At law it is a question of fact in the particular circumstances whether the disclosure of information will cause damage to its owner, and whether the information would be protectable in the absence of express written contractual provisions.

> 'Confidential information is like ... an ice cube ... Give it to the party who undertakes to keep it in a refrigerator and you still have an ice cube ... Give it to the party which has no refrigerator or who will not agree to keep it in one and by the time of the trial you just have a pool of water which neither party wants. It is the inherently perishable nature of confidential information which gives rise to unique problems'[3].

An injunction by the courts to prevent further disclosure will often be too late to retrieve the harm already caused. If the disclosure of information is in breach of contract, damages will be available as for other breaches, on the basis of compensation. However, damage resulting from disclosure of information is always difficult to prove and to quantify. An 'account of profits' can be called for, but this is often difficult to determine. An order can be made for destruction or return of the confidential material.

In American non-disclosure agreements, the recipient is sometimes required to agree that damages would be a wholly inadequate remedy for disclosure. This reads oddly where English law is concerned, and is inappropriate. A judge in the courts of England and Wales is in a position to assess from the evidence presented at the time, and according to the circumstances, what the remedy would be, whether to grant an injunction and whether damages should be awarded.

4. Procedures

There is a growing trend for suppliers and customers alike to demand the signing of non-disclosure agreements, to cover both pre- and post-contract information exchanges. When such agreements are not really necessary, they should not be signed, and a requirement for reciprocal agreements can help to curb over-enthusiastic drafting by one party when an agreement is justified. Once signed, proper attention should be given by the recipient to monitoring the use of the confidential information and its safe custody. This principle applies not only to paper documents but also to material provided electronically, on-screen or by means of disk.

There is too often a cavalier approach to the monitoring and enforcement of obligations. Few organisations would be able to produce evidence of any sort of tracking system if called upon to do so.

A non-disclosure agreement must be executed *before* the parties disclose or receive confidential information. Attempts to apply it to previously received information will normally be ineffective as a matter of law and, in any event, it will be difficult to identify such information accurately.

There may be situations in which a company refuses to sign a non-disclosure agreement. If proprietary information has to be provided to a company in such situations, it should be marked 'confidential'. This will at least give its owners certain limited rights in attempting to protect the information at law without a written agreement.

One exposure for employers and indeed employees, often overlooked, is the situation where a supplier's employee is required by a customer to sign some sort of confidentiality or non-disclosure statement before being admitted to a customer site. Service and support engineers are especially vulnerable to such requests and, perhaps through ignorance or, more positively, motivated by a desire to help the customer and get the job done, they co-operate, sometimes without reporting the matter to their employer. This is a bad practice on the part of customers, because there has been no opportunity for the employee to obtain advice about the implications of the document, and the matter will not have been the subject of any discussions between the customer and the supplier. Suppliers should make a point of positively instructing their employees not to sign any such document without first referring it back for approval. If this involves a delay in the provision of services, it should serve to discourage customers from such practices beyond what has been agreed in the contract for maintenance and support.

5. Information or techniques

Information cannot be 'stolen' as money or machines can. This was established where a student took examination papers, copied and returned them. The university had not been 'permanently deprived' of the papers[4]. It is not transferred out of the owner's possession by being imparted. Information disclosed in confidence will not necessarily be protected by law.

One difficulty in the IT industry lies in distinguishing what actually is confidential information, such as software source code (which can be protected[5]) and what is an employee's know-how (which cannot).

An employee has an obligation of 'good faith' in relation to information he obtains and uses as an employee. However, information which becomes part of the employee's skill and knowledge will not be protectable unless an enforceable agreement is signed. Employers often wish to restrict the future use of employees' know-how, their 'methodology', their approaches of structuring and organising their ways of solving problems. But skills acquired from carrying out the work, in the course of employment, however valuable these may be to the employer, are part of the worker's competence and practical abilities and not readily amenable to protection by confidentiality constraints.

145

6. Employment practice in relation to confidentiality

Good employment practice in relation to the management of confidential information is part of the management of risk. The law tries to strike a balance, in terms of the 'public interest'. Employers must have rights to prevent the unauthorised spread of information which contributes to the prosperity of their enterprise; employees must also have rights to use their skills and expertise to further their career development. This dilemma is acute in the IT industry, where specialised skills are in such short supply and where novelty is at a premium.

Although industrial espionage is reportedly on the increase, the spread of trade secrets would at least be restricted if employees always stayed in the same place. The secret formula for blending Chartreuse liqueur has been guarded for more than 250 years by a small group of Carthusian monks based in the French Alps, working from an already 'ancient' recipe. Only three monks are said to know the secret at any one time, and only they are allowed to carry out the blending process of the dried herbs, in the secret combination used in making the liqueur.

But the religious order is not noted for its job mobility, in contrast to the UK IT industry, where employees change jobs more frequently than in any other sector of employment except for hotel and catering, in order to earn more money from using experience needed by another employer, in order to widen expertise and to work their way up through a myriad of job titles.

Contracts of employment with express restraint provisions are essential as a preliminary step towards protecting business secrets and consequently the business. The more precise the restraints, the better the prospects will be that they can be enforced.

Any employee who in the course of employment may learn the trade secrets of the employer or the employer's suppliers or customers, should have an express term of confidentiality in the employment contract. The employer may even reasonably require a separate confidentiality agreement to be signed by the employee to highlight the importance of the information to which the employee has access, and to demonstrate that it is more than a blanket requirement generally applicable. Again, the obligations should be clear, and the confidential information concerned should be delimited as much as possible, relating to customer or supplier affairs which the employee may learn about as well as to the employer's own affairs. As a matter of good practice, the employee's attention should be drawn to what is regarded as being confidential at any time during the course of employment, to avoid any possibility of doubt.

As a separate issue, an employment contract should include a provision that software should not be copied without authorisation (to conform with the licences of third party software used by the organisation) or used without authorisation (to protect against the introduction of viruses).

B. The structure of a non-disclosure agreement

The structure for this example agreement covers the situation where the owner of confidential information is disclosing it to the recipient.

Terms and conditions

- Definition of 'Confidential Information'*
- Recipient's Undertakings*
- Confidential Information Co-ordinator*
- Exceptions*
- Limitations on Recipient's Liability*
- Intellectual Property Rights, Warranties and Disclaimers*
- Non-conflicting Activities*
- Termination and Time Limit*
- Publicity*
- General
    - Severability
    - Waiver
    - No rights of third parties
    - Law and Jurisdiction

Schedules

- Description of areas covered by the Confidential Information
- Business Purpose (reason for disclosing the Confidential Information)

C. Specific clauses

In the clause examples discussed below, which are those above marked with an asterisk, the parties are referred to as 'Owner' and 'Recipient', denoting the disclosing party, who either owns or is authorised to disclose the information, and the receiver respectively of the confidential information.

1. Definition of 'Confidential Information'

> In consideration of the disclosure to the Recipient of information relating to [proprietary, technological, business and technical] matters of the Owner including but not limited to [documents, drawings, diagrams, models and programs] or any part or copy of such information as more specifically identified in Exhibit A attached to and forming part of this Agreement ('Confidential Information'), the Recipient agrees:

This defines the scope of the information covered by the agreement.

So that there is no doubt between the parties over what is to be regarded as confidential information, the definition should be as specific and as descriptive as possible. The recipient must avoid the possibility of innocent and accidental breach. If information is so important to the owner that it should be treated with great care, the owner must be able to identify it as such.

The recipient may be able to introduce the following optional clause in respect of information disclosed orally. However, this is not always practicable, especially for highly sensitive data. This wording requires the information to be defined in writing as 'confidential' within a short period following its disclosure.

> If the Owner orally discloses Confidential Information to the Recipient, the Owner agrees that the Confidential Information will be identified at the time of disclosure as confidential, and will be confirmed in writing within seven days, referencing the place and date, the names of those persons to whom oral disclosure was made, and the general nature of the subject matter disclosed.

Sometimes attempts are made to find middle ground. Owners of confidential information are nervous about a requirement that oral information will be protected only if it has been confirmed in writing, arguing that in the cut and thrust of intensive commercial activity, procedural niceties will be overlooked. Moreover, they may be anxious about committing confidential information to print. A suggested compromise may be to extend confidential information to include information which, by its very nature and the circumstances of disclosure, the receiving party should have realised was confidential. Unfortunately, there can be no certainty that information claimed to fall within this category would be accepted as such by a court of law. Clear and unambiguous criteria are always to be preferred. If particular information is considered to be confidential by its owner, the owner should be willing to co-operate in procedures intended to assist the recipient to meet its obligations of confidentiality. It is often forgotten that the individual representatives of the parties who make these agreements will have moved on while the agreements are still in force. How are those who follow able to continue the monitoring and enforcement process if no information is available about the disclosures previously made?

2. Recipient's Undertakings

The Recipient undertakes:

(a) to receive and hold the Confidential Information in the strictest confidence and to take all reasonable security precautions in the safekeeping of the Confidential Information and in preventing its unauthorised disclosure to third parties [applying no lesser reasonable security measures to it than to its own confidential information];

(b) not to disclose the Confidential Information to any third party without the Owner's prior written consent [excluding professional advisers];

(c) to use the Confidential Information solely for the Business Purpose specified in Exhibit A;

(d) to make copies of the Confidential Information only as strictly necessary [with the prior written consent of the Owner] [and not to copy or store the Confidential Information electronically or transmit it outside its usual place of business];

(e) to ensure that its employees are given access to the Confidential Information only on a 'need to know' basis for the purposes of dealing with the Owner, and that these employees are informed of the confidential nature of the Confidential Information [and are contractually bound to safeguard the Confidential Information].

These undertakings can be extended in great detail but these particular paragraphs cover the issues concerned.

The first difficulty in negotiation is to be found in the concept of 'reasonable security precautions' in paragraph (a). This is a subjective test and different organisations will have different standards of security. The recipient will wish to avoid giving an absolute undertaking because this allows no leeway, even for genuine oversights in security procedures. However, the owner of the information may need more than the qualified assurance in this paragraph, particularly if the information is very sensitive or valuable. As it stands, in the event of a dispute, it will be for a court or other arbiter to decide whether or not reasonable security precautions were in fact taken. The alternative is for the parties to stipulate expressly the way in which the confidential information will be held, for example in a safe or locked drawer, and with a procedure for regular review to check that the information is still intact, has not been copied, has been returned by an authorised user, and so on.

Any exemption of professional advisers from the category of third parties requiring the owner's prior written consent should be considered on a case-by-case basis. Only where the circumstances require it should disclosures be made to third party advisers, and in those situations there is no reason why the third parties concerned should not themselves be required to enter into non-disclosure agreements. Solicitors may be a justifiable exception because of their general obligations of confidentiality towards their client and the law of professional privilege whereby a solicitor is not obliged to divulge certain information passing between solicitor and client. However, in a significant commercial transaction, an owner could be forgiven for not wishing solely to rely on rules of professional conduct, even where they have the force of law.

There should always be a specified purpose – the 'Business Purpose' mentioned at (c) – for which the confidential information is being supplied to the recipient. It forces the parties to think about what is being agreed and indeed to confirm that use of the information is actually necessary to achieve their business objectives. This will restrict the use which the recipient may make of the information, in particular for its own benefit alone and not in any sense for competition or other exploitation. It should be specified at Exhibit A.

It is not easy for an owner to check whether copies are made, and the undertaking in paragraph (d) is principally a safeguard, so that the owner will have a remedy if in fact it is discovered that unauthorised copies have been made. However, the owner can make copying difficult by supplying the information on a medium not amenable to successful copying, for example, red paper or read-only discs. These days it is becoming common to hold information only electronically, bringing with it additional control and enforcement difficulties for the owner. The words in square brackets may be appropriate in some cases.

There is something to be said for requiring a 'need to know' undertaking from the owner in the sense of the owner promising not to divulge confidential information unnecessarily. There are far too many general non-disclosure agreements around which purport to cover everything said, written or done between the parties, whether needed or not, and without any time limitation. Such an undertaking could be incorporated into the definition of 'confidential information'.

Paragraph (e) goes on to consider the confidential information which should be imparted to employees and an 'employee's need to know' test is useful here because it obliges the recipient employer to think about the areas of information which individuals should know. In sensitive situations the words in square brackets may be used to impose a requirement to bind employees contractually, whether this should be in the form of a general clause in their employment contracts or a specific undertaking covering the particular information. An absolute guarantee that employees will not breach the obligation of confidentiality should be avoided on the grounds that it is impossible to control.

It is worth questioning how reasonable it is to expect employees to enter into individual personal undertakings in relation to confidential information. Employers control their employees and should not generally be willing to permit any direct form of contractual relationship between their customer or supplier and their employees. Certainly any departure from this principle should be an exception reserved for the most serious and sensitive of projects.

It is unfortunate that information protected under the Official Secrets Act 1989 does not necessarily fall into this category. Information received under the umbrella of this Act covers an extremely wide range, often including information of a character which would not be regarded as confidential in normal commercial circumstances, and carries with it an absolute obligation of confidentiality within the precise terms of disclosure. Breach may result in criminal sanctions. An appropriate level of security clearance for the recipient is generally required before information is released under the Act. However, companies wishing to do business with some government departments will find it a non-negotiable prerequisite that the employees involved must first undergo appropriate levels of security vetting and individually sign the Official Secrets Act.

3. Confidential Information Co-ordinator

> The Recipient appoints the person so designated in Exhibit A as its Confidential Information Co-ordinator for the receipt and dispatch of the Confidential Information, or any other person who may be designated by the Recipient to the Owner in writing.

A co-ordinator, who will limit and monitor access to the confidential information by the recipient's staff, should be specially appointed by the recipient of confidential information under the terms of a non-disclosure agreement, whether or not this is a contractual requirement.

The co-ordinator must ensure that the staff who are permitted access understand that the information is confidential and are aware of the agreement itself. The co-ordinator should be given personal responsibility for safeguarding the documents or other media on which the information is stored. Copies of information – in so far as copying is permitted under the agreement – should be made only by the co-ordinator who will be responsible for keeping track of them. When no longer required by the recipient, the information should be returned to the owner with a covering letter or destroyed and its destruction certified to the owner.

If it is not feasible to restrict the description and objective of supplying the confidential information, the means of communicating the information to the recipient should be clearly identified.

The confidential information co-ordinator alone will receive the confidential information from the owner and this will restrict what is to be regarded as confidential. The co-ordinator should be provided with procedures for logging, monitoring and securing the confidential information until it is returned.

4. Exceptions

The parties agree that information is not to be regarded as Confidential Information and that the Recipient will have no obligation with respect to any information which the Recipient can demonstrate:

(a) is already known to, or in the possession of, the Recipient prior to its receipt from the Owner or which is publicly available at the time of disclosure; or

(b) is or becomes known to the public through no wrongful act of the Recipient; or

(c) is received from a third party who is not in breach of any obligation of confidentiality; or

(d) is used or disclosed with the prior written authorisation of the Owner; or

(e) is disclosed by the Recipient in compliance with a legal requirement of a governmental agency or otherwise where disclosure is required by operation of law; or

(f) is developed independently by the Recipient; or

(g) relates to general concepts of information technology.

This clause is important for the recipient.

The recipient should not be placed in a worse position than anyone else who happens to know of the confidential information without being bound by confidentiality requirements, and should ensure that the list of exceptions covers all the situations which ought to be regarded as falling outside the scope of confidentiality. In the event of a claim for breach of confidentiality, the burden of proof will fall on the recipient to prove that one of the exceptions applies.

Nor should the recipient be placed in any better position.

Confidential information must be received subsequent to the date of the agreement. It should not be information which the recipient did not know to be confidential at the time of receipt. Some agreements attempt to extend confidentiality obligations to such information, but there is an obvious danger for the recipient in agreeing to obligations which may already have been broken.

Paragraph (e) is sometimes accompanied by a requirement that notice should be given of any intended disclosure in complying with a legal demand. Legal demands can arise in several ways, generally associated with some form of court action in the course of commercial litigation or statutory enforcement proceedings, where the information is required as evidence. This is to give the owner of the information the opportunity to challenge the demand and to obtain an interim order preventing disclosure pending adjudication on the legitimacy of the demand.

Paragraphs (f) and (g) are broad in scope but are intended to cover the situations where different expressions of similar ideas may exist or where general industry know-how needs to be distinguished from genuinely confidential information owned by the discloser.

5. Limitations on Recipient's Liability

The Recipient will not be liable for:

(a) inadvertent disclosure or use of the Confidential Information provided that:

    (i) it uses the same degree of care in safeguarding such Confidential Information as it reasonably uses for its own confidential information, and

    (ii) upon discovery of such inadvertent disclosure or use, it will endeavour to prevent any further inadvertent disclosure or use; or

(b) unauthorised disclosure or use of Confidential Information by employees or former employees unless it fails to:

    (i) inform its employees about the obligations of confidentiality,

    (ii) supervise the use of the Confidential Information, or

    (iii) supervise the operation of security procedures applicable to the Confidential Information as required by this Agreement[, or

    (iv) conduct exit interviews with departing employees].

This clause, favouring the recipient, is included for the sake of completeness but is unlikely to be acceptable to owners of sensitive confidential information who would not themselves include such a provision in drawing up a non-disclosure agreement. It is one thing to impose a positive requirement to use at least the same degree of care in safeguarding the information as would be reasonably used for the recipient's own confidential information. But it is another matter actually to exclude liability if inadvertent disclosure occurs when the safeguards have been observed. Aside from the fact that exclusions of liability are contrary to the spirit of a confidentiality agreement, the exclusion effectively moves the burden of proof from the recipient to the owner if confidential information is alleged to have been leaked.

A recipient of confidential information may instinctively want to place some limits on liability. Strict open-ended obligations are difficult, and sometimes impossible, to police. However, faced with an example clause like this, an owner should be seeking to strengthen the obligations and place the onus firmly on the recipient to justify any departure from the obligations.

Most owners would certainly expect the obligations of confidentiality to extend to employees. There would be little point in the agreement otherwise. The exclusion is more reasonable when it relates to ex-employees.

In these circumstances, an obligation to conduct exit interviews will be of some comfort to the owner. Owners should also expect the requirements in paragraphs (b)(i), (ii) and (iii) to constitute positive obligations in the agreement.

The parties' views on these issues may be influenced by whether or not the agreement is reciprocal, when the clause is more likely to be acceptable. Negotiations of reciprocal agreements tend to result in milder obligations.

The concept of maintaining the same degree of confidentiality as for the recipient's own information is tending to be adopted more frequently, but it does raise difficulties. There may be considerable incompatibility between the standards observed by each organisation and the requirement that the care used should be reasonable is still going to leave the owner in a state of uncertainty. It is therefore essential that, before agreeing to a clause of this nature, the owner satisfies itself about the security arrangements made by the recipient. Again, the level of sensitivity of the information to be disclosed will also be a factor.

6. Intellectual Property Rights, Warranties and Disclaimers

(a) The Owner retains all intellectual property rights in the Confidential Information at all times and for all purposes [including the copyright in any material(s) produced by the Recipient relating to the Confidential Information].

(b) Nothing contained in this Agreement is to be construed as granting or conferring any rights by licence or otherwise, expressly, or by implication, for any invention, discovery or improvement made or acquired by the Owner before or after the date of this Agreement relating to the Confidential Information.

(c) The Owner gives no warranty, express or implied, in respect of the Confidential Information.

(d) The Owner accepts no responsibility for any expenses or losses incurred or actions undertaken by the Recipient as a result of the Recipient's receipt of the Confidential Information. It is understood by the Recipient that the Owner does not warrant or represent that it will enter into any further contract with the Recipient in connection with the development or supply of any product or service to which the Confidential Information relates.

This clause is important. In disclosing confidential information, owners should never intend to convey any rights in the information to the recipient, warrant the information in any way, or enter into any implied obligation to transact further business. If any of these things are required, they should be the subject of other agreements expressly dealing with those matters and incorporating all of the terms and conditions of the transaction, including the consideration for whatever is conferred or supplied.

The words in square brackets in paragraph (a) are desirable for the owner so that there can be no risk to an owner that anything produced by the recipient infringes the owner's copyright. The recipient should not regard this as unreasonable because it would be in an uncomfortable position if any of its own materials could be subject to third party challenge for infringement of copyright or any other intellectual property right. Any invention developed by the recipient as a result of using the confidential information would be open to challenge on infringement grounds by the owner.

The commercial circumstances are relevant. For example, if the recipient is responding to an invitation to tender and provides detailed designs in response to a confidential set of data, both parties will perceive that they have interests to protect. The owner will object to another party's ownership of any material which incorporates its confidential information. The recipient will consider that its ideas, in which it may have invested much resource, have a commercial value which should not be made available to the owner without charge. Alert to the perceptions of both sides, the parties must negotiate an acceptable compromise – in this example perhaps by agreeing joint ownership of the resulting materials, so that neither party can exploit them without regard to the rights of the other. The terms and conditions of such an arrangement would be negotiated as a separate agreement.

7. Non-conflicting Activities

(a) This Non-Disclosure Agreement will not limit developments by the Recipient which involve processes, techniques or technology of a similar nature to that disclosed, provided that such development is accomplished without the use of the Confidential Information.

(b) It is acknowledged that both parties are free to enter into similar agreements with third parties, provided that the obligations of this Agreement are not breached.

A clause such as this is not often seen in non-disclosure agreements but, certainly in fast moving high technology industries, it is a sensible safeguard.

Paragraph (a) is aimed at the recipient who develops and supplies products and who cannot afford to be fettered in its activities.

Paragraph (b) is useful to both parties because it confirms freedom to deal with others and sets an expectation that such dealings do not imply any breach of the confidentiality obligations.

Sometimes a party may have a concern about a particular competitor and, while there can be legal difficulties in prohibiting competitive activities, the owner can think in terms of strengthening the confidentiality obligations undertaken by the recipient before being willing to disclose information.

8. Termination and Time Limit

(a) This Agreement may be terminated at any time by written notice of termination served by either party on the other.

(b) Upon request, and in any event upon termination for whatever reason, or in the event of any breach of these terms by the Recipient, the Recipient will immediately return all tangible materials in its possession relating to the Confidential Information including, but not limited to, drawings, documents, hardware, disks, and tapes, destroying or erasing any copies, notes or extracts, so that no Confidential Information is retained by the Recipient.

(c) This Agreement is in addition to and not instead of any other written agreements between the parties. The parties' obligations under this Agreement will survive the termination of this Agreement [for a period of [5] years from the date of first disclosure of the Confidential Information to the Recipient].

It is unusual to see a period of notice prior to termination in a non-disclosure agreement. This is one type of agreement where, if either party wants to bring it to an end, it should be able to do so with immediate effect. From the owner's point of view, the need for a termination provision is to trigger the return of its confidential information. The recipient's motive in terminating will be to prevent the receipt of further information: it will already have obligations in respect of information received up to the date of termination.

The arguments in favour of a time limit are that at some time the information will be obsolete and no longer important to the owner and, since the recipient is following special procedures to ensure confidentiality, it should be obliged to do so only to the extent to which it actually matters.

It is also easier for evidential purposes because the boundaries of the obligations are defined.

Five years, or whatever period is agreed, is a maximum. If there is going to be some confidential information which the owner anticipates will need to remain confidential beyond a foreseeable period, it may be preferable not to insert any time limit.

However, given the problems associated with monitoring and policing the security of the confidential information, particularly as time goes by and the individuals involved change, open-ended obligations should be reserved for exceptionally sensitive information which is unlikely to become desensitised over the foreseeable future. Even a longstop fixed period, say ten or even 20 years, if this is genuinely deemed necessary, is to be preferred to an open-ended obligation presumably left to fade into the mists of time.

Fixed periods of time may vary from one industry to another. If the pace of change is slow, a longer period of confidentiality can be better justified. Another point to be negotiated is whether the period selected should run from the date of first disclosure, as in the example, or from termination of the agreement.

The right to use the information will end with the expiry of the contract, but the obligation of confidentiality will continue for the agreed period.

9. Publicity

> The existence of this Agreement and of any relationship between the parties concerning the Confidential Information is confidential and neither party will publish or permit to be published any information about their relationship [or about the Business Purpose], unless that information has first been approved for publication by the other party.

It is consistent with the spirit of non-disclosure that the parties also treat their relationship as confidential. If there are other commercial agreements between them, which are known to the outside world, it may be necessary to tailor this clause so that there is no conflict. It will not be appropriate to make the optional reference here to the business purpose if that purpose has in fact been publicised, or is intended to be.

1   *Mars UK Ltd v Teknowledge Ltd* [2000] FSR 138.
2   *Campbell v Mirror Group Newspapers Ltd* [2004] UKHL 22, [2004] 2 All ER 995.
3   Lord Donaldson *AG v Guardian Newspapers Ltd (No 2)* [1989] 2 FSR 27.
4   *Oxford v Moss* (1979) 68 Cr App Rep 183, [1979] Crim LR 119.
5   *Cantor Fitzgerald International v Tradition (UK) Ltd* [2000] RPC 95.

CHAPTER 9

Computer product supply contracts

A. Introduction

These contracts provide for the supply of computer hardware products, or for hardware and software products in combination as systems.

A 'system' can also represent a complete solution to a problem, with only a partial computer content, but for the purposes of this chapter its meaning is limited to a combination of computer products.

Supplies may be on either a sale or lease basis and may specify the inclusion or exclusion of elements such as installation, training and warranty. There may be associated discount arrangements, for example an agreement for a defined period of time during which a quantity or value discount is provided based upon cumulative purchases – see Section D below.

Suppliers of computer products generally tend to present standard terms and conditions which they apply to all of the products they supply. Thus, as well as often comprising stand-alone agreements, these standard terms are also incorporated, directly or by reference, into their various special-purpose agreements, such as end user or reseller discount agreements, distribution agreements, and umbrella agreements for system supply and support.

Customers, particularly large organisations, likewise try to impose their own standard terms and conditions of purchase, usually by reference on their orders. Alternatively, they may attempt to create a special one-off contract, particularly when they are purchasing a turnkey system or going to a single source of supply. Their legitimate concerns include reliable delivery dates, acceptance procedures, payment terms, warranties and indemnities.

Where a customer intends to acquire its computer system through a lease arrangement, the normal procedure is for the customer to conclude its contract negotiations with the supplier. The selected leasing company will then scrutinise the arrangement and, if satisfied, buy the equipment from the supplier on the basis of the contractual terms of supply negotiated between the supplier and the customer. The leasing company will pay the supplier promptly, following receipt of a signed form of acceptance from the customer, and the customer will make periodic payments to the leasing company through the mechanism of a separate finance agreement.

Delivery will be to the customer's site, and installation, warranty cover and maintenance, training and other services included in the supply contract will be provided by the supplier to the customer direct. In the event of the supplier's default, however, the customer will look first to the leasing company for its remedies. As a means of overcoming this somewhat illogical situation and in order to link the various elements of the transaction together, a short-form tripartite agreement between the supplier, the finance company and the customer may be appropriate and one such agreement is discussed in Section E below. More comprehensive forms of leasing agreements are discussed in **CHAPTER 10**.

Computer equipment is sometimes supplied to customers on a demonstration or loan basis. The motivations are either to stimulate and confirm a sales opportunity or to provide post-sales support to a customer in difficulty. Generally, some sort of charge is involved but, whether or not this is the case, the supplier will need to ensure that any software content is adequately licensed. The supplier should also be concerned to ensure that insurance protection is sufficient and effective and that clear title (that is, ownership) is retained so that the equipment can be recovered at the end of the demonstration or loan period.

Agreements for demonstration or loan usually include an option for the customer to convert to an outright purchase, with some or all of any payments made being applied against the purchase price. Often, the supplier's full standard terms and conditions of supply are incorporated into the demonstration or loan agreement, expressed to apply to the extent that they are not inconsistent with that agreement.

B. The structure of a comprehensive form of computer product supply contract

This contract may be treated as a stand-alone agreement, the details and signatures on the front – or back – page being sufficient to constitute a complete contract document, or it may serve as an individual contract based on a customer order, in the context of an overriding discount agreement designed to govern the supplier-customer relationship for a defined period of time. In either case, the terms and conditions within will apply to all products supplied.

There are many possible variations, but the skeleton structure below includes the majority of provisions to be found in any computer supply contract. The order of clauses is intended to have a logical sequence and some of the clauses will apply only some of the time. For example, the software provisions will apply only when software is included in the supply.

From the supplier's perspective, the terms and conditions which follow will tend to be presented as standard terms of supply. They will thus appear on the reverse side of quotation forms, advice notes, order acceptances and invoices, and will also be incorporated into contract document sets or orders. These latter will also contain variable information on the front page and/or in schedules or attachments.

Front page contents and/or schedules

- Names and Addresses of the Parties (including delivery and invoice addresses)

- Agreement Reference Number

- Order Number

- Product and Service Descriptions

- Quantities

- Delivery Date(s); Special Delivery Instructions

- Installation

- Training

- Warranty Period

- Prices, Extensions and Totals

- Applicable Discount Rates

- Special Payment Terms

- Other Special Conditions

- Limited Liability Statement

- Offer and Acceptance Statements (including reference to the terms and conditions within)

- Authorised Signatures.

It is worthwhile paying careful attention to the general presentation and layout of front pages and attachments. The aim should be to end up with documents which are clear and easy to understand. There will then also be less likelihood of error when these forms are completed by the supplier's sales personnel.

Terms and conditions

- Introduction*

- Definitions*

- Associated Agreements*
- Substitutions and Modifications*
- Cancellation, Rescheduling and Change Orders*
- Delivery*
- Hardware*
- Software*
- Prices and Payment Terms
- Price Changes*
- Indemnities and Limits of Liability
- Intellectual Property Rights Indemnity
- Confidentiality
- Export and Re-export Limitations
- Telecommunications Requirements*
- Maintenance and Support Services*
- Life-endangering Applications*
- General Contract Provisions.

A number of the above provisions, such as the statement on the front page or in the Introduction clause dealing with limited liabilities, and the clauses on Delivery, Software, Indemnities and Limits of Liability, Export and Re-export Limitations, and Telecommunications Requirements, plus aspects of the clause on Hardware, relate to supplier requirements and will not often be initiated by customers, although customers will have strong views on some aspects.

C. Specific clauses

In the clause examples considered below, which are those above marked with an asterisk, the parties are referred to as the 'Supplier' and 'Customer', denoting the seller and the buyer respectively of the computer products.

1. Introduction

(a) These terms and conditions govern the sale to the Customer of the Supplier's Products, subject only to any additional terms and conditions contained in a current discount or other special written agreement between the parties. No other terms or conditions will apply except as provided below.

> (b) THE CUSTOMER HEREBY DECLARES THAT IT HAS ACCEPTED THESE TERMS AND CONDITIONS IN THE KNOWLEDGE THAT THE LIABILITY OF THE SUPPLIER IS LIMITED AND THAT THE PRICES AND CHARGES PAYABLE FOR PRODUCTS HAVE BEEN CALCULATED ACCORDINGLY.

Paragraph (a) of this clause is intended to establish the terms and conditions as the sole basis for the commercial supply transaction between the supplier and the customer. It is in the best interests of both parties that the terms and conditions in their final post-negotiation form of this statement should be referenced clearly on the front page and should be regarded as a complete statement of the parties' business together. However the limitations of any 'Entire Agreement' clause, discussed in **CHAPTER 6**, must be kept in mind.

The capitalised statement in paragraph (b) is included to put the customer on notice that the terms and conditions, and in particular the supplier's various limited liabilities, are important factors in the determination of product prices. The implication is that negotiated variations may cost money and that the supplier is reserving its position in this regard. Sometimes a short form of this statement can be found on the front page of the Agreement.

Customers who consider themselves to be in a strong negotiating position will wish to see this provision deleted, since they will not willingly accept the logic that any negotiated concessions obtained from the supplier are necessarily going to result in higher prices.

2. Definitions

> '*Contract*' means any agreement between the parties resulting from a Customer order for the supply of Products, which expressly or by implication incorporates these Terms and Conditions.
>
> '*DDP*' means 'delivered duty paid' as that expression is defined in the International Chamber of Commerce INCOTERMS 2000 Edition.
>
> '*Hardware*' means the hardware components of the Supplier's products including all ancillary equipment, accessories, spares, supplies and related documentation.
>
> '*Licence Agreement*' means the terms and conditions governing the supply of Software whether the Supplier's own software or third party software which the Supplier is authorised to supply to the Customer.
>
> '*Products*' means the Supplier's standard Hardware and Software products appearing in the current edition of its Standard Product Catalogue. Non-standard products, including products to be specially developed or adapted to

meet the Customer's particular requirements and all services offered by the Supplier, including maintenance and support, training and education, and consultancy services are not Products to which these terms and conditions apply, but are supplied on the terms and conditions contained in the Supplier's applicable service-related agreements.

'*Site*' means the installation site(s) in the United Kingdom to which any item of Hardware or Software is delivered.

'*Software*' means any operating system, utility or applications software delivered by the Supplier in machine-readable object, printed or interpreted form and either incorporated with Hardware or separately supplied, including related documentation.

The definition of 'Contract' is an attempt by the supplier to ensure that any supply of products to the customer will constitute a contract provided that it can be construed as being subject to the supplier's standard terms and conditions. It is intended to encompass circumstances where, although a formal order acceptance has not been sent out by the supplier, or the customer's order has referred to its own standard terms and conditions of purchase, acceptance has occurred and a contract has consequently been made, as a result of the customer's taking delivery of the products. Where there is no associated ongoing agreement in place, such as a discount agreement, the supplier will seek to rely on the terms and conditions having been successfully applied to the contract because, for example, they were printed on the quotation which preceded the customer's order, or they were otherwise notified to the customer in previous dealings. The 'Battle of the Forms' is discussed in **CHAPTER 22**. The resulting uncertainties for suppliers if they are not sufficiently careful about their order administration should encourage them to give proper attention to this area. Customers also risk losing some important contractual benefits if there is any argument about the terms and conditions governing the supply.

While customers might think it worth arguing that their own general procurement terms and conditions, or at least the general rules of contract law, should apply to a specific contract, this is not really advisable, because in a specialist technical supply area such as this, it is likely to mean that important contractual provisions for the customer will be insufficiently clear, or even omitted altogether.

'INCOTERMS' referred to in the 'DDP' definition is a very useful collection of commercial trading terms, of particular relevance to international contracts but also useful in national contracts. The meanings ascribed to the various terms have gained a good measure of international acceptance and they facilitate a consistent approach to the various ways in which goods can be delivered, paid for and insured. INCOTERMS detail the obligations of both buyer and seller if particular definitions are employed in contracts and many trading organisations are familiar with them.

'DDP', as the definition suggests, requires the seller to deliver the goods to the buyer at a designated buyer address, with all duties and carriage charges paid and any necessary export and import licences in place. The seller must insure the goods until the point of delivery. It is useful for a computer products supplier, who will frequently be a foreign entity or the subsidiary of a foreign corporation, to use INCOTERMS to define its delivery responsibilities. Alternative arrangements to 'DDP' are 'Ex-Works', meaning that the buyer will collect the goods, at its expense, from the seller's designated manufacturing facility, and be responsible for any export arrangements and for insurance of the goods from the time of their collection; or 'FCA', meaning that the seller will deliver the goods into the hands of the buyer's carrier at a designated place, which may be the seller's premises, insuring them until that time and sometimes bearing any initial carriage charges. Whichever definition is offered by the supplier, it enables the customer to know precisely what the obligations of each party are going to be.

Some suppliers will not have an adequate infrastructure to be able to offer 'DDP' terms and even for those who can do so, there will be price implications. For the customer, there is some scope here for negotiation of the delivery terms being offered as part of the product price.

The definitions of 'Hardware', 'Software' and 'Products' are self-explanatory. The important point for the supplier to ensure is that 'Products' adequately describe the hardware and software intended to fall within the scope of this supply contract, rather than some alternative contract. Where the supplier does not have some form of product catalogue to refer to, more detail may be needed. Customers also need to be clear about which of their supplier's products are going to be covered by the supply contract.

'Site' is defined because the parties need to be clear about the delivery location. Later in the contract there will be terms and conditions relating to the site, including whether or not delivery to the site is included in the price, who is to pay any expenses associated with the delivery and arising from the physical features of the site, such as it being on the seventh floor of a building with no adequate internal access, and which party is to bear the expenses of delivery to a remote site. The only criterion is one of cost and any negotiation will relate to the apportionment of that cost.

3. Associated Agreements

If these terms and conditions are incorporated by reference into any other form of agreement between the Supplier and the Customer and that other agreement is currently in effect at the time the Contract is made, so that the Contract constitutes a contract for the purposes of that agreement, the terms and conditions of the agreement will apply and will prevail in the event, but only to the extent, of any conflict of meaning with these terms and conditions.

This is a simple provision, intended to link the supply contract into any existing discount or other form of periodic agreement between the parties, in order to enable the application of the discount and/or other varied terms to the supply terms. A clause of this nature is generally to be found only in supplier standard form contracts.

Since 'Customer' may mean a distributor, reseller or large volume end user, such customers should always take care to ensure that any special terms they have negotiated do apply to the supply contract in question.

4. Substitutions and Modifications

> The Supplier reserves the right to make improvements, substitutions or modifications to any part of the Products, provided that such improvements, substitutions or modifications will not materially and adversely affect the capability of the Hardware or Software or overall Products to perform and function in accordance with the Supplier's applicable test procedures.

The supplier's objective in this clause is to allow scope for changes to its product range, some of which will not have been known about when the customer's order was placed.

A significant characteristic of the computer industry is the pace of change. The environment is fiercely competitive and enormous sums are invested in research and development. This results in a constant stream of product improvements and innovative developments. The clause is therefore a legitimate requirement: in major supply organisations, many design or manufacturing changes will be at the detailed technical level and will not be formally announced, for example to the UK subsidiary of an American manufacturing parent, until they are already implemented. The majority of changes made will improve the product being purchased by the customer.

Despite this, customers still need to be alert. In the above example, performance and functionality will not have been prejudiced, but the clause does not address entirely the issue of 'form, fit and function'. Some changes may involve alterations to physical dimensions or positions of input and output ports. While these would be inconsequential to most customers, they could be critical to, for example, an Original Equipment Manufacturer using the products as components within a larger product.

Negotiation here can be difficult. It may not be possible or commercially profitable for the supplier to provide adequate safeguards. The customer can consider requesting the supplier to provide reasonable notice of any changes and may wish to incorporate a right of termination in the event of changes to physical dimension.

However, the supplier may genuinely have difficulty in complying with such a requirement, at least where minor and routine engineering changes are concerned, and should want to limit the availability of any right of termination to circumstances where the customer cannot itself resolve difficulties arising from product changes (after demonstrating reasonable efforts to do so).

5. Cancellation, Rescheduling and Change Orders

> (a) If the Customer cancels all or any part of an order, or requests changes to the date of shipment or to the configuration ordered at least 30 days before the scheduled delivery [ex-factory shipment] date or requested delivery date, whichever is the later, there will be no cancellation or rescheduling charges. But if such cancellation or rescheduling or change of configuration request is less than 30 days from the scheduled or requested delivery date, the Customer agrees to pay a cancellation, rescheduling or reconfiguring charge of 25% of the purchase price agreed with the Customer at the time the order was placed.
>
> (b) In the event of any configuration changes, if these require the supply of additional items, the purchase price will be increased in accordance with the Supplier's price list but subject to any applicable discounts and the Supplier also reserves the right to extend the scheduled shipment date. The purchase price will be reduced in respect of cancelled items.
>
> (c) Where delivery is postponed by the Supplier, the Customer will be entitled to cancel all or part of the affected order without charge if the Supplier is unable to give a revised delivery date, or within 7 days of notification by the Supplier of a revised delivery date.
>
> (d) The Customer agrees that the charges set out in this clause are reasonable and are intended as liquidated damages and not as penalties, recognising that the Supplier's costs in these various circumstances will be difficult to estimate or calculate precisely.

The question of whether or not to provide contractually for the possibility of cancellation is a difficult one. These days, few computer products are in such high demand that loss of profits would inevitably be treated by the courts as a head of damage, in the event of cancellation; on the other hand, suppliers and customers alike tend to prefer the certainty of a pre-estimated sum of liquidated damages in case of this eventuality. It is quite common in the same clause to provide for the possibility of requests for rescheduling of product deliveries and amendments to the order by the customer.

Negotiation is rarely about the merits of including a clause such as this. Instead, discussion tends to focus on matters of detail such as the amount of liquidated damages and the maximum length of notice required for a rescheduling or other change.

The percentage set out in this clause as 'liquidated damages' must represent a genuine estimate of the vendor's potential losses resulting from the cancellation. What constitute 'penalty payments' are matters of fact, whatever the labels applied in contractual documents. To the extent that there is a demonstrable penalty element to so-called liquidated damages, there is a real risk that the provision will be unenforceable, particularly in standard form terms and conditions or contracts with individual customers, imposing an implied requirement for it to be reasonable in the particular circumstances[1].

A proposal by either party to delete a cancellation clause if the liquidated damages figure cannot be agreed, thereby forcing the other to assess the likely outcome of the court's determination of damages for breach of contract, and the related time and expense, should bring a sense of reality to the negotiation of the amount. Sometimes a scale of liquidated damages charges is appropriate, the sum rising as the notice period shortens. If the product to be delivered is being specifically manufactured and there is no alternative buyer in prospect, a supplier will probably wish to make the order non-cancellable once manufacturing resources have been irrevocably committed.

The agreed position in relation to cancellation and rescheduling is often negotiated alongside delivery commitments, discussed in clause 6 (Delivery) below. A supplier who has had to agree to liquidated damages in the event of late delivery is arguably more entitled to require certainty that the order will not be cancelled unless the maximum reasonable compensation becomes payable if it then is cancelled, as a matter of contractual agreement.

If rescheduling is to be permitted, this will involve the supplier in storage costs, at least where notice is given near the delivery date. It may be worthwhile for the customer to try and negotiate a differential between the costs resulting from cancellation and those arising from a request to reschedule or reconfigure. It will often be difficult for a supplier to demonstrate that storage costs equate to cancellation costs, and the administration associated with a reconfiguration should not of itself be significant. Even if there is a net reduction in the order value as a result of the reconfiguration, this is unlikely to be equivalent to the supplier's losses on cancellation of the entire order. Paragraph (d) becomes much more credible if paragraph (a) contains a scale of charges appearing to reflect the different circumstances, and it may also be appropriate to vary the charges in each category to take into account the notice period; the closer to the scheduled delivery date, the more expensive the change. Such an approach also reduces the risk of the whole clause being struck down as unreasonable if the Unfair Contract Terms Act applies to the supply.

6. Delivery

(a) Delivery will be DDP.

(b) The Customer will make the Site available for inspection by appropriate Supplier staff at an agreed time during a period of 30 days before the scheduled delivery date shown in the Supplier's Order Acceptance, if so required by the Supplier.

(c) The Customer will furnish the necessary labour (if the Supplier so requires under the Supplier's direction) for taking any Hardware into its designated operating point, unpacking it and placing it in the desired location.

(d) Unless otherwise specified by the Customer, delivery will be made to the Site shown on the front of this document or otherwise referred to in the Contract.

(e) Delivery date(s) referred to in the Contract or in any quotation, or in any order acknowledgment, order acceptance or elsewhere are approximate only and not of any contractual effect. While the Supplier will use all reasonable endeavours to meet any scheduled delivery date so referred to in the Contract, it will not be liable for any loss or damage (including but not limited to loss of use, loss of contract or loss of profits) incurred by the Customer as a result of any failure to deliver on any particular date.

(f) Each delivery of Products under this Agreement will be deemed to constitute a separate enforceable contract to which these terms and conditions will apply.

(g) If the Customer refuses or fails to take delivery of Products tendered in accordance with this Agreement, delivery will nevertheless be deemed to have taken place for the purpose of the Supplier's rights to payment and the Supplier will be entitled to store the Products at the Customer's risk and expense, including all transportation charges.

(h) On delivery at the entrance to the Site, the Customer will be responsible for, and will bear, the entire risk of loss or damage to Hardware or to Software media, regardless of when acceptance occurs. If the Customer wishes to make any claims for shortages or for damaged Products, full particulars must be notified to the Supplier within 7 days of delivery.

(i) Title to Hardware will pass to the Customer upon receipt of payment in full. TITLE TO SOFTWARE WHETHER THE SUPPLIER'S PROPRIETARY SOFTWARE OR SOFTWARE LICENSED BY THE SUPPLIER WILL NOT PASS TO THE CUSTOMER UNDER ANY CIRCUMSTANCES.

This is always a problematic clause. There are many contingencies which each party wants to have included, and in major purchasing situations there will inevitably be considerable negotiation over this clause.

It is important for the parties to establish which acts constitute delivery (particularly where delivery is used as the trigger for invoicing), who is to pay for carriage and insurance (this example is DDP, 'delivered duty paid', discussed at clause 2 (Definitions) above) and who is responsible for arranging and paying for installation into the actual operating environment (which can sometimes involve the use of cranes, building alterations, special wiring and the like). Site availability and suitability can become significant factors when a physically large system is being supplied, which is intended for use several floors up in a high-rise building. Paragraphs (a) to (c) should be reviewed in this context.

The moments when risk and title pass also need to be unambiguous. In England and Wales, it is common for suppliers to retain title until they have been paid in full. Sometimes clauses dealing with this subject are extremely complex, attempting to trace the proceeds of any sale on by the customer if the customer goes into liquidation without having paid for products already delivered. Retention of title is intended to defeat the claims of receivers and liquidators. Without such security, or a rarely encountered charge by the supplier over the customer's assets, the supplier will be an ordinary creditor with the usual prospect of little or no pay-back at the end of the winding up. As discussed in **CHAPTER 7** at clause 6, the courts have not tended to look very favourably on some of the more complex devices: if an attempt is going to be made to cover any contingency, great accuracy and attention to detail is essential or the procedures will fail. There is much to be said for the simple approach in paragraph (i), which should suffice if the customer is the end user. Where the customer is a reseller, its customers will usually acquire good title to goods by operation of law. Rather than seek to trace the actual money received from the customer's customers, suppliers should concentrate their attention on their credit evaluation and control procedures, and be prepared to act swiftly at the first evidence of a reseller in financial difficulties.

Although risk will usually pass on delivery, as in paragraph (h), a prudent supplier will maintain its own insurance arrangements until all deliverables have been paid for. Sometimes, clauses require the customers to insure and to produce evidence of insurance on request and occasionally even to have the supplier's interest noted on the policy, but all this is heavy-handed and will not be appropriate or even negotiable in the majority of contract situations.

Negotiation of the consequences of late delivery is probably the most commonly encountered issue in computer contract negotiations. Because computer systems so often perform critical applications in a business, other operations are frequently developed around them and if the system is not available to go live on or by a pre-determined date, there can be a considerable knock-on effect. Notwithstanding this, both parties are often guilty of not paying sufficient attention to the delivery circumstances: the customer may have unrealistic expectations, set by itself or by the supplier, and the supplier may have under-estimated the development task, or sold 'futures', that is, products which are not yet on its product list, but are anticipated to be available by the delivery date. Production difficulties or

169

last-minute technical hitches or shortages from third party component manufacturers whose own delivery dates may be uncertain or problematic, can, and often do, delay the release of new products, but sales representatives tend to take chances on the basis of their employer's forthcoming product announcements in order to win business against fierce competition – today's offering may be less powerful but tomorrow's is going to set new industry standards!

This background knowledge, in the minds of most suppliers but not necessarily their customers', causes suppliers to offer terms of delivery based on all reasonable efforts to meet a scheduled delivery date, but with no contractual consequences if they fail to do so (paragraph (e)). 'All reasonable' rather than 'best' endeavours is a less severe, and arguably more realistic standard. 'Best' leaves very limited scope indeed for a failure to perform: outside of 'force majeure' type reasons, discussed in **CHAPTER 6**, a supplier might succeed in establishing that it met the standard only if it had applied virtually the whole of its resources in its efforts to resolve the problem. 'All reasonable', by implication, qualifies and contains the effort which would be expected.

However, a delivery date may be crucial to the customer. There may be linked delivery of products from other suppliers, or an implementation deadline, which may well depend upon a time schedule being met, or the customer may itself be liable for liquidated or open damages to its customer in circumstances where the supplier's product is a key element of the customer's own final product. If the delivery date matters, for these or any other reasons, the customer must be sure to deal with this in the contract, making the objective of the purpose clear to the supplier, together with the reasons for having defined delivery dates. If the customer is in the stronger bargaining position, it will also negotiate a provision for postponing the delivery schedule at its option, and rights of cancellation if any delay by the supplier is excessive, together with rights to recover damages caused by the delay. It may be reasonable for any customer to insist on an obligation by the supplier to give the customer notice in advance of probable delays.

More demanding customers ask for 'time of the essence' deliveries, but this is not generally reasonable, or even necessary, to expect in the particular circumstances. In the absolute legal sense, failure to achieve delivery by a contracted 'time of the essence' date entitles the customer to terminate the contract, recover any sums already paid and sue for losses caused in consequence of the late delivery. A supplier will rarely be willing to expose itself to such extensive liability on top of the loss of the business and the parties will typically try to negotiate a compromise acceptable to them both. The formula which is most widely used provides for a stated percentage of the contract price to be paid or credited for each period, usually a week, of delay, to a stated maximum, for example half of one per cent per week to a maximum of five per cent.

Negotiation then focuses on the amount of each percentage and whether or not a period of grace beyond the contractual delivery date should be agreed before these 'liquidated damages' commence. It still remains necessary for the parties to think ahead – at what point will a late delivery be wholly unacceptable? The supplier will seek to express the liquidated damages as the sole remedy for late delivery, but should also provide for a right of the customer to cancel if the maximum agreed damages have been reached without a genuine imminent delivery. The customer may argue that in these circumstances other liabilities should also arise for the supplier. However, it is recommended that, whatever is finally negotiated, it takes the form of an absolute quantifiable liability so that neither party is in any doubt about the position if late delivery does occur. It should also be remembered that the supplier's obligation to deliver on time will constitute a condition of the contract in any event. In the absence of express provisions dealing with late delivery, after the expiry of a reasonable notice period, the contract can be cancelled and the products rejected by the customer, if this 'final chance' delivery date is not met. Similarly, if delivery is late and the customer takes no action, or telephones to ask when the products will be arriving, its rights may be deemed to have been waived because a continuing intention to accept the products may be implied. The customer will then be obliged to accept them when they are finally delivered.

A delivery clause also needs to deal with the question of partial deliveries. Are these to be permitted or not and, if they are, will each partial delivery constitute a separate contract enforceable in all respects even if, for whatever reason, the delivery originally contracted for is never completed (paragraph (f))? Partial deliveries, even if permitted, should not constitute separate contracts where a system is being purchased which will be satisfactory only in its entirety. On the other hand, if the customer is a reseller purchasing multiple quantities of components or systems, there is no reason why partial deliveries should not have contractual effect in their own right.

Refusals to take deliveries also need to be addressed. Most attention in connection with delivery dates tends to fall on the supplier's obligations, but the customer is also capable of failing to perform: circumstances may range from non-readiness of the delivery location, a reseller's lack of storage space, delays in customer development work, to customer financial difficulties. Paragraph (g) addresses this issue.

An issue which is sometimes dealt with as a paragraph or two in a delivery clause, and sometimes in a separate clause altogether, is that of quality control. It is becoming increasingly topical and there is much focus currently on the international quality standard ISO 9000:2000 series. Aside from official quality standards, and numerous others dealing with product safety, major purchasers of computer equipment seek compliance with production standards set or subscribed to by their own organisations. Quality provisions in contracts may therefore reference specific standards or customer safety and quality publications, but may also provide customer rights of pre-delivery inspection at the manufacturing location(s) and at the distribution premises. It is usual for suppliers to agree to such provisions (given the implications of declining to do so) but they should ensure that they do indeed meet the stipulated standards and they should ensure that any inspections are carried out by prior appointment at times convenient to the supplier and at the customer's expense. If quality failures are discovered on inspection, the contract will need to provide for the consequences of this in terms of time to remedy, re-inspection, expenses and ultimate rights of rejection. The following is one comparatively simple example of a quality control clause:

> All products supplied under this Agreement are certified by the Supplier to comply with IEC 950 concerning safety of information technology equipment, including electrical business equipment, and the Supplier also holds and complies with ISO 9000:2000 as part of its total quality management policies. The Customer is entitled at its own expense, directly or through a nominated independent test agency acceptable to the Supplier, to inspect the Supplier's manufacturing and distribution processes so far as they relate to the Products, by prior appointment during normal business hours. All Products are constructed and delivered in a safe condition and will remain safe provided that they are correctly installed and maintained in accordance with the Supplier's recommendations.

It is frequently forgotten that official quality standards have more to do with efficient and thorough procedures than with the production of a quality product. A badly designed or manufactured product may still be produced in compliance with quality procedures, and customers should not rely solely on the officially recognised standards in making their judgments about supplier quality. This is especially valid in connection with software products because no one has yet worked out an acceptable method of measuring the way software is written or the effectiveness of the results. (There are a number of recognised project management standards, such as the Pathway II project management methodology. These are helpful, and no doubt effective project management does contribute to good quality results, but their focus is really on efficient project management in order to achieve time and cost targets.) Software is unique amongst engineering disciplines in this respect.

7. Hardware

> (a) Where installation – or training – is not included in the purchase price and not ordered by the Customer, the Customer will be solely responsible for these items, and the Supplier disclaims all liability in connection with them.
>
> (b) Where the Hardware includes data communications equipment and data transmission speeds are given in relation to any item of Hardware, these are at all times subject to any conditions of the applicable telecommunications utility company relating to the use of the relevant modem at the speeds indicated, and to the capability of any of that company's equipment to which the Hardware is linked.
>
> (c) Acceptance will be accomplished by using test procedures and/or programs established by the Supplier which are applicable to the Products. Acceptance will take place at the Site when the Supplier demonstrates that the

applicable diagnostic and/or verification programs work properly. If the Supplier's demonstration of the test procedures and/or programs at the Site is delayed for more than 5 working days other than through any fault of the Supplier, the Products will be deemed to be accepted. In the event that any item of Hardware or Software fails the acceptance procedures the Supplier will at its option, replace or repair that item.

(d)

    (i)   The Supplier warrants that it has good title to or the legal right to supply all Hardware supplied to the Customer. Hardware is warranted against defects in workmanship and materials for a period of 90 days from the date of delivery, or 90 days from the date of acceptance, whichever is earlier. Where the Supplier has not installed the Hardware, the warranty under this clause is subject to final approval of the installation by the Supplier at the Customer's expense. Where the Supplier has installed the Hardware, the Supplier's sole responsibility under this warranty will be, at its option, either to repair or replace during its normal working hours, any component which proves defective during the warranty period. All replaced Hardware or parts will become the Supplier's property. The warranty service will be performed at the Supplier's repair facility, or on Site (except in the case of minor component repairs) if the Supplier has installed the Hardware or if the Customer has a current Support Agreement with the Supplier covering the Hardware. Returns will be in accordance with the Supplier's shipping instructions, freight prepaid, but return freight costs will be paid by the Supplier. In any case where the Supplier reasonably determines that the Hardware is not defective within the terms of the warranty, the Customer will pay the Supplier all costs of handling, transportation and repairs at the Supplier's then prevailing rates.

    (ii)   The stated warranties apply only to the initial end user of the Hardware and are contingent upon proper treatment and use of the Products with no unauthorised modifications and maintenance, at a safe and suitable Site.

(e) All proprietary rights in all patents, designs, copyrights, engineering details, schematics, drawings and other similar data relating to the Hardware are and will at all times remain vested in the Supplier. The sale of Hardware to the Customer does not convey any ownership or licence to exploit any of the proprietary rights of the Supplier in the Hardware. Any such proprietary rights granted to the Customer by the Supplier will be granted only subject to a separate restrictive, non-transferable, non-exclusive licence agreement. All operating instructions, manuals and other documentation referencing the Hardware and supplied by the Supplier are the copyright of the Supplier and will not be copied or disclosed to any third party without the prior express written consent of the Supplier.

Alternative approaches are possible here. Some contracts do not distinguish hardware and software, but deal with the various issues covered by this clause in separate subject-matter clauses, such as Acceptance, Warranty, Telecommunications, Proprietary Rights. However, since different considerations apply to hardware and software products (for example, title is commonly passed in hardware and not in software; warranty descriptions and performance measurements are not the same, and so on) it is convenient to group all the relevant matters under the generic heading of 'Hardware' and 'Software' respectively. The example clause illustrates this.

The most frequently negotiated aspects relate to acceptance testing and the length and extent of any warranty. With standard products, suppliers tend to insist on the performance of their own tests by successfully running their diagnostic software as the sole criterion for acceptability. Complete failure of such tests would entitle the customer to reject the product, but generally the supplier is able to resolve the situation by repair or replacement at its option. After all, the customer expects the product to work and it will not be in the supplier's interest to avoid replacement where this is the most practicable solution in the circumstances, when it has to fulfil its continuing warranty obligations, often as well as an ongoing maintenance contract. Satisfactory repairs are often achieved simply by substituting printed circuit boards. Where the customer is able to negotiate special acceptance tests (and suppliers should not readily agree to such tests where standard products only are being supplied), it is extremely important for the supplier that these be agreed and documented in detail, including periods of time for conducting the tests and for dealing with problems and re-testing, prior to entering into the contract. There should, in particular be no ambiguity about what must be demonstrated in order for acceptance to be determined. From the supplier's point of view it is also advisable either for the supplier to conduct the tests or certainly to be permitted to be present at any time during testing, all at the customer's expense if this can be agreed as a concession for the special testing arrangements.

Where hardware is being supplied as part of a complete system or solution, it is becoming common practice for the customer to require the whole system to remain continuously operational for a defined period, before acceptance can be considered complete. Hardware suppliers will only want to agree to this type of condition if the hardware has no discrete value to the customer outside the specific system or solution, and it is advisable to seek to exclude minor or non-material errors which are encountered during testing.

Warranty is a difficult area. The duration of warranties offered varies a good deal, typically between 90 days and 12 months. Suppliers need to be confident that the warranties they offer (or failure to offer warranties) will not breach the Unfair Contract Terms Act by being judged unreasonable. Customers need to understand what warranty actually means and how it can be distinguished from the protection afforded by a maintenance contract. If warranty work is to be carried out wholly or partially on- or off-site this needs to be stated clearly, together with ancillary matters such as responsibility for payment of freight charges detailed appropriately. If a 'Day One' maintenance contract is taken out with the supplier, there should be some price reduction to reflect the duplication with the warranty. Similarly, it should not be difficult to negotiate an extended warranty period for a price consideration. Paragraph (e) has been included as an option because it underlines the ownership of proprietary rights in the hardware. Such rights are not conferred by this paragraph and they will neither be diminished nor much enhanced by its use, but it does put the customer on formal notice of the existence of the rights, and it prohibits the unauthorised copying of manuals and other documentation. It may be appropriate to include this provision, especially if the products in question incorporate exceptionally valuable technology.

8. Software

(a) Copyright subsists in all Software and all related documentation (whether printed or stored electronically) and whether it is the Supplier's proprietary Software or Software supplied by the Supplier under licence. All Software and related documentation is supplied to the Customer only under the terms and conditions of the applicable Licence Agreement (whether this has been signed and/or returned to the Supplier or not). No part of the Software may be copied, reproduced or utilised in any form by any means without the prior approval of the Supplier. Title or ownership to Software does not transfer to the Customer under any circumstances.

(b) Where the Customer has not signed the applicable Licence Agreement in advance, the Customer undertakes to return the Licence Agreement supplied with each item of Software, duly signed by the Customer's authorised representative, prior to the Customer using that item of Software. It is the sole responsibility of the Customer to comply with all of the terms and conditions of the Licence Agreement, and the Customer is hereby notified that any failure to comply with such terms and conditions may result in the revocation of its licence to use the Software.

(c) Software is warranted in accordance with the terms of the Licence Agreement governing its supply. The sole obligation of the Supplier under such warranty will be limited to the use of all reasonable efforts to correct any failure of the Software to conform to its user manual current at the date of delivery and to supply the Customer with a corrected version of the Software as soon as practicable after the Customer has notified the Supplier of any defects.

(d) The Customer is not authorised to sub-license the Software to any third party except where the Customer is an OEM or VAR of the Supplier when the terms and conditions relating to such sub-licensing in the OEM or VAR Agreement signed by the Customer will apply.

In some systems supply contracts a full set of software licensing provisions would be found here, at least to cover the operating system software. Unless the related hardware products are comparatively low-value high-volume standard items, this is not a particularly satisfactory approach. Hardware is freely re-saleable by its purchaser whilst any transfer of software is generally subject to licence conditions. A separate licence document emphasises the importance a supplier attaches to its software and, in the event of any dispute concerning the adequacy of enforceability of terms and conditions of software supply, can be considered independently. Thus, the example clause merely emphasises that the software supplied is the copyright of the supplier or a third party, and is licensed subject to separate terms and conditions.

Paragraph (b) as drafted is increasingly unrealistic these days. Pre-signed Licence Agreements should always be required where the hardware being supplied is a 'high end' system. PCs and other desktop systems/workstations tend to be delivered with shrink-wrap licences for their operating system software. Notwithstanding the widespread use of such licences they are not often read before being discarded by users, and there is little chance of their being signed and returned. This is not satisfactory from a purely legal perspective, but it is the commercial reality.

Software licences are more fully considered in **CHAPTER 12**. Since operating systems software and standard applications packages are often licensed separately by the 'shrink-wrap' technique, the potential shortcomings of this method of licensing should be particularly noted. **CHAPTER 4** also refers at section B.

The clause does deal with warranty and, particularly in the case of package software, it is common to limit this to conformity with a user guide or manual, or published specification or product description. Suppliers will not generally negotiate over this, but as with hardware, the duration of the warranty may be negotiable. Standard software warranties tend to be short: either the package does or does not conform to the stated standards. The supplier's own warranty will be limited in respect of third party software. The supplier may be willing to provide a somewhat less restricted warranty under its own licence terms and conditions separately supplied to the customer. Faulty media is discovered on first attempt at use.

The meanings of 'OEM' and 'VAR', particular kinds of intermediary distributors and resellers referred to in paragraph (d), are discussed in **CHAPTER 11**.

End user contracts will normally prohibit any form of sub-licensing, at least without first obtaining special consent.

9. Price Changes

The Supplier reserves the right, by giving notice to the Customer at any time before delivery, to increase the price of the Products to reflect any increase in the cost to the Supplier which is due to any fact beyond the Supplier's control,

> such as, but not limited to, any foreign exchange fluctuation, currency regulation, alteration of duties, significant increase in the costs of labour, materials or other costs of manufacture, any change in delivery dates, quantities or specifications for the Products which is requested by the Customer, or any delay caused by any instructions of the Customer or by the Customer's failure to give the Supplier adequate information or instructions.

Whenever this clause is included in a contract, it tends to provoke customers. The usual expectation is for prices to be fixed, at least from the time of contract if not from the time of quotation. Sometimes the prices in effect at the time of delivery are stipulated, especially in on-going agreements which are designed to encompass successive supplies of products by separate orders, or the delivery of services, over a defined period. In these instances, customers should expect to see references to supplier price lists and seek to negotiate their continuation without increase for at least a year, increases thereafter being limited to not more than once per year, where appropriate by not more than any increase over that period in a designated index, such as the Retail Prices Index or an industry-related index.

Arguably, a clause such as this example can be justified only when the supply is high-volume, with a long delivery lead time, involving a product manufactured wholly or substantially in another country. The clause is included to illustrate the sorts of issues which parties need to consider in appropriate circumstances. That part of the clause which allows pricing amendments to reflect customer-requested changes is reasonable in any event.

10. Telecommunications Requirements

> When computer equipment is connected to a public network, ie a switchboard or telephone network, certain regulations of the telecommunications provider apply. It is the sole responsibility of the Customer to ensure compliance with all such regulations.

Systems are increasingly purchased for use in networks and, except in the case of local area networks within one site location, this will involve connection to the public telephone system. Suppliers will wish to provide that any such connections, including compliance with relevant statutory regulations, are the responsibility of the customer. Customers should at least ensure that their suppliers' equipment can be connected to the telephone system without undue difficulty, before committing themselves to contracts. Where the customer is placing full reliance on a supplier's experience, it will be an entirely reasonable negotiating stance to expect more active assistance from the supplier.

11. Maintenance and Support Services

The Hardware and Software warranties in this Agreement are provided to ensure that all Products delivered to the Customer operate in accordance with their specification following initial installation and commissioning. Customers with complex or significant computer installations or whose requirements for up-time are above average are likely to require much greater maintenance and support for their Products from the date of delivery than is provided for under warranty. Accordingly the Customer is recommended to contract for hardware maintenance and software support in respect of all of the Hardware and Software from their date of delivery to the Customer and in any event immediately upon the expiry of any warranty periods. Full descriptions of the Supplier's maintenance and support services and the related terms and conditions are contained in the applicable maintenance and support agreements.

OR

The Supplier will assist the Customer in arranging maintenance and support agreements but the Supplier will not be party to any of these contracts and does not accept any liability to the Customer in respect of maintenance and support services.

This is an example of a contractual provision which informs instead of stipulating an obligation. Some lawyers would argue that such advisory provisions have no place in the body of a contract, but if such provisions assist in the interpretation of the contract by emphasising its scope and/or limitations, it is helpful to include them. Here, on the one hand the clause makes clear that the scope of the contract does not extend to maintenance and support services; on the other hand it informs the customer that such services are available from the supplier by separate contract. The alternative provision obligates the supplier to help the customer make its maintenance and support arrangements whilst disclaiming any liability in relation to the performance of such services.

12. Life-endangering Applications

The Products are designed for standard commercial use and are not intended to be installed or used in hazardous or life-threatening environments or for potentially life-endangering applications, including but not limited to environments or applications involving safety critical systems in the nuclear industry or the control of aircraft in the air. The Customer undertakes not to use or supply the Products for any of these purposes and agrees to indemnify and hold the Supplier harmless from and against all liabilities and related costs arising out of the use of any of the Products for any of these purposes.

This clause has been included because it illustrates a stance adopted by many of the computer industry's major hardware suppliers. It arises from a long-standing concern that even where wrongdoing has been established – and this is no longer necessary in several jurisdictions including the UK in relation to some of the consequences of product failures – liability can become too astronomical for a commercial organisation to be reasonably expected to bear. The argument for the supplier runs that where the public interest is served by using computers to enhance the safety and performance of high technology equipment for the general good, such as in the control of aircraft or in the production of nuclear energy, liabilities for failure should be kept at reasonable commercial levels and any further sums which might be recoverable by the victims of product failure should be by means of some form of government indemnity scheme. Levels of damages awarded in many jurisdictions, notably the US, are such that if a product failure resulted in the collision of two crowded giant airliners over a major area of population or, worse still, a nuclear detonation within range of a heavily populated area, the financial consequences of the combined claims which could be made would be enough to wipe out even the largest of corporations. Insurance cover of sufficient magnitude would be impossible, or at least impossibly expensive, to obtain. It is not only equipment designed specifically for the purpose which is affected; many standard products can be used as component parts of safety-critical systems. The tragic events of 11 September 2001 in the US illustrate dreadfully the enormous scale of losses and consequences that a catastrophic disaster can have in pure economic terms and, where the cause is a defective product rather than a deliberate criminal act, liability for such losses would be far beyond the means of any commercial entity.

The clause points out to the customer that the products supplied have not been designed for use in high-risk situations and incorporates an undertaking by the customer not to use the products in such circumstances, together with an indemnity from and against the effects of breach of this undertaking. In reality, even this clause is of limited value to the supplier in the absence of an insurance requirement whose existence and maintenance is validated and monitored. Many of a large supplier's customers will have even less net worth than it has itself. It is a 'comfort' clause, but any challenge by a customer should put the supplier on notice to investigate the intended use of its products very carefully.

D. Discount agreements

Whether a computer product supply contract is being made with an end-user customer or with a distributor customer, such as an OEM or a reseller, volume purchases will attract discount arrangements. These are usually the subject of a separate signed agreement which is either linked by appropriate reference to a supply contract, or incorporates the general terms and conditions of supply within it. The former is the more common method and the one illustrated here. A typical discount agreement would include the following provisions:

- Term and Termination

- Scope*

- Discount Structure*

- Discountable Items*

- Discount Rates*

- Reconciliations and Mid-Year Reviews*

- 'Most Favoured Customer'*

- General Contract Provisions.

To these might be added 'Supplier Obligations', for example to supply standard products on standard terms, to provide minimum quotation periods and to provide advice and assistance, and 'Customer Obligations', for example to promote sales, to provide services, to observe the supplier's software licensing requirements, to maintain demonstration equipment and facilities, to provide forecasts and reports, not to infringe the supplier's trade marks and to submit to inspections. These additional clauses will be appropriate when the customer is a reseller of the supplier and not an end user. Then the discount agreement effectively becomes a distribution agreement, as considered in **CHAPTER 11**.

1. Scope

> For the purposes of this Agreement discounts will be computed from the aggregate qualifying purchases of the Customer and the other Customer participating companies listed in the Schedule, in consideration for which the Customer guarantees the performance by all such participating companies of all of the Customer obligations contained in this Agreement and in any related supply contracts, so far as the same relate to any purchase by a participating company which is eligible for discount under this Agreement. If a participating company defaults in any of its obligations to the Supplier the Customer undertakes to carry out such performance.

If a customer is one of a number of related companies which order from the same supplier, it will be worth an approach to see if all their purchases can be aggregated for the purpose of accumulating and applying discount rates.

Where it is agreed that more than one company's purchases will contribute to an aggregated total for the purposes of discount calculation, it is necessary to identify all of the participating companies. This clause is comparatively simple in its structure and it may be appropriate for the parties to include far more detailed qualifying criteria for participation, such as voting control over each participating company by the customer, minimum purchasing values for each participating company, satisfactory financial status in its own right of each participating company, no previously experienced trading difficulties in any particular case, and so forth. Purchasers in certain countries may also need to be excluded as a matter of regulation to which the supplier is subject or as a matter of supplier policy, perhaps because of lack of a satisfactory support capability in certain territories.

A more controversial condition, nevertheless often found in reseller discount agreements, is to the effect that neither the reseller nor any participating company will engage in competitive practices to the potential detriment of the supplier by manufacturing or selling competitive products alongside the supplier's products. The supplier's principal justification is that, notwithstanding its legal rights in its products, which will be viewed as largely theoretical given the cost, time and difficulties of enforcement, its business could be badly damaged. In addition, any undermining or dissipation of effort in relation to the supplier's products reduces the distribution opportunity, may adversely affect support services, and does not justify the cost of offering the discount when compared with the results which might reasonably be expected from a dedicated reseller. It is also unfair to the dedicated reseller.

The requirement for a guarantee may be contentious. The customer will want to avoid this, particularly where each participating company is a substantial entity in its own right, whilst the supplier may wish to go even further and provide for an actual indemnity to cover any matters not generally falling within the scope of a performance guarantee, such as the consequences of contractual infringements by a participating company. Even where a performance guarantee is agreed, a customer should seek to make it a last resort for the supplier, only to be invoked after all reasonable commercial means of enforcement have been exhausted against the participating company directly.

It may also be the case that the supplier itself is defined to include various sister companies and even its official distributors. If so, the customer can reasonably require performance guarantees from the supplier in return for its own guarantees.

It should be noted that performance guarantees in this context mean the parent effectively standing in the shoes of its subsidiary or associate company, taking over that entity's performance of the contract: to be contrasted with a bank negotiated performance bond which involves cost, the tying up of capital or credit, and which is generally used in circumstances where a small supplier company with limited resources undertakes a major transaction.

2. Discount Structure

(a) To be eligible for discount, each Product Order must refer to the Supplier's reference number on this Agreement, must request delivery within 15 months of the commencement of the applicable one-year ordering period and must have a list price value of at least £500.

(b) Subject to (a) above, all Products ordered within a one-year ordering period from the Commencement Date or from any anniversary of the Commencement Date, will accumulate at list price value and by total unit quantities purchased to determine the initially applicable discount rates.

(c) In the first year of this Agreement, the forecasted total sterling values and unit quantities shown in the Schedule will be used to determine the initially applicable discount rates.

(d) In the second and subsequent years of this Agreement, the applicable discount rates will be determined by reference to the actual total sterling values and unit quantities ordered in the preceding year, unless the parties agree to different rates because there is reason to anticipate a material change (upwards or downwards) in the Customer's ordering patterns from those of the previous year.

This describes the basis of discount computation and any qualifying criteria. Where agreements are international in scope, discount is computed on accumulated purchases over a period of time across national boundaries. The example anticipates that both value and numbers of units purchased will influence discount rates, although many discount agreements will utilise only one of these criteria.

3. Discountable Items

Discountable items are so indicated in Quotations and in the Supplier's applicable Price Lists.

Suppliers are not able to apply their full discounts to all of the products they supply. For example, cables and printers may be bought in from third-party suppliers on very tight margins and there will be little or no scope for discounting. Again, special order items which do not form part of the supplier's general product range are likely to be priced on a one-off basis. The purpose of this clause is to clarify to the customer which products are available for discount, and whether at the full or at a reduced level.

4. Discount Rates

> The discount rates are applied to discountable items and are determined by reference to:
>
> (a) either the total sterling values or total unit quantities (whether calculated on forecast or on past actual figures) in accordance with the discount table shown in the Schedule. The commencing discount rates are set out in the Schedule;
>
> (b) where any discount rate based on unit quantities is greater than a discount rate based on total sterling value, the Customer is entitled to the higher rate.

Most discount structures are tiered and correlated with performance in terms of unit quantities or values purchased. For high value purchasers, this is a very negotiable area but suppliers should be careful to adopt a consistent approach to such negotiations. There is often enough at stake financially for a disgruntled customer to consider making an allegation of anti-competitive practice if any unfairness in treatment is suspected. Employees changing jobs are just one way in which such practices can come to light and, in the international context particularly, penalties can be heavy – see **CHAPTERS 3 AND 4** for further discussion of restrictive trade practices and competition law.

Some major suppliers of hardware equipment seek to use discount rates as a means of giving incentives to their OEMs or other resellers to add value to the products before selling them on. At one time, an absolute requirement to add value as a pre-condition of sale was quite usual, but developments in European Union law in particular have cast doubt on the legality of such restrictions. As a result, the safer course is not to restrict a reseller's right to resell in prescribed circumstances, or only subject to prescribed conditions, but rather to use additional discounts to incentivise or reward the reseller for particular courses of conduct, for example adding value, or concentrating sales effort in particular geographic areas, or within particular product lines. Thus, to encourage and extend product distribution, resellers tend to receive higher discounts than even high volume end users whose purchasing activities could be equal or greater, theoretically because resellers require much less support and therefore reduce the supplier's costs of supply. Further discounts still are then granted if there is acceptable added value, because the more the number of applications which utilise the basic product, the greater will be the overall sales opportunities.

5. Reconciliations and Mid-Year Reviews

(a) Six months after the commencement of each Ordering Year, the Supplier will carry out a review of actual orders placed by the Customer during the half-year just completed. If the accumulated total sterling value or unit quantity of discountable items is then running at more than twice the year-to-date level anticipated for each applicable discount rate, that discount rate will be increased for the remainder of the year to the percentage shown in the Discount Table for an assumed annual total sterling value or unit quantity of twice that used to determine the original discount rate.

(b) A similar method of calculation will decrease a discount rate for the remainder of the year if, at the half-year point, the accumulated total sterling value or unit quantity is running at less than half the year-to-date level anticipated by that discount rate, so that the revised discount rate will be based on an assumed total annual value or unit quantity of half that used to determine the original discount rate.

(c) At the end of each Ordering Year the Supplier's auditors will be requested to compare the discount rates applied to Orders with the values and quantities for those discount rates shown in the Discount Table and to prepare a reconciliation statement. The Supplier will provide the Customer with a copy of this statement. If excess or insufficient discounts have been granted, the party who has benefited from the over- or under-calculation will make the necessary balancing payment to the other party within 30 days of receipt of the reconciliation statement.

Discounts are generally offered to customers on the basis of predicted or forecasted purchasing levels over a set period, at least initially when there is no historical data available. Some suppliers seek to incorporate retrospective adjustment mechanisms at defined points during or at the end of each contract year. Paragraph (c) is an example of this. These rarely work well in practice: they are administratively cumbersome and expensive. Ironically, it is often not easy for a major purchasing entity to receive money back if it has been under-discounted, and there is invariably a resistance to finding more money for a supplier when too much discount has been claimed. Some parties try to deal with the problem by means of credits or goods in lieu (barter) but there are always complications. The simplest and most convenient approach after the initial year of an agreement, is to allow the preceding year's experience to determine the discount level for the next year and leave it at that, but always allowing an opportunity for either party to introduce convincing evidence in support of a different approach. This general area, after the discount itself, tends to be the most negotiable aspect of discount agreements.

6. 'Most Favoured Customer'

> The Supplier warrants to the Customer that the discount rates shown in the Discount Table are its standard rates offered to all of its customers purchasing the values and volumes of discountable items applicable to those discount rates. If any more favourable rates are offered at any time during the term of this Agreement to any other customer of the Supplier when all of the other terms and conditions of supply are substantially similar to those contained in this Agreement, those more favourable discount rates will be offered to the Customer.

This is an optional clause because it is usually required in agreements with government bodies, central and local, and most statutory authorities. Increasingly, it is requested by large commercial customers. It is another example of a 'comfort' clause because, in the practical circumstances of a complex agreement, there will be a sufficient number of material distinguishing features for the supplier to be able to demonstrate that an allegedly unfavourable discount rate compared with that granted to another customer is not an 'apples for apples' comparison.

The supplier also needs to be wary about undesirable side effects of such a clause, for example in a multi-national discount agreement, where a participating customer in one country, whose own volume purchases are small, receives a much higher discount in that country on the aggregation principle, than a large domestic customer in the same country. In a jurisdiction such as the US this could result in a legal liability under anti-trust legislation, and an indemnity from and against such possible liability should be sought from the customer in such circumstances.

E. Tripartite leasing agreements

In circumstances where the lease is negotiated prior to any contract with the supplier, documentation for equipment leasing is usually put forward by the leasing company. In the way of financial organisations, requests for changes tend to be resisted, but suppliers need to ensure that their retained rights in their products are not compromised. There is little difficulty about hardware products but software requires some care. Usually, it is intended that title to software should not pass under any circumstances and, where software is included in the leasing arrangement, this can give rise to problems in relation to capital allowances which in turn affect leasing rates, as well as limiting the value of the finance company's security in the event of the customer's default. Some finance companies try to overcome this by placing guaranteed repurchase obligations on the supplier at sums which reflect the unpaid value of the lease to the finance company rather than the generally very much lower market value of the products. Similar obligations can apply if there are unresolved disputes between the customer and the supplier, or if the supplier fails to provide maintenance and support for any reason. Suppliers should not be so seduced by the promise of prompt payment in full on behalf of otherwise financially risky customers that they fail to read the small print of finance company documents with the utmost care.

Provided that there is no potential for rebound back to the supplier, the supplier does not need to be particularly concerned about the terms of lease between its customer and the finance company, unless perhaps it was responsible for the introduction and is concerned to ensure that its customers are well treated. Similarly, the finance company is not much interested in the general terms of supply beyond securing title to hardware and ensuring that products are delivered in a state acceptable to the customer. Thus, while some finance companies will insist on their own comprehensive documentation, including master agreements with suppliers with whom they deal regularly (**CHAPTER 10** considers leasing documentation from the perspective of establishing an infrastructure which enables a supplier to offer leasing facilities to prospective customers as a matter of course, as a vehicle for expanding its sales opportunities), a simple form of tripartite agreement can actually bring together all of the essential elements of the transaction in a structure along the following lines, suitable for use in 'one-off' situations where the customer decides it wishes to lease, often after the order for products has actually been placed:

- Definitions*
- Scope*
- Supply of Products*
- Payment*
- Intellectual Property Rights*
- General Contract Provisions.

1. Definitions

These will include the 'Supplier's Terms' being the supplier's standard terms and conditions for the supply of computer products and the 'Leasing Terms', being the finance company's standard form leasing or lease purchase agreement, both appended to and forming part of the agreement.

2. Scope

(a) This Agreement governs the sale and licensing of Products in response to an Order from the Lessor on the basis of, and referencing, a Quotation.

(b) All deliveries of Products listed in the Order will be made direct to the Customer but the Supplier's invoices for these will be submitted to the Lessor.

(c) The Customer is obliged to reimburse the Lessor for the Products listed in the Order in accordance with the Leasing Terms.

(d) In the event of any conflict between the Supplier's Terms, the Leasing Terms and the Terms and Conditions of this Agreement, the order of priority will be this Agreement, then the Supplier's Terms in connection with matters arising from the supply of the Products or the Leasing Terms in connection with matters arising between the Lessor and the Customer.

(e) Neither the Supplier nor the Lessor is the employee, agent, representative or partner of the other and neither has authority to bind or obligate the other in any way towards the Customer or towards any third party.

This sets down the basis of the arrangement. In the event of any conflict in terms, the order of priority is the tripartite agreement first and then the supplier's terms in relation to the products, or the finance company's terms in relation to the lease. Deliveries will go directly to the customer but the supplier's invoice will go to the finance company. There is no direct relationship between the supplier and the finance company and neither has any authority to act on behalf of the other.

3. Supply of Products

(a) The Supplier's supply of Products will be made on the Supplier's Terms except that:
   (i)   the Supplier's invoice(s) will be submitted to the Lessor on delivery of the Products listed in the Order to the Customer;
   (ii) if required by the Lessor, the Customer will sign the Lessor's acceptance form to confirm receipt and acceptance of the Products promptly after installation of the Products by the Supplier or the Customer as the case may be;
   (iii) title to Hardware Products will pass to the Lessor only when all of the Price for the Products as defined in the Supplier's Terms has been paid to the Supplier in full. Title to Software Products will remain vested at all times in the Supplier or other third party owners as the case may be. The Lessor agrees that title to the Hardware Products will be passed to the Customer immediately following receipt by the Lessor of the final payment due to the Lessor from the Customer under the Leasing Terms.

(b) The Customer undertakes to observe all of the obligations of the Customer contained in the Supplier's Terms except that the payment terms will not apply to the Customer in respect of any Products (but not related services separately chargeable unless otherwise first agreed to in writing by the Lessor) delivered.

> (c) The Lessor undertakes to observe all of the obligations of the Customer contained in the Supplier's Terms in the event that the Lessor takes possession of the Products for any reason.
>
> (d) Except as stated in this Agreement, all of the obligations of the Supplier contained in the Supplier's Terms will be undertaken for the Customer and not for the Lessor unless the Lessor directs otherwise in writing.
>
> (e) If both the Customer and the Lessor have any claims against the Supplier in connection with the Supplier's agreement to supply the Products listed in the Order, any limitations of liability contained in the Supplier's Terms will apply cumulatively to the combined claims of the Customer and the Lessor.

The purpose of this clause is to establish the supplier's terms as the terms which govern the supply of the products. Even if the customer is in a position to negotiate modifications, the important point is that the supply document which is finally agreed between them is the appended document which constitutes the 'Supplier's Terms'. Those customer obligations which relate to payment will not apply to the customer, but the finance company is expected to honour all of the customer's obligations if it recovers possession of the products from the customer for any reason. This is to safeguard the supplier's interests, because the principal customer obligations other than payment are designed to maintain the confidentiality of any software products and not to infringe the supplier's retained intellectual property rights (ie patents, designs, copyrights and the like). There may also be some restrictions on use in high-risk applications and a requirement to comply with export regulations, as in the example clauses discussed in Section C of this chapter.

This clause also makes it clear that all of the supplier's obligations will be undertaken for the customer and not for the finance company, unless otherwise stated. This reflects the reality of the situation, that the customer is the party who will be using the products.

The final paragraph in the example is extremely important to the supplier. The limitations of liability contained in its terms of supply are not to be implicitly doubled because of the addition of the finance company as a party to the transaction.

4. Payment

> (a) The Lessor will pay the Supplier's invoice(s) for the Products in accordance with the Payment Clause in the Supplier's Terms and, for the avoidance of doubt, the Lessor is not entitled to delay payment beyond 30 days from the invoice date if the Customer fails to sign the Lessor's acceptance form for any reason unless, and only for as long as, any valid claim for shortages or damage to Products made in accordance with the Supplier's Terms remains unresolved.

> (b) The Customer will make the repayments due to the Lessor in accordance with the requirements of the Leasing Terms and agrees to abide by all of the terms and conditions in the Leasing Terms which apply to 'the Lessee'.
>
> (c) The Lessor agrees to abide by all of the terms and conditions in the Leasing Terms applicable to the Lessor.

Here, the finance company accepts the obligation to pay the supplier for the products. The supplier's standard payment terms are invoked, but in practice most finance companies are happy to accept seven-day terms once the acceptance certificate has been signed by the customer. The example anticipates the possibility that this form may not be signed for reasons other than a valid claim of an incomplete or damage delivery, and imposes the supplier's 30-day terms in any event.

As this is a tripartite agreement, the clause also includes an undertaking by the customer to repay the finance company in accordance with the leasing terms and for completeness reiterates the finance company's obligations in the lease agreement.

5. Intellectual Property Rights

> (a) The Lessor is not licensed or otherwise entitled to use any Software Product under any circumstances without the express prior approval of the Supplier. The Supplier reserves the right to charge its applicable licence fee to the Lessor before approving such use.
>
> (b) If the Lessor sells Hardware Products to any entity other than the Customer, any Software Products loaded onto the Hardware Products must be deleted and all copies and related documentation returned to the Supplier, unless the Supplier first consents to grant a transfer of the licence for the Software Products to a third party on its standard terms of Software licence. The Supplier reserves the right to charge its current licence transfer fee to such third party before consenting to the transfer.

This clause addresses the supplier's concern that if the finance company takes possession of or resells the hardware products, it can do the same with the software unless the supplier first consents, reserving the right to charge a fee. Since it is very often the case that software is licensed only for use on designated hardware by a named licensee it is essential to prevent a financing arrangement from overcoming these restrictions. There is some difficulty about seeking to charge a full new licence fee before consenting to a transfer. Provided the original licence fee has been paid (in respect of software installed on the hardware when it was first sold), it could be viewed as an unfair trading practice to seek to prevent the 'sale on' of such software products. This is a similar issue to that of an outsourcing provider taking over the management and use of a computer system on behalf of the licensed end user, although there the risk is arguably greater for the supplier as the outsourcing provider will most probably have other clients who could make use of the same software. This issue is further considered in **CHAPTER 17**.

The agreement above may not be acceptable as presented to a finance company, but it does highlight the issues which the parties need to resolve. Suppliers have the most to lose if they accept the standard leasing documentation of most finance companies.

1   Unfair Contract Terms Act 1977 (discussed further at **CHAPTER 4, SECTION C**).

CHAPTER 10
Leasing agreements

A. Introduction

Tripartite leasing agreements were discussed at Section E in **CHAPTER 9**. This was in the context of 'one-off' leasing arrangements, where a contract to supply goods already existed between the supplier and its customer, and the customer subsequently decided that it would prefer to lease equipment, rather than purchase it outright. The Tripartite Agreement was presented as a means of bringing a finance company into the contractual arrangements, retaining the supplier's terms and conditions relating to the supply of the goods, but introducing the finance company's terms and conditions to govern the finally agreed payment terms.

This chapter is concerned with leasing as a fundamental option to be offered by a supplier to its customers as an alternative to outright purchase.

A customer's motivation for leasing, and/or the way this financing option is sold, will vary. Sometimes it will be for the obvious reason of spreading the cost over time; sometimes it will afford an opportunity to acquire a more advanced and more highly specified, and thus more expensive, system; sometimes the appeal will be a relatively simple and flexible means of replacing obsolescent technology on a regular basis. Often it will be a combination of these reasons.

Information technology leasing is a huge worldwide market, well in excess of ten billion dollars per annum and, in Europe, financing at least 20 per cent of hardware supplies. Traditionally, it was an important means of financing high cost mainframe computers, but today leasing is as likely to finance networks of multiple desktop systems, as well as small consumer transactions (to which consumer credit legislation will also apply). Customer demand for the inclusion of software products and a variety of support services embedded within leases has resulted in fewer, more specialised finance companies willing to support the IT sector. Some manufacturers, with funds available, have also seen financing as a lucrative means of generating and facilitating additional sales.

A major difficulty in the lease financing of computer systems is the lack of meaningful equity in the items financed. Residual values were never very high in the mainframe era, and in the PC world they are almost non-existent. And of course there is rarely any residual value to a lessor in software or services. This has led to the development of innovative leasing agreements, with the associated financial algorithms being based on full amortisation of acquisition cost in the primary period of a lease.

Leasing can facilitate a supplier's opportunity to 'bundle' products, services (for example, installation, commissioning, maintenance, support, configuration design, system tuning) and regular system update plans into offerings that present customers with simple monthly or quarterly payment schemes, intended to cover the complete cost of acquisition, use and replacement. This can be very appealing to customers as can be the opportunity, depending on the type or structure of lease used, to 'expense' the transaction thereby keeping it off the balance sheet. There is not much attraction in having assets on a balance sheet which depreciate heavily in a very short period of time. Customers also have less incentive to replace obsolete systems if they effectively own rather than rent them, and IT managers keen to keep pace with the latest technologies can be subject to internal pressures to use equipment longer in order to support slower rates of depreciation.

The Leasing Agreements considered here are structured on the basis that the owner of the products to be leased is the lessor, who may be the supplier itself, or a finance company to which the supplier has first sold the products. (In the case of software products, ownership in this sense can be taken to mean the right to supply licences, without prejudice to the ultimate ownership of the intellectual property rights in the software.) The customer is the lessee. Most major computer hardware suppliers will also have one or more other Master Agreements with finance companies (sometimes several) setting out the basis of the finance offerings and the respective rights and responsibilities of those parties in the event of either customer dissatisfaction or customer default. Frequently, suppliers will establish a corporate vehicle especially for leasing purposes so that their brand name can be associated with the leasing activity or, alternatively, may permit or require finance companies to 'badge' the leasing product so that it is perceived to be part of their brand offering.

However, customers should bear in mind that there will be, in theory at least, more impartiality if an independent finance company is engaged to finance an IT purchase. It should circumvent any opportunity the supplier might otherwise have to manipulate or hide 'financial risk' costs by incorporating a wide range of services whose costs are difficult to quantify or analyse in the context of all-embracing periodic payments. On the other hand, suppliers financing transactions themselves may be willing to take bigger credit risks with customers in order to secure business.

Customers need to adopt a very cautious approach when leasing IT systems. Leasing agreements should be studied very carefully. 'Buy-back' type provisions, the condition and configuration of equipment to be returned, the costs of disconnecting systems from networks and returning them precisely as supplied can be much more difficult than might at first appear, and such considerations are seldom thought through before a lease is signed.

Finance arrangements are complex and varied, but fundamentally, there are two distinct types of leases offered to customers. They have a variety of labels, but one type is generally known as a capital, or finance, or fixed term lease, and the other is often referred to as an operating, minimum term or rental agreement. For the purposes of this review, the terms 'capital lease' and 'operating lease' will be used to represent the two types.

1. Capital leases

Goods leased by this means are treated, for accounting purposes at least, as being tantamount to outright purchases. Eventual purchase by the lessee is anticipated. Although title to the goods remains with the lessor during the lease period, because the lessee has exclusive use of the goods, and will effectively pay for them during the primary term of the lease (at least 90 per cent of the financial value of an asset at the commencement of a capital lease is the requirement of the relevant UK GAAP accounting standard[1]), the goods are included as assets on the lessee's balance sheet, the corresponding liability being the debt, and depreciation being applied at a steady rate over the life of the asset. The profit and loss account will also reflect interest charges, which will be high at the beginning of the lease and much lower at the end, because they are calculated on the net investment in the lease. The lease will include an option to purchase at the end of the primary term, often for a nominal sum, for example ten pounds, although an option to purchase might alternatively be for a sum which equates to the pre-calculated and agreed residual value of the goods. Once the option is exercised, title in the goods passes to the lessee at that time.

The financial details shown in this type of lease are specific. Both capital and finance elements will be shown, often supported by a schedule itemising all of the costs of the individual goods and services being supplied. The capital element is also used to determine the insurable value, which is a lessee responsibility. An initial payment will be specified which may include a deposit element or down-payment, but which is more often just the first periodic payment (for example, monthly or quarterly), plus the VAT due on the total purchase price of the goods. Then there will be a specified ongoing periodic payment, which will be payable throughout the primary term of the lease. The APR[2] rate may also be shown – and must be if the lease is to a 'consumer' lessee rather than a business lessee.

Capital leases can be popular with government departments, other statutory bodies and some commercial organisations, who have unused capital budgets at their financial year-ends which have to be utilised or will otherwise be lost, with

193

the added difficulty that budgets in the following year may also be reduced to reflect a lower spending pattern than had been previously estimated.

2. Operating leases

These leases are more in the nature of rental agreements (and sometimes so called), usually with a minimum term so that the lessor can be sure of recovering enough of the original purchase value to stay ahead of the fall in value of the asset over time. This type of lease is structured to continue automatically beyond the minimum term, until terminated by a notice from the lessee. Generally, there is no right to buy, and operating leases are structured on the basis that the subject assets will never be owned.

With this type of lease, VAT is charged on each periodic (monthly) payment. The APR is generally not stated, nor is the capital value of the goods and services being leased. Insurance is usually paid by the lessor and factored in, although a minimum sum may be stipulated for insurance purposes where the lessee is also required to insure. Return conditions can be onerous and need to be understood thoroughly by lessees before such leases are agreed. For instance, disengaging a system or key components from a network, restoring it to its original configuration (including removal of software), detaching any peripheral items, and re-cabling, can be complicated and expensive, and might have an adverse impact on the system(s) which remain.

Operating leases are shown in lessors' profit and loss accounts as expense items, the cost being expensed evenly during the term of the lease. They appeal to organisations with cash shortages or suffering from capital expenditure freezes. Lessees tend to focus on the monthly costs of such leases and can fail to require (or sometimes even care about) detailed explanations of their composition. Although in theory lessors are taking a greater financial risk with these types of leases, in practice such lease agreements rarely end early. However, their cost tends to be higher, reflecting the additional financial risk to the lessor.

3. Negotiating factors

The scope for negotiating leases is limited, but this does not mean that it should not be attempted. Finance companies can be very inflexible and their lease documentation tends to be presented in a very formal and form-orientated manner, often in multiple parts, and with an inference of 'take it or leave it'. The same can be true when equipment suppliers present their own documentation. This formal approach is reflected in the example agreements considered below. Prospective lessees should separate the transaction into two parts, one being the terms and conditions of supply relating to the goods and services intended to be leased, and the other being the financial transaction. The paperwork which is provided will generally cover both aspects quite clearly, but not always.

In negotiating the terms and conditions of supply, the parties should each take into consideration the principles discussed in **CHAPTER 9** for the various categories of supply. Although it may at first appear, and on occasion may even be true, that the supplier has the initiative in these types of transaction because it is providing or sourcing the finance, all the usual motivations to secure business will be present and purchaser lessees should act accordingly. In any event, they should ensure that the terms and conditions and accompanying schedules cover all of their requirements and that all expected maintenance and support needs are also detailed. If goods are faulty or claims arise, although lessees can look to the lessor in the first instance, they will want to be satisfied that the supplier can provide the same level of direct back-up as might be expected in a non-leasing situation.

When reviewing the finance documentation, however formal it may be, prospective lessees should have three objectives in mind:

(1)   to ensure that the financial details of the transaction are correct, particularly in terms of the amounts to be paid, the due dates, the cost of any option to purchase, the minimum lease period and any other costs shown;

(2)   to review the terms and conditions and to challenge any which seem unfair or unreasonable, disregarding any statements to the effect that terms are standard and unchangeable: the lessee should either be consciously willing to accept what is written (that is, make an informed decision about whether or not to accept any particular provision), or walk away; and

(3)   to understand the underlying assumptions behind the lease costs when these are not clear in the document – this is especially the case with operating leases. Prospective lessees should not hesitate to challenge figures which seem excessive or unjustified, whilst also recognising the extent of the benefits to them in the transaction and any genuine risks being taken by the supplier or lessor in the particular situation.

Leasing is a complex subject and this chapter is not attempting to present a detailed analysis and financial explanation of all aspects, but rather to provide an overview of the principal influencing factors which give rise to the two types of lease under discussion.

Presentation and ease of use of the documents referred to is important. Many lessors provide a folder pack containing all of the documents, and often some additional explanatory material and warranty claim information in relation to the goods.

The terms and conditions considered below relate to the actual lease agreement. A lessee would also need to review the Terms and Conditions of Supply Schedule very carefully. Supply issues are considered in **CHAPTER 9**, although **CHAPTERS 12** and **14**, which discuss software licensing, maintenance and support, are also going to be relevant.

B. The structure of a typical capital lease (here called a Fixed Term Lease Agreement)

This Agreement, between lessor and lessee, is intended to be the complete agreement between them in relation to the leasing of the goods. For convenience here, it is an example which assumes the lessor also to be the supplier of the goods but, in theory at least, it may also be used where a finance company is the lessor. However, finance companies will invariably have their own documents, no doubt often in a more formal and comprehensive style, designed to safeguard their interests which will differ in some respects from those of a supplier financer. This example Agreement is structured in several parts, comprising a front page containing variable information applicable to the specific transaction and the signatures of the parties, a schedule listing the goods to be supplied and any special (non-standard) conditions, a schedule containing the terms and conditions of the lease, and a schedule containing the terms and conditions of supply of the goods. Other schedules add data and privacy policies and a direct debit authority.

Front page contents and schedules

- Lessee details (including delivery and invoice addresses)
- Basic information about nature of business, number of years trading and company registered number
- Financing Details
  - Fixed Term
  - Payment Intervals
  - Total Cash Price of Leased Goods and separately shown VAT
  - Minimum Initial Payment
  - Minimum number of Further Payments
  - Option to Purchase Fee
- References to Schedules
- Alert to circumstances where Additional Charges may be incurred
- Authorised Signatures

Schedule One

(a)   Goods

(b)   Special Conditions

Schedule Two – Terms and Conditions of Lease

Schedule Three – Terms and Conditions of Supply

Terms and conditions (Schedule Two)

- Definitions*
- Fixed Term Agreement*

196

- Goods*

- Maintenance*

- Payments*

- Insurance*

- Warranties, Limitations and Exclusions of Liability

- Termination of Lease

- Remedies*

- Ownership of Goods and Exercise of Option to Purchase*

- General Contract Provisions

C. Specific clauses

In the clause examples considered below, which are those above marked with an asterisk, the parties are referred to as the 'Lessor' and the 'Lessee', denoting in this instance the supplier/financer on the one hand and the customer on the other. (Note that the schedule containing the terms and conditions of supply, not further considered here, will still use terms like 'supplier' or 'vendor' and 'customer' or 'purchaser'. The lessee will be the customer for the purposes of those terms and conditions.)

1. Definitions

(a) '*Agreement*' means this Fixed Term Lease Agreement including the front page and all of Schedules One, Two and Three appended to this Agreement and any other attachments expressly stated to be part of this Agreement and signed by an authorised representative of each party.

(b) '*Commencement Date*' means the date of commencement of the Fixed Term of this Lease Agreement, being the date of delivery of the Goods to the Lessee.

(c) '*Facility Fee*' means a one-time administrative fee of £95 or such other fee as may be notified to the Lessee in writing prior to it entering into this Agreement.

(d) '*Fixed Term*' means the total period of time for lease of the Goods to the Lessee, expressed in months and shown on the front page of this Agreement.

(e) '*Further Payments*' means the second and subsequent payments due in each Payment Interval for the duration of the Fixed Term.

(f) '*Goods*' means all of the computer products (hardware and software, including all additions and modifications and replacement parts), and other products, supplies, and services listed in Schedule One, which are leased to the Lessee on the terms and conditions of this Agreement.

(g) *'Lessee'* means the entity shown as the Lessee whose details appear on the front page of this Agreement, and who is responsible for the leasing of the Goods from the Lessor.

(h) *'Lessor'* means the entity shown as the Lessor whose details appear on the front page of this Agreement.

(i) *'Minimum Initial Payment'* means the first monthly or quarterly payment plus the Value Added Tax applicable to the Total Cash Price, as detailed on the front page of this Agreement, plus the Facility Fee.

(j) *'Payment Interval'* means 'MONTHLY' or 'QUARTERLY' as shown on the front page of this Agreement.

(k) *'Previous Agreement'* means, if applicable, an earlier agreement between the Lessor and the Lessee in respect of any of the Goods, the reference number for which is shown in Schedule One.

(l) *'Special Conditions'* means any terms and conditions agreed between the Lessor and the Lessee, as shown in Schedule One, which are additions or variations to the terms and conditions in Schedules Two and Three. IN THE EVENT OF ANY CONFLICTS OF MEANING, SPECIAL CONDITIONS PREVAIL OVER THE TERMS AND CONDITIONS IN SCHEDULES TWO AND THREE, AND THE TERMS AND CONDITIONS IN SCHEDULE TWO PREVAIL OVER THE TERMS AND CONDITIONS IN SCHEDULE THREE.

(m) *'Total Cash Price'* means the cumulative value of the Goods excluding Value Added Tax, as listed and totalled in Schedule One and as shown on the front page of this Agreement.

These definitions are generally self-explanatory. Definitions (d), (e), (i), (j) and (m) all relate to items appearing on the front page and are there to help the lessee verify the financial terms of the lease. 'Previous Agreement' is used in the Agreement to deal with the possibility of the lessee taking on a new lease, as many do, which includes some carry over items from a previous lease – see paragraph 2(b) below.

Paragraph (l) provides for the possibility of special non-standard conditions which the parties may negotiate, these being variations, deletions or additions to the terms and conditions in the schedules, making clear that any such conditions will prevail if there is any conflict of meaning, and also establishing that, subject to any special conditions, the finance terms take precedence over the supply terms.

There is not much to negotiate in definitions, but the facility fee defined in paragraph (c) might be challenged – in this instance it is a trivial amount, but if a larger sum is claimed, a lessee should consider making this an issue.

2. Fixed Term Agreement

(a) The Lessor agrees to lease to the Lessee and the Lessee agrees to lease from the Lessor, solely for the internal purposes of its business, the Goods listed in Schedule One for the Fixed Term, which will start on the Commencement Date, even if the Goods have not been at the time fully installed or connected to a network, where applicable. The risk of loss or damage to the Goods will pass to the Lessee on the date of delivery of the Goods to the Lessee.

(b) If Goods are included under this Agreement which were subject to a Previous Agreement, as identified in Schedule One, then on the Commencement Date of this Agreement, and in relation to the retained Goods only, the Previous Agreement will be treated as cancelled and replaced by this Agreement.

(c) This Agreement is for the Fixed Term and the Lessee may not terminate the leasing of the Goods at any time during the Fixed Term.

(d) If in breach of this Agreement the Lessee purports to terminate this Agreement or return the Goods to the Lessor at any time during the Fixed Term, without prejudice to the Lessor's other rights in law or equity or under this Agreement the Lessor will charge the Lessee for:
   (i)   the Minimum Initial Payment and any other sums already due to the Lessor and unpaid;
   (ii)   all Further Payments the Lessee would have paid had the leasing continued for the Fixed Term, discounted at the rate of 3% per annum from the date each Further Payment would have fallen due to the last day of the Fixed Term;
   (iii)   the Lessor's reasonable administration costs; and
   (iv)   interest charged at the rate of 2% per month compound in respect of any late payments, until the date of actual receipt of such payments, whether before or after any judgment.

Paragraph (a) makes clear that the lessee may only lease the goods for its own business purposes. The goods may not be sub-let, even if that is a normal business activity of the lessee, because it would not be an 'internal' purpose. As the insurance clause will require (clause 6 below), the Lessee will need to insure from the moment the goods arrive at its premises and it will also be responsible for payment of the leasing costs from the date of delivery (which is defined to be the Commencement Date) even if it is not ready for any reason to start using the goods. It follows that if any of these circumstances are a concern to the lessee they should be discussed and resolved prior to execution of the lease document.

As mentioned earlier, paragraph (b) covers the possibility of goods already leased under an earlier agreement with the lessor being carried forward into the new lease. This is a logical and convenient way of keeping paperwork to a minimum, but the lessee will need to be satisfied that (a) the cost component for carried forward goods is a reasonable reflection of their then depreciated value, and that (b) the older goods are likely to be required for the whole of the new fixed term.

Paragraph (c) is essential from the lessor's perspective, because the lessor will be expecting to recover the full value of the goods plus interest and operating costs during the fixed term, and will almost always suffer a notable loss if the agreement is terminated early for any reason. Computer equipment is one of the worst depreciating capital assets a business can acquire, primarily due to the continuing trend for such equipment to double in power and halve in cost every 18 months or so.

Paragraph (d) elaborates on what the lessee must pay for premature termination. There are some aspects which a lessee should consider challenging here. Is the discount rate for what is, in effect, early payment a fair and reasonable one in the economic circumstances of the time? If the lessor is recovering its administration costs, why should it seek to contract for a higher sum in the event of late payment than is provided for by statute under the Late Payment of Commercial Debts (Interest) Act 1998?

3. Goods

The Lessee agrees that until such time as ownership of the Goods is transferred to it or the Goods are returned to the Lessor in accordance with the termination procedures in this Agreement, the Lessee is solely responsible for:

(a) selecting the Goods listed in Schedule One;

(b) ensuring that the Goods are suitable for its requirements in every way;

(c) ensuring that once it has taken possession of the Goods they are in good working order;

(d) ensuring that the Goods are used only in the normal course of business and in accordance with the manufacturer's instructions and/or guidelines and in compliance with all health and safety legislation, AND THE LESSEE AGREES TO INDEMNIFY THE LESSOR FROM AND AGAINST ANY LOSS, DAMAGE OR INJURY TO PEOPLE OR PROPERTY CAUSED BY THE GOODS OR THEIR USE, EXCEPT FOR DEATH OR PERSONAL INJURY CAUSED BY THE LESSOR'S NEGLIGENCE;

(e) keeping possession of the Goods, and not doing anything that will interfere with the owner's interest in the Goods, including without limitation not selling the Goods or claiming or allowing any other entity or person to claim capital allowances on them;

(f) ensuring that the Goods remain at the delivery/installation address specified. If the Lessee wishes to relocate the Goods it must first obtain the Lessor's written consent;

(g) connecting and disconnecting the Goods;

(h) installing the Goods unless installation is included in Schedule One;

(i) keeping the Goods in good working order, condition and repair;

(j) ensuring that the Goods are not altered or modified in any way without the Lessor's prior and specific written consent;

(k) bearing the risk of any loss or damage to the Goods, however caused;

(l) complying with all of the Customer's responsibilities in the Terms and Conditions of Supply in Schedule Three, except to the extent that they are varied by provisions in this Schedule Two;

(m) notifying the Lessor immediately if the Goods are lost, stolen, damaged or confiscated;

(n) not removing or defacing any notices of ownership of the Lessor or any other party on any of the Goods, and ensuring that the Goods do not become affixed to any land or building.

If the Lessee has any complaints upon taking delivery of the Goods concerning delivery errors, shortfalls, condition of the Goods or any other matter, it must notify the Lessor immediately of its complaint with as much information as possible, and provide the Lessor with a detailed written statement of the complaint within 5 working days of the delivery. The Lessor is entitled to assume that the Lessee is completely satisfied with the Goods if it has not received any such written statement.

This clause sets out the lessee's responsibilities. It is always important for clauses of this type to be reviewed very carefully because any failures in compliance will cause the lessee to incur costs, directly or indirectly. Although in this example, the lessor is also the supplier of the goods, this clause emphasises the financial role and requires the lessee to take responsibility for ensuring that the goods are exactly what are wanted, that they are in good working order, and that they will be properly looked after and correctly used – all risks of loss being borne by the lessee. This is exactly the sort of clause that can be found in any finance company's lease terms. If the goods are faulty or of poor quality or not fit for any contracted purpose, the lessee will need to rely on the terms and conditions in the supply schedule in order to obtain a remedy from the lessor as supplier, rather than as financer. Does the lessor have a conflict of interest? Not really, because the two functions of supply and finance are distinct ones and, if anything, a lessor supplier may find it more difficult to avoid supply-related obligations than would a pure finance entity.

The final paragraph of this clause is an acknowledgment by the lessor that, even as the financer of the transaction, it cannot completely escape responsibility for any problems with the goods. However, it is vital for a lessee to identify and escalate problems as soon as they become apparent, especially in cases where the finance company is an independent entity.

4. Maintenance

(a) *Hardware*

Except to the extent such maintenance services are included in this Agreement during the Fixed Term, as shown in Schedule One, the Lessee is solely responsible for ensuring that the hardware Goods are kept in optimum operating condition at all times, except only for fair wear and tear, and for obtaining any maintenance services required by the Lessee for the hardware Goods.

(b) *Software*

The Lessee is solely responsible for entering into and complying with the terms of the licences to use any software Goods and for obtaining any maintenance or support on software Goods and if the Lessee is unable to obtain such maintenance or support for any reason it will not be entitled to terminate this Agreement or to withhold any payments.

This clause continues the theme of clause 3, making the lessee responsible for making whatever arrangements it considers necessary for purposes of maintaining hardware goods and licensing and supporting required software applications. Aside from the lessee's responsibility for ensuring that goods are properly maintained, non-availability due to equipment failures or software problems will not be grounds for withholding lease payments. It is, therefore, essential that full consideration be given to maintenance and support requirements before a lease is agreed. Whether or not such maintenance and support is 'bundled' into the lease payments, the need for proper arrangements must not be overlooked. If the lessee's business requires it, an out-of-hours maintenance contract may be required. In other cases, it may be that 'time and materials' arrangements will suffice. These matters must be sorted out with the supplier (whether or not this is also the lessor) before contractual commitments are made.

5. Payments

(a) The Lessee undertakes to pay the Lessor the Minimum Initial Payment on or before the Commencement Date and thereafter the Further Payments on the first day of each following Payment Interval throughout the Fixed Term.

(b) All payments must be made by Direct Debit unless the Lessor otherwise agrees in writing. If the Lessee does not make payments by Direct Debit an extra 5% of the amount of the payment will be charged on each payment to cover the Lessor's increased costs of administration.

(c) All payments must be paid in full and on time and time is of the essence for this purpose. IF PAYMENTS ARE SENT BY POST, THIS IS AT THE LESSEE'S OWN RISK.

(d) All payments must be made free of any set-offs, deductions or withholdings.

(e) The Minimum Initial Payment and Further Payments are calculated on the assumption that there will be no changes in the rate of Corporation Tax during this Agreement. If there is an increase in Corporation Tax of 5 or more percentage points the Lessor is entitled, on giving the Lessee 7 days' notice, to increase the Minimum Initial Payment and/or such Further Payments as the Lessor may specify by 8 percentage points for each 5 point increase, and pro rata for different amounts of increase.

(f) The Lessee will be responsible for any costs incurred by the Lessor in recovering money owed to it (including collection agents' fees), plus interest on all overdue amounts at the rate of 2% per month calculated on a daily basis or £25.00, whichever is the greater, until payment is actually received whether before or after any judgment. The Lessor will also charge the Lessee the sum of £25.00 each time an unpaid Direct Debit or cheque is required to be re-presented. In addition, the Lessor will be entitled to impose an administrative charge of £10.00 per item of correspondence in respect of each payment that falls overdue.

This is not the boilerplate payments clause which is discussed in **CHAPTER 7**, although it covers much of the same ground and to that extent the discussion in clause 7 is still relevant. This clause is tailored to the leasing situation, and lessees should consider those elements of this clause which allow the lessor to impose additional charges. Such charges may be reasonable in some circumstances, and may prove very difficult to negotiate in others, but if a lessee cannot be satisfied about the justification for any of the charges in paragraphs (b), (e) or (f), it should certainly challenge them.

6. Insurance

(a) Unless the parties have agreed in writing that the Lessee is permitted to self-insure, the Lessee must insure the Goods against any loss (including total loss) or damage from all risks and against third party risks. The amount of such insurance must be at least the full cost of replacing the Goods as new, as shown in Schedule One.

(b) If the Lessee is permitted to self-insure, it must nevertheless keep the Goods insured at all times, until either ownership of the Goods has been transferred to it or the Goods have been returned to the Lessor, against loss or damage by fire and water for their full replacement value shown in

Schedule One and against third party risks. Provided the Lessee complies at all times with all statutory requirements relating to the Goods and their insurance, it may act as self-insurer in relation to the other risks.

(c) Unless the Lessee is permitted to self-insure, it must arrange for the Lessor's interest in the Goods to be endorsed on any policy of insurance and show proof whenever the Lessor requests it. If the Lessee does not provide this proof promptly the Lessor may, at the Lessee's expense, arrange for the insurance of the Goods. In such circumstances the Lessor will add an amount equal to the insurance premium to the Minimum Initial Payment or the next due Further Payment. If the Lessee has to make an insurance claim for the Goods it must inform the Lessor immediately. The Lessee is not authorised to agree a settlement of a claim without written permission from the Lessor. The Lessee agrees to appoint the Lessor as its agent for the purposes of managing any claim and authorising the insurance company to pay any settlement of claims on the Goods directly to the Lessor.

It is usual for lessees of goods to incur insurance costs. Sometimes insurance will be arranged by lessors and the costs passed on to the lessee in the lease, and sometimes the lessee will be expected to make these arrangements directly, on the basis that the lessee is going to be responsible for the value of lost, stolen, destroyed or damaged goods, insured or not. But in those cases where the lessee must insure, as here, it is not always easy or even practical to have the interests of another party noted on a policy especially where the policy in question is non-specific to one set of goods and the lessee could potentially have multiple sets of interests to register. It is all a question of degree: the value of the goods (the greater the value, the better the case for a registered interest), the nature of the lessee's business and the financial status of the lessee.

This clause does provide for the possibility of self-insurance, which wealthier organisations often prefer, as also do government departments and public authorities. There is scope for discussion here and the clause should be adapted to meet the needs of both parties. As usual, the small lessee customer will find it much more difficult to negotiate any changes, and from the lessor's perspective it may not be cost-effective to spend much time on the matter, although goodwill is also a factor. A sense of realism should be maintained. The lessor needs to know that if the goods are lost or damaged, it will be compensated with minimal fuss.

7. Remedies

(a) On termination of this Agreement for any reason, at the Lessor's option but at the Lessee's expense the Lessee will either de-install and return the Goods to a UK address designated by the Lessor within 10 working days together with any ancillary equipment originally supplied, all in good operating condition fair wear and tear excepted, or store the Goods at the Lessee's risk for a maximum period of 30 days and then deliver them to a UK address designated by the Lessor, or allow the Lessor to collect the Goods from the Lessee during normal business hours. Any costs incurred by the Lessor in collecting the Goods and/or in restoring them to normal operating condition will be borne by the Lessee and payable to the Lessor on demand. If the Lessee fails to deliver up the Goods for any reason, it will be liable to the Lessor for their replacement cost, being the higher of the outstanding sums owing under this Agreement or the then fair market value of the Goods, without prejudice to any other rights or remedies available to the Lessor in law or equity or under this Agreement.

(b) If the Lessor recovers the Goods and is able to sell them, it will apply any proceeds of sale, after deducting any Value Added Tax and its costs in repossessing and selling the Goods, in the following order:

    (i)   towards any amounts due but not paid by the Lessee pursuant to paragraph (a) above;

    (ii) towards such anticipated future value of the Goods and the end of the Fixed Term, discounted at the rate of 2% per annum from the last day of the Fixed Term to the date of receipt by the Lessor of the proceeds of sale; and

    (iii) if any balance remains, the Lessor will rebate this to the Lessee.

A prospective lessee should consider the implications of this type of clause very carefully. Most lessees in capital leases will exercise their option to purchase, but if they do not, the cost of detaching and returning goods in their original state (fair wear and tear excepted) could be considerable, as discussed in the introduction above.

The costs and inconvenience of storage may also be a problem for a lessee, and the time to negotiate that position is of course prior to contract. A lessee should question the right of the lessor to have a return or storage option. Similarly, costs, or at least the basis of them, should be agreed in advance.

8. Ownership of Goods and Exercise of Option to Purchase

(a) During the leasing of the Goods, the Goods will be and will remain at all times the moveable, personal and chattel property of the Lessor. Other than a right to quiet possession and enjoyment of the Goods during the Fixed Term (provided and for so long as the Lessee is not in breach or default of this Agreement) and subject to (b) below, the Lessee will not have any right, title or interest in the Goods except as Lessee and as set out in this Agreement.

(b) If the Lessee wishes to exercise the option to purchase the Goods at the end of the Fixed Term (in their then existing state and condition), it may do so:

> (i) at any time during the Fixed Term by paying to the Lessor such sum as will, with the payments previously made, amount to the aggregate of all of the sums payable by the Lessee during the Fixed Term (less a discount for the acceleration of the payment at a rate of 3% per annum) plus the Option to Purchase Fee specified on the front page of this Agreement;
>
> (ii) at the expiration of the Fixed Term (and provided all sums due from the Lessee have been paid in full) by payment of the Option to Purchase Fee specified on the front page of this Agreement.

The option to purchase is a particular characteristic of a capital lease. Paragraph (a) emphasises that ownership and related rights do not pass to the lessee prior to exercise of the option to purchase and the lessee's rights are limited to 'quiet possession and enjoyment'. An important point here is that such quiet enjoyment is subject to the proviso that the lessee is not in breach of the lease. This is not satisfactory because there can be a huge number of possibilities for minor technical breaches of any lease. If lessees cannot negotiate an unqualified right to quiet possession (which may be difficult to achieve) they should at least seek to qualify any provision of this kind by limiting it to material breaches or defaults.

Paragraph (b) sets out the basis for exercising the option to purchase. This can be done at any time during the fixed term of the lease provided that all the costs are paid as described. Generally, option fees are nominal and most lessees will exercise and take over ownership of the goods at the end of the lease – it will usually be far cheaper than decommissioning and returning the goods.

D. The structure of a typical operating lease (here called a Minimum Term Rental Agreement)

The clause examples below mirror similar clauses in the Fixed Term capital lease considered above. The differences reflect the fact that this is an operating lease and the term 'Renter' is used here instead of 'Lessee' to remind the reader that this type of lease is much more in the nature of a rental agreement, and often called one. The comments made in Section C in relation to each clause will apply where there is no additional commentary.

Front page and schedule contents

- Lessee details (including delivery and invoice addresses)

- Basic information about nature of business, number of years trading and company registered number

- Rental Details
  - Minimum Term
  - Payment Intervals

     —   Monthly/Quarterly Rental and separately shown VAT
     Total Periodic Rental including VAT

- References to Schedules

- Alert to circumstances where Additional Charges may be incurred

- Authorised Signatures.

Terms and conditions

- Definitions

- Minimum Term Agreement*

- Goods

- Maintenance

- Payments*

- Insurance*

- Warranties, Limitations and Exclusions of Liability

- Termination of Rental Agreement

- Remedies

- Ownership of Goods and Continuation beyond the Minimum Term*

- General Contract Provisions.

E. Specific clauses

1. Minimum Term Agreement

(a) The Lessor agrees to rent to the Renter and the Renter agrees to rent from the Lessor solely for the internal purposes of its business the Goods listed in Schedule One for the Minimum Term, which will start on the Commencement Date, even if the Goods have not been at the time fully installed or connected to a network, where applicable. The risk of loss or damage to the Goods will pass to the Renter on the date of delivery of the Goods to the Renter.

(b) If Goods are included under this Agreement which were subject to a Previous Agreement, as identified in Schedule One, then on the Commencement Date of this Agreement, and in relation to the retained Goods only, the Previous Agreement will be treated as cancelled and replaced by this Agreement.

(c) As this Agreement is for a Minimum Term, the Renter may not terminate the leasing of the Goods at any time prior to the expiry of the Minimum Term.

(d) If in breach of this Agreement the Renter does purport to terminate this Agreement or return the Goods to the Lessor at any time during the Minimum Term, without prejudice to the Lessor's other rights in law or equity or under this Agreement the Lessor will charge the Renter a total of:

    (i) the Minimum Initial Payment and any other sums already due to the Lessor and unpaid;

    (ii) all Monthly/Quarterly Rental payments the Renter would have paid had the renting continued for the Minimum Term, discounted at the rate of 3% per annum from the date each Monthly/Quarterly Rental payment would have fallen due to the last day of the Minimum Term;

    (iii) the Lessor's reasonable administration costs; and

    (iv) interest charged at the rate of 2% per month compound in respect of any late payments, until the date of actual receipt of such payments, whether before or after any judgment.

As discussed above, the renter must examine the numbers very carefully in this type of lease. The lessor has a greater risk because it is much less likely to recover all or most of the capital cost of the goods during the minimum rental period and will be relying on the likelihood of the lease continuing well beyond in order to have a really profitable transaction. Nevertheless, high interest charges and other ancillary costs can be factored into the periodic payments and it is advisable to understand how the numbers have been arrived at and what they include and exclude.

2. Payments

(a) The Lessee must pay the Lessor the Minimum Initial Payment on or before the Commencement Date and thereafter the Monthly/Quarterly Rental payments on the first day of each following Payment Interval throughout the Minimum Term.

(b) This Agreement will continue automatically after the Minimum Term unless or until the Renter serves the Lessor with a minimum of one month/quarter's notice of termination to expire on the expiry date of the Minimum Term or at the end of a subsequent month/quarter (the month or quarter in each case to be in accordance with the Payment Interval shown on the front page of this Agreement). The Renter's Monthly/Quarterly Rentals will continue to be payable until the earlier of the termination date of this Agreement for any reason on or after the Minimum Term, or the Lessor's notice to the Renter of any reduction the Lessor is willing to agree in the Monthly/Quarterly Rental (in which event the revised amount will be substituted as the continuing Monthly/Quarterly Rental).

(c) All payments must be made by Direct Debit unless the Lessor otherwise agrees in writing. If the Renter does not make payments by Direct Debit the Lessor will charge the Renter an extra 5% of the amount of the payment on each payment to cover the Lessor's increased costs of administration.

(d) All payments must be paid in full and on time and time is of the essence for this purpose. IF PAYMENTS ARE SENT BY POST, THIS IS AT THE RENTER'S OWN RISK.

(e) All payments must be made free of any set-offs, deductions or withholdings.

(f) The Minimum Initial Payment and Monthly/Quarterly Rental payments are calculated on the assumption that there will be no changes in the rate of Corporation Tax during this Agreement. If there is an increase in Corporation Tax of 5 or more percentage points the Lessor will be entitled, on giving the Renter 7 days' prior notice, to increase the Minimum Initial Payment and/or such Monthly/Quarterly Rental payments as the Lessor may specify by 8 percentage points for each 5 point increase, and pro rata for different amounts of increase.

(g) The Renter will be responsible for any costs incurred by the Lessor in recovering money owed to it by the Renter (including collection agents' fees) plus interest on all overdue amounts at the rate of 2% per month calculated on a daily basis or £25.00, whichever is the greater, until payment is actually received whether before or after any judgment. The Lessor will charge the Renter the sum of £25.00 each time an unpaid Direct Debit or cheque has to be re-presented. In addition, the Lessor will be entitled to impose an administrative charge of £10.00 per item of correspondence in respect of each payment which falls overdue.

The important new point to note here is that this agreement continues automatically after the minimum term (paragraph (b)) and the renter should consider the implications of this and the length of the required notice period. It is also advisable to establish the principle at the outset of a significantly reduced rental for any continuing rental period beyond the minimum.

3. Insurance

(a) Unless the Lessor has agreed in writing that the Renter is permitted to self-insure, the Renter must insure the Goods against any loss (including total loss) or damage from all risks and against third party risks. The amount of the insurance must be at least the full cost of replacing the Goods as new, as shown in Schedule One.

(b) If the Renter is permitted to self-insure, it must nevertheless keep the Goods insured at all times until either ownership of the Goods has been transferred to it or the Goods have been returned to the Lessor, against loss or damage by fire and water for their full replacement value shown in Schedule One and against third party risks. Provided the Renter complies at all times with all statutory requirements relating to the Goods and their insurance, it may act as self-insurer in relation to the other risks.

(c) Unless the Renter is permitted to self-insure, it must arrange for the Lessor's interest in the Goods to be endorsed on any policy and show proof of the same whenever the Lessor requests it. If the Renter does not provide this proof promptly the Lessor may, at the Renter's expense, arrange the insurance for the Renter. If the Lessor arranges the insurance it will add an amount equal to the insurance premium to the Minimum Initial Payment or the next due Monthly/Quarterly Rental. If the Renter has to make an insurance claim for the Goods it must inform the Lessor immediately. The Renter is not authorised to agree a settlement of a claim without written permission from the Lessor. The Renter agrees to appoint the Lessor as its agent for the purposes of managing any claim and authorising the insurance company to pay any settlement of claims on the Goods directly to the Lessor.

This clause is very similar to the one discussed for the capital lease. Even though the lessor here requires the renter to insure, the lessor will be wise to keep the goods insured on its own policy, at least as a secondary back-up. If a renter fails to insure and goods are lost, the mere presence of a contractual liability for breach may not suffice: the renter might have gone out of business.

4. Ownership of Goods and Continuation beyond the Minimum Term

(a) During the renting of the Goods, the Goods will be and will remain at all times the moveable, personal and chattel property of the Lessor. Other than a right to quiet possession and enjoyment of the Goods during this Agreement (provided and for so long as the Renter is not in breach or default of this Agreement) the Renter will not have any right, title or interest in the Goods except as Renter and as set out in this Agreement.

(b) If this Agreement continues beyond the Minimum Term all of the terms and conditions in this Agreement will remain in full force and effect until its actual date of termination.

There is no option to purchase in operating leases, although terms for purchase may of course be agreed at some point if this is what the parties want. In this version of the clause, the objective is simply to ensure that the terms and conditions of the agreement continue to apply for as long as the rental continues. It follows that if the renter has succeeded in negotiating any variations (of pricing or any other terms) these should be properly recorded and the agreement amended accordingly.

1   GAAP is a Generally Accepted Accounting Practice, and preparation of accounts in accordance with UK GAAP has been a statutory requirement under UK tax law since 1998. GAAP rules are used to determine trading profits. From 2005, companies may elect to apply International Accounting Standards ('IAS') instead.
2   APR is the Annual Percentage Rate, used to enable 'level playing field' comparisons of lease offerings from different lenders.

CHAPTER 11

Distribution and reseller agreements

A. Introduction

The computer industry is characterised by extensive distribution methods, facilitating access to a wide range of customers. The small software house may need the resources of a professional sales organisation to get its products to a wider market than it can address directly, either because it lacks the necessary experience, or because it does not have sufficient financial resources. A company which wants to introduce its products into foreign markets without incurring the expense of establishing local operations in a country will usually consider the appointment of a distributor as a first step, at least until a strong foothold has been established.

In the UK, as in the industry worldwide, far more sales of computer products and services are achieved through indirect channels of distribution than from manufacturers directly. A large number of small manufacturers in the computer industry develop hardware and software products and components but need external channels of distribution. Major manufacturers also sell through multiple channels, both direct and indirect. Direct sales forces give these manufacturers the best opportunities of presenting their offerings to large or strategically significant end-user customers, as well as servicing the overall requirements of original equipment manufacturers ('OEMs') and resellers, and developing particular vertical markets. In times of economic prosperity, the large manufacturers will also rely heavily on indirect channels to help satisfy demand (although now and again their internal structures can lead to unnecessary and unwelcome duplication of effort through competition between the direct and indirect channels).

However, resellers can be amongst the first to go in economic downturns, a point which needs to be borne in mind when negotiating agreements. Certainly, there must be no false expectations about automatic renewals at the end of agreement terms whatever the words may say.

A typical business situation could involve the sale of computer products to an intermediary organisation, which incorporates those products into its own products, adding value for onward supply to end users. Such organisations might be other technology companies, installing their applications software on to a standard hardware product including operating systems software, and selling the whole package on as a complete computer solution to the end-user marketplace, or manufacturers of products which incorporate computer systems as an integral part of their design, such as flight simulators and automated testing equipment, which are then sold as complete systems to end users.

In contrast, other types of resellers do not 'add value' as such, but merely act as intermediaries distributing computer products in volume to smaller end users who would not have the sort of purchasing capabilities to justify the direct attention of the manufacturer. Resellers to these sorts of end users are frequently associated with particular vertical markets where they have developed expertise, eg banking, pharmaceuticals or specific retail sectors.

A third example is the indirect distribution of software products from multiple vendors using the web. This affords one of the purest examples of e-commerce, considered in **CHAPTER 20**, because products can be reviewed, compared, tried, ordered, paid for and delivered electronically over the Internet.

The distribution infrastructure through which computer products and services are distributed consists of distributors who may be called resellers, value added resellers, OEMs, third party vendors, software houses, system integrators, dealerships, commission agents and other labels which are intended to present the role in a manner which is considered appropriate for each type of market, ultimately defined by its target customers.

One label, which has gained enormous popularity in recent years, in both Europe and the United States, is 'partner'. Lawyers find this unfortunate because to the uninformed third party, use of such terminology in certain circumstances may imply a legal partnership, making manufacturer and reseller jointly and severally liable if one of them causes loss to a third party. But 'partner' is perceived to imply a warm and supportive relationship, and the industry is not easily dissuaded from use of the term. It is to be hoped that there is now sufficient common usage of this term to support a defence argument that no third party could reasonably infer a legal partnership from its use without additional evidence.

There is one other dynamic, which can influence the distribution model of computer product suppliers. Powerful multinational customers can demand that a supplier service their requirements a particular way, regardless of its normal direct/indirect sales channel structures. They may demand direct servicing of their requirements for perceived cost savings (fewer parties in the supply chain), or they may wish to be directed to appropriately qualified, accredited resellers with priority access to the supplier whenever required, and across national boundaries. If added value services are needed, these will have to be sourced from somewhere.

Such services can be very broad, and can include consultancy, on-site support, technical support, training, implementation, system integration and optimisation, network management and vertical market expertise. However, this chapter is concerned principally with the straightforward supply of computer products by indirect means (other than via the web, which is considered in **CHAPTER 20**) and further discussion about the provision of related specialist services can be found in **CHAPTERS 15 AND 18** in particular.

1. Distribution or agency?

One of the principal distinguishing features which contrasts distribution agreements from agency arrangements is that a distributor is an independent business organisation, the distributor buying on its own behalf as a principal from the supplier and reselling accordingly. The original vendor does not have a direct relationship with the end user through the distribution contract, although any software supplied by the vendor may be separately licensed. (There may be other legal implications however, arising from the vendor's negligence or from product liability, outside the terms of the contract.) Suppliers will differ greatly in the amount of trouble they take in selecting their distributors. Some will be so concerned to get their products out into the market place as quickly as possible that they will pay little regard to the quality, resources, reputation and experience of their chosen distributors. This frequently proves to be a costly mistake. At the other extreme, numerous checks and enquiries will be made before a prospective distributor is chosen.

However, once the relationship is in place, the distributor will have a contract with its supplier governing its responsibilities and the terms and conditions on which it can acquire the supplier's products. It will then enter into separate contracts of supply with its own customers in relation to the products it is authorised to distribute.

In contrast to this, the agent is a channel facilitating direct contractual relationships between end-user customers and the product manufacturer. The precise nature of the agent's responsibilities can vary greatly, in one case enabling the agent to receive commissions for making introductions but not doing much more and in another case undertaking a large number of responsibilities including pre- and post-sales support, order administration, credit control, and so forth. The latter type of agent begins to look very much like a distributor.

The relationship between the agent and supplier principal consists of rights and obligations implied by law as well as those defined in the contract. Computer product manufacturers tend to shy away from agency relationships because of two fundamental disadvantages. First, whatever the actual authority granted by the agreement between them, the agent has implied legal authority to bind its principal. So, too, in many instances do employed sales staff, but the latter are subject to much closer supervision and control and are also likely to be dependent on their employer for their livelihood. The second disadvantage derives from statute. Agents whose appointments are terminated without cause may be entitled, as of right, to compensation under the provisions of the UK Regulations on Commercial Agents 1993, which are discussed in relation to the last example clause below, on the effects of termination. Distributors do not enjoy similar protection in most jurisdictions. It is not the purpose of this chapter to consider the legal aspects of agency any further.

In order to draw up effective and relevant commercial distribution contracts, it is necessary to be aware of the different kinds of distribution and remarketing channels and to identify correctly the channel which is most appropriate for the products and marketplace.

2. Different distribution definitions and categories

The labelling conventions for distributors and resellers are changeable and the same organisation may give itself a different title depending on the business being transacted. OEMs are not always manufacturers as such. They tend to be hardware-orientated, but they do not generally supply entire products or systems which they have themselves been solely responsible for designing and manufacturing. Some OEMs will design all the hardware components in systems for onward supply, but will obtain software from third parties for incorporation into the systems. Others will use other suppliers' standard products and sub-assemblies, typically incorporating computer systems as the control element in some broader-based system, for example mechanised stock control or computerised assembly production lines for manufacturing industries. The system may carry the OEM's badge even though the OEM has manufactured none of the individual elements.

VAR denotes 'Value Added Reseller' who 'adds value' to the products acquired from third parties for onward supply. A VAR may use hardware as the base for developing specialist software or it may be involved only with software, developing and enhancing its own or third parties' (or both) standard applications packages.

A VAR may specialise in a particular horizontal market sector such as financial systems or retail systems. Alternatively it may service a particular vertical sector, for instance by supplying different kinds of systems to the health care area or to the insurance industry. As specialists, and by adding their own expertise, VARs will reach markets that the manufacturers would not have the opportunity of selling into directly. They will put products and services together for customers, perhaps representing a number of suppliers in doing so. The sales model of such VARs is the 'practitioner' one, where they combine product expertise, in-depth vertical market knowledge, and a track record of successful implementations, giving them credibility with prospective customers.

Systems integrator is another term, often applied to major companies who assemble and co-ordinate all the value-added skills, and hardware too if required, in the design and assembly of large customised systems as complete solutions projects. They may or may not contribute their own applications software to the final product.

The principal expertise of software houses, software developers, or independent software vendors, lies in developing software. They may also undertake systems integration work, or supply applications expertise to systems integrators. As software product manufacturers in their own right they will have direct relationships with end-user customers or utilise distribution channels to sell licences for the use of these software products.

Application service providers ('ASPs') combine a number of roles, some of which may involve the online reselling of hardware and software products, as well as system design, implementation, support and even hosting. ASPs are the subject of **CHAPTER 18**.

Distributors as such have tended to be identified as dealers in fast moving commodity products with large comprehensive catalogues. Such dealers or commodity resellers act as wholesalers and retailers for standard computer products, frequently with high volumes and low price margins. Magazine advertising and direct mailings form part of their sales techniques. However, there is no longer a profitable future for box shifting alone, unless this is done on a large scale, as in computer superstores. An informed customer, particularly at the consumer end of the market or in relation to personal computers, may be interested in comparing different models and prices by dealing with a supplier who can offer a variety of merchandise.

None of the terms mentioned in this section is necessarily used exclusively of the others and a company may describe itself in more than one of these ways. The terms are not a complete list and new terms evolve from time to time.

The manufacturer or software developer will not necessarily be providing products as standard to OEMS, VARs or system integrators. It may itself have to modify or customise its products to meet particular distributor specifications, or the requirements of the distributor's end-user customers.

Software and services are the fastest-growing markets, and consultancy and customised services are growing in importance as attributes of the successful VARs, system integrators, and especially ASPs. The adding of value and customisation of products has increased in significance over the years, the market-led need being for complete 'solutions'. In the last decade, the world's leading manufacturer of computers, IBM, has developed its software and services business to achieve the sort of leadership role in this area which it has always had in mainframe hardware but which it failed to achieve during the emergence of the personal computer.

A special comment needs to be made about distributors in the most complete sense of the term. Although a reseller is a form of distributor, sharing many of the characteristics which derive from an independent business which buys and resells products, there is a high level distinction which can be made. A 'distributor' in the fullest meaning of that expression is a manufacturer's representative in a market or territory, particularly the latter. A manufacturer selling or extending international outlets for its products will often elect to 'test the water' through a distributor before taking the expensive decision to establish a full subsidiary operation. This distributor will have additional responsibilities to those of a 'mere' reseller. As well as direct selling within its assigned 'territory', it may be responsible for establishing and managing a local reseller network. It will generally undertake responsibility for local homologation of the manufacturer's product, to ensure that the product is compliant with the standards of that country in such matters as electrical supply and safety, and telephone connectivity. It will also be responsible for general compliance with local laws and import/export regulations, as well as keeping the manufacturer advised about such matters. These responsibilities are all in addition to the standard types of reseller responsibilities in such areas as marketing, business plans, sales targets, trained staff, adequate resources for local sales and support to the manufacturer's standards, and so forth. It follows that prospective distributors need to think carefully about what is to happen if the manufacturer decides eventually to establish a subsidiary, and to negotiate appropriate provisions in their agreement.

3. Exclusive or sole

Some distribution arrangements are termed 'exclusive' and some are termed 'sole'. This terminology is not consistently applied and it is important that any agreement intended to be sole or exclusive should spell out what the expression is actually intended to mean. The conventional interpretation is that if a distributor is granted exclusive rights, no one else, including the supplier, can have similar rights within a specified geographical area. On the other hand, a sole arrangement reserves the right of the supplier to undertake direct distribution through its own sales force, but prevents it from appointing another third party distributor within the territory. Exclusive distribution arrangements are subject to competition law, discussed in **CHAPTER 3**. Competition law may also be a relevant consideration for features of any distribution agreements, such as pricing or restrictions on the distributor's sales activities.

4. Licensing or sub-licensing end users

The software distributor will be licensed either to copy a master disk or image and distribute copies of the software to end users by licences or sub-licences or to supply software received from the manufacturer in conjunction with obtaining the end user's agreement to be a party to a licence agreement arranged directly with the manufacturer. For this aspect of the distribution activity, if no other, the distributor will be acting as an agent. In high volume situations, the distribution delivery vehicle these days will often be a boxed package containing a CD with the software burned in or an Internet download.

Sometimes a distributor may be granted a licence to the source code by the software owner in order to carry out the support work or at least first-line support for end users.

5. Governing law

Some distribution arrangements are localised, for example assigned districts within a national boundary. Others are broad in scope, the specified territories being countries or even continents.

Generally, the governing law in a distributor or reseller agreement will be stipulated in the agreement to be that of the manufacturer's home country. The manufacturer will perceive itself as having the most to protect and, in particular, will want to depend on familiar law for the protection of its intellectual property rights. But a major-name distributor representing multiple vendors may be able to negotiate its own choice of law.

International distribution arrangements can involve more than one legal system, for example distribution agreements where one or both parties reside in the EU fall within the scope of EC law as well as the applicable local country laws. The relevant legislation is considered in **CHAPTER 3**.

6. Negotiability

By way of preliminary comments on the negotiability of distribution agreements, it has to be said, as usual, that the relative size of the parties is going to be a determining factor in the content of the final agreement. A major hardware manufacturer, which enjoys a sustained demand for its products, is in a position to be highly selective in its choice of distributors and very firm about the terms and conditions of the relationship. Nevertheless, even a small manufacturer can make most of the running if its product is one for which there is heavy demand and therefore a significant marketing opportunity. The same holds for the manufacturers of the larger software applications, and if a product has achieved a prominent reputation in the marketplace, this will usually have a strong influence on the distribution terms finally negotiated. But sometimes the initiative comes from the opposite direction when experienced and well-established distribution companies offer their resources pretty much on their own terms to small manufacturers. This is illustrated by the leading distributors of software component products on the web.

Most product manufacturers should expect to take the initiative in proposing the terms on which their products are to be distributed. Whichever party proposes the first draft of the agreement and however strong a position that party appears to be in, there is always going to be some scope for negotiation about issues such as exclusivity, length of the agreement, marketing and technical support, prices and discounts and so on. Where the parties are more equally balanced, there can be considerable discussion about their respective responsibilities.

If the proposed arrangement is a new one for the party who initiated the discussions, or where there are significant time pressures, it is useful, after the initial exploratory meetings, to draw up 'Heads of Agreement', effectively a checklist of headings of the key elements of the transaction, which can then be refined and developed into the full form agreement as negotiations progress.

If Heads of Agreement are used, it is generally advisable to include a statement declaring them not to be legally binding (except in respect of the continuing confidentiality of the proposed arrangements and any information exchanged). Legal commitment is best reserved until all the terms of a relationship have been negotiated. It is important to make a specific statement about the parties' intentions concerning the degree of legally enforceable agreement, because of the danger otherwise of unwittingly creating an unintended contractual relationship by appearing to include all of the core terms necessary to create a legal agreement. This is further discussed in **CHAPTER 4**.

7. Administration

Good administration is particularly important for both parties in a distribution relationship. It facilitates both legal and commercial efficiency and contributes to the success of the relationship. The supplier should maintain well-organised and up-to-date records on the selection criteria it uses to choose its distributors. It should have efficient systems in place to provide its distributors with information about itself, its products (existing and planned) from both commercial and technical standpoints, marketing and advertising materials, demonstration products and so forth. It should also have good quality administrative records so that it can monitor the performance of its distributors and ensure that its practices towards each one are consistent and fair. As part of their obligations to their suppliers, as well as to be prudent in the management of their businesses, distributors will have to keep records of all aspects of their activities which entitle them to payments or other benefits from their suppliers or which are necessary to demonstrate compliance with their obligations, for example by maintaining a register of software sub-licensees. Many agreements will include rights of independent audit.

8. Variety of distribution terminology and arrangements

There is overlap in the meanings given to different expressions used. A hardware and software distribution agreement may refer to distribution of a manufacturer's computer systems including operating software, but will not necessarily include applications software, although it could.

With the enormous variety and scope for indirect supply, distribution agreements will themselves differ widely, reflecting the particular arrangements made, although they will have certain legal and commercial features in common. The structure which appears in the example below would be typical of a system distribution arrangement, involving hardware and software products used in combination. The specimen also incorporates sole distribution rights linked to performance and is intended to operate in only one EU country. There are many other possible permutations, for example, limiting the products to hardware or software items only, linking added value to discount arrangements, extending to multiple countries inside and outside the EU, granting exclusive or non-exclusive rights and so on.

By way of complete contrast, an example of a software distribution agreement where the emphasis is on the distributor as a major web-based supplier of software products, offering the prospect of international distribution of such products, is considered in **CHAPTER 20**. These products are often created by small companies operating from a single location and lacking the resources and know-how to target an international market. The distributor offers them a solution, often lending its own reputation to a product validation service, on the basis of which it is able to offer its customers first-line (call centre) and second-line (basic technical advice and fixes) support, reverting to the software manufacturer for third-line technical support, if appropriate.

B. The structure of a distribution agreement

The particular features of the structure of this example are that it is a sole distribution agreement, subject to the achievement of performance targets. Products are supplied on the supplier's standard terms and conditions, including software licensing provisions. The distributor is licensed to supply the supplier's hardware and software products to end users, and to add value by adding its own applications and providing second-line support.

Terms and conditions

- Definitions*
- Term
- Distributor's Appointment and Rights*
  - Appointment
  - Independent Contractor
  - Territory
  - Activities
  - Distributor's Licence
  - Marks
  - Products and Applications

- Distributor's Responsibilities*
  - Promotion and Marketing
  - Pre-Sales Activities
  - Performance
  - Training
  - Premises
  - Market Potential and Trends
  - Competing Products
  - Sales Targets
  - Support for End Users
  - Translations
  - Inventory
  - Forecasts and Records
  - Marks
  - Training and Consultancy
  - Compliance with Local Laws and Regulations
  - After Sales

- Supplier's Responsibilities*
  - Supply of Master Disks
  - Information to the Distributor
  - Training
  - Promotional Literature and Further Developments
  - Good Faith
  - Support
  - Continuing Development
  - Bespoke Work
  - Source Code Deposit Agreement

- Advertising and Merchandising Fund*

- Supply of Products*

- Software Licensing*

- Charges*

- Payment Terms

- Confidentiality

- Indemnities and Limits of Liability

- Termination*

- Effect of Termination*

- General Contract Provisions

Schedules

- Charges

- Commencement Date
- Products
- Sales Targets
- Supplier's Order Address
- Supplier's Distribution Price List
- Territory
- Trade Marks

Agreements appended to this Agreement

- Source Code Deposit Agreement
- Supplier's Terms and Conditions of Supply
- Supplier's Software Licence and Support Agreement.

C. Clauses specifically relating to distribution agreements

In the clauses considered below, which are those above marked with an asterisk, the parties are referred to as the 'Supplier' and the 'Distributor'.

1. Definitions

'*Application*' means the Distributor's value-added applications software identified as such in the Products Schedule or subsequently approved in writing by the Supplier and which is marketed by the Distributor in conjunction with the Equipment.

'*Charges*' means the Supplier's Charges set out in the Charges Schedule.

'*Commencement Date*' means the date shown as such in the Commencement Date Schedule.

'*End User*' means a customer of the Distributor.

'*Equipment*' means the hardware items and related operating system software identified in the Price List.

'*Licence and Support Agreement*' means the Supplier's licence and support agreement appended to this Agreement under the terms and conditions of which the software is licensed to End Users.

'*Marks*' means the trade marks and service marks of the Supplier, whether used individually or collectively and whether registered or unregistered, listed in the Trade Marks Schedule.

'*Master Disk*' means one or more compact disks on which the Software is supplied by the Supplier to the Distributor, incorporating the Supplier's copyright notices, serial numbers and proprietary notices.

'*Order Address*' means the Supplier's address for receipt of orders, set out in the Supplier's Order Address Schedule.

'*Price List*' means the current published 'Supplier Distribution Price List' for the United Kingdom appended as the Price List Schedule and any subsequent amendments notified to the Distributor by the Supplier.

'*Products*' means the Software and Equipment supplied in combination under this Agreement, as listed in the Products Schedule.

'*Sales Targets*' means the sales targets set out in the Sales Targets Schedule.

'*Schedule*' means a schedule applicable as identified in this Agreement and which is incorporated into this Agreement.

'*Software*' means the object code versions of the hardware operating systems software and the applications software products of the Supplier and their related documentation and any updates or enhancements to them, listed as such in the Products Schedule.

'*Source Code Deposit Agreement*' means the terms and conditions for source code escrow deposit appended to this Agreement.

'*Terms and Conditions of Supply*' means the document containing the supplier's standard terms and conditions of supply appended to this Agreement under the terms and conditions of which the Products are supplied to the Distributor.

'*Territory*' means the geographical area to which this Agreement and the appointment of the Distributor applies, specified in the Territory Schedule.

The definition of 'Application' in this Agreement means the value-added software developed by the distributor and thus distinguished from 'Software' which consists of the software products supplied under this Agreement, and which may comprise the operating systems software to be used with the hardware supplied, and also additional supplier-sourced applications software.

The definition of 'Equipment' refers to 'Price List', defined as a Schedule to this Agreement because products become obsolete quickly. The distributor does not want to be left with products identified in a schedule which end users are no longer buying. The distributor may want to negotiate information and supply rights to future products and services at the same time as the right to deal in the current products and services, or at least, for the Agreement to extend to successor or replacement products and services. The supplier wants to limit the products to be supplied to this distributor without committing itself over future versions which may be in greater demand, or where it can obtain better terms by dealing through another distributor.

A schedule listing the products is one way of clarifying the issues, but the distributor must be wary of a supplier whose enhanced products bear different names, model or release numbers.

Old product lines may still be marketed even when new product lines come on to the market. Allowing for 'replacement versions' in the agreement definitions, may not be a sufficient answer for the distributor.

One approach, as adopted here for hardware, is to incorporate by reference all the products on the supplier's price list. This must be a document unambiguously applicable to the distributor. This allows for updated standard price lists of products, yet enables the supplier the discretion to omit new non-standard products and to delete obsolescent products.

A precise definition of 'Territory' is essential. For example, 'Europe' is not definite enough. A list of countries or regions set out in a schedule is preferable, which can be amended in the future if necessary. If the distributor is being awarded special rights in respect of a particular area, it is important that the supplier should not inadvertently transgress them or make an arrangement with another distributor in contravention of them. At the outset, the supplier is often only too pleased to get a distribution arrangement working. As the product or service becomes more successful, non-exclusive rights to distribute anywhere the first distributor chooses will restrict the supplier's right to offer exclusive arrangements later with regard to a particular territory where another distributor may have an established reputation and the expertise and experience to exploit the products or services to best advantage.

Territorial exclusivity should be linked to termination on notice or by time limit, or to continuing achievement of targets.

2. Distributor's Appointment and Rights

(a) *Appointment*
The Supplier appoints the Distributor as its sole distributor for the Products in the Territory provided that, and for so long as, the Distributor achieves the Sales Targets and otherwise continues to observe and perform all of its obligations set out in this Agreement.

(b) *Independent contractor*

The relationship between the Supplier and the Distributor is that of independent contractor. Neither party is agent for the other, and neither party has authority to make any contract, whether expressly or by implication, in the name of the other party, without that other party's prior written consent for express purposes connected with the performance of this Agreement.

(c) *Territory*

For the avoidance of doubt the Supplier is entitled to engage in direct sales activities in the Territory but will not appoint any other person, firm or company to be a distributor or agent for the Products in the Territory provided that the Distributor continues to meet the requirements in sub-clause (a) above.

(d) *Activities*

Any Products purchased will be for resale or licence to End Users in the Territory. The Distributor undertakes to refer any enquiries for Products made from outside the Territory to the Supplier, and the Supplier agrees to refer any enquiries for Products made from inside the Territory, which it decides not to sell direct, to the Distributor. It is understood by the parties, although not a binding condition on the Supplier, that the Supplier will generally confine its direct sales activities to large corporations, institutional and government-related End Users. From time to time and by agreement on a case-by-case basis, the parties may agree to collaborate in order to achieve a sale of Products, in which event half the value of any such sale will count towards the Sales Targets. The Distributor further undertakes not to seek to distribute the Software outside the Territory by indirect means, through subsidiaries, affiliates, arrangements with End Users or third parties, or otherwise.

(e) *Marks*

The Supplier grants the Distributor the right to use the Marks on all literature, advertising, promotional material, publications or any other communications used or developed by the Distributor and which refer to the Products. Any such use of the Marks by the Distributor will include an acknowledgment of the proprietary rights of the Supplier. The Supplier reserves the right to issue guidelines on the use of the Marks from time to time, and the Distributor agrees to comply with such guidelines.

(f) *Products and Applications*

The Distributor confirms that it will purchase Products for supply to End Users as part of a system which includes Applications, and the Distributor acknowledges that the Price List is a discounted price list for the Products, applicable to purchases by the Distributor intended for onward supply to End Users together with the Applications, as a means of extending the range of applications available to End Users which utilise the Supplier's Products. If Products are resold without Applications, the Supplier's standard published prices for the Products will apply to the Distributor. Nothing

> in this Agreement is intended to prevent the Distributor from setting its own prices for the supply of Products to End Users.

Paragraph (b) is included because if the agreement is between two parties each acting independently, this fact should be stated, to avoid any implication that one party is an agent for the other.

This matters because an agent, representing his or her principal, has the authority to create contracts between the principal and other parties, and thus obligations which the principal has to abide by, whether or not the principal was aware of these in advance. An agency may be inferred by another party whether it in fact exists or not.

Distribution agreements in particular may give rise to this implication, but many kinds of agreements may be made where subsequent actions might lead an outsider to assume that there was an agency relationship when this is not in fact the case.

It is therefore useful when there is no question of agency or other connected relationship for this to be made clear between the parties to the contract, for the benefit of each of them.

The example clause grants 'sole' distribution rights but, because of the different interpretations given to this sort of terminology, as discussed in the Introduction, paragraph (c) makes it clear that the terms do not preclude direct sales activities within the territory by the supplier. Whenever privileged rights are granted, be they sole or exclusive, it is useful for suppliers to consider what the consequences should be of failure by the distributor to achieve agreed sales or other performance-related targets. It would be unusual and unwise in terms of market development to grant privileged rights without requiring minimum levels of performance in return. As an alternative to termination of the agreement for breach by the distributor's failure to achieve the required performance, a supplier could use the intermediate sanction of withdrawal of the privileged rights so that the distributor would become non-exclusive. This would have the advantage of preserving relationships and exploiting such inroads as the distributor has been able to make, but it would prevent similar privileged rights being made available to a new distributor. A judgment should be made on whether the interests of the development of the territory are best served by a new sole or exclusive arrangement or by appointing multiple distributors. Another alternative could be to start sub-dividing the territory so that the privileged distribution rights are restricted to a smaller geographical area.

In a sole distribution situation, there is bound to be negotiation about the precise nature of the supplier's proposed activities inside the territory. Paragraph (d) provides one example of a compromise, which focuses but does not bind the supplier's activities in the territory to major accounts. It may be that the nature of the collaboration, according to each party's expertise, would need to be spelled out more precisely to ascertain the relative values of the contributions to the collaboration.

The right to display the supplier's trade marks, granted at paragraph (e), should not be included as a matter of course. The supplier needs to be satisfied that it is necessary or beneficial to do so in the particular circumstances. It may be desirable to include a requirement that any material which is to make reference to the supplier's trade marks or, indeed, to the supplier in any other way, is first subject to written approval. If the supplier insists on having an absolute right to accept or reject proposed users without a test of 'reasonableness', the distributor should ensure that any consent is not unreasonably delayed.

If a trade mark is not presented in a manner consistent with the basis on which it was obtained, this can diminish its enforceability. Thus it is not uncommon for major suppliers with multiple logos, trade and service marks, to issue guidelines setting out the names and presentation styles of these marks and rules relating to their use. The wording in the example paragraph makes the observance of such guidelines a matter of contractual obligation.

Paragraph (f) will not always be appropriate, but in some instances the whole point of the distribution arrangement from the supplier's perspective is to encourage applications activities and the development of new vertical markets for its products. This is the value-added requirement that has given rise to the expression 'value-added reseller'. The VAR is receiving a special discount as an incentive to combine the supplier's products with other products, hardware or software in order to sell an applications solution to the end user. The supplier will be concerned that its products should not be resold individually, directly competing with and restricting its own market, but that the distributor should be incorporating them into an integrated system.

However, a distributor is still likely to require the ability to supply spare parts or additional software modules without further added value to its customers at a later date.

Although the distributor must not be prevented from carrying out activities that would be in breach of competition law discussed in **CHAPTER 3**, certain requirements may be specified as part of the distributor's obligations, to lessen the possibility of interference with the sales activities of the supplier's other distributors. For instance, it is legitimate to require the product inventory to be kept within the defined territory, and not to permit the distributor to sell on the products indirectly, and to refer enquiries about the products outside the territory to the supplier. But price fixing will not be permitted.

3. Distributor's Responsibilities

The Distributor agrees:

(a) *Promotion and Marketing*
To use its best efforts to promote and market the Products in association with the Applications in the Territory including the provision of demonstrations to prospective End Users, and generally to act diligently, ethically and in good faith in the best interests of the Supplier in connection with the distribution of the Products, but the Distributor is not entitled to sell, license or enter into any contracts on behalf of the Supplier or to bind the Supplier in any way.

(b) *Pre-Sales Activities*
To carry out pre-sales activities, including qualifying prospective End Users for the Products, conducting demonstrations and preparing quotations and proposals for submission to prospective End Users after the Distributor has approved their content and generally to keep the Distributor informed about enquiries received from prospective End Users.

(c) *Performance*
To perform its duties under this Agreement in such manner as it thinks fit having regard to all of the terms and conditions of this Agreement and to any directions which the Supplier may properly give from time to time, and to conduct the promotion and marketing of the Products with all due care and diligence, cultivating and maintaining good relations with End Users and prospective End Users.

(d) *Training*
To ensure that its relevant employees and representatives are adequately trained and have sufficient expertise to be able to represent and demonstrate the Products and to market the Distributor's related services.

(e) *Premises*
To maintain a computer centre for End User demonstrations at its main place of business and to keep this centre up to date for the prominent display of the Products and for their demonstration and to employ a sufficient number of suitably qualified administrative, technical and support personnel to enable the Distributor to perform its obligations in this Agreement satisfactorily, and further to take reasonable account of any opinion of the Supplier that an identified member of the Distributor's staff is incapable of or unsuitable for dealing in the Software.

(f) *Market Potential and Trends*
To keep the Supplier advised about market potential and trends in the Territory, competitive information, changes of regulations and practices governing the supply of the Products, and to provide the Supplier with

copies of all Distributor-generated promotional materials relating to the Products for them to be approved by the Supplier prior to their use by the Distributor.

(g) *Competing Products*
Not to be involved, directly or indirectly, in the manufacture or distribution in the Territory of any products which compete with the Products, and not to seek to distribute the Products outside the Territory by indirect means, through subsidiaries, affiliates, arrangements with End Users or third parties or otherwise.

(h) *Sales Targets*
To use its best endeavours to achieve the Sales Targets shown in the Schedule, and the Distributor acknowledges that if in any year of this Agreement the aggregate net invoice value of Products ordered from the Supplier by the Distributor is less than the Sales Target value for that year shown in the Schedule the Distributor's sole distribution rights are liable to be withdrawn, without prejudice to any other rights of the Supplier under this Agreement.

(i) *Support for End Users*
To use all reasonable endeavours to achieve contracted delivery, installation, training and consultancy commitments, and to provide information to End Users about the Supplier's hardware maintenance services and to provide an efficient second-line support service for the Software to End Users who have a current Licence and Support Agreement.

(j) *Translations*
To provide translations of:
(i) all material or prospective End User correspondence into the English language and to maintain file copies in the End User's language of all approved English language quotations and proposals, for review by the Supplier at any time. For the avoidance of doubt, correspondence with the End User relating to terms and conditions of contracts or to Product performance is an example of material correspondence;
(ii) the Supplier's standard terms and conditions in the End User's language.

(k) *Inventory*
To maintain an appropriate inventory in the Territory of stocks, spare parts, components and supplies for the Products to ensure prompt delivery and maintenance services to End Users.

(l) *Forecasts and Records*
To provide the Supplier with copies of forecasts for supply of the Products in the Territory at monthly intervals, including a rolling annual forecast, showing estimated delivery volumes by Product and by value, estimated percentage probability of future business, anticipated delivery dates and actual performance achievements against forecasts on a cumulative basis during each year of this Agreement, and further to maintain records of all

Software licences granted and of all fault calls and complaints relating to the Products including response times and remedial actions taken, and to make all of those records available for the Supplier's inspection by prior appointment during the Distributor's normal business hours twice each year during this Agreement.

(m) *Marks*

Not to infringe the Supplier's rights in its Marks, not to alter, remove or conceal any Marks or copyright notices on the Products or their packaging and not to attempt to modify the Products without the prior written consent of the Supplier, and in any event not to make any reference to the Supplier in its publications without first obtaining the Supplier's approval to the form and context of the reference.

(n) *Training and Consultancy*

To offer training and consultancy services to End Users in relation to the Products.

(o) *Compliance with Local Laws and Regulations*

To comply with all local laws and regulations relating to the nature, method of manufacturing, packaging, labelling, sale or licensing of the Products in the Territory and to keep the Supplier fully and promptly advised of all changes to such laws and regulations which could affect the Supplier's Products in the Territory.

(p) *After-Sales*

To inform the Supplier promptly of:

(i)   any complaint or after-sales enquiry concerning the Products which is received by the Distributor;

(ii) any matters coming to its notice which are likely to be relevant in relation to the manufacture, sale, use or development of the Products in the Territory.

The extent of a distributor's responsibilities can vary widely. The supplier will include anything which it perceives as being relevant and necessary to the effective development of its business opportunities in the territory. This clause contains a selection of typical responsibilities, and in deciding on those that are appropriate, a supplier should keep in mind its own long-term goals. Does it intend ultimately to establish a legal presence itself in the territory or to move exclusively to direct selling? If the latter, appropriate thought must also be given to the termination provisions of the agreement. The distributor should also understand the supplier's long-term goals, because this is going to influence both the willingness to become a distributor and the investment to be made in people, premises, support facilities and so on.

Promotion and marketing are always going to be key responsibilities. Some suppliers may have specific requirements in addition to the typical general statement at paragraph (a), perhaps expecting a distributor to attend certain exhibitions, to advertise generally or in specific publications, and to maintain a suitably trained sales force. If the parties have negotiated an advertising budget, a supplier will often agree minimum contributions as a proportion of sales revenues (gross or net). Clause 5 (Advertising and Merchandising Fund) takes this further.

The supply of computer systems often involves pre-sales activities. If the distributor is to have a role in these, which would be normal, this needs to be clearly defined in the agreement.

Every responsibility can be the subject of negotiation, balancing the supplier's requirements and the distributor's resources against the overall background of supply and demand for the distribution opportunity with the particular supplier. A prominent supplier with an established product range and strong reputation will be in a better position to dictate the terms of the distributorship than a new supplier with a product range which is an unknown quantity. All suppliers will want to achieve consistent terms with their distributors wherever possible: to avoid any inference of unfairness as between distributors (with its anti-competitive undertones) and sometimes to comply with express contractual undertakings to treat distributors equally (subject to legal or regulatory differences between territories).

Paragraph (g) is a simple statement of non-competition. It may be necessary to have more detailed provisions, perhaps defining the products of concern to the supplier by listing them in a schedule. The parties will need to keep in mind any rules of competition law as discussed in **CHAPTER 3** which might apply to the proposed arrangements.

Sales targets were discussed earlier in the context of privileged distribution rights, sole or exclusive. Paragraph (h) does give the supplier the right to withdraw these rights if the targets are not met. If it is essential to have a major sole or exclusive distributor in the territory, failure to meet sales targets over a reasonable period should be a ground for termination.

Maintenance of an inventory in the territory can be a costly business for a distributor who should seek more definition of what constitutes an 'appropriate inventory' and should explore the possibility of a sale or return-type arrangement, and agree what is to happen if the supplier changes prices, up or down, in respect of unsold stock.

In paragraph (h) 'best endeavours' are required, as being effort which is both in the distributor's own interests and within its power to control. This is a higher level of commitment than 'reasonable endeavours' used in paragraph (i), and it may be appropriate to make the commitments consistent.

In paragraph (l), reporting requirements could extend to business plans and monthly reports on promotional and marketing activities. The supplier ought to make provisions for audits, annually and whenever it has cause to suspect inaccurate reporting. Payments for audits are usually agreed to be borne by the supplier unless a defined error margin is exceeded when that payment will become the distributor's responsibility.

The use of trade marks on products marketed by the distributor will be a question of strategy for the supplier. If it is keen to build a reputation, the supplier will insist that its trade marks remain on its component products to identify them. This is the stance adopted in paragraph (m). However, the supplier may permit the distributor to market its products under the distributor's name and badging to protect it from any claims by disgruntled end users for any reason.

Paragraph (o) requires the distributor to comply with local laws. This may involve the need to obtain licences or other forms of written authorisation. Some suppliers are concerned to ensure that the form and substance of any such documents are acceptable to them on the grounds that the supplier has a worldwide market for its products and must guard its reputation. When they encounter requirements of this nature, distributors should question their purpose and agree to them only if the supplier can make a justifiable case for them. If the distributor has in fact complied with local regulatory requirements, why is it necessary for their form and substance also to be subject to the supplier's approval? Officiousness should have no place in contracts.

Paragraph (p), which deals with after-sales, can be elaborated and should, in practice, deal with any ongoing responsibility perhaps tying in more with after-sales support for end users. Sub-paragraph (ii) is broad and a distributor should seek to qualify the obligation by such words as 'in the Distributor's opinion'.

4. Supplier's Responsibilities

The Supplier agrees:

(a) *Supply of Master Disks*
To supply a Master Disk for each Software Product.

(b) *Information to the Distributor*
Promptly after the Commencement Date, to provide the Distributor with written information in the English language to enable the Distributor to market, distribute, maintain and support the Products within the Territory, including all current technical information relating to or affecting the use, performance or operation of the Products, and to keep the Distributor fully informed of any additions or modifications to the Products and to supply to the Distributor a copy of any additional or modified Software and any written information at the same time as it is made available to the Supplier's own direct sales personnel or to other distributors of the Products, including up-to-date Supplier's Terms and Conditions of Supply and all current technical information.

(c) *Training*

To provide at the Supplier's premises in the UK such number of the Distributor's employees as the Distributor reasonably requests with such training in the functionality and use of the Products and any subsequent versions, upgrades or enhancements to enable the Distributor to understand the Products fully, the training to take place at the Supplier's premises at no charge to the Distributor except that the Distributor will be responsible for all travel, accommodation and subsistence expenses of its employees.

(d) *Promotional Literature and Further Developments*

To provide the Distributor with adequate quantities of its current promotional literature relating to the Products and to keep the Distributor advised about further developments of the Products, including anticipated release dates, competitive information and any other information that may assist the Distributor in the successful promotion and distribution of the Products.

(e) *Good Faith*

To act in good faith at all times towards the Distributor, and generally to co-operate with the Distributor and to provide as much assistance to the Distributor relating to the Products as the Distributor reasonably requests, including free telephone assistance during the Supplier's normal working hours to the Distributor's employees trained on the Products.

(f) *Support*

To provide a second-line support service for the Software and otherwise to fulfil its obligations in each Licence and Support Agreement with End Users, and to provide an efficient and effective help desk during normal business hours in the Territory, together with an emergency out-of-hours contact service.

(g) *Continuing Development*

To continue to develop, upgrade and enhance the Products to maintain their marketability and competitiveness and to supply a new version of the Master Disk whenever a new version of the Software becomes available.

(h) *Bespoke Work*

To carry out bespoke work to the Software at the Distributor's request from time to time at the time and materials charge rates shown in the Charges Schedule.

(i) *Source Code Deposit Agreement*

To enter into a Source Code Deposit Agreement within 30 days of the Commencement Date, if required by the Distributor, and to ensure that a copy of the latest version of the source code of the Software issued to the Distributor is held in escrow at all times with the party named as escrow custodian in the Source Code Deposit Agreement.

The considerations discussed in relation to the distributor's responsibilities apply equally here. In the nature of these agreements, a list of the supplier's responsibilities tends to be shorter than that of the distributor's, but this should not deter the distributor from seeking to ensure that everything needed from the supplier to make the arrangement successful is negotiated in. Aside from the provision of information and training, it is important that the scope of support to be provided is clearly defined. It may be appropriate to state expressly which services constitute second-line support and which services constitute first-line support for software. Where the supplier is the author of the software being distributed, provision may need to be made for third-line specialist support: the important thing is to define what constitutes each level of support and to set out the responsibilities of each party in relation to the provision of that support. For example, if the distributor is to have any role at all in the process, such as receiving and monitoring fault calls, this needs to be stated.

This agreement anticipates that hardware maintenance will be a separate contract to be entered into directly between the hardware supplier and end user. 'Normal business hours' may require clarification.

Paragraph (a) illustrates one way of facilitating distribution of the supplier's software, by supplying a master disk which the distributor is then licensed to copy and supply under licence to end users, or to the next lower tier in the distribution chain as applicable. The alternative is for the distributor to place orders for software with the supplier, who will supply the product including documentation in its own packaging, or sometimes in re-packaging bearing the distributor's name and logo. 'Badging' of software products is relatively unusual but possible. Where the supplier is providing software to order, clause 6 on product supply and the software licensing clause 7 will require additional provisions to allow for this.

At paragraph (g), the distributor may require an entitlement to a new Master Disk as soon as any permanent change is made to the software, whether or not the change is substantial enough to amount to a new version.

The reference to 'bespoke work' in paragraph (h) is brief, because such work is not generally a feature of distribution agreements. However, if much software development, or even configuration work, is anticipated, at the very least the supplier's development terms and conditions should be appended to the Agreement. As work of this sort is probably going to be done for the distributor's end-user customers, attention will also need to be paid to setting out the respective roles of the supplier and the distributor vis-à-vis the end user, including the extent of their liabilities and ongoing end-user support. All in all, it will be far more appropriate to have a separate specific agreement to deal with such matters.

If the distributor does not have access to source code, a source code deposit agreement is a recommended safeguard for the ultimate benefit of the distributor's end-user customers, as discussed in **CHAPTER 13**.

5. Advertising and Merchandising Fund

(a) The Supplier will establish an advertising and merchandising fund for the purposes of financing advertising matter and literature appropriate for use in marketing the Products in the Territory. Each party will contribute equally to this fund from the proceeds of sale of the Products in amounts to be agreed at each anniversary of the Commencement Date, expressed as a percentage of the net proceeds, and interest accruing to the fund will be added to it. The Distributor will be entitled to draw on this fund for the purposes of purchasing, advertising and merchandising in the Territory, subject to obtaining the Supplier's consent in advance of any expenditure, such consent and the release of monies from the fund not to be unreasonably withheld or delayed. The Supplier will provide audited details of the fund for verification by the Distributor at least once a year and in the event of termination of this Agreement for any reason the then remaining balance in the fund, including interest accrued and unspent, will be withdrawn and repaid in equal proportions to the parties.

(b) The Distributor will not use any advertising or promotional materials in relation to the Products except those supplied or approved by the Supplier.

This needs to link in to any obligations agreed by either party to advertise. There are no specific commitments in this clause but, if a fund is to be established, the parties should ensure that there are clear arrangements for its use, and for approvals to programmes and content.

6. Supply of Products

(a) All of the Products are supplied on the terms and conditions of the Terms and Conditions of Supply and, in addition, in the case of Software on the terms and conditions of the Licence and Support Agreement. Amongst other things, these terms and conditions provide that title to Software does not pass to the Distributor or to those claiming under the Distributor, in any circumstances.

(b) Written orders for Products must be submitted to the Supplier's Order Address and must include for each order the name and address of the End User so that serial numbers can be allocated by the Supplier, together with the location for installation of the Products, the full configuration, requested delivery dates and shipping instructions. No contract for ordered Products will come into being until the Supplier has issued its order acceptance confirming price and delivery details. The Supplier will not unreasonably withhold acceptance of any order.

(c) The Supplier has the right to delete any Product from the Schedule by giving the Distributor 90 days' notice of the deletion. All orders already accepted by the Supplier for any deleted Product will be honoured by supply of the deleted Product or its functional equivalent. Products may be added to this Agreement by means of an amendment signed in accordance with the provisions of this Agreement.

[(d) Each order for Products will constitute a separate contract, and in the event of a material unremedied breach by either party in relation to a single order, the other party will not be entitled to terminate this Agreement.]

The terms on which the supplier's products are supplied to the distributor are an important element of the agreement. Because the supplier is providing its products on its standard terms and conditions of supply, the distributor should give careful thought to the implications in its dealings with end users. It should examine the standard terms and be satisfied that each one is fair and reasonable, and capable of use in the territory. If any term is likely to be a problem or the probable subject of frequent negotiation, it would be as well to discuss this with the supplier at the outset and, if possible, agree a suitable amendment. The distributor should also seek to negotiate a right to review any term or condition with the supplier for the purposes of a specific end-user contract, the supplier not unreasonably to withhold or delay consent to an amendment which will facilitate the distributor's negotiations, without compromising the interests the supplier is trying to protect.

Depending on the way the definitions of 'Product' and 'Price List' have been drafted, the distributor needs to consider the minimum periods of notice needed before a product is materially modified or removed from the product list. The distributor should consider negotiating for the provision of spare parts, and for support to remain available for a minimum period of time which is consistent with its own contractual obligations to end users. It follows that if those obligations are in any way onerous or unusual, it would be prudent to discuss them first with the supplier before entering into them. Distributors all too often overlook the fact that if they grant contractual concessions to end users in connection with product supply, they will be exposed to liabilities which go beyond the terms of supply they have negotiated with the supplier.

Paragraph (d) is an option which, if adopted, would not allow a single instance of breach of contract in relation to an order to provide a ground for termination of the whole agreement. A supplier will need to consider carefully the overall circumstances of its market and the importance of the products being distributed when deciding whether or not to use it.

7. Software Licensing

(a) The Distributor is granted a licence to copy the Master Disk and related Software documentation and to use and demonstrate the Software for the purposes of securing orders from End Users and in order to fulfil deliveries of Software orders only.

(b) The Distributor undertakes:

(i) to use the Software only for demonstration, marketing, and installation and only in accordance with the terms and conditions of this Agreement unless such use is extended by the Distributor obtaining a separate licence to use the Software for the purposes of its business;

(ii) to distribute the Software and its related documentation to End Users only after each End User has signed and returned to the Distributor a Licence and Support Agreement;

(iii) not otherwise to copy the Software without the prior written permission of the Supplier; and otherwise than as permitted under this clause, to keep the Software confidential;

(iv) to use all reasonable endeavours to safeguard the intellectual property rights of the Supplier in the Software, and to report promptly to the Supplier any third party claim relating to the intellectual property rights in the Software after such claim comes to the attention of the Distributor, directly or indirectly, and to co-operate with the Supplier, at the Supplier's expense, in any enforcement or other protective action taken by the Supplier and to report to the Supplier any breaches or suspected breaches of the Software Licence and Support Agreement by End Users which could adversely affect the Supplier's intellectual property rights in the Software.

This clause is structured to confine the distributor's licence to those activities necessary and ancillary to the distribution and marketing of software to end users. If the distributor is itself to be a user, as can apply, for example, if the software is an accounting package, the distributor would need to acquire a separate licence for its own use.

Paragraph (b)(ii) requires the distributor to obtain a signed copy of the supplier's software licence and support agreement before taking delivery of and thus gaining access to the software. Under its responsibilities the distributor is then required to account for these end-user licences. Alternative approaches are possible: rather than the distributor effectively acting as the supplier's agent in licensing the software, a sub-licensing arrangement can be put into place, as discussed in **CHAPTER 12**. The sub-licence could be in a form designated by the supplier, or based on the distributor's own licence, subject to this first being approved by the supplier, so that the supplier can verify that the licence contains equivalent provisions to those in its own licence. Significant factors in the decision about licensing are going to be the distributor's size, experience and apparent administrative capabilities.

Further considerations arise if the software in question is likely to reach the end user through multiple layers of distribution. Suppliers need to treat such arrangements cautiously because there is an inevitable diminution in control, the more intermediaries there are.

This clause presupposes that the software is of sufficient value for shrink-wrap licensing not to be appropriate because of the disadvantages discussed in **CHAPTERS 4 AND 12**.

8. Charges

> (a) The one-time licence fee payable by the Distributor to the Supplier for each copy of the Software licensed to an End User is shown in the Charges Schedule together with discounts applicable to orders for multiple copies for multi-user sites.
>
> (b) The Supplier's charge per End User for its second-line support services is shown in the Charges Schedule together with discounts applicable to multiple End Users and the Supplier's various charge rates for any other services to be provided under this Agreement.
>
> (c) The Charges payable to the Supplier under this Agreement will apply during the first 12 months of this Agreement and cannot then be increased more than once in any 12 months. No increase will exceed the amount of any price increase in the Supplier's local currency, after which it will be subject to conversion to £ sterling at the then prevailing rate of exchange.

This is an additional set of provisions to the standard pricing and payment clause reviewed in **CHAPTER 7**, to illustrate some further specific issues relevant to distribution agreements.

A distributor, being an independent business in its own right, buys products from the supplier at a price and sells them on at a higher price, thus achieving its gross margins. This is in contrast to an agent who is selling on behalf of its supplier principal, usually on a commission basis. Some agreements seek to impose ground rules about pricing policy in relation to the products being distributed. Minimum sale-on pricing requirements are contrary to law, but a supplier can ensure that end-user prices do not *exceed* a given figure. It may perhaps wish to do this as part of a strategy to achieve a given level of market penetration.

This clause is comparatively simple, but distribution prices can in practice become complex. Incentive discounting, designed to steer distributors in the direction of the supplier's business goals is not uncommon, for instance to encourage added value, to persuade a distributor to focus its attention on particular markets or geographical areas, to carry minimum facilities and so on. As long as the structure is of a voluntary nature, leaving the distributor free to make choices, there is unlikely to be any risk of infringement of competition law. Conversely, a dictatorial approach may have implications of anti-competitive practices. It follows that the parties need to consider their arrangements carefully if these are mandatory in nature.

Another area that is frequently the subject of negotiation is the basis for notification of price changes, the scope and frequency of such changes and whether or not they can be applied to existing orders and stocks. Payment terms are discussed in **CHAPTER 7**. Aside from the usual influence of the creditworthiness of the distributor as the supplier's customer, foreign distribution arrangements may require special payment methods. Outside the European sphere (the European Union and the European Free Trade Association ('EFTA')), or areas such as North America and Australasia, it is quite common to see requirements for payment by irrevocable confirmed letters of credit drawn on major banks acceptable to suppliers. In such situations, suppliers often undertake to assist their distributors to comply with local customs formalities and other applicable local regulations.

Consideration should also be given to incorporating a provision enabling price amendments to counter currency fluctuations. These can be confined to movements above or below an agreed level. A 'snake' device' such as this is discussed with reference to the clause on variation of charges in **CHAPTER 7**.

9. Termination

The standard form termination clause, which appears in **CHAPTER 7**, can be used in this agreement but requires elaboration to cover the following concerns which may arise. The standard clause deals with the contingencies of unremedied material breach and insolvency. Further paragraphs may include:

> (a) infringement or threatened infringement by the Distributor of any Mark, trade name, copyright, patent right or other industrial or intellectual property right of the Supplier;
>
> (b) failure by the Distributor to ensure that all payments due to the Supplier in accordance with letters of credit drawn or endorsed by the Distributor in the Supplier's favour are met in full and on time;
>
> (c) in the event of the direct or indirect taking over or assumption of control of the Distributor or substantially all of its assets by any governmental authority or other third party, the Supplier will have the right to terminate this Agreement forthwith.

Paragraphs (a) and (b) are really to reinforce two important areas. Even in the standard clause, an infringement of any of the conditions relating to rights granted or a failure to pay would constitute a material breach. The additional paragraphs are intended to draw specific attention to issues of particular relevance in a supplier/distributor relationship.

It is paragraph (c) that is likely to cause most concern to a prospective distributor. The argument may be raised that the mere fact of being taken over by a third party, in the absence of any evidence that the distributor's ability to discharge its obligations would be adversely affected, should not of itself justify termination. Particularly in circumstances where the distributor is making significant investments in its business in order to comply with the supplier's requirements, there is some merit in this argument. One solution would be to limit the scope of the clause so that the right to terminate is put in the context of the supplier's legitimate concerns. Examples might be where the new owner is a competitor of the supplier or of questionable financial stability, or where there is a history of previous dealings with the supplier which were unsatisfactory, or where the new owner's business reputation or experience could be viewed as potentially detrimental. Whatever qualifications are negotiated, this is not an area where suppliers should readily agree to compromise their subjective judgments with any test of reasonableness.

10. Effect of Termination

(a) On termination of this Agreement for any reason:
  (i) the Distributor will be entitled to fulfil all existing orders for Products to the date of termination;
  (ii) the Supplier will co-operate with the Distributor to enable the Distributor to honour its commitments to End Users for so long as the Distributor has support obligations to End Users;
  (iii) the Source Code Deposit Agreement will continue in full force and effect for so long as the Distributor has support obligations to Customers;
  (iv) no Software Licence and Support Agreements signed and returned by End Users will be affected;
  (v) the licence rights granted to the Distributor under this Agreement will end on termination of this Agreement except as necessary to fulfil existing commitments to provide support services to End Users.

(b) Each party will promptly return to the other party all materials in its possession or control which belong to the other party except to the extent necessary to enable either party to fulfil its continuing obligations.

(c) The Distributor will cease to make any reference to the Supplier or to use the Marks in its promotional materials or otherwise and will cease to hold itself out as an authorised distributor of the Supplier.

(d) No compensation of any kind will be payable by the Supplier to the Distributor, without prejudice to any accrued rights of the parties to the date of termination.

It is important for the parties to give careful thought to the effects of termination. Suppliers will be concerned to ensure that the needs and interests of the end users of their products are safeguarded when a distributor relationship is terminated, particularly if the territory in question is a long way from the supplier's base, and even more so if the distributorship is exclusive.

Distributors in their turn will want to preserve relationships and their reputation on what will be their home ground, and will wish to ensure appropriate support and co-operation from the supplier so that they can meet all their outstanding obligations to end users.

The position becomes much more difficult if the termination is as a result of breach of the agreement, because one or both parties will have lost confidence in the ability or inclination of the other to perform. The issues covered in this clause are representative examples. Other matters may also be relevant, such as the supply of spare parts for a period of time, or the provision of second-line support by the supplier while the distributor continues to have primary support obligations.

It is probably wise for suppliers to ensure that end users are informed of the terminated distributor relationship and of the extent of any remaining rights and authorities of the distributor. It may be appropriate to include a provision that the nature and content of any such notification is subject to agreement by both parties. The requirement in paragraph (c) is an important one and a supplier will wish to ensure that its former distributor does not hold itself out as having a continuing relationship. It is just as appropriate to have an 'exit interview' with the distributor as with a departing key employee.

The issue of compensation often arises, essentially because of the capital investment which may have been made by the distributor relating specifically to the supplier's products and the loss of future revenues. It is often mistakenly believed that, in several jurisdictions, such compensation is a mandatory legal requirement. In fact this highlights another distinction between distributors and agents in most countries.

Under the EC Directive on Self-Employed Commercial Agents[1], commercial agency agreements to which the Directive applies are subject to a number of mandatory provisions to protect the agent. This includes requirements for compensation for terminated agencies. Termination payments may be on either an indemnity or a compensation-for-damage basis. Other matters which are covered include remuneration, exchange of information and notice of termination. The Directive applies to individuals or companies who carry out agency activities in respect of goods (not services alone) within the EU. There are also provisions for compensation in certain other countries, for example Switzerland.

Termination payments can be expensive and suppliers should always take care to understand the prevailing rules in each country where they intend to appoint either a distributor or an agent. Of course, claims for damages for termination in breach of the distribution agreement are another matter, treated like any other breach of contract under the applicable law.

---

1   Directive on Self-Employed Commercial Agents (EC) 86/653, OJ 1986 L 382/17 implemented in the UK by the UK Regulations on Commercial Agents 1993, SI 1993/3053 as amended by SI 1993/3173; www.dti.gov.uk/ccp/topics1/business.htm is a helpful reference site.

CHAPTER 12

Software licences

A. Introduction

Software is an intangible asset which is protected by copyright. The owner has the right to authorise or prohibit copying, as a means of controlling the various ways in which the copyright work may be commercially exploited. 'Copying' includes storing work in any medium by any means and in any form – including storage in computer memory or the uploading and downloading of copyright material over the Internet. There are limited exceptions to software copyright owners' rights: thus a lawful user is entitled to make a back-up copy of a program if this is necessary for its lawful use or to convert from a low level language to a higher level language[1]. Nevertheless, from a user's standpoint, without some sort of agreement with the software owner, or at least an implied consent, it is almost impossible to use software legitimately without infringing the owner's copyright.

Functions of licensing

The law governing copyright and confidentiality offers some basic protection of proprietary rights, but is unlikely to provide the safeguards which a software owner will typically want. This is particularly significant for software which may be used internationally, since copyright law varies from jurisdiction to jurisdiction. The owner will therefore normally grant a licence, that is, a permission to use the software product, to the user, the 'licensee'. A licence does not have to be in formal wording, or even in writing. If the owner hands over a disk containing the program, or displays code on a website without any further limitations, this may be construed as an informal licence.

There are two principal reasons why the owner should control use of software through a written licence. One reason is clarity. As with all agreements, if there is any subsequent argument, it is preferable for the precise terms that have been agreed to be a matter of record. The second reason is that the owner can assert the ownership rights, setting out the conditions for permitting the software to be used with some practical restrictions. The remedy for unauthorised copying or use will then be against the licensee who is in breach of the licence agreement. In this way, the owner preserves the rights of ownership and will be able to enhance, develop and exploit the software product further. It also enables the software to be used by numbers of users.

Licensing and distribution

The 'licensor' party to a licence agreement is not necessarily the owner. The licensor may itself have been granted rights to sub-license or to distribute the software in accordance with terms and conditions which the owner will have set out in the distribution agreement. The licensor should include in any licence agreement a warranty to the effect that it is either the owner of the software product being licensed or is properly authorised to grant the licence. The licensor will also be concerned that a limited form of warranty is provided about the performance and quality standards of the software and that liability limits agreed with the owner are not exceeded. The user should be equally interested in considering the extent of the warranties and limitations of liability contained in a software licence.

If the software is to be distributed through a third party channel, the owner of the software will decide whether each end user is to enter into a licence agreement directly with the owner through the distributor acting as agent for that purpose, or whether the intermediary distributor should be empowered to grant sub-licences to end users on terms approved by the owner. The latter option will reduce the owner's administration efforts, particularly in a situation where the distributor is dealing with many end-user licensees. Many of the owner's interests, including reasonable control over the whereabouts of its software, can be secured by appropriate provisions and indemnities in the distribution agreement. Sometimes multiple layers of distribution are involved, and careful consideration should always be given to the various practical licensing options. Volumes, values and actual distribution channels will all be part of the equation.

Whatever the circumstances, it should be clear that the selection criteria for distributors will be important factors in determining whether to permit software distribution by sub-licensing, and the extent to which the owner is adequately protected, particularly in relation to the financial standing, experience, facilities and quality controls of the distributor. Distribution agreements are discussed in **CHAPTER 11**.

Licensing arrangements

Different kinds of software, and different kinds of business circumstances involving the supply of software, will affect the style of the licence and the licensing method.

Operating software, which governs the way in which the computer will perform its instructions and includes various utility routines to assist the operator in using the systems, will typically be integrated with the hardware supplied by the computer supplier. Commercial application software is rarely written entirely from scratch now. Much is supplied in standard packaged form, with standard licensing terms and conditions. At one extreme, this could be low-priced software products licensed in high volume, as shrink-wrap software, obtained by mail order or off the shelf in a store, generally for personal computers for business or home use, with shrink-wrap licences; or provided online with a click-wrap licence. The other extreme is the individual business solution involving a combination of packaged products, together with extensive customisation of the application software. Here the software licences may be provided as separate documents or assimilated within the services or development contract, as discussed in **CHAPTER 15** or **CHAPTER 16** respectively (unless the contractual arrangements provide that the party commissioning the software is going to be its owner).

In general, licences have become more standardised over the last decade. Opportunities for negotiation of the terms and conditions for shrink-wrap or standard online click-wrap software are unlikely to arise, either because the software is not acquired directly from the licensor, or because the licensor is unwilling to spend time and incur expense without there being a significant financial or strategic incentive. The focus of shrink-wrap licences is on the terms and extent of the permitted uses, and the procedures to be satisfied in order to have the benefit of any warranties that are provided. As stated in **CHAPTER 4**, there are a number of difficulties in legal terms about shrink-wrap licences, notwithstanding that their use is widespread. Yet owners of higher value software products should be circumspect about relying on a licensing system that does not provide evidence of a prospective licensee's agreement to the terms of the licence, or even a clear acknowledgment that they have been read in the first place.

The software will increasingly be supplied online, or on media such as compact discs or tapes to be installed on the machine by the licensee, or for more complex software, to be loaded on to the computer by the supplier. It will usually be accompanied by documentation which may be provided electronically or which consists of a set of user manuals, describing the features of the software product and the instructions for use. It will have been tested by the licensor for performance benchmarks within specific parameters, in terms of its operation on particular computer configurations and systems, and its achievement of the criteria set out in the functional specification or user manual.

The licence will limit the use of the software, and may do so in various ways to cater for a variety of circumstances. It may therefore restrict usage to a maximum number of users at any one time; a maximum number of users of one or more computers within a single geographic location; unlimited use at one site only; several users of different computers in several geographic locations; system licences for networks with limited or unlimited numbers of users; and so on. The licence will normally prohibit any modifications being made to the software, which is to be used as it is supplied or installed.

Source code

Source code is the high level programming language in which software may be written, which uses words as well as symbols and is known as 'human readable'. Source code is generally compiled or translated into object code, which is machine code appearing as a sequence of numbers, for it to work electronically.

In the case of some systems programmed in high level languages, applications developers may supply the software in source code, because the system translates the source code as it is run. This does not fundamentally affect the intended terms of licence, but it does remove from the licensor the additional level of security inherent in most users' inability to convert object code into source code. However, licensing is infrequently of source code since this reveals the secrets of the intellectual property which is the essence of the software's value, that is, it enables the technically conversant to understand how the problem which the software has been supplied to solve, has actually been solved. It follows that the provision of this information carries with it a much greater risk of misappropriation. Object code can be analysed by someone with the appropriate level of technical skill, in order to work back to the source code, but most users will not have this level of expertise and, for complex software, consisting of millions of lines of code, the task would prove uneconomic in most situations.

Source code is also needed in order to carry out any significant modifications to software, and to enable it to be fully maintained. This is why many users who are licensed to use object code are keen to see an escrow arrangement in place when they license software crucial to their businesses to ensure that they can access source in the event of the software supplier's insolvency. Such arrangements are considered in detail in **CHAPTER 13**. Some software suppliers will not be prepared to license their source codes under any circumstances. Others will place a premium price on such a licence, to reflect the fact that the software in question is a significant asset of their business.

A source licence will mirror the provisions of the object licence in many ways: it is simply a 'beefed-up' version, intended to bring into consideration the additional factors, which apply to the supply of sources. A prerequisite to a source licence will often be the existence of a current, valid object licence. Sources are often supplied 'as is', without any form of warranty or support on the basis that the licensee is being supplied with source code as a tool to be used for the purposes of maintaining, modifying and perhaps further developing the software. It would therefore be possible for changes to be made outside the scope of any warranty. Licensors will generally confine the use of the software to the user's business and there will be obligations of confidentiality, coupled with restrictions on any form of commercial exploitative use. Sometimes there will be a requirement for these obligations to be underwritten by insurance. Supplemental source provisions are set out at Section D.

Certain software known as 'open source software' is provided on the basis that it is freely available to use and share, and therefore to modify. It is rarely the case that the owner has waived all rights. It is distributed with a source licence or at least with an explanation of how to access the source code. The Open Source Institute's website[2] sets out some criteria for permitted distribution under its own proposed terms for open source licensing. Normally there will be a disclaimer of warranties and liabilities as for source code generally, and also because there is no payment to the licensor. There is likely to be a requirement for derivative software, ie software developed from the open source software, to be distributed on precisely the same terms as the original open source licence, including the availability of all the source code for examination, use and modification. There may be a positive obligation in future distribution of the software to publish notices of modifications and their dates, a copyright notice and disclaimer of warranty. A fee may sometimes be charged for licensing a software product based on open source software subject to the original source licence, but such software is more likely to be supplied on a different footing, since the source code will be freely available. For example, the Linux open source operating system, an alternative to Microsoft, is essentially supplied free of charge, but users purchase associated services. The example clauses given in this chapter will not be applicable to open source licences, which are not considered further.

Exploiting software commercially

There are various methods of making a profit from software. Conventionally there has been a one-off licence fee, with annual support charges. Rental or subscription charging is growing, as suppliers perceive this to be a more secure and perhaps more profitable revenue stream, charging by individual numbers of users or other basis by which users may vary their requirements over time. Software may alternatively be supplied for a low fee or without charge as a means of supplying other more profitable products and services.

The importance of software licensing for profit is illustrated by the operating system for the first IBM PC. In 1980, IBM was in search of an operating system for the PC it was developing. Bill Gates had already bought the rights to an operating system for his company's use. Microsoft developed the system further and renamed it MS-DOS. IBM became the first licensee, calling the system PC-DOS, for a one-time fee of approximately $80,000, giving IBM the royalty-free right to use the operating system for ever. This is one of the earliest examples in the software industry of promoting strategic value by means of a give-away bargain, and was the foundation of Microsoft's success. IBM had not bought the rights. IBM did not have an exclusive licence. Subsequent makers of machines similar to the IBM PC, like Dell and Compaq, also needed MS-DOS. Again, Microsoft licensed it to them – on Microsoft's terms[3].

246

Demonstration and evaluation licence

A user may wish to try software out before deciding whether or not to purchase a licence, to see if the product in question meets its requirements. It is in the owner's interests to grant an express licence to permit use for a trial period, however short, in order to control and restrict the basis on which the software can be used. It may be in a simple form and considerably limit the owner's obligations. There will otherwise be a significant risk to the owner if the user decides not to take the software after the trial but has meanwhile taken full advantage of its availability. The software may be a demonstration version and the owner may, for security purposes, deliberately stop it working after it has run a specified number of times.

Users' requirements

Prospective licensees should look carefully through the wording of the licence being offered. A user will not want to acquire software to help run some critical aspect of its business, only to find that the licensor reserves the right to withdraw use of the software at a later stage. If a user is not itself licensed to use the source code, it must also investigate the nature of any support being provided by the licensor to maintain and update the software. This is the time to think about arrangements for the user to gain access to the source code if the owner becomes insolvent, or if other circumstances arise which prejudice the user's continuing ability to use the software effectively in its business.

B. The structure of a typical object licence agreement for standard software products

An examination of a comprehensive form of object licence will illustrate most of the material issues which should be thought about by licensors and licensees alike. All of these issues should be considered whenever a software licence is drafted or negotiated, whatever type of licensing arrangement is contemplated. At Section D, source licence clauses are considered.

Terms and conditions

- Definitions*
- Licence to use the Software*
- Duration*
- Supply, Installation and Acceptance*
- Rights in the Software*

247

- Licensee Undertakings*

- Licence Fee

- Payment Terms

- Licensor's Warranties*

- Modifications*

- Escrow*

- Intellectual Property Rights Indemnity

- Indemnity and Limits of Liability

- Termination

- General Contract Provisions.

Schedules

- Licensed Computer System details

- Software descriptions

- Software Development Agreement title and date, if applicable

- Third Party Software

- Fees and charges

C. Specific clauses

In the clause examples considered below, which are those above marked with an asterisk, the owner or supplier of the software will be described as the 'Licensor', and the user as the 'Licensee'.

1. Definitions

'*Licensed Computer System*' means the computer configuration and operational environment specified in the Schedule on which the Software is licensed to run.

'*Software*' means the software products listed in the Schedule, including all their subsequent modifications, upgrades, new versions and releases, which shall form part of the software products, and their related documentation [including where applicable Third Party Software].

'*Software Development Agreement*' means the terms and conditions of the agreement applicable to the development and customisation of the Software if so indicated in the Schedule.

'*Third Party Software*' means all Software owned by a third party, but legally licensed for distribution by the Licensor as part of the Software, as specified in the Schedule.

The purpose of the definition of the 'licensed computer system' is in order to identify where the software is entitled to be used, or to confine it to a particular environment, if this is important. For example, the licence fees for a software product may differ for different sized configurations, and may also be site-related. Special pricing arrangements often exist to take account of multi-user sites and multi-sites. Broadly speaking, software producers seek to amortise their investment in the development of the software by licensing its use and by closing loopholes in what might otherwise lead to open-ended use. This is generally a non-negotiable area, although large volume situations will often give licensees opportunities to negotiate discounts.

The identification of specific central processing units ('CPUs') is often incorporated in the specified details of the licensed computer system so that licensors can reserve their rights to seek additional fees if larger capacity CPUs are subsequently added to licensed computer systems. This is a reasonable requirement where software is being priced to reflect the extent to which it is used. Expanding organisations could otherwise be accused of obtaining something for nothing at the expense of the supplier. In contrast, some software products are more appropriately licensed solely by reference to their numbers of users, regardless of the CPU: this approach is more appropriate for networking and also helps to keep software prices attractively low for small user numbers, but suppliers then need to resolve the problem of control. Can all users be adequately identified and will there be sufficient fee income to generate the required minimum level of profit? This may be linked to payment 'per use' or 'per user'. Automated software can detect what packages are used within organisations, determine usage patterns and match with discounts. For each situation, would-be licensors need to carry out a careful analysis of a market place for the particular product to be able to construct a business case for the most appropriate licensing method.

It is important to identify the software which is the subject matter of the agreement precisely, normally set out in an integral Schedule, so that it is clear what is being paid for and licensed. The licensing provisions should cover any documentation associated with the software and any modifications or upgrades, so that a new licence does not have to be issued with every enhancement. The simplest way of achieving this is to ensure that the definition is comprehensive.

Where software is customised, there should be a software development agreement to cover the development itself. Certain aspects of the transaction will be dealt with in that agreement separately from the licence for standard software, such as the acceptance process, and therefore the software development agreement may need to be cross-referenced in this licence agreement.

The definition of 'third party software' covers the situation in which the licensor is supplying its own software together with another supplier's software. The licensor's terms and conditions need to be consistent with the conditions under which the licensor is licensed by its third party supplier. In paragraph 6(b) below there is a corresponding provision requiring the licensee to have a current valid licence for any third party software it runs on the licensed computer system.

2. Licence to use the Software

(a) The Licensor grants the Licensee a non-exclusive, non-transferable licence to use the Software in object code, including where appropriate Third Party Software, in accordance with these terms and conditions including its termination provisions.

(b) The Licensee is licensed to use the Software [only for its own internal purposes] [at the Licensee's business premises] [for the number of users] [on the Licensed Computer System] [and at the address] [specified in the Schedule to this Agreement] [for its employees and sub-contractors who need to access and use the Software].

(c) The Licensee may use the Software temporarily on an alternative processor to the Licensed Computer System for the purposes of disaster recovery, and not more than twice a year for the purposes of testing disaster recovery procedures.

(d) The Licensee may transfer the Software to an alternative processor forming part of the Licensed Computer System or may relocate the Licensed Computer System [within the country of supply] provided that written notice is given to the Licensor. Any transfer of the Software to a processor outside the Licensed Computer System requires the prior written consent of the Licensor and may be subject to an additional licence fee.

(e) Should the Licensee wish to upgrade or change the Licensed Computer System, notice must be given to the Licensor. The details in the Schedule to this Agreement will be amended accordingly and an upgrade licence fee paid by the Licensee to the Licensor for the upgraded or changed Licensed Computer System, to enable the Licensee to continue to use the Software.

(f) If the Licensee sells or disposes of the Licensed Computer System, it will ensure that all copies of the Software have previously been deleted.

(g) The Licensee agrees to comply with any additional Third Party Software conditions notified to it on or before delivery of any Third Party Software (including if so required the execution and return of a Third Party Software

Licence) and to indemnify the Licensor against any action by a Third Party Software owner as a result of any breach by the Licensee of such conditions.

This statement expressly reserves the licensor's own proprietary rights over the software, and at paragraph (a) entitles the licensee alone to use the software. Sometimes the right of use is specifically extended to associated companies of the licensee, but this should not be agreed to by the licensor without considering the implications and consciously deciding to accept them. There will be a cost implication for the licensor, who might lose out on the extension of the licence by default. There is also the control aspect in that third party associated companies are not themselves parties under this arrangement and the licensee must procure that the associates comply with the terms and conditions. This is far less satisfactory than a direct licence. Moreover, the licensor is entitled to know who is using its software.

Software licences are normally 'non-exclusive'. An exclusive licence implies that no other licence will be granted, usually for a particular territory or other defining domain, such as a particular business sector, and that the licensor itself will not use the software. It is more often encountered in software distribution agreements or in publishing literary content.

The restrictions on the use of the software in these example clauses are common. The options in paragraph (b), governed by the inclusion or exclusion of some or all of the words in square brackets, determine the scope of the licence. The licence may be restricted to a limited number of users, or to an identified computer system located at a specified site as discussed in clause 1 above. Some licences also restrict usage to the licensee's employees, but this would effectively prevent the software being used in legitimate circumstances by external consultants or contractors. Most licensees will readily accept use which is confined to their business premises and which is limited to their own internal business requirements coupled with restrictions on any form of commercial exploitative use.

The tighter restrictions which arise by linking use to an identified computer system (or systems) located at a specified site (or sites) and, in paragraphs (d) and (e), by requiring notification of changes of processor, licensed system or location are at the root of the licensing issue: should there be unrestricted use once the licence fee has been paid, or at least use limited only by a defined number of users, or should use be much more closely controlled? Licensors frequently opt for the latter approach in order to safeguard their anticipated revenues from software products and, when they do so, negotiation of a broader approach will be feasible only if a very large contract is in prospect.

Software is expensive to develop and owners price their licences to recoup and profit from their investment. It follows that there will be a minimum number of licences needed to achieve the desired level of profit, and owners will not wish to

251

see their financial opportunities eroded because their licences fail to take account of the possibility of multiple use. Where large numbers of users are involved, costs are likely to be significant and there is often some scope for negotiation in these situations.

It is difficult to enforce restrictions on use of the software and the licensor may wish to reserve the right to enter the licensee's premises or to access the licensee's systems via a modem, to check on the number of users. However, there are security implications from the licensee's point of view in this approach. It would be reasonable for a licensee to require advance notice, which could, of course, lessen the impact.

Paragraph (c) allows for disaster recovery either for testing purposes or because of an actual emergency at third party sites, without either party suffering the administrative overhead of seeking or giving permission on each occasion. For a real disaster recovery, proper licensed use of software is not going to be the first thing on the licensee's mind, and yet is strictly a short-term extension of use.

A licence that is too restrictive will cause increased negotiating effort and extra administrative needs for notification when a licensee is seeking permission to move from the original terms.

Along with clause 5 (Rights in the Software) below this is the most important part of the licence because it is in these areas that disputes are most likely to arise.

3. Duration

(a) This licence commences on the date of installation of the Software and will subsist for a minimum term of one calendar year. It will then continue in effect unless terminated by the Licensee on 90 days' notice of termination, given on the last day of such minimum term or at any time afterwards, subject to the other termination provisions in this Agreement.

(b) The Software licence provisions are independent of any Software provisions, to the extent that the Licensee's licence to use the Software will survive any termination of the Licensor's obligations to support the Software. Similarly Software supplied without support will be validly licensed.

(c) Termination of these licence provisions will automatically terminate any support obligations by the Licensor for the Software.

This clause states the duration of the licence. It may be stated to be for an initial term and then continue in existence with provisions for termination, or it may be for a limited period of time. There are numerous variations in the wording. Major software suppliers certainly favour limited initial term licences, and some offer

252

their customers a range of term options (for example, one, three or five years, with discounted licence fees available if the longer term options are taken up at the outset). Such licences generally provide for successive renewals on equivalent terms, but at the then current licence fees. Automatic renewals may be subject to a right of either party to decline renewal – a point that prospective licensees should be wary of, and seek to negotiate around if their business is significant enough to give them a negotiating position.

Another growing trend is towards software support being bundled in with licences. The ultimate position is for the two aspects to be inseparable: the licence terms include support of the product for so long as the licence remains in effect. In other cases, while support is incorporated into the licence agreement, it is a severable part and a licensee can elect to continue to use the software without support. The provisions of competition law apply here: an obligation to pay for support irrespective of service being provided as a precondition to keeping the right to use the software would be unacceptable, and thus there should be a choice for the licensee to continue the licence without the support service. This may seem to be an attractive option to the licensee from the perspective of saving on costs, once the software has become fully stabilised on the licensee's computer system, so that the licensee feels confident enough to purchase ongoing support on an occasional, ad hoc, time and materials basis. There is a danger in this, however, because many software suppliers will not maintain a guaranteed support capability for more than one or two immediately previous versions of a software product, and new versions are normally released to users as part of the support arrangements. A licensee who does not keep the support option going may find that its software becomes out of date and can no longer be supported.

Thus, paragraphs (b) and (c) in the example above are necessary only if the agreement is also going to cover an option for support provisions. These paragraphs then entitle the licensee to continue to use the software even if the licensor has ceased to support it. If the software is going to be important to the licensee's business, the licensor should not be able to prevent the licensee's continuing normal use for so long as the licensee complies with all the licence conditions (even if the licensor goes out of business). Termination for cause is dealt with as a general administrative provision in **CHAPTER 7**.

4. Supply, Installation and Acceptance

(a) The programs comprising the Software will be supplied in object code, together with one copy of any related documentation.

(b) Supply of the Software will be made to the address of the Licensee shown in this Agreement [on the date agreed between the parties]. [The Licensor will make all reasonable efforts to keep to the installation date agreed with the Licensee but under no circumstances will the Licensor be liable for damages or costs arising from any delay in delivery.]

> (c) [If the Licensor is responsible for installation of the Software, it will run such commissioning tests as it considers necessary to ensure that the Software is installed correctly, and when these tests are completed, the Licensee will be deemed to have accepted the Software. This is applicable to Software, and also to new releases and new versions of the Software.] [The Software is deemed to be accepted as of the date of installation (provided that such acceptance is subject to the satisfactory performance by the Software during the seven days following installation).] [However, this provision does not apply to any Software to which the Software Development Agreement applies, which sets out separate acceptance procedures.]
>
> (d) Use of the Software is conditional on payment of the licence fee together with any other charges, as shown in the Schedule.

Other than the provision at paragraph (a) clarifying what is being supplied, this clause is not necessary for software collected or sent by post or transmitted electronically, and which can be installed without any difficulty. In more complex situations, this wording provides terms controlling the delivery situation, any conditions about the installation of the software, and the criteria for acceptance.

The alternatives in the square brackets in paragraph (b) will determine whether the licensor is prepared to commit to a specific date and whether it is critical for the licensee for there to be a definite date for the arrival of the software. A licensor will often be reluctant to be precise about an installation date, especially if time is made of the essence. The nature of the software will be a determining factor. There is bound to be an element of unpredictability about an actual date if the software is still under development and/or its documentation is still not finalised at the time of order acceptance. Unless the contract is a high value or strategically important one, the licensor may well be dictatorial, confining its contractual commitment, for example, by delivery of the product on uncorrupted media and dealing through its warranty and support procedures with any problems which arise afterwards. If much more is at stake, the licensee acquires a negotiating position and might, for example, gain agreement to liquidated damages for late delivery. These are considered in **CHAPTER 9**.

Paragraph (c) concerns the point at which the software is accepted by the licensee. As drafted, the licensor makes the decision about the licensee's acceptance of the software. Particularly where the software being supplied is expensive and complex, licensees should expect to participate in these decisions, to run their own acceptance tests and to retain rights of rejection if the software is not finally acceptable. The event of acceptance can be used as a benchmark for various purposes: failure to achieve acceptance by an agreed date can trigger rights of rejection; the date of acceptance is often expressed to be the date of commencement of the warranty period; payment terms are sometimes geared to acceptance. Where specific acceptance tests are agreed, whether these are controlled by the licensor or the licensee, it is vital that they are clearly and unambiguously defined and incorporated in a schedule to the licence agreement. Acceptance tests are more fully considered in connection with software development agreements in **CHAPTER 16**.

5. Rights in the Software

(a) No title or rights of ownership, copyright or any other intellectual property in the Software, including all upgrades, modifications, new versions and releases of the Software, is or will be transferred to the Licensee.

(b) The Licensee understands that the Software contains proprietary information and agrees that [except in accordance with an express written authority signed by an authorised signatory of the Licensor,] it will not provide or otherwise make any of the Software and/or related documentation available for any reason to any other person, firm, company or organisation [whether for outsourcing purposes or otherwise].

(c) The Licensee will not copy or permit the Software to be copied, except for reasonable security and backup purposes. Any copies made shall include all copyright or other proprietary notices.

(d) The Licensee will ensure that all of its relevant employees, agents and sub-contractors are advised that the Software constitutes confidential information and that all intellectual property rights in it are the property of the Licensor, and the Licensee will [use all reasonable endeavours to] ensure that its employees, agents and sub-contractors comply with all of the terms and conditions of this clause.

(e) Recognising that the Software has significant commercial value to the Licensor, the Licensee agrees to indemnify the Licensor in respect of any losses or expenses incurred by the Licensor as a result of the unauthorised use of the Software by any third party, whether through misuse of the Software object code by the Licensee or through any other breach by the Licensee of this Agreement or through the negligence of the Licensee or through any other cause.

Negotiation of this clause is likely to focus on the outsourcing issue in paragraph (b), the control of employees issue in paragraph (d) and the general indemnification in paragraph (e). As with the other provisions, these will be non-negotiable unless the proposed contract is a significant one for the licensor.

The outsourcing issue has proved contentious, if a licensee, either from the commencement of a licence or at some later stage, decides to have its IT systems managed by a specialist third party. This may involve the use of the same or alternative IT systems, at the licensee's premises or remotely, and with or without the continued involvement of the licensee's IT staff.

Some outsourcing providers have their own licence for certain software used by a number of their customers, However, a growing number of software suppliers are requiring additional or supplemental licence agreements to cater for this situation, for which additional fees may be required. Licensees and outsourcing providers contend that nothing has changed and that the software is still going to be used as originally contemplated and licensed: solely for the purposes of the licensee's business. To overcome the concern about access to the software by a third party (namely, the outsourcing provider), an offer to sign a confidentiality undertaking is often made. This will not usually satisfy the licensor who will want an outsourcing provider to accept all of the terms and conditions of the licence agreement whilst ensuring that these continue to bind the licensee.

The licensor's requirement for a fee is a commercial matter governed by the usual considerations which determine pricing policies. Licensors have to become involved in additional administration in order to establish the new arrangements and thereafter to monitor adherence to the licence terms, and they frequently experience a surge in support requests following the implementation of outsourcing. Additionally, licensors face the perceived risk that less scrupulous outsourcing providers might abuse such arrangements, in breach of the licence terms, by using software for their own benefit or that of their other customers, when no such uses are licensed and paid for. It is often difficult to discover such breaches and licensors should not be criticised if they appear reluctant to widen the scope of their licensing terms. Outsourcing agreements are the subject of **CHAPTER 17**.

Paragraph (c) covers permitted copying for security and back-up purposes. Licensees may wish to consider specifying audit and insurance purposes in addition. Making necessary back-up copies cannot lawfully be prohibited by the licensor.

Licensors always worry about employees of their licensees leaving their employment with unauthorised copies of software in their possession. The provisions in paragraph (d) are designed to protect the licensor who is also the owner of the software, by imposing on the licensee an obligation to control and constrain those of its employees who are likely to gain access to the software. However, licensees should resist the imposition of an absolute requirement and at least seek to contain it to 'reasonable endeavours'.

The indemnity in paragraph (e) is not unreasonable as drafted. Much stronger and more comprehensive wording is often used. If the licensor is not also the owner of the software, the indemnity may extend to the third party owner. However, open-ended indemnities will not be satisfactory to licensees, who are naturally concerned to limit their exposure to risk, and this paragraph is one where there may be some scope for negotiation, to define more precisely the indemnity circumstances and possibly to cap the liability.

The intellectual property rights indemnity, discussed in **CHAPTER 7**, should always be included in a software licence from the licensor's point of view.

6. Licensee Undertakings

(a) The Licensee acknowledges that it is licensed to use the Software only in accordance with the express terms of this Agreement.

(b) The Licensee undertakes:

   (i)   to satisfy itself that the Software meets the needs of its business. It is the sole responsibility of the Licensee to determine that the Software is ready for operational use in the Licensee's business before it is so used;

   (ii) to allow the Licensor to study its information and data used with the Software for the purpose of rectifying any problems with the Software;

   (iii) to ensure that the operating system and compiler and any other software with which the Software will be used is either the property of the Licensee or is legally licensed to the Licensee for use with the Software. The Licensee shall indemnify the Licensor in respect of any claims by third parties and all related costs, expenses or damages in the event of any alleged violation of third party proprietary rights which results in any claims against the Licensor.

(c) The Licensee warrants that the Software and all copies will remain under its control and that it will take all reasonable precautions to safeguard the Software against unauthorised use.

(d) The Licensee hereby acknowledges that it is the best judge of the value and importance of the data held on the Licensed Computer System and that it takes sole responsibility for instituting and operating all necessary back-up procedures (for its own benefit) to ensure that data integrity can be maintained in the event of loss of data for any reason.

(e) If the Licensee intends to attempt the decompilation of any of the Software for error correction or any other purpose in the exercise of derived statutory rights, the Licensee will first give reasonable notice to the Licensor of its intention.

This gives the licensee clear obligations with regard to the correct use of the software in addition to those elsewhere. Paragraph (b)(i) assumes a knowledgeable licensee and proper acceptance procedures, and also that the licensee is not relying on specialist consultancy advice from the licensor, such as might be given in connection with customised software.

Paragraph (e) reflects the UK Regulations[4] which gave effect to the 1991 EC Software Directive. Those regulations entitle a lawful licensee to attempt its own error correction by copying or adapting, but, unlike the prohibition on restriction of decompilation or reverse engineering, this entitlement may be excluded by contract. It is arguable that error correction is capable of contractual prohibition if it involves a need to decompile object code software, which will be the usual case.

To give a licensor the opportunity of providing the code required or of testing the position at law, notice is required of any intention to decompile for error correction or other purposes.

7. Licensor's Warranties

(a) The Licensor warrants that it has good title or is otherwise authorised to license the Software to the Licensee.

(b) The Licensor represents and warrants to the Licensee that at the time of delivery of the Software to the Licensee it is a complete, accurate and up-to-date copy of the current release.

(c) The Software is designed to conform to the Software product specification [user guide] applicable at the time of the Licensee's order. However the Licensor does not warrant that the Software will work without interruption or that it is error-free.

(d) The Licensor's sole obligation in the event of non-conformity will be:

   (i) in the case of Software developed or owned by the Licensor to remedy any non-conformity of the Software to its specification [or user guide]; and

   (ii) in the case of Third Party Software to obtain and supply a corrected version where there is a demonstrated non-conformity to specification,

provided in either case that the Licensor has been notified of the non-conformity within 90 days of the date of delivery to the Licensee, or if any commissioning tests are begin carried out by the Licensor, the date on which they are completed, whichever is the later. This warranty does not apply to Software developed under the terms of the Software Development Agreement, which is subject to any warranty and related provisions set out in that Agreement.

(e) The above constitutes the only warranties provided by the Licensor in respect of the Software. The obligations and liabilities of the Licensor set out in this Agreement replace all implied guarantees and warranties, including without limitation, any warranty of satisfactory quality or fitness for a particular purpose which is the Licensee's responsibility to determine.

(f) The Licensee acknowledges that:

   (i) the Software has not been produced to meet individual Licensee specifications;

   (ii) the Software cannot be tested in advance in every possible operating combination and environment;

   (iii) it is not possible to produce Software known to be error-free in all circumstances.

(g) The Licensor recommends, and will provide if so requested, support and maintenance for the Software.

The first warranty confirms the licensor's right to license the software. This right will be set out in conjunction with the provision discussed in **CHAPTER 7** in relation to indemnification in respect of infringement claims.

The licence defines the commitments the licensor is prepared to give about the software and especially to exclude warranties given under statute, such as 'fitness for purpose'. Ninety days is fairly standard within the industry as a software warranty term. The licensor will not want an open-ended commitment, and it would be normal for a software support agreement to come into effect on expiry of the warranty.

CHAPTER 4 includes some discussion on statutory liabilities. Software is arguably not goods but should be assumed to be so for safe drafting purposes. The industry norm is to resist any 'fitness for purpose' obligations, principally because of the impossibility of foreseeing all the potential application uses of most hardware and software products, and because the licensor has no control over how the software might be used. Conformity to a specification or technical description is a normal warranty requirement that the licensor should be able to meet, particularly since the contents of the specification will have been produced by the licensor in the first place. Conformity to a user guide is another common, although often much less precise, warranty standard.

The licensee should make sure of having the opportunity to check the specification before entering into the agreement. Some licensors limit the warranty to 'substantial' or 'material' conformity to specification. Licensees should resist this. Since the specification is within the licensor's control, it is reasonable to expect the software to conform in all respects to the covering documentation.

Paragraph (c) is appropriate for standard software. The licensor asks the licensee to recognise that the software has not been developed to individual requirements and may not be perfect. This is not an unreasonable limitation on complex software which may be licensed to a number of users.

8. Modifications

The Licensor reserves the right to make improvements, substitutions, modifications or enhancements to any part of the Software [provided that the functionality and performance of the Software will not as a result be materially affected to the Licensee's detriment].

The licensor will want to reserve the right to introduce a new version of the software or to amend or enhance it between the time the contract is made and the time of delivery. The definition of 'software' includes modifications made after delivery, but this clause also enables the licensor to introduce them prior to initial installation, with the safeguard for the licensee that it will not have to forgo any features which might have influenced its decision to purchase the licence. Where support is contracted and often also during warranty periods, the software definition would be extended to include upgrades.

It will not be in either party's interest for rights of modification to be excluded. However, the licensee must ascertain that its use of the software will not be made more difficult because of any amendments. For example, functionality and performance may not be impaired, but are there any significant operational changes, or adverse effects on its ability to interface with other products?

This clause is not relevant if the software has been customised to meet an individual customer's requirements.

9. Escrow

> The Licensor has established certain source code deposit ('escrow') arrangements covering the source code and documentation for the Software with an escrow custodian. While this Agreement continues to exist, the Licensee will be entitled to receive the protection of such escrow arrangements subject to entering into a separate written escrow agreement with the Licensor and the escrow custodian.

The licensor may not have any escrow arrangements in force and may not want the trouble and cost of introducing them.

However, it is becoming increasingly common as a reasonable requirement by the licensee for complex software important to its business, which needs updating continually, if source code is not being obtained. This protection should therefore be considered by the licensee, at least in the event of the licensor's insolvency, to enable it to make arrangements for the continued support of the software.

The nature and purpose of source code deposit agreements are discussed in **CHAPTER 13**.

D. Supplemental provisions required for a source code licence

1. Definition

> 'Source' means any Software in a form designated by the Licensor as a 'source' option and/or 'listings' option in its Software product description and any related materials, including without limitation flow charts, logic diagrams, binaries and object codes, source codes and listings whether in machine or human readable form and all improvements, modifications or updates to any of these materials provided to the Licensee.

This is a reasonably comprehensive definition of 'source', which embraces object code and is intended to include every written or machine-produced material which constitutes or relates to the software, in essence, all of the 'know-how' which exists in connection with the software.

2. Supplemental licence terms

> The terms and conditions of the applicable Object Licence continue to apply to the Software, together with the following additional provisions in respect of Source.
>
> (a) Source is provided without warranty or support services of any kind, other than provision of documentation at the Licensor's sole option.
>
> (b) The Licensee will have the right to modify any Source provided by the Licensor in order to further the development of proprietary products of the Licensee, provided that such proprietary products do not infringe any of the legal or equitable rights of the Licensor relating to its proprietary information or trade secrets or copyrights and further provided that all unmodified portions of Source remain subject to the terms of the Software Object Licence.
>
> (c) The Licensor will not be obliged to provide warranty or support services in respect of any object code versions of modified Source.
>
> (d) Source may be used in any computer system for which the Software is currently licensed for use by the Licensor.
>
> [(e) The Licensee will insure the Source against theft or misuse in an amount agreed with the Licensor, and arrange for the Licensor's interest to be noted on the policy of insurance, and will provide evidence of such insurance to the Licensor at any time upon request.
>
> [(f) The Source is licensed to the Licensee for an indefinite term, subject to the termination for cause provisions in the Software Object Licence.

> (g) The Licensee undertakes that it will use the Source only for the purposes of its business and not for any form of commercial exploitation, and that it will not supply any copy of all or any part of the Source to any third party for any purpose without the prior written consent of the Licensor.

It is generally desirable to have a source licence agreement which is a self-contained document incorporating all of the terms of licence, but for illustrative purposes the above supplemental terms emphasise the very issues which need to be considered in addition to the terms of the object licence. 'Object Licence' will thus have been defined. For the most part, these terms are self-explanatory. In this example, the licensee's use of source remains confined to the purposes of its business: it is not being handed a product which it can freely market for its own commercial benefit. There will be occasions, however, when a source licence might be negotiated to permit more or less unrestricted use. The paragraphs and square brackets also tend to be negotiable areas, and some licensors will wish to expand paragraphs (e) and (g) to include fairly comprehensive indemnities where the source is a high value asset of the licensor.

An indefinite licence term may risk being regarded as a sale, and the use of paragraph (f) needs to be viewed in this context. If a source is being supplied for a very high price, the licensor may be prepared to take this risk.

It should be noted that a source licence which has been negotiated commercially and paid for will usually be much wider in scope than one which is granted by operation of an event of release in a source code deposit agreement. The latter will usually confine the licensed use to maintenance for the purpose of running the object code version of the software only.

1   Copyright (Computer Programs) Regulations 1992, SI 1992/3233; Copyright Designs and Patents Act 1988, ss 50A, 50B and 50C.
2   www.opensource.org.
3   The story is related in *The Road Ahead* by Bill Gates, Penguin 1996, and in *Accidental Empires* by Robert X Cringely, Penguin 1996.
4   Copyright (Computer Programs) Regulations 1992, SI 1992/3233; Copyright Designs and Patents Act 1988, ss 50A, 50B and 50C.

CHAPTER 13

Source code deposit 'escrow' services

A. Introduction

Software licensing contracts require licensees to conform to specified restrictions in their use of the software, such as a requirement to keep the software confidential, in order to protect the owner's asset and the investment made in developing and exploiting the software. The majority of software is licensed to users in object code only, that is, a machine-readable format which is unintelligible to lay people. This is a simple and effective way of limiting unauthorised use. As long as the licensee can rely on the supplier for support and enhancement of the software, it will not require access to the source code of the software, which can easily be understood by programmers familiar with the language and the application in question. The software owner will retain the source code, which will often constitute its most valuable asset, keeping it secret and secure.

Sometimes source code licences are available from suppliers under more stringent licensing conditions and at prices, which are higher than for object code versions. But more frequently suppliers will decline to license source code under any circumstances.

Bona fide users will not be interested in a supplier's source codes for ulterior purposes. Indeed, many of them would lack the expertise to do anything with them if they did have them. But astute users do worry about the position they might find themselves in if their supplier ceased business for any reason or failed to support software important to their business in a satisfactory manner.

1. Regular support and enhancement

Some software needs regular support and enhancement to keep working accurately, such as a payroll system, which will need to be modified whenever there are changes in taxation principles or other regulatory matters, or because changes in operating systems and environments can lead to the need to change application programs.

The problem for users lies in being able to continue to use software important to their business where it needs constant support by a supplier who goes out of business and leaves the user stranded. In recent years there have been numerous examples of the apparently safest companies going into receivership and liquidation.

If a supplier of software on which a user is dependent disappears or becomes ineffective, the user may wish to be able to take the source code to alternative computer experts, either in-house or externally, so that the software can be understood for the purposes of support or enhancement. In reality, particularly where very complex and specialised software is concerned, the comfort of being able to make effective use of sources will often be illusory. But it does at least present a chance to get out of difficulty.

Of course, many software products, particularly of the low-value high-volume package variety, are used continually without being modified. They are not critical to the success or failure of a business, or they are not particularly complex, and for these, escrow arrangements are irrelevant.

2. Use of 'Escrow'

Users may ask their suppliers to place a copy of source code on deposit with a neutral third party custodian for release to the user in prescribed situations. The agreement governing these arrangements is known as a 'source code deposit' or 'escrow' agreement and is usually a tripartite agreement between the licensor, the licensee and an independent third party 'escrow custodian' who holds a copy of the source code.

The arrangement enables the software owner to protect the confidentiality of the software by giving the end user access only to object code under normal conditions, yet at the same time giving the user perceived security by allowing a licence to the source code to be released by the escrow custodian for continuing support in certain clearly defined circumstances.

The principal situation for which the escrow arrangements are effected is that, if the supplier goes out of business, the user is entitled to obtain the source code from the escrow custodian for the sole purpose of continuing to use the software, supporting and enhancing it as required. This will not solve all the problems associated with insolvency, but will at least allow the user an opportunity it would not otherwise have for continuing to make use of the software.

The escrow agreement may also be used in other circumstances. The user may obtain source code under an escrow agreement in order to take over support of the software if the supplier is still active as a business but defaults under the terms of the support agreement between the supplier and the user.

The advantage of escrow for owners is in the assurances that can be given to prospective customers. The benefit for users lies in the confidence of being able to run software successfully in the long term.

A clause in the licence agreement to state that the user could have the source code in the event of the supplier's insolvency would not be effective in itself. On liquidation, the licensor company would have no further rights itself to supply source code. Under the terms of the Insolvency Act 1986, the ownership of any remaining assets of the licensor, including source code, will automatically pass to the receiver or liquidator who will be under no obligation to hand it over to anyone. Moreover, the user will have no guarantee that the source has been kept up to date and in a format which would be of any use.

3. Background

'Escrow' is the legal term often used for these agreements. It means that a third party holds something (traditionally this has always been a deed) until certain circumstances agreed between the two principal parties occur. Then the third party delivers it to the designated party. The item is held 'in escrow' until the specified event occurs.

Historically, a deed was delivered by being physically handed over. This meant that the person who handed it over considered himself bound by it. But in property matters, a deed was regarded as being delivered when it was signed and sealed. Yet the signing and sealing would take place before the transaction was completed, for example when the money for the land was paid. Once a document had been delivered, it could not be taken back, but there was still the risk that completion might not happen. This is how the concept of 'escrow' evolved. The document was signed and sealed and therefore irrevocably delivered – but subject to the specified conditions, so that it did not take effect until those conditions had been met.

The concept has also been extended to 'escrow accounts', referring to the deposit of funds in a bank. The funds are held on the basis that if a third party can produce evidence that the depositor has an obligation which cannot be discharged from any other fund or in any other way; there is authorisation to release the funds to that third party. This is analogous to the use of the word 'escrow' to apply to certain circumstances in which software is held.

Here, the conditions which trigger delivery to the designated party, the licensee, of the software held 'in escrow' by the third party, the escrow custodian, will usually be the licensor's insolvency, although the circumstances may be extended to other conditions to trigger the release of the source code.

4. Negotiating factors

The client of the software owner should consider, at the time of negotiating the licence agreement or the software development agreement, whether escrow arrangements should be included in the transaction.

A clause is sometimes found in one of these types of agreements recording the supplier's intentions to put the source code on deposit. The supplier should take care that it is not going to be bound by provisions, which it has not taken the opportunity to consider in the heat of the moment, when trying to get the principal transaction finalised. The customer should ensure that if the clause reflects an intention, the intention is put into effect.

The user will expect to gain access to source code in the event of the supplier's bankruptcy or liquidation as a matter of course, following procedures put in place to safeguard the owner's interests.

However, discussion may be extended to focus on other release contingencies, and here both parties can make legitimate points.

The ability of a user to secure a source code deposit agreement from its supplier is going to be heavily influenced by the value of the business to the supplier. For unique software commissioned by the user, who is paying for the design itself, where copyright is to be retained by the supplier, the user will be in a stronger position to insist on escrow. Where this has been established, the parties move on to discuss the terms of the agreement. The supplier will be concerned to restrict the circumstances of release and also to restrict the authorised uses to which the sources can be put in the event of release.

Sometimes there will be additional considerations. These can be the subject of lengthy negotiations, justifiable only if high value or unique software is involved. There is the added difficulty that, whoever the selected escrow custodian is, it will be difficult to vary the wording of an arrangement which is already in place between the escrow custodian, the software owner and other licensees, and any variations will need the agreement of the escrow custodian as the third party to the contract.

Escrow custodians and licensors will often resist the negotiation of amendments to an agreement which is not satisfactory to the licensee. The escrow custodian may be running a system for many different source codes, and thus want to standardise. For packaged software, the licensor may claim that the system will be less manageable with individually negotiated agreements than where there is one deposit of source code by the licensor made under the terms of a master agreement, each licensee entering into a related subsidiary agreement with the escrow custodian and the licensor.

Where strength lies in the negotiating process will depend on the original licensing transaction itself. At one extreme, if the software is packaged, already in escrow, and there are many users, the supplier will be less likely to concede to individual representations for amendment of existing terms and conditions. However, if the software is being developed for an individual and important customer who is insisting on source code deposit as part of the overall arrangements, that customer will be able to influence significantly the terms and conditions of the deposit agreement. The rights and obligations between the owner, the licensee and the software custodian must be adequately balanced.

Once set up, the agreement can be terminated unilaterally by the owner only if a replacement custodian has been appointed on similar terms, which are reasonably acceptable to the user – unless the original escrow custodian becomes insolvent, when it will be in the immediate interest of the owner to terminate the agreement in any case.

5. Different types of arrangements

There are different forms of escrow agreements. A software developer may have designed software specifically for a single user, and have licensed it, keeping the copyright in the materials and retaining all rights to the source code. The software covered by the escrow agreement will be unique and the agreement will be between the software owner, the licensee and the escrow custodian.

Alternatively, the software may be packaged, standardised, software with many users. In this case, the supplier should deposit the standard software once, under the terms of a master agreement between the supplier and the escrow custodian. Subsidiary agreements will be executed between the supplier, the escrow custodian and each participating licensee, related to the master agreement.

If the software is packaged but significantly enhanced for individual users, it will be a matter for negotiation between the supplier and user whether a source code with the separate enhancements should be deposited individually for that user.

Even where the user succeeds in broadening the circumstances of release beyond liquidation, an escrow custodian is desirable. The source code deposit agreement should be drafted so that the escrow custodian is not called upon to make any decisions but merely to hand over the source code on receiving a sworn statement from the user. If the supplier wanted to question the truth of the statement, this would be a matter to be decided by the courts. Meanwhile the user will be able to continue to use the software. The use of an escrow custodian removes the possibility of arguments between the supplier and the user about whether or not the source should be released by the escrow custodian.

Problems may occur where a relationship of parent and subsidiary exists. Quite often, software will be supplied by an English subsidiary of a foreign company who is the owner. It must be the owner who is party to the agreement. It may prove difficult to obtain an escrow agreement from the parent company, or any escrow arrangement which is made will be based in the parent's country. This may complicate the prospects of a speedy release if the circumstances for release are triggered.

The parties may prefer to have a contractual arrangement whereby the licensor's parent steps into its shoes in order to fulfil its obligations instead of offering an escrow service.

Some source code deposit arrangements are between the escrow custodian and software owner only. These will give users the opportunity to identify themselves to an escrow custodian and claim source software in the prescribed circumstances but they will not have a direct contractual relationship with the escrow custodian. This is an unsatisfactory form of protection, because if the escrow custodian does not release the software, the licensee will have no direct means of enforcement. Nevertheless, it is sometimes used where there are a large number of licensees and the values of individual licences do not justify individual agreements.

6. Escrow custodian

One of the difficulties encountered by suppliers is to find an acceptable escrow custodian. Its characteristics must include reliability, integrity, knowledge and experience. Although it will be exercising a neutral role, it should be a party who understands both the legal and the information technology requirements, and who is also trustworthy and reliable. Even when the evidence of insolvency or of default in supporting software will be available, a decision that the required conditions for handover have been met in every respect has to be made by the escrow custodian.

The NCC Group has long supplied IT escrow services, and is the best known organisation for this purpose in the UK, although its services are not confined to UK companies[1].

Banks sometimes agree to hold source code as escrow custodians but banks are not in the business of understanding the legal requirements of escrow agreements or IT industry practices. What is more significant for both licensor and licensee is that since a bank acts in a professional capacity for the supplier and may be lending it money, in the event of insolvency it might exercise a banker's lien over the source code. This would put the bank in an untenable position over the release of the source code to the user.

Solicitors with specialised knowledge of the IT industry may be prepared to act as escrow custodians, if they are able to obtain the requisite insurance cover. Licensees may raise objections if the solicitor acts for the supplier, as the question of being a creditor might arise in the same way as for a bank.

7. Liquidators' rights

The effect of a source code deposit agreement has not yet been tested in the courts. In general, under the law on insolvency, as set out in the Insolvency Act 1986, liquidators are not bound by a company's existing contracts. Under s 178, a liquidator has extensive powers to 'disclaim', that is to disown, contracts which are unprofitable or contracts which may give rise to a liability to pay money; or which have been entered into within six months of liquidation at less than their genuine value.

The liquidator is concerned that any assets of the insolvent company should not be further reduced.

Regular annual payments under a contract by the licensor could define the contract as 'giving rise to a liability to pay money', which the liquidator could therefore disclaim. A source code deposit agreement is typically structured so that the licensee makes annual payments but the licensor pays only when updating the source code being held.

There is no definition of an 'unprofitable contract'. An agreement where the software owner is paying a fee to store its source code could, in isolation, be regarded as 'unprofitable'. But it is not clear whether the courts would be prepared to link such an agreement to its related contracts, principally the software licence, so as to construe the escrow agreement as being profitable within the context of a particular transaction.

In any event, s 178 specifically states that a disclaimer operates only so as to determine the rights, interests and liabilities of the company in liquidation. It does not affect the rights and liabilities of any other party to the contract except as necessary to release the company in liquidation from any liability. Therefore, as a source code deposit agreement is tripartite, any disclaimer of the contract by a liquidator should not affect the rights and obligations as between the licensee and the escrow custodian. The disclaimer could therefore be said merely to insulate the company from its own particular rights and obligations rather than nullifying the contract as a whole, and the escrow custodian would not be prevented from releasing the source code.

The risk of the arrangements not working would be greater if the deposit with the escrow custodian was of the only source code in existence and if on the licensor's insolvency this sole source code itself were to be transferred to become the licensee's property and of no further value to the liquidator or creditors. However, the terms of the source code deposit agreement should make it absolutely clear that it would be a copy of the source code to be licensed to the licensee in confidence for very limited and specific purposes. There would thus arguably be no reduction in the licensor's assets available for distribution to unsecured creditors.

Even if the agreement had been for storage of the one and only source code and even if a disclaimer on the basis of the contract being unprofitable did operate so as to deny the licensee the right of access, s 181 of the Insolvency Act 1986 enables an application to be made to the court for an order vesting any property which is the subject of such a contract in any person entitled to it under the contract.

8. Materials other than software

While the focus here is on deposit of software source code, the agreement can be used as the basis for a broader range of deposited materials, such as for technical drawings or plans or other manufacturing know-how. If a computer manufacturer is supplying both hardware and software products under a long-term agreement in large volumes for cumulative high values, the terms in the supply contract may require the deposit of hardware manufacturing know-how so that the customer can be assured of a means of obtaining products and spares if the supplier ceases to trade, or even simply decides no longer to produce the product in question. In such circumstances the source code deposit agreement considered below would need a number of modifications, for example changing 'source code' to 'licensed materials', and providing a mechanism for payment; if products and spares are being supplied by the customer to an end-user marketplace, or even distributed within its own organisation, the supplier or its receiver or liquidator is going to expect some payment for the know-how which has enabled the products to be produced. This is in contrast to conventional source code deposit, where the customer is not extending the use of the software but is merely being granted a limited licence to facilitate the ongoing support of the software which it or its own customers are already using, and where no commercial case can reasonably be made for a payment to the licensor. Suppliers are inclined to resist fiercely the extension of the deposit concept to hardware manufacturing know-how, not least because of the difficulty in establishing an appropriate pricing mechanism, which will produce a fair return on the assets to shareholders or creditors as the case may be.

The use of a source code deposit agreement removes the need for the user to rely on trust by having to assume the ongoing soundness of the software owner's business. The user can safeguard its own commercial interests. Most suppliers are reasonably relaxed about the involvement of escrow custodians in cases of insolvency, provided that they have proven reputations, but will insist on their licence and support agreements governing all aspects of access and use by the licensee while the supplier remains in business.

B. The structure of a typical source code deposit agreement

Terms and conditions

- Definitions*

- Deposit of Source Code*

- Custody of Source Code*

- Release of Source Code*

- Licensee's Undertakings*

- Escrow Custodian's Undertakings*

- Licensor's Warranty*

- Verifying the Source Code*

- Ownership and Confidentiality of Source Code*

- Liability of Escrow Custodian*

- Charges*

- Termination*

- Disputes*

- General Provisions.

Schedule contents

- Licence Agreement details

- Distribution Agreement details

- Support Agreement details

- Charges*.

C. Specific clauses

In the clause examples considered below, which are those asterisked above, the owner and supplier of the software source code will be described as the 'Licensor'; the user who is licensed to use the software in its business as an end user, or as a distributor if so validly licensed, will be described as the 'Licensee'; and the party who will hold the software will be described as the 'Escrow Custodian'.

1. Definitions

'*Distribution Agreement*' means the distribution agreement between the Licensor and Licensee, identified in the Schedule.

'*Licence Agreement*' means the licence agreement for the Software between the Licensor and the Licensee, identified in the Schedule.

'*Software*' means the software products and their related documentation licensed to the Licensee, specified in the Schedule.

'*Source Code*' means a copy of the source code version of the Software, including any modifications, enhancements, revisions or updates in versions as supplied to the Licensee from time to time by the Licensor, together with all related listings, flowcharts and associated documentation and details of any software not owned by the Licensor, as necessary for translating into executable code accessible for modification or enhancement.

'*Support Agreement*' means the support agreement for the Software between the Licensor and the Licensee, identified in the Schedule.

The licensor party to the agreement must be the owner of the software and must have an unarguable right to deposit the source materials, excluding any programs or modules belonging to other licensors. Licensees should take care, when third party elements are an important part of the software they wish to secure, to require licensors to obtain appropriate authorities so that these third party elements can either be obtained when the principal sources are released, or be protected by separate source code deposit arrangements with the third parties.

There have also been instances where subsidiary companies have entered into these agreements as licensors without having the title rights they purport to have. There is no value to a licensee in arrangements which cannot be enforced at the end of the day. It is equally important for the use of this source code deposit agreement that the licensor remains the owner of the software and thus a valid party to this agreement. If the licensor sells its rights in the software, arrangements must ensure that the licensee continues to receive the protection of this agreement, for so long as it remains validly licensed. If the purchaser of the rights in the software is not prepared to continue these escrow arrangements or others which are equivalent, this in itself should be a trigger event for release of the source code to the licensee. The threat of this should be enough for the new owner to participate willingly.

The licensee party to the agreement must be an individual licensee. It is not appropriate for it to be a whole user group. The value of the source materials to the licensor makes it important that individual confidentiality undertakings and covenants on limitation of use should be received for each licensee by the escrow custodian.

If the user is not validly licensed to use the software, a source code deposit agreement will be irrelevant. From the user's point of view, negotiations for the source code deposit agreement should take place at the same time as negotiating the licence agreement, when its bargaining position will be at its strongest. If the software has been specially developed for the user, and the supplier will be retaining the source code and continuing to support it for the user, these negotiations should be taking place when the software development agreement is being negotiated. From the supplier's point of view the source code deposit agreement should be dependent on a licence agreement for the software remaining in force with the licensee.

The licence agreement should therefore be identified in a schedule, by its date and the software products concerned, for the purposes of confirming the licensee's continuing right to use the software under conditions ensuring that the licensor's asset value in the software is retained.

The definition of 'Distribution Agreement' by reference to its identification in the Schedule, like the licence agreement, by its date and the software products concerned, will be included only in those situations where the licensee is also the distributor of the software, and where the licensee may need to provide support for the software to end users in the event of the licensor's insolvency, where the end users are not individually entering into source code deposit agreements. It is referred to in the clause on the licensee's covenants. In normal circumstances, the licensee will covenant not to use the software for the benefit of any other party, but there must be an exception so far as end users of a licensee distributor are concerned.

The definition of 'Support Agreement', similarly identified in the Schedule by its date and the software products concerned, will need to be included if the supplier's failure to support is one of the conditions triggering release of source code. If so, the support agreement must be current at the time of failure to support.

It is important that the software that is the subject of this agreement, likely to be a series of programs, should be properly identified in the Schedule.

The definition of 'Source Code' should state exactly what should be deposited. It will be one copy of the source code and will include modifications, enhancements, revisions or updates, related listings and associated documentation, everything that would be necessary to enable the user to support and enhance the software should this be required. It may be stored on magnetic tape, CD-Rom or disk, with listings and manuals as appropriate.

There are practical reasons for the agreement to require a 'copy' of the source code. It is not wise for a licensor who is solvent at the time the agreement is made to pass the only source code over to the escrow custodian – although it is not unknown for this to happen. It also means that in the event of insolvency the escrow custodian is not putting the insolvent company's assets at risk by releasing the only extant version of the source code to a licensee, which could amount to a clean transfer of the owner's assets on insolvency to which the creditors could validly object.

2. Deposit of Source Code

(a) Following the execution of this Agreement, the Licensor shall ensure that the Source Code, clearly identified, is promptly deposited with the Escrow Custodian.

(b) Whenever a new version of the Software is made available to the Licensee, the Licensor shall promptly deposit with the Escrow Custodian a new version of the Source Code, and notify the Licensee in writing that the deposit has been made.

(c) If no new version has been deposited in any 12-month period, the Licensor shall deposit a replacement copy of the then current version of the Source Code with the Escrow Custodian and will notify the Licensee in writing that the deposit has been made.

The licensor should deposit one copy of the source code with the escrow custodian as soon as the agreement is signed and should of course retain a copy for its own purposes; the escrow custodian should not be expected to take charge of the only source in existence, particularly as the licensor does not actually have the right to ask for it back.

A further deposit of source code should take place whenever a new version is issued. If no new version has been issued, the source code should be renewed at defined intervals, to ensure that its quality does not deteriorate, particularly on electronic media.

The licensor should notify the licensee of the new deposit on each occasion, preferably also providing the licensee with a copy of the escrow custodian's receipt, although some licensors will be reluctant to undertake this additional administration. This can be checked by the licensee as far as new versions are concerned, as object code will have been supplied.

The deposit requirements should strike a reasonable balance. Licensors will not want the administrative burden of making deposits too frequently. It may be helpful to define what a 'version' constitutes so that a licensor is not necessarily required to deposit every single bug-fix. Licensees should be satisfied by reference to their object code version and the notification from the licensor pursuant to paragraph (b) above that the source code on deposit is current and capable of being used for the purposes of support.

These arrangements emphasise the importance of administrative procedures by all parties. The licensee will get greater value from the agreement by drawing up its own review procedure to ascertain that a renewed copy of the source code has been deposited, containing the changes reflected in the object code it has been supplied with.

The licensor also needs suitable administrative procedures to remember to forward the current source code version on every occasion to the escrow custodian and to ensure that all deposits are clearly identified with the version, the product name and, if applicable, the identity of an individual licensee. It is often the case with complex products that, while they may have a common standard core, they are tailored to meet the specific requirements of individual licensees, or they will be made up of different modules, and different licensees will take individually customised combinations of modules. The licensor would need to be able to supply these separately.

There is a practical problem for the escrow custodian, who deals with different source codes from a number of suppliers, if the source code is not clearly marked so that it can be instantly identified on its arrival. This difficulty is amplified where software from one supplier is deposited in various versions for different licensees.

3. Custody of Source Code

(a) Whenever the Source Code is deposited, the Escrow Custodian will arrange for its safe and secure storage in accordance with its standard procedures, and send written confirmation that it has been received and stored to the Licensor and the Licensee respectively.

(b) Upon receiving a new version of the Source Code two versions later than the earliest version held by the Escrow Custodian, the Escrow Custodian will return the earliest version to the Licensor.

(c) On receiving a replacement Source Code, the Escrow Custodian will return to the Licensor the Source Code which it replaces.

It is important for the escrow custodian to have proper fireproof storage facilities, secure and atmospherically suitable for electronic media in whatever format. The source code must be kept in conditions where it will not deteriorate, and so that it will not be lost or mislaid. Details of the agreement must be recorded in licensor sequence, cross-referenced to licensee. The escrow custodian should monitor the licensor's obligations in respect of the deposit of the source code. The licensee must be informed by the escrow custodian whenever the source code update has been received as a confirmatory check that the licensor has carried out its obligations.

The escrow custodian will sometimes have the problem of persuading the licensor to provide updates at the appropriate times. It should keep a renewal calendar for administering the procedural requirements of the agreement, as part of its records in which an agreement can be identified by date of renewal for the licensor and licensee so that formal reminders can be sent out as necessary. Where the licensor does not have its own suitable administrative procedures, there will be little incentive on its part to ensure that the updates are correctly made.

The escrow custodian's remedy would be to ask a court for specific performance of this contract, to make an order for the source to be updated.

This raises an interesting question which frequently arises when prospective escrow custodians are being considered. Good escrow custodians are not yet thick on the ground and there are some who, whilst being able to offer the requisite security and reliable administration, will be unwilling to undertake any sort of interventionist role or even to exercise any judgment about whether or not they should respond to a request from either of the parties to implement any of their rights under the agreement. Such escrow custodians will expect the agreement to be framed in absolute terms with no discretionary elements.

It will be in the escrow custodian's own interests to run the deposit system efficiently and keep a renewal calendar, as it must ensure that the licensor and licensee are invoiced, whenever the source code is updated or renewed, or for the annual payments, respectively.

The deposit of source code should be in the UK, as this is an agreement drafted under English law. This does not prevent either licensor or licensee being resident abroad. The National Computing Centre as escrow custodian has deposits of source code from other countries worldwide. Delivery of source code can be efficiently carried out by using air services if necessary in these circumstances. Licensees will look for the simplest and most convenient accessibility, although sometimes they will be offered an escrow facility in, say, the United States, because that is where the owner of the software resides.

Depending on the provisions of their licences and support agreements, licensees may not be obliged to use a new version immediately and may be entitled to continue using versions of the software which have been superseded. In such cases, more than one version of the software should be kept on deposit. Nevertheless, the licensor is unlikely to be supporting older versions indefinitely, and the escrow custodian will not be expected to hold an ever-accumulating series of versions. By actually returning the oldest version to the licensor, the escrow custodian will be demonstrating that it has been kept safely and that it belongs to the licensor.

276

The escrow custodian must have reliable and competent staff, who are aware that release to the wrong party or unauthorised disclosure would be serious. They must appreciate that although the source code is the property of the licensor, it is not entitled to ask for it back, except under certain very specific circumstances. This emphasises the importance of a well-administered system for dealing with source code deposit.

A further reason for proper administration is to permit immediate access at the appropriate time. If the source code were to be lost or mislaid by the escrow custodian while the licensor was still in a position to provide a replacement, it would be unsatisfactory but remediable. But if the loss was discovered only when the trigger event had occurred, and the licensee was expecting to receive the source copy promptly for urgent support or enhancement, it would be calamitous.

4. Release of Source Code

(a) If the Licensor becomes or is at serious and substantial risk of becoming subject to any form of insolvency, administrative receivership or receivership or anything analogous to such event occurs in any applicable jurisdiction or if the Licensor ceases or threatens to cease trading [or if the Licensor has defaulted substantially in any obligation to provide support of the Software Products under the Support Agreement and has failed to remedy such default notified by the Licensee to the Licensor under the terms of such Agreement] then the Licensee will notify both the Escrow Custodian and the Licensor.

(b) Unless within ten working days of this notification, the Licensor delivers to the Escrow Custodian and to the Licensee a counter-notice signed by an authorised officer of the Licensor that no such failure has occurred or that any such failure has been rectified then in order to obtain the release of the Source Code the Licensee will submit to the Escrow Custodian a statutory declaration which will:
  (i) be sworn by an authorised officer of the Licensee;
  (ii) set out the facts and circumstances for seeking release;
  (iii) state that the documents attached to it comprise all relevant supporting documentation in the Licensee's possession.

(c) Upon receipt of this statutory declaration, the Escrow Custodian shall arrange for the release of a copy of the Source Code to the Licensee.

This clause is about the circumstances in which the licensee will gain the right of access to the software and the related formalities. The 'trigger event' must be unambiguously ascertainable.

This clause is where the interests of the licensor and the licensee differ most. Both have legitimate concerns. The licensor will be starting from a position of not really

277

wanting its sources to be available under any circumstances. This will be particularly true when the software in question is high value in terms of the investment made to produce it and the revenue which must be generated to provide a profit.

Insolvency rules differ depending on the jurisdiction under which the licensor carries on business and the first part of the clause allows for this. It has been drafted to provide a triggering event at an early stage in the process of a supplier getting into serious financial difficulties. While some suppliers will argue that a release should not occur so long as they remain alive and with at least a theoretical prospect of financial recovery, it can take a very long time for the position to become finally resolved one way or another. If in the meantime, as is likely to be the case, the supplier cannot effectively support the software, the user will be in an untenable position if it cannot obtain the source.

When they think about this issue, licensees want to broaden the circumstances of release. Their concerns are not confined to the prospect of licensors going out of business. They are anxious about how to ensure that software is maintained if there is no question of the licensor's insolvency, but the licensor fails to support it. Sometimes, therefore, licensees seek to extend the circumstances of release to any unremedied material breach of the support agreement by the licensor, as illustrated by the second part of this example clause.

When the parties negotiate this clause, relevant factors will include the relative strength of the parties' bargaining positions; the value of the software to the licensor and the level of importance to the licensee's business. They should also include the perceived likelihood of expertise available to the licensee to be able to support the software itself and the likely need to have to do so.

A reasonable argument for a licensor is that if there is a breach of the support agreement, the licensee should look to its rights under the support contract. The remedies for breach of contract always include damages and if a licensor is slow to react to a serious problem, this is going to increase the exposure to damages. From the licensee's point of view, a pertinent consideration here will be the financial worth of the licensor in the event of a substantial claim.

If the licensee negotiates successfully for this support condition to be included, the licensor will seek some protection within the terms of the support contract itself against it being invoked. Normally, notice of breach will be required, so that there is an opportunity for the licensor to remedy the situation. The licensee will be able to obtain the source code only if the licensor has not taken the opportunity to rectify the failure once notice has been given. This is most contentious and the definition of the failure not as clear-cut as in insolvency. The terms of the support agreement should be unambiguous and clearly drafted if the licensee is going to be entitled to access the source code because the licensor is not complying with a provision of the agreement. In any case, an expert opinion may be necessary.

If licensees are not capable of supporting a software product themselves, they may use the services of a consultant expert in the software or they may want to go to a third party maintenance software house for this purpose. Appropriate controls need to be imposed in the source licence which is an integral part of this agreement in respect of third party access, making the licensee fully responsible for any breaches of the source licence terms.

A statutory declaration by the licensee with appropriate evidence should be sent to the escrow custodian. A court order is the clearest evidence but the licensee may not be prepared to wait for the time that this will take.

The final part of the clause is intended to provide the escrow custodian with a black-and-white situation, to enable the source code to be released to the licensee.

For some licensees, the arrangements for release presented by the above example will never be enough. They recognise the essential weakness of the escrow device, namely that the process is bound to take time when their needs for having the software supported may be much more immediate. Even in critical software applications, the usual form of source code deposit agreement will probably suffice if the software in question has been in use for some time and can be considered to be stable. However, when the software is comparatively untried and prone to new bugs, and the application is critical to the operation of the licensee's business, there is an understandable wish to act first and ask questions later.

Negotiation can translate this wish into reality by providing a mechanism which will meet the respective needs of the parties: immediate access to sources for the licensee and an adequate security interest for the licensor in the case of a false alarm. Thus, the solution might be for the licensee who reasonably believes that a triggering event for the release of source code has occurred to have the right to call for the immediate release of those sources in return for placing an agreed sum of money in escrow, or providing for payment of this sum by bank guarantee on agreed terms with an acceptable bank. In due course it will be determined (by arbitration or by an independent expert) whether or not a triggering event had in fact occurred. If it had, the deposited sum would be returned to the licensee or the bank guarantee would be cancelled and the licensee would keep the source code on the limited licence terms provided for in the source code deposit agreement. If the triggering event had not occurred, the licensor would be entitled to the deposited sum or would have the right to call on the bank guarantee. The licensee would also be obliged to return the source materials without delay and to provide a certificate that no copies had been retained or passed on.

5. Licensee's Undertakings

Upon receipt of the Source Code, the Licensee shall:

(a) use and copy the Source Code solely for the purposes of supporting or enhancing the Software and/or alleviating or correcting any failure of the Software to conform to any software description or specification contained in the Licence Agreement, copying for security and back-up purposes only as reasonably necessary, and in any event including the Licensor's copyright notice and any other proprietary information;

(b) limit access to the Source Code to those of its employees, agents, contractors or sub-contractors who are directly engaged in the support or enhancement of the Software;

(c) not assign, transfer, sell, lease, rent, charge or otherwise deal in or encumber the Source Code nor use it on behalf of or for the benefit of any other party [except, where the Licensee is an authorised distributor of the Software, to use it for the benefit of end users to whom the Licensee is authorised to supply the Software under the terms of the Distribution Agreement between the Licensee and the Licensor]; and

(d) without prejudice to the generality of the foregoing, will take any other steps necessary from time to time to protect the confidential information and intellectual property rights of the Licensor in the Source Code and to ensure the compliance with the provisions of this clause by its employees, agents, contractors, and sub-contractors.

These days most licensors are pragmatic and recognise that it is reasonable for licensees to require access to the source code for software which is regularly updated if the licensors go out of business. However, even here, the extent of the access needs to be carefully controlled.

The licensor's objective in this clause will be to limit the licensee's use of the software solely for the purposes of support or enhancement and for the licensee to protect the source code and not to treat it as its own property, or under any circumstances for commercial development or exploitation.

The licensee may not itself be maintaining or enhancing the software. It may find a third party who can technically support it so that an extension to those personnel permitted to access it in paragraph (b) may be necessary. Nevertheless, the licensee must take responsibility for protecting its confidentiality and restricting access to it.

Another important reason for this clause limiting use of the source code is to ensure that the liquidator cannot claim that handing over source code to a licensee would lessen the intellectual property rights acquired in the liquidation from the owner. The asset value of the software must be preserved for the benefit of the licensor's creditors and shareholders. There must be no risk of the property in the source code passing to the licensee.

6. Escrow Custodian's Undertakings

> The Escrow Custodian undertakes to the Licensor not to use the Source Code for its own purposes, or on behalf of any other party, or to release it except in accordance with the provisions of this Agreement.

The purpose of this clause is for the licensor to be confident that the escrow custodian will deal with the source code only under the limited terms of this agreement, not for its own uses or in collaboration with anyone else. The clause must therefore be non-negotiable.

7. Licensor's Warranty

> The Licensor represents and warrants to the Licensee that the Source Code deposited with the Escrow Custodian will at all times be a complete, accurate and up-to-date copy of the source code version of the current version of the Software together with all relevant complete, accurate and up-to-date listings, logic manuals and flowcharts.

A licensee is entitled to expect that the source code held by the escrow custodian is complete, accurate and up to date, to match the latest object code version supplied to the licensee, together with all relevant documentation. This clause provides an express warranty for the licensee and thereby the basis for a remedy if these obligations of the licensor are not met.

8. Verifying the Source Code

> (a) On receiving a written request from the Licensee, the Escrow Custodian shall arrange for an independent expert to carry out tests in order to establish whether the Licensor is in compliance with the warranty set out in this Agreement.
>
> (b) If, in the independent expert's reasonable written judgment, the Licensor is in breach of the warranty under [the warranty clause above], then upon receiving notice of this from the Escrow Custodian, the Licensor must deposit with the Escrow Custodian within 14 days of receipt of this notice

those revisions to the Source Code which will be necessary to ensure its compliance with such warranty, and the Escrow Custodian will then arrange to have further tests carried out as specified in this clause, the charges for such further tests to be paid for by the Licensor.

(c) If, in the independent expert's reasonable written judgment, the Licensor is in breach of the warranty under [the warranty clause above], then the Escrow Custodian's charges for arranging the tests and for the independent expert carrying out the tests and reporting on the results will be paid by the Licensor. If, in the independent expert's reasonable written judgment, the Licensor is not in breach of the warranty, then the Escrow Custodian's charges for arranging the tests and for the independent expert carrying out the tests and reporting on the results will be paid by the Licensee.

(d) The Escrow Custodian and the independent expert whom it appoints will be entitled to charge in respect of this clause in arrears on a time-and-materials basis at their prevailing rates. Such charges will be payable (together with any applicable Value Added Tax by the Licensor or the Licensee (as the case may be)) within 20 days of receiving the invoice.

At the point at which the licensee requires the source code, if it is not to the expected standard as warranted by the licensor, it will be too late for the licensee to take any effective action to recover the situation. By this time, the supplier would be out of business, or if the triggering event were failure to support, there would already be one dispute.

So the agreement should allow for testing by an independent expert.

The escrow custodian and independent expert's charges should be paid for by the user requesting the tests. If as a result of the tests the source code is shown to be inadequate, the supplier should pay the charges as well as promptly remedying the situation. Such testing could be costly, but will be in the licensee's interest.

The licensee may want to reserve the right to negotiate in respect of the independent expert's rates, or to agree them before permitting the escrow custodian to go ahead.

The independent expert must be subject to the same confidentiality requirements as the escrow custodian. It will be the escrow custodian, as the neutral third party, who will instruct the independent expert to act. The independent expert can convert the source code to object code and directly compare with the current object code in use. They should be identical.

As previously discussed, not all escrow custodians will be prepared to undertake obligations such as instructing an independent expert. A way round this might be for the licensor's own technical specialist to conduct the tests under the supervision of the licensee, the escrow custodian's only role being to produce the source code for the purposes of the test.

For packaged software, a group of licensees could arrange to share the cost of verification. Another alternative where the organisation would need to be synchronised would be for the licensee or its representative to go to the licensor's premises and actually watch the object code being generated from the source, and the source handed to a courier for transporting to the escrow custodian.

Tests by the independent expert should not be allowed to run indefinitely. Licensors may wish to consider negotiating a time limit, for example one working day during which the licensee or the independent expert may carry out such tests as they deem appropriate.

9. Ownership and Confidentiality of Source Code

(a) Notwithstanding the deposit and release of the Source Code in accordance with the terms of this Agreement, no property in it will be transferred to the Licensee or to the Escrow Custodian.

(b) The Licensee and the Escrow Custodian shall treat the Source Code and all information coming to either party's knowledge or into its possession under this Agreement in the strictest confidence and secrecy, and this obligation and the Licensee's undertakings given in clause [5] above shall survive the termination of this Agreement.

(c) The Escrow Custodian will procure that any independent expert authorised under this Agreement to access the Source Code will sign a written undertaking to treat the Source Code in the strictest confidence and secrecy, so far as possible upon the same terms as those imposed on the Escrow Custodian and the Licensee.

The licensor's objective is to prevent property in the source code from passing to the licensee or escrow custodian. In liquidation it would become the property of the liquidator, as an asset, and there must be no risk of its value being reduced.

This agreement grants a specific form of licence, solely for support and enhancement purposes by the licensee or the licensee's agent.

10. Liability of Escrow Custodian

(a) The Escrow Custodian will not itself be under any obligation to examine, enquire into or inspect the relevance, accuracy or completeness or any other aspect of the Source Code or to determine that whatever is deposited is or is not the Source Code.

(b) The Escrow Custodian will not be under any obligation to examine, enquire into or check the accuracy, completeness or authenticity of any statutory declaration submitted by the Licensee.

(c) The Escrow Custodian will not be liable either to the Licensor or to the Licensee or to any third party for any indirect or consequential loss or loss of profits resulting from any breach or non-performance by the Escrow Custodian of any of its obligations under this Agreement, and the Escrow Custodian's liability under this Agreement will in any event be limited to £100,000.

(d) The Licensor hereby grants a licence to the Escrow Custodian to have as many copies of the Source Code made as the Escrow Custodian may in its reasonable opinion consider necessary to comply with its obligations under this Agreement.

Because the escrow custodian is acting as custodian, it should not be expected or permitted to access the source code itself to check out its accuracy or to ascertain that it is not defective. This is not the escrow custodian's responsibility, even if it were to possess the expertise to be able to do so. It should remain strictly neutral. The provision for testing the source code for verification is open to the licensee, when it will be passed over to an independent expert, under the restricted conditions defined in clause 8 above.

If the escrow custodian releases source code other than to an independent expert or licensee under the agreed terms, the owner of the source code will have a valid claim against the escrow custodian. However, the escrow custodian will be concerned to limit its exposure. Liability is something that both licensees and licensors will wish to negotiate with the escrow custodian. Clauses sometimes seek to protect the escrow custodian from any liability other than that for 'gross negligence'. There may be an attempt to include a joint indemnity by both licensor and licensee in favour of the escrow custodian against loss, damage or liability in general, and untoward release of the source code in particular, in connection with the services being provided. Neither of these clauses should normally be accepted, unless the licensor and licensee have to find ways of encouraging a reluctant escrow custodian. A 'force majeure' clause will normally form part of the general provisions, which will cover the escrow custodian for failure to perform its obligations for reasons beyond its reasonable control.

There will in any event be an implied provision which is imposed by the terms of the Supply of Goods and Services Act 1982 that the escrow custodian will be acting with reasonable care and skill in providing its services.

The escrow custodian must be permitted to copy the source code where the same software is licensed to a number of users, and only one source code version is stored. If the licensor should become insolvent, all its users will need copies.

11. Charges

> The Licensor and the Licensee will each pay the Escrow Custodian's charges in the amounts and at the times set out in the Charges Schedule. All invoices will be payable 30 days from receipt except for the release fee specified in the Schedule which will be payable subject to the presentation of an invoice immediately prior to and as a condition of the release by the Escrow Custodian of the Source Code.

Each party has rights and obligations under the agreement. The licensee and licensor each make payments to the escrow custodian who has the responsibility of holding the source code.

The amounts should be specified in a schedule and there must be provision to increase the charges by a reasonable amount from time to time for the escrow custodian's benefit. The licensor and licensee should not allow increases to be open-ended. However, the standard provisions on charges and payment terms, as discussed in **CHAPTER 7**, must be included here, too, for example concerning VAT.

The licensor will be charged an administrative registration fee by the escrow custodian at the time of the initial deposit of source code. When an update or fresh copy is deposited, there will be a further administrative charge to the licensor. The licensee will pay an annual fee in advance to continue to receive the protection of the agreement, and a release fee should the trigger event occur. The escrow custodian will insist for its own protection that the release fee is payable before the software is released.

Negotiations may take place between the licensor and licensee as to which party should pay the fees due to the escrow custodian. This is discussed further in the comments on the Charges Schedule. The licensor who is not keen on escrow arrangements may expect the licensee to pay all charges.

Clearly, the escrow custodian must maintain accurate records of all transactions including payments made and due.

12. Termination

> (a) This agreement may be terminated:
>   (i)   by the Escrow Custodian upon giving not less than 90 days' notice to the Licensor and to the Licensee; or
>   (ii) jointly by the Licensor and the Licensee upon giving not less than 30 days' notice to the Escrow Custodian;
>   (iii) by the Licensee alone upon giving not less than 30 days' notice to both the Escrow Custodian and the Licensor;

(iv) by the Licensor alone upon giving not less than 30 days' notice to both the Escrow Custodian and the Licensee provided that the written consent of the Licensee has first been given, or upon giving not less than 120 days notice to both the Escrow Custodian and the Licensee provided that it has appointed a replacement custodian of the Source Code on terms and conditions as nearly as possible identical to those set out in this Agreement that will be reasonably acceptable to the Licensee.

(b) This Agreement will be terminated forthwith by the Licensor if the Escrow Custodian becomes or threatens to become or is at serious and substantial risk of becoming subject to any form of insolvency administration or receivership, or is in fundamental breach of its obligations under this Agreement.

(c) Promptly upon receiving notice of termination under clause (a)(i) or (b) above, the Licensor and the Licensee agree to use their respective best endeavours to appoint a mutually acceptable replacement custodian of the Source Code on terms and conditions as nearly as possible identical to those set out in this Agreement.

(d) This Agreement will be terminated immediately if the Licensee attempts to make an assignment for the benefit of creditors, or if a receiver, trustee in bankruptcy or similar officer is appointed to take charge over all or part of its property, or if the Licensee is adjudged a bankrupt, or fails to comply with any other provision of this Agreement, and such failure is not remedied within 10 days after notice of the failure has been given to the Licensee.

(e) If this Agreement is terminated under this clause 12, the Escrow Custodian will return the Source Code to the Licensor, provided that all fees and charges have been paid.

(f) This Agreement will terminate upon the release of the Source Code by the Escrow Custodian to the Licensee as provided for in this Agreement.

(g) If the Licence Agreement is rightfully terminated by the Licensor because of the Licensee's unremedied default under the terms of that Licence Agreement, this Agreement will terminate immediately.

Each party should be permitted to terminate the agreement but only by giving sufficient notice for the arrangements to be continued by other parties. If the licensee goes out of business, the agreement will be terminated.

If the licence agreement is terminated through the default of the licensee, then this agreement should also come to an end. The licensee will no longer be entitled to use the software under any circumstances.

A provision could be included for the term of the agreement to be for a fixed period of time such as ten years, after which the source code material would be returned to the licensor. The term of the software licence will be the principal influencing factor here.

If the source code is correctly released to the licensee, the agreement will come to an end. Otherwise, on termination, the source code must be returned by the escrow custodian to the licensor, provided that all fees have been paid.

13. Disputes

(a) Any dispute arising at any time between the parties to this Agreement in respect of the release of the Source Code or the testing of the Source Code will be referred to such independent party as the parties unanimously nominate.

(b) If the parties should fail to nominate an independent party unanimously within 10 working days of the date of the dispute, then such dispute will be referred at the instance of any party to an independent party appointed by the President for the time being of the British Computer Society or the Society for Computers and Law.

(c) The independent party will act as an expert whose decision (including a decision in respect of costs) will, except in the case of manifest error be final and binding upon the parties.

If there is any dispute over the testing or the release of the source code, the matter must be referred to an expert, an independent party, acting as an expert who understands the technicalities, not merely as an arbitrator, and who can act quickly if there is any information technology element to the dispute. This will be important where 'failure to support' is the trigger event. Argument can become complicated over the issue of whether there has in fact been a breach of the support contract. An appropriate expert will be able to assess the matter more effectively for the resolution of the dispute than an arbitrator.

14. Charges Schedule

	Payable by
1. Initial fee (payable on execution of the agreement)	Licensor
2. Registration fee (payable on execution of the agreement)	Licensee
3. Annual Renewal Fee	Licensee
4. Further Deposit Fee	Licensor
5. Release fee	Licensee

Expenses will be payable in addition in respect of media, courier charges, and other reasonably and necessarily incurred items.

Sometimes the release fee is related to the escrow custodian's hourly rate or charge, for example a number of hours being specified.

There is probably as much discussion in practice about who should pay which charges as about any other element of a source code deposit agreement. The one fact is that the escrow custodian will be the recipient of the fees paid.

The charges tend to be very low in comparison with the cost of the applicable software licences, usually amounting only to a few hundred pounds per annum. Most licensees accept that they should pay a fee for the benefit of what is in effect an insurance policy, but some will expect the licensor to pay for everything. Yet some licensors feel that they should co-operate in an arrangement of this kind only if the licensee bears the full expense. As always, market forces and commercial experience will determine the outcome. However, it is important to remember that enforceability of an agreement depends on the parties' rights and obligations, and payment is the simplest way of demonstrating the obligations of both the licensor and licensee.

1   www.nccglobal.com.

CHAPTER 14

Maintenance and support agreements

A. Introduction

These agreements cover the provision of services relating to the maintenance and support of hardware and software. Their substance consists of defining the services that will be provided.

The agreement will almost invariably be drawn up by the maintenance and support provider. It may apply directly to the end-user customer, or it may be with the reseller or distributor selling on to end users, including in the latter case first-line customer responsibility to the end users for their maintenance requirements.

Maintenance and support are intrinsic to information systems work. Although users are often reluctant to budget properly for support, such costs now form a large part of an IT manager's budget, particularly as systems have increased in size, scale and complexity. Maintenance and support costs can often be as high as 20 per cent per annum of the initial expenditure on the system. Systems get old, but still have to run, and the longer a system is in place the more maintenance it is likely to need.

In any event, complex software can never be guaranteed to be error-free. Whether it has been specially developed or whether it is a standard package, after its acceptance a customer should arrange for an agreement for support to be provided. Without an agreement, the developer would have no obligation or incentive to continue to spend time and effort in supporting the software and enhancing it for the customer's benefit.

A support agreement will be for the purposes of correcting faults where the system does not conform to specification. But support tends to go further than this. Enhancements may be made to the software to make the system more efficient or more user-friendly without altering its features or functions. The supplier should reserve the right to carry out such work at its own option as to time and extent. It will be in the supplier's long-term interest to enhance the software, to give itself a better competitive position, creating new releases.

Proposed changes involving features or functions beyond the original specification, changes in ways that were not envisaged when the software was first supplied, should be agreed by both parties, the supplier to cost the work, and the customer to accept or reject it.

A support agreement can also ensure that as new improved versions of the software are generally released, they can be made available to the individual customer.

Hardware needs regular checking. A maintenance service should correct any faults which prevent effective operation of the equipment. There should also be scope for preventative maintenance.

1. Standard or individual agreements

Standard maintenance and support agreements cover all normal repairs and maintenance and negotiation tends to be limited. The providers of these services will often be reluctant to entertain any variation of their procedures, because to do so could become a management nightmare. Maintenance and support are resource-intensive, and it is difficult for a supplier to estimate the resources necessary to respond quickly to all users' telephone calls. Typically, a supplier will not employ numerous technical specialists, but will have staff who are trained to provide the basic range of support, so that the response times for investigation can be met. Indeed it is increasingly common for suppliers to receive service calls at call centres provided to them on an outsourced basis and in locations far away from their operation centres.

Many of the larger manufacturers tend to offer a range of options to supplement standard services and it is becoming more usual for major users to negotiate complex agreements to cover all maintenance and support issues.

Individual contracts for large companies or systems can be tailor-made, and the user who is negotiating support at the same time as the procurement of a new, customised system is going to be in the best position to obtain variations to a standard agreement.

2. Original supplier or third party

The supplier of the services may be the original manufacturer of the hardware or the software developer. However, the customer may opt for a third party maintenance organisation, which may offer simple diagnostic tools, or also act in a consultancy role, or as a one-stop shop, because the cost savings on offer may be significant.

Third party maintenance is a sensitive issue so far as some suppliers are concerned. Many suppliers would like to exclude the possibility of third party maintenance but are conscious of the pitfalls of acting in restraint of trade or in an anti-competitive manner. For hardware maintenance, they will focus attention on promoting the benefits of dealing directly with the manufacturer of the products, with the most immediate access to technical developments and the broadest range of field experience for the user of hardware products. The situation is not much different from that of the motorist's car being serviced by a main dealer or by a non-franchised garage. In the same way as the motorist, the computer user will certainly verify that satisfactory levels of experience, know-how, equipment and other resources exist before taking a decision to use a third party maintenance organisation.

Although manufacturers are interested in deriving regular income from maintenance, they may be reluctant to continue to maintain older equipment, and want to sell new lines and products. Independent maintainers may offer more competitive pricing for these older products, particularly where they can provide experience in a specialised vertical market.

If special arrangements outside the standard maintenance service are sought, third party maintainers may be able to offer a competitive service or a specialist service, by dealing with a particular range of equipment. Their service will then be directly comparable to the service offered by the manufacturer itself.

Third party maintenance organisations are good at handling large volumes of business at low margins, useful for PC hardware maintenance and packaged software.

Alternatively, more users are choosing to contract with a third party maintainer for a single maintenance source covering equipment from various suppliers, perhaps including support of networks, communications and PC software.

3. Software and intellectual property concerns

Third party software support is less usual, not least because the full support of a software product requires access to source code, and source licences are not always available from software suppliers. However, smaller software houses that develop software often lack the resources and backing to be able to provide necessary levels of support for successful software products. In these circumstances, there is a tendency for them to contract this service out to larger third party organisations to provide support for the users of the software.

Software suppliers may be using a legitimate wish to protect their valuable intellectual property rights as a cloak to deter would-be third party maintainers. It may well be that developments in European law will lead to a more even balance between the interests of suppliers and those of third party organisations. However, many software products involve huge amounts of up front investment, and it is understandable that the vendors of these products want to be able to recover their outlay and to produce a good commercial return by a combination of licence fees and ongoing support revenues to fund the continuing development of the product.

4. Software support

The kind of support available will depend upon the complexity of the software and upon its importance to the licensee customer. The support will include investigation of reported errors, bug-fixing, updating documentation, technical advice and issuing new releases of the software. Issues of new versions may also be covered. It may be by means of telephone consultancy, online investigation and fixing, or by on-site visits. The customer must be prepared to assist the supplier by giving clear and accurate details of any fault, backed up by any printouts which will help a diagnosis. If on-site attendance is made, the customer should provide proper access to the computer system and somewhere suitable for the supplier's staff to work. The supplier may want enquiries to be channelled through a known representative who understands the software and will not waste time on matters which are not faults.

5. Hardware maintenance

The maintenance supplier will need details of: the equipment; its location; its age; the systems of which it forms part; planned development; the requirement for maintenance and the response times to have it put right. Agreement should be reached on the extent to which the customer's maintenance needs are normal or will need fast or out-of-normal working hours service with an appropriate expense tag. Manufacturers will generally be prepared to offer cover extending ultimately to '24/7' at a premium.

Most discussions centre on issues of price, long-term eligibility of products to be maintained or supported, long-term availability of spares, and whether or not replacement hardware parts are new or 'as new'. The shorter the response time limit for the supplier to investigate the problem, the more expensive the contract will be. A strong user can also negotiate for liquidated damages for late response or delayed repair, and for temporary replacement of equipment removed for repair.

292

6. Exclusions

It is of equal importance to note what is specifically disclaimed and excluded from the services to be provided, including those services which may be provided at the maintenance supplier's discretion and charged for separately. The customer will be expected to assume certain responsibilities in respect of its use of the computer products, for example not to tamper with equipment or to misuse it.

7. Warranty and maintenance

Strictly speaking, maintenance should be necessary only when the warranty on the products or software supplied ceases. The user should be entitled to the warranty period for the products in the licence, software development agreement or in the supply terms and conditions. A relative price reduction in the maintenance charges may be negotiated for the first 12 months where the commencement date coincides with installation or implementation. However, the supplier may claim to be offering over-and-above warranty provision through maintenance.

Whatever is agreed between a supplier and customer, there will always be some users who need the maximum support available. A supplier may find that a different payment structure is necessary for such customers. The risk is that they will be utilising the supplier's entire staff at the expense of the supplier's obligation to other customers. It is in the supplier's interests to monitor and prioritise the calls upon its services, to become aware of who are its most demanding customers. They will not necessarily be the largest users but they may well be the least computer literate.

8. Charges and increases

From the customer's point of view, some ceiling should be set on maintenance charge increases. One method is to relate changes to list price, maintenance charges usually being set between 10 and 20 per cent of the list price of the maintained product. Another is an automatic percentage increase or an increase related to inflation from year to year. Sometimes charges are kept low while the products are new, increasing with their age and more extensive repair requirements.

Payment is usually required in advance, often annually, and it is important that increased charges be notified to the customer in time for the customer to withdraw from the agreement if the increase is unacceptable. The mechanism for this will be that price increases should be on a number of days' notice greater than the number of days' notice which a customer is obliged to give in order to terminate the agreement. Cases of debt collection are not unusual on maintenance and support agreements. Often no use will have been made by the customer of the service for some time. The customer does not appreciate that payment has to be made annually in advance and that the agreement may be terminated only in accordance with the notice provisions stipulated in it.

9. Other considerations

Confidentiality is an important consideration in these agreements. Whether the maintenance staff are on-site or accessing the systems remotely, they may easily come into contact with confidential information, as input, printed out, or visible on screens.

An employment restriction may need to be imposed because the supplier's maintenance staff will be working closely on the customer's systems and could be valuable to the customer. This is not exclusively one way, however, and the supplier may be keen to take note of those customer's staff who have a good understanding of the products being maintained.

10. Operations guide

It is easy for terms and conditions in this type of agreement to become over-elaborate because of the natural concern to ensure that every possible contingency and qualification is expressly covered. This can result in excessively long and complex agreements which can be difficult to follow for reference purposes by users of the services, as opposed to their contracts specialists. An effective way of resolving this dilemma can be for the supplier to prepare an operations guide written in lay terms, setting out in some detail the practical steps which should be taken by end users in order to obtain the maximum benefit from the services, and to help them to comply with their obligations under the agreement. The resulting document provides the supplier with a sales and marketing opportunity in relation to the services, and it should be sufficiently straightforward for the users of the products to read and follow. The guide may be referred to in the agreement but would not have contractual status. In this way it can be written and updated without the need to consider the precise legal effects of the words used. The purpose of the guide is to expand on and explain elements of the legal agreement, not to be a substitute for it.

It makes sense for a supplier to understand its customers' businesses and systems, to keep its customers loyal, and to develop a reputation in the market concerned – which will also generate new business for the supplier.

It is good advice to any user of computer products to investigate the maintenance and support issues carefully before making a purchasing decision. If a user has any choice available, it should check out the maintenance supplier's financial soundness and experience in maintenance; find out what resources are available in terms of expertise and numbers to meet requirements; what training facilities there are for personnel to keep up to date; and follow up reference site details.

B. The structure of a maintenance and support agreement

This example focuses upon an agreement by a supplier with its reseller to provide maintenance and support to the reseller or directly to end users who are customers of the reseller in respect of products which combine hardware and the supplier's own software – on-site for hardware maintenance and remotely for software support. No third party products are included.

Terms and conditions

- Definitions*
- Term
- Schedules*
- Cover*
- Eligibility for Hardware Services*
- Hardware Services*
- Hardware Services Exclusions*
- Software Services*
- Additional Software Services*
- Software Services Exclusions*
- Disclaimers*
- Customer Responsibilities*
- Additional Customer Responsibilities (Software)*
- Charges, Expenses and Payment Terms
- Variation of Charges
- Confidential Information
- Employment Restriction
- Indemnities and Limits of Liability
- Termination
- General Contract Provisions

Schedules

- Service Schedules for specific service and product combinations

C. Specific clauses

In the clauses considered below, which are those above marked with an asterisk, the provider of the services is described as the 'Supplier' and the user of the services is described as the 'Customer'.

1. Definitions

'*End Users*' means those customers of the Customer supplied with Products.

'*Hardware*' means the hardware items listed in the Schedule.

'*Products*' means the Hardware and/or Software items to which the Services will apply according to the terms and conditions of this Agreement.

'*Schedule*' means one or more Schedules attached to this Agreement and which form part of this Agreement.

'*Services*' means the Hardware maintenance and/or Software support services provided by the Supplier to the Customer on the terms and conditions of this Agreement and more particularly detailed in this Agreement.

'*Site*' means the locations where the Products are installed as agreed by the Supplier, which may be either the Customer's location or the End Users' locations.

'*Software*' means any software supplied by the Supplier and incorporated in the Products listed in the Schedule or listed separately as Software Products in the Schedule.

'*Supplier Maintenance and Support Centre*' means the Supplier's address and telephone number details specified in the Schedule.

'*System*' means Products manufactured or supplied by the Supplier for use in combination with each other.

2. Schedules

(a) The Customer will ensure that each of its End Users has a copy of this Agreement and, without prejudice to its overriding responsibility for the performance of all of its obligations in this Agreement, the Customer will use all reasonable endeavours to ensure that each of its End Users performs those Customer obligations in respect of every Site referenced in any Schedule signed by the End User.

(b) Each Schedule must be fully completed and signed by the Customer or an End User and by the Supplier before it will take effect as part of this Agreement. By their signatures the Customer and/or End User confirm that the contents of the Schedule are accurate and that the Supplier is entitled to invoice the Customer at the invoice address specified in the Schedule, for maintenance of the Products listed in the Schedule. The Customer will be responsible for monitoring payment of such invoices in accordance with the terms and conditions of this Agreement.

(c) Where Products are added to, or deleted from, a Schedule during an operating year of this Agreement, this will be confirmed to the Customer and to the relevant End User in a letter from the Supplier, and invoicing will take account of such additions or deletions. A revised Schedule will not be issued until the next following renewal date shown on the Schedule.

(d) Any terms and conditions contained in a Schedule prevail over the terms and conditions in this Agreement.

This clause is specifically intended for a reseller with end users, but may be adapted for direct customers if appropriate.

The product schedules are an important part of maintenance and support agreements, where hardware product maintenance is involved. They are in effect the controlling documents for such agreements because they are the basis for invoicing under the agreement and they should also contain any special terms and conditions peculiar to individual sites. As well as catering for customers' own maintenance and support requirements, this example extends to a distributor reseller customer with its own end users. Whilst ensuring that the ultimate responsibility for performance of all customer obligations rests with the customer, most negotiation of this clause focuses on paragraph (c) and the method of dealing with invoicing additions and deletions. This clause provides for these to be invoiced as and when they occur, even though the schedule would not be amended until the next renewal date. Many customers seek to postpone any invoicing amendments until the next renewal date, arguing on a 'swings and roundabouts' basis. Suppliers may be less confident that this will lead to a fair balance, because the tendency is for installations to expand, and thus for additions to exceed deletions. It is sometimes possible to achieve a compromise by agreeing to the renewal date adjustment in return for a longer fixed-term agreement before notice can be given. Compromises may involve quarterly or half-yearly reconciliations as a bridge between instant adjustment and the possibility of waiting for 12 months to effect changes.

3. Cover

> All Services will be performed within the Supplier's normal working hours of 9.00 am to 5.30 pm, Monday to Friday excluding public holidays, for both remedial and maintenance Services. Out-of-hours Services can be provided by arrangement and will be charged for at the Supplier's then current UK extended cover rates. Where out-of-hours Services are provided on a permanent basis, the Supplier's applicable extended cover charges will be payable, which are detailed in the relevant Schedule.

This clause effectively provides a cheaper way for customers to pay for overtime when required regularly, because suppliers will be able to demonstrate a crossover point where their extended cover charges (for example, until 7.30 pm on Monday to Friday or '24/7') become less expensive than their special rates. Large customers may be able to influence the point at which the crossover occurs. But, generally speaking, suppliers will expect to offer the same arrangements to their entire customer base, and are likely to be equally insistent upon operating their basic agreements within their normal working hours rather than those of their customers. This is not unreasonable given that their employees are paid in respect of their publicised normal working hours. Movement outside those hours will incur overtime payments to the supplier's staff, which will be passed on to the customers.

4. Eligibility for Hardware Services

> (a) In order to maintain effective networking and optimum performance levels of interconnected equipment, all Supplier products networked at a Site must be included as Products in the relevant Schedule.
>
> (b) The Products must be in normal operating condition as determined by the Supplier and be at a Supplier-supported revision level. Unless the Products are still under the Supplier's warranty when added to a System, they will be subject to inspection and approval by the Supplier before becoming eligible for coverage. This inspection will be charged to the Customer at the Supplier's then current rates, together with any travel and other expenses necessarily incurred. The Supplier will then provide the Customer with a quotation at its prevailing time-and-material service rates for any repairs and adjustments deemed necessary by the Supplier to return a Product to its normal operating condition or specified revision level, and the Customer will authorise the Supplier to proceed with such repairs and adjustments as a pre-condition to the Supplier's inclusion of the Product in the relevant Schedule for coverage.

Paragraph (a) applies in networked environments and is included because suppliers are expected to maintain equipment to optimum performance levels. These can be compromised if parts of the network are not being maintained to a consistent standard which the supplier is in a position to control. Some suppliers may go further and incorporate some form of disclaimer in the event that any third party equipment on the network not maintained by the supplier is identified as causing or contributing to diminished performance by the supplier-maintained products.

Paragraph (b) is sometimes contentious, particularly the element which provides for inspection charges. Negotiation can lead to such charges not being imposed in cases where hardware is accepted for maintenance, and maintenance is then contracted. Another concession area can be where there is only a comparatively short gap between the expiry of warranty and the commencement of maintenance if this was not agreed at the stage of supply.

5. Hardware Services

The Supplier will provide the following Hardware Services:

(a) The Supplier will use all reasonable endeavours to provide attendance at the Site for the purposes of Hardware Product repair or maintenance within [8] working hours from the time of receipt of the Customer's call. Other response options are available at additional cost and the Customer's selections of these options are noted in the Schedules for the selected Products. In all instances, the Customer's calls for Services will receive priority of response over calls from other customers of the Supplier who have not entered into any agreement with the Supplier for the provision of Services.

(b) The Supplier will supply all labour during the contracted cover time, and the parts and materials necessary to maintain the Products in good working condition.

(c) Services include the diagnosis and correction of equipment malfunctions and failures. Remedies may consist of temporary procedures to be followed by the Customer while a permanent repair or remedy is being sought. If the Supplier determines that additional parts or resources are required, provision of the Services may be interrupted and will resume as soon as such parts or resources are available.

(d) Replacement parts are provided to the Customer either on an interim loan, or on an exchange basis. Such parts may be new or functionally equivalent to new. Where parts are replaced, the replaced parts become the property of the Supplier and the replacement parts become the property of the Customer.

(e) Throughout the term of this Agreement, the Supplier will perform preventative maintenance routines on all Products where such routines are applicable. At the Supplier's option, such preventative maintenance calls may be performed in conjunction with a Customer-requested call for remedial maintenance. All preventative maintenance will be performed during the Supplier's normal working hours, although if requested by the Customer and agreed to by the Supplier, preventative maintenance outside normal working hours may be provided at the Supplier's then current charge rates for such out-of-hours Services.

(f) A telephone 'help-line' support facility is available to the Customer during the Supplier's normal working hours or agreed extended hours of cover, for the purposes of reporting equipment malfunctions.

(g) At the Customer's request, the Supplier will move any Product from its existing Site and install it at a new Site subject to the Customer giving the Supplier reasonable notice and agreeing to pay the Supplier's then current charges for this service, the Customer remaining responsible for any shipping arrangements, insurance and other charges or expenses required in order to move the Product. Moving a Product to a different site may result in an increased maintenance charge for that Product. In this event, the Supplier will notify the Customer of the new charge and the Customer will have the option, within 14 days of such notification, to remove the Product from this Agreement, subject to remaining responsible for payment of any outstanding maintenance charges applicable to the Product during the current operating period of this Agreement. Where the Customer moves a Product without utilising the Supplier's removal and installation services, the Supplier may require a Product inspection at the Customer's expense to re-determine the eligibility of the Product for the Services, prior to the resumption of the Services.

The hardware services described here represent a typical offering from a supplier. It is of course possible to extend the range of services considerably and it really comes down to a question of commercial policy for a supplier to decide what it is willing to provide for the price. Major influencing factors are going to be the complexity of the hardware concerned and the competitive situation in that particular marketplace. As an alternative to an extensive list of services, the supplier who wishes to demonstrate to its customers the broad range of services which could be included can separate those services which are to be provided as part of the standard maintenance fee from those which can optionally be provided on the basis of additional time-and-materials charges, or alternatively by referencing a tiered fee structure.

Other services which could fall into this secondary category might include: investigation and correction of errors; incorporation of amendments; updating documentation; technical advice and assistance; system enhancements; system tuning; and a telephone helpline. The latter may range from advice on operational matters to a comprehensive consultancy service designed to maximise the performance of the system.

From the customer's perspective, there is a growing requirement to see some sort of statement about quality, in particular indicating the supplier's commitment to the international quality standard ISO 9001:2000, or more specifically to the world's first formal standard for IT service management, BS 15000, which specifies a set of management processes.

Prudent suppliers will not be willing to guarantee a solution to a problem in advance or to be committed to a maximum period of time for completion of the investigation and resolution of a problem. The most that a customer can reasonably expect is that contracted times for initiating a response are achieved and that, at least for severe and moderate problems, support will be continuous – during the working hours to which the agreement applies – until the problem is cleared.

From the customer's point of view, the response time should not merely be for visiting the site but also to fix the problem. The level of service will be determined by what the customer requires, what the customer will pay, and the supplier's ability to meet the response times. If the application is critical, then better support provision will be needed by the customer than if the application is not fundamental to the customer's business. If the supplier's response is via a dial-up modem, a shorter response time will be viable.

A typical way of categorising problems according to their severity is:

- *Severe* – a problem which has stopped operations – either the total system or a critical task for which there is no circumvention or fix available to the customer;

- *Moderate* – a problem which is disruptive but not catastrophic, for which there is no fix available to the customer. A circumvention may be available, but the customer considers it to be inconvenient or difficult to implement;

- *Irritant* – an intermittent problem which is not disruptive or which may be circumvented or is a general, technical or user question, or an error of documentation or prompting;

- *Feedback* – other information or observations which the customer is passing on to the supplier.

For critical applications, customers should satisfy themselves that suppliers have the capacity to provide a full out-of-hours service if necessary, including adequate cover if the normal engineers are unavailable for any reason.

Another area which is becoming of increasing interest to customers is to see a range of maximum response times which are related to the severity of the problem being experienced. The levels of support provided will depend on the level of importance of the problem. In the case of the most severe categories of problems, some commitment to remain on-site until the problem is solved will be expected.

It is becoming common practice to impose performance disciplines on suppliers in response to the increasing need for 'uptime guarantees' – complex formulae are used to trigger service credits, that is, automatic reductions in service charges when, for example, responses are late, fixes or repairs take too long, and system availability falls below an agreed average. A strong user can also negotiate for liquidated damages for late response or delayed repair, and for temporary replacement of equipment removed for repair, which will be particularly appropriate where a guaranteed uptime falls below the minimum end of its range. For example, there may be a 99 per cent uptime guarantee with service credits if less, but liquidated damages in addition if the time falls below 95 per cent.

Paragraph (e) focuses on preventative maintenance. This is becoming less of a standard requirement but, where it is necessary, some customers will wish to have such maintenance carried out by prior appointment and not necessarily in conjunction with a call for remedial maintenance.

6. Hardware Services Exclusions

(a) The Supplier's obligation to provide the Services is contingent upon the proper use of the Products and the System, and does not cover Products which have been moved without the Supplier's prior approval or which have been subjected to unusual physical or electrical stress.

(b) The Supplier will be under no obligation to furnish the Services where, in the Supplier's reasonable opinion, these are required because of:
  (i) failure of a Product because of accident, neglect, misuse, failure of electrical power, air conditioning or humidity control;
  (ii) damage occurring during transport of a Product except where the Supplier is responsible for the transport;
  (iii) modifications or attempts to repair a Product made without the Supplier's prior written approval;
  (iv) causes external to a Product including but not limited to failure or modification of electrical power, inadequate cooling, fire, flood or other natural disasters;
  (v) failure by the Customer to maintain software on the Product at the Supplier's specified release level, unless otherwise specifically agreed in advance by the Supplier.
  If service is required, in the Supplier's reasonable opinion, as a result of such causes, such service will be charged at the Supplier's normal hourly rates.

(c) The Supplier reserves the right not to provide the Services and to charge for costs and expenses incurred if a call is not warranted, access to the System is hindered or the environmental conditions at the Site are considered by the Supplier to be unsafe or hazardous.

(d) The Services do not include:
  (i) operating supplies and accessories and other consumables, which must be paid for by the Customer;
  (ii) electrical or cabling work external to the System, or maintenance of

> accessories, alterations, attachments or other devices not furnished
> by the Supplier, or installation, removal, relocation or reconfiguration
> of Products, unless specifically provided for in the Schedules;
>
> (iii)   equipment not covered by this Agreement.
>
> (e) The Supplier reserves the right at any time after the initial term of this
>   Agreement to give 90 days' notice to the Customer that a Hardware
>   Product cannot continue to be properly or economically repaired because
>   of excessive wear or deterioration. In this case, the Supplier will provide
>   the Customer with an estimate of reconditioning charges, and if the
>   Customer does not elect to have the Product reconditioned, the Supplier
>   may delete the Product from the Schedules.

It is unusual for a supplier to be willing to negotiate its stated exclusions and any flexibility is likely to be confined to major customers. This should not deter customers from examining the clause carefully and questioning any aspects which appear to be unreasonable or uncompetitive when compared with those of other possible maintainers. It may well be that any costs incurred by a customer because of paragraph (b) circumstances will be recoverable under an insurance policy.

The most contentious element in the example above is the reserved right of the supplier to give notice that a product requires reconditioning if it is to be kept under maintenance (paragraph (e)). Some customers find it difficult to understand how such a situation can come about if a product has been kept under continuous maintenance, but of course almost all products have a shelf life (although some, for example memory, can carry a lifetime guarantee) and will eventually arrive at a point where they simply become uneconomical to maintain without substantial refurbishment. Indeed the latter may itself be uneconomic when compared with the price of a replacement product, particularly in the computer industry where the trend in hardware products is for performance capabilities to double whilst prices halve every 18 months or two years. Negotiating a minimum product life may be fruitful, although the supplier will point out that product life varies considerably in different user environments.

From the customer's point of view, exclusions should be so phrased that, even if a product or service falls into an excluded category, servicing can be carried out at a reasonable charge if required. Paragraph (b) refers.

7. Software Services

> The Software Services comprise and are limited to the following:
>
> (a) [Remote] fault diagnosis and where possible recommendations for correc-
>   tion [subject to the limitations imposed by contractual restrictions of any
>   third party], following the reporting of any Software problem by telephone

by the Customer to the Supplier Maintenance and Support Centre. The Supplier undertakes to investigate the problem within [4] working hours of receiving the Customer's call. The Supplier will classify any problem as critical or non-critical to the fundamental operation of the Software and the following procedure will apply:

Critical Problems: The Supplier will attempt to generate a fix by modifying the Software to conform to its specification and [sending] [transmitting] the modification to the Customer as soon as possible. The Supplier will use all reasonable endeavours to correct any defect in the Software by reason of which it does not conform to its specification, or to modify the Software to obviate or mitigate the effect of the defect.

Non-critical Problems: The Supplier will attempt to generate a fix for incorporation in the next release of the Software. Where feasible, the Supplier may provide a temporary workaround to the Customer.

The Supplier will determine what action, if any, it proposes to take, based, amongst other things, on the importance of the problem to the Customer, and the likely general benefit of any solution.

In no event will the Supplier be required to correct a problem reported by the Customer, and the Supplier reserves the right to abandon attempts at a fix where the costs are likely to be excessive or the general benefits to the Supplier's customers at large are likely to be negligible.

(b) Diagnosis and solution of operational problems will generally be carried out remotely from the Site [but where circumstances require, the Customer is entitled to up to two visits by the Supplier in each year that this Agreement continues in force]. If it becomes necessary to carry out the Services at the Site, such work will be chargeable at the Supplier's then prevailing daily rate, payable monthly in arrears in accordance with the payment terms stated in this Agreement.

(c) Telephone support on the routine use and operation of the Software.

(d) Telephone advice and assistance on user procedures and on ideas and methods intended to assist the Customer in obtaining the best possible use from the Software.

(e) One copy of any new version of the Software released by the Supplier, including related documentation if appropriate.

When should support properly commence? Products usually carry a warranty and customers should need to be persuaded that there are material benefits to be gained from 'Day One' support. The services provided under a support agreement will normally be wider than those offered by the licence warranty. However, there is scope for negotiating a reduced initial charge for support, taking the warranty period into account.

The categorisation of faults into 'critical' and 'non-critical' by the supplier at paragraph (a) is in contrast to the customer-determined categories considered under hardware services. Suppliers alone are in a position to judge whether a particular software bug, once identified, is easily corrected or is one which is going to involve a substantial rewrite. Customers are not aware of the difficulties which may be caused by a request for an apparently straightforward amendment, which may have hidden ramifications affecting various parts of the system concerned. The supplier's judgment relates to the specification, to which the software will have been warranted to conform. Yet customers may still wish to use their own categorisation so that they obtain support when a software fault classified as non-critical by the supplier is deemed by the customer to have a severely detrimental effect on its business.

Customers should insist on some contractual assurance that work will at least commence on resolving a problem within a given time of reporting the fault. Suppliers should be willing to commit to investigation within a specified time, but should avoid promising to resolve a problem by a deadline, especially before they are aware of what the problem is, but in any case for complex software where not all problems may be readily amenable to resolution. The supplier must also take into account resources available.

As with hardware services, the range of services provided within the standard fee will vary greatly from supplier to supplier. There is particular scope with software to present a range of extra services to be supplied on a 'time and materials' basis, many of these having consultancy characteristics. Examples include training, modem support advice and the hours of support coverage. The customer has two tasks: to understand the scope and extent of the services included; and to see what possibilities there are for converting any of the extras into standards. Where a newly developed product is being supported, there may be some prospect of persuading the supplier to add to the list of standards, at least for an initial period, especially if the product in question was developed uniquely for the customer. As so often stated, the value of the contract to the supplier is going to be an important influencing factor, as also is the method of software development where applicable: if a fixed price has been agreed, some support services can be bundled in.

Paragraphs (c) and (d) are illustrations of services which will not always be offered as standard features of support agreements. Suppliers should be wary of granting open-ended access to telephone advice because inevitably some customers will abuse the position. Negotiable areas may include one or more of: the imposition of cumulative time limits per week or month, after which a defined charge is incurred; confining the non-chargeable service to areas not explicitly covered in the documentation; and requiring the customer to have a suitably experienced designated person who alone would be authorised to access those services (paragraph 11(b) refers).

On the other hand, it may be to the supplier's advantage for marketing and business development purposes to encourage use of a telephone helpline in order to find out from customers new ways in which the software could be used.

305

The automatic supply of new versions of software, as at paragraph (e), is frequently included in software support contracts. For some software products, for example payroll and invoicing packages, the services can be stated to include, specifically, revisions to be supplied promptly following changes in taxation. The customer certainly needs to know whether or not it can rely on such a service. The frequency of new releases may also be material. In circumstances in which the supplier will support only the latest and perhaps immediately previous versions of the software, and where implementation involves extensive acceptance testing including testing interfaces with other systems, a customer may need to negotiate a limit to the rate of supply of new versions. Clause 12 also refers to this matter.

In negotiation, the customer should also seek safeguards in the form of a warranty that replacement software will continue to meet or exceed the original specification, and perhaps an agreed minimum period of time during which the supplier undertakes to maintain a capability of supporting the previous version. A virus-free warranty may also be sought, although few suppliers will be willing to guarantee a situation which they can argue is not within their complete control (unless they themselves load and install the software on the system).

Some customers will seek to make failure to support the software grounds for release of source code under a source code deposit agreement. However, suppliers should resist this, which can turn into a back-door excuse for obtaining the source code. Failure to provide the services defined in this agreement would constitute breach of this contract, and customers should seek appropriate remedies accordingly. This is discussed further in **CHAPTER 13**.

8. Additional Software Services

> The Supplier will also offer the Customer the following services at such charges and on such terms as the parties may agree from time to time:
>
> (a) consultation for the resolution of those problems experienced by the Customer in operating the System and not covered by the Services;
>
> (b) on-site services to carry out such work at the Site as the parties may agree from time to time;
>
> (c) consultation about enhancement of the Software.

The supplier will have resource limitations. This clause clarifies what it is prepared to provide and charge for outside the contracted services. There is of course overlap here with clause 7. The important point for suppliers is to ensure that, between the two clauses, all of their available service offerings are described.

9. Software Services Exclusions

(a) The Supplier is not obliged to support the Software if the Customer is not using the versions of the operating system software as specified by the Supplier from time to time, or if the Customer fails to maintain the Software at the Supplier's specified release level unless specifically agreed in advance by the Supplier.

(b) The Supplier will undertake responsibility for Software on a designated hardware system only if the hardware is covered by this Agreement or is the subject of a separate hardware maintenance agreement with the manufacturer of the hardware or with a reputable third party maintainer.

(c) On-Site Software support services are not included as a standard feature of this Agreement.

(d) The Services do not include service in respect of defects or errors resulting from any modifications or enhancements to the Software not made by the Supplier or made without the Supplier's prior written consent, or resulting from incorrect use of the Software.

(e) The Supplier is not obliged to support the Software if malfunctions are due to incorrect use of the Software, or for any reason external to the Software including, but not limited to, failure or fluctuation of electrical supplies, hardware failures, accidents, or natural disasters.

Paragraph (b) contains a potentially contentious requirement. Many customers balk at any apparent suggestion of tie-in type arrangements, in this instance requiring a hardware maintenance agreement as a prerequisite to software support.

However, it is not such an unreasonable requirement because there is no doubt that hardware which performs poorly or a badly tuned system can have an adverse effect on software performance. The example given above does allow the customer the alternative possibility of hardware maintenance by a third party supplier and this should defuse the main thrust of the tie-in objection.

10. Disclaimers

(a) The Supplier will use its reasonable endeavours to perform the Services promptly but no warranty is given in respect of any times for response or performance by the Supplier and time will not be of the essence.

(b) The Supplier is not liable for delay arising from any industrial dispute or any cause outside its reasonable control and any agreed timescale will be subject to reasonable extension in the event of such delay.

(c) Provision of the Service does not imply any guarantee or representation that the Supplier will be able to assist the Customer in achieving any results from any Products which are not technically feasible. Subject to this, any services that are outside the scope of this Agreement will, at the Customer's request and at the Supplier's option, be provided at the Supplier's then current rates for such services.

(d) Provision of the Services does not imply any guarantee that the Supplier will be successful in correcting Software malfunctions and the Supplier does not accept any liability in this connection.

(e) The Supplier reserves the right to refuse to provide the Software Services at any time without refunding any sums paid by the Customer:

  (i) if any attempt is made, other than by the Supplier, to remove any defects or deal with any errors in the Software; or

  (ii) if any development, enhancement or variation of the Software is carried out other than by the Supplier; or

  (iii) if the Customer has failed to pay a Supplier's invoice in accordance with the provisions of this Agreement; or

  (iv) where, in the reasonable opinion of the Supplier, the Customer's system has ceased to be capable of running the Software successfully for any reason; or

  (v) where modifications are made to the Customer's computer system without the prior agreement of the Supplier; or

  (vi) where, in the reasonable opinion of the Supplier, the System requires tuning in order to facilitate the proper functioning and performance of the Software.

This is an important clause. It sets out the limitations on the services to be provided. Any modifications will involve some sort of increased risk for the supplier and are therefore likely to be resisted, or at least made subject to an increase in costs. For major suppliers, there is the usual added difficulty of assimilating one customer's special needs into an automated system so that calls received are flagged up as requiring extraordinary attention.

Customers will find negotiation more fruitful in areas such as response times and commencement of remedial action than in seeking some form of guarantee that a software fault will be fixed. With the possible exception of very well-established software packages, it is a practical impossibility for a supplier to make such a commitment.

In a major negotiation, there will be a good deal of scope for discussion about paragraph (e)(iv)–(vi). Customers may at least wish to build in a mechanism for independent assessment in the event that they cannot agree with their supplier's opinions about the continuing capabilities of their computers to run the supported software.

11. Customer Responsibilities

The Customer or, at its direction, End Users, will:

(a) use the Products correctly and in accordance with their Supplier operating instructions and with suitable operating supplies;

(b) designate primary and secondary contacts appropriately qualified and trained to an acceptable standard authorised to request Services, and inform the Supplier accordingly. Authorised use of the telephone helpline is limited to these designated contacts;

(c) maintain procedures to facilitate reconstruction of any lost or altered files, data or programs to the extent deemed necessary by the Customer, and the Customer agrees that the Supplier will not be liable under any circumstances for any consequences arising from lost or corrupted data, files or programs. The Customer and/or End Users are solely responsible for carrying out all necessary back-up procedures for their own benefit, to ensure that data integrity can be maintained in the event of loss of data for any reason;

(d) be solely responsible for the security of its confidential and proprietary information, and not disclose such information to the Supplier except on a 'need to know' basis for the purposes of the Supplier's performance of the Services;

(e) notify the Supplier promptly of any Product malfunction;

(f) control the environmental conditions of the Site in accordance with any environmental operating ranges specified by the Supplier or other Product manufacturer;

(g) regularly perform the various routine and preventative maintenance and cleaning operations described in the applicable user guides or as advised by the Supplier including but not limited to any operating and diagnostic checks. The cost of rectifying any damage caused to the System by not observing this undertaking will not be covered by this Agreement;

(h) keep records of the System's usage and performance if requested by the Supplier, in a mutually agreed format;

(i) observe appropriate safety precautions in replacing parts provided under this Agreement;

(j) provide the Supplier with access to and use of such of the Customer's or End User's information and facilities reasonably necessary to service the Products;

(k) make all the relevant Hardware freely available to the Supplier during any agreed preventative maintenance period to enable the Supplier to carry out the Services;

> (l)   have a Customer or End User representative present at all times during the performance of remedial and preventative maintenance Services;
>
> (m) provide ready access to a telephone at the Site on which external calls connected with the Services can be made and received by the Supplier's personnel;
>
> (n)   ensure that only properly trained employees operate or use the System in accordance with the operating instructions and manuals supplied;
>
> (o)   not make any modification or addition to the Software or System, except with the Supplier's consent, which shall not be unreasonably withheld.

This clause is linked to clause 10 above in that, in detailing the customer's responsibilities relating to hardware and software, it is also setting up a situation whereby the supplier can disclaim responsibility and/or make additional charges for services. While many of these responsibilities are really a matter of common sense to a prudent customer, it is appropriate to question some of them.

For instance, customers should ensure that user instructions are clear and sufficiently detailed, referring to paragraphs (a), (f) and (g); that any data disclosed is appropriately protected by the confidentiality provisions in the agreement (paragraphs (d) and (j)) and that there is some control over the use of customer-provided services: are international calls to be permitted under paragraph (m) if a non-UK manufactured product is involved?

Paragraph (b) gives the supplier the option of handling support and maintenance only through a customer-designated person. The supplier will then be certain that the call is from someone who understands the system and who is therefore reporting a genuine fault, or for multiple sites, rather than someone who is ignorant of how the system ought to operate. The customer should not have different people replicating work. An alternative possibility is to insist that only experienced customer staff, trained in the system concerned, are entitled to contact the supplier. Trained users take many less resources in support.

At paragraph (c), data responsibility is often a contentious issue. Some customers have difficulty with the concept that a supplier should not be responsible for lost or corrupted data, even if caused by the supplier's negligence. Such a customer will expect the supplier to back up any data put at risk by its operations in a situation where the supplier would be more likely than the customer to appreciate that there was such a risk. They will at least want the supplier to provide a warning of the risk before going ahead. On the other hand, it is true that if back-up procedures are in place which are appropriate to the importance and sensitivity of the data concerned, the consequences of losing the operational data, for whatever reason, will be minimal.

Paragraph (l) is aimed at the health and safety responsibilities of the customer. These are, of course, also covered by statute. It is questionable whether it is really necessary to have a customer representative on hand throughout what may be a long visit. The environment in which the equipment is located should be an influencing factor.

Notwithstanding the widespread use of mobile telephones, paragraph (m) remains appropriate. Batteries can lose their charge, and there are health and safety issues associated with the prolonged use of mobile telephones.

It is, however, reasonable for customers to seek to confine suppliers, to say, not more than two major revisions per annum, fearing the potential disruption that ongoing installation may cause.

12. Additional Customer Responsibilities (Software)

The Customer or, at its direction, End Users will:

(a) provide modem facilities to the Supplier's requirements for remote investigation of Software defects;

(b) ensure that the Software licences authorising the Customer's use of the Software are in effect throughout the term of this Agreement and that the Software is used only as permitted by the terms of the applicable licences;

(c) use only the current version of the Software as specified by the Supplier from time to time;

(d) install the latest applicable software revisions and enhancements to the Software as soon as reasonably practicable, and in any event within 6 months, unless the parties agree for a particular release an implementation plan with a longer timescale;

(e) copy and use any updates, modifications, corrections or enhancements to the Software only in accordance with the licence granted for the Software. Under no circumstances is title to any Software, including updates, modifications, corrections or enhancements, granted under this Agreement.

This clause is an extension to clause 11, adding some responsibilities in relation to the software elements of the system.

With reference to paragraph (b), a supplier should ensure that the software it is supporting is legally licensed to the customer. A supplier will be concerned to avoid entanglement in an enforcement action by the software owner and it is not uncommon to see a provision whereby the customer indemnifies the supplier in the event of such an action.

Software suppliers are always concerned to ensure that the current version of the software is in use, often supplied as part of the support services. Although some customers are reluctant to install different software, fearing the introduction of problems on a system that is satisfactory in its current state for their purposes (the comments relating to (e) at clause 7 are relevant), it is difficult for suppliers to retain the capacity to support older software. Their staff change or lose touch with the features and performance characteristics at a detailed level. It is, however, reasonable for customers to seek to restrict new versions to, say, not more than two major revisions a year, fearing the potential disruption that ongoing installation may cause.

Customers sometimes object to paragraph (e) and try to negotiate assignment of copyright for enhancements provided to them. However, copyright is of no particular benefit to them. They cannot make economic use of the enhancements separate from the software itself. The software licence should include modifications and enhancements. Paragraph (e) confirms that the conditions of the software licence are extended to updates and enhancements.

CHAPTER 15

Consultancy

A. Introduction

Traditional consultancy assignments used to be clear-cut. Either 'bodies' were needed on a temporary basis, or some sort of project needed to be carried out beyond the resources or capabilities of the internal workforce. Distinctions now are becoming more blurred. Professional Services Agreements are, in effect, a form of consultancy, but tend to have a more permanent character relating to the objective for which the services are required, such as outsourcing (see **CHAPTER 17**).

Whatever the label, there is no doubt that consultancy services cover a wide variety of requirements, whether for programming or analysis services, or for other special expertise, project management, education and training. There may be a requirement for a single person's unique expertise. Alternatively, personnel may be provided to undertake defined tasks.

The motivation which prompts a client to enter into a consultancy agreement may be a requirement for work which arises only on an occasional basis, or one where skills are needed which the client does not possess within its organisation, or where the client's organisation is overloaded and there is a need to obtain additional short-term support.

It is now more common to bring in specialist contractors for their expertise relevant to a particular project, rather than to keep a large pool of staff on the permanent payroll with experience of the business but with less up-to-date knowledge of practical applications in the technical area concerned. Where an organisation is cutting back, 'rationalising' or 'streamlining', consultancy can provide a useful short-term temporary solution.

1. Individual or company arrangement

Often the arrangement appears to be made with one particular individual consultant, but frequently it will be made with the consultant's employer. While sometimes this will mean a company of substance there are many examples of one-person businesses, that is, individuals offering their services through the mechanism of a limited company in which they are the principal shareholder, or as sole traders. It follows that clients requiring such services ought to take care to ensure that adequate protection against liability is in place, including in particular professional indemnity insurance of sufficient value to cover the potential losses which could result from negligent or incompetent work. Consultants themselves must watch the extent of their potential liability to their clients. Realistically speaking, professional indemnity insurance can sometimes be prohibitively expensive for an individual consultant or small firm, who may nevertheless be able to provide specialist skills in short supply.

Whilst individual consultants providing services on their own behalf are actually working, they will expect to be paid more highly than if they were in regular employment as employees. However, they have to balance against this the uncertainty of periods of not being employed, insurance to cover health, lack of corporate fringe benefits and a new meaning to 'holidays' as being days for which they have chosen not to be paid. But they also enjoy the advantages of flexibility, the attraction of new work challenges, changes of working environment and the independence of being answerable only to themselves.

Against these advantages, consultants may have to work away from home, fit into different corporate cultures, which will not necessarily be congenial working environments, and probably suffer financial insecurity. They will have to do their own marketing to promote knowledge of their services and availability. They will have to catch up with administrative tasks at times when they are not at work, which often means at weekends.

An essential characteristic of computer consultancy agreements, sometimes called professional services agreements, is that professionally qualified individuals are being supplied to the client for the purposes of a project, or for ongoing services, whatever these may be. If a project is a self-contained one that the consultant is asked to undertake in its entirety, for instance to develop a computer system or specialised program, then the consultancy agreement will not be the most appropriate agreement to use. A software development agreement would be preferable.

2. Consultancy v employment

Whatever the contract is called, whether it is for the *supply of services* or is a *contract of service*, the latter being an employment contract, is a question of fact in the circumstances. It is important that the distinction is clear, because a contract of service has tax and employment implications which neither party will want if the consultant is self-employed.

The first test to apply is whether the consultant is engaged full-time on the client's work. The second test is the extent of the client organisation's control in the role of employer over the consultant. The more that control is exercised over what the individual is told to do and how and when it is to be done, the more likely it is that it will be regarded as a contract of employment by tax authorities and others, under the terms of which the consultant, as a deemed employee, is obliged to provide a service. Other factors will be the extent to which the consultant is regarded as part of the organisation, whether the consultant uses equipment of his or her own, whether payment is made to cover periods of illness and holidays, the extent of the risk of loss undertaken, and how permanent the management is. For long-term contracts, it is therefore especially important to differentiate the contractor as such from the client organisation's employees by means of the wording in the consultancy terms of agreement. The courts tend to favour confirmation that the relationship is that of employer and employee if there is any room for ambiguity.

In an IT environment, the primary 'control' test is not clear-cut as the consultant may well have to work to quality and security standards imposed by the employer, and produce work in a way which fits in with existing systems and software. The consultant is certainly more likely to be using the client's equipment in the form of the hardware and working on the client's software systems, and to be required to do so, rather than to be able to provide such hardware or software.

Nevertheless, employers need to take care that employee status is avoided in respect of agency workers. The test of 'control' may be key. In a case before the Employment Appeal Tribunal[1], it was decided that a temporary employee, Mr Davidson, under a contract for services with an agency, Melville Craig Group Ltd, who worked at Motorola's plant, could legitimately pursue an unfair dismissal claim against Motorola (rather than against the agency). Mr Davidson had been employed for over two years and had been assigned to work exclusively for Motorola.

The issue concerned the extent of control over Mr Davidson, and whether this gave rise to an employer-employee relationship between Motorola and Mr Davidson.

The factors regarded as significant by the Employment Appeal Tribunal lay in the realities of day-to-day control by Motorola. Motorola decided 'the thing to be done, the way in which it shall be done, the means employed doing it, the time when and the place where it shall be done'. Mr Davidson used Motorola's tools, wore Motorola's uniform, and had to book holidays and raise grievances through Motorola. It was Motorola who had suspended Mr Davidson from work and terminated the relationship. It was not relevant for these purposes that the agency had similar or greater control over Mr Davidson.

However, it is the actual reality of the individual situation which counts. No single isolated factor will necessarily determine the definition in practice of the relationship. Care is therefore needed in drafting a consultancy agreement so that a relationship of employment is not created inadvertently, making each party thereby liable for inappropriate payments, whether tax, national insurance or anything else.

If a self-employed consultant operates through a limited company, able to render invoices and probably VAT-registered, there may be no difficulty. But the Inland Revenue is now taking a much more robust approach, essentially creating a presumption of employment rather than self-employment, and leaving the individual consultant with a very high hurdle to jump in order to establish self-employment. Even the device of a limited company is no guarantee that self-employed status will be accepted[2]. A sole trader should be required to produce confirmation of self-employed status from his or her local tax office. If this is not done, the client who fails to deduct income tax from payments made may run the risk of having to pay this element again if the consultant fails to account for personal taxes to the Inland Revenue. A client in real doubt about the position might consider offering the consultant a short fixed-term employment contract, which can exclude some of the benefits provided to permanent employees, although even here it must be recognised that developments in employment law are moving towards the extension of all benefits pro rata to both part-time and temporary employees.

3. Conflicts of interest

Consultants should be impartial and independent. The client should be aware of other interests of the consultant which are likely to cause potential conflicts of interest. For example, an organisation for whom a consultant's report on the feasibility of outsourcing had been submitted should consider whether it would be appropriate for the resulting outsourcing work to go to the consultant company recommending this approach, without any invitations to tender or independent evaluations of what that company would be providing. Conversely, a former employee of a manufacturer or a company offering special expertise in that manufacturer's products might be the best choice where technical experience of that manufacturer's products was a prerequisite for carrying out the work.

There are several specific issues which need careful attention when a consultancy agreement is being prepared. Very few consultancy organisations are so big that they will be likely to adopt a rigid stance in negotiation. Potentially all required terms are obtainable, and usually the balance of power in negotiating a consultancy agreement will be weighted towards the client requiring the services, if only because the client will often be a much larger organisation.

4. Contractual issues

The contractual issues which arise most often are the following:

- **Levels of service**
  It must be clear to both parties what the consultant's role and functions are to be. Where a number of different consultants are providing services to the client, it is important that the different inputs are successfully matched, so that work is not duplicated, there are no gaps in the results and there are no conflicts over interpretations of what is needed.

- **Copyright ownership**
  Who is to own the work performed by the consultant? In the absence of a contractual provision to the contrary, the consultant will own it.

- **Location**
  Are the services ones which necessarily need to be performed at the client's site and, if so, do consultancy hours allow for travel times?

- **Decision making**
  To what extent is the consultant expected to participate in project management and decision making in relation to the project? Is attendance at project meetings expected?

- **Named individual consultants**
  Is there a requirement for one or more named individual consultants? Are there arrangements to cater for unexpected non-availability or sudden unacceptability of consultant staff to the client?

- **Fees**
  Are these to be based on agreed charge rates related to the experience and seniority of each consultant, or is a fixed rate more appropriate for the services to be provided?

- **Tax**
  This is a matter often overlooked but organisations should be cautious in employing self-employed consultants who could be regarded by the Inland Revenue as, albeit short-term, employees of the client. As discussed above, the tax status is determined by the actual situation as interpreted by established tax law and cases and not by the descriptions which the parties give to their relationship.

5. Agreement structure

An effective way of structuring a consultancy agreement is to establish an overall agreement setting out the normal terms and conditions and then incorporating one or more schedules describing the work or purposes for which the consultant will be employed including all other variable details of the description of work, charge rates, timescales, reporting requirements and other specific conditions relating to the project and its administration.

317

B. The structure of a consultancy agreement

A typical structure for a consultancy agreement is set out below. It does not include software development assignments, which are considered in **CHAPTER 16**. This includes project management services to be provided by a consultant company with a number of employees.

This agreement sets out the overall terms and conditions of consultancy, so that it can continue in existence for so long as there is the possibility of the client business using the services of the consultant. Each specific project will be the subject of an agreed project statement between the parties to be attached to the agreement as a schedule to be incorporated into it as it is drawn up.

Terms and conditions

- Definitions*
- Term
- Consultancy and Project Management Services*
- Consultant's Obligations and Warranties*
- Client's Obligations*
- Consultant's Employees*
- Proprietary Rights*
- Intellectual Property Rights Indemnity
- Charges, Expenses and Payment Terms
- Confidentiality
- Indemnities and Limits of Liability
- Termination*
- General Contract Provisions

Schedule

- Project Statement*

C. Specific clauses

In the clauses considered below, which are those above marked with an asterisk, the organisation which commissions work from a contractor is described as the 'Client', and the contractor who carries out the work is described as the 'Consultant'.

1. Definitions

'*Agreement*' means this Agreement and each Project Statement together or separately. In the event of any conflict of meaning between this Agreement and a Project Statement, the Project Statement prevails.

'*Authorised Representative*' means the person designated by each party whose identity is notified in writing to the other party, who is vested with the authority of the appointing party to communicate all of that party's decisions and representations to the other party in connection with the Services, who will act as the prime point of contact with the Authorised Representative of the other party, and who is authorised to receive the decisions and representations of the other party in connection with the Services.

'*Project*' means the work undertaken as described in a Project Statement.

'*Project Management Services*' means the services identified as such in a Project Statement.

'*Project Results*' means all products designed, developed, written or prepared by the Consultant in respect of the Project and all related documentation including but not limited to any specification, graphics, programs, data, reports, and all other deliverables, written materials or computer output produced in the course of providing the Services.

'*Project Statement*' means a description of a Project utilising some or all of the Services and forming a Schedule to this Agreement, including:

- the title and description of the Project;
- the time schedule for undertaking and completing the Services;
- the time and other resources which the Consultant will commit to achieve the performance of the Services;
- the amount and/or method of calculation of the Consultant's charges.

'*Proprietary Rights*' means all intellectual property rights including but not limited to copyrights, database rights, patents, design rights, trade marks and confidential information.

'*Services*' means the general consultancy, computer systems analysis, programming, training, project management and all related services to be provided by the Consultant and more particularly described in each Project Statement, including as appropriate, the Project Management Services.

2. Consultancy and Project Management Services

(a) The Consultant agrees to provide and the Client agrees to take and pay for the Services described in the Project Statement at the rates or for the sum set out in the Project Statement.

(b) The Consultant is not generally authorised to carry out any work for the Client which is not the subject of a properly executed Project Statement. However, if the Consultant carries out any work at the Client's request which is not the subject of a Project Statement then, unless the parties otherwise agree in writing, the provisions of this Agreement will apply to the work undertaken and if no fee is agreed for this work, the Consultant will be paid on a time and materials basis at its standard published rates of charges, or otherwise at a reasonable rate.

(c) This Agreement is personal to the Consultant who will not be entitled to assign or sub-contract any of its rights or obligations.

(d) This Agreement is not an exclusive arrangement, and subject to the Consultant's obligations in this Agreement, including but not limited to the obligation to avoid any conflicts of interest, nothing in this Agreement will operate to prevent the Consultant from engaging in other consultancy or project management activities.

(e) The Services are provided at the Client's request and the Client accepts that it is responsible for verifying that the Services are suitable for its own needs.

(f) The Client acknowledges that times scheduled in the Project Statement specifications are estimates only of the amount of time required by the Client for the provision of the Services, and the Client will be invoiced for the actual time spent in providing the Services to the Client.

(g) To facilitate the provision of the Project Management Services the Client and the Consultant will meet to discuss and review the Project on a regular basis and will jointly identify, prepare and agree in writing all relevant aspects of the Project including but not limited to:
  (i) the structure and content of the Project team and assignment of functions, including any employees of the Client to be assigned to or work with the Consultant;
  (ii) a provisional programme indicating the sequence and timetable for carrying out the Project, providing the Project Management Services and the period likely to be required for its completion;
  (iii) the frequency at which the Consultant and the Client will meet to review the progress of the Project;
  (iv) where appropriate to the nature of the Project Management Services to be provided, the form and method of presentation of the results of these Project Management Services;
  (v) any parts of the Project to be carried out by third parties and the

authority of the Consultant to engage third parties on behalf of the Client for this purpose, the Client alone being party to any agreement with third parties for the performance of the work or the supply of any goods but by prior agreement, the Client may authorise the Consultant to engage such third parties on behalf of the Client.

The parties will agree upon the services to be performed by any third party. Notwithstanding any suggestions or recommendations which the Consultant makes, the Client must satisfy itself as to the suitability of any third party to perform any work in connection with the Project, and the Consultant will be under no liability in respect of any act or omission of any third party.

(h) The Consultant is authorised to have access to those computer systems identified in the relevant Project Statement to the extent to which this is necessary for the performance of the Services.

(i) The Consultant makes no representations and gives no warranties, guarantees or undertakings concerning its performance or non-performance of the Services except as expressly set out in this Agreement. All other warranties, express or implied, by statute or otherwise, are excluded from this Agreement. There will be no obligation on the Consultant to correct or re-perform any of the Services except at the direction of the Client in accordance with the terms and applicable charge rates set out in this Agreement.

Paragraph (b) seeks to ensure that the consultant does not do any work without proper authority. Particularly in a situation where several personnel are involved and there is a lot of interaction between the parties, it can be difficult to track all of the work being carried out and to validate applications for payment. Ideally the situation referred to in the second sentence should not arise, but if there are likely to be circumstances in which work is going to be required without there being time to create a proper project statement, there needs to be an agreed basis for payment for work which has been requested.

The consultant may be a sole trader or a large computer services supplier. The client organisation should insist on a provision such as the example at paragraph (c), without any supplemental wording giving the consultant a right to assign or sub-contract, even where this is qualified by a requirement for consent, and even if such consent is not to be unreasonably withheld. The client will have selected the consultant on the basis of his or her professional reputation or previous track record, and the company will be unlikely to receive full value by agreeing to an alternative consultant. There is more scope for adopting a flexible attitude if the consultant is a large organisation with alternative high quality resources at its disposal and the obvious ability to underwrite the work that is done.

Some large consultants will be unwilling to offer consultancy services without such an option because they will not think it reasonable to focus the delivery of their consultancy services either through any one individual, or even by their own full-time personnel if their resources become stretched at some point during the time the agreement is in effect. Even if the client is persuaded by such an argument, it should at least retain the right to withhold consent so that it can take a considered view about the precise scope and extent of what is proposed when the time comes.

Consultants are always going to be reluctant to agree to any provisions which limit their ability to obtain other engagements, and paragraph (d) is designed to protect their interests in this respect. This is not unreasonable, but it may be appropriate in some cases for a client to insist upon a constraint to prevent its consultants from acting for any of its competitors for a minimum agreed period, particularly if the consultant is engaged on a project which relates to an aspect of the client's business where the client is seeking to establish or maintain a competitive advantage. Where time is important, some clients will also be concerned to secure priority of service over their consultant's other commitments.

Paragraph (e) serves to emphasise that this agreement is client-driven. The services are required because the client does not have appropriate in-house resources available. However much freedom a consultant is given to perform the services, they remain the ultimate responsibility of the client. Thus, even if the services are so comprehensive that they involve the development of a product, it will be appropriate to use this agreement rather than a development agreement if there has been no handover of, or a shared part of, this responsibility.

A less obvious benefit of paragraph (e) for the self-employed consultant is that it may help to convince the tax inspector that the engagement as a consultant is a genuine business contract, and not a disguised form of employment.

It is usually the case that consultancy services are paid for on the basis of time spent, because for this kind of arrangement, tasks will rarely be so self-contained and completely specified for it to be possible for the consultant to calculate and offer a fixed price. However, if a fixed price is nevertheless agreed, the parties will be wise to include a very clearly defined change control process, having first precisely defined the services included in the fixed price.

This one agreement embraces two distinct types of services, one being consultancy activities which can take a variety of forms, and the other being the provision of project management skills. The latter are one form of consultancy but it is possible to identify some specific responsibilities which fall within the scope of project management. These are described in paragraph (g). The parties will need to agree and record all of the specific project management tasks required in a given situation, as envisaged by the first part of the paragraph, and the list which follows at (i)–(v) is intended to serve as an aide-mémoire to guide them in the construction of the agreed brief. It is important to note that the engagement of

322

third parties referred to here does not constitute sub-contracting. It is merely an aspect of the consultant's project management duties, and there is no conflict with paragraph (b).

Whether the consultant is accessing or modifying the company's computer systems as part of the services being provided, specific authorisation should be included as at paragraph (h). This will also help to support any claim for self-employed status. Unauthorised access and modification are crimes under the Computer Misuse Act 1990. In addition, as part of the company's security procedures, it will be logical to provide for express authorisation.

Paragraph (i) of this clause emphasises that the consultant is giving only the express warranties and undertakings contained in clause 3 below or otherwise specifically stated. A large client may put pressure on a small consultant to remove this provision, but the consultant should insist on its retention and focus any discussion on particular warranties or undertakings which the client wishes to see incorporated. This will allow proper debate and will enable the consultant to decide whether it is capable of, or is commercially justified in conceding, additional commitments.

3. Consultant's Obligations and Warranties

The Consultant warrants and undertakes:

(a) to apply all reasonable professional skill, care and expertise to the performance of the Services in accordance with the terms of this Agreement;

(b) to ensure that all Project Results are of satisfactory quality and fit for their purpose;

(c) to provide suitably qualified personnel to carry out the Services and related tasks (including attendances at meetings and travel) assigned by the Client's Authorised Representative;

(d) to provide the Services in a timely and efficient manner and to a professional standard in accordance with any time schedules stipulated in the Project Statement and which will conform to the standards generally observed in the industry for similar services, and to co-operate with employees and other independent consultants where this is necessary for the performance of the Services;

(e) to ensure that the normal working day is equivalent to seven working hours (excluding travel time to and from the Client's place of business), any requirement for overtime, weekend or holiday working to be specially arranged between the parties upon the terms specified in the Project Statement or on such other terms as they may agree;

(f) to maintain accurate time sheets for approval and endorsement by the Client's Authorised Representative;

(g) that the Project Results so far as they do not comprise material originating from the Client are original works created by the Consultant, and the use or possession of them by the Client will not subject the Client to any claim for infringement of any Proprietary Rights of any third party;

(h) not to make any announcement concerning this Agreement or any Project or any ancillary matter or to publicise this Agreement or Project in any way without the prior written consent of the Client;

(i) to conform to the Client's normal codes of staff and security practice;

(j) to maintain professional indemnity insurance in effect while this Agreement is in force;

(k) to provide evidence to the Client that it is regarded by the Inland Revenue as a bona fide independent business for the purposes of income tax and National insurance liabilities.

In agreements of this nature, there is always going to be scope for negotiating particular obligations which are considered to be necessary by the client in the context of the work to be undertaken. There should not be many objections on the grounds that individual client changes cannot be accommodated because they would compromise established operating procedures in a large consultancy organisation. This clause is intended to anticipate the sorts of requirements which are likely to be considered important by most clients.

The warranties in (a) and (b) are not unreasonable when professional experience is being engaged. They give effect to statutory warranties, although for 'satisfactory quality' and 'fitness for purpose' to apply: (i) the project results would have to involve the production of some sort of physical work product which could be regarded as 'goods' for the purposes of the legislation[3]; and (ii) the client would have to be sufficiently specific about its requirements for the purpose to be clear.

Conformity to general industry standards, referred to in paragraph (d), may be considered vague, but it is arguable that there are no established quality standards which can be used. Those that do exist have more to do with documenting and defining processes than with the quality of deliverables. In the event of a dispute relating to the quality of work produced, it would be necessary to introduce expert evidence to demonstrate what might reasonably be expected. Experts in this area are renowned for disagreeing, but at least the consultant is acknowledging in this paragraph that work of acceptable quality is required. Where the consultant will be working alongside other independent consultants or employees, this paragraph also includes a requirement for working together, and co-operating in order to carry out the work successfully.

Paragraph (d) requires timeliness but time is not expressed to be 'of the essence'. If clients seek this, they are likely to meet resistance, because IT projects are notorious for missing deadlines, as often because of unforeseen difficulties or misinterpretations or misstatements of requirements as for any lacunae in performance. Time can always be made 'of the essence' later on if the consultant is shown to be in breach of this clause.

In paragraph (e) travel to and from the client's premises is excluded. This is reasonable but travel to and from other places on behalf of the client is justifiable, although determined clients may succeed in negotiating a reduced hourly rate for such journeys.

Paragraph (g) contains an important warranty for the client. If significant intellectual property is being created by the consultant, the client should also consider requiring an indemnity in the event of a third party claim, and the Agreement in this example does include such an indemnity, as discussed in more detail in **CHAPTER 7**.

The requirement for professional indemnity insurance in paragraph (j) is important. Standard public liability policies do not extend to cover negligent advice and any purely economic losses which would be likely to result. However, professional indemnity policies are expensive to obtain. Although the chances of being held liable in negligence, especially in respect of advice causing purely economic loss to third parties, are relatively small, the potential damages could be high if liability were to be established. The insurance market seems to be heavily influenced by the experience of the US in this area, where there is ever more readiness to litigate, with the likelihood of more substantial damages awards than are generally experienced in comparable UK cases. Consequently, some consultants do not have this sort of insurance cover because of the cost involved. If there is any reason to doubt the position in cases where professional advice constitutes an important element of the consultancy services, clients should reserve the right to require consultants to carry current and adequate levels of insurance. They are likely to find that their own professional indemnity cover will not extend to work performed by independent businesses.

Paragraph (k) is a prudent inclusion if the consultant is an individual. Payments without income tax and National Insurance withholdings to persons not accepted by the Inland Revenue as genuinely self-employed can result in a tax claim on the client as the deemed employer.

4. Client's Obligations

The Client undertakes:

(a) to pay for the Services together with associated expenses under the terms of this Agreement;

(b) to provide the Consultant and its employees designated to perform the Services with all necessary information, support and co-operation that may reasonably be required to enable the Consultant to carry out its obligations to the Client under this Agreement;

(c) for the purpose of co-ordination, to designate one individual as its Authorised Representative as first notified in writing to the Consultant, who will be responsible for controlling, in consultation with the Consultant, all aspects of the Consultant's assigned work on the Project under the terms of this Agreement;

(d) to provide, at no charge to the Consultant, adequate office accommodation, a secure work space, telephone services and other facilities including access to the applicable computers and systems of the Client, all as reasonably necessary to enable the assigned employees of the Consultant to perform the Services at the Client's sites, and further to allow full access to the areas in which the Services are to be performed at the Client's sites;

(e) to take all reasonable steps to ensure the health and safety of the Consultant's employees while they are at the Client's sites, and to ensure that such employees are provided with copies of all applicable safety information and site regulations;

(f) that the computer and operating system and any other software, information or data which the Consultant's employees are asked to access, use or modify for the purpose of the Services are either the property of the Client or are legally licensed to the Client or otherwise in the lawful possession of the Client for the uses intended, and to indemnify the Consultant in respect of any claims against the Consultant by third parties including all related costs, expenses or damages in the event of any actual or alleged violations of third party (including the Client's employees) proprietary or data rights or software licences;

(g) to ensure that its employees and other independent consultants co-operate fully with the Consultant in relation to the provision of the Services;

(h) to furnish the Consultant promptly with such information and documents as the Consultant may reasonably request for the proper performance of its obligations under this Agreement;

[(i) to provide or arrange at its expense for any specialist training in the Client's methods or products which it requires to be undertaken by the Consultant. Time spent in such training will be invoiced at the daily rate shown in the Schedule;]

[(j) if any perceived performance failure occurs, to inform the Consultant immediately, confirming in writing within seven days. Where no such written confirmation is received, the Consultant's performance will be deemed to be satisfactory.]

This clause is intended to anticipate general requirements appropriate to this sort of agreement. Unless the contract is comparatively small and the services are being provided by a well-established company offering consultancy as part of a range of products and services, there will be scope in negotiation for making this clause more precise where required by the circumstances. In particular, the consultant will wish to have all that it needs to be able to perform the services successfully. Paragraphs (b) to (e) provide examples of some of the most obvious requirements, to which other more specific requirements may be added as necessary.

The indemnity at paragraph (f) is a safeguard for a consultant who is going to have direct access to any of the client's systems, especially having regard to such statutory developments as the Computer Misuse Act in the UK. It is also intended to protect the consultant if the services involve the handling and/or use of individuals' personal data.

At paragraph (g), the reference to 'other independent consultants' will be relevant in cases where the client is using the services of more than one consultancy firm. The consultant should verify that there is consistency in all areas where work is likely to be affected by other outside contractors' work. The client will require consultants' contractual obligations to include provisions such as those stated in this paragraph to work in a spirit of co-operation with other independent consultants, and indeed with the client's employees themselves where this will help achieve effective performance of the services.

Paragraph (i) is an optional provision for inclusion when the nature of the task demands an amount of specialist instruction in the client's business or the intended applications before the services can be rendered effectively.

Paragraph (j) is also optional, intended to afford the consultant some certainty that its work will not be subjected to any claims later on. However, while this may provide some comfort, it will not save the consultant from the consequences of breaches of contract which could not reasonably have come to light at such an early stage.

5. Consultant's Employees

(a) Each of the Consultant's employees assigned to perform the Services will be appropriately qualified and experienced for such assignment. The Client will have the right to interview and approve or reject any employee of the Consultant intended by the Consultant to perform the Services, and the Client will also have the right to request the replacement of any employee of the Consultant engaged in the performance of the Services without having to state a reason, subject to the Consultant being granted a reasonable period of time to allocate a replacement employee.

327

(b) Employees of the Consultant designated to perform the Services will remain under the overall control of the Consultant at all times during the term of this Agreement, although they will be responsible to the Client's Authorised Representative for the performance of the Services and will at all times be responsive to the reasonable requirements of the Client in connection with the performance of the Services.

(c) The Consultant's employees designated to perform the Services will be entitled to take their annual or other leave and to attend the Consultant's internal company meetings as reasonably required by the Consultant but not more than once each month.

(d) If the Consultant's employees designated to perform the Services propose to be absent on short-term leave or at a Consultant company meeting, they will inform the Client's Authorised Representative and if the Client so requires, the Consultant will use all reasonable endeavours to furnish a replacement employee during such absences. In the case of long-term annual leave, the Consultant undertakes to advise the Client at least two weeks in advance of such leave and to replace its designated employee for the leave period if so requested or otherwise to extend any term of this Agreement at the option of the Client.

(e) The Consultant will use all reasonable endeavours to replace promptly any designated employees who leave the Consultant's employment or who are absent through illness or incapacity.

(f) During the term of this Agreement and for a period of 12 months from its termination for any reason, the Client will not employ either directly or indirectly or through any associated company or offer employment to any person employed by or acting on behalf of the Consultant who has worked for the Consultant for a continuous period of six months or more in the preceding 12 months and who has provided Services to the Client in connection with this Agreement. If the Client is in breach of this condition, the Client (recognising that the Consultant will suffer substantial damage) will pay to the Consultant by way of liquidated damages and not by way of penalty a sum equal to the current annual salary of the employee concerned.

(g) *Conflicts of Interest*
Although the Client recognises the non-exclusive nature of this Agreement and the other consulting interests of the Consultant, the Consultant will use all reasonable endeavours to ensure that no conflict with the Client's interests (in terms of performance, obligations, duties and engagements by similar or competitive businesses of the Client) arises at any time during this Agreement.
[If and to the extent agreed in any Project Statement, the Consultant will not (whether directly or indirectly or whether on its own account or the account of any other person, firm or company, or as agent, director, partner, manager, employee, consultant or shareholder of or in any other person,

firm or company) at any time from the date of commencement of the Project specified in that Project Statement to the expiry of a period of 12 months after the completion of the Project, for any reason and in any way, work on any project similar to the Project for any other person or organisation.]

Paragraph (a) often presents difficulties in negotiation. The relative sizes of the parties and the nature of the project are bound to be influencing factors. If senior specialist people are employed on a project, a consultant is not going to be happy to face demands for replacement without reason. The allowance of extra time for the project will not be helpful if other projects in which the consultant has an interest risk being held up as a result. It may be argued that, unless a genuine issue of security is involved, reasons should be tabled and discussed.

Paragraph (b) again seeks to underline both the self-employed status of the consultant and the ultimate responsibility of the client for the services.

The provisions dealing with absences at paragraphs (c) to (e) are relevant for long-term provision of services. In the short term, the client should not expect absenteeism except in emergencies.

A standard version of paragraph (f) is discussed in detail in **CHAPTER 7**. However, as it is relevant for many kinds of IT contracts, a version is included here to emphasise its importance to consultants and clients in an agreement for professional services. It places a restriction on the client to prevent poaching the consultant's staff. As with all such provisions, this will be enforceable only to the extent that it can be considered fair and reasonable in the context of overriding public interest. In practice, difficulties tend to arise over whether or not a consultant has applied for a job rather than having been approached, but paragraph (f) would attempt to prohibit employment in either situation. The consultant who is an employee of the staff assigned to the project should also ensure that the client has similar agreements with its other consultancies, and the consultant employer should have appropriate provisions in its staff employment terms and conditions.

The optional provision in square brackets at paragraph (g) of 'Conflicts of Interest' represents a still more restrictive condition, at least in terms of its post-contractual effect, and enforcement will be correspondingly more difficult. It will be a question of what is reasonable in the circumstances and whether the restriction is likely to affect the consultant's future business opportunities materially. A client who has just funded a project would have good reason for wanting to prevent its competitors benefiting at its expense. Where possible, a safer form of restriction would be to name the principal competitors for whom the consultant should not provide services for a reasonable limited period of time following the termination or expiry of the consultant's services rather than to attempt to rely on a general restriction. The first part of paragraph (g) is a reasonable expectation of a client and defines the spirit in which an agreement of this nature should be undertaken.

6. Proprietary Rights

(a) If compliance with the Client's designs, specifications or instructions results in the Consultant being subject to any claim for infringement of any Proprietary Rights or any third party rights, the Client will indemnify the Consultant against any claims, demands, damages, costs and expenses made against or suffered by the Consultant as a result of any such claim or action.

EITHER

(b)

   (i) The Consultant acknowledges that all Proprietary Rights in the Project Results shall at all times and for all purposes vest and remain vested in the Client. Notwithstanding the foregoing, all Proprietary Rights which the Consultant might otherwise acquire as a result of its performance of the Services are hereby irrevocably assigned to the Client.

   (ii) At the request and expense of the Client, and as required, the Consultant will do all such things including signing all documents or other instruments reasonably necessary in the opinion of the Client to confirm or vest in the Client the rights assigned or otherwise transferred to the Client under this Agreement.

   (iii) Upon request by the Client and in any event upon the expiry or termination of this Agreement, the Consultant will promptly deliver to the Client all copies of materials relating to the Project then in the Consultant's possession.

   (iv) The Consultant will be fully entitled to use in any way it deems fit any skills, techniques, concepts or know-how acquired, developed or used in the course of performing the Consultancy Services, and any improvements to the Consultant's products made or developed during the course of the Services will belong exclusively to the Consultant.

OR

(b)

   (i) The Project Results and the Proprietary Rights relating to them shall be and shall remain the exclusive property of the Consultant.

   (ii) The Client is hereby granted a [non-exclusive] [perpetual] [non-transferable] licence to use the Project Results for its own internal business purposes.

   (iii) The Client undertakes to keep the Project Results confidential and not to make copies of them available to any third party for any purpose.

Paragraph (a) indemnifies the consultant in the event of third party claims alleging breach of intellectual property rights arising from client design, specifications or instructions. As drafted, the clause provides an unconditional indemnity and clients should consider negotiating other elements into the provision, for example to give them sole control of the defence of a third party action and stipulating other conditions and exceptions to the indemnity. The intellectual property indemnity clause in **CHAPTER 7** considers these points from a supplier's perspective, but some of the arguments might also apply in circumstances where the client is supplying the indemnity.

The intellectual property rights in any work produced by the consultant will belong to the consultant as a matter of law unless the Agreement provides otherwise, as in the first alternative of paragraph (b) above. There is a case for client ownership in a consultancy agreement, which may concern consultancy services taking place in the development of various elements of a project.

If any project for which the client is using the consultant's services is for a third party, the client may itself have obligations in terms of assigning copyright. Although it may be the case that the consultant will not want to limit its use of skills by being unable to use again software which has been developed under the terms of this Agreement, and may possibly also make use of standard function programming routines, the actual outcome may depend more on the balance of commercial power between the company and consultant. The consultant may be working in conjunction with other independent consultants and where software is being developed in this way there is a strong argument in favour of establishing ownership of the constituent parts in the client, whether or not the client has conceived the overall design.

Paragraph (b)(iv) in the first alternative may require more definition in any particular circumstances. Whilst it is not possible to restrict the future use of further skills invariably developed as individuals increase their experience, particular techniques or concepts in the form of program sub-routines or problem solving may extend to areas which a client would wish to acquire in some way. If the consultant is a supplier of a range of computer products or services, it is certainly going to want to retain ownership of any improvements to its products.

In paragraph (b)(ii) of the second alternative, an amplified form of licence may be appropriate, depending on the complexity, exploitability and value of the work being produced. Software licences are discussed in **CHAPTER 12**. Indeed it may be appropriate for the parties to discuss the whole question of exclusivity because, even when it is agreed that one party will own the intellectual property arising from performance of the agreement, the other party may have a commercial case for some sort of royalty or commission arrangement in relation to third party transactions involving that intellectual property.

7. Termination

> (a) If the Consultant is unable to carry out its obligations under this Agreement including but not limited to reasons of illness or accident, and such incapacity continues for more than 60 days, the Client will be entitled to terminate this Agreement forthwith by written notice to the Consultant given at any time while such incapacity continues.
>
> (b) The Client may terminate this Agreement forthwith by written notice to the Consultant if the Consultant or any employee of the Consultant engaged in the performance of the Services:
>
> > (i) is guilty of any fraud, dishonesty, or serious misconduct;
> >
> > (ii) is guilty of any conduct which may tend to bring it or the Client into disrepute or is convicted of a criminal offence;
> >
> > (iii) becomes incapable by reasons of mental disorder of performing the Services under this Agreement.

These provisions are additional to those contained in the termination clause in **CHAPTER 7** and are included to cover particular circumstances which may apply to a consultant who is an individual rather than a corporate entity.

When considering paragraph (b)(ii), the client may wish to reserve the right in general to enable it to make a decision according to the nature of the offence. The consultant may wish to negotiate a provision which requires any breach of paragraph (b)(ii) in relation to criminal convictions to exclude those such as minor traffic or regulatory offences.

8. Schedule: Project Statement

> Further to the rights and obligations of each party contained in the Agreement, the parties agree as follows:
>
> (1) Consultant's Responsibilities, Consultancy and/or Project Management Services
>
> (2) Project Results
>
> (3) Acceptance Criteria
>
> (4) Period of Agreement or Estimated Time Schedules
>
> (5) Resources
>
> (6) Fees and Payment Schedules
>
> (7) Computer Systems to which the Consultant is entitled to have access
>
> (8) Other Conditions.

The project statement must clarify as far as possible the extent of the consultant's responsibilities and functions. The objective should be to try to avoid disputes about the nature and content of the services. This is particularly so when the consultant is one of a number brought in by the client to work together on a project. The detail in a project statement should be sufficient to achieve clarity, over and above the framework of the standard terms and conditions of the agreement itself. On a large project, the project statement may be a long document. Consultants should aim to make any specification of time, or other performance criteria targets or objectives, rather than absolute contractual commitments unless they are confident that, allowing for all foreseeable contingencies, they can safely achieve the dates or results stated. Large clients may exert pressure in this area, but the making of unrealistic commitments can only lead to problems later on.

The overriding objective should be to set out the consultant's responsibilities (including any acceptance criteria) completely and unambiguously. This is often difficult to achieve, but too many assignments founder on mismatches of expectations caused or contributed to by inadequate documentation.

Both parties should avoid any temptation to commence performance of services before all the requirements have been finally specified and agreed, documented and signed off. If circumstances dictate otherwise and there is an imperative to start a project so that a chance remains to meet a critical deadline, the consultant would be wise to insist, when entering into the Agreement, that a statement be included to the effect that, until the Project Statement is finally agreed and signed, any work undertaken will be chargeable on a time and materials basis (possibly limited to a stated maximum sum), without any obligation on the part of the consultant to deliver any specific project results. This is obviously a very undesirable and risky way to proceed for the client, and the best advice to the client must always be not to commence a project until all contractual details have been finalised, no matter how intense the external pressures may be to do so.

1   *Motorola v Davidson and Melville Craig Group Ltd* [2001] IRLR 4, EAT.
2   Inland Revenue news release IR35, 1999 Budget, now commonly referred to as 'IR35'.
3   Sale of Goods Act 1979, Sale of Goods and Services Act 1982 and all subsequent modifications and re-enactments.

CHAPTER 16

Software development

A. Introduction

A client organisation may commission a supplier to plan, write and implement a computer system. It may be for a project requiring special expertise, or because the customer has enough other system development and support work to keep its own IT staff busy for the foreseeable future, or because it has only a small number of IT personnel, not enough for large development projects. Almost all user organisations with computing resources suffer an applications backlog, meaning that there is more work for the foreseeable future than can be attended to by the analysts and programmers available.

The contract may well be of high value to both parties, concerning perhaps several resource years of effort by the supplier based on the customer's requirements for the system. Any large system development, whether in-house or commissioned, will also carry high risks. In the worst cases, control of the project development is lost, costs escalate, the timetable is not kept to and the project has to be abandoned, perhaps after the expenditure of several millions of pounds.

A report published jointly by the Royal Academy of Engineering and the British Computer Society notes that significant numbers of complex software and IT projects still fail to deliver key benefits on time and to target costs and specification[1]. It states that a striking proportion of project difficulties stem from failure by both customer and supplier organisations to implement best practice. It considers that the most pressing problems relate to the people and the processes involved in complex IT projects but that further developments in methods and tools to support the design and delivery of such projects could help to raise success rates. It makes a number of practical recommendations. 'The terms of the contract,' it says, 'should reflect the uncertainty associated with a particular project and must also apportion the risks appropriately. In addition it is vital that the contract incorporates disciplines and constructive procedures for dealing with the project if it goes off course'.

Even in less extreme circumstances, statistics suggest that the majority of software development, whatever the method, ends up costing more, and often far more, than was originally budgeted or estimated. The central issue for customers commissioning outside their organisation should therefore be to find suppliers genuinely capable of operating in an efficient and ethical way with all the requisite know-how and experience. The sales representations of such suppliers should be carefully examined and there should be diligent follow-up of reference sites – with the customer insisting on the freedom to talk to anyone on the supplier's customer list rather than being steered to particular reference sites. Sometimes a combination of the two is beneficial because suppliers may have one or more existing customers using the same or very similar applications, with comparable volumes of activity, to those being considered by the prospective customer.

1. Two approaches

Two approaches to software development will be contrasted in this chapter, and will be referred to as 'conventional', sometimes known as 'waterfall' or 'traditional', and 'prototype', which is sometimes called 'Rapid Application Development' ('RAD'). The conventional method is customary for centralised operating environments, for large systems using mainframes or large servers for corporate data management and where high availability is a requirement. Prototyping is often suitable where use of components enables prototype systems to be developed quickly for the users to work out their requirements themselves in concert with the developer as they go.

The customer is always going to suffer if the chosen supplier falls short of the expected standards of quality, or lacks the proper level of expertise, or is unscrupulous about the accumulation of costs, and in these circumstances the development methodology is not really going to make much difference to the final unsatisfactory outcome. However, on the assumption that the chosen supplier is ethical, trustworthy and responsible, possessed of the necessary resources, computing expertise and, where this has been a factor in selection, appropriate experience of the market or application, it is worth examining the comparative merits and claimed disadvantages of both the conventional and prototyping methods of software development. The implications for the development contract are significant because a number of clauses will need to be drafted in a different way, depending on the development method selected.

Initially both conventional and prototype methodologies adopt a similar approach. An analysis of the requirements for a new system and an assessment of the feasibility for development will result in one or more preliminary documents. The 'feasibility study' or 'user requirements' will form the basis of discussions which will eventually evolve into the detail for development of the system.

There is a proliferation of 'big-name' consultants who offer services at this stage. Considerable expense can be involved for the customer, and these consultancy arrangements themselves require careful negotiation of scope and deliverables required. Consideration also needs to be given to the retention of such consultants throughout the system development process in order to ensure that the system which is designed fully meets the user requirements. A word of warning here: it often transpires that during system development, major oversights are discovered in the statement of user requirements. Customers should seek to negotiate appropriate safeguards in their consultancy agreements, as discussed in **CHAPTER 15**, so that they do not end up in effect paying twice for the same service.

The development may mean the creation of new original software or the detailed adaptation of a complex standard software package.

At the next stage – the functional requirements or specification stage – the parties are talking to each other, discussing the requirements of the project with each other in some detail and defining objectives within the costs parameters. The parties will normally continue to communicate harmoniously and it is easy to incorporate changes as thinking develops.

Under the conventional method, the specification will be a long and detailed document, intended to be a definitive statement about what is required. At the end of this process, the specification is signed off.

The supplier who created the specification may then be asked to produce the software. Sometimes the customer will go to tender to have the software produced from the specification.

There are inherent dangers in this approach of going to tender for this phase of a project in isolation because, even where the specification is extremely detailed, the techniques and styles of suppliers and individual analysts and programmers vary and, if a different group develops the software from the group which specified it, this may be a source of problems.

It is essential that the development structure provides for a comprehensive and well-administered change control system to cater for the inevitable changes and thinking which will arise during the software development. It is equally essential for customers to maintain tight internal discipline over those in the customer organisation who expect to benefit from the new system. There is a strong temptation for such prospective users to impose their 'wish lists' into the system specification where such functionality had not been anticipated or intended. This can greatly add to costs. Practices change and much is learned internally which can render the design less useful. Software as finally implemented is rarely in the form originally specified. Both parties learn about the application as a project proceeds, and will discard some features and introduce others. During the course of a large and lengthy project, the customer's business practices may also change, affecting the objectives or methods of the application and thereby necessitating changes to the development of the project.

In contrast, the prototyping method will have produced a much shorter, less detailed, specification or concept document setting down the requirements in a series of broad statements which programmers will be free to interpret as creatively as possible and with the close involvement of the customer, stage by stage. This is the first distinction between the two methodologies. The concept document guides the parties as they work together to develop the new system. The supplier contributes its system engineering and technology expertise and the customer contributes its applications know-how in an effort to obtain the best possible results with close co-operation between the parties throughout the course of the development work. It is perceived as a more risky approach by many because of an apparently open-ended exposure to costs, but this need not be the case if the contract terms are properly drawn.

The second potential distinction is that with the prototyping method, the programmers will always be part of the same team which produced the initial specification or concept document. This need not be the case under the conventional method, when the teams may even have different backgrounds and methods of interpreting specification statements.

The third and major distinction, and the most significant advantage claimed for the prototyping methodology, is the nature of the continuing involvement of the customer. The prototyping advocate argues that the conventional process for design and development of software has become over-structured and inflexible. It involves a tedious serial process of specifying requirements, functionality, design, and then coding, testing and installing. It is a logical process but difficult to adapt to a dynamic commercial environment which is not totally definable. Further, the argument continues, the conventional method induces an underlying adversarial contest. Whether the parties only meet occasionally, the customer expectation being that the specified system will be delivered in a fully operational form by the contracted delivery date, or whether they hold regular progress meetings so that the project can be closely monitored by the customer throughout, the supplier's instinctive business objective will usually be to do the minimum work necessary to achieve the specification in order to maximise its profits. The customer's business objective will be to obtain maximum value for the agreed price. The supplier will seek to charge extra for every deviation from the specification and the more complex the project, the more changes there will be. Meetings tend to address only agenda items and militate against the creative process which demands experimentation with, and adaptation to, new ideas as they arise. These agenda items will also inevitably concentrate on problems where the development did not go smoothly, rather than on those areas where it did. This will contribute to an adversarial and disenchanted atmosphere. There will be no scope for compromise in the process: ideas cannot be 'swapped' because the specification is part of the contract. Any deviation is going to have a cost implication.

With the prototyping method, the constant dialogue between the parties, started when the specification was being prepared, continues. The parties are working jointly to a budget and the process encourages compromise. The customer is closely involved at all stages and gains the level of understanding which allows it to make a continuing series of informed choices between features and, if this is preferred, to pay more for additional features. There is thus always the potential to achieve both cost and delivery date targets. Documentation is kept to a minimum, the argument being that good software should be largely self-documenting via the screen, physical user documentation being for augmentation. Where it is agreed that additional features will be incorporated, this tends to be after careful evaluation: the right business decisions are taken on a value-for-money basis in the context of the customer's close working involvement with all facets of the project. The result should be a working system which meets the essential commercial requirements of the customer's business, with a shared understanding of any costs and time variations agreed. One risk, however, to which those involved in prototyping should be alert, is the danger of the teams identifying with each other rather than with their parent organisations. Tension may then arise internally.

Prototypers argue that modern software development aids, languages and database products make prototyping a much more logical choice when development speed and a tight budget are significant constraining factors, but ultimately, the issue is one of trust. Prototyping depends on it; conventional development seeks to achieve results with the aid of detailed specifications and tightly-worded contracts, so that there is less need for it[2].

Several other features of software development deserve special mention at this stage.

COMPONENTS

There has been something of a revolution in the world of software development, born out of increasing levels of concern at the seemingly unstoppable escalation of costs and delays on major project after major project, too many of which end in costly litigation. There is growing recognition among software developers of the need for compromise in development processes. Many customers in the modern business world cannot afford the luxury of commissioning software projects which require all aspects of the software to be written from the ground up in order to cater in every detail for the customer's individual requirements. Many small software houses and organisations with large development teams invest time and effort in developing specific components which are capable of re-use with little adaptation, for example an e-commerce invoicing process, a currency conversion routine or a worldwide addressing capability. There are thousands of such components (or sub-routines in major software suites) which are capable of being component-ised. Developers are appreciating that if they focus their attention on solving the core business problem of their customer or employer, they can save considerable time and expense by plugging on a huge number of components which provide essential functionality and which have already been created by others. The availability of useful data and analysis demonstrating the returns on investment which individual components can represent to a developer is also

338

helping to encourage a steady increase in the use of components. As a result, distributors of components are making their presence felt in the marketplace. The ordering and delivery of these items lend themselves to online trading (along the lines discussed in **CHAPTER 20**) and the immediate availability of components when required is attractive to more and more developers.

WARRANTY

Customers generally expect the system they are acquiring to be warranted so that defects are fixed free of charge for a reasonable period of time. It is logical to expect a warranty arrangement when the conventional approach is employed, because the customer has not had a close involvement in the development process. The supplier who is developing by the prototyping method will argue that a warranty is inappropriate because, at the time of acceptance, the customer has agreed that the product is exactly as wanted at that point in time and it is reasonable for further changes and problem solving to be paid for on a similar basis to the original development work. However, there should at least be warranties that the software meets the specification agreed between the parties and that it does not infringe third party proprietary rights. It is also appropriate to ensure that there is a warranty to exercise a proper degree of skill and care.

PRICING

The options on pricing are fixed-price or time-and-materials. Customers naturally seek certainty and will generally demand fixed prices so that they can budget satisfactorily. Suppliers need to be wary of fixed prices, because particularly in cases of applications which tread new ground, it is difficult to make an accurate assessment of costs. It is not in the customer's best interests for a supplier to start working to a price when the costs start to escalate, if the result is going to be a less satisfactory end product or, at worst, risk the supplier's ability to continue in business. A reasonable solution is to employ estimated pricing based upon an assessment of the time and materials costs for the development, with a margin for error. The supplier is then obliged to alert the customer if the limits are being approached or if radical changes in thinking as the application unfolds are going to result in significant cost increases. The customer can then make an informed decision about whether to have more or fewer features and functionality. Changes will incur costs. Customers should remember that on complex projects, some suppliers may view fixed-price contracts as licences to print money. It is not possible to get through a major development without invoking substantial change control. Each change will involve costs of one sort or another, whether actual financial costs, extensions of time or both. In competitive bids, 'value for money' is often synonymous with 'lowest fixed price'. A common unsatisfactory experience today, especially on major projects, is to complete the tendering process but then require short-listed candidates to submit 'best and final offers' even though their bids have already gone in. However, customers should bear in mind that if they exert too much pressure in negotiation to achieve a low fixed price, suppliers keen to obtain the business will often accommodate such demands, in quietly confident expectation that they will recover the situation through change control after they have secured the business.

OWNERSHIP

An important point relates to the difficult question of ownership of the software to be developed. Customers will often expect ownership, because they instinctively feel that if they have paid for something they should own it, even when in reality they are not likely to benefit from ownership, because they are not in a position to exploit it, because they lack the skills, or because it bears no relation to their main business. It is not even always easy to take the source code that belongs to another supplier for maintenance purposes, particularly if the software is complex, because of the amount of learning that will have to take place to understand the product sufficiently to maintain it effectively.

On the other hand, the supplier will argue that what the customer has paid for has been simply to have a product it can use for the benefit of its business at a fair market price. That price does not include an entitlement to own the know-how deriving from the considerable skills and experience of the development team, and the supplier would not wish to dispossess itself of techniques and know-how gained from that particular project. Similar new knowledge from previous projects will benefit this customer and future customers will benefit from the present development experience. The situation is arguably no different from that which would apply to the engagement of any other professional services.

The end results tend often to relate to an implied formula which suggests that there is a correlation between ownership of intellectual property rights and the price to be paid. At the bottom of the scale, the cheapest price buys a non-exclusive licence to use, possibly for a limited time. At the top end of the scale, the highest price may buy complete ownership, possibly with a licence back to the developer to use for support purposes only. In between there are degrees of licensing, providing options for exclusivity, perpetuity, joint ownership, royalty arrangements, and so on. In connection with their use of components, customers must recognise that transfer of ownership of components is not possible. The essential feature of a component is its ability to be used in multiple situations, which represent the revenue opportunity of the developer.

QUALITY

The quality of the system which is produced also needs to be considered. There are no generally accepted standards or measurement techniques which can be readily identified for use in contracts at present. Some contracts stipulate 'professional standards' or 'standards common in the software industry' or 'industry best practice' but these kinds of expressions are likely to prove meaningless in the event of disputes, each side's experts being unlikely to agree on specific quality measurements or their interpretation.

The British Standard BS ISO/IEC 18019: 2004 'Software and System Engineering; Guidelines for the Design and Preparation of User Documentation and Application Software' has replaced earlier standards for software documentation.

2. Complexity, change and co-operation

Software development projects can be enormously complex technically and commercially, involving much intricate detail and with great capacity for uncertainty and change. In these respects, they can be regarded as having some similarities to complex construction projects. Taking as an analogy one famous City of London construction project from the 1660s, when Christopher Wren's advice was sought on repairing the old St Paul's church, he proposed altering the Gothic design to incorporate a dome, a form of church building not then known in England – a feasibility study.

After the Great Fire of London, he was commissioned to build the new St Paul's in terms that would please any contractor: to 'frame a design, handsome and noble, and suitable to all the Ends of it, and to the Reputations of the City and the Nation and to take it for granted the Money will be had to accomplish it' – a specification of requirements.

He designed an exotic cathedral based on the Greek cross with a great central dome, to be as grand as any cathedral in Europe. King Charles was so taken with the design that he agreed the construction of a Great Model of the proposed structure, 18 feet long, made of oak and lime wood, which itself took a year to build and cost £600, as much as a London town house – a prototype.

When people saw the Great Model, they objected to its resemblance to Continental Catholic style. Acceptance testing was unsatisfactory. Christopher Wren had to revise the design back to replace the centralised Greek cross with a Gothic style of a long nave leading to an altar at the end. However, he managed to get a change control condition built into his agreement with King Charles who finally allowed the architect to 'make some variations ... as from Time to Time he should see proper' – and left 'the Whole to his own Management' – the project management side.

The end result was quite different in many particularities from the initial concept. It had been subject to changes of direction, increased costs and management differences of opinion. Yet it still succeeded in meeting its original overall objective and in some ways magnificently surpassed it.

A large-scale software development project may encounter similar obstacles, and with a proper development structure and contract in place can overcome them to the satisfaction both of the customer and the supplier. Co-operation between the parties, whatever the development method, is essential for the successful implementation of a dependable system.

B. The structure of a typical software development agreement

In relation to the parties' obligations, alternative approaches are illustrated in this example to provide a feel for the contrasting styles of 'conventional' and 'prototype'.

Terms and conditions

- Definitions*
- Term (for prototyping agreements)
- Supplier's Obligations*
- Customer's Obligations*
- Charges*
- Payment*
- Payment Terms
- Variation of Charges
- System and Acceptance Testing*
- Training
- Variations*
- Late Completion*
- Supplier's Staff*
- Employment Restriction
- Progress Review*
- Intellectual Property Rights (and Licence)*
- Intellectual Property Rights Indemnity
- Confidentiality
- Non-Competition*
- Supplier's Warranties*

- Indemnities and Limits of Liability
- Post-implementation Support*
- Termination and Effects of Termination
- General Contract Provisions

Schedules

- Charges
- Competitors
- Documentation
- Designated Representatives
- Equipment
- Implementation Plan
- Staff
- Third Party Software
- Training

Appendices

- Functional Specification/Concept Document
- Support Agreement

C. Specific clauses

In the clauses considered below, which are those above marked with an asterisk, the parties are referred to as 'Supplier' and 'Customer', denoting the supplier of the commissioned software and the organisation commissioning the software, respectively.

1. Definitions

'*Acceptance Tests*' means tests using Test Data to test the System for acceptance.

'*Change Order*' means a written record of any change to the System.

'*Charges*' means the charges payable for the Project.

343

['*Concept Document*' means the document which outlines the requirements for the System incorporated into this Agreement as the Concept Document Appendix.]

['*Documentation*' means the documentation to be provided by the Supplier for the System, listed in the Documentation Schedule.]

'*Equipment*' means the hardware and operating systems at the Customer's site as listed in the Equipment Schedule, on which, and in combination with which, the Software will run.

'*Estimated Price*' means the price estimated for the Project as set out in the Charges Schedule.

['*Implementation Plan*' means the development plan for the Project specifying the dates for completion of each phase of the Project, forming the Implementation Plan Schedule, as it may be varied from time to time.]

'*Milestone*' means a phase comprising a set of tasks shown in the Implementation Plan.

'*Progress Meeting*' means a meeting held between the parties to discuss progress of the Project.

'*Project*' means the work to be undertaken and services to be performed by the Supplier to develop and implement the System.

'*Project Manager*' means the designated representative appointed by the Supplier or the Customer respectively as initially specified in the Designated Representatives Schedule.

'*Schedules*' means the schedules identified in this Agreement and incorporated into this Agreement.

'*Software*' means the software content of the System developed in accordance with these terms and conditions.

'*System*' means the business system required by the Client[, using the Equipment and Software in combination].

'*System Completion Date*' means the date specified in the Implementation Plan for completion of the System.

'*Test Data*' means data supplied by the Customer for the purpose of testing the System to demonstrate that it works, in order for the System to be accepted by the Customer.

344

'*Third Party Software*' means all third party software owned by a third party but legally licensed to the Supplier for its use in developing the Software.

'*Training*' means the training in using the System to be provided by the Supplier as described in the Training Schedule.

The above definitions represent a typical selection from agreements of this type.

For the conventional method, the original user requirements or functional specification (in its final agreed form), together with any other relevant and unambiguous documentation, should be incorporated into the agreement. It is critical for both parties that the specification should contain enough details of the requirements which they expect the project to meet. For instance, if response times are a significant part of these requirements, they should be made part of the contract by incorporating them into the specification.

For the prototyping method, the concept document will replace the functional specification as the initiating document.

2. Supplier's Obligations

The Supplier undertakes to:

(a) provide its services diligently, expeditiously and with reasonable skill and care;

(b) provide suitably skilled and appropriately experienced personnel to carry out the Project;

(c) provide the Training;

(d) make all reasonable efforts to ensure that the Project is performed in a timely and efficient manner;

(e) maintain accurate time sheets [and make all reasonable efforts to complete the Project within any Estimated Price. If the Supplier foresees a situation where any Estimated Price is likely to be exceeded, it undertakes to draw the Customer's attention promptly to such situation];

Paragraphs (f) onwards below are presented to reflect the two alternative approaches, the first set being used for the conventional method of software development, and the second set for the prototyping method.

(f) develop, write and deliver the Software and Documentation for the Equipment and at the Site in accordance with the Functional Specification;

[(g) comply with the Implementation Plan and meet the System Completion Date.]

An alternative prototyping approach for sub-clauses (f) onwards would delineate the Supplier's obligations as follows:

(f) write the Software and complete the Project utilising such elements of the following procedural framework as may be deemed by the Supplier to be appropriate in the particular circumstances:
    (i) creating with the Customer's assistance the Concept Document;
    (ii) agreeing with the Customer the limitations of the System;
    (iii) agreeing with the Customer the order in which the modules of the Software will be written;
    (iv) discussing and agreeing with the Customer the contents of the first Software module;
    (v) coding the first Software module, testing it and obtaining the agreement of the Customer that the results meet the requirements of the Project;
    (vi) where necessary, redefining and rewriting the first Software module, retesting it and obtaining the agreement of the Customer that the results meet the requirements of the Project;
    (vii) discussing and agreeing with the Customer the contents of the second and subsequent Software modules in the sequence stated in the Concept Document or such amended sequence as the parties may agree;
    (viii) coding the second and subsequent Software modules in the sequence stated in the Concept Document or such amended sequence as the parties may agree, installing them on the Customer's Equipment, testing them, and carrying out such redefinition and rewriting as may be required by the Customer in order to obtain the agreement of the Customer that the results meet the requirements of the Project;

(g) where the Software is located on a Supplier's site, re-install the Software at the Customer's Site;

(h) make all reasonable efforts to ensure that the System meets the needs of the Customer's business.

Dependent upon the requirements of the Project some of the above procedures may be performed by the Supplier in parallel.

Paragraphs (a)–(e) cover areas which will be common ground whichever development approach is being used. Some customers seek to stipulate higher standards of care and experience than is set out in paragraphs (a) and (b), using expressions such as 'in accordance with the best industry standards'. The difficulty lies in establishing what those standards might be. Two experts would probably not be in complete agreement. A better approach is to make straightforward statements which can be tested more objectively in the event of a dispute.

Paragraph (e) relates to charging on a time and materials basis only. It would be irrelevant to the customer if a fixed-price arrangement had been made.

Paragraphs (f) onwards can be expanded depending on the project requirements. Their purpose is to spell out the performance obligations that the supplier must meet in order to complete the project successfully. Thus under the conventional method there can be a requirement in accordance with the functional specification, as in the example. Or it can be expanded to cover every key element of the development, possibly including interim phases, further refinements and versions of the specification, identification and achievement of critical milestones, and so on.

Under the conventional approach, paragraph (g), shown in square brackets, is for the customer who wants the obligation to meet the system completion date included. The supplier will wish to avoid an absolute commitment. From a customer's standpoint, paragraph (g) should apply because an open-ended development period will not be acceptable. However, the supplier will be unwise to commit to a definite obligation in a development contract unless the supplier can be certain that the work will be straightforward and wholly consistent with previous similar projects. Disputes can arise when commitments are made to unrealistic dates. Customers with commercial strength to force the position may be creating significant future problems for their businesses if they coerce suppliers into unrealistic completion date commitments. It is also increasingly the case that when development is component-based, development times can be more confidently predicted.

Under the prototyping approach, paragraph (f) illustrates the co-operative style of this method of development and shows the customer's involvement at every stage. The process is iterative and continues until the customer's requirements are met, in the context of the expenditure which the customer is prepared to allocate to the development. This paragraph refers to software 'modules'. A module is often understood to consist of an identifiable unit of a thousand lines or less of program code. 'Build' is an alternative word which might be used, a familiar term to programmers, used as a noun. 'Version' or 'release' are also possible, but imply whole programs or combinations of programs, and are terms usually used post-implementation.

It is important for customers to understand the prototyping methodology and their own role because, at the end of the process, they are effectively signing off the development and cannot expect to receive a warranty of performance to a specification because there will not be a detailed specification. They will have verified performance to their satisfaction as the development evolved, checking and testing each module and the groups of modules and then the system as a whole.

Sometimes individual modules will even go live if they are discretely capable of benefiting the customer's business without this depending on integration into the overall system.

3. Customer's Obligations

The Customer undertakes:

(a) to pay for the System subject to the performance by the Supplier of its obligations;

(b) to provide where applicable, adequate office accommodation and other facilities, including access to the applicable computer systems of the Customer, to enable the designated employees of the Supplier to carry out the Project;

(c) to take all reasonable steps to ensure the health and safety of the Supplier's employees while they are working at Customer sites;

(d) to comply with any additional Third Party Software conditions notified to it on or before delivery of any Third Party Software (including if so required the execution and return of a Third Party Software Licence);

(e) to ensure that the operating system and any other software with which the Software will be used is either the property of the Customer or is legally licensed to the Customer and to indemnify the Supplier in respect of any claims against the Supplier by third parties and all related costs, expenses or damages, in the event of any actual or alleged violations of third party proprietary rights or software licences;

(f) to take sole responsibility for determining that the System is ready for operational use in the Customer's business before it is so used;

The following obligations represent the conventional approach:

(g) to provide guidance to the Supplier [on the interpretation of the Functional Specification and]about the Customer's business practices which affect the design and construction of the Software;

(h) to recognise the collaborative nature of the Project, and to use its best endeavours to co-operate with the Supplier in order to enable the Supplier to carry out the Project;

(i) to accept the Supplier's advice on the technical feasibility of the Project, having regard to the applicable Customer environment.

The following obligations represent the prototyping approach:

> (g) to recognise that the Project is a joint endeavour between the parties;
>
> (h) to co-operate with the Supplier in defining the Project and in adopting the Supplier's methodology in producing the Software in order to facilitate timely completion of the Project;
>
> (i) to contain its expectations from the Project to technically feasible solutions as advised by the Supplier, having regard to the applicable Customer environment and the Estimated Price;
>
> (j) to create an appropriate test environment in order to satisfy itself that the System meets the needs of its business;
>
> (k) to recognise that the Software is provided without warranty as to function or fitness for purpose because of the collaborative nature of the Project.

The two methodologies involve quite different approaches as discussed in some detail in the Introduction. They are not so much a matter of negotiation as of choice. The supplier will generally offer only one methodology because of the technology in which it specialises and the sorts of projects it handles, and because its organisation will be structured to operate in that way. The customer will need to make a decision about which methodology it prefers and go to a supplier who works in that way. The factors in the decision should take account of the advantages and disadvantages of each method in terms of cost and cost control, speed, certainty of finished product and the degree to which the customer feels the need to have a certain and predictable sequence of events. Most important of all, the customer must be satisfied that it is dealing with a supplier of repute and with the requisite experience to achieve a successful result.

The first six paragraphs, which are common to both methodologies, deal with the facilities which the customer is obliged to make available. Each contract needs to make precise reference to the actual facilities and equipment being provided in the specific circumstances, but these paragraphs incorporate some sensible protections for the supplier. Paragraph (c) contractually requires the customer to have regard to the health and safety of the supplier's employees, underlining the statutory duties which apply to all businesses. Paragraphs (d) and (e) are designed to ensure that any software with which the developed software will be used is properly licensed, the supplier being indemnified if this should prove not to be the case in circumstances which result in a claim being made against the supplier. Presented with such a clause, a customer should at least seek to restrict liability to successful rather than alleged claims specifically confined to third party software which is actually used in conjunction with the developed software – a fine point but illustrating the sorts of detailed comments which often arise during negotiations.

Paragraph (f) places the responsibility firmly on the customer to decide when the system is ready for operational use in its business. This is not an unreasonable requirement. In the conventional approach the customer carries out acceptance testing with this objective. In prototyping, the customer will have been closely involved in every aspect of development and testing and will be fully aware of the features and functions of the finished product.

The paragraphs illustrating the conventional approach nevertheless preserve some level of responsibility of the customer towards the supplier. Some development contracts adopt a much more 'hands off' approach, minimising all customer involvement until a product is ready for acceptance testing. This is short-sighted because it is almost impossible to achieve a satisfactory result when customer and supplier operate in relative isolation. Collaboration and involvement by the customer can only benefit the final result.

Under the prototyping methodology, the customer's close and continuous involvement in the development is emphasised, paragraph (h) cross-referencing the supplier's production methodology. Paragraph (i) cautions the customers to have realistic expectations for the end result having regard to the principal influencing factors. Paragraph (k) is potentially contentious because no warranty is offered but, allied to an ongoing maintenance or support contract, there should not be any exposure for the customer. The supplier will argue that a warranty is inappropriate when both parties have joint responsibility for the end result. But the customer should insist that there is at least a warranty that the software will be written in a professional manner by developers who have demonstrated expertise and a track record of relevant experience to justify their assignment to the project.

Negotiation of this clause will invariably be on matters of detail rather than substance.

4. Charges

EXAMPLE OF FIXED-PRICE CLAUSE

The Charges payable by the Customer for the Project are set out in the Charges Schedule. These Charges constitute a fixed price and will be increased only if the Customer requires the Supplier to carry out other work under a Change Order in which case either the fixed price agreed or (if it is to be done on such basis) the time and materials charges applicable will also be payable. The Charges Schedule sets out how the fixed price has been allocated between the different parts of the Project.

EXAMPLE OF TIME AND MATERIALS CLAUSE

If an Estimated Price has been stated for the Project, it is shown in the Schedule. This Estimated Price is only a non-binding estimate of the likely cost. The work will be carried out on a time and materials basis and will be charged at the Supplier's rates set out in the Charges Schedule. The Supplier may review any Charges not more often than once every 12 months. The Supplier will be entitled to increase such charges by [the percentage increase in the Retail Prices Index published by the Department of Employment] [the percentage difference in the Computer Economics Limited annual survey] [the Supplier's salary inflation] in the preceding 12 months.

The clause is important for the structure of this contract and therefore appears early on, as there are different bases for costing system development.

As with all other forms of contracts, however much a supplier wishes to steer customers to standard price lists and standard charge rates, the price is one of the most negotiable areas. The size of the contract, the urgency of it from the customer's standpoint and the prestige and need for it from the supplier's standpoint, are going to be key factors in what is finally agreed. Again, daily rates should be viewed as negotiable. Even when times are buoyant, a customer may have a short-term project which the supplier can use as a 'fill-in' to increase its average manpower utilisation rate. (Rather like hotel occupancies, business plan profitability of software development organisations is based on target manpower utilisation percentages. This means that there are deals to be done even in good times. In bad times, there will always be downwards pressure on daily rates, driven by competitive forces with too many developers chasing too few projects.)

No two development contracts are entirely alike, and in creative negotiations the supplier and customer should always be able to distinguish their own contractual circumstances from previous situations they may be asked to consider.

In the time and materials example, the estimated price condition links with clause 2(f) of the supplier's obligations. The reference to the supplier's salary inflation is worth noting. The software industry has often been through periods where the demand for really competent software professionals has outstripped supply. At times this has had the effect of forcing salaries, which are likely to be the highest overhead in the supplier's business, above the prevailing rate of inflation. Customers want to know in what circumstances costs are likely to rise, rather than have an open-ended possibility, and the limitation to the supplier's salary inflation provides a measurable number (by reference to the supplier's annual published accounts) while preserving the supplier's objective of maintaining the profitability of the project. However, if the supplier is a very small business, this may not be acceptable to the customer.

A fixed fee can be realistically quoted only after much preparation by the supplier. Most suppliers are reluctant to take on fixed-price contracts because it is very difficult for them at the outset to be aware of all the variables which will influence the development. They prefer to charge on a time and materials basis, which gives more certainty for their finances.

It is common in either form of contract for stage payments to be payable at timed intervals or, more normally, on reaching milestone stages in the project, linked to acceptance tests, and often subject to a retention figure at the completion date, until the system has been working satisfactorily for some days or weeks.

Change orders must be costed. They will apply more to the conventional than to the prototyping methodology, because the latter accepts the notion of a constantly evolving project under the umbrella of a final estimated price with procedures for review if the estimate is likely to be exceeded. However, with the conventional method, it is important to define the processes giving rise to change orders and the methods of costing.

A customer should be aware that with fixed-price contracts, additions and modifications during the course of the project development are likely to be more expensive than if the basis of the work is the effort expended.

The customer will seek to pay only on successful completion of each phase of the project. The customer will seek financial redress whatever the terms of payment consist of, if the system does not meet its completion and acceptance dates. Contractual provision should be made for progress meetings, for both sides to monitor the development stages and the way the project is going. Early action can be taken if the timetable is not being met. This is further discussed in clause 10 below.

If the value of the contract is not sufficient or if there is an unwillingness to depart from standard terms, there will not be much scope for negotiation. It should be one of the objectives of a negotiator in these circumstances to generate sufficient interest in the project to overcome such stonewalling by the other side.

5. Payment

(a) Each invoice will be sent to the Customer by the Supplier [monthly][following completion of a Milestone]. All invoices are payable 30 days from the date of the invoice.

(b) If the Supplier does any work [under a Change Order] on a time and materials basis, the Supplier will during the term of this Agreement and for at least the following 12 months keep accurate and up-to-date records of the time spent on the work and of all materials used. The Customer will by

> its authorised representative on reasonable notice be entitled at all reasonable times to inspect such records and to obtain copies of them.
>
> (c) The payment by the Customer of any invoices will not be deemed to be approval and/or acceptance by the Customer of any work or matter in respect of which such invoice is issued and will be without prejudice to the Customer's rights and remedies under this Agreement or at law or in equity in respect of any failure or delay on the part of the Supplier to perform its obligations.

This is an area where the conventional method tends to be favoured by customers because payment is linked to completed stages of the project development. If the detailed requirements are not met, payment cannot properly be claimed. This places an onus on the supplier to carry out its responsibilities.

Straightforward time-based invoicing as the project progresses, which is a feature of prototyping contracts, is simple, being governed by the need for the customer to measure progress against any quoted estimates for the complete job.

The standard payments terms clause discussed in **CHAPTER 7** should also be included to provide for normal safeguards for the supplier.

6. System and Acceptance Testing

This example will not generally be appropriate for prototyping development agreements.

> (a) When the Supplier has system tested the System, the System will be handed over to the Customer for acceptance testing to be carried out by the Customer using Test Data for the Customer to test that the System conforms to the Functional Specification for use in its business, together with other requirements agreed between the parties.
>
> (b) The Customer will carry out the Acceptance Tests in respect of the System as set out in the Acceptance Tests Schedule over the number of days set out in the Implementation Plan for Acceptance Testing.
>
> (c) If there are failures in the Acceptance Tests, the Customer will inform the Supplier while the Acceptance Tests are in progress, and the Supplier shall promptly use all reasonable endeavours to correct such failures.
>
> (d) The Customer's Project Manager will notify the Supplier's Project Manager promptly in writing of any material failure of the System to pass the Acceptance Tests.
>
> (e) The System will be deemed to be accepted by the Customer after the Acceptance Tests have demonstrated that it is in accordance with the

> Functional Specification, or after a period of one month of being submitted to the Customer for acceptance testing if the Supplier has not been notified of any material failure of the System to pass the Acceptance Tests, whichever is the earlier.
>
> (f) If material failures or omissions remain at the System Completion Date such that the System does not conform with the Specification, the Customer will have a right to terminate this Agreement.
>
> (g) The Supplier reserves the right to amend the Charges and Implementation Plan to the extent that the Project is affected by any delay in the supply of Test Data. If the Test Data includes any data which necessitates any amendments to the Functional Specification, then such amendments will be charged to the Customer at the Supplier's then current rates in addition to the amount set out in the Charges Schedule. Any assistance requested by the Customer in the preparation of Test Data will be chargeable by the Supplier at its then current rates.
>
> (h) Implementation of the System in the Customer's business is the responsibility of the Customer.

System testing will first be carried out by the supplier, but it is strongly recommended that the customer should take responsibility for acceptance testing. This will be the last opportunity to put anything right before the system goes live and payment will depend on formal acceptance by the customer. If the customer does not have enough staff of its own who can carry out acceptance testing, it should consider employing the services of consultants for this specific purpose.

Agreement must be reached on whether the system is to be written and tested at the supplier's premises and on its computer facilities or at the customer's premises with the customer's own machines. There must be certainty that all the testing time required will be available on the hardware, whether the supplier's or the customer's. There must be some final testing at the customer's premises where the system is to run when it is implemented.

Formal acceptance procedures are superseded to a large extent with the prototyping method. There does need to be formal acceptance of the final product but the process of acceptance will actually have been ongoing as the customer agrees that each module or phase meets its requirements. Final acceptance here means obtaining the customer's agreement that all the parts satisfactorily make up the whole. If they do not for some reason, the project simply continues until they do.

The conventional method can be constricting when it comes to the question of acceptance tests. To try to visualise what is going to be required before the project has commenced can be extremely difficult and acceptance tests which have been defined in detail may need to be redefined as often as the functional specification is changed. If there are no changes in either, it may be possible to demonstrate that the software meets the requirements of the functional specification but the finished product may no longer be suitable for the customer's needs. Suppliers will be concerned to assume that the acceptance process is not unduly long because satisfactory completion of the tests will often trigger a claim for the largest element of the price.

Conversely, the prudent customer will want to see a minimum period of continuous running without critical or major defects before signing off. (To extend this to minor defects which do not materially affect functionality would be unreasonable. By its very nature no software is likely to be completely error-free without a considerable period of refinement and experience in use and it may simply be uneconomic to fix some of these errors.)

However, customers typically look for the reassurance that comes from a prolonged period of testing under as wide a variety of conditions as possible. One commonly agreed compromise is to have a phased final acceptance, the major payment being due when the principal operating features and functionality can be demonstrated and a small sum retained for a defined period to allow for a more thorough testing process. This is a safer solution for customers than paying the full contract sum and then seeking either a claw back or warranty-related support services, but most suppliers will negotiate hard to minimise any deferred payment arrangements.

This issue is a less sensitive one with the prototyping method because there should not be any real surprises about the capability or suitability of the software when the development work has been completed. Ongoing refinement will fall under the umbrella of the supplier's support services, which may be provided on a time and materials basis.

The parties need to decide the point at which a system is deemed to be accepted. Under the prototyping method, this is straightforward: it is when the customer is satisfied that the software can go live. A broader range of alternatives is needed under the conventional methodology. Acceptance may be by means of a formal document signed by the customer. However, the supplier should not be in a position of waiting for payment due to be made on acceptance where the software has been handed over and yet has not been implemented nor formally accepted, although no further work remains to be done. Many customers fail to appreciate the distinction between installation of an acceptable system (which is the supplier's responsibility) and its implementation in their business (which is their responsibility unless they have contracted with the supplier for this additional service, usually on a time and materials basis). A common formula is to allow the customer a period of time following delivery in which to accept or reject the software. Failure to respond within that time will result in a deemed acceptance. There may also be a deemed acceptance if the product is used live. A repeat testing opportunity should be provided after rejected software has been modified and it will be a matter for negotiation if repeat testing is required beyond any agreed delivery dates.

355

7. Variations

This example will not generally be appropriate for prototyping development agreements.

(a) Either party may at any time up to 60 days before the System Completion Date formally request in writing any changes to the System.

(b) Within ten working days of receiving such a request from the Customer, or at the time of making its own request, the Supplier will inform the Customer in writing whether such change is technically feasible and of its impact and of any other consequent changes to the System, the Implementation Plan and the System Completion Date that it reasonably judges necessary. For any change requiring additional work, the Supplier will give the Customer either a fixed-price quotation or the Supplier's reasonable estimate for doing that work on a time and materials basis.

(c) If the Customer chooses to proceed with a Change Order, then the Implementation Plan and the System Completion Date will be amended as quoted by the Supplier, and the changes requested by the Customer and any other consequent necessary changes to the System, the Implementation Plan and the System Completion Date will be recorded in a Change Order signed by the Customer, and the Supplier will also issue a written revised price variation, or its estimate of such price variation for work to be done on a time and materials basis.

(d) Changes resulting from Change Orders will be deemed to be incorporated in the Functional Specification, and will be effected by the Supplier, at a time judged to be suitable by the Supplier before the System Completion Date.

(e) The Customer may vary the Implementation Plan by extending it by issuing a Change Order to take account of any delays on the part of third party suppliers or unforeseen operational needs, and will endeavour to give the Supplier reasonable notice of any extension. If the extension exceeds 30 days, the Customer will discuss the extension with the Supplier and any consequent impact caused to the Supplier's obligations. Any resulting changes which are necessary will be agreed between the parties.

(f) The Customer will bear all costs and expenses associated with any variation requested by the Customer including the cost of any feasibility study.

Under the conventional method, a formal procedure for variations must be established, taking into account all the consequences of amendments by the customer. For any large system development, there are bound to be changes. The customer will modify its requirements throughout the life of the development of the system. The agreement should lay down controls for this. Although the controls may seem pedantic, and under stress they will not be easy to comply with, working in accordance with them will save later misunderstandings and difficulties. The customer will make the request in writing and the supplier will evaluate and cost it, according to a set procedure involving the use of forms and time limits. Both parties should formally agree on the effect on price, timescales and other parts of the system before the supplier proceeds to carry out the change. They should also provide for an escalation procedure in the event of failure to agree.

At paragraph (b) the number of days should be agreed between the parties according to what is reasonable for the particular project. For a really large-scale system in its later stages of development, ten days may be insufficient.

At paragraph (d) the supplier is given flexibility about when to work on the change. It will be important for the supplier to control this so as not to jeopardise implementation. It is sensible to have a moratorium on permitting enhancements or modifications within a certain time before the system completion date, when there will be pressure to implement the known, existing requirements.

Whereas paragraph (e) is one which favours the customer, paragraph (f) is one the customer may negotiate to exclude.

8. Late Completion

This example will not generally be found in prototyping development agreements.

(a) If the Supplier fails to complete the System development by the System Completion Date, unless such failure demonstrably results from the Customer's default in performing its obligations under this Agreement or from an agreed extension of time relating to Change Order work, the Customer will notify the Supplier accordingly, and if such failure is not remedied within 10 working days, the Supplier, recognising the loss caused to the Customer, will pay to the Customer a sum calculated at the rate of 1% of the value of the contract in respect of every 7 days which elapse from the System Completion Date to the actual date of completion of the System, any period of less than 7 days to be calculated pro rata. Such sums of money will be paid by the Supplier to the Customer not as a penalty but as and for the ascertained and liquidated damages owing and payable by the Supplier to the Customer by reason of such failure to meet the System Completion Date.

(b) If the Supplier fails to complete the System by the end of the tenth week after the System Completion Date then the Customer (unless such failure demonstrably results from the Customer's default in the performance of its obligations under this Agreement) will be entitled without prejudice to any other rights or remedies it may have under this Agreement or at law or in equity to terminate this Agreement immediately by written notice.

(c) If any delay in meeting the System Completion Date is demonstrably due wholly or mainly to the Customer's fault, the Supplier will nevertheless, if the Customer so requests, continue with the work on the Project with a view to completing it as soon as reasonably possible in the circumstances, and the Implementation Plan will be adjusted accordingly. In such circumstances, the Supplier will be entitled to charge for the additional time at [its then current standard] [the agreed] daily rates.

It would be unusual for a customer to commission a development project without being concerned to ensure that an outside completion date was agreed as part of the contractual arrangement. The development or implementation plan should identify an end date and the parties then need to consider what is to happen if this date is not achieved. In some instances, they will also wish to extend their thinking to key milestone dates along the way. If the contract is silent about the consequences for later delivery, failure to meet an absolute date will constitute a breach of the contract entitling the customer to claim damages and also to serve a notice requiring completion within a reasonable time from the date of the notice ('reasonable' itself producing a different result according to the circumstances: one month may be appropriate in one type of contract but three months might be necessary for a long-term complex contract). If this later date is also not met, the customer will be entitled to end the contract as well as pursue a damages claim.

At the other end of the spectrum, the completion and key milestone dates could be agreed to be 'time of the essence' dates, when failure to meet them would entitle the customer to terminate the contract immediately and claim damages.

Most suppliers in most situations will be unhappy about agreeing 'time of the essence', particularly if the development project is large. There are likely to be all kinds of variables which cannot be anticipated or quantified at the time the contract is made.

The compromise solution tends to be an agreement for pre-agreed liquidated damages to be paid in the event of late delivery. The example clause follows this approach and highlights a number of issues which the parties will need to negotiate. The main decisions are on the amount of liquidated damages, the length of time for which they are to be paid, and whether or not they should constitute the exclusive remedy of the customer for late delivery.

The supplier will also want to be certain that no liability can arise where a customer's actions have caused or contributed to the delay.

Another question is whether the liquidated damages should be in monetary form as an absolute amount or as a percentage, or in the form of credits against future requirements or for substitute products or services, for example free hardware of an equivalent value. There must be no implication that any monetary amount could be construed as a penalty, which would not be enforceable.

358

Where the customer can be shown to be at fault, it may not be sufficient for the supplier to be allowed an appropriate extension of time. Rescheduling and other consequential costs may be incurred by the supplier and should be recoverable from the customer in such circumstances.

In practice, it often happens that the parties become embroiled in disputes over the reasons for implementation delays. It is advisable to link any consequences of late implementation to that part of the agreement which deals with project supervision so that a mechanism for escalation is invoked automatically and the agreed negotiating procedures exhausted before a claim for liquidated damages is made. Arbitration or Alternative Dispute Resolution procedures, discussed in **CHAPTERS 4** and **6**, may also need to be invoked.

Unless the relationship between the parties has deteriorated to the point where all confidence in the supplier has been irrevocably lost, it is of no great long-term benefit to the customer to seek unreasonably high payments from the supplier in the event of late implementation. This may even have the unwanted effect of putting a small but basically competent supplier out of business. The fundamental contractual goal is to provide the customer with a system which works and which is capable of carrying out the intended functions. It is not just a matter of expense for a customer to terminate an agreement and start again with another supplier. It is necessary to consider whether it is in the best interests of the customer's business to persevere until a system is operating satisfactorily, albeit later than intended.

9. Supplier's Staff

(a) The Supplier will use the staff identified in the Staff Schedule to perform its obligations under this Agreement. The Supplier will not without the consent of the Customer (such consent not to be unreasonably withheld or delayed) change the staff allocated to perform its obligations unless it has to do so because of reasons beyond its control.

(b) Each party will procure that its employees and sub-contractors comply with the other party's site regulations [including its working arrangements with outside contractors] and other reasonable instructions of the other party whilst at the other party's premises.

(c) The Supplier will be fully responsible and liable for the acts and omissions of its employees, sub-contractors and any employees of such sub-contractors arising out of the Project.

At first sight it would seem sensible from a customer's perspective to ensure consistency of staff engaged on the development project. In most instances, the customer will have got to know some of the supplier's development staff well prior to contract, and may in part have based its purchasing decision on its favourable reaction to those people. However, the clause should not be used without proper thought. It may be inappropriate for a small project. In some cases, the customer's real concern is to secure the continuing involvement of one or more key individuals rather than everyone involved in the project. The more constraints placed upon a supplier, the more difficult it becomes to comply, and the more implications there may be for unwanted consequences for the project. For instance, there may be a cost to the supplier in compliance, which it will need to recover.

It is quite common for customers to require the supplier's employees to comply with their site regulations and the example in paragraph (b) also anticipates customer employees visiting the supplier's premises. If there are published site regulations, these should be checked to ensure that there will be no potential difficulties in compliance, and if feasible, included as an appendix to the agreement. The customer may wish to go further, to have the right to exclude any member of the supplier's staff from its premises, possibly without having to give a reason. Before agreeing to this, the supplier should at least ensure that, in the absence of demonstrated reasonable cause, any consequential delay or costs will be accepted and met by the customer.

Paragraph (c) contains an open-ended liability for a supplier. Responsibility for the acts and omissions of those engaged on the project should be confined to acts and omissions arising in the proper course of their terms of engagement on the project and not extend to actions undertaken independently and beyond the reasonable control of the supplier. For example, if an employee of the supplier commits a criminal act whilst on the customer's premises, liability should not be accepted by the supplier as a matter of course. It is yet another item for negotiation, taking into account such considerations as the nature and sensitivity of the project and the availability and cost of insurance.

The structure of this example set out above at Section B includes an employment restriction clause, which can be relevant to this type of agreement, and such a clause is discussed in **CHAPTER 7**.

10. Progress Review

(a) The Supplier and the Customer will each nominate a Project Manager authorised to make and communicate decisions relating to the Project, who will be responsible for:
  (i) organising monthly Progress Meetings at which they will both review the progress of the Project and attempt to resolve any problems;
  (ii) providing all information reasonably required by the other for the performance of its obligations.

(b) The Supplier's Project Manager will prepare a monthly progress report in writing and deliver it to the Customer's Project Manager in time for discussion at the Progress Meeting. This report will include a report on the progress of the Project together with other matters as the Customer's Project Manager may reasonably require.

(c) The minutes of the Progress Meeting will be distributed within 7 working days and signed before commencement of the business of the next Progress Meeting by both Project Managers.

(d) If the Supplier has reason to believe that any estimate of any time and materials charges which may be payable for Change Order work is likely to be exceeded or that it is likely that the Implementation Plan will not be complied with, the Supplier will immediately inform the Customer's Project Manager by written notice.

Development projects which fail on account of unpredicted and excessive costs, late implementation and, at worst, unusability, often do so more through mis-management than through inadequate or inappropriate hardware or software. The larger the project and the bigger the company, the greater the risk. Therefore, whichever methodology is adopted, it is essential for each party to establish management and progress meeting procedures and to appoint a project repre-sentative through whom all decisions can be communicated. In each case, that individual should be empowered to make day-to-day decisions during the course of the project, although the supplier may wish to prevent its project manager personally taking immediate decisions on changing any of the contract terms.

Nevertheless, the level of formality will vary according to the complexity and length of the project. It is not in the interests of either party for the supervisory process to become so bureaucratic and time-consuming that it takes significant effort away from the development activity itself, nor for all the details discussed at a meeting to be recorded in the minutes.

11. Intellectual Property Rights (and Licence)

Example of clause for the Customer's benefit.

(a) All right, title and interest of whatever nature (including but not limited to copyright, design right, database right and patent rights) in the System and its related documentation will vest in and belong to the Customer at all times free from any interest of the Supplier or any third parties. The Supplier will do anything the Customer may reasonably require in order effectively to vest such rights in the Customer or to evidence the same (whether before or after the termination of this Agreement).

(b) The Source Code will be delivered to the Customer at the System Completion Date.

Example of clause for the Supplier's benefit.

(a) The Customer acknowledges that all proprietary rights in the Software, including but not limited to any title or ownership rights, patent rights, copyrights and trade secret rights, will at all times and for all purposes vest and remain vested in the Supplier.

(b) The Supplier grants to the Customer a non-transferable, non-exclusive licence to use the Software for an indefinite term and for its own internal purposes ('Licence'), provided that:

    (i)   the Customer does not provide or otherwise make available the Software or any part or copies or any related documentation in any form to any third party; and

    (ii) the Customer does not transfer or assign this Licence without the Supplier's prior written consent.

(c) The Customer undertakes as a condition of this Licence not to copy, adapt, vary or modify the Software without the Supplier's prior written consent.

Intellectual property rights are discussed in **CHAPTER 3**.

If the software consists of modifications to software already licensed under a supplier's software licence agreement, then the terms of the licence should be expressed to form part of this contract and termination of the software licence will terminate the right to use the modified software.

Copyright is first owned by the author or, if the author is an employee, by the employer. Copyright of the system will therefore effectively belong to the supplier if nothing contractual is stated. It is strongly recommended that the position is established contractually, for the avoidance of all doubt.

The customer may be keen to own the copyright. However, the supplier will not want to limit its use of skills acquired while it was under contract to the customer. It may also make use of programs for standard functions. The supplier will therefore wish to retain rights of ownership in the system and license the customer to use it. The customer can agree terms for the system not to be supplied to anyone else – especially a competitor (see discussion on the next clause) – and enter into an escrow agreement if, for some reason, it is not taking over the source code.

Therefore, the considerations include whether title is to pass to the customer and if so, at what point, and terms for delivery of the source code to the customer on completion of the project must be agreed.

Alternatively, licence terms and escrow arrangements need to be agreed. The customer should acknowledge that all proprietary rights will vest and remain vested in the supplier. The customer should automatically be granted a non-transferable non-exclusive licence to use the software for its own internal purposes, termination by the supplier being possible only if the customer fails to remedy any non-compliance with the licence, and the normal terms set out in **CHAPTER 9** relating to the grant of the licence should apply.

The supplier should give an intellectual property rights indemnity in the standard terms set out in **CHAPTER 7**.

The customer may also have to give a limited indemnity that any software or data owned and supplied by it to the supplier does not infringe any third party intellectual property rights.

12. Non-Competition

Recognising that the development of the System will be carried out at the Customer's expense and using knowledge of the Customer's specific type of business, the Supplier agrees from the date of this Agreement until the expiry of a period of 12 months from the System Completion Date not to design or develop or be involved in the design or development of a similar system for any company engaged in the specific type of business listed in the Competitors Schedule.

This is a contentious provision, fraught with potential difficulties. The customer's argument is that it does not wish to invest what could be an enormous sum in software development for its business, only to find that the supplier then uses the know-how thereby gained, in order to market similar solutions to the customer's direct competitors. The customer may suggest that its ownership of the software or an exclusive licence to use it would be an insufficient protection against this eventuality.

The supplier has a number of counter-arguments. Firstly, the expertise in developing software for specialised applications is such that it cannot be inhibited by passing ownership or exclusivity to the customer, at least not without significant price incentives for the supplier. There may be no possibility of amortising development costs if there is going to be only a single user.

Secondly, the supplier may be operating within limited vertical markets and cannot agree to a provision which will effectively prevent it from developing within its specified spheres.

Thirdly, there are competition implications because this provision is essentially anti-competitive and may, in particular circumstances, constitute an illegal restraint of trade giving rise to substantial penalties. If the parties are able to agree some form of non-competition provision which they are both satisfied is reasonable in the circumstances and not of a character likely to be judged illegal, then a clause along the lines of this example may be justified. The significance of any difference between the parties themselves or between the parties and the regulatory authorities will diminish the more narrowly the clause is drawn. For example, a minimum number of direct competitors of the customer and a prohibition on actual design only without trying to extend it to all possible forms of broader-based activities may be acceptable.

It should further be borne in mind that this sort of clause cannot be considered in isolation. There will need to be corresponding provisions in the employment contracts of those engaged in the development and in any non-disclosure agreement between the parties.

13. Supplier's Warranties

The Supplier warrants that:

(a) it is either the sole and exclusive owner or an authorised licensee or user of all intellectual property rights and interests in the Software and that no third party has or is entitled to claim any intellectual property right or interest in any of the Software which is inconsistent with any undertakings of the Supplier made in this Agreement;

(b) the Software will be developed in a skilled and professional manner by personnel who have adequate and relevant expertise and experience commensurate with their assigned roles;

[(c) the Software will for 90 days from the System Completion Date conform in all respects with the Functional Specification, provided that no changes to the Software are made other than by the Supplier or with the Supplier's written consent.]

Paragraph (a) above is a sensible warranty to seek, regardless of the development methodology. The third paragraph is shown in square brackets because, under the prototyping methodology, clause 3(j) on Customer Obligations earlier expressly requires the customer to recognise the absence of warranty for function or fitness for purpose. As discussed there, a warranty that the software will at least be written in a professional manner remains appropriate, and paragraph (b) is an example. The warranty in paragraph (c) is certainly associated with the conventional methodology and the actual period of warranty will be the main point of negotiation. Suppliers may also wish to negotiate a certain amount of in-built latitude in the event of warranty claims. There is no such thing as 'bug-free' software and therefore reasonable opportunities to resolve problems are appropriate before any formal warranty claim for damages is made.

14. Post-implementation Support

(a) Without prejudice to the Supplier's warranty or other obligations, the Supplier agrees to provide the Customer promptly with all assistance from time to time reasonably requested by the Customer for 12 months from the System Completion Date, to permit the Customer to use and operate the System to full advantage. Such support will include but not be limited to software support and modifications. This support will be charged by the Supplier on a time and materials basis at the Supplier's standard rate then in force.

(b) The Supplier will, if the Customer chooses, enter into a Support Agreement on or before the expiry of 12 months from the System Completion Date, the terms of which are [to be agreed between the parties] [appended as an Appendix].

(c) The Supplier undertakes to the Customer (without prejudice to the Customer's rights of termination) that the Supplier will continue to make a support service available to the Customer in accordance with terms to be agreed, and technical support as described above on a time and materials basis at the Supplier's standard charges then in force for not less than [5] years following the System Completion Date.

An alternative, simpler clause is as follows:

The Supplier recommends, or will provide if so requested by the Customer, a separate Support Agreement in the terms appended as an Appendix to cover future support of the System, at its then current charges for such support services.

This is an important provision for the customer who wishes to continue to rely on the supplier's expertise in supporting the system. It also presents an opportunity for ongoing income for the supplier.

Many customers fail to give any thought to the long-term position. They will usually expect some form of warranty and they will generally agree to an annual support agreement, effective from delivery, acceptance or expiry of warranty, as the case may be. However, for some reason, it rarely occurs to them to speculate about their requirements several years later. At that future time they may be dependent on a stabilised software product and they could be in all sorts of difficulties if a serious problem is encountered and the supplier no longer supports the software – or no longer exists. It is sensible to obtain a contractual commitment to a minimum period of support. If the customer is not entitled to receive the source code, an escrow agreement should be considered. Escrow arrangements, or more properly source code deposit agreements, are discussed in **CHAPTER 13**.

1   *The Challenges of Complex IT Projects*, published 2004; available at www.raeng.org.
2   See Table on pp 366–367.

THE CLAIMED ADVANTAGES OF THE PROTOTYPING METHOD OF SOFTWARE DEVELOPMENT

STAGE	ACTIVITY	CONVENTIONAL DEVELOPMENT				PROTOTYPING DEVELOPMENT			
		COMMENT	CUSTOMER RELATIONSHIP	TIME	COST	COMMENT	CUSTOMER RELATIONSHIP	TIME	COST
1.	**Feasibility Study/ User require-ments**	Should be in terms of objectives, not methods	Consensus	Comparatively Slow	Comparatively High	May be shorter than the requirements for conventional development	Consensus	Comparatively Fast	Comparatively Low
2.	**Specifica-tion**	Detailed	Harmonious, changes easily accommo-dated	Slow	High	Loose/concept document. Typically one tenth length of full detailed specification	Harmonious, changes easily accommodated		
3.	**Commis-sioned Program-ming**	Same or different team	Tight contract terms		Fixed Price	Same team	Flexible contract		Time and mat-erials

THE CLAIMED ADVANTAGES OF THE PROTOTYPING METHOD OF SOFTWARE DEVELOPMENT

4.	Development phase	Inflexible: conflicting objectives. Very structured Formal change control to permit any variation	Conflicts may arise at this stage			Joint objectives – both parties working to a budget	Close co-operation; always talking; refining specification. Continuous joint testing. Changes may easily be accommodated	On target	On target
5.	Interpretation	Different – no compromise incentive	Changes require agreement. Potential for exploitation	Increases	Rises	Compromise	Making the right business decisions		
6.	Project meetings	Agenda driven; issues missed	May become confrontational			Flexible and problem orientated	Working systems being produced		
7.	Product	May be not what is really wanted	Often unsatisfactory	Long	High	Exactly as expected	Good	On target	On final budget

CHAPTER 17

Outsourcing services

A. Introduction

It has always been common practice for a business to commission external contractors to assist with IT work. Over the last decade, the ways in which the services are delivered by third parties have evolved.

1. Terminology

The terminology 'provider' and 'client' identify respectively the company providing the outsourcing services and the company or other organisation paying for the services. Other terms frequently found are 'vendor' or 'supplier' for the former and 'customer or 'user' for the latter.

The term 'outsourcing' is used in this chapter as meaning that defined IT activities, or services, are contracted out by a client to a provider to *manage* and run to agreed standards to achieve specified results over an agreed period of time using service level agreements. The outsourcing provider may take over existing computing facilities to enable the client to concentrate on its core business strategy, or it may be responsible for setting up new facilities. The provider's staff may carry out the services at the client's site or remotely, using communications links. Thus outsourcing may encompass the transfer to the provider of the client's staff and/or associated fixed assets and/or premises used in the provision of the services, the client buying back the services.

The outsourcing may be selective or wholesale. Limited functions or processes may be outsourced, to the same or to different providers: perhaps a single system (such as payroll) or set of operations (such as PC support). Selective outsourcing may involve different parts of the business contracted out to different service providers. Alternatively, the entire management services or IT function of an organisation may be the subject of the agreement. This latter kind of outsourcing is high value and high risk.

'Facilities management' used to be a term used interchangeably with outsourcing, but is now generally used in a more literal sense, for management of buildings, logistics or distribution, such as catering or transport, managed for an organisation externally by a third party or by an internal appointment of a facilities manager.

'Outsourcing' is a fashionable term, and consequently is often applied rather indiscriminately to simpler IT situations, such as those for the provision of resources for a development project, or where specialist skills in limited supply are called for, or where the arrangement is simply for support and maintenance services by a third party.

This chapter does not address the ASP (application service provider/provision) model of outsourcing, which is discussed at **CHAPTER 18**. An ASP offers managed software application capabilities and services on a rental basis which may be according to agreed service levels. Software and services are delivered on a one-to-many basis remotely and accessed online. An ASP does not take over the client's existing IT infrastructure or staff. It does not operate locally on the client's premises.

The outsourcing market is continuing to grow, however it is defined. Local authorities and other organisations in the public and utility sectors have been required by the public procurement regime to put various kinds of services out to competitive tender. But all businesses are looking at how they can streamline what they do and become more efficient, and outsourcing is seen as a means of achieving this. Many contracts are now for second and third generation outsourcing, and both providers and clients have learned more sophistication as a result of early mistakes.

2. Reasons for outsourcing

There are many different reasons for an organisation to consider outsourcing, whether selective or wholesale. IT departments are expensive to run, with specialised employees who are difficult to find and retain, hardware which is obsolescent and systems which need continuous attention.

Costs may be escalating. Outsourcing can provide economies of scale in resources. It can give a more flexible costs budget, where service requirements can be added or removed at short notice. It can overcome problems of staffing. It can improve operational cover, planning and accountability.

Outsourcing is often perceived as a straightforward and immediate route to operational cost savings. It is obviously attractive to try to justify it to the Board of Directors with this argument. Yet this is a dangerously simplistic approach. The driver should be value for money, rather than a cost-cutting exercise.

Outsourcing may be used as a prelude to the running down of a particular computer or system, placing the obsolescent machines with the provider who can sell off excess capacity over three years, perhaps while the client is moving to new hardware or new systems.

For new areas, outsourcing may be a way of dealing with lack of expertise in a particular business sector. Its use may enable an organisation to save on having to make capital investment in technology before moving to a different level of processing power or migrating to another provider.

However, outsourcing can be part of the management of change. Movement to outsourcing often goes hand in hand with a fundamental strategic change of direction in an organisation.

The reasons may be mainly political. The company may be relocating, or undergoing some other significant change. Outsourcing may be perceived as transitional or more long term, or as offering more flexibility. It may enable a user company to concentrate more on its core business primary activities. It may result from a management buy-out.

Whatever the reasons for the choice of outsourcing by the client, the final decision should be in terms of quality of service and quality control rather than cost savings. Savings made by outsourcing can also be made without outsourcing.

3. The client/provider relationship

The client needs to look carefully in advance at the viability of the provider, considering the provider's experience, other clients, financial status and ownership. The financial soundness of the provider should be investigated, to minimise the risks of take-overs, mergers and management buy-outs. If a provider is a subsidiary company within a larger group, it will be in the client's interests to consider a guarantee or bond from the parent company, so that if the subsidiary looked as if its business might founder, the parent company would take over entire responsibility from the subsidiary.

Competence is naturally also a prerequisite. Moreover, it is also essential for the success of the relationship that there is a good cultural match between the provider and the client: attitudes to security, working environments, management style, are factors to bring into account.

Outsourcing should be a means, not an objective in itself. Some control should always remain with the business being outsourced. It is not a partnership, strategic or any other kind, between the provider and the client, who have different business goals and do not share the same risks.

370

Nevertheless, as for other IT arrangements, a good working relationship is crucial to the success of the contract. The provider must understand the client's business and have the ability to respond to its needs. However, strategic control should be retained by the client. There are different ways in which this may be achieved, with one or more people or teams. It may be necessary for a client to make a new appointment of a liaison services manager, or to buy in consultancy management for the process. On both sides representation for management liaison should be at a senior level.

4. Service levels

Service level agreements are the key to successful outsourcing for both providers and clients. These are the performance guarantees, translating the sales talk into performance standards. Service level agreements should define precisely and in detail what is required in terms of availability, timeliness and maximising through-put. The service levels will specify what is acceptable and agreed by both sides, and the contract will define what is to happen if the levels are not met. It is important for both sides that the outsourcing provider should recognise the quality of service expected by the client. Compensation levels in the event of failure or delay can be included.

5. Charges

Costs will typically be based on agreed charges for defined services, normally related to performance parameters, such as numbers of transactions or reports, or queries, or timescales, or the resources used in processing.

There are various ways of structuring the charges, and there may be a combination of methods. Some services may be provided at a fixed charge – banded according to volumes, numbers of users or accounts, etc. An alternative is to have rates based on time, activity or volumes. This may extend to open-book accounting where the provider's agreed costs of running the services are then charged together with an additional charge as profit for the provider, as a fee or percentage. If the profits turn out to be greater than expected, there may be an arrangement for them to be split between the provider and the client. The trends today are towards open-book accounting and shared risk/rewards.

Where the provider acquires equipment and staff from the client, this will release capital and other financial resources. It will have an immediate effect of removing fixed cost capital from the client's balance sheet, so that the ongoing costs of IT staffing and investment in new technology become variable. A sum may even be paid by the provider to the client, for the acquisition of hardware assets from the client, or on the transfer of staff.

Whether the charges imposed during the life of the contract are as predicted at the outset, and whether savings are achieved, will be affected by the way the contract is negotiated and finally worded, and the extent of any changes made to the services during the life of the contract.

In principle, the costs should become more transparent and therefore more controllable. Initial prices may be lower, on account of economies of scale, or for increased efficiencies, or for other reasons. The concomitant risks are that the level of service will be lower than before and that changes will cost more to implement. Sometimes users become more selective in justifying their requirements when the relationship between payment and service provision becomes apparent.

6. Business assets and human resources

Special considerations arise in contracts where the premises, equipment and staff are to become the provider's responsibility. Expert corporate, employment, taxation and property legal advice will be required. These matters will generally fall to be dealt with in the Business Transfer Agreement and other contracts rather than the Services Agreement. The focus in this chapter is on the Services Agreement.

Staff issues can be considerable. A significant amount of a business's costs are attributable to IT staffing. The simplest means of cost reduction is to reduce head count. Outsourcing provides an apparently attractive solution to facilitate this, where staff are transferred from the client to the provider. The personnel may at some point probably have the chance of developing their careers by working on systems other than those which were the subject of the outsourcing arrangement, and with more extensive prospects for promotion.

Both the provider and the client need to understand the position of employees affected by the change to outsourcing under their contracts of employment and statutory employment law generally, including the Transfer of Undertakings Regulations[1] ('TUPE') which apply wherever a commercial business in whole or in part, is transferred through legal transfer or merger as a going concern. The question whether a business transfer is a 'relevant transfer' for the purposes of TUPE is more complicated than is immediately apparent. Case law, both in the UK and in other European Union countries, has determined that the Regulations will generally apply to outsourcing where any staff are transferred, even though this may be only part of a business. These Regulations implement the EC Acquired Rights Directive[2] in UK law. Case law in this area is developing, and specialist employment law advice is essential.

If TUPE applies, the employees affected must be transferred on at least their existing terms and conditions of service and they retain the benefit of their previous continuous service. The Regulations also provide for the transfer of collective rights. The possible transfer of pension rights and insurance benefits can cause much difficulty. The transferred employees will be deemed for most purposes to have been employed by their new employer company since their original start date of employment with the client organisation. Entitlement to redundancy in the event of dismissal or a claim for unfair dismissal will be determined as though employment had started on the date on which the employee was first employed by the transferring client company. Dismissals of the outsourced company's employees occurring at the time of transfer for a reason connected with the transfer will be regarded as unfair, unless it can be demonstrated by the employer that they were made because of economic, technological or organisational reasons entailing changes in the workforce.

For the contract, the provider must evaluate its risk and the likelihood of any legal claims, for example, for unfair dismissals. The charges will reflect the cost of this risk, and the provider should also take indemnities in the contract in this respect.

If the premises are to be rented or sold to the provider, a separate property contract will be required. Assets, that is, the computer equipment, might be transferred within this separate contract. A sale, a lease or a licence to occupy would be negotiated covering the term, cost and duration, with options in the event of changes in the service provision.

If the client's IT equipment is to be transferred to the outsourcing provider, all the assets will need to be identified and listed, including computer hardware and communications together with all software for running it. Transfer of ownership and ongoing maintenance will require separate agreements including terms for payment to third parties. These contracts will identify whether the assets are to be transferred to the provider or whether there is simply a licence to use them. A transfer will involve a valuation which may be part of the overall financing. The hardware may already be leased and the leasing contract will identify the rules for assignment. Leasing arrangements can often be complex and should be sorted out at an early stage, to allow for the fact that the lessors may have no incentive to move matters forward quickly. It should be the responsibility of the outsourcing provider to secure the transfer.

If the hardware is not transferred to the provider, the contract should identify the allocation of risk and the insurance requirements and responsibilities.

The agreement may need to deal with the purchase of new equipment by the provider, and the extent of any consultation with a client about the terms of the purchase. It may also need to allocate responsibility for repair and renewal.

7. Intellectual property

One major issue relates to the intellectual property involved, including the software used for the services. The ownership of software and databases needs to be ascertained, to ensure that all the correct permissions are in place. This may

373

involve additional third party licence fees if the outsourcing provider does not have its own licence for running clients' software. This typically involves much negotiation with third party licence holders, who will normally seek extra payment. The client will also be likely to have software of its own, which it must license to the provider.

Some providers will use their own software in running the systems or in development. This is an area where the client must have a licence entitling it to continuing use if the outsourcing contract expires or is terminated. It may be that the provider's proprietary source code should be held in escrow in the event of termination or default in providing the services.

8. Catering for changes

The environment of the outsourcing contract is as subject to change as the general business environment in which the client organisation operates. Even where the outsourcing is not for the declared purpose of business process re-engineering, robust change control procedures must be established. A procedure needs to be agreed in order to enable variations to be made in a controlled way.

Changes which fall within the change control procedure may be those resulting from abandoning obsolete systems, technological advances, amendments as a consequence of new legislation, new service and capability requirements, and changes arising from business strategy shifts.

There should be a separate procedure for co-ordinating the process of changes required to the terms of the contract itself rather than to the substance of the services, the service levels or the technology.

9. Service continuity and transition management

It may be difficult for a client to envisage the failure of an outsourcing arrangement at a time when so much effort is being invested in selecting the provider and working out the contract details. Yet it is essential to plan and document exit routes for termination or expiry at the time the contract is being negotiated. If the mechanics of termination and the consequences are not clearly specified, there can be considerable problems.

At the end of the term, the choices for the client will be to:

- renew the contract – on the same or re-negotiated terms;

- choose another service provider – the current provider may be asked to re-tender; or

- take the service back in-house.

There must be provisions for the outsourcing provider to hand back or hand over the services competently, and preferably gracefully, if the contract is not to be renewed. The client cannot afford to risk ongoing dependence on the outsourcing provider. It will no longer have its own operational staff, its systems will be integrated with the provider's, and the provider will be in control of information critical to any other bidder.

10. Variability of scope of outsourcing agreements

Outsourcing agreements may take months to negotiate. They have to be tailor-made, and can be very complex to take account of all the elements, possibly including arrangements in respect of premises and staff as well as the hardware and systems. It may be appropriate to have other contracts separate from the main services contract, for individual applications or functions, or logically independent services.

The changeover needs careful preparation. Ill-considered outsourcing agreements which are badly managed will be fertile ground for litigation in the years ahead, but the availability of legal remedies will be of little consolation to a company whose business has been seriously damaged by the failure of the arrangement.

These concerns will be addressed in a properly drawn up and well-negotiated contract.

New ways of putting transaction terms together, of charging, of selective outsourcing and of handling the functions being outsourced, mean that contract formats and contents are evolving in order to accommodate developing outsourcing business practices.

The focus of this chapter is on the Services Agreement. Example clauses are also provided for the linked schedule for compensation payments in the event of service failures.

B. The structure of an outsourcing agreement

The structure of an outsourcing agreement is likely to comprise more than one single agreement in an arrangement of any complexity and will be customised to the particular set of circumstances. One typical structure for the overall contract is to have separate agreements for business transfer and staff transfer, the latter incorporating the human resources issues. Each agreement would have its own detailed schedules incorporated. There may be other discrete agreements for individual applications or functions, or logically independent services such as disaster recovery.

In this scenario, the business transfer agreement would deal with:

- the provisions concerning the sale and purchase of assets included in the transfer and any land or premises matters;

- the associated charges and taxes, which may include apportionments and pre-payments;

- insurance and guarantees;

- each party's obligations during the time between the execution of the contract and cut-over to the service provision; and

- human resources concerns.

The services agreement, illustrated below, will then deal with the ongoing service provision, ie:

- the duration of the arrangement;

- the services and service levels;

- the charges;

- software and other intellectual property licensing;

- management liaison, change control and contract review;

- security and contingency planning; and

- termination and exit strategy.

An example of clauses to be included in a schedule covering service level failure compensation follows.

Services Agreement terms and conditions

- Definitions*

- Term of Agreement*

- Services and Service Levels*

- Provider Responsibilities*

- Client Responsibilities*

- Contract Monitoring Arrangements*

- Contract Management*

- Client Software, Data, Information and Know-how*

- Third Party/Provider Software*

- Relations with Third Party Suppliers*

- Change Control Procedure*

- Charges and Payment Terms*

- Employment Restriction

- Confidentiality

- Data Protection

- Audit Requirements*

- Security and Disaster Recovery*

- Warranties

- Indemnity, Insurance, Limits on Liability

- Dispute Resolution Procedure*

- Termination

- Exit Management*

- General Contract Provisions.

Schedules

- Charges

- Disaster Recovery Plan

- Key Personnel

- Service Level Failure Compensation*

- Service Level Agreement(s)

- Services

- Software (Client Software and Third Party Software)

- Technical Requirements

- Transition Plan.*

C. Specific clauses

In the clause examples considered below, which are those above marked with an asterisk, the provider of the services is described as the 'Provider' and the client transferring the services is described as the 'Client'.

1. Definitions

'*Achieved Service Levels*' means the Service Levels which are actually achieved in any month.

'*Annual Review*' means a formal review carried out every 12 months of all aspects of the Services and the Service Levels [and the outsourcing strategy].

'*Business Transfer Agreement*' means an agreement between the Provider and the Client relating to assets and resources connected with the outsourcing arrangements.

'*Change Control Procedure*' means the procedure described in clause [...] for controlling Variations requested or recommended to the Services [or to the Agreement].

'*Charges*' means the charges, fees, prices, rates and formulae and special payment terms set out in the Charges Schedule.

'*Client Liaison Manager*' means the Client's authorised representative.

'*Client Software*' means the Client's software listed in the Software Schedule, including its documentation and all modifications and enhancements to it.

'*Commencement Date*' means [the commencement date identified in the Services Schedule] [dd/mm/yy][the date on which this Agreement is executed].

'*Contract Management Group*' means a group formed of senior representatives of the Provider and the Client.

'*Disaster*' means an event or circumstances specified in the Disaster Recovery Schedule.

'*Disaster Recovery Plan*' means the plan for restoring the Services in the event of a Disaster, attached to this Agreement as the Disaster Recovery Schedule.

'*Dispute Resolution Procedure*' means the procedure for dispute resolution set out in clause [...].

'*Equipment*' means the computer and communications equipment listed in the Technical Requirements Schedule.

'*Key Personnel*' means those employees identified as such in the Key Personnel Schedule.

'*Know-how*' means information which the Client owns or possesses, which the Provider requires for the provision of the Services.

'*Monitoring Meeting*' means the meeting held regularly to monitor the provision of the Services.

'*New Outsourcing Contractor*' means a third party provider whom the client appoints to provide services similar to the Services on termination of this Agreement including any provider invited by the Client to provide proposals for providing such services.

'*Provider Services Manager*' means the Provider's authorised representative.

'*Schedule*' means a schedule identified in this Agreement and incorporated into this Agreement, which will take precedence over the body of this Agreement in the event of any conflict.

'*Services*' means the services provided by the Provider described in [clause ... and] the Services Schedule.

'*Service Failure Compensation Schedule*' means the schedule which sets out the terms on which compensation payments will be made.

'*Service Levels*' means the standards and/or measures agreed by both parties for the provision of the Services, as detailed in the Service Level Agreement or as otherwise expressly agreed between the parties from time to time.

'*Service Level Agreement*' means the document specifying the Service Levels, attached to this Agreement as a Schedule and thereby incorporated into this Agreement.

'*Software*' means the software used in the provision of the Services.

'*System*' means all hardware and operating system software which runs the Software and which may comprise one or more computer systems.

'*Technical Requirements*' means the technical requirements set out in the Technical Requirements Schedule.

'*Third Party Software*' means the third party software listed in the Software Schedule.

'*Third Party Supplier*' means an external supplier, other than the Provider, of products, material and services in connection with the Services.

'*Transfer Date*' means [dd/mm/yy] [the date set out as such in the Services Schedule from which the Services are to be supplied by the Provider].

'*Transition Plan*' means the requirements to be carried out on termination, [set out] [outlined] in the Transition Plan Schedule.

'*Variation*' means a variation to the Services, Service Levels or Charges.

The expanded definitions of certain terms may be found within later clauses of the Agreement, but in certain instances may more conveniently be set out in a Schedule. The Schedules will be incorporated into, and therefore form part of, the Agreement.

2. Term of Agreement

(a) This Agreement will come into effect upon the Commencement Date [and execution of the Business Transfer Agreement. In the event of any conflict between the Business Transfer Agreement and this Agreement the terms and conditions of the Business Transfer Agreement will prevail].

(b) The Provider agrees to provide the Services to the Client from the Transfer Date for a period of [five] years.

(c) The Client will be entitled at its sole option to extend the Agreement for a further two years by written notice to the Provider at least six months before the fourth anniversary of the Commencement Date.

(d) [Either party][The Client] may terminate this Agreement on at least 12 months notice to expire on the [third] anniversary of the Commencement Date or subsequently, and this Agreement will be subject to the other termination provisions contained in it.

If there is to be a separate business transfer agreement to define the arrangements for the assets and resources of the client, paragraph (a) will provide the connection. Ideally both the agreements should be executed at the same time. A statement should be made as to which agreement should prevail in the event of any conflict.

Performance of the services commences from the defined transfer date, which may be a date later than the commencement date when this agreement comes into force. On the transfer date, the parties formally start working together to transfer the services to the provider. Other future dates are related to the defined commencement date of the agreement, such as the date by which the transition plan should be drawn up.

The term of the agreement is important to negotiate. The evidence on outsourcing indicates that shorter contracts have been found to work better than longer contracts. A short term may be appropriate where no major architectural changes are anticipated or where an obsolescent system is being run down. Otherwise, while ten-year terms and sometimes far longer are not unknown, the risks involved are greater than under a more typical length of time of five years. Some of the computer press reports of large outsourcing transactions which have been terminated early may indicate the difficulties of long-term outsourcing in the context of business change.

How far can an organisation look ahead and make reasonable predictions as to its business and service capacities, its structure and business goals? Almost every business has changed in its organisation, procedures and processes from even five or ten years ago, for example in terms of:

- numbers of people employed;

- use of technology: e-mail and Internet are obvious illustrations;

- business conditions;

- compliance requirements, especially for organisations in sectors such as financial services.

The term may be automatically renewable or it may be for a fixed term. The length of any notice period should be thought about carefully. Early termination options on notice by either party, for example, six years into a nine-year term, may be built in, but the greater the flexibility, the greater the cost to the client. However, the contract charges would be balanced to reflect the risk to the provider, so that profits are made earlier, or compensation payable. In some way, the provider will factor the potential loss of profit into the charges. Yet an early termination by the provider will cause immense difficulties to the client, if the exit management strategy is unclear.

It is always possible in practice for either party to try to re-negotiate the contract during the term. In a few well publicised cases the provider has initiated the re-negotiation of the contract where there have been difficulties preventing it carrying out the service profitably.

There will also be the normal built-in clauses for termination in the event of insolvency or material breach – if the service is consistently not being carried out effectively so that service levels are not being met or there is other negligence, and internal remedies and escalation procedures are not working.

No termination option will be exercised lightly for a major outsourcing.

3. Services and Service Levels

(a) In consideration of payment of the Charges by the Client, the Provider will provide the Services in accordance with the terms of this Agreement, to meet the objectives set out at clause 3(b) below, and to comply with the Service Levels.

(b) The objectives in requiring the provision of the Services are:
    (i)   [purpose of outsourcing];
    (ii)   cost savings in running the Services;
    (iii) efficiency in providing the Services;
    (iv) data integrity;

(v)   operational business continuity;

(vi)   responsiveness to changing operational strategy.

(c)   The provision of the Services as further described in the Services Schedule will include but not be limited to:

    (i)   dealing promptly with queries or problems relating to the use or performance of the Software and correcting all material program errors;

    (ii)   identifying the location of any fault on the System, and where it appears in the Equipment or in software not being supported by the Provider, liaising with the applicable Third Party Suppliers to ensure the continuing satisfactory operation of the System, taking all appropriate actions to ensure that the System maintains its full functionality;

    (iii) providing or procuring minor enhancements to the Software, including but not limited to updating data and formulae to ensure that any changes in tax or other statutory regulations or law are incorporated into the Software;

    (iv) ensuring that the documentation in respect of the System is always adequate for use and up to date;

    (v)   meeting the Technical Requirements.

(d)   The Provider will provide the Services in compliance with all relevant legislation, regulations, codes of practice, guidance and other requirements of any relevant government or governmental agency.

(e)   The Provider will provide reports of usage statistics for the Monitoring Meeting which record and summarise the Achieved Service Levels as required by the Service Level Agreement and will provide further statistics of performance in meeting Service Levels within five working days of a request for such statistics by the Client Liaison Manager.

(f)   In agreeing any further Services or any Variations, the parties will act in accordance with the Change Control Procedure (any such Variations affecting Service Levels to be included in the Service Level Agreement when agreed).

(g)   The Service Levels will be subject to review at any time by agreement between the Provider Services Manager and the Client Liaison Manager, and in any event will be reviewed as part of the Annual Review.

(h)   Without prejudice to the Client's rights of termination under this Agreement, in the event of failure to meet the Service Levels so identified as key in the Service Level Agreement, the provisions of the Service Levels Failure Compensation Schedule will apply, and the payments specified in that Schedule will become payable to the Client by the Provider on the terms set out in that Schedule.

The contract must lay down a structure for achieving quality of service by identifying the services to be provided and the performance requirements.

The services schedule will deal with the principles on which the services are being provided, identifying the services and perhaps the associated configuration and equipment, environmental and system aspects, defining and differentiating development from operational and support services, as distinct from the operational and detailed service level agreements.

Paragraph (b) sets out the objectives of the outsourcing, which will consist of the client's specific identified requirements. Paragraph (c) sets out the services which are needed in order to meet those requirements.

It will be an overhead for the provider to produce reports as set out in paragraph (e), and negotiation will focus on content, frequency and scope for revision.

Service levels are always a major feature of an outsourcing contract. The reasons for the client to insist on specific levels of service as well as expecting the provider's 'reasonable skill and care' are logical and practical. Service levels demonstrate the performance of 'reasonable skill and care' in the context of a particular situation. They are ongoing. They are at the heart of the commercial relationship, delineating the criteria by which the objective of achieving quality service is demonstrated.

The service level agreement is therefore a key document, setting out with certainty and precision descriptions of the services together with individual objective and realistically achievable performance levels and standards, in terms of quantity and quality in objective terms for the purposes of effective monitoring.

An analysis of the installation to identify and quantify the key activities will be necessary. It is easy to omit an important service which has always been taken for granted. Whether this analysis is carried out by the client and verified by the provider or whether the process is a joint exercise, both the provider and the user must be satisfied with the results. Perfect performance is not a realistic criterion. What is to be treated as reasonable? Numbers and frequencies of outputs and whether the reports are critical or not, must be identified. If input or information is missing through the client's default, that must constitute an exception. A combination of legal and technical skills will be necessary to draw up the requirements.

Negotiation of service levels will involve a compromise between the client's ideal list of requirements and the need to prioritise these in terms of what is realistically achievable. Performance measurement can entail considerable negotiation. A balance needs to be struck so that the desired levels of performance can be secured without imposing restrictions on the provider which are so tight that they inhibit the development of a creative and effective working relationship. It may even be appropriate to frame certain performance aspects in the service level agreement as targets or objectives which the client desires and the provider will try to achieve, but which will not attract breach of contract consequences if for some reason they are not achieved. In this way, contractual remedies can be focused on the essential features of the outsourcing from the client's point of view whilst also retaining some broader goals which the client would like to achieve if possible.

Once the service levels have been ascertained, the impact of failure to meet them and the level of compensation must be defined. The service level failure compensation schedule at Section D sets out further details in respect of the remedies for service level performance failure where the contract is still operational. Negotiations will focus on what key services should be included and the extent of compensation payable for service failure by the provider. There may well be negotiation over whether the compensation precludes the right of the client to terminate for continual service failures. The schedule sets out proposed circumstances in which termination becomes an option.

4. Provider Responsibilities

(a) The Provider will ensure that the Services are provided by employees who are suitably qualified, experienced and competent for the tasks they perform, and who will have undergone suitable training prior to working on the Services.

(b) *Provider Services Manager*
    (i) The Provider will appoint one of its senior managers as the Provider Services Manager. The appointment will be made on notice in writing, subject to approval by the Client [such approval not to be unreasonably withheld or delayed]. [Such approval will be deemed to have been given if no objection is raised within five working days of receiving notice of appointment.]
    (ii) The Provider Services Manager will oversee the performance of the Provider's obligations under this Agreement, act as its liaison with the Client, co-ordinate all matters relating to the Services, and will have the authority on behalf of the Provider to decide all questions of a day-to-day nature that may arise under this Agreement in relation to the Services.
    (iii) The Provider will be entitled to appoint an alternate to act temporarily if the Provider Services Manager is temporarily unable to fulfil the functions of the Provider Services Manager's role for any reason. Such alternate will have the same rights, responsibilities and obligations under such temporary appointment.

(c) The Provider warrants that for six months immediately following the Commencement Date, it will use all reasonable endeavours to retain the Key Personnel to provide the Services.

(d) The Provider will provide the Provider Services Manager and staff and (at no additional cost to the Client) such other resources as may be necessary for the Provider to fulfil its obligations under the terms of this Agreement.

(e) The Provider will replace any person involved in the Services on request made on reasonable grounds by the Client.

(f) The Provider will draw up the Transition Plan within three months of the Commencement Date, in consultation with the Client, and will be responsible for keeping it up to date in accordance with the Change Control Procedure.

(g) The Provider will continuously review developments and innovations in technology, business processes, help desk services, and industry practice, in order to determine whether such developments would benefit any of the Services, and will promptly bring to the Client's attention at the next Monitoring Meeting all opportunities for improving Service quality or reducing Service cost.

(h) The Provider will promptly advise the Client whenever the Provider has reasonable grounds to believe that it will fail to carry out its obligations under this Agreement.

(i) The Provider will promptly advise the Client whenever it believes that any failure on the Client's part to carry out its obligations under this Agreement will have a detrimental effect on the quality of the Services.

Paragraphs (a) to (e) are about the provider's staff. The client should consider whether specific levels of experience of the provider's staff should be agreed in advance as a contractual commitment. The negotiation of the contract is a different function from day-to-day management, and the client must get a commitment by the provider at paragraph (c) to provide ongoing experience and continuity, with experienced managers who will understand the client's requirements. The potential difficulty for the client is that the provider will replace the staff originally proposed for carrying out the services or their management with different, less experienced or fewer staff. Moreover, the provider may have a career structure whereby its best performers are promoted and moved on to greater responsibilities in a different environment.

The provider's services manager, referred to at paragraph (b), is an essential role as a means of formal contact between the parties. There is a strong case for the client to be consulted on the appointment, where ongoing liaison is so important to the success of the arrangements.

Paragraph (f) refers to the transition plan responsibilities. The outsourcing should be working in practice before the transition plan can usefully be drafted. It is likely to be a problematic area to agree the contents, in advance and in producing the results, but will be enormously important at termination or expiry of the agreement.

At paragraph (g), proposals by the provider for innovation, quality improvement or cost reduction may be made formally to the client through the medium of the regular meetings for monitoring progress. Alternatively, the proposals might be made in writing to members of the contract management group, or perhaps this route should be reserved for those which concern strategic change. The precise aspects to be covered by the continuous review will depend upon the nature of the services provided.

5. Client Responsibilities

(a) To enable the Provider to provide the Services, the Client will at its own expense:
  (i) provide the Provider with access to all relevant information and documentation reasonably required by the Provider;
  (ii) make available to the Provider at reasonable times, for consultation and guidance, staff who are familiar with the Client's organisation, operations, procedures and business practices;
  (iii) provide all input data required to be prepared by the Client for the provision of the Services [and be responsible for the accuracy and completeness of this data];
  (iv) notify the Provider of any special features relating to the input data which the Provider needs to know in order to provide the Services.

(b) The Client will appoint a Client Liaison Manager as its primary point of contact for the Provider[, subject to the approval of the Provider, which will not be unreasonably withheld or delayed]. The Client Liaison Manager will monitor the performance of the Services, and will have the authority on behalf of the Client to decide all questions of a day-to-day nature that may arise under this Agreement in relation to the Services. The Client will be entitled to appoint an alternative to act temporarily in the event that the Client Liaison Manager is temporarily unable to fulfil the functions of the Client Liaison Manager role. Such alternate will have the same rights and responsibilities under such temporary appointment.

(c) *Equipment and Software*
  (i) The Client will be responsible for ensuring that all consents and licences are obtained and maintained in respect of the Equipment and the Software necessary for the performance of the Services.
  (ii) The Client warrants that the Equipment and the Software will, by the Commencement Date, be in reasonable working order and condition for the purpose of performing the Services. The Client's liability in respect of breaches of this warranty is limited to claims notified by the Provider within 12 months of the Commencement Date.

(d) The Client will assist the Provider in drawing up the Transition Plan.

This clause can be wide in scope and the example is merely representative. The important point is that the parties should give careful thought to the nature and extent of the responsibilities which the client will be expected to undertake.

Since the client remains responsible for the delivery of the services, it therefore still needs to retain or acquire relevant expertise.

At paragraph (b) the client's representative and the provider's representative do not have the same functions within the outsourcing relationship. The client's representative may be perceived as having more of a controlling role. The equivalent provision in respect of the provider's representative is set out as part of the provider's responsibilities. Continuing co-operation is essential to successful outsourcing, however, and it may be regarded as reasonable that the client's representative should be acceptable to the provider.

Paragraph (c) may be relevant where the client's equipment is being used in the provision of the services. It may be a matter for negotiation as to whose responsibility it should be to bring the equipment up to standard and to deal with any problems.

The transition plan at paragraph (d) is the provider's responsibility in these example clauses, but the client will have requirements which must be met, and will accordingly need to assist the provider.

6. Contract Monitoring Arrangements

(a) The Client's Client Liaison Manager and the Provider Services Manager will attend the Monitoring Meetings which will be held at least once in each month at the Client location and at a mutually convenient time, to discuss work in progress, any problems or issues requiring decisions, resource requirements, anticipated work and any other relevant matters.

(b) Decisions, together with actions agreed to be undertaken and any other relevant matters, will be recorded as minutes of the Monitoring Meeting by the Provider Services Manager. Such minutes will be forwarded within ten working days of the Monitoring Meeting to the Client's Client Liaison Manager for approval, such approval not to be unreasonably withheld or delayed. It is acknowledged that in the event of a dispute such minutes may be presented as evidence in any formal or informal action.

(c) The usage statistics and any other statistics and reports available relating to the Services and Service Levels will be discussed at each Monitoring Meeting. If the Service Levels are not being achieved, the Client's Client Liaison Manager and the Provider Services Manager will agree the actions to be taken by the Provider to improve the Services, and draw up a plan of action to define the respective responsibilities of the Client and the Provider to be carried out in order to meet the Service Levels.

(d) Either party will have the right to refer to the Contract Management Group any matters arising at a Monitoring Meeting which have not been resolved to its satisfaction.

The contract should set out details on the formal channels of communication between the parties, normally through meetings and reports.

The management of the continuing relationship between provider and client is critical to the success of the contract, for the client to know that the charges are reasonable and that the services are being maintained. The purpose of the meetings is to review service achievements by noting and discussing the reports and statistics, to identify specific difficulties or trends and decide on necessary action. Quality assurance is an important function in this respect. Regular meetings can also provide a useful early warning system, and a means of proposing action to overcome foreseeable problems – as opposed to having to react to problems which have already arrived. The provider should have feedback that it is providing what is required under the contract. Actions can be agreed in the event of failure to achieve service levels or other shortfalls.

7. Contract Management

(a) The Contract Management Group will comprise five representatives appointed by the Client and three representatives appointed by the Provider.

(b) The primary functions of the Contract Management Group will be:
   (i)   to agree the Annual Review;
   (ii) to review the Transition Plan annually; and
   (iii) to resolve any disputes which are referred to it pursuant to the Dispute Resolution Procedure.

(c) The Contract Management Group will meet whenever the representatives or the parties deem appropriate, in order to carry out the functions conferred by this Agreement or otherwise delegated to it by the parties from time to time.

(d) Any appointment of a representative to, or a removal of a representative from, that Contract Management Group, will be made on notice in writing by the relevant party, subject to approval by the other party. Such approval will be deemed to have been given if no objection is raised within five working days of receiving the notice of appointment.

Different levels of meetings with attendance by different personnel may be necessary for a large-scale contract: for example, one model would comprise operational monitoring meetings as discussed in the previous clause; business management meetings to oversee the contract; separate functional steering groups for strategic decisions. In this example the contract management group takes on strategic functions.

The balance and numbers of representation at paragraph (a) will be a matter for negotiation. Sometimes it will be appropriate to set out voting procedures and a quorum for this meeting according to the contractual formality required. It will depend to some extent on the scale of the outsourcing.

It is right that paragraph (d) should be reciprocal, to reflect the importance of the parties working closely together.

8. Client Software, Data, Information and Know-how

Client Software

(a) The Client owns or is authorised to sub-license all copyright and other intellectual property rights in the Software.

(b) The Client grants a non-transferable, non-assignable, non-exclusive licence to the Provider to use the Client Software during this Agreement on the terms and conditions set out in this clause (the 'Licence') for the purposes of providing the Services.

(c) The Provider agrees that:
   (i) the Client Software and all copies of it will remain at all times the property of the Client and that the Provider is not entitled to any rights or interests in the Client Software other than those expressly granted in this Licence;
   (ii) copyright and all other intellectual property rights made by the Provider in any modifications or enhancements to the Client Software will vest absolutely in the Client;
   (iii) the Client Software is confidential information of the Client and it will not disclose any of the Client Software or supply any copies of any of it to any person other than in the performance of the Services under the terms of this Licence, including appropriate express obligations of confidentiality;
   (iv) it will not use any Client Software directly or indirectly otherwise than in connection with providing the Services;
   (v) it will not permit any copy of the Client Software to be made except for reasons of providing the services, security and back up.

(d) The Client will indemnify the Provider against any expense, loss or damage incurred by the Provider as a result of any claim or allegation that the Provider's licensed use of the Client Software infringes the intellectual property rights of a third party.

(e) Upon termination of this Agreement, the Licence will terminate, and the Provider will return the Client Software to the Client.

Data, Information and Know-how

(f) The Client grants the Provider a non-exclusive, royalty-free licence to use Know-how for the purposes of fulfilling the Provider's obligations to provide the Services. The Provider undertakes not to use or otherwise deal with the Know-how for any other purpose.

(g) For the avoidance of doubt, the parties agree that all data and information passed to the Provider by the Client or generated in the course of the Services will be at all times the property of the Client. The Client grants to the Provider a non-exclusive, royalty-free licence to use the Client's data, information and Know-how as necessary for the purpose of fulfilling the Provider's obligations under this Agreement.

(h) The Provider will not acquire any right in the Client's data and information. The Provider will take all necessary steps to ensure that it will not use nor reproduce any such data, information or Know-how which comes into its possession or control except as required by this Agreement.

(i) The Provider will be responsible for maintaining secure copies and backups of all data and information.

Where the provider will be taking over and using software developed by the client, the client must license the provider to use its software. This client software must be identified, by means of inclusion in the relevant schedule.

It is in the client's strategic interest to retain ownership of its software and information and to license the provider's use. The software is a business asset – and the outsourcing arrangement is not necessarily going to be permanent.

In most situations, a client will never have had to do this before. It will be important that the actual licence terms completely cover the particular circumstances. This clause contains the minimum essential elements, but each situation needs to be treated on its own merits. It may be useful to consider the licensing provisions set out in **CHAPTER 12**.

9. Third Party/Provider Software

(a) The [Client/Provider] warrants that Third Party Software is validly licensed for running by the Provider for the term of the Agreement.

(b) The Provider will fully indemnify the Client in respect of all damages, costs and expenses incurred by the Client resulting from any act or default of the Provider in respect of the Third Party Software.

(c) If the Provider proposes to use its proprietary Software in the provision of the Services, the Provider will not introduce such proprietary Provider's Software without the prior consent of the Client, such consent not to be unreasonably withheld or delayed. The Provider will grant the Client a non-exclusive, non-terminable, royalty-free licence to the Provider's Software on its standard and reasonable terms. At all times thereafter the

Provider will, at the cost of the Client, support the Software so licensed to the Client for the benefit of the Client.

(d) If the Provider creates any Software or other intellectual property in the course of providing the Services, it will assign the intellectual property rights in such Software to the Client on such creation with full title guarantee and execute such documents as the Client may require from time to time in this connection.

(e) The Provider hereby undertakes and warrants to the Client that the Software provided in connection with the Services does not infringe the intellectual property rights of any third party and agrees to indemnify and keep the Client indemnified against all costs, claims, expenses and liabilities arising out of or in connection with any claim inconsistent with the warranty.

The third party software must all be identified in its relevant schedule.

Outsourcing implies direct use of software at a site or on a computer system no longer under the client's direct control. This is in contrast to consultancy arrangements, where the agreement is only about the provision of services, and the consultant assigns or retains rights in software it develops and is permitted to access systems for performance of the services. Because the provider will be taking over the client's systems, licences will be required from third party software licensors. Existing licences to the client will normally prevent assignment and limit the use of the software, often to a designated configuration and sometimes at a particular location. It will depend on the circumstances whether the provider or the client takes the responsibility for acquiring the licences. The responsibility is likely to lie with the client initially, as part of a due diligence exercise in ensuring that all relevant third party software is identified for the provider. However, the situation will be familiar to the outsourcing provider who may therefore be prepared to take the initiative in negotiating with third party software owners on this account.

The outsourcing provider should take over the licences, pay annual support and upgrade fees, implement the upgrades, and generally indemnify the client. The outsourcing provider may well have its own licences for certain commonly used software.

Licensors should be informed well in advance of the commencement of the outsourcing, to give the provider appropriate permissions to run the software. Frequently, further fees are demanded from the outsourcing provider, but if these are material (ie more than a reasonable administration charge) they should be challenged and their reasonableness justified. If any third party licensor tries to charge excessively because of the outsourcing arrangements, it is an appropriate time for the client to consider whether that particular software is really essential, or whether an alternative is available. It may also be open to the client to threaten to take legal action on the grounds of unfair trading or unfair competition. Nevertheless, matters should be sorted out at this stage, rather than allowing them to be ignored and risking legal action by the third party owner. A client who licenses software and anticipates the possibility of eventual outsourcing should negotiate permission for this and any related terms into the licence from the outset.

The parties should therefore co-operate in making appropriate arrangements for use of the third party software by the provider for the purpose of performing the services, with the third party software owners. The client should be willing to execute any related transfer or novation or new licence agreements for the third party software required by third party software owners, so that the provider can assume responsibility for all matters in relation to the third party software including the payment of ongoing licence and support fees.

Paragraphs (c) and (d) propose arrangements in connection with the provider's own software, including a provision for assignment of any software created specifically in the provision of the services. A client should be wary of provider software which is not publicly available and which could not easily be replaced. If it will be useful on an ongoing basis, then it should be licensed to the client in terms permitting its use beyond any possible termination of the provider's services. Otherwise it is not wise for the client to have to rely on this proprietary software. In this case, the client should expect the source code of the software to be held by an escrow agent so that it would be available to the client in the event of failure of the provider's business. There may be a case for escrow arrangements, as discussed in **CHAPTER 12** to protect the client if the provider were to default in providing the services, or following termination or expiry of the agreement.

It is reasonable for the client to expect the normal intellectual property infringement indemnity to be provided by the provider, as discussed in **CHAPTER 7**.

10. Relations with Third Party Suppliers

(a) The Client acknowledges that the Provider is the primary supplier of Services to the Client. However, nothing in this Agreement gives the Provider an exclusive right to supply the Client with software, equipment or services of any particular description.

(b) The Provider will co-operate with Third Party Suppliers and will:

   (i) provide such access to information, documentation and premises as such relevant Third Party Supplier will reasonably require at such notice as is reasonable in the circumstances, and subject to the Third Party Supplier complying with such reasonable conditions as to confidentiality as the Provider may require;

   (ii) be responsible for co-ordinating with such Third Party Suppliers to

> ensure that software, equipment, and services provided by the Third Party Suppliers are integrated into the provision of the Services;
>
> (iii) attend any meetings with Third Party Suppliers called by the Client at the Provider's expense.
>
> (c) Where network, communications, computer or other equipment provided by a Third Party Supplier is required to interface with the Equipment, the Provider will be responsible for ensuring that the interface is successfully achieved. For the avoidance of doubt, the Provider remains responsible for meeting Service Levels in spite of any failure of any interface, whether through hardware, software, or any defect in the network, communications or other equipment attached to such interface or for any other reason whatsoever.

This clause will be relevant in selective outsourcing where the client is co-ordinating the supply of various services and products. It clarifies the provider's scope of responsibilities in this respect.

11. Change Control Procedure

> (a) At any time during the term of this Agreement the Client Liaison Manager may request, or the Provider Services Manager may recommend, a Variation by means of a 'Change Request' notice in writing served on the other party.
>
> (b) The Provider will investigate the likely impact of any Variation upon the Services, the Charges and other aspects of this Agreement and will report accordingly to the Client by the next Monitoring Meeting.
>
> (c) Any fundamental Variation requested or recommended such as a Variation which affects the terms of this Agreement itself will be discussed at a meeting of the Contract Management Group before it is agreed or rejected.
>
> (d) If the parties agree at a Monitoring Meeting or otherwise that a Variation should be implemented and on the terms such as any costs attached to such Variation, a 'Change Control Note' will be drawn up by the Provider within seven days of such agreement containing at least:
> - the details of the Variation;
> - the date of agreement to proceed;
> - any impact of the Variation on the Services, Service Levels and Charges;
> - any price to be charged for implementing the Variation;
> - a timetable for implementation and payment if relevant;
> - signatures of both parties.
>
> (e) Neither party will be obliged to agree to any Variation, except that the Provider will not unreasonably refuse to provide any additional services requested by the Client.

(f) Until any Variation has been mutually agreed in writing, the parties will continue to perform their respective obligations without taking it into account.

(g) For the avoidance of doubt, improvements in the Services or the Service Levels which are achieved by the Provider in the course of providing the Services efficiently, or which otherwise arise from the obligations imposed on the Provider under this Agreement, will not be deemed to be a Variation.

(h) All costs incurred by the Provider in connection with the preparation, investigation and negotiation of Variations will be borne by the Provider unless otherwise agreed in writing by the Client Liaison Manager or minuted at a Monitoring Meeting or meeting of the Contract Management Group.

This example clause highlights a dilemma for the parties. Rigid change control procedures may not be desirable when the outsourced services are subject to business process engineering and some flexibility is fundamental to the contractual arrangements. But in general, the client should be able to promote changes to the quality and scope of the services as time passes and it learns more and more about the most effective ways to benefit from outsourcing. The advisability, according to the particular circumstances, of including paragraph (f) should be considered.

It will repay prospective clients to satisfy themselves that the provider they propose to use is of sufficient size and resource to be able to match the client's aspirations, particularly when the client has a fast-growing business. More detailed procedures giving time limits for changes being proposed, considered and costed may be prescribed. Some changes whose effects are predictable will be simple to cost and implement. Others may affect the scope of the services and the contract itself. If the parties are concerned about controlling these aspects, they should refer substantial change requests to the contract management group for authorisation.

12. Charges and Payment Terms

(a) The Charges payable by the Client for the Services will be calculated according to the formulae set out in the Charges Schedule. Charges payable for specific projects or additional services will be agreed as part of the Change Control Procedure.

(b) The Charges will be revised on each anniversary of the Commencement Date during the term of this Agreement to take account of changes in the Service Levels, additional or fewer projects or services resulting from the Change Control Procedure and in any other factors included in the formulae, as more specifically described in the Charges Schedule.

(c) The initial set up fee will be paid to the Provider by the Client on the Commencement Date on receipt of a properly drawn invoice.

(d) Invoices for Services will be submitted monthly in arrears and will [represent one twelfth of the expenditure agreed in advance for the 12-month period concerned][be calculated on the basis of actual usage in the month preceding the month in which the invoice is submitted. Actual usage will be reconciled against initial forecast requirements and any differences identified]. [Invoices will be subject to approval by the Client Liaison Manager and will be due and payable 30 days after the date of the meeting at which the approval is given.]

The actual pricing and payment arrangements can be structured in many different ways and are likely to be features unique to any particular outsourcing agreement. These example clauses are likely to be simpler than those which will be agreed for any particular agreement of any complexity. The more comprehensive the services being transferred, the more complicated the charging mechanisms will be. A forecast of requirements may be made annually or at shorter intervals, to assist planning by the provider, but the client may be charged for actual usage, and any excess or shortfall may be priced at an adjusted rate. Different kinds of costing formulae and alliances are developing.

The review of fees is important as the client needs to be assured that it does not become locked into a provider who can then increase fees at its discretion. It is normal for the fees to be index-linked and, as staff costs are probably the principal part of the increase and expenses, a split index averaging the Retail Prices Index and a mutually agreed computer salaries index is often used as discussed in **CHAPTER 7**. However, this assumes a static service, which is not likely to be the case. There will need to be specific arrangements to cover changes in service levels over the duration of the agreement. The client must ensure that what was originally agreed in terms of charges does not expand unreasonably as a result of such changes.

There may be annual (or other) formal reviews of the pricing and benchmarking at regular intervals by comparing them with rates and charges derived from an agreed source. The basis of comparison must be fair and analogous for the services and both the client organisation's sector, complexity and size, and the provider's size and general features.

Payment methods need to be identified. The last option at paragraph (d) may be appropriate for a powerful client with complex service requirements where the change control procedure is frequently invoked and where there is effective communication through regular meetings between the parties.

13. Audit Requirements

(a) The Provider will permit the Client [at any time without notice] or any third party qualified auditor appointed by the Client on reasonable notice by appointment during normal business hours [but without notice in case of emergency including any reasonably suspected breach of any of the Provider's obligations contained in this Agreement] to observe the carrying out of the Services and to examine and take copies of information relevant to the Services, including any associated Client records and documentation under the Provider's control, subject in any case, [other than in emergency] to such third party entering into such confidentiality agreement as is reasonably required by the Provider.

(b) If, in the reasonable view of the Client, the audit indicates that the Provider's controls or performance are unsatisfactory, it will inform the Provider, and the Contract Management Group will agree on the improvements required and a timetable for achieving them. The Provider will comply with the timetable to implement the improvements.

It will be difficult for a provider to object to an audit requirement. Nevertheless, a provider may wish to control the situation to some extent, for example by limiting the number of visits per year.

The desirability of short-cutting the procedures in emergency situations as proposed in clause 13(a) may not appeal to the provider.

14. Security and Disaster Recovery

(a) The Provider will be responsible for ensuring that all documents, data and software are kept under secure conditions with back up arrangements satisfactory to the Client, to protect them effectively from unauthorised access and so that they can be recovered promptly from any malfunction of the System.

(b) The Provider will take all reasonable precautions to minimise the impact of any Disaster affecting the Services.

(c) In the event of a Disaster, the Provider will implement the Disaster Recovery Plan, in order to restore the provision of the Services affected by the Disaster.

Security and confidentiality issues are clearly important in this kind of agreement. A contingency plan must be agreed. These disaster recovery example clauses will be in addition to data protection and confidentiality clauses.

Clients should ensure that providers have made suitable disaster recovery arrangements, sufficient to cope with any contingency or disaster which might arise, having regard to the nature of the client's business. The clauses will be specific to a client's particular requirements. Disaster recovery agreements are often appended separately to outsourcing agreements and can themselves entail a good deal of negotiation. These agreements are discussed in **CHAPTER 21**.

15. Dispute Resolution Procedure

(a) Except where this Agreement expressly provides to the contrary, any dispute arising in connection with this Agreement will be dealt with in accordance with the Dispute Resolution Procedure which is set out in these clauses (a)–(f).

(b) Neither party will be entitled to commence legal proceedings under the jurisdiction of the courts in connection with any such dispute until 21 days after the Dispute Resolution Procedure is deemed to be exhausted in respect of such dispute.

(c) Notwithstanding clause (b) above, a party is in any event entitled to apply for injunctive relief in the case of breach or threatened breach of confidentiality or infringement or threatened infringement of its intellectual property rights or those of a third party.

(d) The Provider Services Manager or the Client Liaison Manager or any member of the Contract Management Group for the time being will be entitled to call a meeting of the Contract Management Group by written notice of at least 14 days in the event that such person considers that a dispute has arisen. At least two of the nominees of either party from the Contract Management Group will attend such meeting and will use all reasonable endeavours to resolve the dispute.

(e) If such meeting fails to resolve a dispute within seven days of the referral of the dispute to it, the Dispute Resolution Procedure will be deemed exhausted in respect of the dispute in question.

(f) During the progress of the Dispute Resolution Procedure, if the Client has an obligation to make payment to the Provider, the sum relating to the matter in dispute will be paid into an interest-bearing deposit account to be held in the names of the parties at a clearing bank and such payment-in will, for the time being, be a good discharge of the Client's payment obligations under this Agreement. Following final determination of the dispute, the principal sum and interest held in such account will be paid in accordance with such determination. The interest from the account will discharge the liability of the Client to pay interest to the Provider in respect of the period when the money was in the account.

The escalation procedure in this clause is an attempt to enable the outsourcing to continue whilst the dispute is being dealt with. A further level of escalation may be included, to give senior directors the opportunity to resolve the dispute.

Provision to bring in an expert, or independent conciliator or mediator may also be set out here.

The time periods to allow the chance of convening the meeting and resolving the dispute need careful consideration. If the dispute is not resolved in this way, there will be a consequent delay in initiating legal proceedings and the outsourcing services will continue to be delivered in an atmosphere which may be difficult.

Paragraph (f) suggests a procedure to enable payment to be continued while the dispute resolution procedure is under way. The definition of 'dispute resolution procedure' is confined to the procedure set out in this clause and does not extend to litigation.

16. Exit Management

On notice of termination or six months prior to expiry of this Agreement:

(a) the Transition Plan will come into effect, and the parties agree to comply with its provisions. The Provider will co-operate fully with the Client, any New Outsourcing Contractor, and Third Party Suppliers in order to ensure an orderly transfer of the Services to a New Outsourcing Contractor or to the Client;

(b) the Provider will liaise with the Client, making available for such purposes such Provider liaison staff as the Client may reasonably require, and acting in good faith, to ensure a mutually satisfactory handover to the Client or to the new Outsourcing Contractor. The period of transition will commence as soon as notice has been given of termination of this Agreement, and will continue for a minimum period of three months after termination;

(c) the Provider will:
   (i) provide information on the Services in sufficient detail to form the basis of an invitation to tender for services;
   (ii) allow the Client or any New Outsourcing Contractor to conduct a due diligence process in respect of the Services;
   (iii) promptly answer questions about the Services which may be asked by the Client or any New Outsourcing Contractor;

(d) the Provider will, if so requested by the Client, continue to provide the Services or such Services as the Client selects, for a period of up to 12 months from the date of termination, as specified by the Client, on the same terms as applied to the provision of the Services immediately prior to such termination;

(e) except where subject to separate contract, all rights of access, occupation and use granted to the Provider in respect of the Client's premises will cease when the provision of Services ceases in accordance with this Agreement and the Transition Plan;

(f) where assets used in the Services are located on the Provider's premises, the Provider will grant reasonable rights of access to enable the Client or the New Outsourcing Contractor to remove such assets transferred to the Client or the New Outsourcing Contractor in a reasonable time;

(g) the licences to the Provider to use any Client Software will continue after termination of the Services to the extent necessary to enable the Provider to perform its obligations under this Agreement;

(h) on termination of this Agreement [and on satisfactory completion of the Transition Plan], the Provider will procure that all Equipment and materials and all Client Software and documentation, will be returned to the Client or deleted as appropriate from the System, and the Provider shall certify full compliance with this clause;

(i) the Client will have the right to use and to license any New Outsourcing Contractor to use all the Provider's intellectual property required in providing the Services for such transitional period after termination of the Services as may reasonably be required in order to effect the seamless transfer of the Services;

(j) if the Client so requires, the Provider will use its best endeavours to procure the transfer at the Client's expense, to the Client or to a third party nominated by the Client at the Client's sole discretion, of any Third Party Software licences the Provider may have obtained in its own name in order to provide the Services.

If the mechanics of termination and its consequences are not clearly specified, problems are certain to arise. Time and effort spent at this stage may prove an invaluable insurance at some time in the future.

This clause is indicative and general, and will be in addition to the standard wording for termination for breach or insolvency as illustrated in **CHAPTER 7**. Clients, in particular, should give careful thought to the whole question of termination, trying to visualise and ascertain all the implications for their business. If the outsourcing provider's business should fail, planned transition arrangements may prove difficult or impossible to achieve. If specific problems can be identified in advance, solutions can be devised and, to the extent that they need actively to involve the outsourcing provider, they can be negotiated into the agreement.

The euphoria of finding a suitable provider and reaching agreement on running outsourcing services should not blight the client's objective view of a long-term outsourcing arrangement in a dynamic business environment, where a situation will not necessarily stay predictable or satisfactory. The more complex the range of services, the more difficult it is to ensure a smooth transition to another provider or back into the client's organisation.

The situation concerning staff transfer will require addressing in accordance with legal compliance and the wishes of the staff concerned. An indemnity should be sought on termination from the provider in respect of any claims by the provider's employees or former employees that employment or its liabilities have transferred to the client or new outsourcing contractor, where employment offers have not been made.

Paragraphs (a) to (d) may be contentious and their inclusion dependent upon the relative negotiating strengths of the client. The question of reasonable payment for the provider in meeting these obligations will need to be agreed.

Paragraphs (e) and (f) are effectively a reminder, in respect of premises and assets. There may well need to be more detail, if these are elements involved in termination.

The client will need to use relevant software throughout the process of termination, and the issues are exemplified in paragraphs (h) to (j). Software and know-how must be transferable as far as possible yet if the provider has been using its own proprietary software, which is not publicly available or not easily replicable, this may raise complications on termination. This is more likely to be the case if the provider has been involved in business process re-engineering, system development and project management.

D. Service level failure compensation schedule – specific clauses

This Schedule is illustrative only. It will apply only to certain high priority services. It would be unmanageable to cover all service levels.

There will be considerable scope for negotiation over the terms.

1. Scope of Schedule

> This Schedule sets out the calculation processes for Service Credits and/or Liquidated Damages as defined below, and the circumstances in which they will become payable by the Provider.

2. Definitions

For the purposes of this Schedule, in addition to the terms defined in the Definitions clause of the Services Agreement, the following terms have the following meanings:

'*Actual Costs*' means the figure comprising actual costs incurred by the Client in connection with the delivery of the Services in any single Year, excluding, for the avoidance of doubt, capital expenditure, depreciation or alternative means of funding capital expenditure, and including, but not limited to, the expenditure of:

- all such sums as the Client is obliged to pay to the Provider under the terms of the Agreements between the parties in respect of the Year concerned;

- all such sums as the Client is contractually obliged to pay in respect of the Provider's employees or sub-contractors; and

- any costs incidental to the above.

For the avoidance of doubt, in calculating the Actual Costs, no account will be taken of any Service Credits or Liquidated Damages paid by the Provider to the Client;

'*Key Services*' means any one or more of the following services offered by the Client to end users, each of which comprises a number of Service Levels [*List of specific Services*];

'*Liquidated Damages*' means a payment from time to time in respect of a Service Failure as further specified in clause 5 below;

'*Service Credit*' means a payment from time to time in respect of a Shortfall as further specified below;

'*Service Failure*' means any cessation of, or interruption to, a Key Service as further specified below;

'*Service Hours*' means the hours during which the Service Level is required to be available or in continuous operation;

'*Shortfall*' means a situation occurring when the Achieved Service Level in respect of any Service Level is at least 5% less than the Service Level for that Service Level, except where this is not the fault of the Provider;

'*Working Day*' means 9.00 am to 5.00 pm on Mondays to Fridays excluding public and bank holidays; and

'Year' has the meaning defined in the Services Agreement, being [1st April] to [31st March].

A 'shortfall' allows some leeway beyond the achieved service level. For example if the required service level is 95 per cent, the achieved service level must be below 90 per cent for the Service Credits to be triggered, in this illustration.

Compensation for service level failure may be technically in the form of 'liquidated damages' or as 'service credits'. In neither case is this intended to be simple compensation for the difficulties caused to the client by the service levels not being met. They are a form of guarantee with the aim of reducing conflict by setting realistic expectations of service. Financial recompense for not meeting the service levels is intended to be primarily an incentive for the provider by a bearable reduction in profits through having to make a payment to the client.

3. Service Credits

A Service Credit of [£———] will become payable by the Provider to the Client whenever in any rolling period of six months, two Shortfalls occur in respect of any Service Level.

For service credits or rebates, there is an automatic adjustment if the services are not provided to a pre-agreed level in any agreed period of time. A service credit will be payable separately in respect of each service level but not in respect of each shortfall. For example, if there is one shortfall in respect of a service level, in the second and fourth months of any six-month period, service credits will be payable. The level of service credits will be the same whatever the actual number of shortfalls for that service level in the second or fourth month. This means that no increased sum will be payable if there were more than two shortfalls during that period. However, the calculations may be refined, so that for certain service levels which must be separately defined, service credits will become payable for a different number of shortfalls within the six-month period from the number set for other service levels. There is considerable scope for negotiation of service credit amounts, triggering circumstances and the possibility of an escalation process.

4. Service Failures

A Service Failure will commence in respect of any Key Service if:

(a) that Key Service is unavailable to a majority of end users; or

(b) the internal response time, average internal response time or average first response time (whichever measure is specified as the applicable Service

Level) for a Service Level within the Key Service in question falls to the level specified as a Service Failure in the Service Level Agreement over the specified period of time,

except for any cessation of or interruption to the Key Service which is not the fault of the Provider.

There will be different triggers defining failure of key services which constitute the starting point for measuring service failures.

5. Liquidated Damages

(a) The parties agree that the rates and amounts for Liquidated Damages set out [below] [in the Appendix to this Schedule] have been calculated and agreed between them, and that such figures reflect the loss and damage, whether direct, indirect or consequential which could potentially be suffered by the Client in the event of the Service Failures as specified.

(b) Liquidated Damages will apply to the following Key Services where a single Service Failure has affected each Key Service for at least the specified number of Service Hours or Working Days:
[*The Key Services will be listed, with, as appropriate, the number of Service Hours or Working Days after which Liquidated Damages will be applied.*]

(c) The parties may agree that Liquidated Damages will not apply if so stated within a Change Order.

'Liquidated damages' are a form of pre-estimated compensation, where a cost can be attached to the result of failure to provide the service. The estimate must not be a penalty. That is to say, damages payable should not be disproportionate to the loss suffered. A client should not make a profit out of the provider's failure to meet the service levels.

Paragraph (a) refers to specific rates and amounts which may be set out within this paragraph itself or in an associated appendix.

Paragraph (c) allows for changes made under the change control procedure which drastically affect the services being provided. This may mean that it is unfair to invoke liquidated damages while the variations to the services are being implemented.

6. Measurement and Payment

(a) Either Service Credits or Liquidated Damages will apply, but not both. If Liquidated Damages apply in respect of a Service Failure, no Service Credit will apply in respect of the Shortfalls which contributed to the Service Failure.

(b) The Provider will report to the Client within the first ten Working Days of each month on the Achieved Service Levels for the previous month, and whether any Service Failures have occurred. In such report the Provider will provide a calculation of any Service Credits and Liquidated Damages which are payable in respect of the reported performance.

(c) Such Service Credits and Liquidated Damages will be a debt due from the Provider to the Client payable in cash on the date which falls 30 days after the end of the month following the month in respect of which the report was prepared.

The provider should not be penalised by being required to pay both service credits and liquidated damages in respect of a single service failure for one key service or service level. There may be considerable negotiation to determine how the payments should be made, whether by actual sums paid by the provider to the client, or by a reduction in the sums paid to the provider by the client.

7. Corrective Action and Consequences of Repeated Failure

(a) Where Service Credits or Liquidated Damages become payable in respect of a Service Level, the Provider will promptly take such remedial action as is necessary to correct the performance in respect of the Service Level.

(b) Where:
- the aggregate Service Credits payable in any continuous period of 12 months exceed [2]% of the Actual Costs; or
- a Service Failure in respect of a Key Service lasts for more than 12 consecutive Working Days; or
- Liquidated Damages become payable in respect of the same Key Service in the period of 12 consecutive weeks following the ending of a previous Service Failure in respect of which Liquidated Damages became payable,

then the Client may treat such occurrence as a material breach which is incapable of remedy.

These paragraphs first require the provider to take remedial action rather than to assume that the service failures should continue, and second, entitle the client to take legal action to terminate the Agreement (subject to the escalation rules) if the service failures become consistently unacceptable. This does give another safety net to the provider, in addition to the escalation procedure; until this point, the provider is being given opportunities to put matters right.

Negotiation of the number in square brackets and of the precise conditions which will trigger the right to terminate should be conducted with great care by both parties. Note also in this example that termination is not automatic but becomes a client option when these circumstances arise.

8. Limitation of Liability

(a) Notwithstanding clauses 3 and 6 [*on Service Credits*], the Provider will not be obliged to pay to the Client in respect of any single Year, any excess of the sum for Service Credits which in aggregate exceeds [2.5]% of the Actual Costs for the Year concerned.

(b) Notwithstanding clause 5 [*on Liquidated Damages*], the Provider will not be obliged to pay to the Client in respect of any single Year, any excess of the sum for Liquidated Damages which in aggregate exceeds [£......].

(c) The Liquidated Damages (but not the Service Credits) will be deducted from the ceiling of liability set out in clause [......] of the Services Agreement.

This paragraph ensures that the provider will not be penalised by continuing the outsourcing at a loss in the event of cumulative individual service failures, and that the client is not going inadvertently to be gaining a price advantage rather than being reasonably compensated for its loss. This would not assist the ongoing relationship of the parties. If the number or extent of service failures were sufficiently serious, the client should consider termination.

E. Transition plan schedule contents

Some typical contents of the transition plan are proposed here, but this is not intended to be comprehensive. Even so, it will be easier to identify the tasks which would be useful to include in a transition plan than actually to write it and keep it up to date. It will be a fine art to ensure that it is realistic enough to be implemented effectively.

The Transition Plan will include, but not be limited to, the following contents:

* a programme of the transfer process, including details of the means of ensuring continuing provision of the Services throughout the transfer process;

* plans for communicating with staff, suppliers and customers of each party to avoid any detriment to the Client's business as a result of the transfer;

* plans for the transfer of personnel engaged in the undertaking;

* a list of the security tasks necessary at termination;

* processes and procedures used in the performance and monitoring of the Services;

- details of the contracts relating to software and other intellectual property whether of the Provider or any Third Party Supplier, in the course of providing the Services;

- documentation and source code for any software developed by the Provider in the course of providing the Services for the purposes of the Services;

- up-to-date documentation used in delivering the Services.

1   Transfer of Undertakings (Protection of Employment) Regulations 1981, SI 1981/1794, as amended.
2   Acquired Rights Directive 77/187.

CHAPTER 18

Application service provision

A. Introduction

Application service provision ('ASP') is the term used when service providers deliver and support software applications by hosting and maintaining them on a central system for remote access on a one-to-many basis.

Application software is stored and data held on a central network server and accessed directly by users, with no need for local servers. Access may be over the Internet via an ISDN connection, browser software on PCs, point-of-sale terminal or over a corporate private network by dedicated leased line, simply by key stroke. The application never has to be loaded on the user's system.

The service providers can exploit economies of scale by consolidating the requirements of many users, using the same application infrastructure. The range of suitable applications is wide, such as collaborative working software, routine applications which businesses may conveniently share, such as messaging systems. Other successful examples are in data warehousing; enterprise resource planning; customer relationship management, and for sales forces, customer service management; retail point-of-sale, order entry and accounting; stores inventory control, purchasing and material holding. However, competitive leading-edge bespoke software or heavily customised applications do not fit as well into this model, and there is some resistance in subscribing to applications where confidential information, such as certain financial data, is involved.

Application service providers may own the software which they may have developed themselves, or they may be supplying or combining third party software and/or offering value-added services or software. As part of facilitating the use of the software application, day-to-day operational data backups and software upgrades will usually be included. Optional services which may be found are:

- configuration, customisation and integration services; development and support; application updates; training services;

- management services, such as monitoring and testing, upgrade management.

In addition to the service provider itself, software houses, network service providers, telecommunications providers and data centres, may all be involved – in one or in several different locations.

As ever in IT, there are related services with other labels. Other forms of provision include managed service providers (MSPs), managing the infrastructure of computers and networks for their clients rather than the applications, or storage service providers (SSPs). Mobile telephony service providers or wireless application service providers (WASPs) provide applications to take advantage of those technologies.

Internet service providers (ISPs) provide the Internet connectivity. An ASP is more than an application hosting service. If hosting alone is provided, the application services remain the responsibility of the client, who may choose to use internal staff to deliver these services, or may outsource them – whether for design implementation, operation or ongoing support and management.

ASP and outsourcing

ASP is sometimes regarded as an extension of outsourcing or facilities management services. However, the provision of services and software over the net differs markedly from the outsourcing described in **CHAPTER 17**. For ASP, one or more applications and associated services will be provided to many clients. The mode of operation is quite different. The service provider does not operate locally at the client's premises or take over the client's existing IT infrastructure or applications. Rather, it provides the client with online access to the service provider's IT infrastructure at its site.

Costs

ASP is charged by means of rental or subscription payments according to use rather than by initial capital investment or expenditure in hardware and the purchase of software licences, keeping the costs off the balance sheet. There may be an initial fee, but typically there will be regular payments, although there are different kinds of pricing structures. There may be a flat recurring fee covering services, administration, hardware use and database administration, or payment may be based on variables such as volume throughput or number of users. In any comparison of ASP with different delivery methods, the costs of communication should be taken into account.

Service availability

The framework of the infrastructure enables the performance of the applications being provided to numbers of users to be accurately measured and controlled by means of service levels. Sophisticated software systems have been developed for measuring and managing the capabilities for tracking and recording application usage. Users must be able to access any host applications for guaranteed levels of availability expected. Most providers can offer over 99 per cent uptime of the applications being provided. Service credits may be applied for failures to perform to the agreed standards. However, factors other than the operational running of the applications also affect application availability. Service providers cannot be accountable for those problems beyond their control, whether on account of the client's systems, network availability, Internet performance, unpredicted web traffic overloads or third party input.

Potential advantages for users

Subscribing by regular payments for the use of software delivered online may be cheaper than traditional licensing but this is not an inevitable advantage. It depends on usage and the flexibility and expansion that may be required, and there will be less individual customisation. The charges may be relatively low if an intermittent or limited service is required.

A traditional approach to software procurement might involve expenditure on hardware and software components, and investment in staff time, including training and consulting. The positive differences in ASP from conventional implementation of an application ideally include less effort and risk because the software and its infrastructure are already operating, and there is no need for a traditional IT roll-out. At its simplest, implementation may mean signing up and starting to use the application service. In such cases, there is an advantage of speed and no disruption of existing business processes. Against this, the client must make a formal assessment of the suitability of the application service for its requirements in advance without traditional testing or acceptance procedures.

As a result, fewer resources may be required by the client for running and supporting the application service or for implementing upgrades, and the provider will be carrying out the general technical support for all its clients, perhaps using skills in short supply and not otherwise readily available to the client.

There may, therefore, be greater scope for flexibility. It is often difficult for a user to predict future usage levels or growth. This is unimportant for an ASP service which can be made available as required without long lead times or adverse effects. Access is easy and remote working is consequently feasible, by mobile workers signing on via laptops and local telecommunications, not by specially configured equipment; or the services may be provided at a number of locations nationally or internationally.

Security

Clients need reassurance that proprietary data held on remote shared systems is as secure as their own systems, and safely retrievable as required, especially for sensitive data. The ideal is for data hosted remotely to be stored on hardware specific to the organisation, not shared use. However, this is unlikely to be cost-effective. At least the data should be logically separated by being stored on a separate database within a shared physical server. Clearly the premises housing the servers concerned, which may be the service provider's or may be owned by a third party and used under facilities management arrangements, need to be secure against unauthorised access and physical theft. The provider should have good back-up procedures and disaster recovery plans. Thus, there should be a contractual obligation for the provider to minimise the risks of security breaches. The client may seek escrow arrangements for the application, as discussed in **CHAPTER 13**, to cover the potential situation of the provider's insolvency.

Clients should pay special attention to the risks to their businesses if they propose to adopt an ASP solution for the management of any critical functions. They must evaluate and compare the benefits of potentially significant cost savings and access to special expertise in some complex computing areas against the consequences if the hosted applications fail for any reason. Any decision to proceed should be supported by detailed contingency plans, and of course the ASP provider should be selected on the basis of a track record of relevant experience, excellent client references, demonstrable financial strength, management capability and depth of resources.

ASP contract requirements

The emphasis in constructing an ASP contract is on the delivery of a 'service' to support the software application remotely. Nevertheless, if software is being accessed and used, the user still needs to have the right to use it. It is not intrinsic to the concept of a licence that the software has to be held on the user's own configuration.

Unlike software development or procurement, there will be no formal acceptance procedures. There may still be a requirement for management liaison between client and provider, such as a named service delivery manager, and change control procedures, depending on the complexity of the application being provided.

The differences in what is required from contract to contract relate, amongst other things, to:

- the description of the services, their flexibility in terms of customisation and any value-added features provided, the relationship of the services to the application, and whether they cover development, hosting and support;

410

- whether the provider owns the software itself, or supplies or combines third party software, offering value-added services;

- the extent of the provider's obligations and the allocation of responsibility for the various aspects of the network, hardware, software and services;

- whether the client is an intermediary for end users – and whether the client is active in service provision to end users or in its use of the services itself; for example, online software for paying bills may be provided to a vendor, which may enable bills to be viewed and paid online by customers, for whom it may be irrelevant whether the solution is ASP or not;

- whether levels of performance and availability are guaranteed;

- the significance and extent of security for the application and services;

- whether scalability will be built into the contract, so that usage may increase or decline according to the client's requirements. The ways in which changes to the services or volumes may be effected should be contractually agreed. This will include consideration of how upgrades are provided and managed and paid for;

- whether an exit strategy for the client is required.

B. The structure of an ASP agreement

- Definitions*

- Duration

- Service Provision*

- Licence and Scope of Client's Use*

- Client Obligations*

- Charges*

- Payment Terms

- Security and Information*

- Client Branding and Client Information*

- Service Availability*

- Intellectual Property Rights Indemnity

- Warranties and Exclusions*

- Limitations on Use*

- Limitation of Liability

- Termination

- General.

Schedules

- Charges

- End User Licence

- Services
  Including details of:
  - Services provided
  - Application descriptions
  - Details of any special related services, eg for support, helpdesk, security measures, etc

- Service Level Specification
  Including details of:
  - Service Levels
  - Specification of credit amounts for failures of Service Levels
  - Service Availability

- Technical Environment
  Including details of:
  - Network Specification
  - Client Equipment: hardware and software specifications for use of the Application Services.

C. Specific clauses

In the clause examples considered below, which are those above marked with an asterisk, the provider of the services is described as the 'Provider' and the client receiving the services is described as the 'Client'. The client distributes the application services online to its end users, perhaps after adding content as appropriate. This particular application requires the end user to enter into a simple agreement to access the service. It is assumed that the provider is not supplying any equipment. Support services form part of a separate agreement.

1. Definitions

'*Application*' means the specific hosted application(s) for which the Services are provided, identified and described in the Services Schedule, which may be owned by the Provider or by a third party.

'*Charges*' means the fee payable for the provision of the Services and any other charges payable, as further defined in the Charges clause and the Charges Schedule.

'*Client Branding*' means the Client's corporate branding, such as trade marks or names or logos.

'*Client Equipment*' means the hardware and software which the Client uses to enable the Services and Application to be provided.

'*Client Information*' means data input, created or used by the client or End User in using the Application and Services.

'*Downtime*' means an outage causing interruption or failure to the provision of the Services.

'*End User*' means an entity that at any time has been identified by a Client to the Provider as an authorised End User.

'*End User Licence*' means the agreement between the Provider and an End User in the format and wording set out in the End User Licence Schedule.

'*Intellectual Property Rights*' means all copyrights, patents, registered and unregistered design rights, trade marks and service marks and applications for any of these, together with all database rights, trade secrets, know-how and other intellectual property rights in all parts of the world and for the full term including all rights of renewal.

'*Network*' means a network comprising all or any of the following: modems, leased circuits and other telecommunications hardware and software.

'*Schedule*' means a schedule referenced in, and forming part of, this Agreement.

'*Service Levels*' means the levels of performance to which the Services are to be provided to the Client by the Provider.

'*Service Level Specification*' means the document setting out the Service Levels and any security measures, comprising a Schedule to this Agreement.

'*Services*' means the application services to be provided by the Provider as described in the Services Schedule.

'*Service Procedures*' means procedures [set out in writing][accessible by the Client online] to provide instructions and guidance for the Client's management of the Services, which may be amended and updated from time to time.

'*System*' means the Applications, Services, and the Network as they operate together in the provision of the Services.

'*Technical Environment*' means the Network together with the Client Equipment, and any related equipment and connections, all as specified in the Technical Environment Schedule.

2. Service Provision

(a) The Provider agrees to provide the Application and Services to the Client [and to End Users] in consideration of the payment of the Charges by the Client, subject to the terms and conditions of this Agreement.

(b) The Provider will make available to the Client its Service Procedures and other appropriate support and diagnostic information, and will ensure that updated Service Procedures will be made available to the Client whenever they are re-issued. Information contained in the Service Procedures may include, but is not limited to:

   (i)   technical support offered by the Provider;

   (ii) training offered by the Provider;

   (iii) usage restrictions to prevent unreasonable loads being imposed on the Network;

   (iv) procedures to ensure that the security and integrity of the System are maintained, including encryption details if appropriate, and any procedures which arise from the need to comply with regulations of any data centre facility engaged by the Provider in connection with the Services; and

   (v)   procedures to ensure that any database or other applications which form part of the Services can be used to best effect and within capacity.

(c) The Provider will comply with the Service Levels.

(d) Hosting of the Services, Applications and web servers is provided as set out in the Services Schedule.

(e) If the Client wishes the Provider to perform any service which is not part of the Services, the Provider may carry out that service at its sole option, and the Client will be charged separately for it at its current rates for such services.

This clause begins with the general commitment by the provider to supply the application services in return for payment. All services or support provided by the provider should be identified in this clause, such as any special help-desk services or other means of problem fixing. Information specifying the services should be detailed in the Services Schedule.

Paragraph (b) refers to the service procedures, which may be in hard copy or available online, which provide information about the applicable procedures and restrictions in the operation of the services. They are not in themselves contractually binding, as they are likely to contain various operating details and to require relatively frequent updating. Paragraph (c) is the commitment by the provider to meet the service levels, for which the details will be specified in a separate schedule. For example, they may include response times.

Paragraph (d) refers to the Services Schedule for setting out the details of the hosting provision, which may be by a third party.

3. Licence and Scope of Client's Use

(a)   The Provider grants to the Client a non-exclusive, non-transferable licence to use the Services and Application as set out below for the Client's normal business purposes.

(b)   The Client may use the Services only in the jurisdiction in which the Client is registered as a company only by:
  (i)   accessing the Services in accordance with the procedures set out in the Service Procedures;
  (ii)   entering, editing, transferring or deleting and moving its input comprising Client Information, documents, data, files and other content within the Services; and
  (iii) providing interconnection with End Users who have entered into End User Licences, but only to the extent necessary to enable them to participate legitimately in using the Applications and Services.

(c)   The Client acknowledges that it is its sole responsibility to determine that the Application and Services meet the needs of its business and to satisfy itself that the Application is ready for operational use in its business before it is so used.

(d)   The Client is responsible for maintaining validation, error correction, back up and reconstruction of its own software and Client Information.

(e)   The licence granted to the Client in clause (a) above is personal to the Client and the Client is not permitted to assign, transfer, sub-license, or otherwise dispose of any of the licensed rights to use the Service or any component to a third party. other than to End Users under the terms of this Agreement. Nothing in this Agreement transfers any proprietary rights in the Services from the Provider to the Client.

(f)   End User Licence
  (i)   The Client is granted the right to grant licences to End Users in the form of the End User Licence to permit the End User to access and use the Application and Services only in relation to the Client's business purposes or its own use.
  (ii)   The Client acknowledges its responsibility for ensuring that End Users are properly licensed in order to access and use the Services in advance of such access and use.
  (iii) If the Client learns or suspects that any End User is not complying with the terms of its End User Licence, the Client must notify the Provider immediately.

415

This clause defines the scope of the services and therefore limits access and use by the client and any end users. The sub-clauses in respect of end users may be irrelevant for many application services, and clearly therefore these sub-clauses are optional according to the circumstances. But where the system is being accessed by parties other than the client itself, the provider may wish to impose certain restrictions.

4. Client Obligations

(a) The Client acknowledges and undertakes that it will:
    (i) use the Services only for lawful purposes and in accordance with this Agreement; and
    (ii) comply in every respect with all the instructions which the Provider provides concerning the Services, including the requirements set out in the Service Procedures; and
    (iii) use and adhere to the user names, passwords and any authentication codes or security procedures which the Provider may notify to the Client from time to time: and
    (iv) keep and maintain up to date a list of its licensed End Users and will provide such list to the Provider promptly at the Provider's request.

(b) The Client will not:
    (i) reproduce, disseminate or otherwise disclose the content of any Application except as expressly set out in this Agreement;
    (ii) electronically transmit any Application over a network except as necessary for the Client's licensed use of the Application;
    (iii) use run-time versions of any third party products which may be embedded in any Application, for any use other than the use of that Application;
    (iv) modify, disassemble, decompile, or reverse engineer any Application except to the extent permitted by law, and must first give 30 days notice to the Provider;
    (v) sub-license or otherwise grant or transfer possession of any copy of any Application to any other party outside the terms of this Agreement;
    (vi) use any Application in any way not expressly provided for by this Agreement.

(c) The Client is responsible for using only Client Equipment which is in good working order and in compliance with the specification in the Technical Environment Schedule. The Client must give 90 days' written notice of any changes it proposes to make to the Client Equipment. If any such Client Equipment is not compatible with the Services or Application, the Provider will promptly inform the Client in writing, and the Client must promptly rectify the situation.

(d) The Client is responsible for acquiring and maintaining all licences and permissions necessary in respect of any third party software it may use in connection with the Services. The Client confirms that any Client Equipment, Client Information or other materials provided by the Client to the Provider or utilised by the Client in the Services will not infringe any Intellectual Property Rights of any third party, and will not be obscene or defamatory, and will not violate the laws or regulations of any state which may have jurisdiction over such activity.

(e) If, for the purpose of providing the Services, it is necessary or desirable for the Provider to access or use any Client Equipment, Client Information, facilities or services, the Client will make these available to the Provider for access free of charge to enable the Provider to perform its obligations under this Agreement, and the Client grants to the Provider a non-exclusive, royalty-free licence solely for such purposes.

(f) The Client acknowledges that it is responsible for its input to the Services and for any use that it or its End Users make of the such input, and that the Provider has no responsibility for such input or its use.

(g) The Client licenses the Provider to incorporate items of the Client's corporate branding, such as a trade mark or name or logo, for the purpose of customising its pages and input. If, for this purpose, the Provider needs to become a registered user of any of the Client's branding, the Client undertakes promptly to do everything necessary to procure such registration for the Provider.

(h) If the Client learns about or is informed of any of the components, processes or methods of operating any software comprised in any Service it will treat that knowledge or information as the Provider's trade secret, and not use it to the benefit of any party other than the Provider or convey it in any way to any third party or allow any third party to acquire it.

(i) If the Client is in breach of any of its obligations above, then, without prejudice to the other terms and conditions in this Agreement:
  (i) the Provider cannot be held liable for any failure to meet the Service Levels which arises as a direct or indirect result of such Client breach;
  (ii) the Provider will be entitled to charge the Client for staff time engaged on rectifying any resulting problems at the Provider's standard charge rates for the time being.

(j) If the Provider suffers any loss, damage or expense as a result of:
  (i) any unauthorised access to, or use or misuse of, the Services by any employee, agent or sub-contractor of the Client;
  (ii) any unauthorised access to, or use or misuse of, the Services by any third party if such access, use or misuse was permitted or facilitated by such employee, agent or sub-contractor,
the Client will fully indemnify the Provider in respect of such loss, damage or expense.

These obligations are a combination of requirements for positive compliance and prohibitions. The client needs to comply so as to facilitate the smooth operation of the application and services, and to protect their confidentiality. There are licensing obligations for the client, both in respect of its own and any end user's use of the application and services, and in respect of the provider if the latter needs to access any intellectual property of the client or a third party, or if the corporate branding of the client is a feature of the services or application.

Under paragraph (c), the provider specifies the requirements in the Technical Environment Schedule for the hardware and software which the client is to use for the services. However, this may be of no concern to the provider, if the services are provided over a standard browser, for example, and it may not be necessary either to specify the equipment requirements in detail or at all, or to require notification of any changes to be made.

The final paragraphs specify the consequences for the client if it is in breach of any of the other paragraphs. A client in a strong bargaining position will be concerned to limit its obligations in the last paragraph.

5. Charges

(a) The Client will pay the Provider the Charges in respect of the Services at the rates and according to the payment terms set out in the Charges Schedule, and such Charges may be varied on 90 days' written notice after the initial 12-month period.

(b) Costs which are additional to the Charges and which are also the Client's responsibility include:
  (i)   PCs, modems, printers or other equipment which may be necessary to access and use the Services;
  (ii)   communication charges, access fees, levies, tariffs or other related costs, between the Client and the Provider or its End Users or the Internet host or anyone else;
  (iii) installation and testing of any communications lines, links or interfaces or any equipment or service used in connection with the Services.

(c) If any of the Service Levels are not met to the extent that such failure for any such Service Level is defined in the Service Level Specification, unless any such failure is not the Provider's fault and subject to the exceptions stated in this Agreement, the Provider will credit the Client's account according to the method set out in the Charges Schedule with the sum representing the credit for such failure of the Service Level concerned as specified in the Service Level Specification.

(d) During the term of this Agreement and for five years following its termination both parties agree to keep accurate books and records showing all the information required in the accurate calculation of the Charges. These records must be made available to the other party or its appropriately qualified representative for audit purposes.

There are many different ways to structure the charges, and it is normally convenient to set out the particular payment arrangements in a schedule. An initial fee may be payable, and there may be regular subscription or rental payments. The agreement will also set out the provider's payment terms, and the right will be reserved to increase the charges from time to time.

Usage-based charges will require the ability to measure what is used. This is especially the case if credits for performance failures are to be applied, as allowed for in paragraph (c), which relates to the specific formulas in respect of service level failures and amounts consequently due to the Client, as agreed between the parties.

Paragraph (d) enables an independent check on the calculations of the charges. It may be limited to one of the parties alone, depending on the specific arrangements. The provider may expect to be independently audited in respect of the obtaining of the information on which it bases its charges. However, the charges may be dependent to a certain extent on information supplied by the client, such as the number of users, and the provider may wish to have the right to have this information audited.

6. Security and Information

(a) The Provider will effect and maintain at all times continuous and sufficient security measures, in order to safeguard Client Information from unauthorised access and use, and to minimise the risk of a security breach and, if appropriate, these will be specified in the Service Level Specification.

(b) Encryption techniques will be used for protecting Client Information on input and transmission over the Network, as specified in the Service Procedures.

(c) The Provider will promptly notify the Client of any security attack which it learns of or suspects, which appears to be directed towards the Client Information.

(d) If the Client learns about any of the components, processes or methods of operating any software comprised in any Service, the Client will treat that knowledge or information as the Provider's trade secret and not use it to the benefit of any party other than the Provider or convey it in any way to any third party or allow any third party to acquire it.

Security may be a major issue for the client, and this clause enables the provider to give some assurances, which may be further detailed in the Service Procedures.

These may also document the principles for user identification and authentication, for access, adding or changing access rights.

If the details of the security measures are fundamentally critical to the client and unlikely to change, they may be specified as a direct contractual commitment in the Services Schedule or in its own schedule rather than by reference to the Service Procedures.

7. Client Branding and Client Information

(a) The Client warrants that it is the owner or authorised user of all intellectual property rights and all other rights in the Client Branding. The Client agrees that for the purpose of customising the Application, the Provider may incorporate items of Client Branding, and the Client hereby licenses the Provider to do this. If for this purpose it is necessary for the Provider to become a registered user of any Client Branding, the Client undertakes promptly to do everything necessary to procure such registration.

(b) The Client acknowledges and agrees that it is entirely responsible for its Client Information and any use that it or any End User or third party may make of it for any purposes, and that the Provider shall have no responsibility for the Project Information or such use. Without prejudice to the generality of the previous sentence the Client undertakes:

   (i) to inform itself (and, if appropriate, the Provider) concerning, and in performing its obligations under this Agreement fully to comply with, all laws, regulations, licences or binding codes or standards of practice relevant to personal data (including without limitation the Data Protection Act 1998);

   (ii) not to provide any item of Project Information or upload, transmit or download any message or material that:

   - is defamatory, racist or sexist, threatening or menacing to any person or group of people, or contains any obscene elements (in particular, anything which is or could be interpreted as paedophilia), or which in the Provider's reasonable opinion is likely to cause annoyance or distress to any person; or
   - infringes the copyright or other intellectual property rights of any other person, company or partnership, anywhere in the world.

The client must itself give some guarantees as to the legitimacy of its data, especially when used over a network. If its trade mark or other corporate branding is to be used by the provider in the services, there must be appropriate authorisation for this.

420

8. Service Availability

(a) Subject to the provisions set out in this clause, the Provider will use all reasonable endeavours to make the Services and Application available during the times specified in the Service Level Specification.

(b) Notwithstanding the above, the Services or any particular Service Levels may be suspended for so long as is reasonably necessary subject to prior agreement with the Client, such agreement not to be unreasonably withheld or delayed:

   (i) to enable either party to comply with an order or request from a governmental, or other competent regulatory body or administrative authority; or

   (ii) to enable the Provider to carry out work which is necessary in its reasonable opinion to maintain or improve the Services; or

   (iii) to carry out standard maintenance and support;

provided that the Provider will use all reasonable endeavours to schedule such Downtime during hours of low usage of the Services in order to minimise impact on the Services, and to ensure that there is no permanent material degradation of the Services.

(c) If the Application requires immediate correction to enable it to run effectively or for immediate compliance with a governmental or regulatory requirement, the Provider may suspend that Application without advance warning for so long as reasonably necessary to implement the correction or to ensure compliance.

(d) The Provider will be entitled in its sole discretion to make changes or upgrades to the Application or Services or their accessibility, to the Technical Environment or to the Service Procedures, provided that such changes or upgrades do not cause any material reduction in functionality. The Provider will endeavour to give at least seven days' written notice of any such changes. The Application may be suspended for so long as is reasonably necessary, but the Provider will use all reasonable endeavours to minimise the Downtime that may be caused by such change or upgrade. If as a result of such changes, the Client's ability to use the Services or the cost to the Client of using the Services is materially and adversely affected, the Client may terminate the Agreement on seven days' written notice to the Provider.

(e) In the event of Downtime as specified in sub-clauses (b), (c) or (d) above, the Provider will provide status reports to the Client's representative nominated for such purposes by the Client, at two-hourly intervals by telephone or e-mail during working hours, or as otherwise agreed by the parties.

(f) The Provider will use all reasonable endeavours to comply with a request by the Client for Downtime, provided that such requests are made in

> advance to the extent possible, and such Downtime will not be considered as a break in Service for the measurement of the Service Levels or for any other reason.

The provider will wish to retain as much freedom as possible to suspend the application and services, and must be able to do so in the event of circumstances over which it has no control. Moreover, to the extent that the application and services are standard and may be provided to many clients, the provider will need to keep them up to date and will need to introduce changes from time to time.

Nevertheless negotiation will focus on the amount of notice required for scheduled outages, and what the exceptions should be. The client may want to stipulate how such notice should be given, whether by e-mail or a telephone call, to learn the estimated duration and progress of the outages as a matter of course, and to what extent ongoing status reports should be provided.

There may be occasions when the client needs to request a suspension of service. The client may need to follow an agreed procedure, with an agreed period of notice.

Any procedural requirements for outages for either party may be set out in the Service Procedures.

9. Warranties and Exclusions

(a) The Provider warrants that it is either the sole and exclusive owner or an authorised licensee or user of all intellectual property rights in the Application and Services (including any databases, images, 'applets', graphics, animations, video, audio and text incorporated into them), and reserves all its rights.

(b) The Provider warrants that it will provide the Services using all reasonable skill and care in accordance with the terms of this Agreement, and so that they conform to their current published description and that they operate in accordance with the Service Procedures.

(c) The Provider uses all reasonable endeavours to maintain the Services free of bugs and viruses but the Provider strongly recommends that the Client should have its own effective anti-virus programs.

(d) The Provider does not and cannot control the network on which the technology operates or the flow of data to or from its network. Such flow depends largely on the performance of services provided or controlled by third parties. At times, actions or omissions of such third parties can impair or disrupt connections. Although the Provider will use all commercially reasonable efforts to avoid such events and take all actions it deems appropriate to remedy such events, the Provider cannot guarantee that such events will not occur. Accordingly, the Provider cannot and does not warrant that the Services will be uninterrupted, error-free or entirely secure, and disclaims any and all liability resulting from or related to such events.

(e) The Client acknowledges that the Provider does not provide any back-up software or processing facilities covering equipment, data, operating systems or application software unless any are specified in the Service Procedures, and the Client agrees that the Provider will not be responsible or liable if, for any reason concerning any of these, the Service cannot be provided.

(f) The Provider does not make any other warranties, guarantees or representations concerning the operation or performance of the Services. The Client is entirely responsible for deciding to select the Services for its own business purposes and the Provider accepts no liability for any use to which the Client puts the Services.

(g) The Provider does not accept any responsibility or any liability for enabling the Client to link to any site on the World Wide Web, or the contents of any other site, whether one from which the Client may have been linked to, or to which the Client may link from, other than the Provider's website.

(h) Each party represents and warrants to the other that it has obtained, where required by law or regulatory authority, all registrations, permits, licences and approvals necessary in any relevant country for it to perform its obligations hereunder, or alternatively, that it is exempt from obtaining them. Upon request, each party will provide the other with copies of all such registrations, permits, licences and approvals. Each party further warrants and undertakes to the other that in performing its obligations under the terms of this Agreement it will comply with all applicable national and local laws and regulations.

The provider must limit the commitments which it may properly expect to make. In the first place this is to cover circumstances where it does not have entire control over the network and other external factors. Secondly, the provider must avoid liability on its own account or in respect of any effects on other users because of misuse by the client or its end users. However, it is important for the provider that the clause wording justifies the reasoning behind the limited warranties, so that the standard terms and conditions are perceived to be reasonable and therefore enforceable.

Paragraph (h) may be applicable in circumstances where the services may be accessed from other jurisdictions. It is sweeping in its ambit, and the need for it may depend on the content of the services.

10. Limitations on Use

(a) The Provider reserves the right to deny any End User access to the Services and to direct the Client to terminate an End User Licence and access to the Service on reasonable grounds, including but not limited to such End User being a direct competitor of the Provider, or breach by the End User of any term of its End User Licence, or in the event of termination by the host provider, but the Provider will notify the Client of any such refusal promptly by telephone or e-mail and then confirm it in writing.

(b) If at any time the Client's or any End User's access to, or use of, the Services is not in compliance with any applicable law or regulation, the Client will be in breach of this Agreement, and the Provider will be entitled at its sole discretion to terminate it under the termination clause and to discontinue the Services in respect of the Client and any such End User. The Client acknowledges and agrees that the Provider is entitled to report such a breach or non-compliance to any relevant regulatory body or agency, and that the Provider will not incur any liability to the Client or End User as a result of the breach, the non-compliance, or the Provider's reporting of it.

(c) In addition to any other remedies available at law or in equity and without prejudice to its rights under this Agreement, the Provider will have the right to suspend the Services immediately if deemed reasonably necessary by the Provider in order to protect the proper interests of the Provider or of its other clients. If practicable and depending on the nature of the reason for such suspension, the Provider may, in its absolute discretion, give the Client an opportunity to remedy the situation. In such case, if the Client remedies the situation, the Provider will promptly restore the Services.

The Provider must have the right to terminate the agreement immediately if there is illegal material input as a result of the client's use or misuse, and similarly to stop providing services to an end user for the same reason. The standard termination provision allows for termination in respect of material breach of the agreement, and this clause ensures that any non-compliance by the client with laws or regulations may also lead to termination.

Paragraph (a) will be resisted by clients and will be a matter for negotiation.

CHAPTER 19

Website development and support

A. Introduction

The Internet is easily taken for granted, and it is hard to remember that it is effectively at an early stage of development and use, whether for business, social, charitable or educational purposes. Its potential for transforming communications and for efficiently providing information and entertainment is enormous.

To get the greatest benefits from a website, a business must pay great attention to its creation, structure and design, and ensure that it is always up to date and readily accessible. In the early days it used to be common to develop websites by using the services of technically interested employees, friends and relations. Now that websites have become more sophisticated, and there is greater recognition of the benefits which they can bring to the business, the work is normally outsourced professionally. The website developer may provide various associated support services, such as domain name management, maintenance and content provision. The extent of the services to be provided should always be clarified. It will also be necessary to define the nature of any maintenance and support services which will be provided following the site launch.

Nevertheless, innovative web designers are often small, young and transient businesses. Where this is the case, it may well be in the client's interest to put forward its own contract, especially including various checks and controls to take account of lack of business experience, for example, by relating payments closely to deliverables. However, there is no point in having such overly restrictive conditions, whether on payment terms or on timescales, that the designer will be unable to carry out its tasks effectively, and go out of business as a result.

Costing structure

What is being bought and at what price? A small self-contained project lasting a number of days or weeks may be carried out for a fixed price. Other work may be more appropriately charged at a time-based rate. There may be a monthly retainer or other ongoing arrangement. Charges are occasionally linked to incentives where the actual design and provision of content is a key feature of the services provided, such as the number of visits or the volume of sales. Bespoke solutions will generally, but not inevitably, be more expensive than package-based ones.

Content

Various decisions need to be made about the content of the website. If it is to be provided by the designer, how is it to be defined? How much is to be provided? Is there to be advertising or sponsorship content or is the site to be free from third party advertising? What restrictions should there be on style or format? How often is the material to be updated and how is it to be updated? Is the provider to take over total responsibility for ensuring that the material is up-to-date and accurate?

Where the developer will be managing the site and where there are message board or chat facilities within the website, it will be necessary to apportion responsibility between the owner and the developer-manager for ensuring the prompt removal of any content posted by visitors containing material which is illegal, or which infringes the rights of others (for example, because it is defamatory or breaches copyright).

Ownership of rights

The ownership of content and code needs to be defined: what belongs to the provider as designer; what belongs to or needs to be permanently licensed to the client; and what is owned by third parties and licensed by them for use.

The client's ideal perspective is to own the rights in the bespoke design of its web pages and of the software code for the website, as well as in the contents. A second-best option is to have secure permanent licence rights and exclusive use of a customised design. The client will wish to balance the cost of exclusivity with the objectives for its website (which may include competitive advantage). In any event, the developer will wish to re-use its routines, methodologies and precedent structures and keep the ownership rights in those.

The content may itself be made up of many forms of media each with different rights. Third party licences and consents may be required. Content created by the client's employees or legitimately acquired by the client will be owned by the client. The client needs contractual provisions that provide all necessary consents, licences and permissions to cover the use, transmission and display of content, so that it does not breach third party intellectual property rights. Trade mark and logo permissions may also need to be obtained.

Standards

If the website is being designed for a customer who belongs to a trade or professional association, there may be guidelines which have to be taken into account. There are various guides to best practice. For example, the *Guidelines for UK Government Websites* is available on the web, and has some useful pointers[1].

On the launch of the website, the client should ensure that the site is protected by means of any appropriate disclaimers, privacy statements, copyright and other legal notices, together with any relevant technical controls, such as encryption, time-barring or other devices.

Web Analytics

As with all new technological developments, early adopters and first wave customers have embraced the business opportunities made possible with considerable enthusiasm. In the US and to a large extent in the UK there are now relatively few businesses, from sole traders to multi-national corporations, which do not operate a website. Although many websites still contain only basic information about a business – what it does, where it is located and how it may be contacted – e-commerce is advancing rapidly and is becoming crucial to the overall performance and even continuing viability of many businesses.

However, the quality of many e-trading websites leaves much to be desired. They may not be well designed, they may be confusing to use, information may be scattered about illogically, links may be too slow or not work at all, and numerous other problems may cause visitors to such sites to leave abruptly without buying, or abandoning an attempt to make a purchase.

It is therefore becoming a commercial imperative for businesses to understand how their sites are perceived by visitors and users: what is good and useful; what is not; what sort of content and user-friendly processes will produce optimum results? As a result software packages are being developed and licensed which are capable of monitoring and analysing website activity in order to provide site owners with statistics and reports on visitor numbers and site behaviour. Some of these packages are extremely sophisticated and produce mountains of data. This has given rise to a demand for more refined analysis, homing in on the information obtained, measuring it, comparing it and providing business-critical intelligence which can be used to increase revenue yields from websites engaging in e-commerce.

Some of the more mature website developers are incorporating this type of analytical software into their site designs. Any client who engages a developer to design a website for e-commerce should consider ensuring that the selected developer is knowledgeable about and experienced in the latest software developments in this area. The ability to offer appropriate solutions so that the site design is as fit for its purpose as it reasonably can be within the budget provided will impact directly on the commercial success of the client's e-commerce business.

B. The structure of an agreement for website development and services

The contract for the development and hosting of the website will have many of the features of software development and services agreements. Other aspects will be specific to web development and hosting. The parties are referred to here as 'client' and 'designer'.

Terms and conditions

- Scope of Agreement*
- Definitions*
- Duration
- Website Features and Content*
- Designer's Obligations*
- Client's Obligations*
- Website Development*
- Acceptance Testing and Launch*
- Variations*
- Support Services*
- Service Level Compliance*
- Charges
- Payment Terms
- Confidentiality
- Security*
- Intellectual Property Rights*
- Designer's Warranties*
- Indemnities*
- Limits of Liability
- Acknowledgment*
- Termination

- Obligations on Termination*
- General Contract Provisions

Schedules

- Acceptance Tests
- Charges
- Implementation Plan
- Specification

Appendices

- Service Level Agreement
- Support Services Agreement

C. Specific clauses

In the clause examples considered below, which are those above marked with an asterisk, the parties are referred to as 'Client' and 'Designer' denoting the client for, and the designer of, the website services and contents.

1. Scope of Agreement

(a) The Designer has experience in website services including designing, developing, producing, maintaining [monitoring and analysing] websites.

(b) The Client requires a website to be designed, developed, produced, maintained [monitored and analysed] [for its business of ....].

(c) The Client appoints the Designer to design, produce and implement the Website [to promote its business and] [to manage, maintain and to enhance and refine the Website and to provide new content and further development [together with the management of the Website on a web server]] and the Designer accepts such appointment, on the terms and conditions of this Agreement.

(d) The Client has entered into this Agreement based on its 'Invitation to Tender' dated ... and in reliance amongst other things on the representations made in the Designer's 'Response to Tender' dated ... including but not limited to the technical excellence, experience and track record quoted by the Designer in such response.

This clause should indicate the extent of the agreement to provide services. The subject of the contract may be a single development project, with an implementation plan and specific limited objectives. Alternatively, the agreement may be over a fixed term, which may be renewable, within which a number of projects may be undertaken and the website maintained, and when a clause will be needed to specify the duration of the arrangement.

It cannot be over-emphasised that a client must take considerable time and trouble to get its requirements right and to ensure that they are fully defined in the agreement. Insufficient attention to detail will result in a poor quality website which will fail to meet the business objectives set for it, and which will at worst be a complete waste of money and drive potential customers away.

2. Definitions

'*Acceptance Tests*' means the tests for acceptance of the Website.

'*Client Branding*' means the words, terms and phrases [......, ..., ...].

'*Content*' means materials which may include data, information, text, media content, features, products, services, advertisements, promotions, links, pointers, technology, software and databases for publication on the Website (including without limitation, literary, artistic, audio and visual content), including any publication or information created as a result of the Services.

'*Designer Know-how*' means the Designer's methodology and stylistic conventions, and its own distinctive elements in respect of graphics, design, organisation, presentation, layout, user interfaces, navigation, and the combination, co-ordination and interaction of these elements.

'*Estimated Price*' means the estimated costs for the Project as specified in the Charges Schedule.

'*External Area*' means any online area in or outside the Website including but not limited to any sites on the worldwide web section of the Internet.

'*Implementation Plan*' means the implementation plan for the Project set out in the Implementation Plan Schedule as it may be varied by agreement from time to time.

'*Intellectual Property Rights*' means any and all copyrights, database rights, design rights, domain name rights, patents, trade marks and all other intellectual property rights whether registered or not, and applications for such rights.

'*Launch Date*' means the date specified in the Implementation Plan, which is the date on which the Website is first available live for visitors.

'*Link*' means any hypertext link, pointer, or other linking service.

'*Project*' means [any particular project for] [the work involved in] the development and implementation of the Website, using the Services, the results of which will form part of the Content and System.

'*Proposal*' means any particular proposal put forward by the Designer, setting out the user requirements and the work involved in any Project.

'*Representative*' means the representative appointed by each party respectively, authorised to take decisions on behalf of such party.

'*Services*' means the activities undertaken by the Designer as specified in this Agreement.

'*Service Levels*' means the performance standards for the Services.

'*Service Level Agreement*' means the agreement forming a Schedule to this Agreement which sets out the details of the Services and Service Levels.

'*Software*' means the software further identified in the Software Schedule which may be the Designer's proprietary software or Third Party Software.

'*Specification*' means the specification [of the contents/technical/user requirements] for the Website, identified in the Specification Schedule, as it may be varied in accordance with these terms and conditions.

'*Support Materials*' means materials necessary to facilitate the support and enhancement of the System and the Website, software tools required or useful to manipulate, compile and debug the System, and any keys necessary to decrypt the foregoing excluding any such materials relating to Third Party Software except to the extent that the Designer has access to them.

'*Support Services*' means the activities undertaken by the Designer to support the Website through the Internet hosting platform, including server provision and site maintenance as specified in the Support Services Agreement.

'*System*' means the Software, together with databases and infrastructure of the Website, including updates, enhancements and additions to any part of it.

'*Test Date*' means the date in the Implementation Plan marking the anticipated completion of Acceptance Tests.

'*Third Party Software*' means software proprietary to third parties comprised in the Website, the System, the Support Materials, or in any other products designed, developed or produced by the Designer under this Agreement or used to provide or operate the Website[listed as such in the Software Schedule].

'*Website*' means the network location in hypertext mark-up language format [developed in accordance with these terms and conditions] containing digital text, graphics[, sound, and video] which is the Client's proprietary site stored on a service and accessed via the Internet, being identified as '......' [domain name].

'System' is distinguished from 'Website'. 'System' consists of the software, databases and infrastructure, which the designer will be developing through its services, as a project, for installation at the particular network location of the client which is the 'Website'.

3. Website Features and Content

(a) The parties agree that the objectives for the Website are:
  (i)   to provide a comprehensive and authoritative information resource, to offer practical information and facilitate networking;
  (ii) to create a competitive advantage for the Client.

(b) The Designer will design the System to ensure that the Website has the following characteristics:
  (i)   be a user-friendly, interactive, original site;
  (ii) be accessible 24 hours a day without delay;
  (iii) bring together coherently material from a variety of the Client's publications, and other information relevant to visitors to the Website;
  (iv) promote best practice, offer practical information and facilitate networking for its visitors; and
  (v)   be easy to navigate, up to date and authoritative.

(c) The Designer may not, without the written content of the Client, establish any Link to any External Area except as set out in the Service Level Agreement. Any Link created will be subject to such terms and conditions as the Client may require in the creation or maintenance of the Link, including but not limited to any requirement to pay fees for such Links or obligation to market or provide the website through such External Area. However, if required by the Client, the Designer will provide Links to other websites identified by the Client.

(d) The parties acknowledge that the Specifications represent the minimum requirements for the System, and that they do not constitute a definitive or complete set of requirements.

(e) Each party confirms to the other that it will not transmit, display or otherwise include in the Content:

   (i) any material which is defamatory, offensive, abusive, indecent, obscene, pornographic, threatening or annoying, or which may incite violence, cruelty of any sort or discriminate against people in a way which may be illegal, including but not limited to racial hatred, or which is otherwise illegal;

   (ii) any material which infringes the Intellectual Property Rights of the other party or of a third party.

(f) The Designer undertakes to design the Website so that it will efficiently comply with all applicable laws and regulations in relation to its design, accessibility and purpose, including but not limited to laws and regulations concerning disability and discrimination, data protection and electronic commerce.

The purpose of the website will dictate its characteristics, style and content. Does the client have an economic business case for its development, perhaps in terms of anticipated numbers of visitors, increased sales, 'site stickiness' – repeat visits or retention of visitors over time, reduced costs of traditional marketing?

If the focus of the website is its content, and its provision and updating form a large part of the designer's responsibilities, this will need to be detailed in the agreement. Will the subject matter itself need to be precisely described? Is the length significant? How up to date must it be kept, and how often and in what way will updating take place? Does it need to be in a particular format? The requirements for this may have formed part of the invitation to tender and may be linked as commitments into the contract in that way.

At paragraph (b)(i) the use of the term 'original' emphasises the requirement for material which is not copied from other sites. Site visitors are paradoxically becoming more sophisticated in expecting the site to be convenient and easy to use. They will also want content that is relevant and presented effectively.

Where the designer undertakes some responsibility for the content, paragraph (c) limits the use of links which may be made via hypertext words or images to other websites and documents. The ability to link is an intrinsic element of the Internet. However, the risk of infringing third party rights such as copyright and database right is real.

It may be a legitimate requirement for the particular site to link to other specific sites. Some third party site owners may be pleased that their sites will gain more prominence. However, the best advice is to obtain express permission from the site owners. In any event, the terms and conditions attached to those sites should be reviewed, and advance clearance may be expressly required. Acknowledgment of permission to link to the sites will ensure that users will know that the responsibility for those sites rests elsewhere. The safest principle is also to link to a home page rather than deep linking to the heart of the content. Any use of banners or framing should be resisted, and no blocks of text or data should be copied without unequivocal authorisation.

Paragraph (d) allows for flexibility as the website is developed. The designer may welcome the scope for varying the requirements, or may perceive this as encouraging indecision on the part of the client. The inclusion of such a clause will depend how strictly an implementation plan and budget are being followed.

At paragraph (e), the client as website owner will be legally liable for the content of the site, whether its own or from third parties.

The designer may not wish to take on the responsibility of compliance with laws, codes of practice and regulation that will affect the particular website, but discussion can be opened up on the wording of paragraph (f). 'Efficiently' is an adverb which is important in this context, to design certain features optimally which have to be included as a matter of law. It will depend amongst other things on the purpose of the website and its likely visitors, and whether the visitors will be subscribers or whether there will be electronic trading. The Disability Discrimination Act 1995 requires equal access to goods and services by the disabled, such as those with impaired hearing or who are partially sighted. Information must be included on the site for purchasers of electronic goods and services, whether or not they are consumers or trading in the course of business[2].

4. Designer's Obligations

(a) The Designer agrees to undertake the following services:
- registration and updating of the Website with search engines;
- design of the System to work with the operating systems architecture, configuration and access requirements;
- creative Content design;
- development, enhancements and refinements;
- content provision and updating;
- hosting services;
- management, maintenance and support;
- provision of statistics and analysis;
- such other tasks as the Client may request from time to time.

(b) The Designer will:
  (i) provide the Services with skill and expertise to a professional standard, and in a timely and efficient manner, using suitably experienced personnel, to meet the Client's business requirements, the Specification and in accordance with the Implementation Plan;
  (ii) scope and write the Specification, create, design and implement the Content, provide the System with the features and functions set out in the Specification;

> (iii) customise the architecture of the System appropriately[in reliance on information provided by the Client];
>
> (iv) manage, edit, update and maintain the Website, including but not limited to interactive communication capabilities and interactive tools;
>
> (v) ensure continuing integration with existing websites identified by the Client, and seamless interfaces to the Client's systems;
>
> (vi) be responsible (for the avoidance of doubt) for the procurement of suitable computing and communication hardware, software and services necessary for production of the System and the obtaining of any requisite development licences;
>
> (vii) provide any training necessary for the Client to operate the Website.
>
> (c) The Designer will make all reasonable efforts to ensure that the Project will be completed within any Estimated Price which has been agreed. If the Designer foresees a situation where the Estimated Price is likely to be exceeded, it will promptly inform the Client.
>
> (d) The Designer will co-operate with the Client's employees and other independent consultants whenever necessary or desirable in the performance of the Services.
>
> (e) The Designer will designate a Representative. The Designer may change the identity of the Representative or any of the details of the Representative with the prior written consent of the Client, such consent not to be unreasonably withheld or delayed.
>
> (f) [While this Agreement remains in force][For 12 months from the Launch Date], the Designer agrees that it will not undertake the development and design of any website [in England and Wales] promoting similar business activities to those of the Client in similar style to the Website.

Paragraph (a) sets out the scope of the services to be provided. A selection of the examples given here is likely to be appropriate. Different kinds of services may be needed separately: development of the system itself, consultancy, design, management, installation and configuration, running the site, ongoing support and bug-fixing, and so on. If content is being provided, detailed parameters should be set in a schedule to define what is required, in terms of the subject matter; length; format and appearance; its derivation; and updating provisions.

Paragraph (b) sets out the designer's activities in carrying out the services, linking them to specific documentation.

Paragraph (c) applies only where the designer has agreed to develop a project for an estimated price.

Paragraph (e) does not have an equivalent obligation for the designer to approve any change of client representative (see paragraph 5(d) below). The client's

435

selection of designer may well be dependent on the particular personnel involved, for project management as well as for the development itself, and in such case it would not be unreasonable for the client to want to approve any replacement.

While working for the client under this agreement, the designer may be asked to agree not to be involved with any competitor of the client. It would not be reasonable to bar the designer's activities altogether in circumstances where experience in particular methods or business requirements may be gained for future use, and paragraph (f) gives alternative proposals which may be acceptable to both parties for achieving this. A guiding principle with clauses of this type is that the more restrictively they are worded, the less likely they are to be legally enforceable.

5. Client's Obligations

(a) The Client acknowledges that its close involvement is essential for the development of a System which successfully meets its requirements.

(b) The Client agrees to provide guidance to the Designer on the Client's business practices, which affect the Content or the System.

(c) The Client will pay for the Services in accordance with the terms of this Agreement.

(d) The Client will designate a Representative and inform the Designer of the identity and details of such Representative. The Client may change the identity of the Representative or any of the details of the Representative on written notice to the Designer.

(e) The Client warrants that all intellectual property including but not limited to software, databases, graphics, diagrams, charts, sound, with which the System and Content will be used and/or which is necessary for the Designer to access and use, is either the Client's property or is legally licensed to the Client so as to permit access and use by the Designer.

The first two of these client's obligations are practical, in assisting the designer in producing a relevant site.

The obligation of payment at paragraph (c) is essential.

The appointment of a representative at paragraph (d) will facilitate effective management.

The last obligation at paragraph (e) is in the form of a warranty concerning the client's responsibilities in connection with the intellectual property content of the website. It is reasonable to offer the developer this protection, as it can incur legal liability as a result of misusing third party intellectual property, even if such misuse is inadvertent and innocent.

6. Website Development

(a) The Designer will carry out the Project to meet the Implementation Plan utilising such elements of the following procedural framework, in parallel or in sequence, as appropriate to the particular circumstances:
   (i) discuss and agree with the Client the Content and record the requirements;
   (ii) scope and write the Specification;
   (iii) design the System in accordance with the [technical] Specification[, including but not limited to establishing appropriate architecture, supporting particular protocol, server and browser requirements, and compatibility with client and host software and networks, providing continuous navigational ability and mutually acceptable links];
   (iv) create, design, write and code the materials for the System, installing and testing the materials and providing them to the Client for Acceptance Tests;
   (v) edit, manage, update and maintain the Website in accordance with the Specification[, including but not limited to the operating systems architecture, access requirements, interactive communication capabilities, e-commerce capabilities and interactive tools];
   (vi) carry out such redefinition and rewriting as may be required by the Client, and retesting it;
   (vii) install the System on the Client's network.

(b) Any delay in the provision of the Services which occurs as a result of the Client's actions or omissions to act will be the Client's responsibility, and in the event of such delay the Implementation Plan will be extended accordingly to take into account of such delay.

(c) Any delay in the provision of the Services which is due to factors beyond the responsibility of the Designer, including but not limited to access to staff, delivery or proper functioning of hardware or software, will be acknowledged by the Client, and the Implementation Plan will be extended accordingly.

This clause focuses on the development itself. The same considerations apply to website development as for other software development, and the clauses and associated discussion in **CHAPTER 16** on software development should be reviewed, although the development time for a website project may be much shorter by comparison.

It must be clear *what* is being provided. The specification should describe clearly and unambiguously the aims and objectives of the website, functionality and

437

content, and how data will be collected and processed. It should provide all necessary technical details, eg performance levels, capacity, response times, browser compatibility. It should set out any interfaces required with other systems.

For a well-defined project over a short timescale, the change control procedure specified for software development in **CHAPTER 16** will probably not be feasible. Other means must be found to avoid 'feature creep', for features added which were not originally contemplated. It is important that the specification defines the basic requirements, and that the implementation plan is firmly in the forefront of the parties' concerns. It may be necessary to invoke the development requirements for iterative software development, to ensure that meetings to review the scope are held regularly, and that there are procedures in place for implementing changes and adaptations.

The client needs to ensure a disciplined approach within its organisation. Everyone will have an opinion about the 'look and feel' of the website, and many will have their own agenda for content.

7. Acceptance Testing and Launch

(a) The Designer will carry out system tests on the System, and after all components of the System have been installed and commissioned, will carry out a full integration test on the System. When the Designer has completed the full integration test and thereby demonstrated that all elements of the installed System inter-operate correctly and effectively, the Designer will store the System so that it is available for Acceptance Tests, and will ensure that access for the purpose and duration of the Acceptance Tests is restricted through use of a password or other similar access code to persons approved by the Client.

(b) Acceptance Tests will be [prepared by the Client][prepared by the Designer and approved by the Client] which will test that the System conforms to the Specification, together with other requirements agreed between the parties.

(c) The Client will carry out the Acceptance Tests in respect of the System [in accordance with its standard procedures] [as set out in the Acceptance Tests Schedule] over the number of days set out in the Implementation Plan for Acceptance Testing.

(d) If there are failures in the Acceptance Tests, the Client will inform the Designer while the Acceptance Tests are in progress, and the Designer will promptly use all reasonable endeavours to correct such failures.

(e) The Client's Representative will, within three working days of the Test Date, notify the Designer's Representative in writing of any material failure of the Contents or System to pass the Acceptance Tests. If the Designer's representative receives no such notification, the Acceptance Tests will be deemed to be successfully completed, and the Designer will:

    (i)   install the System [and Content] in time for the Launch Date;

    (ii)   deliver to the Client a copy of the Support Materials on appropriate media and in an appropriate format to ensure that the Client or a third party appointed by the Client will be able to maintain, enhance, modify and change the System;

    (iii)   implement the System on the Launch Date.

(f)   If material failures or omissions remain at the Test Date such that the System does not conform to the Specification, the Client will have the right to terminate the Agreement.

(g)   If this Agreement is terminated under Clause (f) above, the Client will notify the Designer either:

    (i)   to deliver promptly to the Client the Incomplete Materials, in which event the Client will pay to the Designer such reasonable amount in respect of the Incomplete Materials as may be agreed between the parties, and the Designer will be deemed to have granted to the Client a perpetual, royalty free, non-exclusive licence to use and sub-license as the Client may deem fit, any Third Party Software comprised in the Incomplete Materials; or

    (ii)   to retain the Incomplete Materials in which event the Client will not be liable to pay to the Designer the fees or any amount whatsoever under this Agreement.

Various levels of testing will be appropriate, to be carried out by the designer, and also by the client, depending on the purpose and functionality of the website and the extent of the client's involvement. They should ideally be set out to form an acceptance test schedule, so that both parties know (and more importantly agree) what is expected. Compatibility testing will determine how effectively the website works with the range of hardware, components, servers, software applications, cross-browsers and operating system combinations to which it is exposed. Stress testing and load testing will determine the extent of website functionality in relation to thresholds of CPU utilisation, input/output activities, network traffic, memory allocation, response times and so on. The website must be tested in terms of the user interface, the inputs, navigational links, connections with databases, and other activities. Localisation testing may be necessary where the website is available in different languages or with different features according to the cultures to which it is addressed. These are tests on structure and infrastructure. However, there must also be tests on substance, to assess conformity with specification.

There is a danger in the ongoing process of acceptance associated with prototyping where a website is the objective. The performance of a website under acceptance conditions may be very different from a live website with access by multiple users simultaneously.

439

A decision may be taken, for practical reasons or to meet a political requirement, on what is to be the launch date of a new website before a practical assessment of the work involved has taken place. The timetable must be realistic. The implementation plan should set out various milestones during the development process. For website development, the timescales may be relatively short, in weeks or months, but the process still needs positive management, and payment linked to deliverables.

What should happen if there is failure to deliver on time or at all? Should there be payments for delay in the form of liquidated damages? At what point should the client have the right to and perhaps consider recovery of money paid?

It depends on the length of time for acceptance testing, the client involvement and the scale of the project as to what should reasonably happen if there is significant failure which is not corrected during acceptance testing. The example here assumes that the project is short, and that there is no time to reiterate the tests. If the project is longer, then it may be reasonable to give the designer more opportunity for rectification.

Some agreements provide for an implied acceptance on the first date of 'Go Live'. Where this is agreed, it is particularly important to allow sufficient time for a proper acceptance process to be completed.

8. Variations

(a) Either party may at any time up to seven days before the Test Date formally request in writing any variation to the System and discuss such variation with the other party.

(b) The Designer will inform the Client in such discussion whether such variation is technically and practically feasible within the timescale and of its impact, and of any other consequent changes to the System that it reasonably judges necessary. For any change requiring additional work, the Designer will give the Client a quotation for the additional costs of carrying out the variation.

(c) If the parties agree that the variation is to be effected, the Designer will provide a written note as a record of the variation and its impact and any additional charges, which will be signed by both parties and will implement the variation at a time it reasonably judges to be suitable before the Test Date.

(d) If the parties do not agree that the variation is to be effected, it will not be carried out.

This clause allows for a variation to be introduced to the system in a simple yet organised way in what may overall be a short timescale, so that both parties understand what it will comprise. Both parties should formally agree to go ahead with the variation. However, either party may be reluctant to proceed. The client may think that it will cost too much. The designer may think that it will not be able to incorporate the variation into the system in time to meet its obligations under the agreement. Under this example clause, the variation will not be implemented if either one of the parties does not agree. If necessary, a more elaborate change control procedure, such as the one discussed in **CHAPTER 16**, can be incorporated into the agreement.

9. Support Services

(a) Following the launch of the Website, the Designer will be responsible for the Support Services, which will include:
  (i) marketing, launch and continuing promotion of the Website;
  (ii) website maintenance and technical support;
  (iii) system support;
  (iv) service recovery;
  (v) help desk;
  (vi) content update[;
  (vii) hardware update and technology refresh].

(b) The Designer will provide the Support Services so as to ensure that the Site is maintained and operated efficiently and effectively [in accordance with the Specification].

(c) The Designer will give the Client reasonable notice of any maintenance work which will affect availability, and shall plan and carry out such work so as to minimise disruption to the Website availability.

(d) The Designer will update Content to the Website within 24 hours of receiving such updated Content from the Client, and at the request of the Client, the Designer will immediately edit or remove as appropriate any Content which is inaccurate, obscene, defamatory or which the Client requires to be removed at the Client's sole discretion.

(e) The Designer will enter bulletin boards and online chat areas where visitors to the Website may post contributions, at least every 24 hours and more frequently if this seems necessary for the purpose of effective monitoring of contributions. Immediately on becoming aware of any contributions which the Designer reasonably believes could be obscene, defamatory or otherwise unlawful or objectionable, or which are the subject of complaints, the Designer will remove such contributions and inform the Client accordingly. The Designer will inform the Client of any measures it deems advisable to be taken to prevent or stop such contributions, and shall comply with reasonable instructions from the

> Client as to further actions to be taken in this regard. The Designer will keep a record of such monitoring activities and provide copies of such records to the Client every month.
>
> (f) The Designer reserves the right to redesign or modify the organisation, structure, 'look and feel', navigation and other elements of the System, by means of the Designer Know-how, provided that the levels of functionality and service levels are maintained.

This clause is important to define the extent of the ongoing services and post-launch support by the designer. These services may be confined to basic technical error correction, or include content updating, or cover the whole range of support. Note that it is easy for mistakes to be made in information displayed, and bad publicity is fast to spread. Legal liability for errors made in e-commerce, such as incorrect pricing, is discussed in **CHAPTER 4**.

What about marketing services? The website should be registered with search engines and promoted. Is this part of the support services? Is the designer to be responsible for furnishing website statistics and analysis?

The obligation of adding, updating and deleting content may be mainly that of either the designer or the client, although the client will ultimately be responsible for what appears on the website. Content, which is illegal or otherwise objectionable, must be edited or removed. Paragraph (d) is a general obligation, but paragraph (e) gives the designer specific monitoring obligations.

These obligations impose important obligations, and the parties should decide whether to accept the positive role of monitoring and thereby knowledge of, and unequivocal responsibility for, the content. Many deliberately choose not to do so, remaining in ignorance and hoping to avoid liability until they are alerted to any questionable content by a third party.

10. Service Level Compliance

> (a) The Designer will meet the Service Levels as set out in the Service Level Agreement, including but not limited to supporting particular protocol, server and browser requirements, including utilities for non-Web services such as e-mail and newsgroups, and compatibility with client and host software networks, providing continuous navigational ability, service ability, capacity and accessibility, mutual accessible links, response times, services management, housekeeping and updating.
>
> (b) The Designer will measure performance, maintain records and provide statistics and analysis as set out in the Service Level Agreement, for performance reporting of Service Levels, and as otherwise reasonably requested by the Client, with a recommended action plan for under-performing areas of the Website.

> (c) Without prejudice to the generality of the foregoing, the Designer will ensure that the Website is available to [authorised visitors][the public] 24 hours a day, 365 days a year, and will continuously monitor such availability. In the event that the Website becomes unavailable, the Designer will use its best endeavours to remedy the fault.

It is important for the site to be so designed as to be easily accessible at all times. Performance measurements for availability, capacity and accessibility will be agreed for the Service Level Agreement.

What are reasonable levels of performance to expect? It should be borne in mind that a requirement for continuous attention to reliability will be expensive. The designer should be capable of ensuring sufficient capacity in respect of services, the website itself, network and memory, and scope for expansion in line with projected traffic predictions. Any acceptable downtime limits should be contractually agreed for the service levels. However, the requirement for 'best endeavours' in paragraph (c) may be challenged by the designer as unrealistic. The value of the contract in relation to the designer's business as a whole will be a material factor in agreeing the wording here.

Regular reports of the designer's performance should be submitted to the client, and reports of site use may be also routinely called for, the numbers of visitors accessing different parts of the website, sales reports, etc.

What are the sanctions to be for breach of this contractual obligation? There may be a formula for payment of liquidated damages or service credits set out in the service level agreement deriving from regular measurement of the service levels, together with a requirement for corrective action, as discussed in **CHAPTER 17** for service levels in an outsourced environment. Serious or repeated breaches will lead to the right to terminate.

11. Security

> (a) The Designer will:
>   (i) use its best endeavours to keep confidential the passwords or other security information relating to the Software, the Website or any equipment of the Client;
>   (ii) ensure compliance with the Client's strategic and security requirements to protect the authenticity and integrity of the Website, and pro-actively provide security for the Website, ensuring that adequate security protections are in place;
>   (iii) regularly review its security policies and the actual security of the Website, and inform the Client of any additional measures necessary to maximise security of the Website and the integrity of the Content;

> (iv) make a backup copy of the Content [daily][weekly] in an agreed format, and deposit such copy with the Client;
>
> (v) provide and implement when necessary a disaster recovery programme and service for the Client.
>
> (b) The Designer will comply with data protection legislation in respect of any personal data to which it has access or which it may use in providing the Support Services. The Designer will maintain secure records for reporting to the Client of all personal data submitted to the Website in conformity with the Principles of data protection legislation, including, if relevant, details of those visitors who choose to opt in to receive promotional material or other information. Once such records have been reported, the Designer shall not retain a copy of any such personal data.
>
> (c) The Designer will safely destroy and not keep any copy of data provided by the Client for the Website following its use for the purpose for which it was provided.

Website security is extremely important, and the clause here refers to general security requirements for the website and its content. In paragraph (a)(i) the requirement for 'best endeavours' may be justifiable whatever the value of the contract, because the issue of security is arguably of special importance, deserving a higher standard of performance. Paragraph (b) is for those cases where the designer may have ongoing responsibility on behalf of the client for handling personal data submitted by visitors, and in any event the designer must comply with data protection legislation. Paragraph (c) is more general in requiring the destruction of any data provided by the client after use.

12. Intellectual Property Rights

> **Software and System**
>
> (a) The Designer assigns to the Client with full title guarantee, in respect of copyright by way of present assignment of future copyright, all Intellectual Property Rights in the Software, the System and any other materials designed or developed or produced by the Designer for the Website excluding Designer Know-how, Support Materials and any Third Party Software [unconditionally and immediately on the creation of the System] [on successful completion of the Acceptance Tests] [with effect from the Test/Launch Date] [on receipt by the Designer of full payment of the Charges in accordance with the Charges Schedule], and undertakes to execute such deeds and documents and do such things as the Client may require to vest such Intellectual Property Rights in the Client.

(b) The Client grants to the Designer a non-transferable licence to use the System in both source and object code form solely for the purposes of fulfilling the Designer's obligations under this Agreement while this Agreement remains in force.

Content

(c) All Intellectual Property Rights in the Content will at all times vest exclusively in the Client, except for Content owned by third parties, in respect of which the Client will be responsible for ensuring that all necessary consents have been obtained such that it has a licence to use and display, and to authorise the Designer's access and use.

(d) The Client grants to the Designer a non-transferable royalty-free licence to use the Content solely for the purposes of designing, developing, producing and maintaining the Website in accordance with this Agreement, and while this Agreement remains in force.

(e) If either party learns of any claim of infringement of the Client's Intellectual Property Rights in the Content, it will promptly notify the other party. The Designer will do all such things as the Client may reasonably require at the Client's expense to assist the Client in taking proceedings or any other actions the Client may reasonably take to terminate or prevent any such claim.

Client Branding and Domain Name

(f) The Client grants the Designer a non-exclusive non-transferable licence to use and copy the Client Branding, only so far as is necessary for providing the Services under the terms of this Agreement and while this Agreement remains in force.

(g) For the avoidance of doubt, the Client's domain name remains the property of the Client and the Designer may use such name only in the performance of this Agreement.

Designer Know-how and Support Materials

(h) The Designer grants to the Client a perpetual worldwide licence to use the Designer Know-how and Support Materials while this Agreement is in force and subsequently, permitting the ongoing use of the Designer Know-how for the purposes of supporting the Website[, and for using, marketing, licensing, storing, distributing, displaying, communicating, performing, transmitting and promoting the Website], including, but not limited to, use for such purposes by consultants, systems designers, outsourcing providers or disaster recovery suppliers.

(i) The Client will not use the Support Materials unless this Agreement is terminated, and until then will take all reasonable measures to ensure that the Support Materials are securely stored.

(j) For the avoidance of doubt the Designer will be entitled to use the Designer Know-how in the provision of services similar to these Services to other customers of its business.

Third Party Software

(k) The Designer will not include any Third Party Software in the Website, the Support Materials or the System unless the Designer has informed the Client and the Client has given its written consent, and provided that the Designer has procured the right from the relevant third party owner or licensor of the Third Party Software to permit such use.

(l) The Client has sole responsibility for obtaining the appropriate licences or rights required for access and use of any Third Party Software other than as set out in the Third Party Software Schedule and for any Content and is liable for any claim that such use of such Third Party Software infringes the Intellectual Property Rights of any other third party.

These clauses allocate rights and obligations over the various types of intellectual property involved. The types of content and code which will belong to the designer must be distinguished from those which will belong to or be permanently licensed to the client.

For original client material, the client retains the proprietary rights and grants a licence to the designer to use for the purposes of design, development and updating of the content.

The client should expect at least to have rights to the content and design of the pages and specific coding of pages. At paragraph (a) negotiation will focus on the precise point at which it is appropriate for the rights to be assigned, according to the payment structure.

In relation to a claim of infringement concerning the site's content, paragraph (e) allows for the fact that the designer may learn of the claim earlier than the client. It is reasonable for the designer to assist the client in enforcing the client's rights, especially where the designer is itself deeply involved in creating or maintaining the site content.

For the designer's proprietary material a licence must be granted to the client, which should extend beyond the term of this agreement. In the event of termination, the client will normally wish to retain rights to use this material and ensure portability of the website design and strategy. The client should consider negotiating escrow arrangements for this material, as discussed in **CHAPTER 13**.

13. Designer's Warranties

The Designer warrants and undertakes to the Client that:

(a) it will provide the Services with reasonable skill and care, using suitably skilled personnel;

(b) it has sufficient experience of designing, developing and producing websites to be able to undertake its obligations under this Agreement;

(c) any employee, agent or contractor of the Designer will be suitably experienced to perform his or her contribution and conform to the standards, skill and ability to be reasonably expected of such performance;

(d) neither the execution nor the performance of this Agreement will conflict with any agreement or arrangement to which the Designer is party or any legal or administrative arrangement by which the Designer is bound;

(e) it is authorised to use the Third Party Software concerned in connection with its obligations under this Agreement and will remain so authorised for the duration of this Agreement and will remain authorised by the relevant licensors and owners to grant the rights for the Client to use such Third Party Software;

(f) upon termination of this Agreement, the System and the Support Materials will be the only materials required by a person with reasonable knowledge of the design, development and production of websites to be able to maintain enhance and modify the Website;

(g) none of the System, the Support Materials or Content provided by the Designer will include computer viruses, routines, worms, time bombs, or any other such devices or mechanisms of misuse;

(h) the System will conform in all respects with the Specification;

(i) the Services will comply with the Service Levels in the Service Level Agreement;

(j) the System is capable of meeting the transaction volumes set out in the Service Level Agreement and their expansion by at least one third without upgrade, and response times of less than [three] seconds from keystroke irrespective of location;

(k) it has and will maintain in effect all necessary licences and any other authorisations and rights required in providing the Services, including those to the enhancements, modifications and upgrades to Third Party Software or data;

(l) the Software and the System and any other materials designed or developed or produced by the Designer for the Website will not infringe

> any third party's Intellectual Property Rights, will not be obscene or defamatory, and [to the best of the Designer's knowledge, information and belief,] will comply with all applicable laws, regulations and codes of conduct;
>
> (m) for any software or data not being part of the Software used by the Designer or provided by the Designer to the Client for use by the Client pursuant to this Agreement, the Designer warrants that it owns or possesses all necessary licences or rights required to perform its obligations under this Agreement, including those to all enhancements or upgrades to such Third Party Software or data.

The warranty at paragraph (a) is basic, expanded a little at (b) and (c). It would be possible for the client to insist on a higher level of experience and competence, depending on the particular designer selected, and the amount of the charges which have been agreed.

The other warranties confirm the client's requirements for the site, including compliance with specification, service levels and proprietary rights.

Faced with so many warranties, designers should examine and clearly understand each one, and negotiate variations or exclusions on the basis of their genuine ability to comply. If warranties of particular importance to a client cannot be offered, this may influence the client's decision to use that designer. It should be possible to agree compromise wording in most instances.

14. Indemnities

> (a) The Designer will indemnify the Client against all losses, costs and expenses including reasonable legal expenses and third party claims suffered by the Client arising out of any breach by the Designer of the warranties given in this Agreement or any other default of the Designer in connection with this Agreement.
>
> (b) The Designer will not be liable in respect of any loss or damage suffered by the Client resulting from any third party claim that a posting on a bulletin board, online chat area or similar area in which visitors to the Website may legitimately post contributions is obscene or defamatory, provided that the Designer has complied with its obligations in this Agreement in respect of postings.
>
> (c) The Client will indemnify the Designer against all losses, costs and expenses including reasonable legal expenses arising from any third party claim that the Content infringes the Intellectual Property Rights, or is obscene or defamatory, or that any posting on a bulletin board, online chat area or similar area in which visitor to the Website may legitimately post contributions is obscene or defamatory, provided that the Designer:

> (i)   has complied with its obligations in this Agreement in respect of postings;
>
> (ii)   promptly notifies the Client of any claim in respect of which the indemnity is sought;
>
> (iii) gives the Client full conduct and control of any such claim.

The first two indemnities reinforce the designer's warranties. In considering them, the designer should seek to limit its exposure to commercial limits of liability as discussed in **CHAPTER 7**, seeking insurance cover to underwrite the indemnity to the maximum extent possible.

The intellectual property indemnity at paragraph (c) is stronger than the normal standard indemnity set out in **CHAPTER 7**, and negotiation is likely to focus on a lesser commitment by the client.

15. Acknowledgment

> (a) With the prior written consent of the Client, not to be unreasonably withheld or delayed, the Designer may include a statement in the Website, the format, content and position to be approved by the Client at its discretion, to the effect that the Designer has designed, developed and produced the Website. Such statement may not be changed or removed while this Agreement is in force without the written agreement of both parties, not to be unreasonably withheld or delayed.
>
> (b) The Designer agrees not to use the Client's name or issue any announcement about these Services without first obtaining the Client's written consent [not to be unreasonably withheld or delayed].

The designer may wish to have publicity both for its design and for any ongoing relationship. This may be acceptable to the client, on the basis that the website must be expected to be good enough for the designer to want to advertise its authorship. Nevertheless, the client may be more concerned to maintain confidentiality in its relationship, or at least not to publicise it.

16. Obligations on Termination

> On termination of this Agreement for any reason the Designer will co-operate with the Client in that it will immediately:
>
> (a) return all Content to the Client and not retain any part of it in any form whatsoever;

(b) destroy or delete the Client's confidential information under its control or in its possession;

(c) be deemed to have granted to the Client a perpetual loyalty free non-exclusive licence to the Client to use, change, adapt, enhance and sub-license as the Client may deem fit, the Support Materials and all Third Party Software contained in the Support Materials;

(d) if so requested by the Client, provide assistance in transferring the Website to another server at [its standard charges][reasonable charges to be agreed with the Client].

The client cannot afford the risk of lock-in to its designer. It is essential that the structure and content of the website are sufficiently portable to enable its migration either to another designer or to the client itself. The clause on intellectual property rights specifies rights to use copyright material post-termination. Negotiation may take place over whether the designer's obligations should not take effect if the designer terminates the contract because of the client's default. The circumstances of the website development and payments will affect the outcome of this.

1   At www.e-envoy.gov.uk.
2   For example, E-Commerce Regulations 2002, Distance Selling Regulations 2000, Sale of Goods Act 1979 (as amended).

CHAPTER 20

Electronic commerce

A. Introduction

In this introductory section, certain general legal principles relating to e-commerce are discussed. The example agreement, considered at Section B onwards, is an agreement between an online distributor of software products and the authors of the software products, ie a commercial agreement between businesses, both of which are in the IT sector.

There are an increasing number of laws and regulations designed to protect online individual consumers, and to encourage e-commerce transactions with them. Some of these are referred to in this introduction, but e-traders who wish to sell into consumer markets, whether in their own jurisdiction or more widely, are strongly recommended to obtain up-to-date specialist legal advice to ensure that they are in compliance with the law in the geographical and product markets applicable to the areas in which they wish to trade.

The scope of e-commerce, trading electronically in goods or services over the Internet, means that:

- information may be available and business may be conducted on a one-to-many, many-to-one or many-to-many basis;

- the e-trader can provide information visually in an online catalogue or in some other format which may comparatively easily be kept up to date;

- it is possible to trade in different jurisdictions from the e-trader's base;

- the customer has greater choice in making purchasing decisions;

- the e-trader may garner information from the transaction for sophisticated market intelligence purposes.

There is not one single unified global legal regime. Different national and regional commercial laws, consumer protection regulations and tax regimes will affect e-commerce in practice, both within and beyond the EU. This is exacerbated by the speed of legal change in this new area as laws are made, both nationally and by the EU, and as cases reach court.

There is a growing body of EU law relating to e-commerce: some Directives are already effective throughout member states; some are about to be implemented in national legislation; others are still being discussed. There are also voluntary codes of practice and sets of regulations, such as UNCITRAL's Model Law on Electronic Commerce.

It is, therefore, possible that different laws may apparently apply to a single transaction. Trading over the Internet may result in deliberately or inadvertently breaching laws in any part of the world, with associated liability risks.

In order to trade safely, legally and profitably over the Internet, and to manage the risks, a combination of commercial considerations, technical methods, legal awareness and common sense is required. E-traders who wish to trade internationally should positively select the countries in which they are prepared to trade, so that they will be able to comply with the local laws relating to those jurisdictions, and so that they can take active measures to attract customers from those jurisdictions and to exclude those outside. They should have clear and workable standard terms and conditions which are readily available, provide accurate information, display notices and publish disclaimers if appropriate. If consumers form their target market, there are further legal issues to take into account. Various industries, such as financial services, will have additional regulations to conform with. Moreover, intellectual property rights assume greater significance.

Audit trails of the contract process should be kept, together with other records. Appropriate levels of security need to be created and maintained. Insurance cover is important.

Promoting products and services

Goods may be pictured or services described in various ways: in an e-mail, on a website, in a catalogue online or offline. As for other forms of trading, the supplier will be liable for inaccurate information about its products or services, or for false or misleading statements. All advertisements, including website advertisements, are governed by law and regulation. There are special regulations for advertising and sales in certain industry sectors, in the UK as in most jurisdictions, such as those for gambling, alcohol and the pharmaceutical industry.

Statements on a website disclaiming any responsibility for its content are often found. If worded carefully, they can sometimes be useful for a supplier in restricting the ambit of liability. However, the efficacy of disclaimers is questionable and suppliers should not place undue dependence on them. They are likely to be subject to local law in any country, in particular where someone relies on the content and suffers damage as a result – or for the promotion of regulated goods.

Unsolicited marketing and privacy notices

Visitors to websites from whom personal data is collected – and online, data may be collected via cookies or applets without the visitor even realising – must be informed about:

- who is collecting the data;

- what data is being collected;

- the purposes for which the collected data will be used[1].

It is advisable for privacy notices to be displayed on websites, to comply with data protection law. These should state:

- whether cookies or other means are used to collect personal information;

- whether data will be shared with third parties for marketing, such as other group companies, or credit reference agencies;

and give contact details where users can find out more about the data held about them, or ask for their data to be amended or erased.

In most cases, the prior consent of the user must be expressly obtained before sending any direct marketing material by e-mail. Unsolicited e-mails may be sent to existing customers. But consent must be obtained to use visitors' personal data for a reason not associated with the collection of the data; for example, to transfer data to a third party direct marketing company.

The best practice is to design e-mails and web forms to enable website visitors to choose to opt in, eg by actually clicking an 'accept' or 'authorise' box. Visitors should see the privacy notice on the website before any cookie or similar device is activated so that they have the option to leave the site without any of their details being retained.

E-commerce compliance

The Electronic Commerce (EC Directive) Regulations 2002, which implemented the EC E-Commerce Directive applicable throughout the EEA, set out require-ments to be met by all those who provide 'information society' services, essentially electronic services including sales and advertising. For online contracts, these include the following:

- General information about the service provider and the transaction must be provided online for commercial communications, such as business name and other contact details, company registration details, prices, taxes and delivery costs, details of promotional offers.

- Contract terms and general conditions must be provided in such a way that the customer is able to store and reproduce them.

- It must be clear how the contract is made, and the point of commitment, and how input errors may be corrected.

- Receipt of orders placed electronically should be acknowledged.

- Any codes of conduct to which the e-trader subscribes should be advised.

- Out-of-court schemes for dispute settlement should be encouraged.

- Contact points should be established by member states to enable service providers and customers to obtain information on contractual rights and obligations, on remedies available for resolving disputes, and to furnish details of organisations which can assist. These may themselves be electronic.

Further Regulations are specifically applicable to financial services[2].

Providers of online services will be regulated where they are 'established'. This means the place where the operator pursues an economic activity through a fixed establishment – irrespective of the location of its websites or servers.

Consumers and distance selling

Standards for distance selling to consumers (ie not business customers) have been set in the EU[3], and implemented in the UK[4] for contracts concluded when the supplier and consumer are not physically present in the same place and at the same time, for the sale of most goods and services. This therefore covers e-mail and Internet contracts as well as contracts resulting directly from press advertisements, mail-order catalogues or those made by telephone.

There are a number of exceptions. Business-to-business contracts, auctions, automated vending machines or one-off contracts outside an organised distance-selling scheme are exempt. Other exceptions concern the subject matter of the contract – land, deliveries of food or beverages, transport, accommodation, catering or leisure services provided on specific dates.

Consumers have the right to have:

- details in writing about the supplier and the terms of the transaction;

- written confirmation of their orders;

- further information, including a notice of cancellation rights, complaints procedures, after-sales services and guarantees;

- delivery within 30 days unless otherwise agreed.

A consumer is entitled to a cooling-off period of seven working days in which to cancel the contract, starting from when the goods are received, without having to give a reason. (If no details of the cooling-off period have been given by the supplier to the consumer, it is extended to three months.) The right to withdraw can be exercised by the consumer even after the goods have been delivered, or the services have been provided. The consumer is entitled to receive a full refund for a cancelled contract within 30 days.

There are certain realistic exceptions, such as:

- services where performance has begun within seven days;

- goods or services where the price is dependent upon fluctuations in a financial market beyond the supplier's control;

- goods personally specified;

- goods which would deteriorate or where their value would expire – electricity, flowers, newspapers;

- sealed audio or video recordings or software which has been opened;

- contracts for gaming or lotteries.

Retail financial services sold at a distance are regulated similarly but separately[5]. 'Financial services' are defined as banking, insurance, investment or payment services. Consumer purchasers must receive information about the service. They have a 'cooling off' period of up to 30 days, depending on the individual member state's laws. The right of withdrawal does not extend to financial services which could involve speculation – foreign exchange, collective investment schemes, money market instruments, transferable securities, futures, options and exchange and interest rate instruments. Nor does it apply to non-life insurance contracts of less than two months, nor to contracts completed before the right of withdrawal is exercised.

The promotion of financial products and services over the Internet is prohibited unless the promoter is authorised by the Financial Services Authority or the communication is approved by a person or organisation who is so authorised[6]. 'Financial promotion' covers any communication of information which 'might reasonably be expected to lead directly or indirectly to engagement in investment activity'. Only authorised persons may conduct investment business.

Providers of online financial services, such as insurance, banking and investment, need to be aware that restrictions on advertising and service provision may operate not only in their home country, but may also be imposed by national regulators abroad. Money laundering identification procedures and security systems must be implemented in an online environment, as with traditional client relationships.

'Stop Now' orders

The UK Office of Fair Trading, trading standards departments and other consumer bodies themselves have powers to apply to the courts for 'Stop Now' Orders, to stop the trader from failing to comply with the Electronic Commerce Regulations or the Distance Selling Regulations[7]. Companies may have to publish corrections or be required to take down non-conforming websites. Failure to comply with an Order is a contempt of court, punishable by fine or imprisonment.

Forming a contract online

As discussed in more detail in **CHAPTER 4**, there must be an unequivocal offer by one party and acceptance by the other in order to form a binding contract under English law.

There are rules on what legally constitutes 'acceptance'. In the UK, for mail sent by post, there is a rule that acceptance takes place at the time the letter is posted. Otherwise, acceptance occurs when it is received – as for telephone, telex or fax.

Online acceptance is frequently made by keystrokes or pointing and clicking or by a message transmitted to say that acceptance has taken place. Such acceptance may arguably be regarded as analogous to telex or fax. However, where an e-mail message is unopened – or even not received – there could arguably be scope for conflict over whether a contract had in fact been made, or whether, meanwhile, the offer had been withdrawn.

Fortunately, the rules on acceptance can be overridden if the means of contract acceptance are set out in the terms and conditions. It is therefore ideal to have a clear statement on display about how offers and acceptances are to be communicated and received. Websites offering goods for sale should make it clear whether the advertisements displayed are offers capable of acceptance, or whether a customer's order must be acknowledged by the seller before a contract is formed.

From the trader's perspective, rather than by making an offer in legal terms, it is often preferable to invite an offer, that is, a request to buy, by describing the goods available and the procedures for creating the sale, including the terms and conditions which will apply to the sale. The potential customer may then choose to make an offer which the trader can decide to accept or not. In this way, where the trader is not willing or able to accept an offer, the right is reserved to reject it.

The need or preference to reject an order online may arise for all sorts of reasons. The purchaser would normally be expected to register identity, address and any other relevant details. A customer may be under-age or otherwise may not have the legal capacity to enter into a particular contract. A person claiming to be a company representative may not have the authority to enter into the contract. The address may be in a location where there are legal or political restrictions hindering the validity of the contract, or there may be practical difficulties affecting delivery, taxes or payment. The supplier may wish to avoid business-to-consumer transactions, or need to check that there are enough supplies to fulfil the order, or want to check a customer's credit status.

The supplier should state its geographical or other limits. Technical constraints should be built in as far as possible, to prevent access or interaction by potential purchasers who are of no interest to the supplier. A sequence of web-pages may be constructed for particular languages or regions.

If security is a requirement, and for authenticating certain types of contracts, digital signatures and verification will be important. A party to an online contract ought at least to be aware of, and to be willing to accept, when and where the contract is actually made.

A supplier's terms and conditions of business should always be brought to the potential buyer's notice before the contract is made. They should be readily accessible and printable, so that the purchaser is able to understand the context in which the offer and acceptance will be made. There will be some additional built-in legal protection for the purchaser who is a consumer.

When placing the order, the customer should positively affirm that the terms and conditions have been read and understood. This may be achieved by requiring the customer to scroll through the terms and conditions, ideally by participating in some form of dialogue in so doing, before reaching the stage of pointing and clicking to make the order. Alternatively, a hyperlink can be created from the offer-and-acceptance section to separately displayed terms and conditions. This is not recommended, as a customer might be able to deny any knowledge of them.

The 'offer' part of an e-commerce contract may be made in one country and the 'acceptance' in another – and theoretically the services may be carried out or the goods delivered in a third. The rules can become complicated in determining which law applies to a contract and which courts have jurisdiction to deal with a dispute. It will depend on the exact circumstances of forming the contract, the wording in the contract, the effect of the contract, the status of the parties, and the locations involved.

Law and jurisdiction principles for international contracts are discussed in **CHAPTER 3**.

The strongest advice is that the governing law and jurisdiction applicable should always be expressly stated in business-to-business contracts.

B. The structure of an e-commerce distributor/author agreement

This example Agreement is a business-to-business agreement between a distributor of software products online ('Distributor') and the owner of the software products provided ('Author'). In this example it is envisaged that the variable information would be entered on the front page of the Agreement. The clause examples considered in Section C are those marked with an asterisk. Section D goes on to consider the supplementary terms and conditions if the option of a Source Code Escrow Service is taken up. Finally, in Section E there is comment on the Licence Agreement between the supplier and its online end-user customers ('Customers') ('Distributor End User Software Licence Agreement').

Terms and conditions

- Term
- Definitions*
- Services*
- Author Responsibilities*
- Product Submission*
- Fees and Author's Charges*
- Additional Activities*
- Reporting*
- Customer Support*
- Author's Warranties
- Intellectual Property Rights Indemnity
- Limits of Liability
- Termination
- General Contract Provisions.

C. Specific clauses

1. Definitions

'*Author*' means the organisation or individual identified on the front page of this Agreement wishing to supply Products to the market through licence sales using the Distributor.

'*Author's Charges*' means a monthly fee of £...... payable by the Author for marketing its Products on the Website.

'*Author Representative*' means the principal Author representative authorised to make and communicate decisions on behalf of the Distributor identified on the front page of this Agreement or subsequently notified to the Distributor.

'*Customer*' means a customer of the Distributor purchasing licensed Products for its own use or for resale.

'*Materials*' means Product evaluations, demonstrations, documentation, help files, technical information, marketing information and the encrypted full retail current release versions of Products.

'*Media*' means a compact disc or other media containing Products and Materials.

'*Product*' means any software product listed on the front page of this Agreement or Supplement, or any new software product, or new software product version subsequently released by the Author and sold under licence from the Website or Media.

'*Programme*' means the 'Distributor Worldwide Marketing Programme'.

'*Source Code Escrow Service*' means the optional escrow service detailed in the Supplementary Terms and Conditions appended to this Agreement.

'*Supplement*' means any current Supplementary Agreement, identified by its Agreement Number by linking to this Agreement.

'*Website*' means a commercial website owned by the Distributor, URL .... containing Materials for viewing and purchase by Customers.

2. Services

(a) The Distributor is seeking to develop markets and sales of software licences for its Authors through the Programme by owning and maintaining the Website, and by distributing e-mails, a hard copy directory, and/or Media containing marketing information on selected Products linked to the Website.

(b) Materials which are supplied by the Author will be included on the Website, subject to a satisfactory content and quality assurance review by the Distributor, and subject to these terms and conditions.

(c) The Distributor is responsible for updating the Website regularly, producing e-mails at regular intervals as described in the published schedule, and distributing e-mails to a qualified database of software developers. The

459

Distributor will use its reasonable commercial endeavours to improve its Programme and database on a regular basis.

(d) A Customer wishing to purchase a Product licence, or to subscribe to use a Product on a time-limited or usage basis from the Website, will be required to agree to the terms of the Distributor End User Software Licence Agreement. The Distributor will require the Customer to provide valid payment details, and in return will charge the Customer for the usage made of the Product.

(e) Transactions resulting from orders placed on the Website by Customers take place electronically in a securely encrypted form. The Distributor will use encryption/decryption software which is proprietary and proven, and will use all reasonable efforts to keep the encryption technique secret.

(f) Decryption keys are issued to a Customer in return for the provision of its valid payment details. There is a single opportunity to use the decryption keys provided, and if a Customer attempts to use any key again, the decryption process will fail.

(g) After decryption, in order to install the Product, a copy of the full retail version of the Product, as supplied by the Author, is created on the Customer's hard drive as simulated Media.

(h) To enable the marketing of any Product upgrade, the purchase of Product upgrades to qualifying Customers may be restricted on the Website, such that a Customer may enter the order, but must contact the Distributor for verification prior to download.

The business example used in this chapter illustrates the sorts of business opportunities which lend themselves to the exploitation of the Internet. The example chosen is a particularly pure form of e-commerce because an entire transaction can be achieved without human intervention. The software products being offered for licensed sale can be reviewed on the website, demonstrated, trialled, purchased, delivered by downloading, and paid for on any day of the year and at any time of the day or night.

One of the concerns which a distributor of products via a website should have is to do as much as reasonably possible to ensure that product content is accurate and in compliance with statutory warranties such as 'satisfactory quality' and 'fitness for purpose'. The distributor has something of a dilemma here, because it will probably lack the expertise and resources to test exhaustively each product offered for sale. (There are likely to be thousand of products coming from hundreds of sources.) The solution for the distributor is therefore to adopt a two-level approach to the problem. The first is contractually to require the author to comply with appropriate quality standards, supported by an indemnity. The second is to have its own internal system which will have at least a sufficient capability to ensure that products load properly and without obvious glitches, and to be in a position to demonstrate that, in onward supply of products, it has taken reasonable steps to ensure that quality is acceptable and that products are free of viruses.

It will be important to an author to have its products distributed by a distributor whose website is modern, well presented and updated regularly. Paragraph (c) covers this point, but an author may want even more, for example, an undertaking to update the website at least twice yearly and to take reasonable account of author suggestions for improvement.

It is important to mention the terms and conditions, which will apply to a customer for the product. In many instances these days, software products contain built-in licence terms which have to be agreed to before the product can be accessed. However, to cover the situation where there is no built-in licence, and to ensure that licence terms are presented to customers *before* they enter into a contract to purchase the licence (bearing in mind that the basic law of contract requires the parties to know all the material terms before an agreement on those terms can become legally binding) a distributor is well advised to impose its own software licence agreement as part of the sales process from its website. Since no two licence agreements are ever identical, a very broad wording of such a licence will be necessary if it is going to serve a generic purpose. This is discussed further in Section E.

Security is important. A website of this type needs to offer secure data protection for both customer details and payment-related data, and the product itself must be delivered in a secure manner to satisfy the proper interests of the author. High-level encryption and decryption techniques are the means by which security is achieved, and paragraphs (e) and (f) deal with this.

3. Author Responsibilities

The Author agrees in respect of each Product which it submits for inclusion on the Website or Media to:

(a) put only the Author name and/or the Distributor name, web address, e-mail, fax and telephone numbers as the contact information, on the Materials to be included. The Author agrees not to list other dealers, value added resellers or distributors on the Materials for the Website;

(b) provide a short description of the Product of up to 75 words for the Website, to explain why the Product was developed and its use for a developer;

(c) provide a description of the technical details of up to 1,000 words for the Website for each purchase option or edition of the Product, listing the differences from the previous option or edition;

461

(d) complete the 'Product Submission Form' on the Website, each time a new Product or version is submitted to the Distributor, to provide details of the Product such as: architecture, compatibility, system requirements, licensing requirements. Where indicated on the form, these details will appear on the Website;

(e) provide as part of the demonstration environment, and for the Website, Executable, Trial Version, Demonstration, Help (normally from the full retail version), Word, Excel, PowerPoint or PDF files and other such technical information, so that a Customer may download and evaluate the Product and make an informed purchase;

(f) provide the latest full retail version on release for the Website, which will install from a hard disk without error;

(g) provide Materials by e-mail or by download from an 'FTP Site'.

And the Author agrees further for each Product to:

(h) submit Materials when each new Product version is released, in a timely and efficient manner, at least five days prior to any release date for publication on the Website;

(i) allow the Distributor to provide the latest version of the Product free-of-charge to any Customer who has purchased the previous Product version from the Distributor within the last 30 days;

(j) ensure that the Materials accurately reflect the functionality of the full retail version to be encrypted;

(k) make all reasonable efforts to supply the Materials and any subsequent updates virus-free;

(l) mark the Materials being submitted, 'For FREE Download' or 'Full Retail Product' respectively;

(m) provide stock(s) of manuals, Media or boxed Products, if these should be required;

(n) provide a range of serial numbers for any Product which needs further unlocking or authorisation, upon request in a timely and efficient manner;

(o) allow the Distributor to host the Products, where appropriate, on the Website and rent access on a time-limited or usage basis;

(p) put the Distributor name, web address, e-mail, fax, telephone numbers as contact information on the Author's website and in any listing for author-ised licensors, dealers, value added resellers or distributors of the Author's Product;

(q) provide a link to the Website from the Author's website, using a customised link for the Author provided by the Distributor;

(r) assist in providing up-to-date press releases, customer referral letters and case studies about the Product;

(s) allow the Distributor to unlock the Product to official journalists for evaluation, without charge;

(t) provide technical support for the Product to the Distributor via e-mail, fax and telephone, in a timely and efficient manner;

(u) promptly advise the Distributor where a Product version has been withdrawn for technical reasons.

This clause in practice will always be tailored to meet the process requirements of the distributor and, because it is orientated to the distributor's system, there will not be much scope for negotiation by an individual author. However, it is important for an author to satisfy itself that it is fully capable of meeting all the requirements, and to discuss and agree compromise solutions with the distributor if there are practical difficulties in complying with any particular aspects.

The reference in paragraph (g) to 'FTP site' illustrates one particular way for an author to deliver materials to a distributor. 'FTP' means File Transfer Protocol, and is a standard commonly used as a means of transferring complete files from one computer system to another. (Another example is 'http' or the Hypertext Transfer Protocol, used to download web pages.)

Paragraph (k) requires the author to make 'all reasonable efforts' to ensure that materials are delivered virus-free to the distributor. Some distributors may prefer to impose an absolute requirement, although in practice it is difficult to justify such a burden when viruses can be introduced in so many unforeseeable ways.

4. Product Submission

(a) The Author agrees that by submitting its Products for inclusion on the Website, the Distributor may at its option and cost, also include or license the usage of the Materials on other websites or Media that it or other parties may produce.

(b) The Materials will bear the copyright notice, if any, provided by the Author, but so long as they bear such copyright notice, may be distributed by the Distributor without limitation.

(c) The Distributor reserves the right not to include any Product for any reason in its sole discretion, in which event a proportion of the Author's Charges paid by the Author for that period of time will be refunded, except where the Product submitted for inclusion fails to meet the minimum requirements defined above.

(d) The Distributor may make copies of Products and Materials as reasonably necessary for the purpose of providing Customers with machine-readable copies and for back-up purposes and for the efficient and secure operation of its business.

(e) The Distributor will take reasonable care to prevent the unauthorised use of the Materials.

(f) For each Product which is designated as a 'Source Code Escrow Service Product' on the front page of this Agreement, the Author will:

    (i)   promptly enter into the Source Code Escrow Service Agreement with the Distributor as custodian;

    (ii) promptly deposit a source copy of the Product with the Distributor;

    (iii) subject to compliance by the Distributor and relevant Customers with the terms of the Source Code Escrow Service Agreement, authorise the Distributor to release a copy of the source Product to such current Customers for the Product under the terms of such Source Code Escrow Service Agreement.

In this clause, the distributor is seeking to obtain as broad an authority as possible from the author in relation to its dealings with the product. As the distributor is in the distribution business, it will want maximum flexibility so that it can market the products effectively. The distributor's motive in seeking this and the author's reason for agreeing to it is that there is mutual interest in obtaining maximum financial benefit from sales of the product. Thus, provided that the author's copyright notice is retained (paragraph (b)), the distributor can market the products on sites other than its own, or using physical media, without any restriction (paragraphs (a) and (b)).

Paragraph (c) gives the distributor an absolute say in whether or not to include a product on its site, with appropriate adjustment in charges if not all products are included as originally anticipated. It is understandable that a distributor would want such a safeguard because it will want to maintain the integrity of its website, and be in a position to take any unilateral action it deems necessary for this purpose. Whilst an author may be unsuccessful in overcoming this discretion on the part of the distributor, it might wish to gain agreement for any reasons for non-inclusion to be stated, to be notified in advance if reasonably possible, and to require the distributor to take reasonable account of any counter-arguments it might wish to present.

Section D reviews the Source Code Escrow Service, but this agreement is structured so that if the distributor and author reach agreement that one or more products should be offered to customers with the benefit of an escrow of the source code, such products will be identified on the front page of the agreement, and this will have the effect of invoking the supplemental escrow terms and conditions.

5. Fees and Author's Charges

(a) For each licence of the Product or licensed usage of a hosted Product, the Distributor will remit to the Author ...% of the licence fee paid by the Customer excluding any sales, use or value added taxes that the Distributor collects.

(b) The Distributor will pay the Author at the end of the month following the month of sale for all licence fees for Products supplied during that month, less any refunds for returns given as a result of Customer claims.

(c) For the avoidance of doubt, payment will be due to the Author only for copies made for a Customer purchasing the Product.

(d) The Author will pay the Author's Charges in respect of the marketing of each Product via the Website. The Distributor will not make any extra charge for including the encrypted full retail version on the Website but the Author accepts that such inclusion is at the discretion of the Distributor.

(e) Where the total amount payable to the Author for Product licence fees made by the Distributor is equal to or exceeds [£...] in any calendar month, the Author's Charges will be deducted from any payments due by the Distributor to the Author for that month.

(f) For the avoidance of doubt, where the total amount payable to the Author for Product licence sales is less than [£...] in any calendar month, the Author's Charges will not be payable to the Distributor.

(g) The Author's Charges are exclusive of any sales, use or value added taxes.

(h) The Distributor will be entitled to increase the Author's Charges not more than once annually by three months' notice to the Author.

(i) It is agreed that in offering Products for resale, the Distributor is acting as an authorised independent value added reseller for the Author and not as its agent. Neither party has authority to bind or speak for the other party except as permitted by this Agreement or as may be authorised in writing from time to time.

Paragraphs (a) to (c) deal with the author's entitlement to payments arising from the sale of product licences. The basis of payment is that the distributor will take the full licence fee due from the customer, deduct its agreed fee, and remit the balance to the author. These specific arrangements will be supplemented by the general payment terms in the clause following.

There will be scope for negotiating the percentage of the licence fee to be retained by the distributor. While the distributor is likely to be able to dictate this fee, based on a standard it will seek to apply to all its authors, the negotiating advantage will move towards the author where either the products in question are relatively unique, or where sales volumes are likely to be sufficiently large to justify discounted payments according to an agreed formula. All such arrangements should be recorded in the final version of this clause.

Paragraphs (d) to (h) are concerned with the payment which the author is required to make as consideration for the inclusion of not only its products, but more particularly, detailed information and comparative analyses of its products on the distributor's website. There may be circumstances where the author will feel justified in seeking a waiver or reduction of this charge. Does the benefit to the author of coverage on the website outweigh the benefit to the distributor of having that information on its site?

In paragraph (i) it is made clear that the parties are independent business entities. This sort of provision is usually included in the general contract housekeeping provisions. In an agreement of this nature, it is helpful to place the statement in its context.

6. Additional Activities

(a) From time to time the Author may be offered additional marketing opportunities for its Products, such as: component pavilions at exhibitions, co-operative advertising in magazines, e-mail sponsorship, direct mail or third party Media distributions. Additional fees and or terms and conditions will apply in such cases. The Author will sign a Supplement if it agrees to participate in such marketing opportunities.

(b) All Supplements will be incorporated into and form part of this Agreement when executed, and the other terms and conditions of this Agreement will continue to apply. In the event of any conflict between a Supplement and any other terms of this Agreement the Supplement will prevail. Discontinuance of a Supplement does not otherwise affect the continuity of this Agreement.

(c) The Distributor is striving to increase the corporate adoption of the quality software components and Products that it markets. This involves increasing the services that are available to Customers such as: software upgrade, maintenance, enhanced technical support and source code escrow services. By signing this Agreement, the Author also agrees not to withhold unreasonably its support for these other activities.

In any distributorship situation, there will be numerous opportunities to develop the services and broaden the scope of an agreement, especially after the relationship has become established, and the parties will have a better idea of what they can each bring to the relationship. The motivation will always be to maximise the earnings opportunities from the sales activities to the parties' mutual benefit. It should therefore be anticipated that, either at the outset or at some future date, the agreement will be expanded to include the various supplements. As supplementary agreements will have been specially designed and negotiated, it is logical that they should take precedence whenever their wording conflicts with the main agreement, and paragraph (b) covers this point.

7. Reporting

(a) The Distributor will provide to the Author Representatives by e-mail and via secure logon to the Website a sales report giving details of the Customers who have purchased licences. The details will include: Customer name, organisation, country, Product and quantity licensed, with serial numbers allocated, if applicable.

(b) The Author will use these details to register the Customer on its databases, to facilitate efficient handling of Customer technical support requests, but will not make any other use of this data without first obtaining the consent of the Customer via the Distributor. The Author undertakes that no Customer details will be passed on to third parties or used for any purpose other than to give the Customer full access to technical support.

(c) The Distributor will also provide to the Author Representative via secure logon to the Website, a monthly financial report at the end of each month summarising the amounts due to the Author.

This simple clause provides the author with important feedback on the results being achieved by the distributor in terms of both sales analysis and financial summaries. If the parties wish to have a regular amount of defined information, it should be identified by listing the actual reports required and their specific content.

An author should also consider seeking a commitment from the distributor to permit a periodic audit of the distributor's records to validate the accuracy of the information provided in the reports. If such an audit process is agreed, the distributor will wish to have it conducted by an independent auditor by prior appointment during normal business hours, and not more than once annually without reasonable cause, in order to minimise disruption to its business. The parties relative strengths of negotiating position will determine whether or not the distributor can impose an administrative charge for facilitating such audits, and it is quite common for the audit cost itself to be borne by the author unless financial inaccuracies are greater than, for example, two per cent, in which case the cost would be borne by the distributor. Any balancing payments in either direction should be agreed to be paid promptly following the results of the audit.

8. Customer Support

> The Distributor will provide a support service to Customers for a period of 30 days from the date of Product purchase. Any Customer issues which the Distributor is unable to resolve will be passed to the Author Representative who will co-ordinate an attempted resolution in a timely and efficient manner, keeping the Distributor fully informed of progress and of any issues with the Product.

There are several variables to be considered in this clause. The distributor will be expected to offer support to customers, in some instances for considerably longer than 30 days. Given the wide range of products likely to be offered on the distributor's website, it is unrealistic to expect the distributor to do much more than provide some sort of help desk to receive customer calls, possibly to resolve basic and obvious problems. It will be essential for the author to provide a more detailed level of technical support. This clause allows for such requirements to be managed by the author representative. Where complex products are being sold, a more specific level of technical support is likely to be required. The content and cost of such support should be detailed in the final agreement, including any remuneration to the distributor for continuing to provide a first-line help desk, and/or for selling the author's maintenance service. On the other hand, many products will be licensed on the basis that customers can obtain technical support from the author direct.

D. Source code escrow supplementary terms and conditions

As the e-commerce example chosen for this chapter relates to the distribution of software products, it demonstrates an opportunity to add value by offering the option of a source code escrow service. End user licensees of software tend to worry about how that software might be supported in the event that the software author ceases to trade for any reason, or ceases itself to offer any ongoing support for a product. Generally, source code escrow services are provided by specialist organisations such as the NCC Group. However, if the parties are willing, there is no reason why a major distributor should not itself act as escrow agent. This represents an additional earnings opportunity for the distributor, but it also adds value to the sales proposition to customers by giving them the reassurance of availability of source code under an escrow arrangement. (As the service is integrated and easily accessible, many customers will be happy to trade off the theoretical conflict of interest of the distributor as the representative of the author.) In some circumstances, this can enhance sales opportunities, and some authors will recognise this and be willing to opt for this service and lodge source code with the distributor. If the author is unwilling to do so, the option box on the front page of the agreement will not be completed, and demands by customers for escrow facilities will have to be addressed on a case-by-case basis, where the financial value of the business is going to influence the author's willingness to escrow its source codes with either the distributor or another agreed escrow agent. Smaller entities in particular find it convenient to incorporate an escrow arrangement within the overall distribution service. They readily see the sales advantage it presents, and both they and the distributor will benefit from the fee income from those customers who elect to take advantage of the service.

The Supplementary Terms and Conditions will include the following provisions:

- Scope and Authority

- Additional Definitions

- Additional Author Undertakings

- Distributor Undertakings

- Term of Source Code Licence after Release

- Escrow Fees

- Termination before Release of Source Code

- Distributor Escrow Service Liabilities.

Although the terminology will need to be adapted to the circumstances of the main agreement, there is a detailed discussion of escrow services in **CHAPTER 13**, the 'Licensor' in that chapter representing the author, and the 'Escrow Agent' representing the distributor. The one other important difference is that all escrow fees under this arrangement would be payable by the customer and divided (equally) between the distributor and the author.

E. Distributor's end user software licence agreement

CHAPTER 12 discusses software licences, including a review of the contents of a typical licence. The same considerations will apply in this instance, but here there is a need for a comprehensive form of licence, designed to cover all the prospective uses of software products sold from the distributor's website, but which will, at the same time, meet the expectations of multiple authors from multiple countries.

In many cases, the distributor's generic licence will replicate the provisions in an individual author licence, such as the example in **CHAPTER 12**, and there will also be a need to include supplementary terms and conditions to cover those cases where an author has opted to offer the source code escrow service and the customer has elected to purchase it. The same licence is also needed to cover downloads for demonstration and evaluation purposes. An example of the structure of a licence of this sort is as follows:

- Pre-Download Statement of Agreement

- Fees, Order and Payment

- Grant of Licence and Software Use Restrictions
  - Restricted Licence
  - Evaluation Licence
  - Access Licence

- Copying Restrictions

- Ownership of Software and Media

- Transfer Restrictions

- Export Restrictions

- Term and Termination

- Limited Software Warranties and Disclaimers

- Intellectual Property Rights Protection

- General Contract Provisions

- Source Code Supplementary Terms and Conditions.

There is one other issue that merits discussion. E-commerce is a process susceptible to fraud. There will be occasions when the distributor will need to investigate fraudulent transactions, and this will necessitate access to data which would normally be protected. As a matter of prudent practice, just as every properly constructed website involving collection of personal data should contain a privacy policy, an anti-fraud detection notice should be prominently displayed, and an example of such a notice is shown below.

WARNING: ANTI-FRAUD DETECTION NOTICE

To combat fraud, the Distributor may gather identifying information about the computer running the browser software. This information includes, but is not necessarily limited to, the Customer's IP address. The Customer agrees that its IP address may be supplied to prosecuting or regulatory authorities in connection with fraud or other formal investigations, and the Distributor undertakes to keep such information confidential except for disclosure to such authorities in connection with such investigations.

---

1   Privacy and Electronic Communications (EC Directive) Regulations 2003, implementing EU Privacy and Electronic Communications Directive 2002/58/EC.
2   Financial Services and Markets Act 2000 (Regulated Activities) (Amendment) (No 2) Order 2002, SI 2002/1776; Electronic Commerce Directive (Financial Services and Markets) (Amendment) Regulations 2002, SI 2002/2015; Financial Services and Markets Act 2000 (Financial Promotion) (Amendment) (Electronic Commerce Directive) Order 2002, SI 2002/2157.
3   Directive 97/7/EC on the Protection of Consumers in Respect of Distance Contracts.
4   Consumer Protection (Distance Selling) Regulations 2000, SI 2000/2334.
5   Distance Marketing of Consumer Financial Services Directive 2002/65/EC.
6   Financial Services and Markets Act 1998.
7   Stop Now Orders (EC Directive) Regulations 2001, SI 2001/1422.

CHAPTER 21
Disaster recovery agreements

A. Introduction

The concept of 'business continuity' is part of the risk management process to ensure that business can continue unhindered by any interruptions. Disaster recovery is part of business continuity, to restore the operational running of computer systems where normal technology has failed because of the exceptional circumstances of a disaster. Unfortunately there are plenty of real life illustrations of disasters of various magnitudes which have affected computer systems. Terrorist activities, unusually hazardous weather conditions and power outages, are all actual disasters which have destroyed the ability of organisations to continue running their systems at their own premises.

Contingency planning ensures that if a company has prepared for the worst, the consequences of a disaster can be contained. Every company should have properly documented and tested back-up arrangements for its key systems. Copies of software and files should be taken regularly and stored safely. As part of their contingency plans, many organisations invest in expensive standby contracts to provide back-up for their IT systems, one form being an agreement with a disaster recovery service provider for 'hot restart' services, that is, to run high priority systems at a physically remote location with compatible computing equipment available. It is vital for the enterprise to get the terms of this contract right.

An organisation addressing these risks may choose to maintain its own fully replicated computer system at a different site, at least in so far as the key elements are concerned. For many businesses this will be an extravagant option, and they will prefer an alternative option of employing the services of a company offering disaster recovery arrangements for selected systems and data critical to their operations.

A disaster recovery service offered by a third party should be designed to enable its customers to overcome quickly any set of circumstances threatening to disable their key computer systems. This means that key systems must be identified so that they are the ones that receive priority in the event of disaster, to get them back up and running. The object for the customer is for a fast response to enable a return to normal working as soon as possible.

The disaster recovery provider must be able to offer its services immediately, on a 24 hour, seven days per week basis if this is essential for its customers. The computer facilities and office accommodation must be geographically distant from the location of the disaster, yet convenient for customers to secure access. The provider must have compatible hardware and communications, together with security at least as good as that of its customers, and operational support services.

The provider must ensure that it is legally committed only to the back-up services which it is capable of fulfilling. The worst-case scenario would be if all its customers called on its services simultaneously. Its potential liability would be ruinous if it failed to meet its customers' demands for running key systems to meet the strategic needs of each customer's business, so that each customer could carry on as near to normal as practicable. For this reason providers would be wise to limit the numbers of their customers and ensure that they are located well away from each other, policies which vigilant customers should also wish to see adopted.

The disaster recovery contract shares the objectives of an insurance policy in seeking ostensibly to highlight the 'policy' features while being careful to contain the liabilities of the supplier in the actual event of a disaster. Customers therefore need to scrutinise disaster recovery agreements very carefully to ensure that their particular concerns are going to be met without reservation. If not, and if they cannot negotiate the necessary improvements, they should shop around.

From the customer's point of view, in order to enable it to continue its critical operations, a disaster recovery agreement must allow for every contingency which might prevent this. Each customer will have unique computing requirements, but the disaster recovery provider must accommodate the requirements of them all.

The procedure to be followed in the event of a disaster should be known to all key customer staff, and should take into account the possibility of operational personnel not being available. It should allow for the likelihood that the entire building housing the customer's computer systems will not be accessible in a disaster. The customer should therefore keep this disaster recovery contract in an accessible place, separately from its systems and servers. It would also be sensible to keep a map with the contract showing the location of the disaster recovery centre, and telephone numbers for the centre and for staff affected (and to keep this information up to date). At least one employee (and alternate) should be appointed to organise the staff on-site. Firefighters, detectives, surveyors and other officials will take precedence over any IT staff at the scene of the disaster itself.

A disaster recovery agreement should include facilities for the customer's senior managers and other staff responsible for managing a disaster recovery scenario to test these emergency arrangements from time to time. It normally takes more than one attempt to make sure that everything works effectively.

Disaster recovery agreements are therefore important aspects of the security strategy of computing facilities and businesses, and need careful drafting.

B. The structure of a typical disaster recovery agreement

- Definitions*
- Term
- Services*
- Testing*
- Supplier Undertakings*
- Data*
- Customer Undertakings*
- Exclusions*
- Charges
- Payment Terms
- Confidential Information
- Indemnities and Limits of Liability
- Termination
- General Contract Provisions

Schedule contents

- Configuration details
- System details
- Contact details

C. Specific clauses

In these clause examples, which are those above marked with an asterisk, the parties are referred to as 'Supplier' for the company providing the Disaster Recovery Services and 'Customer' for the party requiring the Disaster Recovery Services.

1. Definitions

'*Configuration*' means the Supplier's computer system defined in the Schedule, located at the Site, on which the Services are to be provided.

'*Data*' means the Customer's data [defined in the Schedule] which are processed by the Systems.

'*Data Controller*' means any person so nominated by the Customer.

'*Disaster*' means any event or circumstance which causes the complete or partial loss or non-availability of the Customer's System, or which prevents the normal operation of the Customer's System or the performance of any task or function of the System [in either case which is or may reasonably be expected to be inoperable or inaccessible for at least [24] hours], or any event or circumstance similarly affecting a Subscriber.

'*Media*' means computer input materials and data including but not limited to magnetic tapes and disks.

'*Services*' means those services undertaken by the Supplier for the Customer detailed in this Agreement.

'*Site*' means the site where the Configuration is situated.

'*Subscriber*' means customers of the Supplier for the Services other than the Customer.

'*System*' means the Customer's computer systems defined in the Schedule, to which the Services apply.

The definition of 'Disaster' is probably the most important one because it is going to govern the circumstances which will entitle the customer to access the supplier's computer system. It must be defined in terms of loss or non-availability of key systems. It is tempting to list examples, and more challenging to draft, but there is always scope for an unforeseeable catastrophe – a rat chewing through wiring or an exploding boiler – and the unpredictable is exactly what this agreement should be about. The more mundane disasters may cause the most damage. As there are going to be several other customers, the supplier will probably be unwilling to negotiate this definition. If this is the case, and the definition offered does not adequately meet the customer's requirements, it may be necessary to look for alternative suppliers. For example, the words in square brackets may constitute the criteria for one particular supplier, but others may not make this stipulation. From a negotiating point of view, it may be possible to achieve deletion of the words in square brackets in return for a slightly higher price, the argument being that the opportunity for more immediate access to the configuration can be costed in terms of anticipated greater use of the services. A point such as this is likely to be more important to the customer who has a single vital system than to the one with several, who is prepared to cope with its own emergencies in the short term. A short break in continuous access may be critical to some organisations, such as a currency trading system, where a service gap measured in hours would be too long.

2. Services

(a) The Services consist of making available and maintaining the Configuration at the Site [during normal office hours of 9.00 am to 5.00 pm on normal working days excluding public and other statutory holidays] [for the number of days during any 12-month period as specified in the Schedule] [for 24 hours per day seven days per week throughout the year] [for three days in any 12-month period] [excluding 25 December and 26 December] with telephone facilities, and with normal office space and staffing which the Supplier determines to be reasonably necessary for the sole use of the Customer and Subscribers in Disasters or for Disaster testing purposes.

(b) The Customer's access to the Configuration will at all times be subject to availability, but a Customer's Disaster will always be given priority over testing or other equivalent usage requirements of either the Supplier or Subscribers. If the Services are requested by the Customer when a Subscriber is already using the Services for a similar purpose, that Subscriber will have a higher priority of access to the configuration than the Customer.

(c) The Customer will be entitled to have such members of its own authorised staff attending at the Site as is reasonably necessary during a Disaster or for testing purposes.

(d) Facilities for storage of Media can be made available at the Site for the exclusive use of the Customer at the Supplier's then current charges.

(e) If the Customer so requests, the Supplier will provide peripheral equipment additional to that included in the Configuration, at its then current charges, subject to availability and subject to at least 24 hours' notice from the Customer.

(f) Application by the Customer for access to the Configuration in the event of a Disaster should be made by telephone to any one of the persons listed as contacts in the Schedule or as otherwise advised to the Customer, stating the grounds upon which the application to use the Configuration is based.

(g) The Customer is entitled to inspect the Site at any time on reasonable notice.

(h) The Customer is entitled to three days' use of the Configuration at the Site each year during the term of this Agreement for the purposes of carrying out any tests and trials in relation to the System as the Customer may consider necessary. These days will be arranged by mutual agreement between the Supplier and the Customer.

(i) Where the Customer invokes the Services because of a Disaster, a minimum charge equivalent to one day's use of the Configuration at the daily rate specified in the Schedule will apply.

This clause identifies the basic services to be provided for the charges, and points to supplemental services, which can be provided for additional sums. It is better for services to be defined in terms of need, that is, loss or non-availability of key systems, rather than by a list of possible disaster scenarios such as fires or earthquakes. There is always scope for unforeseen disasters, which is exactly what the agreement should be about.

The key systems should be identified in a schedule, which can be amended by subsequent agreement, should they change. The supplier will need advance indication of the resources which may have to be provided. The supplier may also be interested in providing other services requested by the customer outside the scope of the standard clause, subject of course to the supplier's continuing ability to satisfy the contractual requirements of its other customers accessing the configuration. It may accordingly be possible for the customer to negotiate without much difficulty broader provisions than those set out in the above clause, provided that these do not fall within the scope of the exclusions considered in clause 7 below.

The parties must be in no doubt about the proper order of priorities applicable to any individual customer or subscriber in the event of a disaster. The configuration is a shared facility and scrupulous fairness is needed in the interests of every subscribing customer. This clause seeks to make the supplier's obligations completely clear to all concerned, so that there can be no cause for complaint. It would be difficult for the supplier to agree any variation to this clause without involving all the other participating customers.

The supplier may want to set a limit on the number of the customer's staff entitled to be at the site.

Paragraph (f) of this clause is included because the customer must be entitled to secure access to the computer configuration immediately when it is needed and, by knowing the correct procedure and who should be contacted at the disaster recovery location, be able to ensure this in practice. It is in the interests of both parties for the procedure to be stated clearly and unambiguously. A customer's staff should not be caused added concern at a time of stress by anxiously knocking on locked doors of darkened premises in the middle of the night. Names and telephone numbers should be listed in a schedule.

The customer should review the site from time to time, to check out that the facilities still apply, as permitted at paragraph (g).

An alternative to paragraph (h) is to limit the number of days cover for a disaster to, for example, three in any 12 months, and thereafter at a daily rate specified in the schedule. 'Hours' may be a more appropriate measure of time than 'days' in some cases.

3. Testing

(a) The Services will be made available to the Customer only after completion of tests which establish the compatibility of the Customer's System for running on the Configuration to the Supplier's reasonable satisfaction. These tests will be conducted within 30 days of the date of this Agreement. If these test results are not satisfactory to the Supplier, this Agreement will be terminated immediately and all sums paid by the Customer under the Agreement refunded.

(b) The Customer will institute procedures for testing its System quarterly to ensure maintenance of compatibility of the System with the Configuration. The Customer agrees to book tests at the Site at least 14 days in advance, and understands that such tests may nevertheless be postponed with or without notice if the Configuration becomes unavailable because of a Disaster experienced by a Subscriber. Tests may also be postponed by the Customer for reasons outside the Customer's control.

The requirement of testing is certainly in the customer's best interests. Many contingency plans fail when they are first tried out. There is little point in spending money on a disaster recovery facility if it turns out to be inadequate when it is needed, by definition in crisis circumstances. The customer may negotiate to have the tests carried out earlier than the standard 30 days allowed for here.

The procedural requirements of the supplier are unlikely to be negotiable because the supplier is having to take into account the needs of several subscribers.

4. Supplier Undertakings

The Supplier undertakes that it has good title to or a right to use the Configuration, and further undertakes:

(a) to make all reasonable endeavours at all times to provide the services to the Customer in the event of a Disaster;

477

(b) not to exceed the maximum number of Subscribers stated in the Schedule for the Configuration;

(c) not to register any other customer as a Subscriber for the Services using the Configuration who is located in the same or an adjacent building to the Customer;

(d) [to keep the Configuration in good working order to meet the Customer's requirements, ensuring its regular maintenance, and in the event of failure or breakdown, to restore it to good working order promptly;] [to arrange for the Configuration to be maintained by keeping third party hardware and software maintenance agreements current, which in the case of hardware maintenance agreements will include provision for investigation within a maximum of four hours as one of the terms;]

(e) to provide an experienced manager at the Site during normal office hours and to ensure that the Customer always has a means of contacting a manager who can help to provide access;

(g) to keep the Site secure and to permit only authorised Supplier, Customer and Subscriber personnel to gain access;

(h) to keep an accurate record of the components of the Configuration at all times, including location, serial numbers and maintenance details, and to provide this to the Customer on request;

(i) to ensure that the Site always meets the environmental requirements of the Configuration, that it contains the attendant facilities normally associated with the operation and management of a system of equivalent size and complexity to the Configuration, taking account of the anticipated level of usage, and that it is generally kept clean and tidy;

(j) to indemnify the Customer against any claims by third parties arising out of the provision of the Services to the Customer.

It is important for the customer to ensure that there are provisions to limit the number of other organisations being supported by the disaster recovery services. The customer does not want to find itself in dispute with other subscribers at critical times. It should ensure that no neighbour of its own computer centre is also registered at the same disaster recovery location. The same fire or other disaster could affect them too.

Paragraph (a) is the most important. The example places an 'all reasonable endeavours' requirement on the supplier to provide the services. Customers may wish to make provision of the services an absolute requirement, arguing that if they cannot have a complete guarantee that the services will be available in the event of a disaster, there is not much point in having an agreement. Conversely the supplier will argue that it cannot control all eventualities and is not in a position to offer an absolute guarantee. The compromise on this occasion could be to elevate the standard placed on the supplier to 'best endeavours', essentially relieving the supplier of its obligation only in circumstances beyond its control.

At paragraph (c), it is in the interests of both parties that the service should not be made available to more adjacently situated customers than could be accommodated simultaneously. A disaster is more likely to strike a geographical area than it is to affect similar types of businesses.

There will be few suppliers who will not object to a provision along the lines of the final paragraph of the example clause. It is non-specific and open-ended and, whilst it represents an ideal position from the customer's perspective, the supplier should seek to limit the scope of an indemnity by confining its application to negligent acts or omissions up to a stated limit of liability and excluding consequential losses.

The supplier's undertakings included in this clause are representative of the principal features which should be incorporated into disaster recovery services. There are a number of additional services which some suppliers may offer to provide either as an integral part of the services or for payment of any additional fee. These additional services might include storage of media, storage of object codes of the customer's software (provided that the customer certifies its rights to use the software and indemnifies the supplier from third party claims), data back-up services, archiving creation and reconstruction of databases and day-to-day bureau services.

At paragraph (h) the supplier may wish to limit the reporting of the details of the configuration, or may expect the customer to pay for the effort involved.

5. Data

> (a) The Supplier further undertakes:
> - (i) to act only on instructions from the Data Controller in relation to any personal data which may be comprised in the Data as such 'personal data' is defined by the Data Controller;
> - (ii) that its technical and organisational security measures govern the processing of the Data;
> - (iii) that it will use its best endeavours to prevent any unauthorised or unlawful processing of the Data or any accidental loss, destruction or damage;
> - (iv) that it has taken reasonable steps to ensure the honesty and reliability of its personnel;
> - (v) to indemnify the Customer against any claims by third parties arising out of any breach of the undertakings in this clause.
>
> (b) Data, whether provided by the Customer in human or machine readable form, and any output resulting from processing by the System, remain at all times the property of the Customer, subject to the confidentiality provisions in this Agreement.

The Data Protection Act 1998 regulates the processing of personal data, and defines 'processing' very broadly, to include almost any activity relating to such data; 'obtaining' and 'holding' being two such activities. The Act distinguishes 'data controllers' from 'data processors'. Data controllers take decisions about the processing of personal data. Data processors process the personal data on behalf of the data controller (other than employees). Data controllers have specific responsibilities under the Act when the processing of personal data is carried out on their behalf by another organisation. Such processing is likely to cover the provision of disaster recovery services.

The customer's data controller must comply with the seventh data protection principle:

> 'Appropriate technical and organisational measures shall be taken against unauthorised or unlawful processing of personal data and against accidental loss or destruction of, or damage to, personal data'.

The second Schedule of the Data Protection Act 1998 specifies the requirements incumbent on the data controller in order to ensure that the data processor can guarantee its security governing the processing and otherwise comply with the obligations of the seventh principle. Guidance at the data protection website of the Information Commissioner[1] states that the processing should be carried out under a contract evidenced in writing, for the data processor to act only on instructions from the data controller in respect of personal data, and otherwise to ensure compliance with the seventh principle.

This example clause sets out some simple obligations for the supplier. They might reasonably be extended to any data to be processed, especially since, in these circumstances, the supplier should not normally need to be aware of the nature of the data being processed on behalf of the customer, and should also be following security procedures as a matter of good practice.

Paragraph (b) is a sensible provision from the customer's point of view and is really included for the avoidance of all doubt.

6. Customer Undertakings

(a) The Customer undertakes:
  (i) to provide the Supplier with a list of its personnel authorised to invoke the Services in a Disaster and always to keep this list up to date. The Supplier will not accept any instructions or bookings from any personnel not so listed;
  (ii) to be solely responsible for all transportation and associated costs for Media storage;
  (iii) to be solely responsible for ensuring that all Media kept by the Customer at the Site are compatible with the Configuration. The Customer undertakes to ensure that the Media are supplied and maintained in good condition;

(iv) to use on the Configuration only the versions of any software which are capable of running on the latest version operating system of the Configuration;

(v) to observe, and instruct its staff to observe, the access and security procedures at the Site at all times, and to keep confidential, and take all reasonable measures to ensure that its staff keep confidential, any identification numbers and passwords provided by the Supplier for the purposes of gaining access to the Site;

(vi) to allow the Supplier to study, for the sole purpose of rectifying problems, any of the Data, provided that all such data is treated as confidential by the Supplier, and that the security provisions set out in relation to Data in this Agreement are complied with;

(vii) to ensure that its staff use the Site only for the purposes of this Agreement;

(viii) to take all reasonable measures to ensure that its staff working at the Site comply with any instructions of any supervisory personnel of the Supplier;

(ix) to provide the Supplier and its employees assigned to perform the Services with all necessary information and assistance that may reasonably be required to enable the Supplier to carry out its obligations in this Agreement to the Customer.

(b) The Customer warrants that the System is either owned by or legally licensed to the Customer and is available for use in a Disaster on an alternative computer system to that for which it was supplied, and the Customer fully indemnifies the Supplier in respect of any damages, costs or expenses incurred by the Supplier as a result of any claim against the Supplier from a third party alleging unauthorised use on the Configuration of the System.

These provisions are the essential ground rules for the customer and there will probably be little scope for negotiating reduced responsibilities. The supplier will be likely to take the view that it cannot vary these basic requirements from one customer to another when the overall performance is essential for the good order of the system, configuration and site. Security at the site must include a limit on who will be permitted access. A supplier should ask for confidentiality undertakings from all subscribers to protect everyone.

The warranty and indemnity in paragraph (b) should be regarded as essential by the supplier. Many software licences do not provide for use on an alternative third party system in disaster circumstances. The supplier must avoid the possibility of action by an owner of software based upon unauthorised use of software on the supplier's configuration, perhaps by taking out its own licences where appropriate. It is in the interests of both parties for software and hardware to be accessible at the supplier's site without any possibility of prevention by a third party.

One undertaking which is not included in the above example but which may be acceptable in some situations, is to provide that, in the event of a disaster or series of disasters affecting more than one customer, a customer should be willing to time-share on the configuration, at least until after a reasonable period of time has elapsed, to give the supplier an opportunity to provide adequate alternative or supplemental computer facilities.

7. Exclusions

(a) The Services are subject to availability, and the Supplier will not be liable for any losses, costs or expenses incurred by the Customer and arising from any failure in the provision of the Services for any reason.

(b) The Supplier will not be obliged to maintain compatibility of the Configuration with the System, and reserves the right at all times to make changes or modifications to the Configuration following a minimum of 30 days' notice to the Customer (except in case of emergency) and subject to the Customer's right to terminate this Agreement with effect from the expiry of the notice if the proposed changes or modifications will result in incompatibility with the System.
OR
The Supplier reserves the right to make major changes or modifications to the Configuration subject to continued compatibility with the Customer's requirements and subject to the Customer's agreement, not to be unreasonably withheld or delayed.

(c) The Supplier will use all reasonable endeavours to maintain the Configuration and any changes or modifications to it in full working order, but subject to compliance with this undertaking the Supplier will not be liable in any way under any circumstances to the Customer for any equipment or software failures within the Configuration.

(d) Subject to the other provisions in this Agreement on security of the Data, it is the sole responsibility of the Customer to make appropriate arrangements for the maintenance of the integrity of the Data, including instituting adequate back-up procedures for the Customer's business requirements. The Supplier will not be responsible or liable to the Customer in any way for any lost or corrupted Data however caused.

The exclusions in this example are drafted for the benefit of the disaster recovery supplier. It must not be exposed if the emergency system is not available when needed by a particular customer, and must not be fettered in terms of updating and improving the emergency system when another opportunity to do so arises. Of course the supplier has to be concerned to manage the situation for all of the customers assigned to a particular system, whereas any individual customer will be concerned about its own position. By the very nature and concept of a disaster recovery agreement, several customers are signing up for the same potentially scarce resource. Suppliers offering these services are always going to resist negotiations, because any agreed amendment is almost certain to require consequential adjustments to the agreements of all the other participants. Nevertheless, it behoves customers to check exclusions very carefully so that they can make a properly informed decision about whether or not to subscribe to the particular service being offered. The balance of advantage probably lies with suppliers, in that they are prepared to offer the services only on business terms which they perceive as manageable with a number of subscribers.

The supplier will seek the ability to change compatibility of the configuration provided that notice is given to the customer. This needs care in negotiation. There is no point in the customer having a disaster recovery agreement if it cannot rely on the structure, combination and content of the configuration. The customer should therefore be looking for a commitment from the supplier that the configuration will not be modified too frequently or too significantly without there being some benefit to the customer. On the other hand, the supplier may not want to be committed long term to equipment that is unlikely to remain up to date, particularly having the requirements of several customers to consider.

A major consideration for suppliers is that if they fail to provide the services they have contracted to provide in a disaster, they will almost certainly be responsible for causing considerable consequential harm to the affected customer, in circumstances where the whole point of the agreement is to provide the customer with security in the event of the disaster. A serious failure could therefore amount to a breach of such magnitude that the supplier might not be able to rely on contractual limitations of liability. The customer may well go out of business. Suppliers therefore need to exercise the utmost care in deciding whether or not they are capable of offering a satisfactory disaster recovery service and on what terms. They should also be quite clear about the scope and limitations of insurance cover they seek to rely on in relation to this service. Indeed, in many cases, insurers are insisting on some of the limitations included in standard terms and conditions.

The final element of the clause focuses on the customer's responsibility for maintaining its own data integrity. This is a reasonable requirement. Every customer should be well aware of the importance of its computerised data and should have back-up procedures in place to reflect that importance. Sensitive data should be backed up frequently or moved to a different location at regular intervals. Regardless of any contractual rights, it is going to be of little comfort to any customer if important data is irretrievably lost, or would take so long to reconstitute that the business would founder in the meantime. Therefore, back-up should be sufficient to safeguard against any accidental, negligent or deliberate destruction of the customer's data.

1   www.dataprotection.gov.uk.

CHAPTER 22

Administration and legal risk management

A. Introduction

IT use and development now take place in a business environment that is turbulent and dynamic. The marketplace for suppliers has become aggressively competitive, and users now have a greater knowledge and experience in articulating their requirements and expecting them to be met.

The management of risk in meeting the commercial objectives of IT has become an important function of business in these circumstances. The risks may be technical, eg the extent of security arrangements in controlling access to sensitive data; commercial, eg the potential insolvency of a supplier to whom payment has been made for goods not yet delivered; and legal, eg whether a clause which excludes liability will be valid in a contract based on standard terms and conditions.

Law is unavoidably intrinsic to IT business. For instance, even in the particular structure chosen as the vehicle for conducting entrepreneurial operations, there are legal as well as financial ramifications. What is the most appropriate way for a particular business to be run effectively and to maximise its profitability? Should it be a private limited company, a public limited company, or a partnership with unlimited or limited liability?

B. Managing legal risk proactively

One of the challenges in carrying out commercial activities to make profits lies in identifying a risk, and balancing the cost of managing that risk against the potential losses if it is ignored. In looking at any given activity for the risk involved, an assessment must be made of how much risk, and what kinds of risks, are acceptable.

If loss or damage is caused because of another party's fault, and if informal channels of resolving a dispute do not work, there are legal remedies available. The party claiming the remedy is reacting to the loss or damage by seeking compensation. In this way, legal processes in the commercial marketplace are often regarded as responding reactively and imposing barriers and restrictions.

The alternative to this reactive view of law is to treat it as a strategic resource. In this way, time can be invested in negotiating contracts to mutual benefit; administrative procedures can be set up to keep control of business transactions; compliance with regulatory requirements can be facilitated, the better to service clients.

This proactive approach is both sensible commercial practice and good legal practice – anticipating, deterring and preventing legal and commercial risks.

By analogy, in medicine, vaccination is available against certain diseases to provide relatively cheap and simple protection in advance. Waiting until the disease strikes leads to panic reactions and uncertain outcomes.

C. Legal risk management

How can the legal risks inherent in IT be managed? There are three major ways.

- The first is by means of contracts.

- The second is the use of sound administrative procedures. This is a neglected area of great importance, covering: order administration; contract administration; post-contract administration; insurances and guarantees.

- Finally, there are compliance procedures, to ensure that commercial practice is in accordance with laws, regulations, standards and codes of practice.

Contracts, order and contracts administration and procedures, insurances and guarantees are discussed further below.

D. Contract

A contract enables the parties to achieve their strategic and commercial aims by establishing and reflecting the terms of a trading transaction, regulating the commercial relationship and allocating risks between the parties. It should focus on the parties' respective requirements, defining the terms that represent the commitments and different interests of the parties. The contract therefore sets the context and is a useful structure for stating the business objectives and anticipating important issues.

If the parties' expectations are not met, the contract will provide legal remedies.

The reviews of specific types of contracts in this book deal with the areas which are most likely to cause risk to the parties in the transactions under discussion.

E. Order administration

Order administration is a pre-contractual activity (except in bid or tender situations) culminating in the making of the contract if all the elements are found to be correct and therefore capable of acceptance.

The supplier's objective is to make a contract either on its standard terms and conditions or by negotiation. From this perspective, the supplier's terms and conditions treat, or should seek to treat, the customer's order as the offer.

The customer's objective is to use its order to make a contract on terms and conditions it has negotiated or accepted. Only the larger user organisations can realistically expect to negotiate and contract on the basis of their own terms and conditions, and even then they will need to be able to show that their terms and conditions have taken full account of the special contractual issues to be found in IT contracts, for example, software licensing, protection of proprietary rights, export and re-export regulations, high levels of customer involvement in product development, and so on.

Customers should understand the legal effect of issuing each order: that is, does it constitute an offer or an acceptance of an offer? Which terms and conditions apply to the contract? Are they agreed or acceptable? The technical features which need to be present to create a legally enforceable agreement are discussed in **CHAPTER 4**.

'The Battle of the Forms'

This involves a manipulation of the basic rules of offer and acceptance so that one party's terms and conditions clearly apply to the transaction.

Many arguments turn on which terms and conditions prevail: those of the supplier or those of the customer. Ideally, there needs to be a clear and unambiguous reference to the terms and conditions intended by the parties to apply to the contract.

If the order does not correctly and unequivocally incorporate the supplier's terms and conditions, the supplier should reject it, and rely on its own form of order acceptance, referring to its terms and conditions, as a counter-offer. If this does not produce a response from the customer, the supplier can argue that the customer's subsequent act of taking delivery of the goods constitutes acceptance of the supplier's terms by conduct.

There are potential weaknesses in this argument – for example, previous dealings; the status and thus implied level of authority of persons taking delivery; and the legal principle that silence does not constitute acceptance. Its uncertainty makes it an unsatisfactory way of dealing with important and complex contracts. It is more a basis for argument in the absence of an unequivocal offer-acceptance position.

Handwritten or typed references prevail over pre-printed statements, because they demonstrate evidence of a later intention. Suppliers can be reasonably confident that an order has been placed on their terms and conditions if there is a clear and correct reference by number and date to their quotation, when the quotation has been stated to be subject to the supplier's terms and conditions. Even if the customer's order contains pre-printed terms and conditions, the terms of the quotation are later in time and the supplier's order acceptance will then complete the making of the contract. Some customers use expressions such as 'Quotation number ABC123 applies for pricing purposes'. This implies that for all other purposes, the customer's printed terms will apply. However, this will not necessarily work in this way. There is a strong argument that a price is offered by a supplier on the basis of its terms and conditions contained in its quotation. A customer in these circumstances cannot expect to select only the terms which are favourable to it out of the standard set.

One case on the 'Battle of the Forms' concerned the supply of an industrial ink[1]. Coates Brothers plc, the supplier, supplied Leicester Circuits Ltd, the customer, with an ink 'T1', used in the preparation of circuit boards. An agreement was made in writing to deliver T1 ink in accordance with the supplier's standard terms and conditions of sale. These standard conditions were important for the supplier because they contained an exclusion of liability for consequential or incidental damages. This agreement could be amended only in writing.

The procedure for supply of the T1 ink was as follows:

- Leicester Circuits would fax Coates Brothers an order form with standard terms and conditions on the reverse, stating that they had precedence over the printed conditions of the supplier.

- Coates Brothers would send Leicester Circuits an order acknowledgment form on the front of which was printed: 'Coates's standard conditions of sale shall apply'.

- Upon delivery, Coates Brothers would send Leicester Circuits an invoice containing its standard terms and conditions on the reverse.

However, Coates Brothers began to supply a different ink known as 'T4' without amending the agreement or the supply procedure. Following the changeover to the T4 ink, Leicester Circuits had many complaints and lost customers. In consequence, Leicester Circuits claimed for breach of its standard terms and conditions and, alternatively, breach of the warranty of 'fitness for purpose' which is implied into contracts for the sale of goods (see **CHAPTER 4**).

Coates Brothers said that it was their standard terms and conditions which applied, therefore excluding liability. They used two arguments. They said that the agreement remained in effect after the changeover to the T4 ink. They also said that in the supply procedure, their standard terms and conditions directly applied, because they were the last to be seen.

The decision was:

- the agreement did not apply to the supply of T4 ink, because the definition of 'products' covered by the Agreement was clear and precise, referring to the T1 ink. The definition had not been amended in any way to include T4; and

- neither party's standard conditions applied. This was because the references to the conditions of sale and purchase were contained in documents exchanged in rapid succession, and nobody thought about it once the T4 ink was being supplied.

So only the statutory implied terms as to 'fitness for purpose' applied – and Coates Brothers were held to be in breach of these implied terms.

Thus, if the defaulting party is aware of the appropriate terms and conditions and agrees to make the contract on those terms, they will apply. But it is not satisfactory simply to try and determine which set of terms and conditions were the last to be made available prior to conclusion of the contract, when the sequence of exchange of documents is unclear, or when no attention was paid by either party to the terms and conditions.

F. Order administration procedures

Is there a company policy for order administration – supplier or customer? If not, one should be developed.

It is recommended that a copy of the policy should be included in a manual of contracts policies and procedures to be issued to all those in the company involved in activities connected with the obtaining, processing or administration of business. New sets of standard terms and conditions would also be issued to holders of this manual, as well as any contracting guidelines and business policies of the company. However, negotiating guidelines should not be included in such a manual because, notwithstanding any rules of confidentiality, it is almost inevitable that at some point a copy will find its way into the hands of the other side and prejudice the outcome of a negotiation.

The checking of terms and conditions should be incorporated into the procedures for order placing (customer) or reviewing (supplier).

- Are there any sub-contractors involved and do the terms and conditions and safeguards carry through fully and accurately? Does the main contract permit sub-contracting in the first place? Is any notice required?

- Are there any other contract conditions to be met?

- Are the prices and other variable details correct? A non-obvious mistake can be dangerous. It will probably be incapable of correction in practice without the other party's agreement, and it will not always be possible to rely on the other party's co-operation.

- What is the sign-off procedure, including the members of the management hierarchy required to approve non-standard terms? For example, in non-disclosure agreements, must obligations be confined to 'need to know' information which is written and marked 'confidential'? If not, why not?

It is good practice for each party to follow up the making of the contract by informing all of its relevant personnel about the contract, its purpose and principal features, performance criteria, timings and consequences of delays or failures in performance. Development of a standard form for this purpose encourages the discipline of routine completion, and acts as a checklist to ensure that all required information is included.

G. Contracts administration

(a) The importance of contracts administration to suppliers

What ongoing obligations are there for the supplier? These need to be identified, recorded and monitored. Failures to perform are breaches of contract. Customer remedies include damages and a possible right to rescind or cancel the contract. At the very least, the entitlement to remedies presents an opportunity for negotiating purposes later on.

Sometimes there is legal exposure. For example, the parties may, consciously or unconsciously, engage in anti-competitive practices. This may render them liable to heavy fines, make the contract unenforceable and create unfavourable publicity.

What undertakings has the customer given that the supplier should note? Does the customer gain access to any confidential information or trade secrets of the supplier? Are there stage payments to be monitored? Is there an interest entitlement to be claimed because of late payment?

(b) The importance of contracts administration to customers

Customers need to satisfy themselves that what has been promised in the contract is received in full.

Many computer contracts contain extensive supplier obligations and these should be regularly reviewed until performance is complete. Customers' confidential information must be protected.

What are the customer's own obligations? Are they being met? The customer must be aware of the consequences of breaches of contract in terms of damages, rescission of the contract or finding itself at a negotiating disadvantage in future dealings with the supplier.

H. Contracts administration procedures

(a) Responsibility

The responsibility for the contracts administration procedures is best performed by a legal or contracts department. If this is not possible, adequate training must be given to whoever is appointed to carry out this function. It is important to establish effective liaison between sales or purchasing account managers and contract administrators. Even a small company should not be excused from its obligations on the grounds that it cannot be expected to have much resource in this area: there is a widespread tendency to pay lip service to these responsibilities, but the liabilities incurred in the event of default will not be token liabilities.

(b) Procedures

(i) Create an administration copy file of all signed contracts and agreements separate from the internal files created for other purposes, such as order processing, accounts or credit control.

(ii) In the case of all negotiated or non-standard agreements, create a pro-forma sheet on which can be recorded in summary form all of the material agreed departures from company policy.

(iii) In the case of all negotiated or non-standard contracts and agreements, create a list of *all* ongoing obligations, for example, confidentiality, discount policy, and separately identify both parties' post-contractual obligations. Although standard terms and conditions will minimise ongoing obligations, there will almost always be some such obligations, for example to keep certain information confidential, and therefore even these contracts will require monitoring.
For the procedures outlined above, a database of negotiated contracts will enable fast checking, access to precedent templates, contract lists and general analysis.

(iv) Append related separate documents, such as specifications, non-disclosure agreements, escrow agreements, service agreements, and so on, so that the complete contract package is readily available for inspection.

(v) Establish procedures for checking that each party's obligations have been performed and that any ancillary matters have been dealt with. For example, track renewal dates; check the insurance; carry out regular credit checks; spot-check the contents and whereabouts of confidential documents: have those no longer required been returned? Are specific requirements, such as custody, of certain files in a safe, being met?

(vi) Provide for notification to relevant management if deadlines are not being achieved (by either side). The contract itself may incorporate precise escalation procedures, in which event these should be followed and monitored.

(vii) In the event of termination of the contract for any reason, a review of all immediately consequential obligations should be undertaken, and steps taken to ensure that they are fully actioned. Some contracts stipulate specific transition or exit arrangements. Where these apply, review and monitor them.

(c) Ongoing contract administration

(i) Periodic checks must be recorded and dated during the currency of each contract. In particular, notice must be taken of:
   - time limits for returning documents and materials, and other property of the other party;
   - compliance with policies regarding provision of spares, ongoing support;
   - rights to material in escrow, including regular checks that the materials deposited remain valid and current;
   - obligations of continuing confidentiality;
   - any breaches of other ongoing rights, for example, intellectual property rights; employment restrictions.

(ii) A final sign-off procedure should confirm the completion of all contract performance when all relevant dates have expired.

(iii) A destruction policy should be established, including the earliest dates for disposal of defined categories of information. Some material is required by law to be held for a minimum period of time and it is prudent in any event to keep records until at least a year after the final date for possible legal action. For example, contracts should be retained for at least seven years after performance has been completed.

(iv) Records must be kept efficiently. The most extensive record of Americans who served in the 1939–45 War was unreadable because no resources, either financial or human, were available for the effort of translating the 1,600 reels of microfilm of computer punched cards on which it was stored. Another example is the BBC's 'Domesday Project'. This created a record of British life for the 900th anniversary of the 1085 Doomsday Book (which is still available to read in the Public Records Office). The material was stored on hardware that has since become obsolete, and is no longer accessible as originally intended. Fortunately this was discovered in time for measures to be taken to preserve the digital materials by means of an emulation process. Even so this will need to be reviewed from time to time to ensure the continued preservation of the data and its migration potential.

I. Insurances and guarantees

These can be regarded as a sub-set of the procedures for contracts administration, with periodic reviews and general monitoring forming part of the process.

(a)   Are one party's goods properly protected when on the other party's premises or in transit? Consider a policy to cover any loopholes or gaps, for example goods left in employees' vehicles.

(b)   Does the supplier have satisfactory levels of public liability insurance? If there are sub-contractors, do they have adequate insurance, to cover their indemnities to the supplier in the event of any failures to perform or negligent performance?

(c)   Are the terms and conditions of any performance bonds satisfactory, if applicable? (It is essential to negotiate such bonds in consultation with the issuing bank before the contract is executed if they are a condition of the contract, in order to be certain that the bonds will be acceptable.)

(d)   Are any parent guarantees or other guarantees still adequate? What enforcement difficulties could there be in the case of foreign-based guarantees?

(e)   Is professional indemnity cover in place for a satisfactory sum, if relevant? These policies, which are expensive, need particularly careful scrutiny of their small print. What exclusions apply? What are the rules of aggregation of claims? Does the cover extend to all overseas markets? Cover for US activities is especially difficult to obtain.

(f)   Are there rights of inspection and verification of premium payments?

(g)   Is it appropriate to have an interest noted on a policy of insurance, or at least to obtain the written agreement of an insurer to notify and provide a reasonable opportunity for responding before cancelling a policy?

J. Conclusion

Instilling an appropriate culture of awareness and compliance is a basic requirement in legal risk management. Training may be necessary from time to time. Refresher courses may need to be considered for existing staff as well as induction courses for new recruits. Audits can be implemented at intervals for particular risks, such as for assessing security or for ascertaining intellectual property rights.

It is essential to integrate legal risk management procedures into working practices, ensuring that they are manageable and practicable.

1   *Leicester Circuits Ltd v Coates Bros plc* [2002] EWHC 812 (QB), [2002] All ER (D) 383 (Feb).

CHAPTER 23
Checklists

Introduction

The following are some brief reminders of the principal points which should be considered in connection with negotiation, for developing expertise and obtaining specialist support, and for the construction of a contract. Then, for the general clauses, and for each of the agreements discussed in this book, reminders are given of some of the decisions that may need to be made before contract drafting or negotiation commences. Finally there is a checklist for administration.

A. Key reminders for negotiation

1. Is a negotiation going to be worthwhile?

- What is the value of the transaction?
- What is the status of the other party?
- What is the likely cost going to be?
- What is the timescale going to be?
- Can negotiation be carried out by correspondence or will a meeting progress matters more effectively?

2. Careful preparation

(A) HOMEWORK

- Knowledge of other party/previous history
- Knowledge of own party's principles and objectives
- Knowledge of legal environment and contract law

- Knowledge of product and services: those the subject of the negotiation and (competitive) alternatives

(B) PREPARATION FOR THE NEGOTIATION

- Strategy

- Tactics

- Team

- Leader:
  - criteria
  - ground rules

3. The negotiation

- Have the correct materials to hand

- Make any presentation succinct

- Aim high

- Use time wisely

- Be prepared to adapt to changing circumstances

- Be aware of how to treat others

- The art of silence

B. Developing expertise and obtaining specialist support

1. Likely requirements

- To write terms and conditions

- To draft agreements

- To analyse responses

- To evaluate the contracts or terms of others (against norms/commercial realities)

- To conduct or guide negotiations

2. What might an organisation do for itself?

- Use checklists, framework structure and precedent agreements: its own; others; standard and specials

- Train its sales and purchasing people

- Acquire ready access to expertise:
  - by employment
  - by identification of a part-time source

- Develop administrative systems

- Know when to get help:
  - the need for particular expertise (complex legal areas)
  - the need for objectivity

- External or in-house seminars:
  - the purpose?
  - from whom?

3. The use of specialists

(A) IN-HOUSE HIRING CRITERIA

- A lawyer?

- A one-person department or part of a team?

- Defined role

- Reporting lines

- Understanding intellectual property rights

- Communication skills

- Industry experience

- Negotiating experience (the importance of range: no two negotiations are ever the same)

- Cost

- Benefits: company and product know-how

(B) EXTERNAL ASSISTANCE

- Availability (but what order of precedence?)

- Cost: negotiable (can it be related to turnover or individual contract values?)

- Reputation

- Benefits:
  - objectivity
  - marketplace knowledge
  - insurance
  - weight given to opinions
  - no conflict of interest

(C) LEADERSHIP ROLE

- Agree the ground rules: before and during negotiations

- Avoid uneconomic use of external resources

- Seek a practical and commercial approach

C. Principal points: contract construction

This process applies equally to the preparation of standard terms and conditions and to bespoke agreements.

- Logical approach: to the process; to the contract

- Research

- Find out what happens now commercially

- Understand:
    - what is wanted
    - what is needed
        (These are not necessarily identical objectives)

- Take into account the value and strategic importance of the transaction

- Is it necessary to incorporate another party's terms?

- Define

- Outline

- Detail: attend to drafting techniques

- Obtain agreement at each stage

- Check the law

- Consider the presentation

- Subsequent amendment by agreement (negotiation).

D. Agreement checklists

1. Standard housekeeping provisions (CHAPTER 6)

- Are there any documents, other contracts or information that should be referred to or included?

- Should there be an 'entire agreement' clause?

- Is there any reason for not including provisions on severability and waiver?

- Does the independence of the parties' relationship need to be clarified?

- Might a third party be able to benefit under or to enforce any term of the agreement?

- Is assignment to be prohibited, or permitted subject to consent?

- Are there any special requirements for giving or receiving formal notices?

- Is there any reason for excluding a force majeure provision, or for specifying conditions which will, or will not, apply?

- Should there be any exclusive or non-exclusive jurisdiction provisions?

- Is an arbitration or Alternative Dispute Resolution provision to be included?

2. Administrative provisions (CHAPTER 7)

DURATION

- Should the contract include a duration provision?

- If so, what will be the term of the contract?

- Is renewal automatic?

- Is the contract terminable on notice by either or both parties?

- Is the contract terminable by the customer in the event of notification of a price increase?

- May notice be given at any time after the initial term or at an anniversary?

CHARGES

- Are the charging arrangements clear, eg fixed price or time and materials; single or recurring charge?

- What do they include/exclude?

- Will price variation be a feature? If so, what will the price variation mechanism be?

- Will there be stage payments/retention of money due?

EXPENSES

- Are these to be included in the charges or separately chargeable, and are permitted expenses to be specified?

PAYMENT TERMS

- What contractual sanctions are there for late payment?

TITLE

- What rights before payment for goods does the supplier need to establish?

- What are the trading circumstances?

- What is the value of the average sale?

- Which party should bear risk of loss from when?

INTELLECTUAL PROPERTY RIGHTS INDEMNITY

- Should this provision be included?

- Where are the products to be used?

- What is the territorial scope of the indemnity?

- What are the limits of the indemnity in respect of the customer's continued use of the product, or the supplier's refund if the customer is not able to continue to use the product?

- Does it link in with the licensor's insurance cover?

INDEMNITIES AND LIMITS OF LIABILITY

- What are the financial limits for different liabilities? Are they covered by insurance?

- Are the exclusions legal, justifiable and reasonable?

- Are the limitations justifiable and reasonable?

- Will the party not at fault have its own responsibilities in limiting the scope for things to go wrong?

INTEGRITY OF DATA

- Is it necessary and is it reasonable to include a provision that the responsibility for the customer's data is the customer's alone?

EMPLOYMENT RESTRICTION

- Is it necessary for either or both parties to be subject to a restriction on soliciting employment of the other party's staff?

- To whom should it apply?

- What length of time for the restriction to apply would be reasonable?

- What payment to the injured party would be appropriate as a genuine pre-estimate of loss?

- Is the whole clause as worded reasonable and likely to be enforceable?

CONFIDENTIALITY

- Is one general clause sufficient, or would a non-disclosure agreement be preferable?
- Should the provisions be mutually applicable?
- To what kind of information should the provision apply?
- Should there be a time limit for the information to be kept confidential?
- What exceptions will there be?

PUBLICITY

- Are there any reasons for publicity about the contract to be prohibited or for approval first to be obtained?
- Are there any reasons for the existence of the contract itself to be kept confidential?

INSURANCE AND GUARANTEES

- Does the customer require the supplier to give specific undertakings about its insurance?
- Will the customer require a performance guarantee?

DATA PROTECTION

- Does the transaction involve personal data?
- Is a general provision sufficient or should more detailed requirements be specified?

EXPORT CONTROL

- Is the supplier required to comply with US export control regulations?
- Is an indemnity from the distributor required?

TERMINATION FOR CAUSE

- On what grounds may the contract be terminated? Non-payment by the customer; material or continuing breach; insolvency? Any other grounds specific to the transaction?

- Are there any specific requirements as a result of termination to be carried out by either party?

3. Non-disclosure (**CHAPTER 8**)

- Is the confidentiality obligation to be reciprocal?

- What is the subject matter comprising the 'confidential information'?

- What is the purpose of disclosing the confidential information?

- Is confidential information to be supplied only in writing, or to be confirmed in writing?

- Will either or both parties appoint a confidential information co-ordinator?

- What are the exceptions to confidentiality in respect of people or information?

- Are special procedures appropriate for receiving, holding and using the confidential information?

- Are there to be any exceptions to what is apparently confidential information?

- Should there be a time limit for the confidentiality obligation to be maintained?

- Is existence of the non-disclosure agreement itself to be regarded as confidential?

4. Computer product supply (**CHAPTER 9**)

- Are there any associated ongoing agreements in place, eg a discount agreement?

- Which products are going to be covered by this contract?

- Is software to be included?

- What is the delivery location address?

- What maximum length of notice and amount of damages are to be agreed in the cancellation and re-scheduling provisions?

- Which acts will constitute delivery?

- Who is to pay for carriage and insurance?

- Who is responsible for arranging and paying for installation into the operating environment?

- When are risk and title to pass?

- How critical is the delivery date to the customer?

- Are partial deliveries to be permitted? If so, will each partial delivery constitute a separate contract?

- What are the consequences of failure to accept?

- What are the criteria for acceptance?

- What are the remedies in the event of failure of acceptance or during warranty?

- What is the length of the warranty period to be?

- Does the nature of the supply justify pricing amendment mechanisms?

5. Leasing (CHAPTER 10)

- What type of lease is required: is it intended that the transaction should be on- or off-balance sheet?

- Is the lessor satisfied with the lessee's business stability and creditworthiness?

- What duration and payment intervals are to be applied?

- In the case of a capital lease, is the option-to-purchase fee to be nominal or substantial? If the latter, how much?

- What schedules will be required (determined by the products and services to be included in the lease)?
    - Terms and conditions of supply?
    - Software licences?
    - Maintenance and support agreements?
    - Other services?
    - Direct debit arrangements?

- Are there any special charges relating to the location of, and access to, the system, unusual risks, special insurances etc?

- Is the lessee required to insure the products, and if so, has the insurable amount been agreed, and is there evidence of insurance (or at least an explanation of the insurance arrangements to be put in place for subsequent verification)?

- Are the security arrangements for the products satisfactory?

- Have the checklists in relation to product supply, licensing and services been reviewed as applicable?

6. Distribution (CHAPTER 11)

- Is the relationship that of independent contractors, for which a distribution agreement is appropriate?

- What is the subject of the agreement? Hardware, software, systems?

- Are the products the supplier's own, or is the supplier itself an intermediary?

- Is the distributor adding services/products for onward supply?

- Will the distributor be supplying to end users?

- Is the arrangement exclusive or sole? Is it acceptable under competition law?

- What is the territory?

- Will the distributor have to meet targets? What happens if the targets are not achieved?

- How is the software being distributed? Is the distributor copying a master disk, or is the distributor supplying software direct from the manufacturer?

- What are the distributor's responsibilities?

- What are the supplier's responsibilities?

- Who is responsible for advertising and merchandising?

- Is the distributor carrying out any support work for software: first-line or second-line or all support work?

- Is the distributor separately licensed by the supplier for its own use of software provided by the supplier?

- Identify the distributor's application software

- Identify the trade marks of the supplier

- Are there any specific requirements on termination, to allow for end users' licences or other aspects?

7. Software licences (**CHAPTER 12**)

- What does the software to be licensed comprise?

- Is source code or object code to be supplied?

- Is use to be restricted to a particular environment, computer configuration, business site, multi-site?

- Who is the owner of the software: the licensor or a third party?

- Is the licence to be for a specific term?

- Is support to be provided by the licensor and, if so, will this be as a separate agreement or as part of the licence agreement terms and conditions?

- Is the licence fee to be one-off or by regular payments?

- Will there be specific delivery and installation provisions for the software?

- What are the acceptance provisions?

- Does the licence permit use of the software for testing in disaster recovery circumstances, for use at a remote site in the event of disaster, for use in outsourcing?

- What is the extent of confidentiality required?

- Is escrow a requirement?

8. Source code deposit (**CHAPTER 13**)

- Does the software concerned need regular support and enhancement?

- Is the software so important to the business that a supplier's insolvency would be cause for concern?

- Is only object code being licensed?

- Is the licensor actually the owner of the software?

- Is there a valid licence agreement?

- Is the licensee also the distributor of the software?

- Is the trigger event only to be insolvency, or is it to include failure to support the software?

- What is being deposited comprising the source code?

- What does a 'version' for deposit comprise?

- Does the licensee have its own review procedure to ensure that renewed copies of source code continue to be deposited?

- Does the licensor have administrative procedures to ensure that a new version of source code is deposited as agreed?

- Does the escrow custodian have suitable administrative procedures in order to monitor the licensor's obligations and inform the licensee whenever a source code update has been received?

- Does the agreement restrict the use of the source code by the licensee in the event of legitimate access?

- Are there satisfactory independent procedures for verification of source code?

- Are there sufficient procedures for the escrow arrangements to continue in the event of termination of this particular agreement?

- Are there adequate procedures agreed in the event of disputes?

9. Maintenance and support (**CHAPTER 14**)

- Is the agreement between supplier and customer only, or between supplier and reseller customer with end users?

- What are the hardware products to which the agreement applies?

- What are the software products to which the agreement applies?

- What are the supplier's details for the maintenance and support centre and telephone helpline?

- Are there any special terms and conditions applicable to individual sites where the products are located?

- Will the supplier's normal working hours provide sufficient cover?

- What are the supplier's extended cover charges?

- What are the hardware services to be provided?

- What are the software services to be provided?

- What qualifying and excluding criteria apply?

- Are the exclusions acceptable for the customer?

- What optional services are available?

10. Consultancy (**CHAPTER 15**)

- Is the provision of services for a single self-contained project, for which a software development agreement would be more appropriate?

- What are the services that are to be provided?

- Are project management services required?

- Is the provision of consultancy services to be by an independent consultant or through a limited company? If independent, is the tax status clear and unambiguous?

- Is there a particular resource requirement in terms of numbers, skills or identified named consultants?

- Are the consultant's role and functions clear?

- What is the extent of the consultant's project management and decision-making responsibilities?

- Are specific project results required?

- Can acceptance criteria be defined?

- Are there any timetables or time constraints required by the services?

- Will the results of the services require a decision as to copyright ownership or licensing arrangements?

- Where are the consultancy services to be carried out?

- What is the basis of the charges and how are they to be calculated? Are expenses separately chargeable?

- Are there any specific terms of payment, such as a payment schedule?

- Can the consultancy responsibilities and time schedules be sufficiently defined?

- Which of the client's computer systems is the consultant entitled to access?

11. Software Development (CHAPTER 16)

- Which approach is proposed: 'conventional' or 'prototype' methodology?

- Is the production of the specification to be a separate exercise?

- What warranties will the supplier provide?

- What are the charging methods?

- Has a price been agreed?

- Can payments be related to milestones in the project development?

- Does the software depend on particular equipment?

- Is third party software involved?

- Who is to own the software developed?

- What are the change control mechanisms to be?

- What performance criteria should be defined?

- To what extent can the acceptance testing process be defined at the outset?

- Is there to be a sanction for payments by the supplier in the event of delayed implementation?

- Is the customer able to specify named staff of the supplier to work on the project?

- What are the progress meeting mechanisms to comprise?

- Does the customer wish to restrict provision of similar software to competitors?

- What post-implementation support will be required?

12. Outsourcing Services (CHAPTER 17)

- Define the objectives of the outsourcing

- Define the scope of the outsourcing

- Define the services

- Identify the equipment concerned. Is the provider or the client to provide the equipment and is a separate agreement required?

- Are there any technical requirements to be specified?

- Where are the services to be carried out? Are the customer's premises being transferred?

- Identify the relevant employees. Will the Transfer of Undertakings Regulations apply?

- What separate agreements will be required (Business Transfer, Employee Transfer, Services, Service Levels)?

- Define the service levels and the key service levels

- Are any special security arrangements required?

- Calculate the basis and formulae for the charges

- Are the provider's expenses payable, and on what basis?

- What usage statistics will be regularly required?

- Define the compensation for key service level failures

- Identify the client software concerned

- Identify the third party software concerned

- Is personal data involved?

- Have the third party software owners consented to the arrangements?

- Have change control procedures been agreed?

- Identify the provider's services manager

- Identify the client's liaison manager

- Who are the provider's key personnel?

- Have the monitoring procedures been agreed?

- Who will the Contract Management Group members be?

- Is a contingency/disaster plan agreed?

- Determine the transfer date and the commencement date

- For how long is the agreement initially to run? Is there to be an optional extension or a notice option? How much notice of termination is required?

- What arrangements have been agreed for handover in the event of termination? Can a transition plan be drawn up before execution of the Agreement?

13. Application service provision (CHAPTER 18)

- What services are required/provided?

- How flexible are the services in terms of customisation and value-added features?

- Do the services cover development, hosting and support?

- Who is responsible for the network, hardware, software and services?

- Is the client an intermediary for end users, and if so is the client active in service provision to end users or in its use of the services itself?

- Who owns the application itself?

- What are the provider's obligations?

- Are there separate service procedures to assist in operation?

- Is training required?

- Is there a specific technical environment that needs to be identified?

- Are levels of performance and availability guaranteed?

- Is security important for the application and services, and is it provided as required?

- Does scalability need to be built into the contract, for increasing or declining usage?

- How will changes to the services or volumes be effected?

- How will upgrades be provided and managed?

- How are the services to be paid for?

- What do the charges cover and what do they exclude?

- Is an independent audit required?

- How will outages be handled?

- Is an exit strategy for the client available?

14. Website development and maintenance (CHAPTER 19)

- Are the services to be for a self-contained development project?

- Are ongoing services to be provided, and what will they include: support, hosting, content development?

- What is the domain name for the website?

- What are the objectives for the website?

- Is the website to be integrated with existing websites of the client's?

- How are the services to be paid for?

- Are the charges to be linked to targets or incentives, such as sales or numbers of visitors?

- Is content to be provided by the designer?

- Are there any concerns about the designer working on competitors' websites?

- What restrictions are there on style or format?

- How often is material to be updated?

- Does the designer have responsibilities for the accuracy of the content, and for keeping it up to date?

- Has the ownership of the different aspects been agreed – bespoke design, software code, designer's know-how, support materials, client branding and domain name, content in different media, third party software or data?

- Have third party licences and permissions been obtained?

- Do trade mark and logo permissions need to be obtained?

- Have links to other sites been agreed with the third parties?

- Are disclaimers, privacy notices, opt-in requests, part of the content?

- Will the website comply with regulatory requirements and disability compliance guidelines?

- What security features are there?

- May the designer use the client's name in publicity?

- Are there technical controls such as encryption or time-barring?

- How often is the website to be backed up?

- Are the service levels defined and agreed?

- Has the implementation plan been drawn up and agreed?

15. E-commerce value added reseller agreement (CHAPTER 20)

- Is the supplier/distributor able to provide useful analysis of website activity and how detailed is the information?

- Does the website provide detailed analysis of products, comparisons with competitive products and guidance on use?

- Who will be responsible for support of products and what will be the mechanisms for delivery of that support?

- Are all the author responsibilities, including the procedures for product submission, reasonable for the author to comply with?

- Will the author be able to comply with appropriate quality standards and be willing to give an indemnity?

- Will the supplier/distributor have its own procedures to ensure that quality is acceptable?

- Will additional activities be of interest to the author, such as marketing campaigns, co-operative advertising and direct mailings, and what fees and terms will apply?

- Is the author willing to deposit its source codes in escrow?

- What commissions will be paid for sales of products?

- Is any fee payable for the promotional aspects of the distribution services?

- Are there audit arrangements in place?

- Does the author accept the terms and conditions in the supplier/ distributor's generic end user software licence agreement?

16. Disaster recovery (CHAPTER 21)

- Is the definition of 'disaster' sufficiently comprehensive?

- Is the configuration sufficiently defined?

- Where is the disaster recovery site to be?

- How many other customers will have access to that site?

- Are the services to be provided at all times, or are there to be exclusions?

- Are the procedures for access to the site clear, and does everyone who needs to know about them know where they can be found?

- Are testing facilities available?

- Is there a requirement to process personal data, and thus to ensure that the supplier is registered?

17. Administration and legal risk management (CHAPTER 22)

- Is the significance of administration and legal risk management understood?

- Is the contract used strategically?

- Are procedures in place for order administration and applied strategically?

- Are responsibilities and procedures for ongoing contract administration maintained?

- Are there compliance policies as appropriate?

- For customers, is the legal effect of issuing the order understood?

- Is it clear which set of terms and conditions applies to a transaction?

- Is there a manual of contracts policies and procedures, and is it kept up to date?

- Has a register of non-disclosure agreements been established and is it updated regularly and internally audited from time to time?

- Is there a file for all signed contracts and associated materials, and is it maintained?

- Are departures from company policy in individual contracts recorded and filed?

- Is there a procedure for informing personnel of the relevant parts of the contract, once executed?

- Is there a contract monitoring procedure for monitoring each party's ongoing contractual obligations, to maintain maximum contractual advantage, and to safeguard commercial and financial interests?

- Is there a document destruction policy and is it followed?

- Are the insurance requirements checked each time?

Precedent Agreement Contents

Introduction to Precedents

The following represents a selection of IT contract precedents, many of which are based on the contracts discussed in the individual chapters.

However, they are rarely going to be suitable for any particular transaction as they stand, and they are not intended to be so used. We recommend that they should be referred to as a guide and framework in combination with the commentary in the relevant chapter.

To create a good contract it is essential that the commercial transaction for which it is being drafted is fully understood in the light of its individual requirements, in order to exclude provisions which are immaterial in the context, and to include those terms which do matter and are applicable. The sequence and sense of the terms overall must also be considered, so that the contract is an integrated and comprehensible whole.

Legal advice may also be necessary or helpful, and it must be remembered that the law changes and should be consulted in relation to specific aspects.

NON-DISCLOSURE AGREEMENT

Date of agreement ....

1. Introduction

In consideration of the disclosure to .... ('**Recipient**') whose registered office is at .... of information relating to proprietary, technological, business and technical matters of .... ('**Owner**') whose registered office is at .... including but not limited to documents, drawings, diagrams, models and programs or any part or copy of such information as more specifically identified in Exhibit A attached to and forming part of this Agreement ('**Confidential Information**'), the Recipient undertakes:

1.1 to receive and hold the Confidential Information in the strictest confidence and to take all reasonable security precautions in the safekeeping of the Confidential Information and in preventing its unauthorised disclosure to third parties, applying no lesser security measures to it than to its own confidential information;

1.2 not to disclose the Confidential Information to any third party without the Owner's prior written consent (excluding professional advisers who are bound by client confidentiality obligations);

1.3 to use the Confidential Information solely for the Business Purpose specified in Exhibit A;

1.4 to make copies of the Confidential Information only as strictly necessary [with the prior written consent of the Owner] and not to copy or store the Confidential Information electronically or transmit it outside its usual place of business;

1.5 to ensure that its employees are given access to the Confidential Information only on a 'need to know' basis for the purposes of dealing with the Owner, and that these employees are informed of the confidential nature of the Confidential Information [and are contractually bound to safeguard the Confidential Information].

2. Confidential Information Co-ordinator

The Recipient appoints the person so designated in Exhibit A as its **Confidential Information Co-ordinator** for the receipt and dispatch of the Confidential Information, or any other person who may be designated by the Recipient to the Owner in writing.

3. Exceptions

The parties agree that information is not to be regarded as Confidential Information and that the Recipient will have no obligation with respect to any information which the Recipient can demonstrate:

3.1   is already known to, or in the possession of, the Recipient prior to its receipt from the Owner or which is publicly available at the time of disclosure; or

3.2   is or becomes known to the public through no wrongful act of the Recipient; or

3.3   is received from a third party who is not in breach of any obligation of confidentiality; or

3.4   is used or disclosed with the prior written authorisation of the Owner; or

3.5   is disclosed by the Recipient in compliance with a legal requirement of a governmental agency or otherwise where disclosure is required by operation of law; or

3.6   is developed independently by the Recipient; or

3.7   relates to general concepts of information technology.

4. Intellectual Property Rights, Warranties and Disclaimers

4.1   The Owner retains all intellectual property rights in the Confidential Information at all times and for all purposes [including the copyright in any material(s) produced by the Recipient relating to the Confidential Information].

4.2   Nothing contained in this Agreement is to be construed as granting or conferring any rights by licence or otherwise, expressly, or by implication, for any invention, discovery or improvement made or acquired by the Owner before or after the date of this Agreement relating to the Confidential Information.

4.3   The Owner gives no warranty, express or implied, in respect of the Confidential Information.

4.4   The Owner accepts no responsibility for any expenses or losses incurred or actions undertaken by the Recipient as a result of the Recipient's receipt of the Confidential Information. It is understood by the Recipient that the Owner does not warrant or represent that it will enter into any further contract with the Recipient in connection with the development or supply of any product or service to which the Confidential Information relates.

5. Non-Conflicting Activities

5.1   This Non-Disclosure Agreement will not limit developments by the Recipient which involve processes, techniques or technology of a similar nature to that disclosed, provided that such development is accomplished without the use of the Confidential Information.

5.2 It is acknowledged that both parties are free to enter into similar agreements with third parties, provided that the obligations of this Agreement are not breached.

6. Termination and Time Limit

6.1 This Agreement may be terminated at any time by written notice of termination served by either party on the other.

6.2 Upon request, and in any event upon termination for whatever reason, or in the event of any breach of these terms by the Recipient, the Recipient will immediately return all tangible materials in its possession relating to the Confidential Information including, but not limited to, drawings, documents, hardware, disks and tapes, destroying or erasing any copies, notes or extracts, and any other records containing the Confidential Information, so that no Confidential Information is retained by the Recipient.

6.3 This Agreement is in addition to, and not instead of, any other written agreements between the parties. The parties' obligations under this Agreement will survive the termination of this Agreement [for a period of [five] years from the date of first disclosure of the Confidential Information to the Recipient].

7. Publicity

The existence of this Agreement and of any relationship between the parties concerning the Confidential Information is confidential, and neither party will publish or permit to be published any information about their relationship [or about the Business Purpose] unless that information has first been approved for publication by the other party.

8. General

8.1 **Severability**
If any of the provisions of this Agreement is judged to be illegal or unenforceable, the continuation in full force and effect of the remainder of them will not be prejudiced.

8.2 **Waiver**
No forbearance or delay by either party in enforcing its respective rights will prejudice or restrict the rights of that party, and no waiver of any such rights or of any breach of any contractual terms will be deemed to be a waiver of any other right or of any later breach.

8.3 No rights of third parties

A person, company or other organisation who is not a party to this Agreement has no right to enforce any term of this Agreement.

8.4 Governing Law and Jurisdiction

This Agreement is governed by English Law and the parties submit to the jurisdiction of the English Courts.

Signed by

....

Authorised Representative of Recipient

Name

....

Date

....

Signed by

....

Authorised Representative of Owner

Name

....

Date

....

EXHIBIT A

To the Agreement dated

....

made between .... and

....

Confidential Information:

Business Purpose:

Recipient's Confidential Information Co-ordinator:

COMPUTER PRODUCT SUPPLY TERMS AND CONDITIONS

THE SUPPLIER ....

of ....

....

.... ('**Supplier**')

1. Introduction

1.1   These terms and conditions govern the sale to the customer ('Customer') of the Supplier's Products, subject only to any additional terms and conditions contained in a current discount or other special written agreement between the parties. Unless otherwise expressly agreed by the Supplier in writing, these terms and conditions will apply to any orders from the Customer for Products or Services, and will supersede any other terms and conditions referred to, offered, or relied on by the Customer. No other terms or conditions will apply except as provided for below.

1.2   THE CUSTOMER HEREBY DECLARES THAT IT HAS ACCEPTED THESE TERMS AND CONDITIONS IN THE KNOWLEDGE THAT THE LIABILITY OF THE SUPPLIER IS LIMITED AND THAT THE CHARGES PAYABLE FOR PRODUCTS HAVE BEEN CALCULATED ACCORDINGLY.

1.3   Any order placed with the Supplier by the Customer will constitute an offer to the Supplier subject to these terms and conditions and will be subject to acceptance by the Supplier at its above address.

2. Definitions

'*Contract*' means any agreement between the parties resulting from a Customer order for the supply of Products, which expressly or by implication incorporates these terms and conditions.

'*DDP*' means 'delivered duty paid' as that expression is defined in the International Chamber of Commerce INCOTERMS 1990 Edition.

'*Hardware*' means the hardware components of the Supplier's products including all ancillary equipment, accessories, spares, supplies and related documentation.

'*Licence Agreement*' means the terms and conditions governing the supply of Software whether the Supplier's own software or third party software which the Supplier is authorised to supply to the Customer.

518

'*Products*' means the Supplier's standard Hardware and Software products appearing in the current edition of its Standard Product Catalogue. Non-standard products, including products to be specially developed or adapted to meet the Customer's particular requirements and all services offered by the Supplier, including maintenance and support, training and education, and consultancy services, are not Products to which these terms and conditions apply, but are supplied on the terms and conditions contained in the Supplier's applicable service-related agreements.

'*Site*' means the installation site(s) in the United Kingdom to which any item of Hardware or Software is delivered, identified in the Schedule.

'*Software*' means any operating system, utility or applications software delivered by the Supplier in machine-readable object, printed or interpreted form and either incorporated with Hardware or separately supplied, including related documentation.

3. Associated Agreements

If these terms and conditions are incorporated by reference into any other form of agreement between the Supplier and the Customer and that other agreement is currently in effect at the time the Contract is made, so that the Contract constitutes a contract for the purposes of that agreement, the terms and conditions of such agreement will prevail in the event, but only to the extent, of any conflict of meaning with these terms and conditions.

4. Substitutions and Modifications

The Supplier reserves the right to make improvements, substitutions or modifications to any part of the Products, provided that such improvements, substitutions or modifications will not materially and adversely affect the capability of the Hardware or Software or overall Products to perform and function in accordance with the Supplier's applicable test procedures.

5. Cancellation, Rescheduling and Change Orders

5.1   If the Customer cancels all or any part of an order, or requests changes to the date of shipment or to the configuration ordered at least 30 days before the scheduled delivery [ex-factory shipment] date or requested delivery date, whichever is the later, there will be no cancellation or rescheduling charges. But if such cancellation or rescheduling or change of configuration request is less than 30 days from the scheduled or requested delivery date, the Customer agrees to pay a cancellation, rescheduling or reconfiguring charge of 25% of the purchase price agreed with the Customer at the time the order was placed.

5.2   In the event of any configuration changes, if these require the supply of additional items, the purchase price will be increased in accordance with the

Supplier's price list but subject to any applicable discounts and the Supplier also reserves the right to extend the scheduled shipment date. The purchase price will be reduced in respect of cancelled items.

5.3 Where delivery is postponed by the Supplier, the Customer will be entitled to cancel all or part of the affected order without charge if the Supplier is unable to give a revised delivery date, or within seven days of notification by the Supplier of a revised delivery date.

5.4 The Customer agrees that the charges set out in this clause are reasonable and are intended as liquidated damages and not as penalties, recognising that the Supplier's costs in these various circumstances will be difficult to estimate or calculate precisely.

6. Delivery

6.1 Delivery will be DDP.

6.2 The Customer will make the Site available for inspection by appropriate Supplier staff at an agreed time during a period of 30 days before the scheduled delivery date shown in the Supplier's Order Acceptance, if so required by the Supplier.

6.3 The Customer will furnish the necessary labour (if the Supplier so requires under the Supplier's direction) for taking any Hardware into its designated operating point, unpacking it and placing it in the desired location.

6.4 Unless otherwise specified by the Customer, delivery will be made to the Site.

6.5 Delivery date(s) referred to in the Contract or in any quotation, or in any order acknowledgment, order acceptance or elsewhere are approximate only and not of any contractual effect. While the Supplier will use all reasonable endeavours to meet any scheduled delivery date so referred to in the Contract, it will not be liable for any loss or damage (including loss of use, loss of contract or loss of profits) incurred by the Customer as a result of any failure to deliver on any particular date.

6.6 Each delivery of Products will be deemed to constitute a separate enforceable contract to which these terms and conditions will apply.

6.7 If the Customer refuses or fails to take delivery of Products tendered in accordance with these terms and conditions, delivery will nevertheless be deemed to have taken place for the purpose of the Supplier's rights to payment and the Supplier will be entitled to store the Products at the Customer's risk and expense, including all transportation charges.

6.8 On delivery at the entrance to the Site, the Customer will be responsible for and will bear the entire risk of loss or damage to Hardware or to Software media, regardless of when acceptance occurs. If the Customer wishes to make any claims for shortages or for damaged Products, full particulars must be notified to the Supplier within seven days of delivery.

6.9 Title to Hardware will pass to the Customer upon receipt of payment in full. TITLE TO SOFTWARE WHETHER THE SUPPLIER'S PROPRIETARY SOFT-WARE OR SOFTWARE LICENSED BY THE SUPPLIER WILL NOT PASS TO THE CUSTOMER UNDER ANY CIRCUMSTANCES.

6.10 The Customer is entitled at its own expense, directly or through a nominated independent test agency acceptable to the Supplier, to inspect the Supplier's manufacturing and distribution processes so far as they relate to the Products, by prior appointment during normal business hours. All Products are constructed and delivered in a safe condition and will remain safe provided that they are correctly installed and maintained in accordance with the Supplier's recommendations.

6.11 Risk will pass to the Customer at the time of delivery. Title to Hardware only will pass to the Customer when all prices, taxes and charges due have been paid in full. Software supplied by the Supplier is not sold but is supplied under the terms and conditions set out at clause 8.

7. Hardware

7.1 Where installation or training is not included in the purchase price and not ordered by the Customer, the Customer will be solely responsible for this, and the Supplier disclaims all liability in this connection.

7.2 Where the Hardware includes data communications equipment and data transmission speeds are given in relation to any item of Hardware, these are at all times subject to any conditions of the applicable telecommunications utility company relating to the use of the relevant modem at the speeds indicated and to the capability of any of that company's equipment to which the Hardware is linked.

7.3 Acceptance will be accomplished by using test procedures and/or programs established by the Supplier which are applicable to the Products. Acceptance will take place at the Site when the Supplier demonstrates that the applicable diagnostic and/or verification programs work properly. If the Supplier's demonstration of the test procedures and/or programs at the Site is delayed for more than seven working days other than through any fault of the Supplier, the Products will be deemed to be accepted. In the event that any item of Hardware or Software fails the acceptance procedures the Supplier will at its option, replace or repair that item.

7.4 All proprietary rights in all patents, designs, copyrights, engineering details, schematics, drawings and other similar data relating to the Hardware are and will at all times remain vested in the Supplier. The sale of Hardware to the Customer does not convey any ownership or licence to exploit any of the proprietary rights of the Supplier in the Hardware. Any such proprietary rights granted to the Customer by the Supplier will be granted only subject to a separate non-transferable, non-exclusive licence agreement. All operating instructions, manuals and other documentation referencing the Hardware

521

and supplied by the Supplier are the copyright of the Supplier and will not be copied or disclosed to any third party without the prior express written consent of the Supplier.

8. Software

8.1 Copyright subsists in all Software and all related documentation (whether printed or stored electronically) and whether it is the Supplier's proprietary Software or Software supplied by the Supplier under licence. All Software and related documentation is supplied to the Customer only under the terms and conditions of the applicable Licence Agreement (whether this has been signed and/or returned to the Supplier or not). No part of the Software may be copied, reproduced or utilised in any form by any means without the prior approval of the Supplier. Title or ownership to Software does not transfer to the Customer under any circumstances.

8.2 Where the Customer has not signed the applicable Licence Agreement in advance, the Customer undertakes to return the Licence Agreement supplied with each item of Software, duly signed by the Customer's authorised representative, prior to the Customer using that item of Software. It is the sole responsibility of the Customer to comply with all of the terms and conditions of the Licence Agreement, and the Customer is hereby notified that any failure to comply with such terms and conditions may result in the revocation of its licence to use the Software.

8.3 Software is warranted in accordance with the terms of the Licence Agreement governing its supply. The sole obligation of the Supplier under such warranty will be limited to the use of all reasonable efforts to correct any failure of the Software to conform to its user manual current at the date of delivery and to supply the Customer with a corrected version of the Software as soon as practicable after the Customer has notified the Supplier of any defects.

8.4 The Customer is not authorised to sub-license the Software to any third party except where the Customer is an OEM or VAR of the Supplier when the terms and conditions relating to such sub-licensing in the OEM or VAR Agreement signed by the Customer will apply.

9. Prices and Payment Terms

9.1 The charges for the Products supplied under these terms and conditions will be set out in the Schedule. The charges are exclusive of Value Added Tax, and any similar taxes. All such taxes are payable by the Customer and will be applied in accordance with UK legislation in force at the tax point date.

9.2 Unless and until credit payment terms are established, all Charges are payable in £ sterling in full (without any deduction or set-off) by the Customer to the Supplier on or before delivery, against invoice.

9.3   The Supplier will be entitled without prejudice to its other rights to require payment in advance of delivery in relation to any order if the total amount then owed by the Customer to the Supplier exceeds the credit limit established by the Supplier for the Customer.

9.4   Payments which are not received when payable will be considered overdue and remain payable by the Customer together with interest for late payment from the date payable at the statutory rate applicable as well after as before any judgment, and independent of such judgment. This interest will accrue on a daily basis and be payable on demand.

9.5   Notwithstanding the above provision for late payment, in this event the Supplier may at its option, and without prejudice to any other remedy at any time after payment has become due, terminate or temporarily suspend performance of the Contract.

9.6   If the Supplier becomes entitled to terminate the Contract for any reason, any sums then due to the Supplier will immediately become payable in full.

10. Price Changes

The Supplier reserves the right, by giving notice to the Customer at any time before delivery, to increase the price of the Products to reflect any increase in the cost to the Supplier which is due to any fact beyond the Supplier's control, such as, but not limited to, any foreign exchange fluctuation, currency regulation, alteration of duties, significant increase in the costs of labour, materials or other costs of manufacture, any change in delivery dates, quantities or specifications for the Products which is requested by the Customer, or any delay caused by any instructions of the Customer or by the Customer's failure to give the Supplier adequate information or instructions.

11. Warranties

11.1   The Supplier warrants that it has good title to or right to supply the Products.

11.2 Hardware warranties

(a)   The Supplier warrants that it has good title to or the legal right to supply all Hardware supplied to the Customer. Hardware is warranted against defects in workmanship and materials for a period of 90 days from the date of delivery, or 90 days from the date of acceptance, whichever is earlier. Where the Supplier has not installed the Hardware, the warranty under this clause is subject to final approval of the installation by the Supplier at the Customer's expense. Where the Supplier has installed the Hardware, the Supplier's sole responsibility under this warranty will be, at its option, either to repair or replace during its normal working hours, any component which proves defective during the warranty period. All replaced Hardware or parts will become the Supplier's property. The warranty service will be performed at the Supplier's repair facility, or on Site (except in the case of minor component repairs) if the Supplier has installed the Hardware or if the Customer has a current Support Agreement with the Supplier covering the Hardware. Returns will be in accordance with the Supplier's shipping instructions, freight prepaid, but return freight costs will be paid by the Supplier. In any case where the Supplier reasonably determines that the Hardware is not defective within the terms of the warranty, the Customer will pay the Supplier all costs of handling, transportation and repairs at the Supplier's then prevailing rates.

(b) The stated warranties apply only to the initial end user of the Hardware and are contingent upon proper treatment and use of the Products with no unauthorised modifications and maintenance, at a safe and suitable Site.

11.3 Except for the express warranties stated above, the Supplier disclaims and excludes all other warranties whether express or implied in law or otherwise, and the above warranties are in lieu of all obligations and liabilities on the part of the Supplier for damages arising out of or in connection with the Products, including, without limitation, any warranty of satisfactory quality or fitness for a particular purpose.

12. Indemnities and Limits of Liability

12.1 The Supplier will indemnify the Customer for direct physical injury or death caused solely either by defects in any of the Products or by the negligence of its employees acting within the course of their employment and the scope of their authority.

12.2 The Supplier will indemnify the Customer for direct damage to property caused solely either by defects in any of the Products or by the negligence of its employees acting within the course of their employment and the scope of their authority. The total liability of the Supplier in such circumstances will be limited to £250,000 for any one event or series of connected events.

12.3 Subject to clauses 12.1 and 12.2, the Supplier's liability for any breach of these terms and conditions or the Contract will be limited to a refund of the Charges paid by the Customer for the Products. In no event will the Supplier be liable for any costs of procurement of substitute Products.

12.4 Except as stated in clause 11, this clause 12 and clause 13, the Supplier disclaims all liability to the Customer in connection with these terms and conditions including the Customer's use of the Products, and in no event will the Supplier be liable to the Customer for indirect or consequential damages or for loss of profits or arising from loss of data.

13. Intellectual Property Rights Indemnity

13.1 The Supplier, at its own expense, will defend or cause to be defended or, at its option, settle any claim or action brought against the Customer on the issue of infringement of any United Kingdom intellectual property right by the Products ('Claim'). Subject to the other conditions of this clause, the Supplier will pay any final judgment entered against the Customer with respect to any Claim provided that the Customer:

(a)   notifies the Supplier in writing of the Claim immediately on becoming aware of it;

(b)   grants sole control of the defence of the Claim to the Supplier; and

(c)   gives the Supplier complete and accurate information and full assistance to enable the Supplier to settle or defend the Claim.

13.2 If any part of the Products should become the subject of any Claim, or if a Court judgment is made that the Products do infringe, or if the use or licensing of any part of the Products is restricted, the Supplier at its option and expense may:

(a)   obtain for the Customer the right under the patent, design right, trade secret or copyright to continue to use the Products; or

(b)   replace or modify the Products so that they become non-infringing; or

(c)   if the use of the Products is prevented by permanent injunction, accept return of them and refund an amount equal to the sum paid by the Customer for the Products, subject to straight line depreciation over a five-year period.

13.3 The Supplier will have no liability under this clause for:

(a)   any infringement arising from the combination of the Products with other products not supplied by the Supplier; or

(b)   the modification of the Products unless the modification was made or approved expressly by the Supplier; or

(c)   supplying the Customer with any information, data, service or applications assistance.

13.4 In no circumstances will the Supplier be liable for any costs or expenses incurred by the customer without the Supplier's written authorisation and the foregoing states the exclusive remedy of the Customer in respect of any intellectual property right infringement by the Products.

14. Confidentiality

The Customer will keep confidential and not disclose without the Supplier's written consent any confidential information which it may obtain. The Customer will take all reasonable steps to ensure that its employees and contractors are bound by the same obligation.

15. Export and Re-export Limitation

Having regard to the current statutory or other United Kingdom Government regulations in force from time to time and, in the case of Products manufactured in the United States of America, to the United States Department of Commerce export regulations in force from time to time, and regardless of any disclosure made by the Customer to the Supplier of an ultimate destination for any Products, the Customer will not export or re-export directly or indirectly any Products without first obtaining all such written consents or authorisation as may be required by any applicable government regulations.

16. Telecommunications Requirements

When computer equipment is connected to a public network, ie a switchboard or telephone network, certain regulations of the telecommunications provider apply. It is the sole responsibility of the Customer to ensure compliance with all such regulations.

17. Maintenance and Support Services

The Hardware and Software warranties in these terms and conditions and the applicable Licence Agreements are provided to ensure that all Products delivered to the Customer operate in accordance with their specification following initial installation and commissioning. Customers with complex or significant computer installations or whose requirements for up-time are above average are likely to require much greater maintenance and support for their Products from the date of delivery than is provided for under warranty. Accordingly, the Customer is recommended to contract for hardware maintenance and software support in respect of all of the Hardware and Software from their date of delivery to the Customer and in any event immediately upon the expiry of any warranty periods. Full descriptions of the Supplier's maintenance and support services and the related terms and conditions are contained in the applicable maintenance and support agreements.

18. Life-endangering Applications

The Products are designed for standard commercial use and are not intended to be installed or used in hazardous or life-threatening environments or for potentially life-endangering applications, including but not limited to environments or applications involving safety critical systems in the nuclear industry or the control of aircraft in the air. The Customer undertakes not to use or supply the Products for any of these purposes and agrees to indemnify and hold the Supplier harmless from and against all liabilities and related costs arising out of the use of any of the Products for any of these purposes.

19. General Contract Provisions

19.1 **Variations**

No variation of these terms and conditions will be valid unless confirmed in writing by authorised signatories of both parties on or after the date of this Agreement.

19.2 **Severability**

If any of the provisions of this Agreement is judged to be illegal or unenforceable, the continuation in full force and effect of the remainder of them will not be prejudiced.

19.3 **Waiver**

No forbearance or delay by either party in enforcing its respective rights will prejudice or restrict the rights of that party, and no waiver of any such rights or of any breach of any contractual terms will be deemed to be a waiver of any other right or of any later breach.

19.4 **Rights of Third Parties**

A person who is not a party to this Agreement has no right to benefit under or to enforce any term of these terms and conditions or of the Contract.

19.5 **Notices**

Any notice given under these terms and conditions by either party to the other must be in writing and may be delivered personally or by first-class post, and in the case of post will be deemed to have been given two working days after the date of posting where the addresses of the parties are both within the United Kingdom or seven working days after the date of posting where the notice is addressed to or is posted from an address outside the United Kingdom. Notices will be delivered or sent to the address of the respective party as set out in the Schedule.

19.6 **Force Majeure**

Neither party will be liable to the other party for any delay in or failure to perform its obligations (other than a payment of money) as a result of any cause beyond its reasonable control, including but not limited to any industrial dispute.

19.7 **Governing Law and Jurisdiction**

This Agreement is governed by and construed according to English law and the parties submit to the non-exclusive jurisdiction of the courts of England and Wales.

SCHEDULE CONTENTS

- Names and Addresses of the Parties (including delivery and invoice addresses)

- Agreement Reference Number

- Agreement Date

- Order Number

- Product Descriptions

- Quantities

- Delivery Date(s); Special Delivery Instructions

- Site

- Installation

- Charges, including any discount rates

- Special or Credit Payment Terms

- Other Special Conditions

- Authorised Signatures.

FIXED TERM LEASE AGREEMENT

Agreement No: ....

LESSOR NAME AND ADDRESS

....

....

....

....

LESSEE DETAILS

Full Name ....

Address ....

....

....

.... Postcode ....

E-mail Address ....

Delivery Address
(if different from above)

....

....

.... Postcode ....

Telephone   ....

Fax   ....

Contact Name   ....

Nature of Business   ....

Number of Years Trading   .... years

Company Registered No   ....
(if applicable)

FINANCING
DETAILS

1. Fixed Term   ....
(words)   months

2. Payment Intervals ....
(words)

*(first payment due in
advance of delivery
of Goods)*

3. Total Cash Price   £ ....   VAT @ 17.5% £ ....
of leased Goods

4. Minimum Initial   £ ....   *(Total VAT on Goods + 1st Monthly*
Payment (in   *Payment + Facility Fee)*
advance)

5. Minimum No of Further Payments (words)
(Monthly/Quarterly) *(delete as applicable)* .... each of
£ ....

6. Option to   £ ....
Purchase Fee

#TableE

This is a FIXED TERM Agreement in FIVE parts: (1) this first signature page, (2) the Schedule of Goods being leased and any Special Conditions (Schedule One), (3) the Terms and Conditions of this Agreement WHICH YOU SHOULD READ CARE-FULLY BEFORE SIGNING BELOW (Schedule Two), (4) Lessor Terms and Conditions of Supply (Schedule Three), and (5) Direct Debit Mandate. The Minimum Initial Payment is required on or before the date of delivery of the leased Goods which will also be deemed to be the DATE OF COMMENCEMENT of the lease Fixed Term. All Further Payments are payable by direct debit and will be collected on the 1st day of each month/quarter, commencing on the 1st day of the month/quarter following delivery of the Goods. Additional charges may be incurred under clauses 2.4, 5.2, 5.5, 5.6 and 6.3 of this Agreement.

LESSEE AUTHORISED SIGNATORY	LESSOR AUTHORISED SIGNATORY
	Accepted for and on behalf of Lessor

Signed   Signed

Name   Name

Title   Title

Date   Date

SCHEDULE ONE

GOODS INCLUDED IN FIXED TERM LEASE

Invoice No	PO Number	Value ex VAT	Description of Goods (*denotes part of a Previous Agreement*)

SPECIAL CONDITIONS OF LEASE

No.	Condition

PREVIOUS AGREEMENT DETAILS (IF APPLICABLE)

Reference No:

SCHEDULE TWO

LESSOR TERMS AND CONDITIONS OF FIXED TERM LEASE

1. Definitions

1.1 'Agreement' means this Fixed Term Lease Agreement including the front page and all of Schedule One, this Schedule Two and Schedule Three appended to this Agreement and any other attachments expressly stated to be part of this Agreement and signed by an authorised representative of each party.

1.2 'Commencement Date' means the date of commencement of the Fixed Term of this Lease Agreement, being the date of delivery of the Goods to the Lessee.

1.3 'Facility Fee' means a one-time administrative fee of £95 or such other fee as may be notified to the Lessee in writing prior to it entering into this Agreement.

1.4 'Fixed Term' means the total period of time for lease of the Goods to the Lessee, expressed in months and shown on the front page of this Agreement.

1.5 'Further Payments' means the second and subsequent payments due in each Payment Interval for the duration of the Fixed Term.

1.6 'Goods' means all of the computer products (hardware and software, including all additions and modifications and replacement parts), and other products, supplies, and services listed in Schedule One, which are leased to the Lessee on the terms and conditions of this Agreement.

1.7 'Lessee' means the entity shown as the Lessee whose details appear on the front page of this Agreement, and who is responsible for the leasing of the Goods from the Lessor.

1.8 'Lessor' means the entity shown as the Lessor whose details appear on the front page of this Agreement.

1.9 'Minimum Initial Payment' means the first monthly or quarterly payment plus the Value Added Tax applicable to the Total Cash Price, as detailed on the front page of this Agreement, plus the Facility Fee.

1.10 'Payment Intervals' means 'MONTHLY' or 'QUARTERLY' as shown on the front page of this Agreement.

1.11 'Previous Agreement' means, if applicable, an earlier agreement between the Lessor and the Lessee in respect of any of the Goods, the reference number for which is shown in Schedule One.

1.12 'Special Conditions' means any terms and conditions agreed between the Lessor and the Lessee, as shown in Schedule One, which are additions or variations to the terms and conditions in Schedules Two and Three. In the event of any conflicts of meaning, Special Conditions prevail over the terms and conditions in Schedules Two and Three, and the terms and conditions in Schedule Two prevail over the terms and conditions in Schedule Three.

1.13 *'Total Cash Price'* means the cumulative value of the Goods excluding Value Added Tax, as listed and totalled in Schedule One and as shown on the front page of this Agreement.

2. Fixed Term Agreement

2.1 The Lessor agrees to lease to the Lessee and the Lessee agrees to lease from the Lessor, solely for the internal purposes of its business, the Goods listed in Schedule One for the Fixed Term, which will start on the Commencement Date, even if the Goods have not been at the time fully installed or connected to a network, where applicable. The risk of loss or damage to the Goods will pass to the Lessee on the date of delivery of the Goods to the Lessee.

2.2 If Goods are included under this Agreement which were subject to a Previous Agreement, as identified in Schedule One, then on the Commence-ment Date of this Agreement, and in relation to the retained Goods only, the Previous Agreement will be treated as cancelled and replaced by this Agreement.

2.3 This Agreement is for the Fixed Term and the Lessee may not terminate the leasing of the Goods at any time during the Fixed Term.

2.4 If in breach of this Agreement the Lessee purports to terminate this Agreement or return the Goods to the Lessor at any time during the Fixed Term, without prejudice to the Lessor's other rights in law or equity or under this Agreement the Lessor will charge the Lessee for:
  (a) the Minimum Initial Payment and any other sums already due to the Lessor and unpaid;
  (b) all Further Payments the Lessee would have paid had the leasing continued for the Fixed Term, discounted at the rate of 3% per annum from the date each Further Payment would have fallen due to the last day of the Fixed Term;
  (c) the Lessor's reasonable administration costs, and
  (d) interest charged at the rate of 2% per month compound in respect of any late payments, until the date of actual receipt of such payments, whether before or after any judgment.

3. Goods

The Lessee agrees that until such time as ownership of the Goods is transferred to it or the Goods are returned to the Lessor in accordance with clause 10, the Lessee is solely responsible for:

3.1 selecting the Goods listed in Schedule One;

3.2   ensuring that the Goods are suitable for its requirements in every way;

3.3   ensuring that once it has taken possession of the Goods they are in good working order;

3.4   ensuring that the Goods are used only in the normal course of business and in accordance with the manufacturer's instructions and/or guidelines and in compliance with all health and safety legislation, and the Lessee agrees to indemnify the Lessor from and against any loss, damage or injury to people or property caused by the Goods or their use, except for death or personal injury caused by the Lessor's negligence;

3.5   keeping possession of the Goods, and not doing anything that will interfere with the owner's interest in the Goods, including without limitation not selling the Goods or claiming or allowing any other entity or person to claim capital allowances on them;

3.6   ensuring that the Goods remain at the delivery/installation address specified. If the Lessee wishes to relocate the Goods it must first obtain the Lessor's written consent;

3.7   connecting and disconnecting the Goods;

3.8   installing the Goods unless installation is included in Schedule One;

3.9   keeping the Goods in good working order, condition and repair;

3.10   ensuring that the Goods are not altered or modified in any way without the Lessor's prior and specific written consent;

3.11   bearing the risk of any loss or damage to the Goods, however caused;

3.12   complying with all of the Customer's responsibilities in the Terms and Conditions of Supply in Schedule Three, except to the extent that they are varied by provisions in this Schedule Two;

3.13   notifying the Lessor immediately if the Goods are lost, stolen, damaged or confiscated;

3.14   not removing or defacing any notices of ownership of the Lessor or any other party on any of the Goods, and ensuring that the Goods do not become affixed to any land or building.

If the Lessee has any complaints upon taking delivery of the Goods concerning delivery errors, shortfalls, condition of the Goods or any other matter, it must notify the Lessor immediately of its complaint with as much information as possible, and provide the Lessor with a detailed written statement of the complaint within five working days of the delivery. The Lessor is entitled to assume that the Lessee is completely satisfied with the Goods if it has not received any such written statement.

4. Maintenance

4.1 Hardware

Except to the extent such maintenance services are included in this Agreement during the Fixed Term, as shown in Schedule One, the Lessee is solely responsible for ensuring that the hardware Goods are kept in optimum operating condition at all times, except only for fair wear and tear, and for obtaining any maintenance services required by the Lessee for the hardware Goods.

4.2 Software

The Lessee is solely responsible for entering into and complying with the terms of the licences to use any software Goods and for obtaining any maintenance or support on software Goods and if the Lessee is unable to obtain such maintenance or support for any reason it will not be entitled to terminate this Agreement or to withhold any payments.

5. Payments

5.1 The Lessee undertakes to pay the Lessor the Minimum Initial Payment on or before the Commencement Date and thereafter the Further Payments on the first day of each following Payment Interval throughout the Fixed Term.

5.2 All payments must be made by Direct Debit unless the Lessor otherwise agrees in writing. If the Lessee does not make payments by Direct Debit an extra 5% of the amount of the payment will be charged on each payment to cover the Lessor's increased costs of administration.

5.3 All payments must be paid in full and on time and time is of the essence for this purpose. If payments are sent by post, this is at the Lessee's own risk.

5.4 All payments must be made free of any set-offs, deductions or withholdings.

5.5 The Minimum Initial Payment and Further Payments are calculated on the assumption that there will be no changes in the rate of Corporation Tax during this Agreement. If there is an increase in Corporation Tax of five or more percentage points the Lessor is entitled, on giving the Lessee seven days' notice, to increase the Minimum Initial Payment and/or such Further Payments as the Lessor may specify by eight percentage points for each five point increase, and pro rata for different amounts of increase.

5.6 The Lessee will be responsible for any costs incurred by the Lessor in recovering money owed to it (including collection agents' fees), plus interest on all overdue amounts at the rate of 2% per month calculated on a daily basis or £25.00, whichever is the greater, until payment is actually received whether before or after any judgment. The Lessor will also charge the Lessee the sum of £25.00 each time an unpaid Direct Debit or cheque is required to be re-presented. In addition, the Lessor will be entitled to impose an administrative charge of £10.00 per item of correspondence in respect of each payment which falls overdue.

535

6. Insurance

6.1 Unless the parties have agreed in writing that the Lessee is permitted to self-insure, the Lessee must insure the Goods against any loss (including total loss) or damage from all risks and against third party risks. The amount of such insurance must be at least the full cost of replacing the Goods as new, as shown in Schedule One.

6.2 If the Lessee is permitted to self-insure, it must nevertheless keep the Goods insured at all times, until either ownership of the Goods has been transferred to it or the Goods have been returned to the Lessor, against loss or damage by fire and water for their full replacement value shown in Schedule One and against third party risks. Provided the Lessee complies at all times with all statutory requirements relating to the Goods and their insurance, it may act as self-insurer in relation to the other risks.

6.3 Unless the Lessee is permitted to self-insure, it must arrange for the Lessor's interest in the Goods to be endorsed on any policy of insurance and show proof whenever the Lessor requests it. If the Lessee does not provide this proof promptly the Lessor may, at the Lessee's expense, arrange for the insurance of the Goods. In such circumstances the Lessor will add an amount equal to the insurance premium to the Minimum Initial Payment or the next due Further Payment. If the Lessee has to make an insurance claim for the Goods it must inform the Lessor immediately. The Lessee is not authorised to agree a settlement of a claim without written permission from the Lessor. The Lessee agrees to appoint the Lessor as its agent for the purposes of managing any claim and authorising the insurance company to pay any settlement of claims on the Goods directly to the Lessor.

7. Warranties, Limitations and Exclusions of Liability

7.1 The Lessee declares that it has selected the Goods relying entirely on its own judgment. The Lessor therefore excludes from this Agreement all warranties, conditions or guarantees implied by law to the fullest extent permitted by law, and the express warranties, indemnities and limitations of liability set out in the Terms and Conditions of Supply in Schedule Three, and the benefit of any other warranties or guarantees the Lessor is able to assign to the Lessee from third party manufacturers of the Goods, are the only warranties, guarantees, and indemnities given to the Lessee in relation to the Goods. Accordingly the Lessor's liability to the Lessee in connection with the supply of the Goods (except for death or personal injury caused by the Lessor's negligence), whether in contract or in tort for any loss (including consequential and indirect loss, loss of data, loss of business, loss of use or loss of opportunity), damage or expense which the Lessee may suffer as a result of:
(a) the Goods failing to function properly;
(b) the Goods not being delivered on any provisional delivery date notified to the Lessee; or

(c)   any software failing to function properly, or not being correctly licensed to the Lessee,

is limited as set out in this clause 7.1 and in the Terms and Conditions of Supply in Schedule Three.

7.2   The Lessee acknowledges and agrees that all of the terms and conditions relating to the leasing of the Goods and the scope and extent of any warranties and guarantees in relation to the supply of the Goods are limited as set out in this Agreement.

8. Termination of Lease

The Lessor will be entitled to give the Lessee notice of termination of this Agreement and bring this lease and right to possession of the Goods to an end with immediate effect, and without prejudice to any of its other rights in law or equity or under this Agreement, if:

8.1   the Lessee fails to make the Minimum Initial Payment or any Further Payment or any other payment due under or in connection with this Agreement within seven days of its due date;

8.2   the Lessee fails to comply with any of its other obligations under this Agreement and does not remedy the situation within 30 days of its being notified of the breach;

8.3   the Lessor has reasonable grounds to believe that the Lessee cannot pay its debts as they fall due, or the Lessee is declared or becomes insolvent;

8.4   a petition is presented for the appointment of an administrator, administrative receiver, receiver or liquidator or a like officer or such person is appointed over all or any of the Lessee's assets, or if the Lessee arranges or attempts to arrange a composition or scheme with its creditors or a meeting of creditors, or if any steps are taken against the Lessee for its winding up or dissolution;

8.5   the Lessee is merged with another company and the merged entity does not acknowledge to the Lessor in writing its acceptance of the Lessee's continuing obligations under this Agreement;

8.6   the Goods are stolen or otherwise become a total loss for insurance purposes, or the Lessor has reasonable grounds to believe that the Goods or the owner's interest in them is at risk.

9. Remedies

9.1   On termination of this Agreement for any reason, at the Lessor's option but at the Lessee's expense the Lessee will either decommission and return the Goods to a UK address designated by the Lessor within ten working days together with any ancillary equipment originally supplied, all in good operating condition fair wear and tear excepted, or store the Goods at the Lessee's risk for a maximum period of 30 days and then deliver them to a UK address designated by the Lessor, or allow the Lessor to collect the Goods from the Lessee during normal business hours. Any costs incurred by the Lessor in collecting the Goods and/or in restoring them to normal operating condition will be borne by the Lessee and payable to the Lessor on demand. If the Lessee fails to deliver up the Goods for any reason, it will be liable to the Lessor for their replacement cost, being the higher of the outstanding sums owing under this Agreement in accordance with clause 10.2(a) below or the then fair market value of the Goods, without prejudice to any other rights or remedies available to the Lessor in law or equity or under this Agreement.

9.2 If the Lessor recovers the Goods and is able to sell them, it will apply any proceeds of sale, after deducting any Value Added Tax and its costs in repossessing and selling the Goods, in the following order: (i) towards any amounts due but not paid by the Lessee pursuant to clause 9.1 above; (ii) towards such anticipated future value of the Goods and the end of the Fixed Term, discounted at the rate of 2% per annum from the last day of the Fixed Term to the date of receipt by the Lessor of the proceeds of sale, and (iii) if any balance remains, the Lessor will rebate this to the Lessee.

10. Ownership of Goods and Exercise of Option to Purchase

10.1 During the leasing of the Goods, the Goods will be, and will remain at all times, the movable, personal and chattel property of the Lessor. Other than a right to quiet possession and enjoyment of the Goods during the Fixed Term (provided and for so long as the Lessee is not in breach or default of this Agreement) and subject to clause 10.2 below, the Lessee will not have any right, title or interest in the Goods except as Lessee and as set out in this Agreement.

10.2 If the Lessee wishes to exercise the option to purchase the Goods at the end of the Fixed Term (in their then existing state and condition), it may do so:

(a) at any time during the Fixed Term by paying to the Lessor such sum as will, with the payments previously made, amount to the aggregate of all of the sums payable by the Lessee during the Fixed Term (less a discount for the acceleration of the payment at a rate of 3% per annum) plus the Option to Purchase Fee specified on the front page of this Agreement;

(b) at the expiration of the Fixed Term (and provided all sums due from the Lessee have been paid in full) by payment of the Option to Purchase Fee specified on the front page of this Agreement.

11. Assignment or Novation

11.1 The Lessee is not entitled to assign any of its rights under this Agreement without the Lessor's prior written consent and the Lessor will not agree to a request for a novation arrangement unless it is satisfied that its overall security position in relation to both the Goods and the Lessee's payment obligations in this Agreement will not be prejudiced or diminished in any way.

11.2 The Lessor may assign the benefit of this Agreement to another party and may pass title in the Goods to that party, and if the Lessee is so notified of such an assignment it must make all subsequent payments due under this Agreement to, or as directed by, such party.

12. Entire Agreement

This Agreement constitutes the entire agreement and understanding between the parties and supersedes any previous agreement, representation or understanding between the parties in relation to the lease of the Goods. Each party acknowledges that in entering into this Agreement, it does not rely on and will have no remedy in respect of any statement of fact or opinion not recorded in this Agreement (whether negligently or innocently made), except for any representation made fraudulently. No addition, modification or variation of these terms and conditions will be valid unless confirmed in writing by authorised signatories of both parties on or after the date of this Agreement.

13. Waiver

No forbearance or delay by either party in enforcing its respective rights under or in connection with this Agreement will prejudice or restrict the rights of that party, and no waiver of any such rights or of any breach of any contractual terms will be deemed to be a waiver of any other right or of any later breach.

14. Notices

Any notice given under this Agreement by either party to the other must be in writing and may be delivered personally or by [recorded delivery] [first class] post, and in the case of post will be deemed to have been given two working days after the date of posting [where the addresses of the parties are both within the United Kingdom or seven working days after the date of posting where the notice is addressed to or is posted from an address outside the United Kingdom]. Notices will be delivered or sent to the addresses of the parties on the first page of this Agreement or to any other address notified in writing by either party to the other for the purpose of receiving notices after the date of this Agreement.

15. Governing Law and Jurisdiction

This Agreement is governed by and construed in accordance with the law of England and Wales and the parties submit to the [non-exclusive/exclusive] jurisdiction of the courts of England and Wales.

MINIMUM TERM RENTAL AGREEMENT

Agreement No: .... LESSOR NAME AND ADDRESS

....

....

....

RENTER DETAILS

Full Name ....

Address ....

....

....

.... Postcode ....

E-mail Address ....

Delivery Address
(if different from above)

....

....

.... Postcode ....

Telephone   ....

Fax   ....

Contact Name   ....

Nature of Business   ....

Number of Years Trading   .... years

Company Registered No   ....
(if applicable)

RENTAL DETAILS

1. Minimum Term (words)   .... months

2. Payment Intervals (words)   ....
(*first payment due in advance of
delivery of Goods*)

3. Monthly / Quarterly Rental £ .... VAT £ ....
                               @ 17.5%

(*delete as applicable*)

4. Total Periodic Rental   £ ....
including VAT

This is a MINIMUM TERM Agreement in FIVE parts: (1) this first signature page, (2) the Schedule of Goods being rented and any Special Conditions (Schedule One), (3) the Terms and Conditions of this Agreement WHICH YOU SHOULD READ CAREFULLY BEFORE SIGNING BELOW (Schedule Two), (4) Lessor Terms and Conditions of Supply (Schedule Three), and (5) Direct Debit Mandate. The first Total Periodic Rental payment is required on or before the date of delivery of the rented Goods which will also be deemed to be the DATE OF COMMENCEMENT of the Minimum Term. All further Total Periodic Rental payments are payable by direct debit and will be collected on the 1st day of each month/quarter, commencing on the 1st day of the month / quarter following delivery of the Goods. Additional charges may be incurred under clauses 2.4, 5.3, 5.6, 5.7 and 6.3 of this Agreement.

RENTER Authorised Signatory

LESSOR AUTHORISED SIGNATORY
Accepted for and on behalf of Lessor

Signed .... Signed ....

Name .... Name ....

Title .... Title ....

Date .... Date ....

SCHEDULE ONE

GOODS INCLUDED IN MINIMUM TERM RENTAL

Invoice No	PO Number	Minimum Replacement Insurance Value	Description of Goods (* denotes part of a Previous Agreement)

SPECIAL CONDITIONS

No.	Condition

PREVIOUS AGREEMENT DETAILS (IF APPLICABLE)

Reference No:

542

SCHEDULE TWO

LESSOR TERMS AND CONDITIONS OF MINIMUM TERM RENTAL

1. Definitions

1.1 *'Agreement'* means this Minimum Term Rental Agreement including the front page and all of Schedule One, this Schedule Two and Schedule Three appended to this Agreement.

1.2 *'Commencement Date'* means the date of commencement of the Minimum Term of this Rental Agreement, being the date of delivery of the Goods to the Renter.

1.3 *'Facility Fee'* means a one-time administrative fee of £95 or such other fee as may be notified to the Renter in writing prior to it entering into this Agreement.

1.4 *'Goods'* means all of the computer products (hardware and software, including all additions and modifications and replacement parts), and other products, supplies, and services listed in Schedule One, which are leased to the Renter on the terms and conditions of this Agreement.

1.5 *'Lessor'* means the entity shown as the Lessor whose address and company registration details are shown on the front page of this Agreement.

1.6 *'Minimum Initial Payment'* means the first Monthly/Quarterly Rental detailed on the front page of this Agreement, plus the Facility Fee.

1.7 *'Minimum Term'* means the minimum period of time for rental of the Goods to the Renter, expressed in months and shown on the front page of this Agreement.

1.8 *'Monthly/Quarterly Rental'* means the payments including Value Added Tax due in each Payment Interval for the duration of the Minimum Term.

1.9 *'Payment Intervals'* means 'MONTHLY' or 'QUARTERLY' as shown on the front page of this Agreement.

1.10 *'Previous Agreement'* means, if applicable, an earlier agreement between the Lessor and the Renter in respect of any of the Goods, the reference number for which is shown in Schedule One.

1.11 *'Renter'* means the entity shown as the Renter whose details appear on the front page of this Agreement, and who is responsible for the renting of the Goods.

1.12 *'Special Conditions'* means any terms and conditions agreed between the Lessor and the Renter, as shown in Schedule One, which are additions or variations to the terms and conditions in Schedules Two and Three. **In the event of any conflicts of meaning, Special Conditions prevail over**

543

the terms and conditions in Schedules Two and Three, and the terms and conditions in Schedule Two prevail over the terms and conditions in Schedule Three.

2. Minimum Term Agreement

2.1 The Lessor agrees to rent to the Renter and the Renter agrees to rent from the Lessor, solely for the internal purposes of its business, the Goods listed in Schedule One for the Minimum Term, which will start on the Commencement Date, even if the Goods have not been at the time fully installed or connected to a network, where applicable. The risk of loss or damage to the Goods will pass to the Renter on the date of delivery of the Goods to the Renter.

2.2 If Goods are included under this Agreement which were subject to a Previous Agreement, as identified in Schedule One, then on the Commencement Date of this Agreement, and in relation to the retained Goods only, the Previous Agreement will be treated as cancelled and replaced by this Agreement.

2.3 As this Agreement is for a Minimum Term, the Renter may not terminate the leasing of the Goods at any time prior to the expiry of the Minimum Term.

2.4 If in breach of this Agreement, the Renter does purport to terminate this Agreement or return the Goods to the Lessor at any time during the Minimum Term, without prejudice to the Lessor's other rights in law or equity or under this Agreement, the Lessor will charge the Renter a total of:
  (a) the Minimum Initial Payment and any other sums already due to the Lessor and unpaid;
  (b) all Monthly/Quarterly Rental payments the Renter would have paid had the renting continued for the Minimum Term, discounted at the rate of 3% per annum from the date each Monthly/Quarterly Rental payment would have fallen due to the last day of the Minimum Term;
  (c) the Lessor's reasonable administration costs; and
  (d) interest charged at the rate of 2% per month compound in respect of any late payments, until the date of actual receipt of such payments, whether before or after any judgment.

3. Goods

The Renter agrees that until such time as the Goods are returned to the Lessor in accordance with clause 10, the Renter is solely responsible for:

3.1 selecting the Goods listed in Schedule One;

3.2 ensuring that the Goods are suitable for its requirements in every way;

3.3 ensuring that once it has taken possession of the Goods they are in good working order;

3.4 ensuring that the Goods are used only in the normal course of business and in accordance with the manufacturer's instructions and/or guidelines and in compliance with all health and safety legislation, and the Renter agrees to indemnify the Lessor from and against any loss, damage or injury to people or property caused by the Goods or their use, except for death or personal injury caused by the Lessor's negligence;

3.5 keeping possession of the Goods, and not doing anything that will interfere with the owner's interest in the Goods, including without limitation not selling the Goods or claiming or allowing any other entity or person to claim capital allowances on them;

3.6 ensuring that the Goods remain at the delivery/installation address specified. If the Renter wishes to relocate the Goods it must first obtain the Lessor's written consent;

3.7 connecting and disconnecting the Goods;

3.8 installing the Goods unless installation is included in Schedule One;

3.9 keeping the Goods in good working order, condition and repair;

3.10 ensuring that the Goods are not altered or modified in any way without the Lessor's prior and specific written consent;

3.11 bearing the risk of any loss or damage to the Goods, however caused;

3.12 complying with all of the Customer's responsibilities in the Terms and Conditions of Supply in Schedule Three, except to the extent that they are varied by provisions in this Schedule Two;

3.13 notifying the Lessor immediately if the Goods are lost, stolen, damaged or confiscated;

3.14 not removing or defacing any notices of ownership of the Lessor or any other party on any of the Goods, and ensuring that the Goods do not become affixed to any land or building.

If the Renter has any complaints upon taking delivery of the Goods concerning delivery errors, shortfalls, condition of the Goods or any other matter, it must notify the Lessor immediately of its complaint with as much information as possible, and provide the Lessor with a detailed written statement of its complaint within five working days of the delivery. The Lessor is entitled to assume that the Renter is completely satisfied with the Goods if it has not received any such written statement.

4. Maintenance

4.1 Hardware

Except to the extent such maintenance services are included in this Agreement during the Minimum Term, as shown in Schedule One, the Renter is solely responsible for ensuring that the hardware Goods are kept in optimum operating condition at all times, except only for fair wear and tear, and for obtaining any maintenance services required by the Renter for the hardware Goods.

4.2 **Software**

The Renter is solely responsible for entering into and complying with the terms of the licences to use any software Goods and for obtaining any maintenance or support on software Goods and if the Renter is unable to obtain such maintenance or support for any reason the Renter will not be entitled to terminate this Agreement or to withhold any payments.

5. Payments

5.1 The Renter must pay the Lessor the Minimum Initial Payment on or before the Commencement Date and thereafter the Monthly/Quarterly Rental payments on the first day of each following Payment Interval throughout the Minimum Term.

5.2 This Agreement will continue automatically after the Minimum Term unless or until the Renter serves the Lessor with a minimum of one month/ quarter's notice of termination to expire on the expiry date of the Minimum Term or at the end of a subsequent month/quarter (the month or quarter in each case to be in accordance with the Payment Interval shown on the front page of this Agreement). The Renter's Monthly/Quarterly Rentals will continue to be payable until the earlier of the termination date of this Agreement for any reason on or after the Minimum Term, or the Lessor's notice to the Renter of any reduction the Lessor is willing to agree in the Monthly/Quarterly Rental (in which event the revised amount will be substituted as the continuing Monthly/Quarterly Rental).

5.3 All payments must be made by Direct Debit unless the Lessor otherwise agrees in writing. If the Renter does not make payments by Direct Debit the Lessor will charge the Renter an extra 5% of the amount of the payment on each payment to cover the Lessor's increased costs of administration.

5.4 All payments must be paid in full and on time and time is of the essence for this purpose. If payments are sent by post, this is at the Renter's own risk.

5.5 All payments must be made free of any set-offs, deductions or withholdings.

5.6 The Minimum Initial Payment and Monthly/Quarterly Rental payments are calculated on the assumption that there will be no changes in the rate of Corporation Tax during this Agreement. If there is an increase in Corpora- tion Tax of five or more percentage points the Lessor will be entitled, on giving the Renter seven days' prior notice, to increase the Minimum Initial Payment and/or such Monthly/Quarterly Rental payments as the Lessor may specify by eight percentage points for each five point increase, and pro rata for different amounts of increase.

5.7 The Renter will be responsible for any costs incurred by the Lessor in recovering money owed to it by the Renter (including collection agents' fees) plus interest on all overdue amounts at the rate of 2% per month calculated on a daily basis or £25.00, whichever is the greater, until payment is actually received whether before or after any judgment. The Lessor will charge the Renter the sum of £25.00 each time an unpaid Direct Debit or cheque has to be re-presented. In addition, the Lessor will be entitled to impose an administrative charge of £10.00 per item of correspondence in respect of each payment which falls overdue.

6. Insurance

6.1 Unless the Lessor has agreed in writing that the Renter is permitted to self-insure, the Renter must insure the Goods against any loss (including total loss) or damage from all risks and against third party risks. The amount of the insurance must be at least the full cost of replacing the Goods as new, as shown in Schedule One.

6.2 If the Renter is permitted to self-insure, it must nevertheless keep the Goods insured at all times until either ownership of the Goods has been transferred to it or the Goods have been returned to the Lessor, against loss or damage by fire and water for their full replacement value shown in Schedule One and against third party risks. Provided the Renter complies at all times with all statutory requirements relating to the Goods and their insurance, it may act as self-insurer in relation to the other risks.

6.3 Unless the Renter is permitted to self-insure, it must arrange for the Lessor's interest in the Goods to be endorsed on any policy and show proof of the same whenever the Lessor requests it. If the Renter does not provide this proof promptly the Lessor may, at the Renter's expense, arrange the insurance for the Renter. If the Lessor arranges the insurance it will add an amount equal to the insurance premium to the Minimum Initial Payment or the next due Monthly/Quarterly Rental. If the Renter has to make an insurance claim for the Goods it must inform the Lessor immediately. The Renter is not authorised to agree a settlement of a claim without written permission from the Lessor. The Renter agrees to appoint the Lessor as its agent for the purposes of managing any claim and authorising the insurance company to pay any settlement of claims on the Goods directly to the Lessor.

7. Warranties, Limitations and Exclusions of Liability

7.1 The Renter declares that it has selected the Goods relying entirely on its own judgment. The Lessor therefore excludes from this Agreement all warranties, conditions or guarantees implied by law to the fullest extent permitted by law, and the express warranties, indemnities and limitations of liability set out in the Terms and Conditions of Supply in Schedule Three, and the benefit of any other warranties or guarantees the Lessor is able to assign to the Renter from third party manufacturers of the Goods, are the only warranties, guarantees, and indemnities given to the Renter in relation to the Goods. Accordingly the Lessor's liability to the Lessee in connection with the

547

supply of the Goods (except for death or personal injury caused by the Lessor's negligence), whether in contract or in tort for any loss (including consequential and indirect loss, loss of data, loss of business, loss of use or loss of opportunity), damage or expense which the Renter may suffer as a result of:

(a)   the Goods failing to function properly;

(b)   the Goods not being delivered on any provisional delivery date notified to the Renter; or

(c)   any software failing to function properly, or not being correctly licensed to the Renter,

is limited as set out in this clause 7.1 and in the Terms and Conditions of Supply in Schedule Three.

7.2   The Renter acknowledges and agrees that all of the terms and conditions concerning the leasing of the Goods to you and the scope and extent of any warranties and guarantees in relation to the supply of the Goods are limited as shown in this Agreement.

8. Termination of Rental Agreement

The Lessor will be entitled to give the Renter notice of termination of this Agreement and bring the Renter's right to possession of the Goods to an end with immediate effect, and without prejudice to any of its other rights in law or equity or under this Agreement, if:

8.1   the Renter fails to make the Minimum Initial Payment or any Monthly/Quarterly Rental payment or any other payment due under or in connection with this Agreement within seven days of its due date;

8.2   the Renter fails to comply with any of its other obligations under this Agreement and does not remedy the situation within 30 days of its being notified of the breach;

8.3   the Lessor has reasonable grounds to believe that the Renter cannot pay its debts as they fall due, or the Renter is declared or becomes insolvent;

8.4   a petition is presented for the appointment of an administrator, administrative receiver, receiver or liquidator or a like officer or such person is appointed over all or any of the Renter's assets or if the Renter arranges or attempts to arrange a composition or scheme with its creditors or a meeting of creditors, or any steps are taken against the Renter for its winding up or dissolution;

8.5   the Renter is merged with another company and the merged entity does not acknowledge to the Lessor in writing its acceptance of the Renter's continuing obligations under this Agreement;

8.6   the Goods are stolen or otherwise become a total loss for insurance purposes, or the Lessor has reasonable grounds to believe that the Goods or the owner's interest in them is at risk.

9. Remedies

9.1   On termination of this Agreement for any reason, at the Lessor's option but at the Renter's expense, the Renter will either decommission and return the Goods to a UK address designated by the Lessor within ten working days together with any ancillary equipment originally supplied, all in good operating condition fair wear and tear excepted, or store the Goods at the Renter's risk for a maximum period of 30 days and then deliver them to a UK address designated by the Lessor, or allow the Lessor to collect the Goods from the Renter during normal business hours. Any costs incurred by the Lessor in collecting the Goods and/or in restoring them to normal operating condition will be borne by the Renter and payable to the Lessor on demand. If the Renter fails to deliver up the Goods for any reason, it will be liable to the Lessor for their replacement cost being the higher of the outstanding sums owing under this Agreement. Such replacement cost as will, with the payments previously made, amount to the aggregate of all of the sums payable by the Renter during the Minimum Term (less a discount for the acceleration of the payment at a rate of 3% per annum) or the then fair market value of the Goods, without prejudice to any other rights or remedies available to the Lessor in law or equity or under this Agreement.

9.2   If the Lessor recovers the Goods and is able to sell them, it will apply any proceeds of sale, after deducting any Value Added Tax and its costs in repossessing and selling the Goods towards any amounts due but not paid by the Renter pursuant to Clause 9.1 above.

10. Ownership of Goods and Continuation Beyond the Minimum Term

10.1   During the renting of the Goods, the Goods will be and will remain at all times the movable, personal and chattel property of the Lessor. Other than a right to quiet possession and enjoyment of the Goods during this Agreement (provided and for so long as the Renter is not in breach or default of this Agreement) the Renter will not have any right, title or interest in the Goods except as Renter and as set out in this Agreement.

10.2   If this Agreement continues beyond the Minimum Term all of the terms and conditions in this Agreement will remain in full force and effect until its actual date of termination.

11. Assignment or Novation

11.1   The Renter is not entitled to assign any of its rights under this Agreement without the Lessor's prior written consent and the Lessor will not agree to a request for a novation arrangement unless it is satisfied that its overall security position in relation to both the Goods and the Renter's payment obligations in this Agreement will not be prejudiced or diminished in any way.

11.2   The Lessor may assign the benefit of this Agreement to another party and may pass title in the Goods to that party, and if the Renter is so notified of such an assignment it must make all subsequent payments due under this Agreement to, or as directed by, such party.

12. Entire Agreement

This Agreement constitutes the entire agreement and understanding between the parties and supersedes any previous agreement, representation or understanding between the parties in relation to the lease of the Goods. Each party acknowledges that in entering into this Agreement, it does not rely on and will have no remedy in respect of any statement of fact or opinion not recorded in this Agreement (whether negligently or innocently made), except for any representation made fraudulently. No addition, modification or variation of these terms and conditions will be valid unless confirmed in writing by authorised signatories of both parties on or after the date of this Agreement.

13. Waiver

No forbearance or delay by either party in enforcing its respective rights under or in connection with this Agreement will prejudice or restrict the rights of that party, and no waiver of any such rights or of any breach of any contractual terms will be deemed to be a waiver of any other right or of any later breach.

14. Notices

Any notice given under this Agreement by either party to the other must be in writing and may be delivered personally or by [recorded delivery] [first class] post, and in the case of post will be deemed to have been given two working days after the date of posting [where the addresses of the parties are both within the United Kingdom or seven working days after the date of posting where the notice is addressed to or is posted from an address outside the United Kingdom]. Notices will be delivered or sent to the addresses of the parties on the first page of this Agreement or to any other address notified in writing by either party to the other for the purpose of receiving notices after the date of this Agreement.

15. Governing Law and Jurisdiction

This Agreement is governed by and construed in accordance with the law of England and Wales and the parties submit to the [non-exclusive/exclusive] jurisdiction of the courts of England and Wales.

DISTRIBUTION AGREEMENT

This is an example of a sole distribution agreement. Products are supplied on the supplier's standard terms and conditions, including licensing provisions. The distributor is licensed to supply the supplier's hardware and software products to end users, and to add value by adding its own applications and providing second-line support.

Date of Agreement ....

BETWEEN:

(1)   **THE SUPPLIER** whose registered office is at ....
.... ('**Supplier**');

AND

(2)   **THE DISTRIBUTOR** whose registered office is at ....
.... ('**Distributor**').

1. Introduction

The Supplier agrees to appoint the Distributor and the Distributor agrees to such appointment, subject to the terms and conditions of this Agreement.

2. Definitions

2.1   *'Application'* means the Distributor's value-added applications software identified as such in the Products Schedule or subsequently approved in writing by the Supplier and which is marketed by the Distributor in conjunction with the Equipment.

2.2   *'Charges'* means the Supplier's Charges set out in the Charges Schedule.

2.3   *'Commencement Date'* means the date shown as such in the Commencement Date Schedule.

2.4   *'End User'* means a customer of the Distributor.

2.5   *'Equipment'* means the hardware products and related operating system software identified in the Price List.

2.6   *'Licence and Support Agreement'* means the Supplier's licence and support agreement appended to this Agreement under the terms and conditions of which the Software is licensed to End Users.

2.7   *'Marks'* means the trade marks of the Supplier, whether used individually or collectively and whether registered or unregistered, listed in the Trade Marks Schedule.

2.8   *'Master Disk'* means one or more compact discs on which the Software is supplied by the Supplier to the Distributor, incorporating the Supplier's copyright notices, serial numbers and proprietary notices.

2.9 *'Order Address'* means the Supplier's address for receipt of orders, set out in the Supplier's Order Address Schedule.

2.10 *'Price List'* means the current published 'Supplier Distribution Price List' for the United Kingdom appended as the Price List Schedule and any subsequent amendments notified to the Distributor by the Supplier.

2.11 *'Products'* means the Software and Hardware supplied in combination under this Agreement, as listed in the Products Schedule.

2.12 *'Sales Targets'* means the sales targets set out in the Sales Targets Schedule.

2.13 *'Schedule'* means a schedule applicable as identified in this Agreement and which is incorporated into this Agreement.

2.14 *'Software'* means the object code versions of the hardware operating systems software and the applications software products of the Supplier and their related documentation and any updates or enhancements to them, listed as such in the Products Schedule.

2.15 *'Source Code Deposit Agreement'* means the terms and conditions for source code deposit appended to this Agreement.

2.16 *'Terms and Conditions of Supply'* means the document containing the supplier's standard terms and conditions of supply appended to this Agreement under the terms and conditions of which the products are supplied to the Distributor.

2.17 *'Territory'* means the geographical area to which this Agreement and the appointment of the Distributor applies, specified in the Territory Schedule.

3. Duration

This Agreement commences on the Commencement Date and will continue for an initial period of 12 months, after which it will remain in force until terminated by either party giving at least 90 days' notice of termination to the other party to expire on the last day of the initial term [or on any subsequent anniversary of the Commencement Date], [or at any time thereafter], or by the Distributor giving 90 days' notice within 30 days of receipt of notification of a change in prices by the Supplier as permitted by this Agreement, and otherwise subject to the other termination provisions in this Agreement.

4. Distributor's Appointment and Rights

4.1 Appointment

The Supplier appoints the Distributor as its sole distributor for the Products in the Territory provided that, and for so long as, the Distributor achieves the Sales Targets and otherwise continues to observe and perform all of its obligations set out in this Agreement.

4.2 Independent Contractor

The relationship between the Supplier and the Distributor is that of independent contractor. Neither party is agent for the other, and neither party has authority to make any contract, whether expressly or by implication, in the name of the other party, without that other party's prior written consent for express purposes connected with the performance of this Agreement.

4.3 Territory

For the avoidance of doubt the Supplier is entitled to engage in direct sales activities in the Territory but will not appoint any other person, firm or company to be a distributor or agent for the Products in the Territory provided that the Distributor continues to meet the requirements in sub-clause 4.1 above.

4.4 Activities

Any Products purchased will be for resale or licence to End Users in the Territory. The Distributor undertakes to refer any enquiries for Products made from outside the Territory to the Supplier, and the Supplier agrees to refer any enquiries for Products made from inside the Territory which it decides not to sell direct, to the Distributor. It is understood by the parties, although not a binding condition on the Supplier, that the Supplier will generally confine its direct sales activities to large corporations, institutional and government-related End Users. From time to time and by agreement on a case-by-case basis, the parties may agree to collaborate in order to achieve a sale of Products, in which event half the value of any such sale will count towards the Sales Targets. The Distributor further undertakes not to seek to distribute the Software outside the Territory by indirect means, through subsidiaries, affiliates, arrangements with End Users or third parties, or otherwise.

4.5 Marks

The Supplier grants the Distributor the right to use the Marks on all literature, advertising, promotional material, publications or any other communications used or developed by the Distributor and which refer to the Products. Any such use of the Marks by the Distributor will include an acknowledgment of the proprietary rights of the Supplier. The Supplier reserves the right to issue guidelines on the use of the Marks from time to time, and the Distributor agrees to comply with such guidelines.

4.6 Products and Applications

The Distributor confirms that it will purchase Products for supply to End Users as part of a system which includes Applications, and the Distributor acknowledges that the Price List is a discounted price list for the Products, applicable to purchases by the Distributor intended for onward supply to End Users together with the Applications, as a means of extending the range of applications available to End Users which utilise the Supplier's Products. If Products are resold without Applications, the Supplier's standard published prices for the Products will apply to the Distributor. Nothing in this

Agreement is intended to prevent the Distributor from setting its own prices for the supply of Products to End Users.

5. Distributor's Responsibilities

The Distributor agrees:

5.1 **Promotion and Marketing**

To use its best efforts to promote and market the Products in association with the Applications in the Territory including the provision of demonstrations to prospective End Users, and generally to act diligently, ethically and in good faith in the best interests of the Supplier in connection with the distribution of the Products, but the Distributor is not entitled to sell, license or enter into any contracts on behalf of the Supplier or to bind the Supplier in any way;

5.2 **Pre-sales Activities**

To carry out pre-sales activities, including qualifying prospective End Users for the Products, conducting demonstrations and preparing quotations and proposals for submission to prospective End Users after the Distributor has approved their content and generally to keep the Distributor informed about enquiries received from prospective End Users;

5.3 **Performance**

To perform its duties under this Agreement in such manner as it thinks fit having regard to all of the terms and conditions of this Agreement and to any directions which the Supplier may properly give from time to time, and to conduct the promotion and marketing of the Products with all due care and diligence, cultivating and maintaining good relations with End Users and prospective End Users;

5.4 **Training**

To ensure that its relevant employees and representatives are adequately trained and have sufficient expertise to be able to represent and demonstrate the Products and to market the Distributor's related services;

5.5 **Premises**

To maintain a computer centre for End User demonstrations at its main place of business and to keep this centre up to date for the prominent display of the Products and for their demonstration and to employ a sufficient number of suitably qualified administrative, technical and support personnel to enable the Distributor to perform its obligations in this Agreement satisfactorily, and further to take reasonable account of any opinion of the Supplier that an identified member of the Distributor's staff is incapable of or unsuitable for dealing in the Software;

5.6 **Market Potential and Trends**

To keep the Supplier advised about market potential and trends in the Territory, competitive information, changes of regulations and practices governing the supply of the Products, and to provide the Supplier with copies of all Distributor-generated promotional materials relating to the Products for them to be approved by the Supplier prior to their use by the Distributor;

5.7 Competing Products

Not to be involved, directly or indirectly, in the manufacture or distribution in the Territory of any products which compete with the Products, and not to seek to distribute the Products outside the Territory by indirect means, through subsidiaries, affiliates, arrangements with End Users or third parties or otherwise;

5.8 Sales Targets

To use its best endeavours to achieve the Sales Targets shown in the Schedule, and the Distributor acknowledges that if in any year of this Agreement the aggregate net invoice value of Products ordered from the Supplier by the Distributor is less than the Sales Target value for that year shown in the Schedule the Distributor's sole distribution rights are liable to be withdrawn, without prejudice to any other rights of the Distributor under this Agreement;

5.9 Support for End Users

To use all reasonable endeavours to achieve contracted delivery, installation, training and consultancy commitments, and to provide information to End Users about the Supplier's hardware maintenance services and to provide an efficient second-line support service for the Software to End Users who have a current Licence and Support Agreement;

5.10 Translations

To provide translations of:

(a) all material or prospective End User correspondence into the English language and to maintain file copies in the End User's language of all approved English language quotations and proposals, for review by the Supplier at any time. For the avoidance of doubt, correspondence with the End User relating to terms and conditions of contracts or to Product performance is an example of material correspondence;

(b) the Supplier's standard terms and conditions in the End User's language;

5.11 Inventory

To maintain an appropriate inventory in the Territory of stocks, spare parts, components and supplies for the Products to ensure prompt delivery and maintenance services to End Users;

5.12 Forecasts and Records

To provide the Supplier with copies of forecasts for supply of the Products in the Territory at monthly intervals, including a rolling annual forecast, showing estimated delivery volumes by Product and by value, estimated percentage probability of future business, anticipated delivery dates and actual perform-ance achievements against forecasts on a cumulative basis during each year of this Agreement, and further to maintain records of all Software licences granted and of all fault calls and complaints relating to the Products including response times and remedial actions taken, and to make all of those records available for the Supplier's inspection by prior appointment during the Distributor's normal business hours twice each year during this Agreement;

5.13 **Marks**

Not to infringe the Supplier's rights in its Marks, not to alter, remove or conceal any Marks or copyright notices on the Products or their packaging and not to attempt to modify the Products without the prior written consent of the Supplier, and in any event not making any reference to the Supplier in its publications without first obtaining the Supplier's approval to the form and context of the reference;

5.14 **Training and Consultancy**

To offer training and consultancy services to End Users in relation to the Products;

5.15 **Compliance with Local Laws and Regulations**

To comply with all local laws and regulations relating to the nature, method of manufacturing, packaging, labelling, sale or licensing of the Products in the Territory and to keep the Supplier fully and promptly advised of all changes to such laws and regulations which could affect the Supplier's Products in the Territory;

5.16 **After-sales**

To inform the Supplier promptly of:

(a) any complaint or after-sales enquiry concerning the Products which is received by the Distributor;

(b) any matters coming to its notice which are likely to be relevant in relation to the manufacture, sale, use or development of the Products in the Territory.

6. Supplier's Responsibilities

The Supplier agrees:

6.1 **Supply of Master Disks**

To supply a Master Disk for each Software Product;

6.2 **Information to the Distributor**

Promptly after the Commencement Date, to provide the Distributor with written information in the English language to enable the Distributor to market, distribute, maintain and support the Products within the Territory, including all current technical information relating to or affecting the use, performance or operation of the Products, and to keep the Distributor fully informed of any additions or modifications to the Products and to supply to the Distributor a copy of any additional or modified Software and any written information at the same time as it is made available to the Supplier's own direct sales personnel or to other distributors of the Products, including up-to-date Supplier's Terms and Conditions of Supply and all current technical information;

6.3 Training

To provide at the Supplier's premises in the UK such number of the Distributor's employees as the Distributor reasonably requests with such training in the functionality and use of the Products and any subsequent versions, upgrades or enhancements to enable the Distributor to understand the Products fully, the training to take place at the Supplier's premises at no charge to the Distributor except that the Distributor will be responsible for all travel, accommodation and subsistence expenses of its employees;

6.4 Promotional Literature and Further Developments

To provide the Distributor with adequate quantities of its current promotional literature relating to the Products and to keep the Distributor advised about further developments of the Products, including anticipated release dates, competitive information and any other information which may assist the Distributor in the successful promotion and distribution of the Products;

6.5 Good Faith

To act in good faith at all times towards the Distributor, and generally to co-operate with the Distributor and to provide as much assistance to the Distributor relating to the Products as the Distributor reasonably requests, including free telephone assistance during the Supplier's normal working hours to the Distributor's employees trained on the Products;

6.6 Support

To provide a second-line support service for the Software and otherwise to fulfil its obligations in each Licence and Support Agreement with End Users, and to provide an efficient and effective help desk during normal business hours in the Territory, together with an emergency out-of-hours contact service;

6.7 Continuing Development

To continue to develop, upgrade and enhance the Products to maintain their marketability and competitiveness and to supply a new version of the Master Disk whenever a new version of the Software becomes available;

6.8 Bespoke Work

To carry out bespoke work to the Software at the Distributor's request from time to time at the time and materials charge rate shown in the Charges Schedule;

6.9 Source Code Deposit Agreement

To enter into a Source Code Deposit Agreement within 30 days of the Commencement Date, if required by the Distributor, and to ensure that a copy of the latest version of the source code of the Software issued to the Distributor is held in escrow at all times with the party named as escrow custodian in the Source Code Deposit Agreement.

7. Advertising and Merchandising Fund

7.1 The Supplier will establish an advertising and merchandising fund for the purposes of financing advertising matter and literature appropriate for use in marketing the Products in the Territory. Each party will contribute equally to this fund from the proceeds of sale of the Products in amounts to be agreed at each anniversary of the Commencement Date, expressed as a percentage of the net proceeds, and interest accruing to the fund will be added to it. The Distributor will be entitled to draw on this fund for the purposes of purchasing, advertising and merchandising in the Territory, subject to obtaining the Supplier's consent in advance of any expenditure, such consent and the release of monies from the fund not to be unreasonably withheld or delayed. The Supplier will provide audited details of the fund for verification by the Distributor at least once a year and in the event of termination of this Agreement for any reason the then remaining balance in the fund, including interest accrued and unspent, will be withdrawn and repaid in equal proportions to the parties.

7.2 The Distributor will not use any advertising or promotional materials in relation to the Products except those supplied or approved by the Supplier.

8. Supply of Products

8.1 All of the Products are supplied on the terms and conditions of the Terms and Conditions of Supply and, in addition, in the case of Software on the terms and conditions of the Licence and Support Agreement. Amongst other things, these terms and conditions provide that title to Software does not pass to the Distributor or to those claiming under the Distributor, in any circumstances.

8.2 Written orders for Products must be submitted to the Supplier's Order Address and must include for each order the name and address of the End User so that serial numbers can be allocated by the Supplier, together with the location for installation of the Products, the full configuration, requested delivery dates and shipping instructions. No contract for ordered Products will come into being until the Supplier has issued its order acceptance confirming price and delivery details. The Supplier will not unreasonably withhold acceptance of any order.

8.3 The Supplier has the right to delete any Product from the Schedule by giving the Distributor 90 days' notice of the deletion. All orders already accepted by the Supplier for any deleted Product will be honoured by supply of the deleted Product or its functional equivalent. Products may be added to this Agreement by means of an amendment signed in accordance with the provisions of this Agreement.

9. Software Licensing

9.1 The Distributor is granted a licence to copy the Master Disk and related Software documentation and to use and demonstrate the Software for the purposes of securing orders from End users and in order to fulfil deliveries of Software orders only.

9.2   The Distributor undertakes:

(a)   to use the Software only for demonstration, marketing, and installation and only in accordance with the terms and conditions of this Agreement unless such use is extended by the Distributor obtaining a separate licence to use the Software for the purposes of its business;

(b)   to distribute the Software and its related documentation to End Users only after each End User has signed and returned to the Distributor a Licence and Support Agreement. The Distributor understands and acknowledges the Supplier's requirement to maintain control of its Software and the Supplier reserves the right to terminate any Software licence with a End User where there have been persistent or serious violations of that Software licence;

(c)   not otherwise to copy the Software without the prior written permission of the Supplier; and otherwise than as permitted under this clause, to keep the Software confidential;

(d)   to use all reasonable endeavours to safeguard the intellectual property rights of the Supplier in the Software, and to report promptly to the Supplier any third party claim relating to the intellectual property rights in the Software after such claim comes to the attention of the Distributor, directly or indirectly, and to co-operate with the Supplier, at the Supplier's expense, in any enforcement or other protective action taken by the Supplier and to report to the Supplier any breaches or suspected breaches of the Software Licence and Support Agreement by End Users which could adversely affect the Supplier's intellectual property rights in the Software.

10. Charges

10.1 The one-time licence fee payable by the Distributor to the Supplier for each copy of the Software licensed to an End User is shown in the Charges Schedule together with discounts applicable to orders for multiple copies for multi-user sites.

10.2 The Supplier's charge per End User for its second-line support services is shown in the Charges Schedule together with discounts applicable to multiple End Users and the Supplier's various charge rates for any other services to be provided under this Agreement.

10.3 The Charges payable to the Supplier under this Agreement will apply during the first 12 months of this Agreement and cannot then be increased more than once in any 12 months. No increase will exceed the amount of any price increase in the Supplier's local currency, after which it will be subject to conversion to £ sterling at the then prevailing rate of exchange.

10.4 The Supplier will be responsible for the cost of insurance during carriage within the UK.

10.5 All prices are exclusive of Value Added Tax and any similar taxes. All such taxes are payable by the Customer and will be applied in accordance with UK legislation in force at the tax point date.

11. Payment Terms

11.1 Unless and until credit payment terms are established, all Charges are payable in £ sterling in full (without any deduction or set-off) by the Distributor to the Supplier on or before delivery, against invoice.

11.2 The Supplier will be entitled without prejudice to its other rights to require payment in advance of delivery in relation to any order if the total amount then owed by the Distributor to the Supplier exceeds the credit limit established by the Supplier for the Distributor.

11.3 Payments which are not received when payable will be considered overdue and remain payable by the Distributor together with interest for late payment from the date payable at the statutory rate applicable as well after as before any judgment, and independent of such judgment. This interest will accrue on a daily basis and be payable on demand.

11.4 Notwithstanding the above provision for late payment, in this event the Supplier may at its option, and without prejudice to any other remedy at any time after payment has become due, terminate or temporarily suspend performance of this Agreement. If the Supplier becomes entitled to termi-nate this Agreement for any reason, any sums then due to the Supplier will immediately become payable in full.

12. Confidentiality

The parties recognise that under this Agreement they may each receive trade secrets and confidential or proprietary information of the other party, including but not limited to information concerning products, business accounts, financial or contractual arrangements. All such information which is either marked 'Confiden-tial' or stated at the time of disclosure and subsequently confirmed in writing to be confidential constitutes 'Confidential Information'. Each party agrees not to divulge Confidential Information received from the other to any of its employees who do not need to know it, and to prevent its disclosure to or access by any third party without the prior written consent of the disclosing party.

13. Indemnities and Limits of Liability

13.1 The Supplier will indemnify the Distributor for direct physical injury or death caused solely either by defects in the Products or by the negligence of its employees acting within the course of their employment and the scope of their authority.

13.2 The Supplier will indemnify the Distributor for direct damage to property caused solely either by defects in the Products or by the negligence of its employees acting within the course of their employment and the scope of their authority. The total liability of the Supplier under this sub-clause will be limited to [£1,000,000] for any one event or series of connected events.

13.3 Except as expressly stated in this clause and elsewhere in this Agreement, any liability of the Supplier for breach of this Agreement will not exceed in the aggregate of damages, costs, fees and expenses capable of being awarded to the Distributor the total price paid or due to be paid by the Distributor under this Agreement.

13.4 Except as expressly stated in this Agreement, the Supplier disclaims all liability to the Distributor in connection with the Supplier's performance of this Agreement or the Distributor's use of the Products and in no event will the Supplier be liable to the Distributor for special, indirect or consequential damages including but not limited to loss of profits or arising from loss of data or unfitness for user purposes.

13.5 The Distributor will indemnify the Supplier in respect of any losses or expenses incurred by the Supplier as a result of the Distributor's failure to maintain adequate current licences for the software used with the Products.

14. Termination

14.1 This Agreement may be terminated immediately by notice in writing:
    (a)   By either party:
        (i) if the other party is in material or continuing breach of any of its obligations under this Agreement and fails to remedy the breach (if capable of remedy) for a period of 30 days after written notice by the other party;
        (ii) if the other party is involved in any legal proceedings concerning its solvency, or ceases trading, or commits an act of bankruptcy or is adjudicated bankrupt or enters into liquidation, whether compulsory or voluntary, other than for the purposes of an amalgamation or reconstruction, or makes an arrangement with its creditors or petitions for an administration order or if a trustee, receiver, administrative receiver or manager is appointed over all or any part of its assets or generally becomes unable to pay its debts within the meaning of Section 123 or Section 268 of the Insolvency Act 1986, or equivalent circumstances occur in any other jurisdiction;
    (b)   By the Supplier:
        (i) if the Distributor fails to ensure that all payments due to the Supplier, whether in accordance with letters of credit drawn or endorsed by the Distributor in the Supplier's favour or otherwise, are met in full and on time without prejudice to any other provisions relating to late payment in this Agreement;
        (ii) if the Distributor infringes or threatens to infringe any Mark, trade name, copyright, patent right or other industrial or intellectual property right of the Supplier;

(iii) if the Distributor or substantially all of its assets should be directly or indirectly taken over or its control assumed by any governmental authority or other third party.

14.2 Any termination of this Agreement under this clause will be without prejudice to any other rights or remedies of either party under this Agreement or at law and will not affect any accrued rights or liabilities of either party at the date of termination.

15. Effect of Termination

15.1 On termination of this Agreement for any reason:
  (a) the Distributor will be entitled to fulfil all existing orders for Products to the date of termination;
  (b) the Supplier will co-operate with the Distributor to enable the Distributor to honour its commitments to End Users for so long as the Distributor has support obligations to End Users;
  (c) the Source Code Deposit Agreement will continue in full force and effect for so long as the Distributor has support obligations to Distributors;
  (d) no Software Licence and Support Agreements signed and returned by End Users will be affected;
  (e) the licence rights granted to the Distributor under this Agreement will end on termination of this Agreement except as necessary to fulfil existing commitments to provide support services to End Users.

15.2 Each party will promptly return to the other party all materials in its possession or control which belong to the other party except to the extent necessary to enable either party to fulfil its continuing obligations.

15.3 The Distributor will cease to make any reference to the Supplier or to use the Marks in its promotional materials or otherwise and will cease to hold itself out as an authorised distributor of the Supplier.

15.4 No compensation of any kind will be payable by the Supplier to the Distributor, without prejudice to any accrued rights of the parties to the date of termination.

16. General Contract Provisions

16.1 Entire Agreement
This Agreement constitutes the entire agreement between the parties and supersedes any previous agreement between the parties relating to the subject matter of this Agreement. Each of the parties acknowledges that in entering into this Agreement, it does not rely on and will have no remedy in respect of any statement of fact or opinion not recorded in this Agreement (whether negligently or innocently made), except for any representation made fraudulently.

16.2 **Variations**

No variation of these terms and conditions will be valid unless confirmed in writing by authorised signatories of both parties on or after the date of this Agreement.

16.3 **Severability**

If any of the provisions of this Agreement is judged to be illegal or unenforceable, the continuation in full force and effect of the remainder of them will not be prejudiced.

16.4 **Waiver**

No forbearance or delay by either party in enforcing its respective rights will prejudice or restrict the rights of that party, and no waiver of any such rights or of any breach of any contractual terms will be deemed to be a waiver of any other right or of any later breach.

16.5 **Rights of Third Parties**

A person who is not a party to this Agreement has no right to benefit under or to enforce any term of this Agreement.

16.6 **Assignment**

Neither party will assign, sub-contract or otherwise deal with this Agreement or any rights and obligations under this Agreement without the prior consent of the other party.

16.7 **Notices**

Any notice given under this Agreement by either party to the other must be in writing and may be delivered personally or by first class or registered post, and in the case of post will be deemed to have been given two working days after the date of posting where the addresses of the parties are both within the United Kingdom or seven working days after the date of posting where the notice is addressed to or is posted from an address outside the United Kingdom. Notices will be delivered or sent to the addresses of the parties on the first page of this Agreement or to any other address notified in writing by either party to the other for the purpose of receiving notices after the date of this Agreement.

16.8 **Force Majeure**

Neither party will be liable to the other party for any delay in or failure to perform its obligations (other than a payment of money) as a result of any cause beyond its reasonable control, including but not limited to any industrial dispute. If such delay or failure continues for at least 90 days, either party will be entitled to terminate the Agreement by notice in writing without further liability of either party arising directly as a result of such delay or failure.

16.9 **Governing Law and Jurisdiction**

This Agreement is governed by and construed according to English law and the parties submit to the exclusive jurisdiction of the courts of England and Wales.

SCHEDULES

Charges

Commencement Date

Products

Sales Targets

Supplier's Order Address

Supplier's Distribution Price List

Territory

Trade Marks

AGREEMENTS APPENDED TO THIS AGREEMENT

Source Code Deposit Agreement

Supplier's Terms and Conditions of Supply

Supplier's Software Licence and Support Agreement

Signed ....

FOR AND ON BEHALF OF

Company name ....

Date ....

Supplier

Signed ....

FOR AND ON BEHALF OF

Company name ....

Date ....

Distributor

OBJECT/SOURCE CODE LICENCE AGREEMENT

Date of Agreement ....

BETWEEN:

(1) **THE LICENSOR** whose registered office is at
.... ('Licensor');

AND

(2) **THE LICENSEE** whose registered office is at
.... ('Licensee').

1. Introduction

The Licensor agrees to license software as defined below to the Licensee, in accordance with these terms and conditions and the Licensee acknowledges that it is licensed to use such software subject to these terms and conditions ('Licence').

2. Definitions

'*Licensed Computer System*' means the computer configuration and operational environment specified in the Schedule on which the Software is licensed to run.

'*Software*' means the software products listed in the Schedule including all their subsequent modifications, upgrades, new versions and releases which shall form part of such software products, and their related documentation [including where applicable Third Party Software].

['*Source*' means any Software in a form designated by the Licensor as a 'source' option and/or 'listings' option in its Software product description and any related materials, including without limitation flow charts, logic diagrams, binaries and object codes, source codes and listings whether in machine or human readable form and all modifications, upgrades, new versions and releases to any of these materials provided to the Licensee.]

'*Third Party Software*' means all Software owned by a third party, but legally licensed for distribution by the Licensor as part of the Software, as specified in the Schedule.

3. Licence to use the Software

3.1 The Licensor grants the Licensee a non-exclusive, non-transferable licence to use the Software in object code, including where appropriate Third Party

Software, in accordance with these terms and conditions including its termination provisions.

3.2   The Licensee is licensed to use the Software [only for its own internal purposes][at the Licensee's business premises] [for the number of users][on the Licensed Computer System] [and at the address] [specified in the Schedule to this Licence][for its employees and sub-contractors who need to access and use the Software].

3.3   The Licensee may use the Software temporarily on an alternative processor to the Licensed Computer System for the purposes of disaster recovery, and not more than twice a year for the purposes of testing disaster recovery procedures.

3.4   The Licensee may transfer the Software to an alternative processor forming part of the Licensed Computer System or may relocate the Licensed Computer System [within the country of supply] provided that written notice is given to the Licensor. Any transfer of the Software to a processor outside the Licensed Computer System requires the prior written consent of the Licensor and may be subject to an additional licence fee.

3.5   Should the Licensee wish to upgrade or change the Licensed Computer System, notice must be given to the Licensor. The details in the Schedule to this Licence will be amended accordingly and an upgrade licence fee paid by the Licensee to the Licensor for the upgraded or changed Licensed Computer System, to enable the Licensee to continue to use the Software.

3.6   If the Licensee sells or disposes of the Licensed Computer System, it will ensure that all copies of the Software have previously been deleted.

3.7   The Licensee agrees to comply with any additional Third Party Software conditions notified to it on or before delivery of any Third Party Software (including if so required the execution and return of a Third Party Software Licence) and to indemnify the Licensor against any action by a Third Party Software owner as a result of any breach by the Licensee of such conditions.

[3.8   The Licensee is authorised to sub-license the Software in object code versions only to end users as defined in, and subject to the applicable terms and conditions of, a separate Reseller Agreement between the parties, for so long as such Reseller Agreement is current, and on condition that the Licensee's Sub-Licence with its customer incorporates all of the provisions of this Licence (or their equivalent) except any permission to sub-license the Software further, and any provisions relating to the supply of Source.]

[3.9   If specifically indicated in the Schedule that the Supplemental Source Licence Schedule applies, and if the Supplemental Source Licence Schedule is signed, the Licensor thereby additionally grants the Licensee a non-exclusive, non-transferable licence to use the Source subject to the terms and conditions contained in the Supplemental Source Licence Schedule. In the event of any conflict between this Licence and the Supplemental Source Licence Schedule terms, the latter will prevail in respect of the licence for the Source.]

4. Duration

4.1 This licence commences on the date of installation of the Software and will subsist for a minimum term of one calendar year. It will then continue in effect unless terminated by the Licensee on 90 days' notice of termination, given on the last day of such minimum term or at any time afterwards, subject to the other termination provisions in this Licence.

4.2 The Software licence provisions are independent of any Software support provisions, to the extent that the Licensee's licence to use the Software will survive any termination of the Licensor's obligations to support the Software. Similarly Software supplied without support will be validly licensed.

4.3 Termination of these licence provisions will automatically terminate any support obligations by the Licensor for the Software.

5. Supply, Installation and Acceptance

5.1 The programs comprising the Software will be supplied in object code, together with one copy of any related documentation.

5.2 Supply of the Software will be made to the address of the Licensee shown in this Licence [on the date agreed between the parties]. [The Licensor will make all reasonable efforts to keep to the installation date agreed with the Licensee but under no circumstances will the Licensor be liable for damages or costs arising from any delay in delivery.]

5.3 [If the Licensor is responsible for installation of the Software, it will run such commissioning tests as it considers necessary to ensure that the Software is installed correctly, and when these tests are completed, the Licensee will be deemed to have accepted the Software. This is applicable to Software, and also to new releases and new versions of the Software.] [The Software is deemed to be accepted as of the date of installation (provided that such acceptance is subject to the satisfactory performance by the Software during the seven days following installation).] [However, this provision does not apply to any Software to which the Software Development Agreement applies, which sets out separate acceptance procedures.]

5.4 Use of the Software is conditional on payment of the licence fee together with any other charges, as shown in the Schedule.

6. Rights in the Software

6.1 No title or rights of ownership, copyright or any other intellectual property in the Software, including all upgrades, modifications, new versions and releases of the Software, is or will be transferred to the Licensee.

6.2 The Licensee understands that the Software contains proprietary information, and agrees that [except in accordance with an express written authority signed by an authorised signatory of the Licensor,] it will not provide or otherwise make any of the Software and/or related documentation available for any reason to any other person, firm, company or organisation [whether for outsourcing purposes or otherwise].

6.3 The Licensee will not copy or permit the Software to be copied, except for reasonable security and backup purposes [except that the Licensee may copy the object code version of the Software as necessary to fulfil sub-licence orders in accordance with the terms and conditions of this Licence]. Any copies made will include all copyright or other proprietary notices.

6.4 The Licensee will ensure that all of its relevant employees, agents and sub-contractors are advised that the Software constitutes confidential information and that all intellectual property rights in it are the property of the Licensor, and the Licensee will [use all reasonable endeavours to] ensure that its employees, agents and sub-contractors comply with all of the terms and conditions of this clause.

6.5 Recognising that the Software has significant commercial value to the Licensor, the Licensee agrees to indemnify the Licensor in respect of any losses or expenses incurred by the Licensor as a result of the unauthorised use of the Software by any third party, whether through misuse of the Software by the Licensee or through any other breach by the Licensee of this Licence or through the negligence of the Licensee or through any other cause.

7. Licensee Undertakings

7.1 The Licensee acknowledges that it is licensed to use the Software only in accordance with the express terms of this Licence.

7.2 The Licensee undertakes:
   (a) to satisfy itself that the Software meets the needs of its business. It is the sole responsibility of the Licensee to determine that the Software is ready for operational use in the Licensee's business before it is so used;
   (b) to allow the Licensor to study its information and data used with the Software for the purpose of rectifying any problems with the Software;
   (c) to ensure that the operating system and compiler and any other software with which the Software will be used is either the property of the Licensee or is legally licensed to the Licensee for use with the Software. The Licensee will indemnify the Licensor in respect of any claims by third parties and all related costs, expenses or damages in the event of any alleged violation of third party proprietary rights which results in any claims against the Licensor.

7.3   The Licensee warrants that the Software and all copies will remain under its control and that it will take all reasonable precautions to safeguard the Software against unauthorised use.

7.4   The Licensee hereby acknowledges that it is the best judge of the value and importance of the data held on the Licensed Computer System and that it takes sole responsibility for instituting and operating all necessary backup procedures (for its own benefit) to ensure that data integrity can be maintained in the event of loss of data for any reason.

7.5   If the Licensee intends to attempt the decompilation of any of the Software for error correction or any other purpose in the exercise of derived statutory rights, the Licensee will first give reasonable notice to the Licensor of its intention.

8. Licence Fee and Payment Terms

8.1   The licence fee as set out in the Schedule will be paid to the Licensor on or before installation, against invoice, or as otherwise specified in the Schedule.

8.2   All fees and charges are exclusive of Value Added Tax and any similar taxes. All such taxes are payable by the Licensee and will be applied in accordance with UK legislation in force at the tax point date.

8.3   All invoices are payable 20 days after receipt. Payments which are not received when payable will be considered overdue and remain payable by the Licensee together with interest for late payment from the date payable at the statutory rate applicable as well after as before any judgment, and independent of such judgment. This interest will accrue on a daily basis and be payable on demand.

8.4   Notwithstanding the above provision for late payment, in this event the Licensor may at its option, and without prejudice to any other remedy at any time after payment has become due, terminate or temporarily suspend performance of this Licence.

8.5   If the Licensor becomes entitled to terminate this Licence for any reason, any sums then due to the Licensor will immediately become payable in full.

9. Licensor's Warranties

9.1   The Licensor warrants that it has good title or is otherwise authorised to license the Software to the Licensee.

9.2   The Licensor represents and warrants to the Licensee that at the time of delivery of the Software to the Licensee it is a complete, accurate and up-to-date copy of the current release.

9.3   The Software is designed to conform to the Software product specification [user guide] applicable at the time of the Licensee's order. However, the Licensor does not warrant that the Software will work without interruption or that it is error-free.

9.4 The Licensor's sole obligation in the event of non-conformity will be:

(a) in the case of Software developed or owned by the Licensor to remedy any non-conformity of the Software to its specification [user guide]; and

(b) in the case of Third Party Software to obtain and supply a corrected version where there is a demonstrated non-conformity to specification;

provided in either case that the Licensor has been notified of the non-conformity within 90 days of the date of delivery to the Licensee, or if any commissioning tests are being carried out by the Licensor, the date on which they are completed, whichever is the later. This warranty does not apply to Software developed under the terms of the Software Development Agreement, which is subject to any warranty and related provisions set out in that Agreement.

9.5 The above constitutes the only warranties provided by the Licensor in respect of the Software. The obligations and liabilities of the Licensor set out in this Licence replace all implied guarantees and warranties, including without limitation, any warranty of satisfactory quality or fitness for a particular purpose which is the Licensee's responsibility to determine.

9.6 The Licensee acknowledges that:

(a) the Software has not been produced to meet individual Licensee specifications;

(b) the Software cannot be tested in advance in every possible operating combination and environment;

(c) it is not possible to produce Software known to be error-free in all circumstances.

9.7 The Licensor recommends, and will provide if so requested, support and maintenance for the Software.

10. Modifications

The Licensor reserves the right to make improvements, substitutions, modifications or enhancements to any part of the Software [provided that the functionality and performance of the Software will not as a result be materially affected to the Licensee's detriment].

11. Escrow

The Licensor has established certain source code deposit ('escrow') arrangements covering the source code and documentation for the Software with an escrow custodian. While this Licence continues to exist, the Licensee will be entitled to receive the protection of such escrow arrangements subject to entering into a separate written escrow agreement with the Licensor and the escrow custodian.

12. Intellectual Property Rights Indemnity

12.1 The Licensor, at its own expense, will defend or cause to be defended or, at its option, settle any claim or action brought against the Licensee on the issue of infringement of any [United Kingdom or Republic of Ireland] intellectual property right by the Software ('Claim'). Subject to the other conditions of this clause, the Licensor will pay any final judgment entered against the Licensee with respect to any Claim, and fully indemnify the Licensee in respect of all costs and expenses relating to the Claim provided that the Licensee:

(a) notifies the Licensor in writing of the Claim immediately on becoming aware of it;

(b) grants sole control of the defence of the Claim to the Licensor; and

(c) gives the Licensor complete and accurate information and full assistance to enable the Licensor to settle or defend the Claim.

The costs and fees of any separate legal representation for the Licensee will be the Licensee's sole responsibility.

12.2 If any part of the Software becomes the subject of any Claim or if a court judgment is made that the Software does infringe, or if the use or licensing of any part of the Software is restricted, the Licensor at its option and expense may:

(a) obtain for the Licensee the right under the patent, design right, trade secret or copyright to continue to use the Software; or

(b) replace or modify the Software so that any alleged or adjudged infringement is removed; or

(c) if the use of the Software is prevented by permanent injunction, accept its return and refund an amount equal to the sum paid by the Licensee for the Software subject to straight line depreciation over a five-year period.

12.3 The Licensor will have no liability under this clause for:

(a) any infringement arising from the combination of the Software with other software not supplied by the Licensor; or

(b) the modification of the Software unless the modification was made or approved expressly by the Licensor.

12.4 IN NO CIRCUMSTANCES WILL THE LICENSOR BE LIABLE FOR ANY COSTS OR EXPENSES INCURRED BY THE LICENSEE WITHOUT THE LICENSOR'S PRIOR WRITTEN AUTHORISATION AND THE FOREGOING STATES THE ENTIRE REMEDY OF THE LICENSEE IN RESPECT OF ANY INTELLECTUAL PROPERTY RIGHT INFRINGEMENT BY THE SOFTWARE.

13. Indemnities and Limits of Liability

13.1 The Licensee acknowledges that it has accepted these terms and conditions in the knowledge that the Licensor must limit its liability and that the licence fees and any other charges have been calculated accordingly.

13.2 The Licensor will indemnify the Licensee for direct physical injury or death caused solely either by defects in the Software or by the negligence of its employees acting within the course of their employment and the scope of their authority.

13.3 The Licensor will indemnify the Licensee for direct damage to property caused solely either by defects in the Software or by the negligence of its employees acting within the course of their employment and the scope of their authority. The total liability of the Licensor under this sub-clause will be limited to [£500,000] for any one event or series of connected events.

13.4 Except as expressly stated in this clause 13 and elsewhere in this Licence, any liability of the Licensor for breach of this Licence will not exceed in the aggregate of damages, costs, fees and expenses capable of being awarded to the Licensee the total fees and charges paid or due to be paid by the Licensee under this Licence.

13.5 Except as expressly stated in this Agreement, the Licensor disclaims all liability to the Licensee in contract or in tort (including negligence or breach of statutory duty) in connection with the Licensor's performance of this Licence or the Licensee's use of the Software, and in no event will the Licensor be liable to the Licensee for special, indirect or consequential damages or for loss of profits or arising from loss of data or unfitness for user purposes.

14. Termination

14.1 This Licence may be terminated immediately by notice in writing:
  (a) by the Licensor if the Licensee fails to pay any sums due under this Agreement by the due date without prejudice to any other provisions relating to late payment in this Agreement;
  (b) by either party if the other party is in material or continuing breach of any of its obligations under this Licence and fails to remedy the breach (if capable of remedy) for a period of 30 days after written notice by the other party;
  (c) by either party if the other party is involved in any legal proceedings concerning its solvency, or ceases trading, or commits an act of bankruptcy or is adjudicated bankrupt or enters into liquidation, whether compulsory or voluntary, other than for the purposes of an amalgamation or reconstruction, or makes an arrangement with its creditors or petitions for an administration order or has a receiver or manager appointed over all or any part of its assets or generally becomes unable to pay its debts within the meaning of Section 123 of the Insolvency Act 1986, or equivalent circumstances occur in any other jurisdiction.

14.2 Any termination of this Licence under this clause will be without prejudice to any other rights or remedies of either party under this Licence or at law and will not affect any accrued rights or liabilities of either party at the date of termination.

14.3 On termination of this Licence, the Licensee will be obliged to certify in writing to the Licensor within 14 days of termination that it has erased the Software and all copies of any part of the Software from the Licensed Computer System and from its magnetic media and that it has no ability to reproduce the Software in any way, and it will immediately return to the Licensor all related documentation belonging to the Licensor.

15. General Contract Provisions

15.1 **Variations**

No variation of these terms and conditions will be valid unless confirmed in writing by authorised signatories of both parties on or after the date of this Licence.

15.2 **Severability**

If any of the provisions of this Licence is judged to be illegal or unenforceable, the continuation in full force and effect of the remainder of them will not be prejudiced.

15.3 **Waiver**

No forbearance or delay by either party in enforcing its respective rights will prejudice or restrict the rights of that party, and no waiver of any such rights or of any breach of any contractual terms will be deemed to be a waiver of any other right or of any later breach.

15.4 **Rights of Third Parties**

A person who is not a party to this Licence has no right to benefit under or to enforce any term of this Agreement.

15.5 **Assignment**

Neither party will assign this Licence [or any benefits or interests arising under this Licence] without the prior written consent of the other party [except that assignments to associated companies [of the Licensor/Licensee] will be permitted] [which will not be unreasonably withheld or delayed].

15.6 **Notices**

Any notice given under this Licence by either party to the other must be in writing and may be delivered personally or by first-class post, and in the case of post will be deemed to have been given [two][seven] working days after the date of posting. Notices will be delivered or sent to the addresses of the parties on the first page of this Licence or to any other address notified in writing by either party to the other for the purpose of receiving notices after the date of this Licence.

15.7 **Governing Law and Jurisdiction**

This Licence is governed by and construed according to English law and the parties submit to the exclusive jurisdiction of the courts of England and Wales.

SCHEDULE

Licensed Computer System ....

Software description ....

Third Party Software ....

Software Development Agreement title and date, if applicable ....

....

Fees and charges ....

Does the Supplemental Source Licence Schedule apply?   Yes/No

FOR AND ON BEHALF OF THE LICENSEE	**FOR AND ON BEHALF OF THE LICENSOR**
The Licensee agrees to accept the licence for the Software on the terms and conditions of this Licence Agreement	The Licensor agrees to license the Software on the terms and conditions of this Licence Agreement

Signed ....   Signed ....

Name ....   Name ....

Date ....   Date ....

Licensee Authorised Representative   **Director of the Licensor**

SUPPLEMENTAL SOURCE LICENCE SCHEDULE

The terms and conditions of the applicable Licence of which this Schedule forms part continue to apply to the Software, together with the following additional provisions in respect of Source:

1. Source is provided without warranty or support services of any kind, other than provision of documentation at the Licensor's sole option.

2. The Licensee will have the right to modify any Source provided by the Licensor in order to further the development of proprietary products of the Licensee, provided that such proprietary products do not infringe any of the legal or equitable rights of the Licensor relating to its proprietary information or trade secrets or copyrights and further provided that all unmodified portions of Source remain subject to the terms of the Software Object Licence.

3. The Licensor will not be obliged to provide warranty or support services in respect of any object code versions of modified Source Software.

4. Source may be used in any Licensed Computer System.

5. Source is licensed to the Licensee for an indefinite term, subject to the termination for cause provisions in the Agreement.

6. The Licensee undertakes that it will use the Source only for the purposes of its business and not for any form of commercial exploitation, and that it will not supply any copy of all or any part of the Source to any third party for any purpose without the prior written consent of the Licensor.

FOR AND ON BEHALF OF THE LICENSEE

The Licensee agrees to accept the licence for the Software Source on the terms and conditions of this Schedule.

Signed ....

Name ....

Date ....

Licensee Authorised Representative

FOR AND ON BEHALF OF THE LICENSOR

The Licensor agrees to license the Software on the terms and conditions of this Schedule.

Signed ....

Name ....

Date ....

Director of the Licensor

DEMONSTRATION AND EVALUATION LICENCE AGREEMENT

FOR .... **SOFTWARE** ('Software')

....
registered office: ....
....
('we', the Licensor)
and
....
registered office: ....
....
('you', the Licensee)
Date of agreement: ....

You are entitled to use the Software only if you agree to abide by these terms and conditions.

1. Terms and Conditions

These are the terms and conditions on which we license the Software to you and the staff within your organisation to use.

2. Licence to use the Software

2.1   We grant you a non-exclusive, non-transferable licence to use the Software free of charge subject to these terms and conditions, and limited in time to whichever of the following occurs first:
- six months from the date you receive the disk containing the Software; or
- the date on which you and your staff cease using the Software; or
- until the time limit embedded in the Software takes effect, at which point the Software will no longer work.

2.2   We license you to use the Software only for demonstration, training and education purposes at your business premises. You are not entitled to use the Software for commercial purposes.

2.3   We have the right to grant you this licence. We are not transferring any rights of ownership, copyright or other intellectual property in the Software to you.

3. Conditions of Licence

3.1   Because the Software is supplied to you 'as is' without charge, only for training and demonstration purposes, we do not give any warranties about it, whether express or implied, including, but not limited to, implied warranties of quality and fitness for a particular purpose.

3.2   We will not be providing support and maintenance for the Software.

3.3   Because of the circumstances of the supply of the Software, we will not be liable to you or to any third party for any lost revenues or profits, loss of data or any direct, indirect or consequential damages relating to the Software in any way, or for inability to use the Software for any reason.

3.4

(a)   If you learn of any claim against you that the Software infringes the right of any third party and you inform us of the claim and let us settle or litigate it and do not yourself settle or litigate it, and the claim does not arise from your breach of this licence, we will indemnify you against any damages or costs arising from the claim and we will pay your expenses, provided that you co-operate with us.

(b)   If the Software should become the subject of any claim, or if a court judgment is made that the Software does infringe, or if the use of the Software is restricted, we may withdraw the Software from use, in which case you acknowledge that you will have no claim to it.

(c)   This clause 3.4 states your entire remedy in respect of any intellectual property right infringement by the Software.

4. Your use of the Software

4.1   You agree that:
   * you and your staff will keep the Software confidential;
   * you will not copy the Software or allow anyone else to copy it;
   * you will not make the Software available to anyone else.

4.2   You agree that you have accepted the use of this Software on the basis of this licence, recognising that we must limit and exclude our liability to the extent legally possible.

4.3   You also agree that if we suffer any loss, damage, fine or expenses as a result of unauthorised access to or any use or misuse of the Software because of your breach of any provision of this Agreement, you will indemnify us.

5. Governing Law and Jurisdiction

These terms and conditions are governed by and construed according to English law.

Signed by .... Signed by ....
Authorised Representative of Software *Authorised Representative of Software*
Licensor *Licensee*

Name .... Name ....

Date .... Date ....

SOURCE CODE DEPOSIT (ESCROW SERVICES) AGREEMENT

Date of Agreement ....

BETWEEN:

(1)   **THE OWNER** whose registered office is at ....
.... ('Owner');

(2)   **THE LICENSEE** whose registered office is at ....
.... ('Licensee');

(3)   **THE ESCROW CUSTODIAN** whose registered office is at ....
.... ('Escrow Custodian').

Background

(A)   The Owner has licensed the software described below to the Licensee in object code under certain terms and conditions, and provides support and maintenance services for such software to the Licensee.

(B)   In certain circumstances the Owner may no longer be able to provide support and maintenance services, and the Licensee may require access to the source code to enable the software to continue to be supported and maintained.

(C)   The Owner has therefore agreed to deposit a copy of the source code for such software with the Escrow Custodian, who will release it to the Licensee under the terms and conditions agreed below if certain specified events occur, to enable the software to continue to be supported and maintained.

1. Definitions

'*Distribution Agreement*' means the distribution agreement between the Licensor and Licensee, identified in the Schedule.

'*Licence Agreement*' means the licence agreement for the Software between the Licensor and the Licensee, identified in the Schedule.

'*Software*' means the software products and their related documentation licensed to the Licensee, specified in the Schedule.

'*Source Code*' means a copy of the source code version of the Software, including any modifications, enhancements, revisions or updates in versions as supplied to the Licensee from time to time by the Licensor, together with all related listings, flowcharts and associated documentation and details of any software not owned by the Licensor, as necessary for translating into executable code accessible for modification or enhancement.

'*Support Agreement*' means the support agreement for the Software between the Licensor and the Licensee, identified in the Schedule.

2. Deposit of Source Code

2.1　Following the execution of this Agreement, the Licensor will ensure that the Source Code, clearly identified, is promptly deposited with the Escrow Custodian.

2.2　Whenever a new version of the Software is made available to the Licensee, the Licensor will promptly deposit with the Escrow Custodian a new version of the Source Code, and notify the Licensee in writing that the deposit has been made.

2.3　If no new version has been deposited in any 12-month period, the Licensor will deposit a replacement copy of the then current version of the Source Code with the Escrow Custodian and will notify the Licensee in writing that the deposit has been made.

3. Custody of Source Code

3.1　Whenever the Source Code is deposited, the Escrow Custodian will arrange for its safe and secure storage in accordance with its standard procedures, and send written confirmation that it has been received and stored to the Licensor and the Licensee respectively.

3.2　Upon receiving a new version of the Source Code two versions later than the earliest version held by the Escrow Custodian, the Escrow Custodian will return the earliest version to the Licensor.

3.3　On receiving a replacement Source Code, the Escrow Custodian will return to the Licensor the Source Code which it replaces.

4. Release of Source Code

4.1　If the Licensor becomes or is at serious and substantial risk of becoming subject to any form of insolvency, administrative receivership or receivership or anything analogous to such event occurs in any applicable jurisdiction or if the Licensor ceases or threatens to cease trading [or if the Licensor has defaulted substantially in any obligation to provide support of the Software Products under the Support Agreement and has failed to remedy such default notified by the Licensee to the Licensor under the terms of such Agreement] then the Licensee will notify both the Escrow Custodian and the Licensor.

4.2　Unless within ten working days of this notification, the Licensor delivers to the Escrow Custodian and to the Licensee a counter-notice signed by an authorised officer of the Licensor that no such failure has occurred or that any such failure has been rectified, then in order to obtain the release of the Source Code the Licensee will submit to the Escrow Custodian a statutory declaration which will:

(a)   be sworn by an authorised officer of the Licensee;

(b)   set out the facts and circumstances for seeking release;

(c)   state that the documents attached to it comprise all relevant support-ing documentation in the Licensee's possession.

4.3   Upon receipt of this statutory declaration, the Escrow Custodian will arrange for the release of a copy of the Source Code to the Licensee.

5. Licensee's Undertakings

Upon receipt of the Source Code, the Licensee will:

5.1   use and copy the Source Code solely for the purposes of supporting or enhancing the Software and/or alleviating or correcting any failure of the Software to conform to any software description or specification contained in the Licence Agreement, copying for security and back-up purposes only as reasonably necessary, and in any event including the Licensor's copyright notice and any other proprietary information;

5.2   limit access to the Source Code to those of its employees, agents, contractors or sub-contractors who are directly engaged in the support or enhancement of the Software;

5.3   not assign, transfer, sell, lease, rent, charge or otherwise deal in or encumber the Source Code nor use it on behalf of or for the benefit of any other party [except, where the Licensee is an authorised distributor of the Software, to use it for the benefit of end users to whom the Licensee is authorised to supply the Software under the terms of the Distribution Agreement between the Licensee and the Licensor]; and

5.4   without prejudice to the generality of the foregoing, will take any other steps necessary from time to time to protect the confidential information and intellectual property rights of the Licensor in the Source Code and to ensure the compliance with the provisions of this clause by its employees, agents, contractors, and sub-contractors.

6. Escrow Custodian's Covenants

The Escrow Custodian covenants and undertakes to the Licensor not to use the Source Code for its own purposes nor on behalf of any other party nor to release it except in accordance with the provisions of this Agreement.

7. Licensor's Warranty

The Licensor represents and warrants to the Licensee that the Source Code deposited with the Escrow Custodian will at all times be a complete, accurate and up-to-date copy of the source code version of the current version of the Software together with all relevant complete, accurate and up-to-date listings, logic manuals and flowcharts.

8. Verifying the Source Code

8.1 On receiving a written request from the Licensee, the Escrow Custodian will arrange for an independent expert to carry out tests which will reasonably establish whether the Licensor is in compliance with the warranty set out in clause 7 above.

8.2 If, in the independent expert's reasonable written judgment, the Licensor is in breach of the warranty under clause 7 above, then upon receiving notice of this from the Escrow Custodian, the Licensor must deposit with the Escrow Custodian within 14 days of receipt of this notice those revisions to the Source Code which will be necessary to ensure its compliance with such warranty, and the Escrow Custodian will then arrange to have further tests carried out as specified in this clause, the charges for such further tests to be paid for by the Licensor.

8.3 If, in the independent expert's reasonable written judgment, the Licensor is in breach of the warranty under clause 7 above, then the Escrow Custodian's charges for arranging the tests and for the independent expert carrying out the tests and reporting on the results will be paid by the Licensor. If, in the independent expert's reasonable written judgment, the Licensor is not in breach of the warranty, then the Escrow Custodian's charges for arranging the tests and for the independent expert carrying out the tests and reporting on the results will be paid by the Licensee.

8.4 The Escrow Custodian and the independent expert whom it appoints will be entitled to charge in respect of this clause in arrears on a time-and-materials basis at their prevailing rates. Such charges will be payable (together with any applicable Value Added Tax by the Licensor or the Licensee (as the case may be)) within 20 days of receiving the invoice.

9. Ownership and Confidentiality of Source Code

9.1 Notwithstanding the deposit and release of the Source Code in accordance with the terms of this Agreement, no property in it will be transferred to the Licensee or to the Escrow Custodian.

9.2 The Licensee and the Escrow Custodian will treat the Source Code and all information coming to either party's knowledge or into its possession under this Agreement in the strictest confidence and secrecy, and this obligation and the Licensee's undertakings given in clause 5 above will survive the termination of this Agreement.

9.3 The Escrow Custodian will procure that any independent expert authorised under this Agreement to access the Source Code will sign a written undertaking to treat the Source Code in the strictest confidence and secrecy, so far as possible upon the same terms as those imposed on the Escrow Custodian and the Licensee.

10. Liability of Escrow Custodian

10.1 The Escrow Custodian will not itself be under any obligation to examine, enquire into or inspect the relevance, accuracy or completeness or any other aspect of the Source Code or to determine that whatever is deposited is or is not the Source Code.

10.2 The Escrow Custodian will not be under any obligation to examine, enquire into or check the accuracy, completeness or authenticity of any statutory declaration submitted by the Licensee.

10.3 The Escrow Custodian will not be liable either to the Licensor or to the Licensee or to any third party for any indirect or consequential loss or loss of profits resulting from any breach or non-performance by the Escrow Custodian of any of its obligations under this Agreement, and the Escrow Custodian's liability under this Agreement will in any event be limited to £100,000.

10.4 The Licensor hereby grants a licence to the Escrow Custodian to have as many copies of the Source Code made as the Escrow Custodian may in its reasonable opinion consider necessary to comply with its obligations under this Agreement.

11. Charges

11.1 The Licensor and the Licensee will each pay the Escrow Custodian's charges in the amounts and at the times set out in the Charges Schedule.

11.2 The Escrow Custodian's charges are exclusive of expenses incurred in the performance of this Agreement by the Escrow Custodian, in respect of media, courier charges, and other reasonably and necessarily incurred items, which will be chargeable in addition.

11.3 All charges and expenses are exclusive of Value Added Tax and any similar taxes. All such taxes are also payable and will be applied in accordance with UK legislation in force at the tax point date.

11.4 All invoices will be payable 30 days from receipt except for the release fee specified in the Schedule which will be payable subject to the presentation of an invoice immediately prior to and as a condition of the release by the Escrow Custodian of the Source Code.

11.5 Payments which are not received when payable will be considered overdue and remain payable by the Customer together with interest for late payment from the date payable at the statutory rate applicable as well after as before any judgment, and independent of such judgment. This interest will accrue on a daily basis and be payable on demand.

11.6 The Escrow Custodian will be entitled to increase its charges on the anniversary of the date of execution of this Agreement and thereafter not more than once in any successive period of 12 months while this Agreement is in force by giving not less than 60 days' notice to the Owner and the Licensee provided that any such increase expressed as a percentage does not exceed any percentage increase in the Retail Price Index for the 12 months immediately preceding the date of the notice.

12. Termination

12.1 This Agreement may be terminated:
- (a) by the Escrow Custodian upon giving not less than 90 days notice to the Licensor and to the Licensee; or
- (b) jointly by the Licensor and the Licensee upon giving not less than 30 days notice to the Escrow Custodian;
- (c) by the Licensee alone upon giving not less than 30 days notice to both the Escrow Custodian and the Licensor;
- (d) by the Licensor alone upon giving not less than 30 days notice to both the Escrow Custodian and the Licensee provided that the written consent of the Licensee has first been given, or upon giving not less than 120 days notice to both the Escrow Custodian and the Licensee provided that it has appointed a replacement custodian of the Source Code on terms and conditions as nearly as possible identical to those set out in this Agreement that will be reasonably acceptable to the Licensee.

12.2 This Agreement will be terminated promptly by the Licensor if the Escrow Custodian becomes or threatens to become or is at serious and substantial risk of becoming subject to any form of insolvency administration or receivership, or is in fundamental breach of its obligations under this Agreement.

12.3 Forthwith upon receiving notice of termination under clause 12.1(a) or 12.2 above, the Licensor and the Licensee agree to use their respective best endeavours to appoint a mutually acceptable replacement custodian of the Source Code on terms and conditions as nearly as possible identical to those set out in this Agreement.

12.4 This Agreement will be terminated immediately if the Licensee attempts to make an assignment for the benefit of creditors, or if a receiver, trustee in bankruptcy or similar officer is appointed to take charge over all or part of its property, or if the Licensee is adjudged a bankrupt, or fails to comply with any other provision of this Agreement, and such failure is not remedied within ten days after notice of the failure has been given to the Licensee.

12.5 If this Agreement is terminated under this clause, the Escrow Custodian will return the Source Code to the Licensor, provided that all fees and charges have been paid.

12.6 This Agreement will terminate upon the release of the Source Code by the Escrow Custodian to the Licensee as provided for in this Agreement.

12.7 If the Licence Agreement is rightfully terminated by the Licensor because of the Licensee's unremedied default under the terms of that Licence Agreement, this Agreement will terminate immediately.

13. Disputes

13.1 Any dispute arising at any time between the parties to this Agreement in respect of the release of the Source Code or the testing of the Source Code will be referred to such independent party as the parties unanimously nominate.

13.2 If the parties should fail to nominate an independent party unanimously within ten working days of the date of the dispute, then such dispute will be referred at the instance of any party to an independent party appointed by the President for the time being of the British Computer Society.

13.3 The independent party will act as an expert whose decision (including a decision in respect of costs) will except in the case of manifest error be final and binding upon the parties.

14. General Contract Provisions

14.1 Entire Agreement

This Agreement constitutes the entire agreement and understanding between the parties in respect of source code deposit services, and supersedes any previous agreement between the parties in this connection. Each of the parties acknowledges and agrees that in entering into this Agreement, and the documents referred to in it, it does not rely on, and will have no remedy in respect of any statement of fact or opinion not recorded in this Agreement (whether negligently or innocently made).

14.2 Variations

No variation of these terms and conditions will be valid unless confirmed in writing by authorised signatories of all parties on or after the date of this Agreement.

14.3 Severability

If any of the provisions of this Agreement is judged to be illegal or unenforceable, the continuation in full force and effect of the remainder of them will not be prejudiced.

14.4 Waiver

No forbearance or delay by any party in enforcing its respective rights will prejudice or restrict the rights of that party, and no waiver of any such rights or of any breach of any contractual terms will be deemed to be a waiver of any other right or of any later breach.

14.5 **Rights of Third Parties**

A person who is not a party to this Agreement has no right to benefit under or to enforce any term of this Agreement.

14.6 **Assignment**

None of the parties will assign, sub-contract or otherwise deal with this Agreement or any rights and obligations under this Agreement.

14.7 **Notices**

Any notice given under this Agreement by either party to the others must be in writing and may be delivered personally or by first-class post, and in the case of post will be deemed to have been given two working days after the date of posting. Notices will be delivered or sent to the addresses of the parties on the first page of this Agreement or to any other address notified in writing by either party to the others for the purpose of receiving notices after the date of this Agreement.

14.8 **Governing Law and Jurisdiction**

This Agreement is governed by and construed according to English law and the parties submit to the exclusive jurisdiction of the courts of England and Wales.

SCHEDULE

Licence Agreement

Title, parties and date of Agreement

Distribution Agreement

Title, parties and date of Agreement

Support Agreement details

Title, parties and date of Agreement

Software

Details

CHARGES SCHEDULE

Fee	Payable by	When payable
Initial fee £	Owner	On execution of this Agreement
Registration fee £	Licensee	On execution of this Agreement
Annual renewal fee £	Licensee	Annually in advance
Further deposit fee £	Owner	On deposit of new version or replacement
Release fee £	Licensee	Prior to release of the Software Source Code to the Licensee

SIGNED

....

FOR AND ON BEHALF OF

Company name ....

Date ....

Owner

SIGNED

....

FOR AND ON BEHALF OF

Company name ....

Date ....

Licensee

SIGNED

....

FOR AND ON BEHALF OF

Company name ....

Date ....

Escrow Custodian

HARDWARE MAINTENANCE SERVICES AGREEMENT

This precedent is between a supplier and a reseller customer with end users to whom the services may also be provided.

Date of Agreement ....

BETWEEN:

(1)   **THE SUPPLIER** whose registered office is at
.... ('**Supplier**');

AND

(2)   **THE CUSTOMER** whose registered office is at
.... ('**Customer**').

1. Introduction

The Supplier has experience and expertise in providing hardware maintenance services and the Customer wishes to receive such services.

2. Definitions

'*Commencement Date*' means the date identified as such in the Schedule.

'*End Users*' means those customers of the Customer supplied with Products.

'*Products*' means the hardware items listed in the Schedule to which the Services will apply according to the terms and conditions of this Agreement.

'*Schedule*' means the one or more Schedules of Products attached to this Agreement and which form part of this Agreement.

'*Services*' means the Product maintenance services provided by the Supplier to the Customer on the terms and conditions of this Agreement and more particularly detailed in this Agreement.

'*Site*' means the locations where the Products are installed as agreed by the Supplier, which may be either the Customer's location or the End Users' locations, identified in the Schedule.

'*Supplier Maintenance and Support Centre*' means the supplier's address and telephone number details specified in the Schedule.

'*System*' means Products manufactured or supplied by the Supplier for use in combination with each other.

3. Term

This Agreement commences on the date shown in the Schedule and will continue for an initial period of 12 calendar months after which it will remain in force until terminated by either party giving at least 90 days' notice of termination to the other to expire on the anniversary of the Commencement Date or on any subsequent anniversary, or by the Customer giving 90 days' notice within 30 days of receipt of notification of a change in prices by the Customer pursuant to this Agreement, and otherwise subject to the termination provisions of this Agreement.

4. Schedules

4.1   The Customer will ensure that each of its End Users has a copy of this Agreement and, without prejudice to its overriding responsibility for the performance of all of its obligations in this Agreement, the Customer will use all reasonable endeavours to ensure that each of its End Users performs those Customer obligations in respect of every Site referenced in any Schedule signed by the End User.

4.2   Each Schedule must be fully completed and signed by the Customer or an End User and by the Supplier before it will take effect as part of this Agreement. By its signature the Customer and/or End User confirms that the contents of the Schedule are accurate and that the Supplier is entitled to invoice the Customer at the invoice address specified in the Schedule, for maintenance of the Products listed in the Schedule. The Customer will be responsible for monitoring payment of such invoices in accordance with the terms and conditions of this Agreement.

4.3   Where Products are added to, or deleted from, a Schedule during an operating year of this Agreement, this will be confirmed to the Customer and to the relevant End User in a letter from the Supplier, and invoicing will take account of such additions or deletions. A revised Schedule will not be issued until the next following renewal date shown on the Schedule.

4.4   Any terms and conditions contained in a Schedule prevail over the terms and conditions in this Agreement.

5. Cover

All Services will be performed within the Supplier's normal working hours of 9.00 am to 5.00 pm, Monday to Friday excluding public holidays. Out-of-hours Services can be provided by arrangement and will be charged for at the Supplier's then current UK extended cover rates. Where out-of-hours Services are provided on a permanent basis, the Supplier's applicable extended cover charges will be payable and detailed in the relevant Schedule.

6. Eligibility for Product Services

6.1   In order to maintain effective networking and optimum performance levels of interconnected equipment, all Supplier products networked at a Site must be included as Products in the relevant Schedule.

6.2   The Products must be in normal operating condition as determined by the Supplier and be at a Supplier-supported revision level. Unless the Products are still under the Supplier's warranty when added to a System, they will be subject to inspection and approval by the Supplier before becoming eligible for coverage. This inspection will be charged to the Customer at the Supplier's then current rates, together with any travel and other expenses necessarily incurred. The Supplier will then provide the Customer with a quotation at its prevailing time-and-material service rates for any repairs and adjustments deemed necessary by the Supplier to return a Product to normal operating condition or specified revision level, and the Customer will authorise the Supplier to proceed with such repairs and adjustments as a pre-condition to the Supplier's inclusion of the Product in the relevant Schedule for coverage.

7. Services

The Supplier will provide the following Services:

7.1   The Supplier will use all reasonable endeavours to provide attendance at the site for the purposes of Product repair or maintenance within 8 working hours from the time of receipt of the Customer's call. Other response options are available at additional cost and the Customer's selections of these options are noted in the Schedules for the selected Products. In all instances, the Customer's calls for service will receive priority of response over calls from other customers of the Supplier who have not contracted for the provision of Services by means of a Supplier service agreement.

7.2   The Supplier will supply all labour during the contracted cover time, and the parts and materials necessary to maintain the Products in good working condition.

7.3   Services include the diagnosis and correction of equipment malfunctions and failures. Remedies may consist of temporary procedures to be followed by the Customer while a permanent repair or remedy is being sought. If the Supplier determines that additional parts or resources are required, provision of the Services may be interrupted and will resume as soon as such parts or resources are available.

7.4   Replacement parts are provided to the Customer either on an interim loan or on an exchange basis. Such parts may be new or functionally equivalent to new. Where parts are replaced, the replaced parts become the property of the Supplier and the replacement parts become the property of the Customer.

7.5   Throughout the term of this Agreement, the Supplier will perform preventive maintenance routines on all Products where such routines are applicable. At the Supplier's option, such preventive maintenance calls may be performed in conjunction with a Customer-requested call for remedial maintenance. All preventive maintenance will be performed during the Supplier's normal working hours, although if requested by the Customer and agreed to by the Supplier, preventive maintenance outside normal working hours may be provided at the Supplier's then current charge rates for such out-of-hours Services.

7.6 A telephone help-line support facility is available to the Customer during the Supplier's normal working hours or agreed extended hours of cover, for the purposes of reporting equipment malfunctions.

7.7 Following any request from the Customer, the Supplier will decommission any Product and re-install it at a new location subject to the Customer giving the Supplier reasonable notice and agreeing to pay the Supplier's then current charges for this service, the Customer remaining responsible for any shipping arrangements, insurance and other charges or expenses required in order to move the Product. Moving a Product to a different location may result in an increased maintenance charge for that Product. In this event, the Supplier will notify the Customer of the new charge and the Customer will have the option, within 14 days of such notification, to remove the Product from this Agreement, subject to remaining responsible for payment of any outstanding maintenance charges applicable to the Product during the current operating period of this Agreement. Where the Customer moves a Product without utilising the Supplier's decommissioning/re-installation services, the Supplier may require a Product inspection at the Customer's expense to re-determine the eligibility of the Product for the Services, prior to the resumption of the Services.

8. Service Exclusions

8.1 The Supplier's obligation to provide the Services is contingent upon the proper use of the Products and the System, and does not cover Products which have been moved without the Supplier's prior approval or which have been subjected to unusual physical or electrical stress.

8.2 The Supplier will be under no obligation to furnish the Services where, in the Supplier's reasonable opinion, these are required because of:
(a) failure of a Product because of accident, neglect, misuse, failure of electrical power, air conditioning or humidity control;
(b) damage occurring during transport of a Product;
(c) modifications to or attempts to repair a Product made without the Supplier's prior written approval;
(d) causes external to a Product including but not limited to failure or modification of electrical power, inadequate cooling, fire, flood or other natural disasters;

591

(e)   failure by the Customer to maintain software on the Product at the Supplier's specified release level, unless otherwise specifically agreed in advance by the Supplier.

If service is required, in the Supplier's opinion, as a result of such causes, such service will be charged at the Supplier's normal hourly rates.

8.3   The Supplier reserves the right not to provide the Services and to charge for costs and expenses incurred if a call is not warranted, access to the System is hindered or the environmental conditions at the Site are considered by the Supplier to be unsafe or hazardous.

8.4   The Services do not include:

(a)   operating supplies and accessories such as magnetic media and disk packs and other consumables, which must be paid for by the Customer;

(b)   electrical or signal cabling work external to the System, or maintenance of accessories, alterations, attachments or other devices not furnished by the Supplier, or installation, decommissioning, removal, relocation or reconfiguration of Products, unless specifically provided for in the Schedule;

(c)   equipment not covered by this Agreement.

8.5   The Supplier reserves the right at any time after the initial term of this Agreement to give 90 days' notice to the Customer that a Product cannot continue to be properly or economically repaired because of excessive wear or deterioration. In such event the Supplier will provide the Customer with an estimate of reconditioning charges, and if the Customer does not elect to have the Product reconditioned, the Supplier may delete the Product from the Schedule.

9. Disclaimers

9.1   The Supplier will use its reasonable endeavours to perform the Services promptly but no warranty is given in respect of any times for response or performance by the Supplier, and time will not be of the essence.

9.2   The Supplier is not liable for delay arising from any industrial dispute or any cause outside its reasonable control and any agreed timescale will be subject to reasonable extension in the event of such delay.

9.3   Provision of the Services does not imply any guarantee or representation that the Supplier will be able to assist the Customer in achieving any results from any Products which are not technically feasible. Subject to this, any services which are outside the scope of this Agreement will, at the Customer's request and at the Supplier's option, be provided at the Supplier's then current rates for such services.

10. Customer Responsibilities

The Customer or, at its direction, End Users, will:

10.1 use the Products correctly and in accordance with their Supplier operating instructions and with suitable operating supplies;

10.2 designate primary and secondary contacts appropriately qualified and trained to an acceptable standard authorised to request Services, and inform the Supplier accordingly. Authorised use of the telephone helpline is limited to these designated contacts;

10.3 maintain procedures to facilitate reconstruction of any lost or altered files, data or programs to the extent deemed necessary by the Customer, and the Customer agrees that the Supplier will not be liable under any circumstances for any consequences arising from lost or corrupted data, files or programs. The Customer and/or End Users are solely responsible for carrying out all necessary backup procedures for its own benefit, to ensure that data integrity can be maintained in the event of loss of data for any reason;

10.4 be solely responsible for the security of its confidential and proprietary information, and not disclose such information to the Supplier except on a 'need to know' basis for the purposes of the Supplier's performance of the Services;

10.5 notify the Supplier promptly of any Product malfunction;

10.6 control the Site environmental conditions in accordance with any environmental operating ranges specified by the Supplier or other Product manufacturer;

10.7 regularly perform the various Customer routine and preventative maintenance and cleaning operations described in the applicable user guides or as advised by the Supplier including but not limited to any operating and diagnostic checks and the regular inspection and, if necessary, cleaning, of disk packs and cartridges. The cost of rectifying any damage caused to the System by not observing this undertaking will not be covered by this Agreement;

10.8 keep records of the System's usage and performance if requested by the Supplier, in a mutually agreed format;

10.9 observe appropriate safety precautions in replacing parts provided under this Agreement;

10.10 provide the Supplier with access to and use of such of the Customer's or End User's information and facilities reasonably necessary to service the Products;

10.11 make all the relevant Products freely available to the Supplier during any agreed preventative maintenance period to enable the Supplier to carry out the Services;

10.12 have a Customer or End User representative present at all times during the performance of remedial and preventative maintenance Services;

10.13 provide ready access to a telephone at the Site on which external calls connected with the Services can be made and received by the Supplier's personnel;

10.14 ensure that only properly trained employees operate or use the System in accordance with the operating instructions and manuals supplied;

10.15 not make any modification or addition to the System, except with the Supplier's consent, which shall not be unreasonably withheld.

11. Charges and Payment Terms

11.1 The Customer will be invoiced quarterly in advance for the support charge shown in the Schedule. Expenses and other charges will be invoiced monthly in arrears. All invoices are payable net 30 days from receipt. All charges are exclusive of Value Added Tax and any similar taxes, which will be applied in accordance with prevailing legislation in force at the tax point date.

11.2 Payments which are not received when payable will be considered overdue and remain payable by the Customer together with interest for late payment from the date payable at the statutory rate applicable as well after as before any judgment, and independent of such judgment. This interest will accrue on a daily basis and be payable on demand.

11.3 Notwithstanding the above provision for late payment, in this event the Supplier may at its option, and without prejudice to any other remedy at any time after payment has become due, terminate or temporarily suspend this Agreement.

11.4 If the Supplier becomes entitled to terminate this Agreement for any reason, any sums then due to the Supplier will immediately become payable in full.

12. Expenses

12.1 All prices quoted in this Agreement are exclusive of expenses incurred in the performance of this Agreement by the Supplier, which will be chargeable in addition.

12.2 Expenses include: travel to the Customer's sites when applicable; magnetic media; data connection charges; couriers; freight; accommodation; and any other expenses reasonably incurred by the Supplier in connection with this Agreement.

13. Variation of Charges

The Supplier will be entitled to increase its charges upon the anniversary of the Commencement Date and thereafter not more than once in every successive period of 12 months during this Agreement upon giving not less than 60 days' notice to the Customer provided that any such increase expressed as a percentage does not exceed the rate of the Supplier's salary inflation reported in its accounts for the immediately preceding year.

14. Confidentiality

The parties recognise that under this Agreement they may each receive trade secrets and confidential or proprietary information of the other party, including but not limited to commercial information, products, customers, business accounts, finance or contractual arrangements or other dealings, program source and object codes. All such information which is either marked 'Confidential' or stated at the time of disclosure and subsequently confirmed in writing to be confidential constitutes 'Confidential Information'. Each party agrees not to divulge Confidential Information received from the other to any of its employees who do not need to know it, and to prevent its disclosure to or access by any third party without the prior written consent of the disclosing party.

15. Employment Restriction

While this Agreement is in force and for a period of 12 months from its termination for any reason, the Customer will not actively solicit or canvass the employment of any person employed by or acting on behalf of the Supplier who was assigned to work on the Customer's System over a period of 3 months or more in the preceding 12 months. If the Customer is in breach of this condition, the Customer (recognising that the Supplier will suffer substantial damage) will pay to the Supplier by way of liquidated damages and not by way of penalty a sum equal to the gross annual sum paid to that person as salary or for services by the Supplier in the immediately preceding 12 months.

16. Indemnities and Limits of Liability

16.1 The Customer agrees that it has accepted these terms and conditions in the knowledge that the Supplier's liability is limited and that the prices and charges payable have been calculated accordingly. The Customer is advised to make its own insurance arrangements if it desires to limit further its exposure to risk or if it requires further or different cover. The Supplier will be willing to provide reasonable assistance to the Customer if the Customer requests the Supplier to make enquiries about increasing cover on the Customer's behalf provided that the Customer recognises that this will result in increased charges being passed on to the Customer.

16.2 The Supplier will indemnify the Customer for direct physical injury or death caused by the negligence of its employees acting within the course of their employment and the scope of their authority.

16.3 The Supplier will indemnify the Customer for direct damage to property caused by the negligence of its employees acting within the course of their employment and the scope of their authority. The total liability of the Supplier under this sub-clause will be limited to £100,000 for any one event or series of connected events.

16.4 Except as expressly stated in this clause and elsewhere in this Agreement, any liability of the Supplier for breach of this Agreement will not exceed in the

595

aggregate of damages, costs, fees and expenses capable of being awarded to the Customer the total price paid or due to be paid by the Customer under this Agreement.

16.5 Except as expressly stated in this Agreement, the Supplier disclaims all liability in contract or in tort (including negligence or breach of statutory duty) to the Customer in connection with the Supplier's performance of this Agreement or the Customer's use of the Products including but not limited to liability for loss of profits whether in the course of the Customer's business or otherwise, or arising from loss of data, and in no event will the Supplier be liable to the Customer for special, indirect or consequential damages.

16.6 The Customer will indemnify and defend the Supplier and its employees in respect of any third party claims which arise from any Supplier performance carried out on the instructions of the Customer or its authorised representative.

16.7 The Customer will indemnify the Supplier in respect of any losses or expenses incurred by the Supplier as a result of any failure by the Customer to maintain adequate current licences for the software running on the System.

16.8 The parties agree that the Customer is the best judge of the value and importance of the data held on the Customer's computer system, and the Customer will be solely responsible for:

    (a)   instituting and operating all necessary back-up procedures, for its own benefit, to ensure that data integrity can be maintained in the event of loss of data for any reason;

    (b)   taking out any insurance policy or other financial cover for loss or damage which may arise from loss of data for any reason.

16.9 If the Supplier fails to comply with its obligations during the term of this Agreement then it will be entitled to be given a reasonable opportunity to correct any errors and to perform its obligations.

17. Termination

17.1 This Agreement may be terminated immediately by notice in writing:

    (a)   by the Supplier if the Customer fails to pay any sums due under this Agreement by the due date notwithstanding any other provisions for late payment in this Agreement;

    (b)   by either party if the other party is in material or continuing breach of any of its obligations under this Agreement and fails to remedy the same (if capable of remedy) for a period of 30 days after written notice of the breach by the other party;

    (c)   by either party if the other party is involved in any legal proceedings concerning its solvency, or ceases trading, or commits an act of bankruptcy or is adjudicated bankrupt or enters into liquidation, whether compulsory or voluntary, other than for the purposes of an amalgamation or reconstruction, or makes an arrangement with its creditors or petitions for an administration order or has a receiver or manager appointed over all or any part of its assets or generally becomes unable to pay its debts within the meaning of Section 123 of the Insolvency Act 1986 or anything analogous to such event occurs in any applicable jurisdiction.

17.2 Any termination of this Agreement under this clause will be without prejudice to any other rights or remedies of either party under this Agreement or at law and will not affect any accrued rights or liabilities of either party at the date of termination.

18. General Contract Provisions

18.1 Entire Agreement
This Agreement constitutes the entire agreement between the parties and supersedes any previous agreement between the parties relating to the subject matter of this Agreement. Each of the parties acknowledges that in entering into this Agreement, it does not rely on and will have no remedy in respect of any statement of fact or opinion not recorded in this Agreement (whether negligently or innocently made), except for any representation made fraudulently.

18.2 Variations
No variation of these terms and conditions will be valid unless confirmed in writing by authorised signatories of both parties on or after the date of this Agreement.

18.3 Severability
If any of the provisions of this Agreement is judged to be illegal or unenforceable, the continuation in full force and effect of the remainder of them will not be prejudiced [unless the substantive purpose of this Agreement is thereby frustrated, in which case either party may terminate this Agreement forthwith on written notice].

18.4 Waiver
No forbearance or delay by either party in enforcing its respective rights will prejudice or restrict the rights of that party, and no waiver of any such rights or of any breach of any contractual terms will be deemed to be a waiver of any other right or of any later breach.

18.5 Rights of Third Parties
A person who is not a party to this Agreement has no right to benefit under or to enforce any term of this Agreement.

18.6 Assignment
Neither party will assign, sub-contract or otherwise deal with this Agreement or any rights and obligations under this Agreement without the prior consent of the other party.

18.7 **Notices**

Any notice given under this Agreement by either party to the other must be in writing and may be delivered personally or by first-class post, and in the case of post will be deemed to have been given two working days after the date of posting. Notices will be delivered or sent to the addresses of the parties on the first page of this Agreement or to any other address notified in writing by either party to the other for the purpose of receiving notices after the date of this Agreement.

18.8 **Governing Law and Jurisdiction**

This Agreement is governed by and construed according to English law and the parties submit to the exclusive jurisdiction of the courts of England and Wales.

SCHEDULE(S) OF PRODUCTS FOR EACH END USER/ CUSTOMER

Including details of:

Commencement Date

Products and Charges

Extended Cover Charges

Customer Invoice Address

Supplier Maintenance and Support Centre details.

The Customer agrees to accept the Services on the terms and conditions of this Agreement.	The Supplier agrees to provide the Services on the terms and conditions of this Agreement.
FOR AND ON BEHALF OF THE CUSTOMER	**FOR AND ON BEHALF OF THE SUPPLIER**
Signed	Signed ....
Name	Name ....
Date	Date ....
Customer Authorised Representative	**Director of the Supplier**

SOFTWARE SUPPORT SERVICES AGREEMENT

Date of Agreement ....

BETWEEN:

(1)   **THE SUPPLIER** whose registered office is at
.... (**'Supplier'**);

AND

(2)   **THE CUSTOMER** whose registered office is at
.... (**'Customer'**).

1. Introduction

The Supplier has experience and expertise in providing support services for the software described below, and the Customer wishes to receive such services.

2. Definitions

'*Commencement Date*' means the date identified as such in the Schedule.

'*Schedule*' means the schedule attached to this Agreement, which forms part of this Agreement. In the event of any conflict between a provision in the Schedule and a provision in the main body of this Agreement, the Schedule will prevail.

'*Services*' means the software support services provided by the Supplier to the Customer on the terms and conditions of this Agreement.

'*Site*' means the Customer's location where the software is installed.

'*Software*' means the software products listed in the Schedule to which the Services will apply according to the terms and conditions of this Agreement.

3. Term

This Agreement commences on the date shown in the Schedule and will continue for an initial period of 12 calendar months after which it will remain in force until terminated by either party giving at least 90 days' notice of termination to the other to expire on the anniversary of the Commencement Date or on any subsequent anniversary, or by the Customer giving 90 days' notice within 30 days of receipt of notification of a change in prices by the Customer pursuant to this Agreement, and otherwise subject to the termination provisions of this Agreement.

4. Service Provision

4.1 The Supplier will provide the Services during the Supplier's normal working hours of 9.00 am to 5.00 pm, Monday to Friday, excluding public holidays, or during any other timescales specified in the Schedule. Out-of-hours Services can be provided by arrangement and will be charged for at the Supplier's then current UK extended cover rates as set out in the Schedule.

4.2 The Services are provided subject to the licence agreement for the Software between the Supplier and the Customer remaining in force.

4.3 The Services will be operated by means of a telephone helpline support facility.

4.4 The following services are outside the scope of the Services, but the Supplier is willing to offer them to the Customer at such charges and on such terms as the parties may agree from time to time:

(a) consultation for the resolution of those problems experienced by the Customer in operating the System and not covered by the Services;

(b) on-site services to carry out such work at the Site as the parties may agree from time to time;

(c) consultation about enhancement of the Software.

5. Software Services

The Software Services comprise and are limited to the following:

5.1 remote fault diagnosis and where possible recommendations for correction subject to the limitations imposed by contractual restrictions of any third party, following the reporting of any Software problem by telephone by the Customer to the Supplier's telephone helpline support facility;

(a) The Supplier undertakes to investigate the problem within four working hours of receiving the Customer's call. When the Supplier has diagnosed the fault, it will give an estimate to the Customer how long this fault may take to correct, and will keep the Customer informed of progress on the investigation of the problem from time to time.

(b) The Supplier will classify any problem as critical or non-critical to the fundamental operation of the Software and the following procedure will apply:

Critical Problems: The Supplier will attempt to generate a fix by modifying the Software to conform to its specification and transmitting the modification to the Customer as soon as possible. The Supplier will use all reasonable endeavours to correct any defect in the Software by reason of which it does not conform to its specification, or to modify the Software to obviate or mitigate the effect of the defect.

Non-critical Problems: The Supplier will attempt to generate a fix for incorporation in the next release of the Software. Where feasible, the Supplier may provide a temporary workaround to the Customer.

(c) The Supplier will determine what action, if any, it proposes to take, based, amongst other things, on the importance of the problem to the Customer, and the likely general benefit of any solution. In no event will the Supplier be required to correct a problem reported by the Customer, and the Supplier reserves the right to abandon attempts at a fix where the costs are likely to be excessive or the general benefits to the Supplier's customers at large are likely to be negligible.

(d) Diagnosis and solution of operational problems will generally be carried out remotely from the Site. If it becomes necessary to carry out the Services at the Site, such work will be chargeable at the Supplier's then prevailing daily rate, payable monthly in arrears in accordance with the payment terms stated in this Agreement;

5.2 telephone support on the routine use and operation of the Software;

5.3 telephone advice and assistance on user procedures and on ideas and methods intended to assist the Customer in obtaining the best possible use from the Software;

5.4 one copy of any new version of the Software released by the Supplier, including related documentation if appropriate.

6. Software Services Exclusions

6.1 The Supplier is not obliged to support the Software if the Customer is not using the versions of the operating system software as specified by the Supplier from time to time, or if the Customer fails to maintain the Software at the Supplier's specified release level unless specifically agreed in advance by the Supplier.

6.2 The Supplier will undertake responsibility for Software on a designated hardware system only if the hardware is covered by this Agreement or is the subject of a separate hardware maintenance agreement with the manufacturer of the hardware or with a reputable third party maintainer.

6.3 On-Site Software support services are not included as a standard feature of this Agreement.

6.4 The Services do not include service in respect of defects or errors resulting from any modifications or enhancements to the Software not made by the Supplier or made without the Supplier's prior written consent, or resulting from incorrect use of the Software.

6.5 The Supplier is not obliged to support the Software if malfunctions are due to incorrect use of the Software.

7. Disclaimers

7.1 The Supplier will use its reasonable endeavours to perform the Services promptly but no warranty is given in respect of any times for response or performance by the Supplier and time will not be of the essence.

7.2 The Supplier is not liable for delay arising from any industrial dispute or any cause outside its reasonable control and any agreed timescale will be subject to reasonable extension in the event of such delay.

7.3 Provision of the Service does not imply any guarantee or representation that the Supplier will be able to assist the Customer in achieving any results from any Software which are not technically feasible. Subject to this, any services which are outside the scope of this Agreement will, at the Customer's request and at the Supplier's option, be provided at the Supplier's then current rates for such services or as otherwise agreed between the parties.

7.4 Provision of the Services does not imply any guarantee that the Supplier will be successful in correcting Software malfunctions and the Supplier does not accept any liability in this connection.

7.5 The Supplier reserves the right to refuse to provide the Software Services at any time without refunding any sums paid by the Customer:
    (a)   if any attempt is made, other than by the Supplier, to remove any defects or deal with any errors in the Software; or
    (b)   if any development, enhancement or variation of the Software is carried out other than by the Supplier; or
    (c)   if the Customer has failed to pay a Supplier's invoice in accordance with the provisions of this Agreement; or
    (d)   where, in the reasonable opinion of the Supplier, the Customer's system has ceased to be capable of running the Software successfully for any reason.

8. Customer Responsibilities

The Customer will:

8.1 designate primary and secondary contacts authorised to request Services, and inform the Supplier accordingly. Authorised use of the telephone helpline is limited to these designated contacts;

8.2 ensure that the licences authorising the Customer's use of the Software are in effect throughout the term of this Agreement, and that the Software is used only as permitted by the terms of the applicable licences;

8.3 copy and use any updates, modifications, or enhancements to the Software only in accordance with the relevant licence. Title to such updates, modifications, or enhancements is not granted under this Agreement;

8.4 maintain procedures to facilitate reconstruction of any lost or altered files, data or programs to the extent it deems necessary;

8.5 keep records of usage and performance if requested by the Supplier, in a mutually agreed format;

8.6 provide telephone and modem facilities to the Supplier's requirements for remote investigation of Software defects;

8.7   provide the Supplier with access to and use of such of the Customer's information and facilities reasonably necessary to provide the Services;

8.8   install the latest applicable software revisions and enhancements to the Software as soon as reasonably practicable, and in any event within six months, unless the parties agree for a particular release an implementation plan with a longer timescale.

9. Charges and Payment Terms

9.1   The Customer will be invoiced quarterly in advance for the support charge shown in the Schedule. All support charges are exclusive of expenses reasonably incurred in the performance of this Agreement by the Supplier, which will be payable in addition, and these and other charges will be invoiced monthly in arrears. All invoices are payable 30 days from receipt. All charges are exclusive of Value Added Tax and any similar taxes, which will be applied in accordance with prevailing legislation in force at the tax point date.

9.2   Payments which are not received when payable will be considered overdue and remain payable by the Customer together with interest for late payment from the date payable at the statutory rate applicable as well after as before any judgment, and independent of such judgment. This interest will accrue on a daily basis and be payable on demand.

9.3   Notwithstanding the above provision for late payment, in this event the Supplier may at its option, and without prejudice to any other remedy at any time after payment has become due, terminate or temporarily suspend this Agreement.

9.4   If the Supplier becomes entitled to terminate this Agreement for any reason, any sums then due to the Supplier will immediately become payable in full.

10. Variation of Charges

The Supplier will be entitled to increase its charges upon the anniversary of the Commencement Date and thereafter not more than once in every successive period of 12 months during this Agreement upon giving not less than 60 days' notice to the Customer provided that any such increase expressed as a percentage does not exceed the rate of the Supplier's salary inflation reported in its accounts for the immediately preceding year.

11. Confidentiality

The parties recognise that under this Agreement they may each receive trade secrets and confidential or proprietary information of the other party, including but not limited to commercial information, products, customers, business accounts, finance or contractual arrangements or other dealings, program source and object codes. All such information which is either marked 'Confidential' or stated at the time of disclosure and subsequently confirmed in writing to be confidential constitutes 'Confidential Information'. Each party agrees not to divulge Confidential Information received from the other to any of its employees who do not need to know it, and to prevent its disclosure to or access by any third party without the prior written consent of the disclosing party.

12. Employment Restriction

While this Agreement is in force and for a period of 12 months from its termination for any reason, the Customer will not actively solicit or canvass the employment of any person employed by or acting on behalf of the Supplier who was assigned to work on the Customer's System over a period of three months or more in the preceding 12 months. If the Customer is in breach of this condition, the Customer (recognising that the Supplier will suffer substantial damage) will pay to the Supplier by way of liquidated damages and not by way of penalty a sum equal to the gross annual sum paid to that person as salary or for services by the Supplier in the immediately preceding 12 months.

13. Indemnities and Limits of Liability

13.1 The Customer agrees that it has accepted these terms and conditions in the knowledge that the Supplier's liability is limited and that the prices and charges payable have been calculated accordingly. The Customer is advised to make its own insurance arrangements if it desires to limit further its exposure to risk or if it requires further or different cover. The Supplier will be willing to provide reasonable assistance to the Customer if the Customer requests the Supplier to make enquiries about increasing cover on the Customer's behalf provided that the Customer recognises that this will result in increased charges being passed on to the Customer.

13.2 The Supplier will indemnify the Customer for direct physical injury or death caused by the negligence of its employees acting within the course of their employment and the scope of their authority.

13.3 The Supplier will indemnify the Customer for direct damage to property caused by the negligence of its employees acting within the course of their employment and the scope of their authority. The total liability of the Supplier under this sub-clause will be limited to £100,000 for any one event or series of connected events.

13.4 Except as expressly stated in this clause and elsewhere in this Agreement, any liability of the Supplier for breach of this Agreement will not exceed in the aggregate of damages, costs, fees and expenses capable of being awarded to the Customer the total price paid or due to be paid by the Customer under this Agreement.

13.5 Except as expressly stated in this Agreement, the Supplier disclaims all liability in contract or in tort (including negligence or breach of statutory duty) to the Customer in connection with the Supplier's performance of this Agreement or the Customer's use of the Software including but not limited to liability for loss of profits whether in the course of the Customer's business or otherwise, or arising from loss of data, and in no event will the Supplier be liable to the Customer for special, indirect or consequential damages.

13.6 The Customer will indemnify and defend the Supplier and its employees in respect of any third party claims which arise from any Supplier performance carried out on the instructions of the Customer or its authorised representative.

13.7 The Customer will indemnify the Supplier in respect of any losses or expenses incurred by the Supplier as a result of any failure by the Customer to maintain adequate current licences for the software running on the System.

13.8 The parties agree that the Customer is the best judge of the value and importance of the data held on the Customer's computer system, and the Customer will be solely responsible for:
   (a) instituting and operating all necessary back-up procedures, for its own benefit, to ensure that data integrity can be maintained in the event of loss of data for any reason;
   (b) taking out any insurance policy or other financial cover for loss or damage which may arise from loss of data for any reason.

13.9 If the Supplier fails to comply with its obligations during the term of this Agreement then it will be entitled to be given a reasonable opportunity to correct any errors and to perform its obligations.

14. Termination

14.1 This Agreement may be terminated immediately by notice in writing:
   (a) by the Supplier if the Customer fails to pay any sums due under this Agreement by the due date notwithstanding any other provisions for late payment in this Agreement;
   (b) by either party if the other party is in material or continuing breach of any of its obligations under this Agreement and fails to remedy the same (if capable of remedy) for a period of 30 days after written notice of the breach by the other party;
   (c) by either party if the other party is involved in any legal proceedings concerning its solvency, or ceases trading, or commits an act of bankruptcy or is adjudicated bankrupt or enters into liquidation, whether compulsory or voluntary, other than for the purposes of an amalgamation or reconstruction, or makes an arrangement with its creditors or petitions for an administration order or has a Receiver or Manager appointed over all or any part of its assets or generally becomes unable to pay its debts within the meaning of Section 123 of the Insolvency Act 1986 or anything analogous to such event occurs in any applicable jurisdiction.

14.2 Any termination of this Agreement under this clause will be without prejudice to any other rights or remedies of either party under this Agreement or at law and will not affect any accrued rights or liabilities of either party at the date of termination.

15. General Contract Provisions

15.1 Entire Agreement

This Agreement constitutes the entire agreement between the parties and supersedes any previous agreement between the parties relating to the subject matter of this Agreement. Each of the parties acknowledges that in entering into this Agreement, it does not rely on and will have no remedy in respect of any statement of fact or opinion not recorded in this Agreement (whether negligently or innocently made), except for any representation made fraudulently.

15.2 Variations

No variation of these terms and conditions will be valid unless confirmed in writing by authorised signatories of both parties on or after the date of this Agreement.

15.3 Severability

If any of the provisions of this Agreement is judged to be illegal or unenforceable, the continuation in full force and effect of the remainder of them will not be prejudiced [unless the substantive purpose of this Agreement is thereby frustrated, in which case either party may terminate this Agreement forthwith on written notice].

15.4 Waiver

No forbearance or delay by either party in enforcing its respective rights will prejudice or restrict the rights of that party, and no waiver of any such rights or of any breach of any contractual terms will be deemed to be a waiver of any other right or of any later breach.

15.5 Rights of Third Parties

A person who is not a party to this Agreement has no right to benefit under or to enforce any term of this Agreement.

15.6 Assignment

Neither party will assign, sub-contract or otherwise deal with this Agreement or any rights and obligations under this Agreement without the prior consent of the other party.

15.7 Notices

Any notice given under this Agreement by either party to the other must be in writing and may be delivered personally or by first-class post, and in the case of post will be deemed to have been given two working days after the date of posting. Notices will be delivered or sent to the addresses of the parties on the first page of this Agreement or to any other address notified in writing by either party to the other for the purpose of receiving notices after the date of this Agreement.

15.8 **Governing Law and Jurisdiction**

This Agreement is governed by and construed according to English law and the parties submit to the exclusive jurisdiction of the courts of England and Wales.

SCHEDULE

Including details of:

Commencement Date

Software and Software Support Charges

Extended Cover Charges

Customer Invoice Address

The Customer agrees to accept the Services on the terms and conditions of this Agreement.	The Supplier agrees to provide the Services on the terms and conditions of this Agreement.
FOR AND ON BEHALF OF THE CUSTOMER	**FOR AND ON BEHALF OF THE SUPPLIER**
Signed	Signed ....
Name	Name ....
Date	Date ....
Customer Authorised Representative	**Director of the Supplier**

CONSULTANCY SERVICES AGREEMENT

This structure includes project management services to be provided by a consultant services company with a number of employees. It sets out the overall terms and conditions of consultancy, so that it can continue in existence for as long as there is the possibility of the company using the services of the consultant. Each specific project will be the subject of an agreed statement between the parties to be attached to the agreement as a schedule to be incorporated into it as the statement is drawn up.

Date of Agreement ....

BETWEEN:

(1) **THE CLIENT** whose registered office is at
.... ('**Client**');

AND

(2) **THE CONSULTANT** whose registered office is at
.... ('**Consultant**').

1. Introduction

The Client has agreed to engage the services of the Consultant to provide computer consultancy, programming and related services from time to time as an independent contractor, and the Consultant has agreed to accept such engagement on the following terms and conditions.

2. Definitions

In this Agreement, the following expressions have the following meanings:

2.1 '*Agreement*' means this Agreement and each Project Statement together or separately. In the event of any conflict of meaning between this Agreement and a Project Statement, the Project Statement prevails.

2.2 '*Authorised Representative*' means the person designated by each party whose identity is notified in writing to the other party, who is vested with the authority of the appointing party to communicate all of that party's decisions and representations to the other party in connection with the Services, and who will act as the prime point of contact with the Authorised Representative of the other party, and who is authorised to receive the decisions and representations of the other party in connection with the Services.

2.3 '*Project*' means the work undertaken as described in a Project Statement.

2.4 '*Project Results*' means all products designed, developed, written or prepared by the Consultant in respect of the Project and all related documentation including but not limited to any specification, graphics, programs, data, reports, and all other deliverables, written Results or computer output produced in the course of providing the Services.

2.5 '*Project Management Services*' means the services identified as such in a Project Statement.

2.6 '*Project Statement*' means a description of the Project utilising some or all of the Services and forming a Schedule to this Agreement, including:
- the title and description of the Project;
- the nature of the work and the Consultant's responsibilities;
- the time schedule for undertaking and completing the Services;
- the time and other resources which the Consultant will commit to achieve the performance of the Services;
- the amount and/or method of calculation of the Consultant's charges for the Services.

2.7 '*Proprietary Rights*' means all intellectual property rights including but not limited to copyrights, database rights, patents, design rights, trade marks, and trade secrets.

2.8 '*Services*' means general [consultancy, computer systems analysis, programming, training, project management] and all related services to be provided by the Consultant and more particularly described in each Project Statement, including as appropriate, the Project Management Services.

3. Duration

This Agreement commences on the Date of Agreement specified above and will continue for an initial period of 12 calendar months, after which it will remain in force unless or until terminated by either party giving at least 90 days' notice of termination to the other party to expire at the end of such period or at any time thereafter, and otherwise subject to the other termination provisions in this Agreement.

4. The Consultancy and Project Management Services

4.1 The Consultant agrees to provide and the Client agrees to take and pay for the Services described in the Project Statement at the rates or for the sums set out in the Project Statement.

4.2 The Consultant is not generally authorised to carry out any work for the Client which is not the subject of a properly executed Project Statement. However, if the Consultant does carry out any work at the Client's request which is not the subject of a Project Statement then, unless the parties otherwise agree in writing, the provisions of this Agreement will apply to the work undertaken, and if no fee is agreed for this work, the Consultant will be paid on a time and materials basis at its standard published rates of charges, or otherwise at a reasonable rate.

4.3 This Agreement is personal to the Consultant, who will not be entitled to assign or sub-contract any of his or her rights or obligations.

4.4 This Agreement is not an exclusive arrangement, and subject to the Consultant's obligations in this Agreement, including but not limited to the obligation to avoid any conflicts of interest, nothing in this Agreement will operate to prevent the Consultant from engaging in other consultancy or project management activities.

4.5 The Services are provided at the Client's request and the Client accepts that it is responsible for verifying that the Services are suitable for its own needs.

4.6 The Client acknowledges that times scheduled in any Project Statement are estimates only of the amount of time required by the Client for the provision of the Services, and the Client will be invoiced for the actual time spent by the Consultant in providing the Services to the Client.

4.7 To facilitate the provision of the Project Management Services the Client and the Consultant will meet to discuss and review the Project on a regular basis and will jointly identify, prepare and agree in writing all relevant aspects of the Project including but not limited to:

(a) the structure and content of the Project team and assignment of functions, including any employees of the Client to be assigned to or work with the Consultant;

(b) a provisional programme indicating the sequence and timetable for carrying out the Project, providing the Project Management Services and the period likely to be required for its completion;

(c) the frequency at which the Consultant and the Client will meet to review the progress of the Project;

(d) where appropriate to the nature of the Project Management Services to be provided, the form and method of presentation of the results of these Project Management Services;

(e) any parts of the Project to be carried out by third parties and the authority of the Consultant to engage third parties on behalf of the Client for this purpose, the Client alone being party to any agreement with third parties for the performance of the work or the supply of any goods but by prior agreement, the Client may authorise the Consultant to engage such third parties on behalf of the Client;

(f) the parties will agree upon the services to be performed by any third party. Notwithstanding any suggestions or recommendations which the Consultant makes, the Client must satisfy itself as to the suitability of any third party to perform any work in connection with the Project, and the Consultant will be under no liability in respect of any act or omission of any third party.

4.8   The Consultant is authorised to have access to those computer systems identified in the relevant Project Statement to the extent to which this is necessary for the performance of the Services.

5. Consultant's Obligations and Warranties

The Consultant warrants and undertakes:

5.1   to apply all reasonable professional skill, care and expertise to the performance of the Services in accordance with the terms of this Agreement;

5.2   to provide suitably qualified personnel to carry out the Services and related tasks (including attendances at meetings and travel) assigned by the Client's Authorised Representative;

5.3   to provide the Services in a timely and efficient manner and to a professional standard in accordance with any time schedules stipulated in the Project Statement and which will conform to the standards generally observed in the industry for similar services, and to co-operate with employees and other independent consultants where this is necessary for the performance of the Services;

5.4   to ensure that the normal working day is equivalent to seven working hours (excluding travel time to and from the Client's place of business), any requirement for overtime, weekend or holiday working to be specially arranged between the parties upon the terms specified in the Project Statement or on such other terms as they may agree;

5.5   to maintain accurate time sheets for approval and endorsement by the Client's Authorised Representative;

5.6   that the Project Results so far as they do not comprise material originating from the Client are original works created by the Consultant, and the use or possession of them by the Client will not subject the Client to any claim for infringement of any Proprietary Rights of any third party;

5.7   not to make any announcement concerning this Agreement or any Project or any ancillary matter or to publicise this Agreement or Project in any way without the prior written consent of the Client;

5.8   to conform to the Client's normal codes of staff and security practice;

5.9   to maintain professional indemnity insurance in effect while this Agreement is in force;

5.10   to provide evidence to the Client that it is regarded by the Inland Revenue as a bona fide independent business for the purposes of income tax and National Insurance liabilities.

6. The Client's Obligations

The Client undertakes:

6.1 to pay for the Services together with associated expenses under the terms of this Agreement;

6.2 to provide the Consultant and its employees designated to perform the Services promptly with all necessary information, support and co-operation that may reasonably be required to enable the Consultant to carry out its obligations under this Agreement;

6.3 for the purpose of co-ordination to designate one individual as its Authorised Representative as first notified in writing to the Consultant, who will be responsible for controlling, in consultation with the Consultant, all aspects of the Consultant's assigned work on the Project under the terms of this Agreement;

6.4 to provide at no charge to the Consultant adequate office accommodation, a secure work space, telephone services and other facilities including access to the applicable computers and systems of the Client, all as reasonably necessary to enable the assigned employees of the Consultant to perform the Services at the Client's sites, and further to allow full access to the areas in which the Services are to be performed at the Client's sites;

6.5 to take all reasonable steps to ensure the health and safety of the Consultant's employees while they are at the Client's sites, and to ensure that such employees are provided with copies of all applicable safety information and site regulations;

6.6 that the computer and operating systems and any other software, information or data which the Consultant's employees are asked to access, use or modify for the purpose of the Services are either the property of the Client or are legally licensed to the Client or otherwise in the lawful possession of the Client for the uses intended, and to indemnify the Consultant in respect of any claims against the Consultant by third parties including all related costs, expenses or damages in the event of any actual or alleged violations of third party (including the Client's employees) proprietary or data rights or software licences;

6.7 to ensure that its employees and other independent consultants co-operate fully with the Consultant in relation to the provision of the Services;

6.8 to furnish the Consultant promptly with such information and documents as the Consultant may reasonably request for the proper performance of its obligations under this Agreement;

6.9 to provide or arrange at its expense for any specialist training in the Client's methods or products which it requires to be undertaken by the Consultant. Time spent in such training will be invoiced at the daily rate shown in the Schedule.

7. Consultant's Employees

7.1 Each of the Consultant's employees assigned to perform the Services will be appropriately qualified and experienced for such assignment. The Client will have the right to interview and approve or reject any employee of the Consultant intended by the Consultant to perform the Services, and the Client will also have the right to request the replacement of any employee of the Consultant engaged in the performance of the Services without having to state a reason, subject to the Consultant being granted a reasonable period of time to allocate a replacement employee.

7.2   Employees of the Consultant designated to perform the Services will remain under the overall control of the Consultant at all times during the term of this Agreement, although they will be responsible to the Client's Authorised Representative for the performance of the Services and will at all times be responsive to the reasonable requirements of the Client in connection with the performance of the Services.

7.3   The Consultant's employees designated to perform the Services will be entitled to take their annual or other leave and to attend the Consultant's internal company meetings as reasonably required by the Consultant but not more than once each month.

7.4   If the Consultant's employees designated to perform the Services propose to be absent on short-term leave or at a Consultant company meeting, they will inform the Client's Authorised Representative and if the Client so requires, the Consultant will use all reasonable endeavours to furnish a replacement employee during such absences. In the case of long-term annual leave, the Consultant undertakes to advise the Client at least two weeks in advance of such leave and to replace its designated employee for the leave period if so requested or otherwise to extend any term of this Agreement at the option of the Consultant.

7.5   The Consultant will use all reasonable endeavours to replace promptly any designated employees who leave the Consultant's employment or who are absent through illness or incapacity.

7.6   During the term of this Agreement and for a period of 12 months from its termination for any reason the Client will not employ either directly or indirectly through any associated company or offer employment to any person employed by or acting on behalf of the Consultant who has worked for the Consultant for a continuous period of six months or more in the preceding 12 months, and who has provided Services to the Client in connection with this Agreement. If the Client is in breach of this condition, the Client (recognising that the Consultant will suffer substantial damage) will pay to the Consultant, by way of liquidated damages and not by way of penalty, a sum equal to the current annual salary of the person concerned.

8. Proprietary Rights

8.1   If compliance with the Client's designs, specifications or instructions results in the Consultant being subject to any claim for infringement of any Proprietary Rights or any third party rights, the Client will indemnify the

Consultant against any claims, demands, damages, costs and expenses made against or suffered by the Consultant as a result of any such claim or action. *EITHER*

8.2 The Consultant acknowledges that all Proprietary Rights in the Project Results relating to them will at all times and for all purposes vest and remain vested in the Client. Notwithstanding the foregoing, all Proprietary Rights which the Consultant might otherwise acquire as a result of its performance of the Services are hereby irrevocably assigned to the Client.

8.3 At the request and expense of the Client, and as required, the Consultant will do all such things including signing all documents or other instruments reasonably necessary in the opinion of the Client to confirm or vest in the Client the rights assigned or otherwise transferred to the Client under this Agreement.

8.4 Upon request by the Client, and in any event upon the expiry or termination of this Agreement, the Consultant will promptly deliver to the Client all copies of Project Results relating to the Project then in the Consultant's possession.

8.5 The Consultant will be fully entitled to use in any way it deems fit any skills, techniques, concepts or know-how acquired, developed or used in the course of performing the Consultancy Services, and any improvements to the Consultant's products made or developed during the course of the Services will belong exclusively to the Consultant.
OR

8.2 The Project Results and the Proprietary Rights relating to them will be and will remain the exclusive property of the Consultant.

8.3 The Client is hereby granted a [non-exclusive] [perpetual] [non-transferable] licence to use the Project Results for its own internal business purposes.

8.4 The Client undertakes to keep the Project Results confidential and not to make copies of them available to any third party for any purpose.

9. Intellectual Property Rights Indemnity

[If the Proprietary Rights remain with the Consultant]

9.1 The Consultant, at its own expense, will defend or cause to be defended or, at its option, settle any claim or action brought against the Client on the issue of infringement of any [United Kingdom or Republic of Ireland] intellectual property right by the Project Results ('Claim'). Subject to the other conditions of this clause, the Consultant will pay any final judgment entered against the Client with respect to any Claim, provided that the Client:

(a) notifies the Consultant in writing of the Claim immediately on becoming aware of it;

(b) grants sole control of the defence of the Claim to the Consultant; and

  (c) gives the Consultant complete and accurate information and full assistance to enable the Consultant to settle or defend the Claim.

9.2 If any part of the Project Results should become the subject of any Claim, or if a Court judgment is made that the Project Results do infringe, or if the use or licensing of any part of the Project Results is restricted, the Consultant at its option and expense may:

  (a) obtain for the Client the right under the patent, design right, trade secret or copyright to continue to use the Project Results; or

  (b) replace or modify the Project Results so that they become non-infringing; or

  (c) if the use of the Project Results is prevented by permanent injunction, accept return of them and refund an amount equal to the sum paid by the Client for the Project Results, subject to straight line depreciation over a five-year period.

9.3 The Consultant will have no liability under this clause for:

  (a) any infringement arising from the combination of the Project Results with other Results not supplied by the Consultant; or

  (b) the modification of the Project Results unless the modification was made or approved expressly by the Consultant.

IN NO CIRCUMSTANCES WILL THE CONSULTANT BE LIABLE FOR ANY COSTS OR EXPENSES INCURRED BY THE CLIENT WITHOUT THE CONSULTANT'S WRITTEN AUTHORISATION AND THE FOREGOING STATES THE ENTIRE REMEDY OF THE CLIENT IN RESPECT OF ANY INTELLECTUAL PROPERTY RIGHT INFRINGEMENT BY THE PROJECT RESULTS.

10. Charges, Expenses and Payment Terms

10.1 In consideration of the Services rendered by the Consultant pursuant to each Project Statement, the Client will pay to the Consultant fees in the amounts and at the rates set out in that Project Statement plus Value Added Tax if applicable.

10.2 Unless otherwise agreed in a Project Statement, such fees will accrue monthly and the Consultant will render monthly invoices and approved timesheets to the Client in respect of the fees, and where registered for VAT, the Consultant will show any VAT separately on such invoices.

10.3 All fees will be payable to the Consultant without deductions of any kind except in respect of moneys owed by the Consultant to the Client. The Consultant is responsible for arranging its own tax affairs in an appropriate manner and for accounting to the appropriate authorities.

10.4 The Client will pay or reimburse to the Consultant on production of such vouchers and/or other evidence as it may require all reasonable and proper expenses including accommodation and subsistence arising out of journeys undertaken on the Client's behalf incurred in connection with the Services. No expenses will be incurred while the Consultant is working at the Client's offices.

10.5 All fees payable by the Client will be paid within 30 days of the receipt by the Client of the Consultant's invoice for such fees.

10.6 Payments which are not received when payable will be considered overdue and remain payable by the Client together with interest for late payment from the date payable at the statutory rate applicable as well after as before any judgment. This interest will accrue on a daily basis and be payable on demand.

10.7 Notwithstanding the above provision for late payment, in this event the Consultant may at its option, and without prejudice to any other remedy at any time after payment has become due, terminate or temporarily suspend performance of this Agreement.

10.8 If the Consultant becomes entitled to terminate this Agreement for any reason, any sums then due to the Consultant will immediately become payable in full.

11. Confidential Information

11.1 The Consultant will not use or divulge or communicate to any person (other than to those whose province it is to know or with the authority of the Client):

(a) any of the confidential information concerning the products, customers, business, accounts, finance or contractual arrangements or other dealings, transactions or affairs of the Client which may come to the Consultant's knowledge in the course of providing the Services;

(b) any information concerning any Project;

(c) any of the Project Results,

and the Consultant will use all reasonable endeavours to prevent the unauthorised publication or disclosure of any such information, Results or documents.

11.2 If stipulated in any Project Statement, the Consultant will also enter into a specific confidentiality agreement relating to that Project.

11.3 The provisions of this clause will survive the termination of this Agreement but the restrictions contained in clause 11.1 will cease to apply to any information which may come into the public domain otherwise than through unauthorised disclosure by the Consultant or by anyone on its behalf.

12. Indemnities and Limits of Liability

12.1 The Consultant makes no representations and gives no warranties, guarantees or undertakings concerning its performance of the Services except as expressly set out in this Agreement. All other warranties express or implied, by statute or otherwise, are excluded from this Agreement. There will be no obligation on the Consultant to correct or re-perform any of the Services except at the direction of the Client in accordance with the terms and applicable charge rates set out in this Agreement.

12.2 The Consultant will indemnify the Client for direct physical injury or death caused solely by the negligence of the Consultant in the provision of the Services.

12.3 The Consultant will indemnify the Client for direct damage to property caused solely by the negligence of the Consultant in the provision of the Services. The total liability of the Consultant under this clause will be limited to [£100,000] for any one event or series of connected events.

12.4 The Consultant will [maintain in effect whilst this Agreement is in force professional indemnity insurance] [insure with a reputable insurance company in respect of public liability for at least £1,000,000] [and provide evidence to the Client of such cover at the Client's request].

12.5 The Consultant will indemnify and keep the Client fully and effectively indemnified subject to a maximum of [£500,000] per claim or series of related claims which the Client may sustain or incur or which may be brought against it arising from:
  (a) the negligence, recklessness or wilful misconduct of the Consultant or its staff in the provision of the Services;
  (b) the breach of any of the warranties or obligations contained in this Agreement;
  (c) any unauthorised act or omission of the Consultant or its staff.

12.6 Except as stated in the above sub-clauses the Consultant disclaims all liability to the Client in connection with this Agreement and in no event will the Consultant be liable to the Client for special, indirect or consequential damages or for loss of profits or arising from loss of data or unfitness for user purposes.

12.7 The Client will indemnify the Consultant and keep the Consultant fully and effectively indemnified against any losses, claims, damages, costs, charges, expenses, liabilities, demands, proceedings and actions which the Consultant may sustain or incur which may be brought or established against the Consultant by any person and which arise in relation to any claims by third parties arising from the Consultant's performance pursuant to any instructions by the Client or its authorised representative including but not limited to instructions concerning the performance of the Services for third parties.

13. Termination

13.1 If the Consultant is unable to carry out the obligations under this Agreement because of illness, injury or accident and such incapacity continues for more than 60 days, the Client will be entitled to terminate this Agreement forthwith by written notice to the Consultant given at any time while such incapacity continues.

13.2 The Client may promptly terminate this Agreement by written notice to the Consultant if the Consultant or any of the Consultant's employees engaged in the performance of the Services:

(a) commits any material or persistent breach of the Consultant's obligations under this Agreement, which in the case of a breach capable of remedy shall not have been remedied within 30 days of receipt by the Consultant of notice identifying the breach and requiring its remedy; or

(b) is guilty of any fraud, dishonesty, or serious misconduct; or

(c) is guilty of any conduct which may tend to bring it or the Client into disrepute or is convicted of a criminal offence; or

(d) becomes incapable by reason of mental disorder of performing the Services under this Agreement.

13.3 Either party may terminate this Agreement forthwith by written notice to the other if the other convenes a meeting of its creditors or if a proposal shall be made for a voluntary arrangement within Part I of the Insolvency Act 1986 or a proposal for any other composition, scheme or arrangement with, or assignment for the benefit of, its creditors, or if the other shall be unable to pay its debts within the meaning of Section 123 or Section 268 of the Insolvency Act 1986 or if a trustee, receiver, administrative receiver or similar officer is appointed in respect of all or any part of the business or assets of the other, or if a petition is presented or a meeting is convened for the purpose of considering a resolution or other steps are taken for the winding up of the other, or for the making of an administration order (otherwise than for the purpose of an amalgamation or reconstruction).

13.4 Termination of this Agreement for any reason will not entitle the Consultant to compensation and will be without prejudice to the rights of both parties accrued before such termination.

14. General Contract Provisions

14.1 This Agreement, and the documents referred to in it, constitutes the entire agreement and understanding between the parties and supersedes any previous agreement between the parties relating to the subject matter of this Agreement. Each of the parties acknowledges and agrees that in entering into this Agreement, and the documents referred to in it, it does not rely on, and shall have no remedy in respect of any statement of fact or opinion not recorded in this document (whether negligently or innocently made). Nothing in this sub-clause will, however, operate to limit or exclude any liability for fraud.

14.2 No variation of these terms and conditions will be valid unless confirmed in writing by authorised signatories of both parties on or after the date of this Agreement.

14.3 If any of the provisions of this Agreement is judged to be illegal or unenforceable, the continuation in full force and effect of the remainder of them will not be prejudiced [unless the substantive purpose of this

Agreement is thereby frustrated, in which case either party may terminate this Agreement forthwith on written notice].

14.4 No forbearance or delay by either party in enforcing its respective rights will prejudice or restrict the rights of that party, and no waiver of any such rights or of any breach of any contractual terms will be deemed to be a waiver of any other right or of any later breach.

14.5 The relationship between the Client and the Consultant is that of independent contractor. Neither party is agent for the other, and neither party has any authority to make any contract, whether expressly or by implication, in the name of the other party, without that party's prior written consent for express purposes connected with the performance of this Agreement.

14.6 A person who is not a party to this Agreement has no right to benefit under or to enforce any term of this Agreement.

14.7 Any notice given under this Agreement by either party to the other must be in writing and may be delivered personally or by first-class post and in the case of post will be deemed to have been given two working days after the date of posting. Notices will be delivered or sent to the addresses of the parties on the first page of this Agreement or to any other address notified in writing by either party to the other for the purpose of receiving notices after the date of this Agreement.

14.8 Neither party will be liable to the other party for any delay in or failure to perform its obligations (other than a payment of money) as a result of any cause beyond its reasonable control, including but not limited to any industrial dispute. If such delay or failure continues for at least 90 days, either party will be entitled to terminate the Agreement by notice in writing.

14.9 This Agreement is governed by English Law and the parties submit to the [non-exclusive/exclusive] jurisdiction of the English Courts.

The Client agrees to accept the Services on the terms and conditions of this Agreement.	The Consultant agrees to provide the Services on the terms and conditions of this Agreement.
SIGNED	**SIGNED**
FOR AND ON BEHALF OF	**FOR AND ON BEHALF OF**
Name	Name ....
Date	Date ....
Director of the Client	**Director of the Consultant**

PROJECT STATEMENT

BETWEEN

(1)   **THE CLIENT** whose registered office is at
.... ('**Client**');

AND

(2)   **THE CONSULTANT** whose registered office is at
.... ('**Consultant**').

Further to the rights and obligations of each party contained in the Consultancy Agreement between the parties, the parties agree as follows:

1.   **Consultant's Responsibilities, Consultancy and/or Project Management Services**
....

2.   **Project Results**
....

3.   **Acceptance Criteria**
....

4.   **Period of Agreement or Estimated Time Schedules**
....

5.   **Resources**
....

6.   **Fees and Payment Schedules**
....

7.   **Computer Systems to which the Consultant is entitled to have access**
....

8.   **Other Conditions**
....

Signed ....   Signed ....
FOR AND ON BEHALF OF   **FOR AND ON BEHALF OF**
Name ....   Name ....
Date ....   Date ....
Director of the Client   **Director of the Consultant**

SOFTWARE DEVELOPMENT AGREEMENT

Date of Agreement ....

BETWEEN:

(1)   **THE SUPPLIER** whose registered office is at
.... ('**Supplier**');

AND

(2)   **THE CUSTOMER** whose registered office is at
.... ('**Customer**').

1. Scope of Contract

1.1   The Supplier has experience and expertise in developing and implementing software projects.

1.2   The Customer wishes to procure a software system and related services from the Supplier.

2. Definitions

2.1   '*Acceptance Tests*' means tests using Test Data to test the System for acceptance.

2.2   '*Change Order*' means a written record of any change to the System requested and signed by the Customer.

2.3   '*Charges*' means the charges payable for the Project.

2.4   '*Documentation*' means the documentation to be provided by the Supplier for the System, listed in the Documentation Schedule.

2.5   '*Equipment*' means the hardware and operating systems at the Customer's site as listed in the Equipment Schedule, on which, and in combination with which, the Software will run.

2.6   '*Estimated Price*' means the price estimated for the Project as set out in the Charges Schedule.

2.7   '*Functional Specification*' means the document which specifies the System, incorporated into this Agreement as the Functional Specification Appendix.

2.8   '*Implementation Plan*' means the plan specifying the dates of the completion of each phase of the Project set out in the Implementation Plan Schedule, as it may be varied from time to time.

621

2.9 *'Milestone'* means a phase comprising a set of tasks shown in the Implementation Plan.

2.10 *'Progress Meeting'* means a meeting held between the parties to discuss progress of the Project.

2.11 *'Project'* means the work to be undertaken and services to be performed by the Supplier to develop and implement the System.

2.12 *'Project Manager'* means the designated representative appointed by the Supplier or the Customer respectively as initially specified in the Designated Representatives Schedule.

2.13 *'Progress Meeting'* means a meeting held to discuss progress of the Project.

2.14 *'Schedules'* means the schedules identified in this Agreement and incorporated into this Agreement.

2.15 *'Software'* means the software content of the System developed in accordance with these terms and conditions.

2.16 *'System'* means the business system required by the Customer[, using the Equipment and Software in combination].

2.17 *'System Completion Date'* means the date specified in the Implementation Plan for completion of the System.

2.18 *'Test Data'* means data supplied by the Customer for the purpose of testing the System to demonstrate that it works, in order for the System to be accepted by the Customer.

2.19 *'Third Party Software'* means all third party software owned by a third party but legally licensed to the Supplier for use in developing the Software, listed in the Third Party Software Schedule.

2.20 *'Training'* means the training in using the System to be provided by the Supplier as described in the Training Schedule.

3. Supplier's Obligations

The Supplier undertakes to:

3.1 provide its services diligently, expeditiously and with reasonable skill and care;

3.2 provide suitably skilled and appropriately experienced personnel to carry out the Project;

3.3 provide the Training;

3.4 take steps to ensure that its employees comply with any rules and regulations of the Customer when on Customer sites;

3.5 make all reasonable efforts to ensure that the Project is performed in a timely and efficient manner;

3.6 maintain accurate time sheets and make all reasonable efforts to complete the Project within any Estimated Price. If the Supplier foresees a situation where any Estimated Price is likely to be exceeded, it undertakes to draw the Customer's attention promptly to such situation;

3.7 develop, write and deliver the Software and Documentation in accordance with the Functional Specification;

3.8 comply with the Implementation Plan and meet the System Completion Date.

4. Customer's Obligations

The Customer undertakes:

4.1 to pay for the System subject to the performance by the Supplier of its obligations;

4.2 to provide where applicable, adequate office accommodation and other facilities, including access to the applicable computer systems of the Customer, to enable the designated employees of the Supplier to carry out the Project;

4.3 to take all reasonable steps to ensure the health and safety of the Supplier's employees while they are working at Customer sites;

4.4 to comply with any additional Third Party Software conditions notified to it on or before delivery of any Third Party Software (including if so required the execution and return of a Third Party Software Licence);

4.5 to ensure that the operating system and any other software with which the Software will be used is either the property of the Customer or is legally licensed to the Customer and to indemnify the Supplier in respect of any claims against the Supplier by third parties and all related costs, expenses or damages, in the event of any actual or alleged violations of third party proprietary rights or software licences;

4.6 to provide guidance to the Supplier on the interpretation of the Functional Specification and about the Customer's business practices which affect the design and construction of the Software;

4.7 to recognise the collaborative nature of the Project, and to use its best endeavours to co-operate with the Supplier in order to enable the Supplier to carry out the Project;

4.8 to accept the Supplier's advice on the technical feasibility of the Project, having regard to the applicable Customer environment;

4.9 to take sole responsibility for determining that the System is ready for operational use in the Customer's business before it is so used.

5. Charges

5.1 If an Estimated Price has been stated for the Project, it is shown in the

Schedule. This Estimated Price is only a non-binding estimate of the likely cost. The work will be carried out on a time and materials basis and will be charged at the Supplier's rates set out in the Charges Schedule.

5.2 The Charges in this Agreement are exclusive of expenses reasonably incurred in the performance of this Agreement, including but not limited to travel to Customer sites when applicable, couriers, accommodation and any other expenses reasonably incurred by the Supplier in connection with this Agreement.

5.3 The Charges and all other prices, rates and expenses in this Agreement are exclusive of Value Added Tax and any similar taxes. All such taxes are payable by the Customer and will be applied in accordance with UK legislation in force at the tax point date.

5.4 The Supplier will be entitled to increase its charges on the anniversary of the date of this Agreement and thereafter not more than once in any successive period of 12 months during this Agreement by giving not less than 60 days' notice to the Customer, provided that any such increase expressed as a percentage does not exceed the rate of the Supplier's salary inflation reported in its accounts for the immediately preceding year.

6. Payment

6.1 Each invoice will be sent to the Customer by the Supplier following completion of a Milestone. All invoices are payable 30 days from receipt.

6.2 The Supplier will during the term of this Agreement and for at least the following 12 months keep accurate and up-to-date records of the time spent on the work. The Customer will by its authorised representative on reasonable notice be entitled at all reasonable times to inspect such records and to obtain copies of them.

6.3 The payment by the Customer of any invoices will not be deemed to be approval and/or acceptance by the Customer of any work or matter in respect of which such invoice is issued and will be without prejudice to the Customer's rights and remedies under this Agreement or at law or in equity in respect of any failure or delay on the part of the Supplier to perform its obligations.

6.4 Payments which are not received when payable will be considered overdue and remain payable by the Customer together with interest for late payment from the date payable at the statutory rate applicable as well after as before any judgment, and independent of such judgment. This interest will accrue on a daily basis and be payable on demand.

6.5 Notwithstanding the above provision for late payment, in this event the Supplier may at its option, and without prejudice to any other remedy at any time after payment has become due, terminate or temporarily suspend performance of this Agreement.

6.6   If the Supplier becomes entitled to terminate this Agreement for any reason, any sums then due to the Supplier will immediately become payable in full.

7. System and Acceptance Testing

7.1   When the Supplier has system tested the System, the System will be handed over to the Customer for acceptance testing to be carried out by the Customer using Test Data for the Customer to test that the System conforms to the Functional Specification for use in its business, together with other requirements agreed between the parties.

7.2   The Customer will carry out the Acceptance Tests in respect of the System as set out in the Acceptance Tests Schedule over the number of days set out in the Implementation Plan for Acceptance Testing.

7.3   If there are failures in the Acceptance Tests, the Customer will inform the Supplier while the Acceptance Tests are in progress, and the Supplier will promptly use all reasonable endeavours to correct such failures.

7.4   The Customer's Project Manager will notify the Supplier's Project Manager promptly in writing of any material failure of the System to pass the Acceptance Tests.

7.5   The System will be deemed to be accepted by the Customer after the Acceptance Tests have demonstrated that it is in accordance with the Functional Specification, or after a period of one month of being submitted to the Customer for acceptance testing if the Supplier has not been notified of any material failure of the System to pass the Acceptance Tests, whichever is the earlier.

7.6   If material failures or omissions remain at the System Completion Date such that the System does not conform with the Functional Specification, the Customer will have a right to terminate this Agreement.

7.7   The Supplier reserves the right to amend the Charges and Implementation Plan to the extent that the Project is affected by any delay in the supply of Test Data. If the Test Data includes any data which necessitates any amendments to the Functional Specification, then such amendments will be charged to the Customer at the Supplier's then current rates in addition to the amount set out in the Charges Schedule. Any assistance requested by the Customer in the preparation of Test Data will be chargeable by the Supplier at its then current rates.

7.8   Implementation of the System in the Customer's business is the responsibility of the Customer.

8. Variations

8.1   Either party may at any time up to 60 days before the System Completion Date formally request in writing any changes to the System.

8.2   Within ten working days of receiving such a request from the Customer, or at the time of making its own request, the Supplier will inform the Customer in writing whether such change is technically feasible and of its impact and of any other consequent changes to the System, the Implementation Plan and the System Completion Date that it reasonably judges necessary. For any change requiring additional work, the Supplier will give the Customer either a fixed price quotation or the Supplier's reasonable estimate for doing that work on a time and materials basis.

8.3   If the Customer chooses to proceed with a Change Order, then the Implementation Plan and the System Completion Date will be amended as quoted by the Supplier, and the changes requested by the Customer and any other consequent necessary changes to the System, the Implementation Plan and the System Completion Date will be recorded in a Change Order signed by the Customer, and the Supplier will also issue a written revised price variation, or its estimate of such price variation for work to be done on a time and materials basis.

8.4   Changes resulting from Change Orders will be deemed to be incorporated in the Functional Specification, and will be effected by the Supplier, at a time judged to be suitable by the Supplier before the System Completion Date.

8.5   The Customer may vary the Implementation Plan by extending it by issuing a Change Order to take account of any delays on the part of third party suppliers or unforeseen operational needs, and will endeavour to give the Supplier reasonable notice of any extension. If the extension exceeds one month, the Customer will discuss the extension with the Supplier and any consequent impact caused to the Supplier's obligations. Any resulting changes which are necessary will be agreed between the parties.

9. Late Completion

9.1   If the Supplier fails to complete the System development by the System Completion Date, unless such failure demonstrably results from the Customer's default in performing its obligations under this Agreement or from an agreed extension of time relating to Change Order work, the Customer will notify the Supplier accordingly, and if such failure is not remedied within ten working days, the Supplier, recognising the loss caused to the Customer, will pay to the Customer a sum calculated at the rate of 1% of the value of the contract in respect of every seven days which elapse from the System Completion Date to the actual date of completion of the System, any period of less than seven days to be calculated pro rata. Such sums of money will be paid by the Supplier to the Customer not as a penalty but as and for the ascertained and liquidated damages owing and payable by the Supplier to the Customer by reason of such failure to meet the System Completion Date.

9.2   If the Supplier fails to complete the System by the end of the tenth week after the System Completion Date then the Customer (unless such failure demonstrably results from the Customer's default in the performance of its obligations under this Agreement) will be entitled without prejudice to any other rights or remedies it may have under this Agreement or at law or in equity to terminate this Agreement immediately by written notice.

9.3 If any delay in meeting the System Completion Date is demonstrably due wholly or mainly to the Customer's fault, the Supplier will nevertheless, if the Customer so requests, continue with the work on the Project with a view to completing it as soon as reasonably possible in the circumstances, and the Implementation Plan will be adjusted accordingly. In such circumstances, the Supplier will be entitled to charge for the additional time at its then current standard daily rates.

10. Supplier's Staff

10.1 The Supplier will use the staff identified in the Staff Schedule to perform its obligations under this Agreement. The Supplier will not without the consent of the Customer (such consent not to be unreasonably withheld or delayed) change the staff allocated to perform its obligations unless it has to do so because of reasons beyond its control.

10.2 Each party will procure that its employees and sub-contractors comply with the other party's site regulations (including its working arrangements with outside contractors) and other reasonable instructions of the other party whilst at the other party's premises.

10.3 The Supplier will be fully responsible and liable for the acts and omissions of its employees, sub-contractors and any employees of such sub-contractors arising out of the Project.

11. Progress Review

11.1 The Supplier and the Customer will each nominate a Project Manager authorised to make and communicate decisions relating to the Project, who will be responsible for:
   (a) organising monthly Progress Meetings at which they will both review the progress of the Project and attempt to resolve any problems;
   (b) providing all information reasonably required by the other for the performance of its obligations.

11.2 The Supplier's Project Manager will prepare a monthly progress report in writing and deliver it to the Customer's Project Manager in time for discussion at the Progress Meeting. This report will include a report on the progress of the Project together with other matters as the Customer's Project Manager may reasonably require.

11.3 The minutes of the Progress Meeting will be distributed within seven working days and signed before commencement of the business of the next Progress Meeting by both Project Managers.

12. Intellectual Property Rights and Licence

12.1 The Customer acknowledges that all proprietary rights in the Software,

627

including but not limited to any title or ownership rights, patent rights, copyrights, database rights and trade secret rights, will at all times and for all purposes vest and remain vested in the Supplier.

12.2 The Supplier grants to the Customer a non-transferable, non-exclusive licence to use the Software ('Licence') for an indefinite term and for its own internal purposes, provided that:

(a) the Customer does not provide or otherwise make available the Software or any part or copies or any related documentation in any form to any third party; and

(b) the Customer does not transfer or assign this Licence without the Supplier's prior written consent.

12.3 The Customer hereby undertakes as a condition of this Licence not to copy, adapt, vary or modify the Software without the Supplier's prior written consent.

13. Intellectual Property Rights Indemnity

13.1 The Supplier, at its own expense, will defend or cause to be defended or, at its option, settle any claim or action brought against the Customer on the issue of infringement of any [United Kingdom or Republic of Ireland] intellectual property right by the Software ('Claim'). Subject to the other conditions of this clause, the Supplier will pay any final judgment entered against the Customer with respect to any Claim, and fully indemnify the Customer in respect of all costs and expenses relating to the Claim provided that the Customer:

(a) notifies the Supplier in writing of the Claim immediately on becoming aware of it;

(b) grants sole control of the defence of the Claim to the Supplier; and

(c) gives the Supplier complete and accurate information and full assistance to enable the Supplier to settle or defend the Claim.

The costs and fees of any separate legal representation for the Customer will be the Customer's sole responsibility.

13.2 If any part of the Software becomes the subject of any Claim or if a Court judgment is made that the Software does infringe, or if the use or licensing of any part of the Software is restricted, the Supplier at its option and expense may:

(a) obtain for the Customer the right to continue to use the Software; or

(b) replace or modify the Software so that any alleged or adjudged infringement is removed; or

(c) if the use of the Software is prevented by permanent injunction, accept its return and refund an amount equal to the sum paid by the Customer for the Software subject to straight line depreciation over a five-year period.

13.3 The Supplier will have no liability under this clause for:

(a)   any infringement arising from the combination of the Software with other software not supplied by the Supplier; or

(b)   the modification of the Software unless the modification was made or approved expressly by the Supplier.

13.4   IN NO CIRCUMSTANCES WILL THE SUPPLIER BE LIABLE FOR ANY COSTS OR EXPENSES INCURRED BY THE CUSTOMER WITHOUT THE SUPPLIER'S PRIOR WRITTEN AUTHORISATION AND THE FOREGOING STATES THE ENTIRE REMEDY OF THE CUSTOMER IN RESPECT OF ANY INTELLECTUAL PROPERTY RIGHT INFRINGEMENT BY THE SOFTWARE.

14. Confidentiality

The parties recognise that under this Agreement they may each receive trade secrets and confidential or proprietary information of the other party, including but not limited to commercial information, products, customers, business accounts, finance or contractual arrangements or other dealings, program source and object codes. All such information which is either marked 'Confidential' or stated at the time of disclosure and subsequently confirmed in writing to be confidential constitutes 'Confidential Information'. Each party agrees not to divulge Confidential Information received from the other to any of its employees who do not need to know it, and to prevent its disclosure to or access by any third party without the prior written consent of the disclosing party.

15. Supplier's Warranties

The Supplier warrants that:

15.1   it is either the sole and exclusive owner or an authorised licensee or user of all intellectual property rights and interests in the Software and that no third party has or is entitled to claim any intellectual property right or interest in any Software which is inconsistent with any undertakings of the Supplier made in this Agreement;

15.2   it has all the rights necessary to perform its obligations under this Agreement;

15.3   the Software will be developed in a skilled and professional manner by personnel who have adequate and relevant expertise and experience commensurate with their assigned roles;

15.4   the Supplier makes no representations and gives no warranties, guarantees or undertakings concerning its performance of the Services except as expressly set out in this Agreement. All other warranties, express or implied, by statute or otherwise, are excluded from this Agreement.

16. Indemnities and Limits of Liability

16.1   The Customer agrees that it has accepted these terms and conditions in the knowledge that the Supplier's liability is limited and that the Charges payable have been calculated accordingly. The Customer is advised to make its own insurance arrangements if it desires to limit further its exposure to risk or if it requires further or different cover.

16.2 The Supplier will indemnify the Customer for direct physical injury or death caused solely either by defects in the System or by the negligence of its employees acting within the course of their employment and the scope of their authority.

16.3 The Supplier will indemnify the Customer for direct damage to property caused solely either by defects in the System or by the negligence of its employees acting within the course of their employment and the scope of their authority. The total liability of the Supplier under this sub-clause will be limited to [£one million] for any one event or series of connected events.

16.4 Except as expressly stated in this clause and elsewhere in this Agreement, any liability of the Supplier for breach of this Agreement will not exceed in the aggregate of damages, costs, fees and expenses capable of being awarded to the Customer the total price paid or due to be paid by the Customer under this Agreement.

16.5 Except as expressly stated in this Agreement, the Supplier disclaims all liability to the Customer in contract or in tort (including negligence or breach of statutory duty) in connection with the Supplier's performance of this Agreement or the Customer's use of the System and in no event will the Supplier be liable to the Customer for special, indirect or consequential damages or for loss of profits or arising from loss of data or unfitness for user purposes.

17. Post-Implementation Support

The Supplier recommends, or will provide if so requested by the Customer, a separate support agreement to cover future support of the System, at its then current charges for such support services.

18. Termination

18.1 This Agreement may be terminated immediately by notice in writing:
   (a) by the Supplier if the Customer fails to pay any sums due under this Agreement by the due date notwithstanding any other provisions for late payment in this Agreement;
   (b) by either party if the other party is in material or continuing breach of any of its obligations under this Agreement and fails to remedy the same (if capable of remedy) for a period of 30 days after written notice of the breach by the other party;
   (c) by either party if the other party is involved in any legal proceedings concerning its solvency, or ceases trading, or commits an act of bankruptcy or is adjudicated bankrupt or enters into liquidation, whether compulsory or voluntary, other than for the purposes of an

amalgamation or reconstruction, or makes an arrangement with its creditors or petitions for an administration order or has a receiver or manager appointed over all or any part of its assets or generally becomes unable to pay its debts within the meaning of Section 123 of the Insolvency Act 1986 or anything analogous to such event occurs in any applicable jurisdiction.

18.2 Any termination of this Agreement under this clause will be without prejudice to any other rights or remedies of either party under this Agreement or at law and will not affect any accrued rights or liabilities of either party at the date of termination.

19. General Contract Provisions

19.1 Entire Agreement

This Agreement constitutes the entire agreement between the parties and supersedes any previous agreement between the parties relating to the subject matter of this Agreement. Each of the parties acknowledges that in entering into this Agreement, it does not rely on and will have no remedy in respect of any statement of fact or opinion not recorded in this Agreement (whether negligently or innocently made), except for any representation made fraudulently.

19.2 Variations

No variation of these terms and conditions will be valid unless confirmed in writing by authorised signatories of both parties on or after the date of this Agreement.

19.3 Severability

If any of the provisions of this Agreement is judged to be illegal or unenforceable, the continuation in full force and effect of the remainder of them will not be prejudiced [unless the substantive purpose of this Agreement is thereby frustrated, in which case either party may terminate this Agreement forthwith on written notice].

19.4 Waiver

No forbearance or delay by either party in enforcing its respective rights will prejudice or restrict the rights of that party, and no waiver of any such rights or of any breach of any contractual terms will be deemed to be a waiver of any other right or of any later breach.

19.5 Rights of Third Parties

A person who is not a party to this Agreement has no right to benefit under or to enforce any term of this Agreement.

19.6 Assignment

Neither party will assign, sub-contract or otherwise deal with this Agreement or any rights and obligations under this Agreement without the prior consent of the other party.

19.7 **Notices**

Any notice given under this Agreement by either party to the other must be in writing and may be delivered personally or by first-class post, and in the case of post will be deemed to have been given two working days after the date of posting. Notices will be delivered or sent to the addresses of the parties on the first page of this Agreement or to any other address notified in writing by either party to the other for the purpose of receiving notices after the date of this Agreement.

19.8 **Force Majeure**

Neither party will be liable to the other party for any delay in or failure to perform its obligations (other than a payment of money) as a result of any cause beyond its reasonable control, including but not limited to any industrial dispute. If such delay or failure continues for at least 90 days, either party will be entitled to terminate the Agreement by notice in writing without further liability of either party arising directly as a result of such delay or failure.

19.9 **Governing Law and Jurisdiction**

This Agreement is governed by and construed according to English law and the parties submit to the exclusive jurisdiction of the courts of England and Wales.

SCHEDULES

Charges

Competitors

Documentation

Designated Representatives

Equipment

Implementation Plan

Staff

Third Party Software

Training

Functional Specification Appendix

The Customer agrees to accept the Project on the terms and conditions of this Agreement.

The Supplier agrees to carry out the Project on the terms and conditions of this Agreement.

....

....

FOR AND ON BEHALF OF THE CUSTOMER

FOR AND ON BEHALF OF THE SUPPLIER

Name: ....

Name: ....

Date: ....

Date: ....

Director of the Customer

Director of the Supplier

PROTOTYPE SOFTWARE DEVELOPMENT AGREEMENT

Date of Agreement ....

BETWEEN:

(1)   **THE SUPPLIER** whose registered office is at
.... ('**Supplier**');

AND

(2)   **THE CUSTOMER** whose registered office is at
.... ('**Customer**').

I. Scope of Contract

1.1   The Supplier has experience and expertise in developing and implementing software projects.

1.2   The Customer wishes to procure a software system and related services from the Supplier.

2. Definitions

2.1   '*Charges*' means the charges payable for the Project.

2.2   '*Concept Document*' means the document which outlines the requirements for the System incorporated into this Agreement as the Concept Document Appendix.

2.3   '*Estimated Price*' means the price estimated for the Project as set out in the Charges Schedule.

2.4   '*Progress Meeting*' means a meeting held between the parties to discuss progress of the Project.

2.5   '*Project*' means the work to be undertaken and services to be performed by the Supplier to develop and implement the System.

2.6   '*Project Manager*' means the designated representative appointed by the Supplier or the Customer respectively as initially specified in the Designated Representatives Schedule.

2.7   '*Schedules*' means the schedules identified in this Agreement and incorporated into this Agreement.

2.8   '*Software*' means the software content of the System developed in accordance with these terms and conditions.

2.9 '*System*' means the business system required by the Client[, using the Equipment and Software in combination].

2.10 '*Third Party Software*' means all third party software owned by a third party but legally licensed to the Supplier for use in developing the Software.

2.11 '*Training*' means the training in using the System to be provided by the Supplier as described in the Training Schedule.

3. Duration

This Agreement commences on the date shown in the Schedule and will continue for an initial period of 12 calendar months, after which it will remain in force until terminated by either party giving at least 90 days' notice of termination to the other party to expire on the last day of the initial term or at any time thereafter.

4. Supplier's Obligations

The Supplier undertakes to:

4.1 provide its services diligently, expeditiously and with reasonable skill and care;

4.2 provide suitably skilled and appropriately experienced personnel to carry out the Project;

4.3 provide the Training;

4.4 make all reasonable efforts to ensure that the Project is performed in a timely and efficient manner;

4.5 maintain accurate time sheets;

4.6 write the Software and complete the Project utilising such elements of the following procedural framework as may be deemed by the Supplier to be appropriate in the particular circumstances:
   (a) creating with the Customer's assistance the Concept Document;
   (b) agreeing with the Customer the limitations of the System;
   (c) agreeing with the Customer the order in which the modules of the Software will be written;
   (d) discussing and agreeing with the Customer the contents of the first Software module;
   (e) coding the first Software module, testing it and obtaining the agreement of the Customer that the results meet the requirements of the Project;
   (f) where necessary, redefining and rewriting the first Software module, retesting it and obtaining the agreement of the Customer that the results meet the requirements of the Project;
   (g) discussing and agreeing with the Customer the contents of the second

and subsequent Software modules in the sequence stated in the Concept Document or such amended sequence as the parties may agree;

(h)   coding the second and subsequent Software modules in the sequence stated in the Concept Document or such amended sequence as the parties may agree, installing them on the Customer's Equipment, testing them, and carrying out such redefinition and rewriting as may be required by the Customer in order to obtain the agreement of the Customer that the results meet the requirements of the Project;

4.7   where the Software is located on a Supplier's site, re-install the Software at the Customer's Site;

4.8   make all reasonable efforts to ensure that the System meets the needs of the Customer's business.

Depending upon the requirements of the Project, some of the above procedures may be performed by the Supplier in parallel.

5. Customer's Obligations

The Customer undertakes:

5.1   to pay for the System subject to the performance by the Supplier of its obligations;

5.2   to provide where applicable, adequate office accommodation and other facilities, including access to the applicable computer systems of the Customer, to enable the designated employees of the Supplier to carry out the Project;

5.3   to take all reasonable steps to ensure the health and safety of the Supplier's employees while they are working at Customer sites;

5.4   to comply with any additional Third Party Software conditions notified to it on or before delivery of any Third Party Software (including if so required the execution and return of a Third Party Software Licence);

5.5   to ensure that the operating system and any other software with which the Software will be used is either the property of the Customer or is legally licensed to the Customer, and to indemnify the Supplier in respect of any claims against the Supplier by third parties and all related costs, expenses or damages, in the event of any actual or alleged violations of third party proprietary rights or software licences;

5.6   to recognise that the Project is a joint endeavour between the parties;

5.7   to co-operate with the Supplier in defining the Project and in adopting the Supplier's methodology in producing the Software in order to facilitate timely completion of the Project;

5.8 to contain its expectations from the Project to technically feasible solutions as advised by the Supplier, having regard to the applicable Customer environment;

5.9 to create an appropriate test environment in order to satisfy itself that the System meets the needs of its business;

5.10 to take sole responsibility for determining that the System is ready for operational use in the Customer's business before it is so used;

5.11 to recognise that the Software is provided without warranty as to function or fitness for purpose because of the collaborative nature of the Project.

6. Charges

6.1 The work will be carried out on a time and materials basis and will be charged at the Supplier's rates set out in the Charges Schedule.

6.2 The Charges in this Agreement are exclusive of expenses reasonably incurred in the performance of this Agreement, including but not limited to travel to Customer sites when applicable, couriers, accommodation and any other expenses reasonably incurred by the Supplier in connection with this Agreement.

6.3 The Charges and all other prices, rates and expenses in this Agreement are exclusive of Value Added Tax and any similar taxes. All such taxes are payable by the Customer and will be applied in accordance with UK legislation in force at the tax point date.

6.4 The Supplier will be entitled to increase its charges on the anniversary of the date of this Agreement and thereafter not more than once in any successive period of 12 months during this Agreement by giving not less than 60 days' notice to the Customer, provided that any such increase expressed as a percentage does not exceed the rate of the Supplier's salary inflation reported in its accounts for the immediately preceding year.

7. Payment

7.1 Each invoice will be sent to the Customer by the Supplier monthly. All invoices are payable 30 days from receipt.

7.2 The Supplier will during the term of this Agreement and for at least the following 12 months keep accurate and up-to-date records of the time spent on the work. The Customer will by its authorised representative on reasonable notice be entitled at all reasonable times to inspect such records and to obtain copies of them.

7.3 The payment by the Customer of any invoices will not be deemed to be approval and/or acceptance by the Customer of any work or matter in respect of which such invoice is issued and will be without prejudice to the

Customer's rights and remedies under this Agreement or at law or in equity in respect of any failure or delay on the part of the Supplier to perform its obligations.

7.4   Payments which are not received when payable will be considered overdue and remain payable by the Customer together with interest for late payment from the date payable at the statutory rate applicable as well after as before any judgment, and independent of such judgment. This interest will accrue on a daily basis and be payable on demand.

7.5   Notwithstanding the above provision for late payment, in this event the Supplier may at its option, and without prejudice to any other remedy at any time after payment has become due, terminate or temporarily suspend performance of this Agreement.

7.6   If the Supplier becomes entitled to terminate this Agreement for any reason, any sums then due to the Supplier will immediately become payable in full.

8. Progress Review

8.1   The Supplier and the Customer will each nominate a Project Manager authorised to make and communicate decisions relating to the Project, who will be responsible for:

(a)   organising monthly Progress Meetings at which they will both review the progress of the Project and attempt to resolve any problems;

(b)   providing all information reasonably required by the other for the performance of its obligations.

8.2   The Supplier's Project Manager will prepare a monthly progress report in writing and deliver it to the Customer's Project Manager in time for discussion at the Progress Meeting. This report will include a report on the progress of the Project together with other matters as the Customer's Project Manager may reasonably require.

8.3   The minutes of the Progress Meeting will be distributed within seven working days and signed before commencement of the business of the next Progress Meeting by both Project Managers.

9. Intellectual Property Rights and Licence

9.1   The Customer acknowledges that all proprietary rights in the Software, including but not limited to any title or ownership rights, patent rights, copyrights and trade secret rights, will at all times and for all purposes vest and remain vested in the Supplier.

9.2   The Supplier grants to the Customer a non-transferable, non-exclusive licence to use the Software ('Licence') for an indefinite term and for its own internal purposes, provided that:

(a)   the Customer does not provide or otherwise make available the Software or any part or copies or any related documentation in any form to any third party; and

(b)   the Customer does not transfer or assign this Licence without the Supplier's prior written consent.

9.3   The Customer hereby undertakes as a condition of this Licence not to copy, adapt, vary or modify the Software without the Supplier's prior written consent.

10. Intellectual Property Rights Indemnity

10.1   The Supplier, at its own expense, will defend or cause to be defended or, at its option, settle any claim or action brought against the Customer on the issue of infringement of any [United Kingdom or Republic of Ireland] intellectual property right by the Software ('Claim'). Subject to the other conditions of this clause, the Supplier will pay any final judgment entered against the Customer with respect to any Claim, and fully indemnify the Customer in respect of all costs and expenses relating to the Claim provided that the Customer:

(a)   notifies the Supplier in writing of the Claim immediately on becoming aware of it;

(b)   grants sole control of the defence of the Claim to the Supplier; and

(c)   gives the Supplier complete and accurate information and full assistance to enable the Supplier to settle or defend the Claim.

The costs and fees of any separate legal representation for the Customer will be the Customer's sole responsibility.

10.2   If any part of the Software becomes the subject of any Claim or if a Court judgment is made that the Software does infringe, or if the use or licensing of any part of the Software is restricted, the Supplier at its option and expense may:

(a)   obtain for the Customer the right to continue to use the Software; or

(b)   replace or modify the Software so that any alleged or adjudged infringement is removed; or

(c)   if the use of the Software is prevented by permanent injunction, accept its return and refund an amount equal to the sum paid by the Customer for the Software subject to straight line depreciation over a five-year period.

10.3   The Supplier will have no liability under this clause for:

(a)   any infringement arising from the combination of the Software with other software not supplied by the Supplier; or

(b)   the modification of the Software unless the modification was made or approved expressly by the Supplier.

10.4   IN NO CIRCUMSTANCES WILL THE SUPPLIER BE LIABLE FOR ANY COSTS OR EXPENSES INCURRED BY THE CUSTOMER WITHOUT THE SUPPLIER'S PRIOR WRITTEN AUTHORISATION AND THE FOREGOING STATES THE ENTIRE REMEDY OF THE CUSTOMER IN RESPECT OF ANY INTELLECTUAL PROPERTY RIGHT INFRINGEMENT BY THE SOFTWARE.

11. Confidentiality

The parties recognise that under this Agreement they may each receive trade secrets and confidential or proprietary information of the other party, including but not limited to commercial information, products, customers, business accounts, finance or contractual arrangements or other dealings, program source and object codes. All such information which is either marked 'Confidential' or stated at the time of disclosure and subsequently confirmed in writing to be confidential constitutes 'Confidential Information'. Each party agrees not to divulge Confidential Information received from the other to any of its employees who do not need to know it, and to prevent its disclosure to or access by any third party without the prior written consent of the disclosing party.

12. Supplier's Warranties

The Supplier warrants that:

12.1 it is either the sole and exclusive owner or an authorised licensee or user of all intellectual property rights and interests in the Software and that no third party has or is entitled to claim any intellectual property right or interest in any Software which is inconsistent with any undertakings of the Supplier made in this Agreement;

12.2 it has all the rights necessary to perform its obligations under this Agreement;

12.3 the Software will be developed in a skilled and professional manner by personnel who have adequate and relevant expertise and experience commensurate with their assigned roles;

12.4 the Supplier makes no representations and gives no warranties, guarantees or undertakings concerning its performance of the Services except as expressly set out in this Agreement. All other warranties, express or implied, by statute or otherwise, are excluded from this Agreement.

13. Indemnities and Limits of Liability

13.1 The Customer agrees that it has accepted these terms and conditions in the knowledge that the Supplier's liability is limited and that the Charges payable have been calculated accordingly. The Customer is advised to make its own insurance arrangements if it desires to limit further its exposure to risk or if it requires further or different cover.

13.2 The Supplier will indemnify the Customer for direct physical injury or death caused solely either by defects in the System or by the negligence of its employees acting within the course of their employment and the scope of their authority.

13.3 The Supplier will indemnify the Customer for direct damage to property caused solely either by defects in the System or by the negligence of its employees acting within the course of their employment and the scope of their authority. The total liability of the Supplier under this sub-clause will be limited to [£one million] for any one event or series of connected events.

13.4 Except as expressly stated in this clause and elsewhere in this Agreement, any liability of the Supplier for breach of this Agreement will not exceed in the aggregate of damages, costs, fees and expenses capable of being awarded to the Customer the total price paid or due to be paid by the Customer under this Agreement.

13.5 Except as expressly stated in this Agreement, the Supplier disclaims all liability to the Customer in contract or in tort (including negligence or breach of statutory duty) in connection with the Supplier's performance of this Agreement or the Customer's use of the System and in no event will the Supplier be liable to the Customer for indirect or consequential damages or for loss of profits or arising from loss of data or unfitness for user purposes.

14. Post-Implementation Support

The Supplier recommends, or will provide if so requested by the Customer, a separate Support Agreement to cover future support of the System, at its then current charges for such support services.

15. Termination

15.1 This Agreement may be terminated immediately by notice in writing:

(a) by the Supplier if the Customer fails to pay any sums due under this Agreement by the due date notwithstanding any other provisions for late payment in this Agreement;

(b) by either party if the other party is in material or continuing breach of any of its obligations under this Agreement and fails to remedy the same (if capable of remedy) for a period of 30 days after written notice of the breach by the other party;

(c) by either party if the other party is involved in any legal proceedings concerning its solvency, or ceases trading, or commits an act of bankruptcy or is adjudicated bankrupt or enters into liquidation, whether compulsory or voluntary, other than for the purposes of an amalgamation or reconstruction, or makes an arrangement with its creditors or petitions for an administration order or has a receiver or manager appointed over all or any part of its assets or generally becomes unable to pay its debts within the meaning of Section 123 of the Insolvency Act 1986 or anything analogous to such event occurs in any applicable jurisdiction.

15.2 Any termination of this Agreement under this clause will be without prejudice to any other rights or remedies of either party under this Agreement or at law and will not affect any accrued rights or liabilities of either party at the date of termination.

16. General Contract Provisions

16.1 Entire Agreement

This Agreement constitutes the entire agreement between the parties and supersedes any previous agreement between the parties relating to the subject matter of this Agreement. Each of the parties acknowledges that in entering into this Agreement, it does not rely on and will have no remedy in respect of any statement of fact or opinion not recorded in this Agreement (whether negligently or innocently made), except for any representation made fraudulently.

16.2 Variations

No variation of these terms and conditions will be valid unless confirmed in writing by authorised signatories of both parties on or after the date of this Agreement.

16.3 Severability

If any of the provisions of this Agreement is judged to be illegal or unenforceable, the continuation in full force and effect of the remainder of them will not be prejudiced [unless the substantive purpose of this Agreement is thereby frustrated, in which case either party may terminate this Agreement forthwith on written notice].

16.4 Waiver

No forbearance or delay by either party in enforcing its respective rights will prejudice or restrict the rights of that party, and no waiver of any such rights or of any breach of any contractual terms will be deemed to be a waiver of any other right or of any later breach.

16.5 Rights of Third Parties

A person who is not a party to this Agreement has no right to benefit under or to enforce any term of this Agreement.

16.6 Assignment

Neither party will assign, sub-contract or otherwise deal with this Agreement or any rights and obligations under this Agreement without the prior consent of the other party.

16.7 Notices

Any notice given under this Agreement by either party to the other must be in writing and may be delivered personally or by first-class post, and in the case of post will be deemed to have been given two working days after the date of posting. Notices will be delivered or sent to the addresses of the parties on the first page of this Agreement or to any other address notified in writing by either party to the other for the purpose of receiving notices after the date of this Agreement.

16.8 Force Majeure

Neither party will be liable to the other party for any delay in or failure to perform its obligations (other than a payment of money) as a result of any cause beyond its reasonable control, including but not limited to any industrial dispute. If such delay or failure continues for at least 90 days, either party will be entitled to terminate the Agreement by notice in writing without further liability of either party arising directly as a result of such delay or failure.

16.9 **Governing Law and Jurisdiction**

This Agreement is governed by and construed according to English law and the parties submit to the exclusive jurisdiction of the courts of England and Wales.

SCHEDULES

Charges

Designated Representatives

Equipment

Third Party Software

Training

Concept Document Appendix

The Customer agrees to accept the Project on the terms and conditions of this Agreement	The Supplier agrees to carry out the Project on the terms and conditions of this Agreement
....	....
FOR AND ON BEHALF OF THE CUSTOMER	**FOR AND ON BEHALF OF THE SUPPLIER**
Name:	Name: ....
Date:	Date: ....
Director of the Customer	**Director of the Supplier**

OUTSOURCING SERVICES AGREEMENT

Date of Agreement ....

BETWEEN:

(1)   **THE CLIENT** whose registered office is at
.... ('**Client**');

AND

(2)   **THE PROVIDER** whose registered office is at
.... ('**Provider**').

BACKGROUND

(A)   The Client wishes to receive from the Provider certain information technology and related services [which were previously provided internally].

(B)   The Provider has experience and expertise in providing information technology and related services.

(C)   Under the terms of the Business Transfer Agreement (as defined below), the employees, and certain assets and undertakings which will be used in providing those services which will be undertaken under the terms of this Agreement are transferred by the Client to the Provider.

(D)   The Client wishes the Provider, and the Provider has agreed, to provide certain information technology and related services to the Client on the terms of this Agreement.

1. Definitions

In this agreement the following terms will have the following meanings:

1.1   '*Achieved Service Levels*' means the Service Levels which are actually achieved in any month.

1.2   '*Annual Review*' means a formal review carried out every 12 months of all aspects of the Services and the Service Levels [and the outsourcing strategy].

1.3   '*Business Transfer Agreement*' means an agreement between the Provider and the Client relating to assets and resources connected with the outsourcing arrangements.

1.4   '*Change Control Procedure*' means the procedure described in clause 11 for controlling Variations requested or recommended to the Services [or to the Agreement].

1.5 '*Charges*' means the charges, fees, prices, rates and formulae and special payment terms set out in the Charges Schedule.

1.6 '*Client Liaison Manager*' means the Client's authorised representative.

1.7 '*Client Software*' means the Client's software listed in the Software Schedule, including its documentation and all modifications and enhancements to it.

1.8 '*Commencement Date*' means [the commencement date identified in the Services Schedule] [dd/mm/yy][the date on which this Agreement is executed].

1.9 '*Confidential Information*' means any information of a confidential nature [including trade secrets and information of commercial value] which may become known to either party from the other party and which relates to the other party.

1.10 '*Contract Management Group*' means a group formed of senior representatives of the Provider and the Client.

1.11 '*Disaster*' means an event or circumstances specified in the Disaster Recovery Schedule.

1.12 '*Disaster Recovery Plan*' means the plan for restoring the Services in the event of a Disaster, attached to this Agreement as the Disaster Recovery Schedule.

1.13 '*Dispute Resolution Procedure*' means the procedure for dispute resolution set out in clause 19.

1.14 '*Equipment*' means the computer and communications equipment listed in the Technical Requirements Schedule.

1.15 '*Key Personnel*' means those employees identified as such in the Key Personnel Schedule.

1.16 '*Know-how*' means information which the Client owns or possesses, which the Provider requires for the provision of the Services.

1.17 '*Monitoring Meeting*' means the meeting held regularly to monitor the provision of the Services.

1.18 '*New Outsourcing Contractor*' means a third party supplier whom the client appoints to provide services similar to the Services on termination of this Agreement including any supplier invited by the Client to provide proposals for providing such services.

1.19 '*Personal Data*' means personal data as defined in the Data Protection Act 1998, which may be accessed, processed or created as part of the Services.

1.20 '*Provider Services Manager*' means the Provider's authorised representative.

1.21 '*Schedule*' means a schedule identified in this Agreement and incorporated into this Agreement, which will take priority over the body of this Agreement in the event of any conflict.

1.22 *'Services'* means the services provided by the Provider described in [clause 3 and] the Services Schedule.

1.23 *'Service Failure Compensation Schedule'* means the schedule which sets out the terms on which compensation payments will be made.

1.24 *'Service Levels'* means the standards and/or measures agreed by both parties for the provision of the Services, as detailed in the Service Level Agreement or as otherwise expressly agreed between the parties from time to time.

1.25 *'Service Level Agreement'* means the document attached to this Agreement as a Schedule and thereby incorporated into this Agreement.

1.26 *'Software'* means the software used in the provision of the Services.

1.27 *'System'* means all hardware and operating system software which runs the Software and which may comprise one or more computer systems.

1.28 *'Technical Requirements'* means the technical requirements set out in the Technical Requirements Schedule.

1.29 *'Third Party Software'* means the third party software listed in the Software Schedule.

1.30 *'Third Party Supplier'* means an external supplier, other than the Provider, of products, material and services in connection with the Services.

1.31 *'Transfer Date'* means [dd/mm/yy] [the date set out as such in the Services Schedule] from which the Services will be supplied by the Provider.

1.32 *'Transition Plan'* means the requirements to be carried out on termination, [set out] [outlined] in the Transition Plan Schedule.

1.33 *'Variation'* means a variation to the Services, Service Levels or Charges.

2. Term of Agreement

2.1 This Agreement will come into effect upon the Commencement Date and execution of the Business Transfer Agreement. In the event of any conflict between the Business Transfer Agreement and this Agreement the terms and conditions of the Business Transfer Agreement will prevail.

2.2 The Provider agrees to provide the Services to the Client from the Transfer Date for a period of five years.

2.3 The Client will be entitled at its sole option to extend the Agreement for a further two years by written notice to the Provider at least six months before the fourth anniversary of the Commencement Date.

2.4 [Either party][The Client] may terminate this Agreement on at least 12 months notice to expire on the [third] anniversary of the Commencement Date or subsequently, and this Agreement will be subject to the other termination provisions contained in it.

3. Services and Service Levels

3.1 In consideration of payment of the Charges by the Client, the Provider will provide the Services in accordance with the terms of this Agreement, to meet the objectives set out at clause 3.2 below, and to comply with the Service Levels.

3.2 The objectives in requiring the provision of the Services are:
(a) [purpose of outsourcing];
(b) cost savings in running the Services;
(c) efficiency in providing the Services;
(d) data integrity;
(e) operational business continuity;
(f) responsiveness to changing operational strategy.

3.3 The provision of the Services as further described in the Services Schedule will include but not be limited to:
(a) dealing promptly with queries or problems relating to the use or performance of the Software and correcting all material program errors;
(b) identifying the location of any fault on the System, and where it appears in the Equipment or in software not being supported by the Provider, liaising with the applicable Third Party Suppliers to ensure the continuing satisfactory operation of the System, taking all appropriate actions to ensure that the System maintains its full functionality;
(c) providing or procuring minor enhancements to the Software, including but not limited to updating data and formulae to ensure that any changes in tax or other statutory regulations or law are incorporated into the Software;
(d) ensuring that the documentation in respect of the System is always adequate for use and up to date;
(e) meeting the Technical Requirements.

3.4 The Provider will provide the Services in compliance with all relevant legislation, regulations, codes of practice, guidance and other requirements of any relevant government or governmental agency.

3.5 The Provider will provide reports of usage statistics for the Monitoring Meeting which record and summarise the Achieved Service Levels as required by the Service Level Agreement and will provide further statistics of performance in meeting Service Levels within five working days of a request for such statistics by the Client Liaison Manager.

3.6 In agreeing any further Services or any Variations, the parties will act in accordance with the Change Control Procedure (any such Variations affecting Service Levels to be included in the Service Level Agreement when agreed).

3.7 The Service Levels will be subject to review at any time by agreement between the Provider Services Manager and the Client Liaison Manager, and in any event will be reviewed as part of the Annual Review.

3.8   Without prejudice to the Client's rights of termination under this Agreement, in the event of failure to meet the Service so identified as key in the Service Level Agreement, the provisions of the Service Failure Compensation Schedule will apply, and the payments specified in that Schedule will become payable to the Client by the Provider on the terms set out in that Schedule.

4. Provider Responsibilities

4.1   The Provider will ensure that the Services are provided by employees who are suitably qualified, experienced and competent for the tasks they perform, and who will have undergone suitable training prior to working on the Services.

4.2   **Provider Services Manager**

(a)   The Provider will appoint one of its senior managers as the Provider Services Manager. The appointment will be made on notice in writing, subject to approval by the Client [such approval not to be unreasonably withheld or delayed]. [Such approval will be deemed to have been given if no objection is raised within five working days of receiving notice of appointment.]

(b)   The Provider Services Manager will oversee the performance of the Provider's obligations under this Agreement, act as its liaison with the Client, co-ordinate all matters relating to the Services, and will have the authority on behalf of the Provider to decide all questions of a day-to-day nature that may arise under this Agreement in relation to the Services.

(c)   The Provider will be entitled to appoint an alternate to act temporarily if the Provider Services Manager is temporarily unable to fulfil the functions of the Provider Services Manager's role for any reason. Such alternate will have the same rights, responsibilities and obligations under such temporary appointment.

4.3   The Provider warrants that for six months immediately following the Commencement Date, it will use all reasonable endeavours to retain the Key Personnel to provide the Services.

4.4   The Provider will provide the Provider Services Manager and staff and (at no additional cost to the Client) such other resources as may be necessary for the Provider to fulfil its obligations under the terms of this Agreement.

4.5   The Provider will replace any person involved in the Services on request made on reasonable grounds by the Client.

4.6   The Provider will draw up the Transition Plan within three months of the Commencement Date, in consultation with the Client, and will be responsible for keeping it up to date in accordance with the Change Control Procedure.

4.7   The Provider will continuously review developments and innovations in technology, business processes, help desk services, and industry practice, in order to determine whether such developments would benefit any of the Services, and will promptly bring to the Client's attention at the next Monitoring Meeting all opportunities for improving Service quality or reducing Service cost.

4.8 The Provider will promptly advise the Client whenever the Provider has reasonable grounds to believe that it will fail to carry out its obligations under this Agreement.

4.9 The Provider will promptly advise the Client whenever it believes that any failure on the Client's part to carry out its obligations under this Agreement will have a detrimental effect on the quality of the Services.

5. Client Responsibilities

5.1 To enable the Provider to provide the Services, the Client will at its own expense:
   (a) provide the Provider with access to all relevant information and documentation reasonably required by the Provider;
   (b) make available to the Provider at reasonable times, for consultation and guidance, staff who are familiar with the Client's organisation, operations, procedures and business practices;
   (c) provide all input data required to be prepared by the Client for the provision of the Services [and be responsible for the accuracy and completeness of this data];
   (d) notify the Provider of any special features relating to the input data which the Provider needs to know in order to provide the Services.

5.2 The Client will appoint a Client Liaison Manager as its primary point of contact for the Provider[, subject to the approval of the Provider, which will not be unreasonably withheld or delayed]. The Client Liaison Manager will monitor the performance of the Services, and will have the authority on behalf of the Client to decide all questions of a day-to-day nature that may arise under this Agreement in relation to the Services. The Client will be entitled to appoint an alternate to act temporarily in the event that the Client Liaison Manager is temporarily unable to fulfil the functions of the Client Liaison Manager role. Such alternate will have the same rights and responsibilities under such temporary appointment.

5.3 **Equipment and Software**
   (a) The Client will be responsible for ensuring that all consents and licences are obtained and maintained in respect of the Equipment and the Software necessary for the performance of the Services.
   (b) The Client warrants that the Equipment and the Software will by the Commencement Date be in reasonable working order and condition for the purpose of performing the Services. The Client's liability in respect of breaches of this warranty is limited to claims notified by the Provider within 12 months of the Commencement Date.

5.4 The Client will assist the Provider in drawing up the Transition Plan.

6. Contract Monitoring Arrangements

6.1 The Client Liaison Manager and the Provider Services Manager will attend the Monitoring Meetings which will be held at least once in each month at the Client location and at a mutually convenient time, to discuss work in progress, any problems or issues requiring decisions, resource requirements, anticipated work and any other relevant matters.

6.2 Decisions, together with actions agreed to be undertaken and any other relevant matters, will be recorded as minutes of the Monitoring Meeting by the Provider Services Manager. Such minutes will be forwarded within ten working days of the Monitoring Meeting to the Client Liaison Manager for approval, such approval not to be unreasonably withheld or delayed. It is acknowledged that in the event of a dispute such minutes may be presented as evidence in any formal or informal action.

6.3 The usage statistics and any other statistics and reports available relating to the Services and Service Levels will be discussed at each Monitoring Meeting. If the Service Levels are not being achieved, the Client's Client Liaison Manager and the Provider Services Manager will agree the actions to be taken by the Provider to improve the Services, and draw up a plan of action to define the respective responsibilities of the Client and the Provider to be carried out in order to meet the Service Levels.

6.4 Either party will have the right to refer to the Contract Management Group any matters arising at a Monitoring Meeting which have not been resolved to its satisfaction.

7. Contract Management

7.1 The Contract Management Group will comprise five representatives appointed by the Client and three representatives appointed by the Provider.

7.2 The primary functions of the Contract Management Group will be:
- to agree the Annual Review;
- to review the Transition Plan annually; and
- to resolve any disputes which are referred to it pursuant to the Dispute Resolution Procedure.

7.3 The Contract Management Group will meet whenever the representatives or the parties deem appropriate, in order to carry out the functions conferred by this Agreement or otherwise delegated to it by the parties from time to time.

7.4 Any appointment of a representative to, or a removal of a representative from, that Contract Management Group, will be made on notice in writing by the relevant party, subject to approval by the other party. Such approval will be deemed to have been given if no objection is raised within five working days of receiving the notice of appointment.

8. Client Software, Data, Information and Know-how

Client Software

8.1 The Client owns or is authorised to sub-license all copyright and other intellectual property rights in the Software.

8.2 The Client grants a non-transferable, non-assignable, non-exclusive licence to the Provider to use the Client Software during this Agreement on the terms and conditions set out in this clause (the 'Licence') for the purposes of providing the Services.

8.3 The Provider agrees that:
   (a) the Client Software and all copies of it will remain at all times the property of the Client and that the Provider is not entitled to any rights or interests in the Client Software other than those expressly granted in this Licence;
   (b) copyright and all other intellectual property rights made by the Provider in any modifications or enhancements to the Client Software will vest absolutely in the Client;
   (c) the Client Software is confidential information of the Client and it will not disclose any of the Client Software or supply any copies of any of it to any person other than in the performance of the Services under the terms of this Licence, including appropriate express obligations of confidentiality;
   (d) it will not use any Client Software directly or indirectly otherwise than in connection with providing the Services;
   (e) it will not permit any copy of the Client Software to be made except for reasons of providing the services, security and back up.

8.4 The Client will indemnify the Provider against any expense, loss or damage incurred by the Provider as a result of any claim or allegation that the Provider's licensed use of the Client Software infringes the intellectual property rights of a third party.

8.5 Upon termination of this Agreement, the Licence will terminate, and the Provider will return the Client Software to the Client.

Data, Information and Know-how

8.6 The Client grants the Provider a non-exclusive, royalty-free licence to use Know-how for the purposes of fulfilling the Provider's obligations to provide the Services. The Provider undertakes not to use or otherwise deal with the Know-how for any other purpose.

8.7 For the avoidance of doubt, the parties agree that all data and information passed to the Provider by the Client or generated in the course of the Services will be at all times the property of the Client. The Client grants to the Provider a non-exclusive, royalty-free licence to use the Client's data, information and Know-how as necessary for the purpose of fulfilling the Provider's obligations under this Agreement.

8.8 The Provider will not acquire any right in the Client's data and information. The Provider will take all necessary steps to ensure that it will not use nor reproduce any such data, information or Know-how which comes into its possession or control except as required by this Agreement.

8.9 The Provider will be responsible for maintaining secure copies and backups of all data and information.

9. Third Party/Provider Software

9.1 The [Client/Provider] warrants that Third Party Software is validly licensed for running by the Provider for the term of the Agreement.

9.2 The Provider will fully indemnify the Client in respect of all damages, costs and expenses incurred by the Client resulting from any act or default of the Provider in respect of the Third Party Software.

9.3 If the Provider proposes to use its proprietary Software in the provision of the Services, the Provider will not introduce such proprietary Provider's Software without the prior consent of the Client, such consent not to be unreasonably withheld or delayed. The Provider will grant the Client a non-exclusive, non-terminable, royalty-free licence to the Provider's Software on its standard and reasonable terms. At all times thereafter the Provider will, at the cost of the Client, support the Software so licensed to the Client for the benefit of the Client.

9.4 If the Provider creates any Software or other intellectual property in the course of providing the Services, it will assign the intellectual property rights in such Software to the Client on such creation with full title guarantee and execute such documents as the Client may require from time to time in this connection.

9.5 The Provider hereby undertakes and warrants to the Client that the Software provided in connection with the Services does not infringe the intellectual property rights of any third party and agrees to indemnify and keep the Client indemnified against all costs, claims, expenses and liabilities arising out of or in connection with any claim inconsistent with the warranty.

10. Relations with Third Party Suppliers

10.1 The Client acknowledges that the Provider is the primary supplier of Services to the Client. However, nothing in this Agreement gives the Provider an exclusive right to supply the Client with software, equipment or services of any particular description.

10.2 The Provider will co-operate with Third Party Suppliers and will:
(a) provide such access to information, documentation and premises as such relevant Third Party Supplier will reasonably require at such notice as is reasonable in the circumstances, and subject to the Third Party Supplier complying with such reasonable conditions as to confidentiality as the Provider may require;

(b)   be responsible for co-ordinating with such Third Party Suppliers to ensure that software, equipment, and services provided by the Third Party Suppliers are integrated into the provision of the Services;

(c)   attend any meetings with Third Party Suppliers called by the Client at the Provider's expense.

10.3   Where network, communications, computer or other equipment provided by a Third Party Supplier is required to interface with the Equipment, the Provider will be responsible for ensuring that the interface is successfully achieved. For the avoidance of doubt, the Provider remains responsible for meeting Service Levels in spite of any failure of any interface, whether through hardware, software, or any defect in the network, communications or other equipment attached to such interface or for any other reason whatsoever.

11. Change Control Procedure

11.1   At any time during the term of this Agreement the Client Liaison Manager may request, or the Provider Services Manager may recommend, a Variation by means of a 'Change Request' notice in writing served on the other party.

11.2   The Provider will investigate the likely impact of any Variation upon the Services, the Charges and other aspects of this Agreement and will report accordingly to the Client by the next Monitoring Meeting.

11.3   Any fundamental Variation requested or recommended such as a Variation which affects the terms of this Agreement itself will be discussed at a meeting of the Contract Management Group before it is agreed or rejected.

11.4   If the parties agree at a Monitoring Meeting or otherwise that a Variation should be implemented and on the terms such as any costs attached to such Variation, a 'Change Control Note' will be drawn up by the Provider within seven days of such agreement containing:

- the details of the Variation;
- the date of agreement to proceed;
- any impact of the Variation on the Services, Service Levels and Charges;
- any price to be charged for implementing the Variation;
- a timetable for implementation and payment if relevant;
- signatures of both parties.

11.5   Neither party will be obliged to agree to any Variation, except that the Provider will not unreasonably refuse to provide any additional services requested by the Client.

11.6   Until any Variation has been mutually agreed in writing, the parties will continue to perform their respective obligations without taking it into account.

11.7   For the avoidance of doubt, improvements in the Services or the Service Levels which are achieved by the Provider in the course of providing the

Services efficiently, or which otherwise arise from the obligations imposed on the Provider under this Agreement, will not be deemed to be a Variation.

11.8 All costs incurred by the Provider in connection with the preparation, investigation and negotiation of Variations will be borne by the Provider unless otherwise agreed in writing by the Client Liaison Manager or minuted at a Monitoring Meeting or meeting of the Contract Management Group.

12. Charges and Payment Terms

12.1 The Charges payable by the Client for the Services will be calculated according to the formulae set out in the Charges Schedule. Charges payable for specific projects or additional services will be agreed as part of the Change Control Procedure.

12.2 The Charges will be revised on each anniversary of the Commencement Date during the term of this Agreement to take account of changes in the Service Levels, additional or fewer projects or services resulting from the Change Control Procedure and in any other factors included in the formulae, as more specifically described in the Charges Schedule.

12.3 The initial set up fee will be paid to the Provider by the Client on the Commencement Date on receipt of a properly drawn invoice.

12.4 Invoices for Services will be submitted monthly in arrears and will [represent one twelfth of the expenditure agreed in advance for the 12-month period concerned][be calculated on the basis of actual usage in the month preceding the month in which the invoice is submitted. Actual usage will be reconciled against initial forecast requirements and any differences identified].

12.5 Invoices will be subject to approval by the Client Liaison Manager and will be due and payable 30 days after the date of the meeting at which the approval is given.

12.6 All Charges and other costs are exclusive of Value Added Tax and any similar taxes. All such taxes are payable by the Client and will be applied in accordance with UK legislation in force at the tax point date.

12.7 The Provider hereby acknowledges and agrees that the Client may deduct from the payment next due any sums which the Client is entitled to deduct pursuant to clause 3 as calculated in accordance with the formula[e] set out in the Service Failure Compensation Schedule, or if no advance payment to the Provider is due promptly on receipt of the Client's invoice, the Provider will pay to the Client any sum representing the sum that would have been deducted had a quarterly payment been due.

12.8 For the duration of this Agreement the Provider will maintain on file full records of all Charges, prices, costs and expenses associated with and invoiced in respect of the Services or any other services pursuant to this Agreement. If on receipt of any invoice from the Provider, the Client disputes the sum invoiced in respect of any item in that invoice the Provider will promptly supply to the Client's satisfaction corroborating evidence of the method of calculation in respect of such sum and if this is shown to be incorrect or otherwise unsatisfactory the Provider will promptly remove and deduct such sum from such invoice or, if any payment has been made by the Client in respect of such sum, refund such payment to the Client.

12.9 The Client will reimburse any reasonable expenses reasonably incurred by the Provider which are not comprised in the Charges provided that such expenses are incurred only following (a) notification by the Provider to the Client of its request to incur expenses additional to the Charges accompanied by the Provider's reasons for incurring such expenses, (b) receipt by the Provider of the Client's written permission signed by the Client Liaison Manager to incur such expenses, and (c) presentation to the Client of the Provider's invoice for such expenses accompanied by a full account and any appropriate receipts.

12.10 Apart from the Services, the Client will not be liable for any expense, work or services carried out by the Provider unless the item is referable to a purchase order, which has been signed by way of approval by a relevant signatory of the Client.

12.11 Travel costs and all costs associated with meetings will not be chargeable by the Provider to the Client.

12.12 Payments which are not received when payable will be considered overdue and remain payable by the Client together with interest for late payment from the date payable at the statutory rate applicable as well after as before any judgment, and independent of such judgment. This interest will accrue on a daily basis and be payable on demand.

13. Confidentiality

13.1 Each party agrees and undertakes that during the term of this Agreement and thereafter it will keep confidential and will not use for its own purposes nor without the prior written consent of the other party disclose to any third party any Confidential Information unless such information is public knowledge or already known to such party at the time of disclosure or subsequently becomes public knowledge other than by breach of this Agreement or subsequently comes lawfully into the possession of such party from a third party.

13.2 To the extent necessary to implement the provisions of this Agreement, each party may disclose the Confidential Information to such of its employees, agents or permitted sub-contractors as may be reasonably necessary or desirable provided that, before any such disclosure, each party will make such employees and permitted sub-contractors aware of its obligations of confidentiality under this Agreement and will at all times procure compliance by such employees, agents or permitted sub-contractors.

13.3 The provisions of this clause 13 will remain in full force and effect notwithstanding any termination of this Agreement or its expiry.

14. Data Protection

In providing the Services or any other services to the Client, the Provider will comply with all relevant provisions of the Data Protection Act 1998, and without limitation to the foregoing, the Provider will:

14.1 process Personal Data only in accordance with the instructions of the Client;

14.2 comply with any applicable guidelines and codes of practice issued by the Information Commissioner from time to time;

14.3 take all appropriate measures to ensure that the Personal Data is kept secure and is not subject to any unauthorised processing, loss, destruction or damage;

14.4 ensure that its personnel and contractors are bound by appropriate confidentiality and non-use obligations in relation to the Personal Data;

14.5 provide the Client, at its request, with evidence of compliance with the Provider's obligations under this clause;

14.6 assist the Client to comply with any valid requests for access to Personal Data received by the Client;

14.7 notify the Client if the Provider receives any requests for access to Personal Data and comply with the Client's instructions in this connection;

14.8 notify the Client of any unauthorised or unlawful disclosure or use of Personal Data of which the Provider becomes aware;

14.9 at the request and option of the Client, promptly return or safely destroy all Personal Data in the Provider's possession or control.

15. Audit Requirements

15.1 The Provider will permit the Client [at any time without notice] or any third party qualified auditor appointed by the Client on reasonable notice by appointment during normal business hours [but without notice in case of emergency including any reasonably suspected breach of any of the Provider's obligations contained in this Agreement] to observe the carrying out of the Services and to examine and take copies of information relevant to the Services, including any associated Client records and documentation under the Provider's control, subject in any case, [other than in emergency] to such third party entering into such confidentiality agreement as is reasonably required by the Provider.

15.2 If, in the reasonable view of the Client, the audit indicates that the Provider's controls or performance are unsatisfactory, it will inform the Provider, and the Contract Management Group will agree on the improvements required and a timetable for achieving them. The Provider will comply with the timetable to implement the improvements.

16. Security and Disaster Recovery

16.1 The Provider will be responsible for ensuring that all documents, data and software are kept under secure conditions with backup arrangements satisfactory to the Client, to protect them effectively from unauthorised access and so that they can be recovered promptly from any malfunction of the System.

16.2 The Provider will take all reasonable precautions to minimise the impact of any Disaster affecting the Services.

16.3 In the event of a Disaster, the Provider will implement the Disaster Recovery Plan, in order to restore the provision of the Services affected by the Disaster.

17. Warranties

17.1 The Provider represents and warrants to the Client that it has obtained, where required by law or regulatory authority, all necessary registrations, permits, licences and approvals for it to perform its obligations under this Agreement. Upon request, the Provider will provide the Client with copies of all such registrations, permits, licences and approvals.

17.2 The Provider further warrants and undertakes to the Client that in performing its obligations under the terms of this Agreement it will comply with all applicable laws.

17.3 The Provider warrants and undertakes to the Client that:
   (a)   it will, and will procure that its personnel will, perform the Provider's obligations under this Agreement with all reasonable skill, care and diligence, in a professional manner;
   (b)   it will use appropriately qualified, skilled, trained and experienced personnel to provide the Services.

17.4 The Client warrants that the Client Software is validly licensed to the Client for access and use by the Provider for the term of this Agreement.

18. Limits of liability

18.1 In this clause 'Default' will mean:
   (a)   any act or omission of the Provider, its sub-contractors or any of their respective personnel which results in a breach of this Agreement;
   (b)   any negligent act or omission by the Provider, its sub-contractors or any of their respective personnel;
   (c)   any breach of statutory duty by the Provider, its sub-contractors or any of their respective personnel.

18.2 Except for liability arising from death or personal injury caused by negligence, and except for the indemnity in clause 18.3 below, for each of which no limitation will apply, the Provider's liability for all loss and damage caused by an individual Default will be limited to £1,000,000.

18.3 The Provider will indemnify the Client in respect of all loss, damages, costs and expenses (including without limitation legal expenses) which the Client suffers or incurs as a result of any breach by the Provider, its sub-contractors or any of their respective Personnel, of its confidentiality or data protection obligations or any Intellectual Property Rights infringement of the Client Software.

18.4 Except as expressly stated in this clause 18 and elsewhere in this Agreement, any liability of the Provider in respect of this Agreement will not exceed in the aggregate of damages, costs, fees and expenses capable of being awarded to the Client £5,000,000.

18.5 Except as expressly stated in this Agreement, the Provider disclaims all liability to the Client in contract or in tort (including negligence or breach of statutory duty) in connection with the Provider's performance of this Agreement or the Client's use of the Products and in no event will the Provider be liable to the Client for special, indirect or consequential damages [or for loss of profits].

18.6 The Provider makes no representations and gives no warranties, guarantees or undertakings concerning its performance of the Services except as expressly set out in this Agreement. All other warranties, express or implied, by statute or otherwise, are excluded from this Agreement.

19. Dispute Resolution Procedure

19.1 Except where this Agreement expressly provides to the contrary, any dispute arising in connection with this Agreement will be dealt with in accordance with the Dispute Resolution Procedure which is set out in this clause 19.

19.2 Neither party will be entitled to commence legal proceedings under the jurisdiction of the courts in connection with any such dispute until 21 days after the Dispute Resolution Procedure is deemed to be exhausted in respect of such dispute.

19.3 Notwithstanding clause 19.2 above, a party is in any event entitled to apply for injunctive relief in the case of breach or threatened breach of confidentiality or infringement or threatened infringement of its intellectual property rights or those of a third party.

19.4 The Provider Services Manager or the Client Liaison Manager or any member of the Contract Management Group for the time being will be entitled to call a meeting of the Contract Management Group by written notice of at least 14 days in the event that such person considers that a dispute has arisen. At least two of the nominees of either party from the Contract Management Group will attend such meeting and will use all reasonable endeavours to resolve the dispute.

19.5 If such meeting fails to resolve a dispute within seven days of the referral of the dispute to it, the Dispute Resolution Procedure will be deemed exhausted in respect of the dispute in question.

19.6 During the progress of the Dispute Resolution Procedure, if the Client has an obligation to make payment to the Provider, the sum relating to the matter in dispute will be paid into an interest-bearing deposit account to be held in the names of the parties at a clearing bank and such payment-in will, for the time being, be a good discharge of the Client's payment obligations under this Agreement. Following final determination of the dispute, the principal sum and interest held in such account will be paid in accordance with such determination. The interest from the account will discharge the liability of the Client to pay interest to the Provider in respect of the period when the money was in the account.

20. Termination

This Agreement may be terminated immediately by notice as follows:

20.1 By either party if the other party is involved in any legal proceedings concerning its solvency, or ceases trading, or commits an act of bankruptcy or is adjudicated bankrupt or enters into liquidation, whether compulsory or voluntary, other than for the purposes of an amalgamation or reconstruction, or makes an arrangement with its creditors or petitions for an administration order or if a trustee, receiver, administrative receiver or general officer is appointed over all or any part of its assets or if it generally becomes unable to pay its debts within the meaning of Section 123 or Section 268 of the Insolvency Act 1986;

20.2 By the Client if the Provider undergoes a change in control (where 'control' shall have the meaning ascribed to it in Section 840 of the Income and Corporation Taxes Act 1988 as amended from time to time and any legislation that re-enacts, consolidates and/or replaces it) such that the Provider is placed under the control of a corporation to which the Client may reasonably object;

20.3 By either party if the other party is in material or continuing breach of any of its obligations under this Agreement, (and, for the avoidance of doubt, failure to meet Service Levels will constitute such breach), and where such breach is capable of remedy, fails to remedy it within 30 days of notice specifying the default;

20.4 By the Provider if the Client fails to pay any sums properly due under this Agreement and such sums have not been paid following 30 days' written notice of such failure by the Provider.

21. Exit Management

On notice of termination or six months prior to expiry of this Agreement:

21.1 The Transition Plan will come into effect, and the parties agree to comply with its provisions. The Provider will co-operate fully with the Client, any

New Outsourcing Contractor, and Third Party Suppliers in order to ensure an orderly transfer of the Services to a New Outsourcing Contractor or to the Client.

21.2 The Provider will liaise with the Client, making available for such purposes such Provider liaison staff as the Client may reasonably require, and acting in good faith, to ensure a mutually satisfactory handover to the Client or to the new Outsourcing Contractor. The period of transition will commence as soon as notice has been given of termination of this Agreement, and will continue for a minimum period of three months after termination.

21.3 The Provider will:

(a) provide information on the Services in sufficient detail to form the basis of an invitation to tender for services;

(b) allow the Client or any New Outsourcing Contractor to conduct a due diligence process in respect of the Services;

(c) promptly answer questions about the Services which may be asked by the Client or any New Outsourcing Contractor.

21.4 The Provider will, if so requested by the Client, continue to provide the Services or such Services as the Client selects, for a period of up to 12 months from the date of termination, as specified by the Client, on the same terms as applied to the provision of the Services immediately prior to such termination.

21.5 Except where subject to separate contract, all rights of access, occupation and use granted to the Provider in respect of the Client's premises will cease when the provision of Services ceases in accordance with this Agreement and the Transition Plan.

21.6 Where assets used in the Services are located on the Provider's premises, the Provider will grant reasonable rights of access to enable the Client or the New Outsourcing Contractor to remove such assets transferred to the Client or the New Outsourcing Contractor in a reasonable time.

21.7 The licences to the Provider to use any Client Software will continue after termination of the Services to the extent necessary to enable the Provider to perform its obligations under this Agreement.

21.8 On termination of this Agreement [and on satisfactory completion of the Transition Plan], the Provider will procure that all Equipment and materials and all Client Software and documentation, will be returned to the Client or deleted or removed as appropriate from the System, and the Provider will certify full compliance with this clause.

21.9 The Client will have the right to use and to license any New Outsourcing Contractor to use all the Provider's intellectual property required in providing the Services for such transitional period after termination of the Services as may reasonably be required in order to effect the seamless transfer of the Services.

21.10 If the Client so requires, the Provider will use its best endeavours to procure the transfer at the Client's expense, to the Client or to a third party nominated by the Client at the Client's sole discretion, of any Third Party Software licences the Provider may have obtained in its own name in order to provide the Services.

22. General Contract Provisions

22.1 Entire Agreement

This Agreement including its Schedules sets out the entire agreement and understanding between the parties in connection with the subject matter of this Agreement and supersedes all prior discussions, agreements and under-standings made between them. Each of the parties acknowledges that in entering into this Agreement, it does not rely on and will have no remedy in respect of any statement of fact or opinion not recorded in this Agreement (whether negligently or innocently made), except for any representation made fraudulently.

22.2 Severability

If any of the provisions of this Agreement is judged to be illegal or unenforceable, the continuation in full force and effect of the remainder of them will not be prejudiced.

22.3 Waiver

No forbearance or delay by either party in enforcing its respective rights will prejudice or restrict the rights of that party, and no waiver of any such rights or of any breach of any contractual terms will be deemed to be a waiver of any other right or of any later breach.

22.4 Assignment

(a)   Neither party will without the prior consent of the other party assign, sub-contract or otherwise deal with this Agreement or any rights and obligations under this Agreement.

(b)   A person who is not a party to this Agreement has no right under the Contracts (Rights of Third Parties) Act 1999 to benefit under or to enforce any term of this Agreement.

22.5 Variations to Agreement

No Variation or any change will be made to this Agreement except in writing by authorised signatories of both parties on or after the date of this Agreement.

22.6 Notices

Any notice given under this Agreement by either party to the other must be in writing and may be delivered personally or by [recorded delivery] [first class] post, and in the case of post will be deemed to have been given two working days after the date of posting [where the addresses of the parties are both within the United Kingdom or seven working days after the date of posting where the notice is addressed to or is posted from an address outside the United Kingdom]. Notices will be delivered or sent to the

661

addresses of the parties on the first page of this Agreement or to any other address notified in writing by either party to the other for the purpose of receiving notices after the date of this Agreement.

22.7 **Governing Law and Jurisdiction**

This Agreement is governed by and construed according to English law and the parties submit to the exclusive jurisdiction of the courts of England and Wales.

SCHEDULES

Charges

Disaster Recovery Plan

Key Personnel

Service Level Failure Compensation

Service Level Agreement(s)

Services

Software (Client Software and Third Party Software)

Technical Requirements

Transition Plan

FOR AND ON BEHALF OF *[PROVIDER]*	FOR AND ON BEHALF OF *[CLIENT]*
The Provider agrees to provide the Services on the terms and conditions of this Agreement	The Client agrees to accept the Services on the terms and conditions of this Agreement
Signed	Signed ....
Name	Name ....
Date	Date ....
Provider Authorised Representative	**Client Authorised Representative**

ASP WEB-BASED SERVICES FRAMEWORK AGREEMENT

This Framework Agreement is between the Provider and the Client for the provision of various web-based services set out in one or more Services Schedules, to which the Client will add information for access by its end users

Date of Agreement ....

BETWEEN:

(1) **THE PROVIDER** whose registered office is at
.... ('**Provider**');

AND

(2) **THE CLIENT** whose registered office is at
.... ('**Client**').

1. Introduction

1.1 This Agreement comprises these standard terms and conditions including any Schedule to them, and concerns the supply by the Provider to, and use by the Client of, the web-based project information services identified in the Service Schedules.

1.2 The Service the Provider provides to the Client will be identified in a Schedule in the form set out in the Services Schedule attached to this Agreement with the commencement date applicable to that Service. If there is any direct conflict between any of the provisions in the main body of this Agreement and the Services Schedule, the provision in the Services Schedule will prevail for the period and Service to which it applies. Each Service will be provided for the period identified in its Services Schedule, unless this Agreement is terminated for any reason at a date earlier than the date for the end of Service in any Services Schedule, in which event the provision to the Client of any Service will cease at the termination of this Agreement.

2. Definitions

2.1 '*Application*' means the specific hosted application(s) for which the Services are provided, identified and described in the Services Schedule, which may be owned by the Provider or by a third party.

2.2 '*Charges*' means the fee payable for the provision of the Services and any other charges payable, as further defined in the Charges clause.

2.3 '*Client Branding*' means the client's corporate branding, such as trade marks or names or logos.

2.4 *'Client Equipment'* means the hardware and software which the Client uses to enable the Services and Application to be provided.

2.5 *'Client Information'* means data input, created or used by the client or End User in using the Application and Services.

2.6 *'Downtime'* means an outage causing interruption or failure to the provision of the Services.

2.7 *'End User'* means an entity that at any time has been identified by a Client to the Provider as an authorised End User.

2.8 *'End User Licence'* means the agreement between the Provider and an End User in the format and wording set out in the End User Licence Schedule attached to this Agreement.

2.9 *'Initial Term'* means the initial period of three years from the date of the Agreement specified at the head of this Agreement.

2.10 *'Intellectual Property Rights'* means all copyrights, patents, registered and unregistered design rights, trade marks and service marks and applications for any of these, together with all database rights, trade secrets, know-how and other intellectual property rights in all parts of the world.

2.11 *'Network'* means a network comprising all or any of the following: modems, leased circuits and other telecommunications hardware and software.

2.12 *'Schedule'* means a schedule referenced in, and forming part of, this Agreement.

2.13 *'Service Levels'* means the levels of performance to which the Services are to be provided to the Client by the Provider.

2.14 *'Service Level Specification'* means the document setting out the Service Levels and any security measures, comprising a Schedule to this Agreement.

2.15 *'Services'* means the application services to be provided by the Provider as described in the Services Schedule.

2.16 *'Service Procedures'* means procedures [set out in writing][accessible by the Client online] to provide instructions and guidance for the Client's management of the Services, which may be amended and updated from time to time.

2.17 *'System'* means the Applications, Services, and the Network as they operate together in the provision of the Services.

2.18 *'Technical Environment'* means the Network together with the Client Equipment, and any related equipment and connections, all as specified in the Technical Environment Schedule.

3. Term

This Agreement will come into effect as of its date and will remain in force for the Initial Term and then will continue in force from year to year or until one party gives at least 180 days' notice to the other that it is to end either on the last day of the Initial Term or on any anniversary of that date and otherwise subject to the termination provisions of this Agreement.

4. Service Provision

4.1 The Provider agrees to provide the Application and Services to the Client and to End Users in consideration of the payment of the Charges by the Client, subject to the terms and conditions of this Agreement.

4.2 The Provider will make available to the Client its Service Procedures and other appropriate support and diagnostic information, and will ensure that updated Service Procedures will be made available to the Client whenever they are re-issued. Information contained in the Service Procedures may include, but is not limited to:
  (a) technical support offered by the Provider;
  (b) training offered by the Provider;
  (c) usage restrictions to prevent unreasonable loads being imposed on the Network;
  (d) procedures to ensure that the security and integrity of the System are maintained, including encryption details if appropriate, and any proce-dures which arise from the need to comply with regulations of any data centre facility engaged by the Provider in connection with the Services; and
  (e) procedures to ensure that any database or other applications which form part of the Services can be used to best effect and within capacity.

4.3 The Provider's obligations regarding service levels and response times in support of any Service will be as set out in the Service Level Specification relevant to such Service.

4.4 Hosting of the Services, Applications and web servers is provided as set out in the Services Schedule.

4.5 If the Client wishes the Provider to perform any service which is not part of the Services, the Provider may carry out that service at its sole option, and the Client will be charged separately for it at its current rates for such services.

5. Scope of Client's Use

5.1 The Provider grants to the Client a non-exclusive, non-transferable licence to use the Services and Application as set out below for the Client's normal business purposes.

5.2 The Client may use the Services only in the jurisdiction in which the Client is registered as a company only by:
  (a) accessing the Services in accordance with the procedures set out in the Service Procedures;

(b)   entering, editing, transferring or deleting and moving its input comprising Client Information, documents, data, files and other content within the Services; and

(c)   providing interconnection with End Users who have entered into End User Licences, but only to the extent necessary to enable them to participate legitimately in using the Applications and Services.

5.3   The Client acknowledges that it is its sole responsibility to determine that the Application and Services meet the needs of its business and to satisfy itself that the Application is ready for operational use in its business before it is so used.

5.4   The Client is responsible for maintaining validation, error correction, back up and reconstruction of its own software and Client Information.

5.5   The licence granted to the Client in clause 5.1 is personal to the Client and the Client is not permitted to assign, transfer, sub-license, or otherwise dispose of any of the licensed rights to use the Service or any component to a third party, other than to End Users under the terms of this Agreement. Nothing in this Agreement transfers any proprietary rights in the Services from the Provider to the Client.

5.6   **End User Licence**

(a)   The Client is granted the right to grant licences to End Users in the form of the End User Licence to permit the End User to access and use the Application and Services only in relation to the Client's business purposes or its own use.

(b)   The Client acknowledges its responsibility for ensuring that End Users are properly licensed in order to access and use the Services in advance of such access and use.

(c)   If the Client learns or suspects that any End User is not complying with the terms of its End User Licence, the Client must notify the Provider immediately.

6. Client Obligations

6.1   The Client acknowledges and undertakes that it:

(a)   will use the Services only for lawful purposes and in accordance with this Agreement; and

(b)   will comply in every respect with all the instructions which the Provider provides concerning the Services, including the requirements set out in the Service Procedures; and

(c)   will use and adhere to the user names, passwords and any authentication codes or security procedures which the Provider may notify to the Client from time to time: and

(d)   will keep and maintain up to date a list of its licensed End Users and will provide such list to the Provider promptly at the Provider's request.

6.2   The Client will not:

(a)   reproduce, disseminate or otherwise disclose the content of any Application except as expressly set out in this Agreement;

(b)   electronically transmit any Application over a network except as necessary for the Client's licensed use of the Application;

(c)   use run-time versions of any third-party products which may be embedded in any Application, for any use other than the use of that Application;

(d)   modify, disassemble, decompile, or reverse engineer any Application except to the extent permitted by law, and must first give 90 days' notice to the Provider;

(e)   sub-license or otherwise grant or transfer possession of any copy of any Application to any other party outside the terms of this Agreement;

(f)   use any Application in any way not expressly provided for by this Agreement.

6.3   The Client is responsible for using only Client Equipment which is in good working order and in compliance with the specification in the Technical Environment Schedule. The Client must give 90 days' written notice of any changes it proposes to make to the Client Equipment. If any such Client Equipment is not compatible with the Services or Application, the Provider will promptly inform the Client in writing, and the Client must promptly rectify the situation.

6.4   The Client is responsible for acquiring and maintaining all licences and permissions necessary in respect of any third party software it may use in connection with the Services. The Client confirms that any Client Equipment, Client Information or other materials provided by the Client to the Provider or utilised by the Client in the Services will not infringe any Intellectual Property Rights of any third party, and will not be obscene or defamatory, and will not violate the laws or regulations of any state which may have jurisdiction over such activity.

6.5   If, for the purpose of providing the Services, it is necessary or desirable for the Provider to access or use any Client Equipment, Client Information, facilities or services the Client will make these available to the Provider for access free of charge to enable the Provider to perform its obligations under this Agreement, and the Client grants to the Provider a non-exclusive, royalty-free licence solely for such purposes.

6.6   The Client acknowledges that it is responsible for its input to the Services and for any use that it or its End Users make of such input, and that the Provider has no responsibility for such input or its use.

6.7   The Client licenses the Provider to incorporate items of the Client's corporate branding, such as a trade mark or name or logo, for the purpose of customising its pages and input. If, for this purpose, the Provider needs to become a registered user of any of the Client's branding, the Client undertakes promptly to do everything necessary to procure such registration for the Provider.

6.8 If the Client learns about or is informed of any of the components, processes or methods of operating any software comprised in any Service it will treat that knowledge or information as the Provider's trade secret, and not use it to the benefit of any party other than the Provider or convey it in any way to any third party or allow any third party to acquire it.

6.9 If the Client is in breach of any of its obligations above, then, without prejudice to the other terms and conditions in this Agreement:

(a)   the Provider cannot be held liable for any failure to meet the Service Levels which arises as a direct or indirect result of such Client breach;

(b)   the Provider will be entitled to charge the Client for staff time engaged on rectifying any resulting problems at the Provider's standard charge rates for the time being.

6.10 If the Provider suffers any loss, damage or expense as a result of:

(a)   any unauthorised access to, or use or misuse of, the Services by any employee, agent or sub-contractor of the Client;

(b)   any unauthorised access to, or use or misuse of, the Services by any third party if such access, use or misuse was permitted or facilitated by such employee, agent or sub-contractor,

the Client will fully indemnify the Provider in respect of such loss, damage or expense.

7. Charges

7.1   The Client will pay the Provider the Charges in respect of the Services at the rates and according to the payment terms set out in the Charges Schedule, and such Charges may be varied on 90 days' written notice after the initial 12-month period. All Charges are exclusive of Value Added Tax and any similar taxes, which will be applied in accordance with prevailing legislation in force at the tax point date.

7.2   Costs which are additional to the Charges and which are also the Client's responsibility include:

(a)   PCs, modems, printers or other equipment which may be necessary to access and use the Services;

(b)   communication charges, access fees, levies, tariffs or other related costs, between the Client and the Provider or its End Users or the Internet host or anyone else;

(c)   installation and testing of any communications lines, links or interfaces or any equipment or service used in connection with the Services.

7.3   If any of the Service Levels is not met to the extent that such failure for any such Service Level is defined in the Service Level Specification, unless any such failure is not the Provider's fault and subject to the exceptions stated in this Agreement, the Provider will credit the Client's account according to the method set out in the Charges Schedule with the sum representing the credit for such failure of the Service Level concerned as specified in the Service Level Specification.

7.4 During the term of this Agreement and for five years following its termination both parties agree to keep accurate books and records showing all the information required in the accurate calculation of the Charges. These records must be made available to the other party or its appropriately qualified representative for audit purposes.

8. Payment Terms

8.1 All invoices are payable 30 days from receipt. Payments which are not received when payable will be considered overdue and remain payable by the Client together with interest for late payment from the date payable at the statutory rate applicable as well after as before any judgment, and independent of such judgment. This interest will accrue on a daily basis and be payable on demand.

8.2 Notwithstanding the above provision for late payment, in this event the Provider may at its option, and without prejudice to any other remedy at any time after payment has become due, terminate or temporarily suspend this Agreement.

8.3 If the Provider becomes entitled to terminate this Agreement for any reason, any sums then due to the Provider will immediately become payable in full.

9. Security

9.1 The Provider will effect and maintain at all times continuous and sufficient security measures, in order to safeguard Client Information from unauthorised access and use, and to minimise the risk of a security breach and, if appropriate, these will be specified in the Service Level Specification.

9.2 Encryption techniques will be used for protecting Client Information on input and transmission over the Network, as specified in the Service Procedures.

9.3 The Provider will promptly notify the Client of any security attack which it learns of or suspects, which appears to be directed towards the Client Information.

10. Client Branding and Client Information

10.1 The Client warrants that it is the owner or authorised user of all Intellectual Property Rights and all other rights in the Client Branding. The Client agrees that for the purpose of customising the Application, the Provider may incorporate items of Client Branding, and the Client hereby licenses the Provider to do this. If for this purpose it is necessary for the Provider to become a registered user of any Client Branding, the Client undertakes promptly to do everything necessary to procure such registration.

10.2 The Client acknowledges and agrees that it is entirely responsible for its Client Information and any use that it or any End User or third party may make of it for any purposes, and that the Provider will have no responsibility for the Client Information or such use. Without prejudice to the generality of the previous sentence the Client hereby undertakes:

(a) to inform itself (and, if appropriate, the Provider) concerning, and in performing its obligations under this Agreement fully to comply with, all laws, regulations, licences or binding codes or standards of practice relevant to personal data (including without limitation the Data Protection Act 1998);

(b) not to provide any item of Project Information or upload, transmit or download any message or material that:

(i) is defamatory, racist or sexist, threatening or menacing to any person or group of people, or contains any obscene elements (in particular, anything which is or could be interpreted as paedophilia), or which in the Provider's reasonable opinion is likely to cause annoyance or distress to any person; or

(ii) infringes the copyright or other Intellectual Property Rights of any other person, company or partnership, anywhere in the world; or

(iii) in any way act in a manner that constitutes, or may involve the Provider in, sending any unsolicited e-mail.

11. Service Availability

11.1 Subject to the provisions set out in this clause, the Provider will use all reasonable endeavours to make the Services and Application available during the times specified in the Service Level Specification.

11.2 Notwithstanding the above, the Services or any particular Service Levels may be suspended for so long as is reasonably necessary subject to prior agreement with the Client, such agreement not to be unreasonably withheld or delayed:

(a) to enable either party to comply with an order or request from a governmental, or other competent regulatory body or administrative authority; or

(b) to enable the Provider to carry out work which is necessary in its reasonable opinion to maintain or improve the Services; or

(c) to carry out standard maintenance and support,

provided that the Provider will use all reasonable endeavours to schedule such Downtime during hours of low usage of the Services in order to minimise impact on the Services, and to ensure that there is no permanent material degradation of the Services.

11.3 If the Application requires immediate correction to enable it to run effectively or for immediate compliance with a governmental or regulatory requirement, the Provider may suspend that Application without advance warning for so long as reasonably necessary to implement the correction or to ensure compliance.

11.4 The Provider will be entitled in its sole discretion to make changes or upgrades to the Application or Services or their accessibility, to the Technical Environment or to the Service Procedures, provided that such changes or upgrades do not cause any material reduction in functionality. The Provider will endeavour to give at least seven days' written notice of any such changes. The Application may be suspended for so long as is reasonably necessary, but the Provider will use all reasonable endeavours to minimise the Downtime that may be caused by such change or upgrade. If as a result of such changes, the Client's ability to use the Services or the cost to the Client of using the Services is materially and adversely affected, the Client may terminate the Agreement on seven days' written notice to the Provider.

11.5 In the event of Downtime as specified in sub-clauses 11.2, 11.3 or 11.4 above, the Provider will provide status reports to the Client's representative nominated for such purposes by the Client, at two-hourly intervals by telephone or e-mail during working hours, or as otherwise agreed by the parties.

11.6 The Provider will use all reasonable endeavours to comply with a request by the Client for Downtime, provided that such requests are made in advance to the extent possible, and such Downtime will not be considered as a break in Service for the measurement of the Service Levels or for any other reason.

12. Intellectual Property Rights Indemnity

12.1 If the Client learns of any claim that any Service or part of it infringes any Intellectual Property Rights of any third party in the jurisdiction in which the Client is entitled to use such Service and (a) the Client informs the Provider promptly of the claim and grants sole control of the defence to the Provider to enable the Provider to settle or litigate it, and does not itself settle or litigate it, and (b) the claim does not arise from the Client's breach of this Agreement, the Provider will indemnify the Client and hold the Client harmless against any damages or costs arising from the claim.

12.2 In the event of any claim or if the use of any Service is restricted as a result of any claim, the Provider may at its option and expense: (a) obtain the right for the Client to continue to use the Service; or (b) modify or replace the Service for the Client to use; or (c) if the use of the Service is permanently prevented by the courts, terminate it and refund to the Client a sum equal to the sum the Client will have paid for its use over the 12 months immediately prior to such termination. The Provider will not be liable if any claim is caused by combining the Service with any software, database or information or data of any kind of which the Provider has not approved. These clauses 12.1 and 12.2 state the Provider's entire liability and the Client's entire remedy in respect of any infringement by any Service.

13. Warranties

13.1 The Provider warrants that it is either the sole and exclusive owner or an authorised licensee or user of all Intellectual Property Rights in the Application and Services (including any databases, images, 'applets', graphics, animations, video, audio and text incorporated into them), and reserves all its rights.

13.2 The Provider warrants that it will provide the Services using all reasonable skill and care in accordance with the terms of this Agreement, and so that they conform to their current published description and that they operate in accordance with the Service Procedures.

13.3 The Provider uses all reasonable endeavours to maintain the Services free of bugs and viruses but the Provider strongly recommends that the Client should have its own effective anti-virus programs.

13.4 The Provider does not and cannot control the network on which the technology operates or the flow of data to or from its network. Such flow depends largely on the performance of services provided or controlled by third parties. At times, actions or omissions of such third parties can impair or disrupt connections. Although the Provider will use all commercially reasonable efforts to avoid such events and take all actions it deems appropriate to remedy such events, the Provider cannot guarantee that such events will not occur. Accordingly, the Provider cannot and does not warrant that the Services will be uninterrupted, error-free or entirely secure, and disclaims any and all liability resulting from or related to such events.

13.5 The Client acknowledges that the Provider does not provide any back-up software or processing facilities covering equipment, data, operating systems or application software unless any are specified in the Service Procedures, and the Client agrees that the Provider will not be responsible or liable if, for any reason concerning any of these, the Service cannot be provided.

13.6 The Provider does not make any other warranties, guarantees or representations concerning the operation or performance or the Services. The Client is entirely responsible for deciding to select the Services for its own business purposes and the Provider accepts no liability for any use to which the Client puts the Services.

13.7 The Provider does not accept any responsibility or any liability for enabling the Client to link to any site on the World Wide Web, or the contents of any other site, whether one from which the Client may have been linked to, or to which the Client may link from, other than the Provider's website.

13.8 Each party represents and warrants to the other that it has obtained, where required by law or regulatory authority, all registrations, permits, licences and approvals necessary in any relevant country for it to perform its obligations hereunder, or alternatively, that it is exempt from obtaining them. Upon request, each party will provide the other with copies of all such registrations, permits, licences and approvals. Each party further warrants and undertakes to the other that in performing its obligations under the terms of this Agreement it will comply with all applicable national and local laws and regulations.

14. Limitations on Use

14.1 The Provider reserves the right to deny any End User access to the Services and to direct the Client to terminate an End User Licence and access to the Service on reasonable grounds, including but not limited to such End User being a direct competitor of the Provider, or breach by the End User of any term of its End User Licence, or in the event of termination by the host provider, but the Provider will notify the Client of any such refusal promptly by telephone or e-mail and then confirm it in writing.

14.2 If at any time the Client's or any End User's access to, or use of, the Services is not in compliance with any applicable law or regulation, the Client will be in breach of this Agreement, and the Provider will be entitled at its sole discretion to terminate it under clause 16 and to discontinue the Services in respect of the Client and any such End User. The Client acknowledges and agrees that the Provider is entitled to report such a breach or non-compliance to any relevant regulatory body or agency, and that the Provider will not incur any liability to the Client or End User as a result of the breach, the non-compliance, or the Provider's reporting of it.

14.3 In addition to any other remedies available at law or in equity and without prejudice to its rights under this Agreement, the Provider will have the right to suspend the Services immediately if deemed reasonably necessary by the Provider in order to protect the proper interests of the Provider or of its other clients. If practicable and depending on the nature of the reason for such suspension, the Provider may, in its absolute discretion, give the Client an opportunity to remedy the situation. In such case, if the Client remedies the situation, the Provider will promptly restore the Services.

15. Limitation of liability

15.1 The Client acknowledges that it has accepted these terms and conditions in the knowledge that the Provider must limit its liability and that the Charges have been calculated accordingly.

15.2 If the Client suffers loss or damage as a result of the Provider's negligence or failure to comply with the provisions of this Agreement, any claim by the Client against the Provider arising from the Provider's negligence or failure will be limited in respect of any one incident, or series of connected incidents to, in the case of direct damage to property: £1,000,000 and, in respect of any other loss or damage arising in connection with any Service, the Charges payable by the Client for the supply to the Client of such Service in the 12-month period preceding the month in which the loss or damage occurs (to be calculated pro rata if the period is less than 12 months from the date of this Agreement).

15.3 The Provider will not be liable to the Client for any indirect, special, incidental or consequential loss or damage which may arise in respect of the Client's use of any Service or any component of it, nor for loss of profits or loss of data.

15.4 The Client undertakes that if the Provider suffers any loss, damage, fine or expense as a result of:

(a) any unauthorised access to, or use or misuse of, any Service by any employee, agent or sub-contractor of the Client;

(b) any unauthorised access to, or use or misuse, by any third party (including any End User) if that access or use or misuse was enabled or permitted by such an employee, agent or sub-contractor; or

(c) the ownership or nature or any use made of Client Information;

the Client will fully indemnify the Provider in respect of such loss, damage, fine or expense.

15.5 Nothing in this clause 15 will be construed as attempting to limit the liability of either party in respect of injury to or the death of any person caused by any wilful or negligent act or omission of either party, or its employees or agents.

15.6 The Provider will not be liable for any damages arising from negligence or otherwise unless the Client has established reasonable back up, accuracy checks and security precautions to guard against possible malfunctions, loss of data or Client Information, or unauthorised access, and has taken reasonable steps to minimise any loss.

16. Termination

16.1 This Agreement may be terminated immediately by notice in writing:

(a) by the Provider if the Client fails to pay any sums due under this Agreement by the due date notwithstanding any other provisions for late payment in this Agreement;

(b) by either party if the other party is in material or continuing breach of any of its obligations under this Agreement and fails to remedy the same (if capable of remedy) for a period of 30 days after written notice of the breach by the other party;

(c) by either party if the other party is involved in any legal proceedings concerning its solvency, or ceases trading, or commits an act of bankruptcy or is adjudicated bankrupt or enters into liquidation, whether compulsory or voluntary, other than for the purposes of an amalgamation or reconstruction, or makes an arrangement with its creditors or petitions for an administration order or has a receiver or manager appointed over all or any part of its assets or generally becomes unable to pay its debts within the meaning of Section 123 of the Insolvency Act 1986 or anything analogous to such event occurs in any applicable jurisdiction.

16.2 Any termination of this Agreement under this clause will be without prejudice to any other rights or remedies of either party under this Agreement or at law and will not affect any accrued rights or liabilities of either party at the date of termination.

16.3 On termination of this Agreement for any reason, the Client [and its End Users] must immediately cease all use of all Services and promptly certify in writing to the Provider that this has been done.

17. General Contract Provisions

17.1 Entire Agreement

This Agreement constitutes the entire agreement between the parties and supersedes any previous agreement between the parties relating to the subject matter of this Agreement. Each of the parties acknowledges that in entering into this Agreement, it does not rely on and will have no remedy in respect of any statement of fact or opinion not recorded in this Agreement (whether negligently or innocently made), except for any representation made fraudulently.

17.2 Variations

No variation of these terms and conditions will be valid unless confirmed in writing by authorised signatories of both parties on or after the date of this Agreement.

17.3 Force Majeure

Neither party will be liable to the other for any delay or non-performance of its obligations under this Agreement arising from any cause or causes beyond its reasonable control, including (without limitation) act of God, act of government or regulatory authority, war, fire, flood, explosion or civil commotion, or failure of the Internet. If such delay or non-performance arising from such cause or causes persists for more than 90 days either party may terminate this Agreement on written notice to the other without incurring any further liability under its terms.

17.4 Severability

If any of the provisions of this Agreement is judged to be illegal or unenforceable, the continuation in full force and effect of the remainder of them will not be prejudiced unless the substantive purpose of this Agreement is thereby frustrated, in which case either party may terminate this Agreement forthwith on written notice.

17.5 Waiver

No forbearance or delay by either party in enforcing its respective rights will prejudice or restrict the rights of that party, and no waiver of any such rights or of any breach of any contractual terms will be deemed to be a waiver of any other right or of any later breach.

17.6 Rights of Third Parties

A person who is not a party to this Agreement has no right to benefit under or to enforce any term of this Agreement.

17.7 Assignment

Neither party will assign, sub-contract or otherwise deal with this Agreement or any rights and obligations under this Agreement without the prior consent of the other party.

17.8 Notices

Any notice given under this Agreement by either party to the other must be in writing and may be delivered personally or by first-class post, and in the case of post will be deemed to have been given two working days after the date of posting. Notices will be delivered or sent to the addresses of the parties on the first page of this Agreement or to any other address notified in writing by either party to the other for the purpose of receiving notices after the date of this Agreement.

17.9 Governing Law and Jurisdiction

This Agreement is governed by and construed according to English law and the parties submit to the exclusive jurisdiction of the courts of England and Wales.

SCHEDULES

Charges

End User Licence

Services

Service Level Specification

Technical Environment

FOR AND ON BEHALF OF THE CLIENT

The Client agrees to accept the Services on the terms and conditions of this Agreement.

Signed ....

Name ....

Date ....

Client Authorised Representative

FOR AND ON BEHALF OF THE PROVIDER

The Provider agrees to provide the Services on the terms and conditions of this Agreement.

Signed ....

Name ....

Date ....

Director of the Provider

WEBSITE DEVELOPMENT AND SUPPORT AGREEMENT

Date of Agreement ....

BETWEEN:

(1) **THE DESIGNER** whose registered office is at
.... ('**Designer**');

AND

(2) **THE CLIENT** whose registered office is at
.... ('**Client**').

1. Scope of Agreement

1.1 The Designer has experience in website services including designing, developing, producing and maintaining [monitoring and analysing] websites.

1.2 The Client requires a website to be designed, developed, produced [and maintained] [, monitored and analysed] [for its business of ....].

1.3 The Client appoints the Designer to design, produce and implement the Website [to promote its business and] [to manage, maintain and to enhance and refine the Website and to provide new content and further development [together with the management of the Website on a web server]] [and to monitor and analyse the Website] and the Designer accepts such appointment, on the terms and conditions of this Agreement.

1.4 The Client has entered into this Agreement based on its 'Invitation to Tender' dated ...... and in reliance amongst other things on the representations made in the Designer's 'Response to Tender' dated .... including but not limited to the technical excellence, experience and track record quoted by the Designer in such response.

2. Definitions

2.1 '*Acceptance Tests*' means the tests for acceptance of the Website.

2.2 '*Charges*' means the charges payable by the Client to the Designer for the Services.

2.3 '*Client Branding*' means the words, terms and phrases [......, ..., ...].

2.4 '*Commencement Date*' means the Date of Agreement specified above.

2.5 '*Content*' means materials which may include data, information, text, media content, features, products, services, advertisements, promotions, links, pointers, technology, software and databases for publication on the Website

677

(including without limitation, literary, artistic, audio and visual content), including any publication or information created as a result of the Services.

2.6 *'Designer Know-how'* means the Designer's methodology and stylistic conventions, and its own distinctive elements in respect of graphics, design, organisation, presentation, layout, user interfaces, navigation, and the combination, co-ordination and interaction of these elements.

2.7 *'Estimated Price'* means the estimated price for the Project as specified in the Charges Schedule.

2.8 *'External Area'* means any online area in or outside the Website including but not limited to any sites on the worldwide web section of the Internet.

2.9 *'Implementation Plan'* means the implementation plan for the Project set out in the Implementation Plan Schedule as it may be varied by agreement from time to time.

2.10 *'Intellectual Property Rights'* means any and all copyright, database rights, design rights, domain name rights, patents, trade marks and all other intellectual property rights whether registered or not, and applications for such rights.

2.11 *'Launch Date'* means the date specified in the Implementation Plan, which is the date on which the Website is first available live for visitors.

2.12 *'Link'* means any hypertext link, pointer, or other linking service.

2.13 *'Project'* means [any particular project for] [the work involved in] the development and implementation of the Website, using the Services, the results of which will form part of the Content and System.

2.14 *'Proposal'* means any particular proposal put forward by the Designer, setting out the user requirements and the work involved in any Project.

2.15 *'Representative'* means the representative appointed by each party respectively, authorised to take decisions on behalf of such party.

2.16 *'Services'* means the activities undertaken by the Designer as specified in this Agreement.

2.17 *'Service Levels'* means the performance standards for the Services.

2.18 *'Service Level Agreement'* means the agreement forming a Schedule to this Agreement which sets out the details of the Services and Service Levels.

2.19 *'Schedule'* means a schedule identified in this Agreement, attached to and hereby incorporated into this Agreement.

2.20 *'Software'* means the software further identified in the Software Schedule which may be the Designer's proprietary software or Third Party Software.

2.21 *'Specification'* means the specification [of the contents/technical/user requirements] for the Website, identified in the Specification Schedule, as it may be varied in accordance with these terms and conditions.

2.22 '*Support Materials*' means materials necessary to facilitate the support and enhancement of the System and the Website, software tools required or useful to manipulate, compile and debug the System, and any keys necessary to decrypt the foregoing excluding any such materials relating to Third Party Software except to the extent that the Designer has access to them;

2.23 '*Support Services*' means the activities undertaken by the Designer to support the Website through the Internet hosting platform, including server provision and site maintenance as specified in the Support Services Agreement.

2.24 '*System*' means the Software, together with databases and infrastructure of the Website, including updates, enhancements and additions to any part of it.

2.25 '*Test Date*' means the date in the Implementation Plan marking the anticipated completion of Acceptance Tests.

2.26 '*Third Party Software*' means software proprietary to third parties comprised in the Website, the System, the Support Materials, or in any other products designed, developed or produced by the Designer under this Agreement or used to provide or operate the Website[listed as such in the Software Schedule].

2.27 '*Website*' means the network location in hypertext mark-up language format [developed in accordance with these terms and conditions] containing digital text, graphics[, sound, and video] which is the Client's proprietary site stored on a service and accessed via the Internet, being identified as '......' [domain name].

3. Duration

This Agreement commences on the Commencement Date and will continue for an initial period of 12 calendar months, after which it will remain in force unless or until terminated by either party giving at least 90 days' notice of termination to the other party to expire on the anniversary of the Commencement Date or at any time thereafter, or by the Client giving 90 days' notice within 30 days of receipt of notification of a change in prices by the Designer as permitted by this Agreement, and otherwise subject to the other termination provisions in this Agreement.

4. Website Features and Content

4.1 The parties agree that the objectives for the Website are:
   (a)   to provide a comprehensive and authoritative information resource, to offer practical information and facilitate networking;
   (b)   to create a competitive advantage for the Client.

4.2 The Designer will design the System to ensure that the Website has the following characteristics:
   (a)   be a user-friendly, interactive, original site;
   (b)   be accessible 24 hours a day without delay;

    (c)   bring together coherently material from a variety of the Client's publications, and other information relevant to visitors to the Website;

    (d)   promote best practice, offer practical information and facilitate networking for its visitors; and

    (e)   be easy to navigate, up to date and authoritative.

4.3   The Designer may not, without the written content of the Client, establish any Link to any External Area except as set out in the Service Level Agreement. Any Link created will be subject to such terms and conditions as the Client may require in the creation or maintenance of the Link, including but not limited to any requirement to pay fees for such Links or obligation to market or provide the website through such External Area. However, if required by the Client, the Designer will provide Links to other websites identified by the Client.

4.4   The parties acknowledge that the Specifications represent the minimum requirements for the System, and that they do not constitute a definitive or complete set of requirements.

4.5   Each party confirms to the other that it will not transmit, display or otherwise include in the Content:

    (a)   any material which is defamatory, offensive, abusive, indecent, obscene, pornographic, threatening or annoying, or which may incite violence, cruelty of any sort or discriminate against people in a way which may be illegal, including but not limited to racial hatred, or which is otherwise illegal;

    (b)   any material which infringes the Intellectual Property Rights of the other party or of a third party.

4.6   The Designer undertakes to design the Website so that it will efficiently comply with all applicable laws and regulations in relation to its design, accessibility and purpose, including but not limited to laws and regulations concerning disability and discrimination, data protection and electronic commerce.

5. Designer's Obligations

5.1   The Designer agrees to undertake the following services:

- registration and updating of the Website with search engines;
- design of the System to work with the operating systems architecture, configuration and access requirements;
- creative Content design;
- development, enhancements and refinements;
- content provision and updating;
- hosting services;
- management, maintenance and support;
- provision of statistics and analysis;
- such other tasks as the Client may request from time to time.

5.2   The Designer will:

(a)   provide the Services with skill and expertise to a professional standard, and in a timely and efficient manner, using suitably experienced personnel, to meet the Client's business requirements, the Specification and in accordance with the Implementation Plan;

(b)   scope and write the Specification, create, design and implement the Content, provide the System with the features and functions set out in the Specification;

(c)   customise the architecture of the System appropriately [in reliance on information provided by the Client];

(d)   manage, edit, update and maintain the Website, including but not limited to interactive communication capabilities and interactive tools;

(e)   ensure continuing integration with existing websites identified by the Client, and seamless interfaces to the Client's systems;

(f)   be responsible (for the avoidance of doubt) for the procurement of suitable computing and communication hardware, software and services necessary for production of the System and the obtaining of any requisite development licences;

(g)   provide any training necessary for the Client to operate the Website.

5.3   The Designer will make all reasonable efforts to ensure that the Project will be completed within any Estimated Price which has been agreed. If the Designer foresees a situation where the Estimated Price is likely to be exceeded, it will promptly inform the Client.

5.4   The Designer will co-operate with the Client's employees and other independent consultants whenever necessary or desirable in the performance of the Services.

5.5   The Designer will designate a Representative. The Designer may change the identity of the Representative or any of the details of the Representative with the prior written consent of the Client, such consent not to be unreasonably withheld or delayed.

5.6   [While this Agreement remains in force][For 12 months from the Launch Date], the Designer agrees that it will not undertake the development and design of any website [in England and Wales] promoting similar business activities to those of the Client in similar style to the Website.

[5.7   For the avoidance of doubt the Designer will be responsible for the procurement of suitable communication and computing hardware and services necessary for production of the System and the obtaining of any requisite development licences.]

6. Client's Obligations

6.1   The Client acknowledges that its close involvement is essential for the development of a System which successfully meets its requirements.

6.2   The Client agrees to provide guidance to the Designer on the Client's business practices which affect the Content or the System.

6.3 The Client will pay for the Services in accordance with the terms of this Agreement.

6.4 The Client will designate a Representative and inform the Designer of the identity and details of such Representative. The Client may change the identity of the Representative or any of the details of the Representative on written notice to the Designer.

6.5 The Client warrants that all intellectual property including but not limited to software, databases, graphics, diagrams, charts, sound, with which the System and Content will be used and/or which is necessary for the Designer to access and use, is either the Client's property or is legally licensed to the Client so as to permit access and use by the Designer.

7. Website Development

7.1 The Designer will carry out the Project to meet the Implementation Plan utilising such elements of the following procedural framework, in parallel or in sequence, as appropriate to the particular circumstances:

(a) discuss and agree with the Client the Content and record the requirements;

(b) scope and write the Specification;

(c) design the System in accordance with the [technical] Specification[, including but not limited to establishing appropriate architecture, supporting particular protocol, server and browser requirements, and compatibility with client and host software and networks, providing continuous navigational ability and mutually acceptable links];

(d) create, design, write and code the materials for the System, installing and testing the materials and providing them to the Client for Acceptance Tests;

(e) edit, manage, update and maintain the Website in accordance with the Specification[, including but not limited to the operating systems architecture, access requirements, interactive communication capabilities, e-commerce capabilities and interactive tools];

(f) carry out such redefinition and rewriting as may be required by the Client, and retesting the System as a result;

(g) install the System on the Client's network.

7.2 Any delay in the provision of the Services which occurs as a result of the Client's actions or omissions to act will be the Client's responsibility, and in the event of such delay the Implementation Plan will be extended accordingly to take into account of such delay.

7.3 Any delay in the provision of the Services which is due to factors beyond the responsibility of the Designer, including but not limited to access to staff, delivery or proper functioning of hardware or software, will be acknowledged by the Client, and the Implementation Plan will be extended accordingly.

8. Acceptance Testing and Launch

8.1   The Designer will carry out system tests on the System, and after all components of the System have been installed and commissioned, will carry out a full integration test on the System. When the Designer has completed such full integration test and thereby demonstrated that all elements of the installed System inter-operate correctly and effectively, the Designer will store the System so that it is available for Acceptance Tests, and will ensure that access for the purpose and duration of the Acceptance Tests is restricted through use of a password or other similar access code to persons approved by the Client.

8.2   Acceptance Tests will be [prepared by the Client][prepared by the Designer and approved by the Client] which will test that the System conforms to the Specification, together with other requirements agreed between the parties.

8.3   The Client will carry out the Acceptance Tests in respect of the System [in accordance with its standard procedures] [as set out in the Acceptance Tests Schedule] over the number of days set out in the Implementation Plan for Acceptance Testing.

8.4   If there are failures in the Acceptance Tests, the Client will inform the Designer while the Acceptance Tests are in progress, and the Designer will promptly use all reasonable endeavours to correct such failures.

8.5   The Client's Representative will, within three working days of the Test Date, notify the Designer's Representative of any material failure of the Contents or System to pass the Acceptance Tests. If the Designer's representative receives no such notification, the Acceptance Tests will be deemed to be successfully completed, and the Designer will:

(a)   install the System [and Content] to the Client in time for the Launch Date;

(b)   deliver to the Client a copy of the Support Materials on appropriate media and in an appropriate format to ensure that the Client or a third party appointed by the Client will be able to maintain, enhance, modify and change the System;

(c)   implement the System on the Launch Date.

8.6   If material failures or omissions remain at the Test Date such that the System does not conform with the Specification, the Client will have a right to terminate this Agreement.

8.7   If this Agreement is terminated under Clause 8.6 above, the Client will notify the Designer either:

(a)   to deliver promptly to the Client the Incomplete Materials, in which event the Client will pay to the Designer such reasonable amount in respect of the Incomplete Materials as may be agreed between the parties, and the Designer will be deemed to have granted to the Client a perpetual, royalty free, non-exclusive licence to use and sub-license as the Client may deem fit, any Third Party Software comprised in the Incomplete Materials; or

(b) to retain the Incomplete Materials in which event the Client will not be liable to pay to the Designer the fees or any amount whatsoever under this Agreement.

9. Variations

9.1 Either party may at any time up to seven days before the Test Date formally request in writing any variation to the System and discuss such variation with the other party.

9.2 The Designer will inform the Client in such discussion whether such variation is technically and practically feasible within the timescale and of its impact, and of any other consequent changes to the System that it reasonably judges necessary. For any change requiring additional work, the Designer will give the Client a quotation for the additional costs of carrying out the variation.

9.3 If the parties agree that the variation is to be effected, the Designer will provide a written note as a record of the variation and its impact and any additional charges, which will be signed by both parties and will implement the variation at a time it reasonably judges to be suitable before the Test Date.

9.4 If the parties do not agree that the variation is to be effected, it will not be carried out.

10. Support Services

10.1 Following the launch of the Website, the Designer will be responsible for the Support Services, which will include:
(a) marketing, launch and continuing promotion of the Website;
(b) website maintenance and technical support;
(c) system support;
(d) service recovery;
(e) help desk;
(f) content update;
(g) [hardware update and technology refresh].

10.2 The Designer will provide the Support Services so as to ensure that the Site is maintained and operated efficiently and effectively [in accordance with the Specification].

10.3 The Designer will give the Client reasonable notice of any maintenance work which will affect availability, and will plan and carry out such work so as to minimise disruption to the Website availability.

10.4 The Designer will update Content to the Website within 24 hours of receiving such updated Content from the Client, and at the request of the Client, the Designer will immediately edit or remove as appropriate any Content which is inaccurate, obscene, defamatory or which the Client requires to be removed at the Client's sole discretion.

10.5 The Designer will enter bulletin boards and online chat areas where visitors to the Website may post contributions, at least every 24 hours and more frequently if this seems necessary for the purpose of effective monitoring of contributions. Immediately on becoming aware of any contributions which the Designer reasonably believes could be obscene, defamatory or otherwise unlawful or objectionable, or which are the subject of complaints, the Designer will remove such contributions and inform the Client accordingly. The Designer will inform the Client of any measures it deems advisable to be taken to prevent or stop such contributions, and will comply with reasonable instructions from the Client as to further actions to be taken in this regard. The Designer will keep a record of such monitoring activities and provide copies of such records to the Client every month.

10.6 The Designer reserves the right to redesign or modify the organisation, structure, 'look and feel', navigation and other elements of the System, by means of the Designer Know-how, provided that the levels of functionality and service levels are maintained.

11. Service Level Compliance

11.1 The Designer will meet the Service Levels as set out in the Service Level Agreement, including but not limited to supporting particular protocol, server and browser requirements, including utilities for non-Web services such as e-mail and newsgroups, and compatibility with client and host software networks, providing continuous navigational ability, service ability, capacity and accessibility, mutual accessible links, response times, services management, housekeeping and updating.

11.2 The Designer will measure performance, maintain records and provide statistics and analysis as set out in the Service Level Agreement, for performance reporting of Service Levels, and as otherwise reasonably requested by the Client, with a recommended action plan for under-performing areas of the Website.

11.3 Without prejudice to the generality of the foregoing, the Designer will ensure that the Website is available to [authorised visitors][the public] 24 hours a day, 365 days a year, and will continuously monitor such availability. In the event that the Website becomes unavailable, the Designer will use its best endeavours to remedy the fault.

12. Charges

12.1 In consideration of the Services rendered by the Designer, the Client will pay to the Designer the Charges in the amounts and at the rates set out in the Charges Schedule.

12.2 The Charges are exclusive of expenses incurred in the performance of this Agreement by the Designer. Expenses must be agreed in advance with the Client and must be supported by receipts or other documentary evidence as appropriate.

12.3 The Charges and expenses are exclusive of Value Added Tax and any similar taxes. All such taxes are payable by the Customer and will be applied in accordance with UK legislation in force at the tax point date.

12.4 The Supplier will be entitled to increase its charges on the anniversary of the Commencement Date and thereafter not more than once in any successive period of 12 months while this Agreement is in force by giving not less than 60 days' notice to the Customer provided that any such increase expressed as a percentage does not exceed any percentage increase in the Employment Index published by Computer Economics for the 12 months immediately preceding the date of the notice.

13. Payment Terms

13.1 The Client will be invoiced [monthly in advance][at the times stated in the Schedule] for the Charges. Expenses and other charges will be invoiced monthly in arrears.

13.2 All Charges and other expenses properly due shall be payable by the Client within ten days of the date of the Designer's invoice.

13.3 Payments which are not received when payable will be considered overdue and remain payable by the Client together with interest for late payment from the date payable at the statutory rate applicable as well after as before any judgment, and independent of such judgment. This interest will accrue on a daily basis and be payable on demand.

13.4 Notwithstanding the above provision for late payment, in this event the Designer may at its option, and without prejudice to any other remedy at any time after payment has become due, terminate or temporarily suspend performance of this Agreement.

13.5 Payments which are not received when payable will be considered overdue and remain payable by the Client together with interest for late payment from the date payable at the statutory rate applicable as well after as before any judgment, and independent of such judgment. This interest will accrue on a daily basis and be payable on demand.

13.6 Notwithstanding the above provision for late payment, in this event the Designer may at its option, and without prejudice to any other remedy at any time after payment has become due, terminate or temporarily suspend performance of this Agreement.

14. Confidentiality

The Designer acknowledges that under this Agreement it may receive trade secrets and confidential or proprietary information of the Client identified as 'confidential', including but not limited to information concerning products, customers, security arrangements, and development plans. All such information constitutes 'Confidential Information'. The Designer agrees not to divulge Confidential Information received from the Client to any of its employees who do not need to know it, and to prevent its disclosure to or access by any third party without the prior written consent of the disclosing party.

15. Security

15.1 The Designer will:

(a) use its best endeavours to keep confidential the passwords or other security information relating to the Software, the Website or any equipment of the Client;

(b) ensure compliance with the Client's strategic and security requirements to protect the authenticity and integrity of the Website, and pro-actively provide security for the Website, ensuring that adequate security protections are in place;

(c) regularly review its security policies and the actual security of the Website, and inform the Client of any additional measures necessary to maximise security of the Website and the integrity of the Content;

(d) make a backup copy of the Content [daily][weekly] in an agreed format, and deposit such copy with the Client;

(e) provide and implement when necessary a disaster recovery programme and service for the Client.

15.2 The Designer will comply with data protection legislation in respect of any personal data to which it has access or which it may use in providing the Support Services. The Designer will maintain secure records for reporting to the Client of all personal data submitted to the Website in conformity with the principles of data protection legislation, including, if relevant, details of those visitors who choose to opt in to receive promotional material or other information. Once such records have been reported, the Designer will not retain a copy of any such personal data.

15.3 The Designer will safely destroy and not keep any copy of data provided by the Client for the Website following its use for the purpose for which it was provided without the prior written consent of the Client.

16. Intellectual Property Rights

Software and System

16.1 The Designer assigns to the Client with full title guarantee, in respect of copyright by way of present assignment of future copyright, all Intellectual Property Rights in the Software, the System and any other materials designed or developed or produced by the Designer for the Website excluding Designer Know-how, Support Materials and any Third Party Software [unconditionally and immediately on the creation of the System] [on successful completion of the Acceptance Tests] [with effect from the Test/Launch Date] [on receipt by the Designer of full payment of the Charges in accordance with the Charges Schedule], and undertakes to execute such deeds and documents and do such things as the Client may require to vest such Intellectual Property Rights in the Client.

16.2 The Client grants to the Designer a non-transferable licence to use the System in both source and object code form solely for the purposes of fulfilling the Designer's obligations under this Agreement while this Agreement remains in force.

Content

16.3 All Intellectual Property Rights in the Content will at all times vest exclusively in the Client, except for Content owned by third parties, in respect of which the Client will be responsible for ensuring that all necessary consents have been obtained such that it has a licence to use and display, and to authorise the Designer's access and use.

16.4 The Client grants to the Designer a non-transferable royalty-free licence to use the Content solely for the purposes of designing, developing, producing and maintaining the Website in accordance with this Agreement, and while this Agreement remains in force.

16.5 If either party learns of any claim of infringement of the Client's Intellectual Property Rights in the Content, it will promptly notify the other party. The Designer will do all such things as the Client may reasonably require at the Client's expense to assist the Client in taking proceedings or any other actions the Client may reasonably take to terminate or prevent any such claim.

Client Branding and Domain Name

16.6 The Client grants the Designer a non-exclusive non-transferable licence to use and copy the Client Branding, only so far as is necessary for providing the Services under the terms of this Agreement and while this Agreement remains in force.

16.7 For the avoidance of doubt, the Client's domain name remains the property of the Client and the Designer may use such name only in the performance of this Agreement.

Designer Know-how and Support Materials

16.8 The Designer grants to the Client a perpetual worldwide licence to use the Designer Know-how and Support Materials while this Agreement is in force and subsequently, permitting the ongoing use of the Designer Know-how for the purposes of supporting the Website, [and for using, marketing, licensing, storing, distributing, displaying, communicating, performing, transmitting and promoting the Website] including but not limited to use for such purposes by consultants, systems designers, outsourcing providers or disaster recovery suppliers.

16.9 The Client will not use the Support Materials unless this Agreement is terminated, and until then will take all reasonable measures to ensure that the Support Materials are securely stored.

16.10 For the avoidance of doubt the Designer will be entitled to use the Designer Know-how in the provision of services similar to these Services to other customers of its business.

Third Party Software

16.11 The Designer will not include any Third Party Software in the Website, the Support Materials or the System unless the Designer has informed the Client and the Client has given its written consent, and provided that the Designer has procured the right from the relevant third party owner or licensor of the Third Party Software to permit such use.

16.12 The Client has sole responsibility for obtaining the appropriate licences or rights required for access and use of any Third Party Software other than as set out in the Third Party Software Schedule and for any Content and is liable for any claim that such use of such Third Party Software infringes the Intellectual Property Rights of any other third party.

17. Designer's Warranties

The Designer warrants and undertakes to the Client that:

17.1 it will provide the Services with reasonable skill and care, using suitably skilled personnel;

17.2 it has sufficient experience of designing, developing and producing websites to be able to undertake its obligations under this Agreement;

17.3 any employee, agent or contractor of the Designer will be suitably experienced to perform his or her contribution and conform to the standards, skill and ability to be reasonably expected of such performance;

17.4 neither the execution nor the performance of this Agreement will conflict with any agreement or arrangement to which the Designer is party or any legal or administrative arrangement by which the Designer is bound;

17.5 it is authorised to use the Third Party Software concerned in connection with its obligations under this Agreement and will remain so authorised for the duration of this Agreement and will remain authorised by the relevant licensors and owners to grant the rights for the Client to use such software;

17.6 upon termination of this Agreement, the System and the Support Materials will be the only materials required by a person with reasonable knowledge of the design, development and production of websites to be able to maintain enhance and modify the Website;

17.7 none of the System, the Support Materials or Content provided by the Designer will include:

(a) any executable code which has not been authorised by the Client; or

(b) computer viruses, routines, worms, time bombs, or any other such devices or mechanisms of misuse;

17.8 the System will conform in all respects with the Specification;

17.9 the Services will comply with the Service Levels in the Service Level Agreement;

17.10 the System is capable of meeting the transaction volumes set out in the Service Level Agreement and their expansion by at least one third without upgrade, and response times of less than [three] seconds from keystroke irrespective of location;

17.11 it has and will maintain in effect all necessary licences and any other authorisations and rights required in providing the Services, including those to the enhancements, modifications and upgrades to Third Party Software or data;

17.12 the Software and the System and any other materials designed or developed or produced by the Designer for the Website will not infringe any third party's Intellectual Property Rights, will not be obscene or defamatory, and [to the best of the Designer's knowledge, information and belief] will comply with all applicable laws, regulations and codes of conduct;

17.13 for any software or data not being part of the Software used by the Designer or provided by the Designer to the Client for use by the Client pursuant to this Agreement, the Designer warrants that it owns or possesses all necessary licences or rights required to perform its obligations under this Agreement, including those to all enhancements or upgrades to such Third Party Software or data.

18. Indemnities

18.1 The Designer will indemnify the Client against all losses, costs and expenses including reasonable legal expenses and third party claims suffered by the Client arising out of any breach by the Designer of the warranties given in this Agreement or any other default of the Designer in connection with this Agreement.

18.2 The Designer will not be liable in respect of any loss or damage suffered by the Client resulting from any third party claim that a posting on a bulletin board, online chat area or similar area in which visitors to the Website may legitimately post contributions is obscene or defamatory, provided that the Designer has complied with its obligations in this Agreement in respect of postings.

18.3 The Client will indemnify the Designer against all losses, costs and expenses including reasonable legal expenses arising from any third party claim that the Content infringes the Intellectual Property Rights, or is obscene or defamatory, or that any posting on a bulletin board, online chat area or

similar area in which visitor to the Website may legitimately post contributions is obscene or defamatory, provided that the Designer:

(a) has complied with its obligations in this Agreement in respect of
postings;

(b) promptly notifies the Client of any claim in respect of which the
indemnity is sought;

(c) gives the Client full conduct and control of any such claim.

19. Limits of liability

19.1 The Client agrees that it has accepted these terms and conditions in the
knowledge that the Designer's liability is limited and that the Charges payable
have been calculated accordingly.

19.2 The Designer will indemnify the Client for direct physical injury or death
caused by the negligence of its employees acting within the course of their
employment and the scope of their authority.

19.3 The Designer will indemnify the Client for direct damage to property caused
by the negligence of its employees acting within the course of their
employment and the scope of their authority. The total liability of the
Designer under this sub-clause will be limited to £500,000 for any one event
or series of connected events.

19.4 Except as expressly stated in this clause and elsewhere in this Agreement, any
liability of the Designer for breach of this Agreement will not exceed in the
aggregate of damages, costs, fees and expenses capable of being awarded to
the Client the total price paid or due to be paid by the Client under this
Agreement.

19.5 Except as expressly stated in this Agreement, the Designer disclaims all
liability in contract or in tort (including negligence or breach of statutory
duty) to the Client in connection with the Designer's performance of this
Agreement or the Client's use of the System including but not limited to
liability for loss of profits whether in the course of the Client's business or
otherwise, or arising from loss of data, and in no event will the Designer be
liable to the Client for special, indirect or consequential damages.

19.6 The Designer makes no representations and gives no warranties, guarantees
or undertakings concerning its performance of the Services except as
expressly set out in this Agreement. All other warranties, express or implied,
by statute or otherwise, are excluded from this Agreement.

20. Acknowledgment

20.1 With the prior written consent of the Client, not to be unreasonably
withheld or delayed, the Designer may include a statement in the Website,
the format, content and position to be approved by the Client at its
discretion, to the effect that the Designer has designed, developed and
produced the Website. Such statement may not be changed or removed

while this Agreement is in force without the written agreement of both parties, not to be unreasonably withheld or delayed.

20.2 The Designer agrees not to use the Client's name or issue any announcement about these Services without first obtaining the Client's written consent [not to be unreasonably withheld or delayed].

21. Termination

21.1 This Agreement may be terminated immediately by notice in writing:

    (a) by the Designer if the Client fails to pay any sums due under this Agreement for a period of 30 days after written notice by the Designer without prejudice to any other provisions relating to late payment in this Agreement;

    (b) by either party if the other party is in material or continuing breach of any of its obligations under this Agreement and fails to remedy the breach (if capable of remedy) for a period of 30 days after written notice;

    (c) by either party if the other party is involved in any legal proceedings concerning its solvency, or ceases trading, or commits an act of bankruptcy or is adjudicated bankrupt or enters into liquidation, whether compulsory or voluntary, other than for the purposes of an amalgamation or reconstruction, or makes an arrangement with its creditors or petitions for an administration order or if a receiver or manager is appointed over all or any part of its assets or if it generally becomes unable to pay its debts within the meaning of Section 123 or Section 268 of the Insolvency Act 1986.

21.2 Any termination of this Agreement under this clause will be without prejudice to any other rights or remedies of either party under this Agreement or at law and will not affect any accrued rights or liabilities of either party at the date of termination.

22. Obligations on Termination

On termination of this Agreement for any reason the Designer will co-operate with the Client in that it will immediately:

22.1 return all Content to the Client and not retain any part of it in any form whatsoever;

22.2 destroy or delete the Client's Confidential Information under its control or in its possession;

22.3 be deemed to have granted to the Client a perpetual loyalty free non-exclusive licence to the Client to use, change, adapt, enhance and sub-license as the Client may deem fit, the Support Materials and all Third Party Software contained in the Support Materials;

22.4 if so requested by the Client, provide assistance in transferring the Website to another server at [its standard charges][reasonable charges to be agreed with the Client].

23. General Contract Provisions

23.1 Entire Agreement

This Agreement constitutes the entire agreement and understanding between the parties and supersedes any previous agreement between the parties relating to the subject matter of this Agreement. Each of the parties acknowledges and agrees that in entering into this Agreement, and the documents referred to in it, it does not rely on, and shall have no remedy in respect of any statement of fact or opinion not recorded in this Agreement (whether negligently or innocently made).

23.2 Variations

No variation of these terms and conditions will be valid unless confirmed in writing by authorised signatories of both parties on or after the date of this Agreement.

23.3 Severability

If any of the provisions of this Agreement is judged to be illegal or unenforceable, the continuation in full force and effect of the remainder of them will not be prejudiced.

23.4 Waiver

No forbearance or delay by either party in enforcing its respective rights will prejudice or restrict the rights of that party, and no waiver of any such rights or of any breach of any contractual terms will be deemed to be a waiver of any other right or of any later breach.

23.5 Rights of Third Parties

A person who is not a party to this Agreement has no right to benefit under or to enforce any term of this Agreement.

23.6 Assignment

Neither party will assign, sub-contract or otherwise deal with this Agreement or any rights and obligations under this Agreement.

23.7 Notices

Any notice given under this Agreement by either party to the other must be in writing and may be delivered personally or by first-class post, and in the case of post will be deemed to have been given two working days after the date of posting. Notices will be delivered or sent to the addresses of the parties on the first page of this Agreement or to any other address notified in writing by either party to the other for the purpose of receiving notices after the date of this Agreement.

23.8 Force Majeure

Neither party will be liable to the other party for any delay in or failure to perform its obligations (other than a payment of money) as a result of any

693

cause beyond its reasonable control, including but not limited to any industrial dispute. If such delay or failure continues for at least 90 days, either party will be entitled to terminate the Agreement by notice in writing without further liability of either party arising directly as a result of such delay or failure.

23.9 Governing Law and Jurisdiction
This Agreement is governed by and construed according to English law and the parties submit to the exclusive jurisdiction of the courts of England and Wales.

SCHEDULES

Acceptance Tests

Charges

Implementation Plan

Specification

Documentation

APPENDICES

Service Level Agreement

Support Services Agreement

The Designer agrees to provide the Services on the terms and conditions of this Agreement	The Client agrees to accept the Services on the terms and conditions of this Agreement

FOR AND ON BEHALF OF   **FOR AND ON BEHALF OF**

Name ....   Name ....
Date ....   Date ....
Director of the Designer Limited   **Director of the Client Limited**

E-COMMERCE DISTRIBUTOR/AUTHOR AGREEMENT

Date of Agreement ....

BETWEEN:

(1) **THE DISTRIBUTOR** whose registered office is at
.... ('**Distributor**');

AND

(2) **THE AUTHOR** whose registered office is at
.... ('**Author**').

1. Introduction

1.1 The Distributor is seeking to develop markets and software licence sales on behalf of its Authors, by maintaining a website which allows customers to view and purchase software products.

1.2 The Author wishes to supply materials for inclusion on such website for licence sales using the Distributor.

1.3 The Distributor will include the materials supplied by the Author on such website subject to a satisfactory content and quality assurance review and to the terms and conditions of this Agreement.

1.4 This Agreement is valid only when signed by both parties.

2. Term

This Agreement will come into effect as of its date and will continue in force until one party gives at least 90 days' notice of termination to the other and otherwise subject to the other termination provisions of this Agreement.

3. Definitions

3.1 '*Author's Charges*' means a monthly fee of £...... payable by the Author for marketing its Products on the Website.

3.2 '*Author Representative*' means the principal Author representative authorised to make and communicate decisions on behalf of the Distributor identified in the Schedule or subsequently notified to the Distributor.

3.3 '*Customer*' means a customer of the Distributor purchasing licensed Products for its own use or for resale.

3.4 '*Intellectual Property Rights*' means all copyrights, patents, registered and unregistered design rights, trademarks and service marks and applications for

695

any of these, together with all database rights, trade secrets, know-how and other intellectual property rights in all parts of the world, whether registered or conferred by law.

3.5 'Materials' means Product evaluations, demonstrations, documentation, help files, technical information, marketing information and the encrypted full retail current release versions of Products.

3.6 'Media' means a compact disc or other media containing Products and Materials.

3.7 'Product' means any software product listed in the Schedule, or any new software product, or new software product version subsequently released by the Author and sold under licence from the Website or Media.

3.8 'Programme' means the 'Distributor Worldwide Marketing Programme'.

3.9 'Source Code Escrow Service' means the optional escrow service detailed in the Supplementary Terms and Conditions appended to this Agreement.

3.10 'Supplement' means any current Supplementary Agreement, identified by its Agreement Number by linking to this Agreement.

3.11 'Website' means a commercial website owned by the Distributor, URL .... containing Materials for viewing and purchase by Customers.

4. Services

4.1 The Distributor is seeking to develop markets and sales of software licences for its Authors through the Programme by owning and maintaining the Website, and by distributing e-mails, a hard copy directory, and/or Media containing marketing information on selected Products linked to the Website.

4.2 Materials which are supplied by the Author will be included on the Website, subject to a satisfactory content and quality assurance review by the Distributor, and subject to these terms and conditions.

4.3 The Distributor is responsible for updating the Website regularly, producing e-mails at regular intervals as described in the published schedule, and distributing e-mails to a qualified database of software developers. The Distributor will use its reasonable commercial endeavours to improve its Programme and database on a regular basis.

4.4 A Customer wishing to purchase a Product licence, or to subscribe to use a Product on a time-limited or usage basis from the Website, will be required to agree to the terms of the Distributor End User Software Licence Agreement. The Distributor will require the Customer to provide valid payment details, and in return will charge the Customer for the usage made of the Product.

4.5 Transactions resulting from orders placed on the Website by Customers take place electronically in a securely encrypted form. The Distributor will use encryption/decryption software which is proprietary and proven, and will use all reasonable efforts to keep the encryption technique secret.

4.6 Decryption keys are issued to a Customer in return for the provision of its valid payment details. There is a single opportunity to use the decryption keys provided, and if a Customer attempts to use any key again, the decryption process will fail.

4.7 After decryption, in order to install the Product, a copy of the full retail version of the Product, as supplied by the Author, is created on the Customer's hard drive as simulated Media.

4.8 To enable the marketing of any Product upgrade, the purchase of Product upgrades to qualifying Customers may be restricted on the Website, such that a Customer may enter the order, but must contact the Distributor for verification prior to download.

5. Author Responsibilities

The Author agrees in respect of each Product, which it submits for inclusion on the Website or Media, to:

5.1 put only the Author name and/or the Distributor name, web address, e-mail, fax and telephone numbers as the contact information, on the Materials to be included. The Author agrees not to list other dealers, value added resellers or distributors on the Materials for the Website;

5.2 provide a short description of the Product of up to 75 words for the Website, to explain why the Product was developed and its use for a developer;

5.3 provide a description of the technical details of up to 1,000 words for the Website for each purchase option or edition of the Product, listing the differences from the previous option or edition;

5.4 complete the 'Product Submission Form' on the Website, each time a new Product or version is submitted to the Distributor, to provide details of the Product such as: architecture, compatibility, system requirements, licensing requirements. Where indicated on the form, these details will appear on the Website;

5.5 provide as part of the demonstration environment, and for the Website, Executable, Trial Version, Demonstration, Help (normally from the full retail version), Word, Excel, PowerPoint or PDF files and other such technical information, so that a Customer may download and evaluate the Product and make an informed purchase;

5.6 provide the latest full retail version on release for the Website, which will install from a hard disk without error;

5.7 provide Materials by e-mail or by download from an 'FTP Site'.

And the Author agrees further for each Product to:

5.8 submit Materials when each new Product version is released, in a timely and efficient manner, at least five days prior to any release date for publication on the Website;

5.9 allow the Distributor to provide the latest version of the Product free-of-charge to any Customer who has purchased the previous Product version from the Distributor within the last 30 days;

5.10 ensure that the Materials accurately reflect the functionality of the full retail version to be encrypted;

5.11 make all reasonable efforts to supply the Materials and any subsequent updates virus-free;

5.12 mark the Materials being submitted, 'For FREE Download' or 'Full Retail Product' respectively;

5.13 provide stock(s) of manuals, Media or boxed Products, if these should be required;

5.14 provide a range of serial numbers for any Product which needs further unlocking or authorisation, upon request in a timely and efficient manner;

5.15 allow the Distributor to host the Products, where appropriate, on the Website and rent access on a time-limited or usage basis;

5.16 put the Distributor name, web address, e-mail, fax, telephone numbers as contact information on the Author's website and in any listing for authorised licensors, dealers, value added resellers or distributors of the Author's Product;

5.17 provide a link to the Website from the Author's website, using a customised link for the Author provided by the Distributor;

5.18 assist in providing up-to-date press releases, customer referral letters and case studies about the Product;

5.19 allow the Distributor to unlock the Product to official journalists for evaluation, without charge;

5.20 provide technical support for the Product to the Distributor via e-mail, fax and telephone, in a timely and efficient manner;

5.21 promptly advise the Distributor where a Product version has been withdrawn for technical reasons.

6. Product Submission

6.1 The Author agrees that by submitting its Products for inclusion on the Website, the Distributor may at its option and cost, also include or license the usage of the Materials on other websites or Media that it or other parties may produce.

6.2　The Materials will bear the copyright notice, if any, provided by the Author, but so long as they bear such copyright notice, may be distributed by the Distributor without limitation.

6.3　The Distributor reserves the right not to include any Product for any reason in its sole discretion, in which event a proportion of the Author's Charges paid by the Author for that period of time will be refunded, except where the Product submitted for inclusion fails to meet the minimum requirements defined above.

6.4　The Distributor may make copies of Products and Materials as reasonably necessary for the purpose of providing Customers with machine-readable copies and for back-up purposes and for the efficient and secure operation of its business.

6.5　The Distributor will take reasonable care to prevent the unauthorised use of the Materials.

6.6　For each Product which is designated as a 'Source Code Escrow Service Product' on the front page of this Agreement, the Author will:
(a)　promptly enter into the Source Code Escrow Service Agreement with the Distributor as custodian;
(b)　promptly deposit a source copy of the Product with the Distributor;
(c)　subject to compliance by the Distributor and relevant Customers with the terms of the Source Code Escrow Service Agreement, authorise the Distributor to release a copy of the source Product to such current Customers for the Product under the terms of such Source Code Escrow Service Agreement.

7. Fees and Author's Charges

7.1　For each licence of the Product or licensed usage of a hosted Product, the Distributor will remit to the Author …% of the licence fee paid by the Customer excluding any sales, use or value added taxes that the Distributor collects.

7.2　The Distributor will pay the Author at the end of the month following the month of sale for all licence fees for Products supplied during that month, less any refunds for returns given as a result of Customer claims.

7.3　For the avoidance of doubt, payment will be due to the Author only for copies made for a Customer purchasing the Product.

7.4　The Author will pay the Author's Charges in respect of the marketing of each Product via the Website. The Distributor will not make any extra charge for including the encrypted full retail version on the Website but the Author accepts that such inclusion is at the discretion of the Distributor.

7.5　Where the total amount payable to the Author for Product licence fees made by the Distributor is equal to or exceeds [£…] in any calendar month, the Author's Charges will be deducted from any payments due by the Distributor to the Author for that month.

7.6 For the avoidance of doubt, where the total amount payable to the Author for Product licence sales is less than [£...] in any calendar month, the Author's Charges will not be payable to the Distributor.

7.7 The Author's Charges are exclusive of any sales, use or value added taxes.

7.8 The Distributor will be entitled to increase the Author's Charges not more than once annually by three months' notice to the Author.

7.9 It is agreed that in offering Products for resale, the Distributor is acting as an authorised independent value added reseller for the Author and not as its agent. Neither party has authority to bind or speak for the other party except as permitted by this Agreement or as may be authorised in writing from time to time.

8. Additional Activities

8.1 From time to time the Author may be offered additional marketing opportunities for its Products, such as: component pavilions at exhibitions, co-operative advertising in magazines, e-mail sponsorship, direct mail or third party Media distributions. Additional fees and or terms and conditions will apply in such cases. The Author will sign a Supplement if it agrees to participate in such marketing opportunities.

8.2 All Supplements will be incorporated into and form part of this Agreement when executed, and the other terms and conditions of this Agreement will continue to apply. In the event of any conflict between a Supplement and any other terms of this Agreement the Supplement will prevail. Discontinuance of a Supplement does not otherwise affect the continuity of this Agreement.

8.3 The Distributor is striving to increase the corporate adoption of the quality software components and Products that it markets. This involves increasing the services that are available to Customers such as: software upgrade, maintenance, enhanced technical support and source code escrow services. By signing this Agreement, the Author also agrees not to withhold unreasonably its support for these other activities.

9. Reporting

9.1 The Distributor will provide to the Author Representatives by email and via secure logon to the Website a sales report giving details of the Customers who have purchased licences. The details will include: Customer name, organisation, country, Product and quantity licensed, with serial numbers allocated, if applicable.

9.2 The Author will use these details to register the Customer on its databases, to facilitate efficient handling of Customer technical support requests, but will not make any other use of this data without first obtaining the consent of the Customer via the Distributor. The Author undertakes that no Customer details will be passed on to third parties or used for any purpose other than to give the Customer full access to technical support.

9.3 The Distributor will also provide to the Author Representative via secure logon to the Website, a monthly financial report at the end of each month summarising the amounts due to the Author.

10. Customer Support

The Distributor will provide a support service to Customers for a period of 30 days from the date of Product purchase. Any Customer issues which the Distributor is unable to resolve will be passed to the Author Representative who will co-ordinate an attempted resolution in a timely and efficient manner, keeping the Distributor fully informed of progress and of any issues with the Product.

11. Author's Warranties and Indemnity

11.1 The Author warrants that it is the sole and exclusive owner of all Intellectual Property Rights in the Products (including any databases, images, 'applets', graphics, animations, video, audio and text incorporated into them) and of Materials which it supplies, and that they do not violate any intellectual property rights of any third party. The Author indemnifies the Distributor and holds the Distributor harmless against all damages, costs and expenses arising from any claim relating to the Intellectual Property Rights in the Products and Materials which it supplies.

11.2 The Author warrants that the Products will function properly and in accordance with any marketing and technical information provided by the Author.

12. Limits of Liability

12.1 Subject to clause 11 above, if either party suffers loss or damage as a result of the other party's negligence or failure to comply with the provisions of this Agreement, any claim arising from such negligence or failure will be limited to a maximum of £200,000 in respect of any one incident, or series of connected incidents.

12.2 Subject to clauses 11 and 12.1 above, direct contractual liabilities of each party to the other will be limited cumulatively to the sum of the licence fee for the Product concerned multiplied by the number of copies sold during the 12 months prior to the date of claim (to be calculated pro rata if the period is less than 12 months from the date of this Agreement).

12.3 Nothing in this clause 12 will be construed as attempting to limit the liability of either party in respect of injury to or the death of any person caused by any wilful or negligent act or omission of either party, or its employees or agents.

12.4 Except as expressly stated in this Agreement, each party disclaims all liability in contract or in tort (including negligence or breach of statutory duty) to the other including but not limited to liability for loss of profits whether in the course of the other party's business or otherwise, or arising from loss of data, and in no event will either party be liable to the other for special, indirect or consequential damages.

12.5 Neither party will be liable for any damages arising from negligence or otherwise unless such party has established reasonable back up, accuracy checks and security precautions to guard against possible malfunctions, loss of data or Information, or unauthorised access, and has taken reasonable steps to minimise any loss.

13. Termination

13.1 This Agreement may be terminated immediately by notice in writing:
  (a) by either party if the other party is in material or continuing breach of any of its obligations under this Agreement;
  (b) by either party if the other party is involved in any legal proceedings concerning its solvency, or ceases trading, or commits an act of bankruptcy or is adjudicated bankrupt or enters into liquidation, whether compulsory or voluntary, other than for the purposes of an amalgamation or reconstruction, or makes an arrangement with its creditors or petitions for an administration order or has a Receiver or Manager appointed over all or any part of its assets or generally becomes unable to pay its debts within the meaning of Section 123 of the Insolvency Act 1986 or anything analogous to such event occurs in any applicable jurisdiction.

13.2 Any termination of this Agreement under this clause will be without prejudice to any other rights or remedies of either party under this Agreement or at law and will not affect any accrued rights or liabilities of either party at the date of termination.

14. General Contract Provisions

14.1 Entire Agreement
This Agreement constitutes the entire agreement between the parties and supersedes any previous agreement between the parties relating to the subject matter of this Agreement. Each of the parties acknowledges that in entering into this Agreement, it does not rely on and will have no remedy in respect of any statement of fact or opinion not recorded in this Agreement (whether negligently or innocently made), except for any representation made fraudulently.

14.2 Variations
No variation of this Agreement will be valid unless confirmed in writing by authorised signatories of both parties on or after the date of this Agreement.

14.3 **Force Majeure**

Neither party will be liable to the other for any delay or non-performance of its obligations under this Agreement arising from any cause or causes beyond its reasonable control, including (without limitation) act of God, act of government or regulatory authority, war, fire, flood, explosion or civil commotion, or failure of the Internet. If such delay or non-performance arising from such cause or causes persists for more than 30 days, either party may terminate this Agreement on written notice to the other without incurring any further liability under its terms.

14.4 **Severability**

If any of the provisions of this Agreement is judged to be illegal or unenforceable, the continuation in full force and effect of the remainder of them will not be prejudiced unless the substantive purpose of this Agreement is thereby frustrated, in which case either party may terminate this Agreement forthwith on written notice.

14.5 **Waiver**

No forbearance or delay by either party in enforcing its respective rights will prejudice or restrict the rights of that party, and no waiver of any such rights or of any breach of any contractual terms will be deemed to be a waiver of any other right or of any later breach.

14.6 **Rights of Third Parties**

A person who is not a party to this Agreement has no right to benefit under or to enforce any term of this Agreement.

14.7 **Assignment**

Neither party will assign, sub-contract or otherwise deal with this Agreement or any rights and obligations under this Agreement without the prior consent of the other party.

14.8 **Notices**

Any notice given under this Agreement by either party to the other must be in writing and may be delivered personally or by first class post, and in the case of post will be deemed to have been given two working days after the date of posting. Notices will be delivered or sent to the addresses of the parties on the first page of this Agreement or to any other address notified in writing by either party to the other for the purpose of receiving notices after the date of this Agreement.

14.9 **Governing Law and Jurisdiction**

This Agreement is governed by and construed according to English law and the parties submit to the non-exclusive jurisdiction of the courts of England and Wales.

SCHEDULE

Supplementary Terms and Conditions

Supplement

Source Code Escrow Service

FOR AND ON BEHALF OF THE AUTHOR

The Author agrees to the terms and conditions of this Agreement.

Signed ....

Name ....

Date ....

Author Authorised Representative

FOR AND ON BEHALF OF THE DISTRIBUTOR

The Distributor agrees to the terms and conditions of this Agreement.

Signed ....

Name ....

Date ....

Director of the Distributor

DISASTER RECOVERY SERVICES AGREEMENT

Date of Agreement ....

BETWEEN:

(1) **THE SUPPLIER** whose registered office is at
.... ('**Supplier**');

AND

(2) **THE CUSTOMER** whose registered office is at
.... ('**Customer**').

1. Introduction

The Supplier has experience and expertise in providing disaster recovery services and the Customer wishes to receive such disaster recovery services.

2. Definitions

2.1 '*Charges*' means the charges payable for the Services.

2.2 '*Commencement Date*' means the Date of Agreement specified above.

2.3 '*Configuration*' means the Supplier's computer system defined in the Schedule, located at the Site, on which the Services are to be provided.

2.4 '*Data*' means the Customer's data [defined in the Schedule] which are processed by the Systems.

2.5 '*Data Controller*' means any person so nominated by the Customer.

2.6 '*Disaster*' means any event or circumstance which causes the complete or partial loss or non-availability of the Customer's System, or which prevents the normal operation of the Customer's System or the performance of any task or function of the System [in either case which is or may reasonably be expected to be inoperable or inaccessible for at least [24] hours], or any event or circumstance similarly affecting a Subscriber.

2.7 '*Media*' means computer input materials and data including but not limited to magnetic tapes and disks.

2.8 '*Services*' means those services undertaken by the Supplier for the Customer detailed in this Agreement.

2.9 '*Site*' means the site where the Configuration is situated.

2.10 '*Subscriber*' means customers of the Supplier for the Services other than the Customer.

2.11 'System' means the Customer's computer systems defined in the Schedule, to which the Services apply.

3. Term

This Agreement commences on the Commencement Date, and will continue for an initial period of 12 calendar months, after which it will remain in force unless or until terminated by either party giving at least 90 days' notice of termination to the other party to expire on the anniversary of the Commencement Date or on any subsequent anniversary of the Commencement Date, or by the Customer giving 90 days' notice within 30 days of receipt of notification of a change in prices by the Supplier as permitted by this Agreement, and otherwise subject to the other termination provisions in this Agreement.

4. Services

4.1 The Services consist of making available and maintaining the Configuration at the Site [during normal office hours of 9.00 am to 5.00 pm on normal working days excluding public and other statutory holidays] [for the number of days during any 12-month period as specified in the Schedule] [for 24 hours per day seven days per week throughout the year] [for three days in any 12-month period] [excluding 25 December and 26 December] with telephone facilities, and with normal office space and staffing which the Supplier determines to be reasonably necessary for the sole use of the Customer and Subscribers in Disasters or for Disaster testing purposes.

4.2 The Customer's access to the Configuration will at all times be subject to availability, but a Customer's Disaster will always be given priority over testing or other equivalent usage requirements of either the Supplier or Subscribers. If the Services are requested by the Customer when a Subscriber is already using the Services for a similar purpose, that Subscriber will have a higher priority of access to the configuration than the Customer.

4.3 The Customer will be entitled to have such members of its own authorised staff attending at the Site as is reasonably necessary during a Disaster or for testing purposes.

4.4 Facilities for storage of Media can be made available at the Site for the exclusive use of the Customer at the Supplier's then current charges.

4.5 If the Customer so requests, the Supplier will provide peripheral equipment additional to that included in the Configuration, at its then current charges, subject to availability and subject to at least 24 hours' notice from the Customer.

4.6 Application by the Customer for access to the Configuration in the event of a Disaster should be made by telephone to any one of the persons listed as contacts in the Schedule or as otherwise advised to the Customer, stating the grounds upon which the application to use the Configuration is based.

4.7 The Customer is entitled to inspect the Site at any time on reasonable notice.

4.8 The Customer is entitled to three days' use of the Configuration at the Site each year during the term of this Agreement for the purposes of carrying out any tests and trials in relation to the System as the Customer may consider necessary. These days will be arranged by mutual agreement between the Supplier and the Customer.

4.9 Where the Customer invokes the Services because of a Disaster, a minimum charge equivalent to one day's use of the Configuration at the daily rate specified in the Schedule will apply.

5. Testing

5.1 The Services will be made available to the Customer only after completion of tests which establish the compatibility of the Customer's System for running on the Configuration to the Supplier's reasonable satisfaction. These tests will be conducted within 30 days of the date of this Agreement. If these test results are not satisfactory to the Supplier, this Agreement will be terminated immediately and all sums paid by the Customer under the Agreement refunded.

5.2 The Customer will institute procedures for testing its System quarterly to ensure maintenance of compatibility of the System with the Configuration. The Customer agrees to book tests at the Site at least 14 days in advance, and understands that such tests may nevertheless be postponed with or without notice if the Configuration becomes unavailable because of a Disaster experienced by a Subscriber. Tests may also be postponed by the Customer for reasons outside the Customer's control.

6. Supplier Undertakings

The Supplier undertakes that it has good title to or a right to use the Configuration, and further undertakes:

6.1 to make all reasonable endeavours at all times to provide the services to the Customer in the event of a Disaster;

6.2 not to exceed the maximum number of Subscribers stated in the Schedule for the Configuration;

6.3 not to register any other customer as a Subscriber for the Services using the Configuration who is located in the same or an adjacent building to the Customer;

6.4 [to keep the Configuration in good working order to meet the Customer's requirements, ensuring its regular maintenance, and in the event of failure or breakdown, to restore it to good working order promptly;] [to arrange for the Configuration to be maintained by keeping third party hardware and software maintenance agreements current, which in the case of hardware

707

maintenance agreements will include provision for investigation within a maximum of four hours as one of the terms;]

6.5   to provide an experienced manager at the Site during normal office hours and to ensure that the Customer always has a means of contacting a manager who can help to provide access;

6.6   to keep the Site secure and to permit only authorised Supplier, Customer and Subscriber personnel to gain access;

6.7   to keep an accurate record of the components of the Configuration at all times, including location, serial numbers and maintenance details, and to provide this to the Customer on request;

6.8   to ensure that the Site always meets the environmental requirements of the Configuration, that it contains the attendant facilities normally associated with the operation and management of a system of equivalent size and complexity to the Configuration, taking account of the anticipated level of usage, and that it is generally kept clean and tidy;

6.9   to indemnify the Customer against any claims by third parties arising out of the provision of the Services to the Customer.

7. Data

7.1   The Supplier undertakes:

   (a)   to act only on instructions from the Data Controller in relation to any personal data which may be comprised in the Data as such 'personal data' is defined by the Data Controller;

   (b)   that its technical and organisational security measures govern the processing of the Data;

   (c)   that it will use its best endeavours to prevent any unauthorised or unlawful processing of the Data or any accidental loss, destruction or damage;

   (d)   that it has taken reasonable steps to ensure the honesty and reliability of its personnel;

   (e)   to indemnify the Customer against any claims by third parties arising out of any breach of the undertakings in this clause.

7.2   Data, whether provided by the Customer in human or machine readable form, and any output resulting from processing by the System, remain at all times the property of the Customer, subject to the confidentiality provisions in this Agreement.

8. Customer Undertakings

8.1   The Customer undertakes:

   (a)   to provide the Supplier with a list of its personnel authorised to invoke the Services in a Disaster and always to keep this list up to date. The Supplier will not accept any instructions or bookings from any personnel not so listed;

(b) to be solely responsible for all transportation and associated costs for Media storage;

(c) to be solely responsible for ensuring that all Media kept by the Customer at the Site are compatible with the Configuration. The Customer undertakes to ensure that the Media are supplied and maintained in good condition;

(d) to use on the Configuration only the versions of any software which are capable of running on the latest version operating system of the Configuration;

(e) to observe, and instruct its staff to observe, the access and security procedures at the Site at all times, and to keep confidential, and take all reasonable measures to ensure that its staff keep confidential, any identification numbers and passwords provided by the Supplier for the purposes of gaining access to the Site;

(f) to allow the Supplier to study, for the sole purpose of rectifying problems, any of the Data, provided that all such data is treated as confidential by the Supplier, and that the security provisions set out in relation to Data in this Agreement are complied with;

(g) to ensure that its staff use the Site only for the purposes of this Agreement;

(h) to take all reasonable measures to ensure that its staff working at the Site comply with any instructions of any supervisory personnel of the Supplier;

(i) to provide the Supplier and its employees assigned to perform the Services with all necessary information and assistance that may reasonably be required to enable the Supplier to carry out its obligations in this Agreement to the Customer.

8.2 The Customer warrants that the System is either owned by or legally licensed to the Customer and is available for use in a Disaster on an alternative computer system to that for which it was supplied, and the Customer fully indemnifies the Supplier in respect of any damages, costs or expenses incurred by the Supplier as a result of any claim against the Supplier from a third party alleging unauthorised use on the Configuration of the System.

9. Exclusions

9.1 The Services are subject to availability, and the Supplier will not be liable for any losses, costs or expenses incurred by the Customer and arising from any failure in the provision of the Services for any reason.

9.2 The Supplier will not be obliged to maintain compatibility of the Configuration with the System, and reserves the right at all times to make changes or modifications to the Configuration following a minimum of 30 days' notice to the Customer (except in case of emergency) and subject to the Customer's right to terminate this Agreement with effect from the expiry of the notice if the proposed changes or modifications will result in incompatibility with the System.

OR

The Supplier reserves the right to make major changes or modifications to the Configuration subject to continued compatibility with the Customer's requirements and subject to the Customer's agreement, not to be unreasonably withheld or delayed.

9.3 The Supplier will use all reasonable endeavours to maintain the Configuration and any changes or modifications to it in full working order, but subject to its compliance with this undertaking the Supplier will not be liable in any way under any circumstances to the Customer for any equipment or software failures within the Configuration.

9.4 Subject to the other provisions in this Agreement on security of the Data, it is the sole responsibility of the Customer to make appropriate arrangements for the maintenance of the integrity of the Data, including instituting adequate back-up procedures for the Customer's business requirements. The Supplier will not be responsible or liable to the Customer in any way for any lost or corrupted Data however caused.

10. Charges

10.1 The Charges payable by the Customer to the Supplier for the Services are set out in the Schedule.

10.2 The Charges are exclusive of expenses incurred in the performance of this Agreement by the Supplier. Expenses must be agreed in advance with the Customer and must be supported by receipts or other documentary evidence as appropriate.

10.3 The Charges and expenses are exclusive of Value Added Tax and any similar taxes. All such taxes are payable by the Customer and will be applied in accordance with UK legislation in force at the tax point date.

10.4 The Supplier will be entitled to increase its charges on the anniversary of the Commencement Date Agreement and thereafter not more than once in any successive period of 12 months while this Agreement is in force by giving not less than 60 days' notice to the Customer provided that any such increase expressed as a percentage does not exceed any percentage increase in the Employment Index published by Computer Economics for the 12 months immediately preceding the date of the notice.

11. Payment Terms

11.1 The Customer will be invoiced annually in advance for the Charges shown in the Schedule. Expenses and other charges will be invoiced monthly in arrears.

11.2 All Charges and other expenses properly due will be payable by the Customer within ten days of the date of the Supplier's invoice.

11.3 Payments which are not received when payable will be considered overdue and remain payable by the Customer together with interest for late payment from the date payable at the statutory rate applicable as well after as before any judgment, and independent of such judgment. This interest will accrue on a daily basis and be payable on demand.

11.4 Notwithstanding the above provision for late payment, in this event the Supplier may at its option, and without prejudice to any other remedy at any time after payment has become due, terminate or temporarily suspend performance of this Agreement.

11.5 If the Supplier becomes entitled to terminate this Agreement for any reason, any sums then due to the Supplier will immediately become payable in full.

12. Confidential Information

The Supplier acknowledges that confidentiality is an important feature of this Agreement and that under this Agreement it may receive trade secrets and confidential or proprietary information of the Customer, including but not limited to information concerning products, customers, security arrangements, finance or contractual arrangements, or other dealings, program source and object codes and development plans. All such information constitutes 'Confidential Information'. The Supplier agrees not to divulge Confidential Information received from the Customer to any of its employees who do not need to know it, and to prevent its disclosure to or access by any third party without the prior written consent of the disclosing party.

13. Indemnities and Limits of Liability

13.1 The Customer agrees that it has accepted these terms and conditions in the knowledge that the Supplier's liability is limited and that the prices and charges payable have been calculated accordingly. The Customer is advised to make its own insurance arrangements if it desires to limit further its exposure to risk or if it requires further or different cover.

13.2 The Supplier will indemnify the Customer for direct physical injury or death caused solely either by defects in the Products or by the negligence of its employees acting within the course of their employment and the scope of their authority.

13.3 The Supplier will indemnify the Customer for direct damage to property caused solely either by defects in the Products or by the negligence of its employees acting within the course of their employment and the scope of their authority. The total liability of the Supplier under this sub-clause will be limited to £500,000 for any one event or series of connected events.

13.4 Except as expressly stated in this clause and elsewhere in this Agreement, any liability of the Supplier for breach of this Agreement will not exceed in the aggregate of damages, costs, fees and expenses capable of being awarded to the Customer the total price paid or due to be paid by the Customer under this Agreement.

13.5 Except as expressly stated in this Agreement, the Supplier disclaims all liability in contract or in tort (including negligence or breach of statutory duty) to the Customer in connection with the Supplier's performance of this Agreement or the Customer's use of the Products including but not limited to liability for loss of profits whether in the course of the Customer's business or otherwise, or arising from loss of data, and in no event will the Supplier be liable to the Customer for special, indirect or consequential damages.

13.6 The Customer will indemnify the Supplier in respect of any third party claims which arise from any the Supplier's actions carried out on the instructions of the Customer or its authorised representative.

13.7 The Supplier makes no representations and gives no warranties, guarantees or undertakings concerning its performance of the Services except as expressly set out in this Agreement. All other warranties, express or implied, by statute or otherwise, are excluded from this Agreement.

14. Termination

14.1 This Agreement may be terminated immediately by notice in writing:
  (a) by the Supplier if the Customer fails to pay any sums due under this Agreement by the date payable without prejudice to any other provisions relating to late payment in this Agreement;
  (b) by either party if the other party is in material or continuing breach of any of its obligations under this Agreement and fails to remedy the breach (if capable of remedy) for a period of 30 days after written notice;
  (c) by either party if the other party is involved in any legal proceedings concerning its solvency, or ceases trading, or commits an act of bankruptcy or is adjudicated bankrupt or enters into liquidation, whether compulsory or voluntary, other than for the purposes of an amalgamation or reconstruction, or makes an arrangement with its creditors or petitions for an administration order or if a trustee, receiver, administrative receiver or general officer is appointed over all or any part of its assets or if it generally becomes unable to pay its debts within the meaning of Section 123 or Section 268 of the Insolvency Act 1986, or equivalent circumstances occur in any other jurisdiction.

14.2 Any termination of this Agreement under this clause will be without prejudice to any other rights or remedies of either party under this Agreement or at law and will not affect any accrued rights or liabilities of either party at the date of termination.

15. General Contract Provisions

15.1 Entire Agreement

This Agreement constitutes the entire agreement and understanding between the parties and supersedes any previous agreement between the parties relating to the subject matter of this Agreement. Each of the parties acknowledges that in entering into this Agreement, it does not rely on, and will have no remedy in respect of any statement of fact or opinion not recorded in this Agreement (whether negligently or innocently made), except for any representation made fraudulently.

15.2 Variations

No variation of these terms and conditions will be valid unless confirmed in writing by authorised signatories of both parties on or after the date of this Agreement.

15.3 Severability

If any of the provisions of this Agreement is judged to be illegal or unenforceable, the continuation in full force and effect of the remainder of them will not be prejudiced [unless the substantive purpose of this Agreement is thereby frustrated, in which case either party may terminate this Agreement forthwith on written notice].

15.4 Waiver

No forbearance or delay by either party in enforcing its respective rights will prejudice or restrict the rights of that party, and no waiver of any such rights or of any breach of any contractual terms will be deemed to be a waiver of any other right or of any later breach.

15.5 Relationship of the Parties

The relationship between the Supplier and the Customer is that of independent contractor. Neither party is agent for the other, and neither party has any authority to make any contract, whether expressly or by implication, in the name of the other party, without that party's prior written consent for express purposes connected with the performance of this Agreement.

15.6 Rights of Third Parties

A person who is not a party to this Agreement has no right to benefit under or to enforce any term of this Agreement.

15.7 Assignment

Neither party will assign, sub-contract or otherwise deal with this Agreement or any rights and obligations under this Agreement without the prior consent of the other party.

15.8 Notices

Any notice given under this Agreement by either party to the other must be in writing and may be delivered personally or by first-class post, and in the case of post will be deemed to have been given two working days after the date of posting. Notices will be delivered or sent to the addresses of the parties on the first page of this Agreement or to any other address notified in writing by either party to the other for the purpose of receiving notices after the date of this Agreement.

15.9 **Governing Law and Jurisdiction**
This Agreement is governed by and construed according to English law and the parties submit to the exclusive jurisdiction of the courts of England and Wales.

SCHEDULE

Configuration

System

Contact information

Charges

The Customer agrees to accept the Services on the terms and conditions of this Agreement.	The Supplier agrees to provide the Services on the terms and conditions of this Agreement.
FOR AND ON BEHALF OF	**FOR AND ON BEHALF OF**
Name	Name ....
Date	Date ....
Director of the Customer	**Director of the Supplier**

Index

Index

Index